Language Development from Two to Three

Language Development from Two to Three

Lois Bloom
Teachers' College, Columbia University

with

Joanne Bitetti Capatides, Kathleen Fiess,
Barbara Gartner, Jeremie Hafitz,
Lois (Hood) Holzman, Margaret Lahey,
Karin Lifter, Patsy Lightbown,
Susan Merkin, Peggy Miller,
Matthew Rispoli, Lorraine Rocissano,
Jo Tackeff, Janet Wootten

 **CAMBRIDGE**
UNIVERSITY PRESS

Published by the Press Syndicate of the University of Cambridge
The Pitt Building, Trumpington Street, Cambridge CB2 1RP
40 West 20th Street, New York, NY 10011-4211, USA
10 Stamford Road, Oakleigh, Melbourne 3166, Australia

First published 1991
First paperback edition 1993

Printed in the United States of America

Library of Congress Cataloging-in-Publication Data

Bloom, Lois.
Language development from two to three / Lois Bloom with Joanne
Bitetti Capatides...[et al.].
p.   cm.
ISBN 0-521-40178-X
1. Language acquisition.   I. Title.
P118.B59   1991
401'.93–dc20   90-45644
                                                                   CIP

British Library Cataloguing in Publication Data

Bloom, Lois
Language development from two to three.
1. Children. Language skills. Development
I. Title
401.9

ISBN 0-521-40178-X hardback
ISBN 0-521-43583-8 paperback

Contents

Acknowledgments   *page* vii

1. Introduction   I

Part I. Acquisition of Simple Sentences   37
  2. Categories of Verbs and Simple Sentences   39
  3. Verb Subcategorization and Linguistic Covariation   86
  4. Sentence Negation   143
  5. Verb Subcategorization and Inflections   208
  6. *Wh*-Questions   240

Part II. Acquisition of Complex Sentences   257
  7. Connectives and Clausal Meaning Relations   259
  8. Infinitive Complements with *to*   290
  9. *Wh*- and Sentence Complements   310
  10. Forms and Functions of Causal Language   333
  11. Causal Meanings and the Concept of Causality   375

Part III. Studies of Process and Interaction   395
  12. Imitation and Its Role in Language Development   397
  13. Development of Contingency in Discourse   434

References   473
Author Index   497
Subject Index   504

Acknowledgments

First, I thank the children. Eric, Gia, Kathryn, and Peter are now in their adult years, but they will always be 2-year-olds to me. Through their words and the details of that time in their lives they unwittingly enriched the study of child language. In appreciation, I dedicate this book to them. In their honor and because of all I learned from them, beginning with my own dissertation research, the royalties from the sales of this book have been assigned to the American Speech–Language–Hearing Foundation to support graduate students' research in early child language and its development.

I am fortunate to have had the collaboration of my coauthors in the last 20 years, and many have become valued colleagues and friends. The success of the project's early years owed much to the enthusiasm and good-natured industry of Patsy Lightbown and Lois (Hood) Holzman; they were the first in a succession of women who contributed in countless ways to the intellectual and personal life of the research. Peg Lahey, as my counsel and my friend, shared much of what happened both inside and outside the lab over the years, and I am grateful for her. Karin Lifter's support and devotion to the project and to me made an important difference in all that we did together. Joanne Bitetti Capatides, Jeremie Hafitz, Peggy Miller, and Lorraine Rocissano made many contributions to more than just those studies for which they appear as coauthors. Ira Blake, Lorraine Harner, and Bambi Schieffelin do not appear as coauthors, but they enriched our context and influenced our thinking. And Lila Braine's good judgment and friendship over the years could always be counted on when it mattered most. Finally, Marie Bauza and Gazetta Murray made it possible for me to do the research in this book by doing much of the work that had to be done at home.

The individual studies benefited from discussions and consultations with many colleagues. Richard Beckwith's input to the later studies was especially valuable, and he also helped make the connections between this research and other research in the field. I thank, in particular, Ruth Gold, Tory Higgins, Donald Hood, William Labov, Annick Mansfield, Michael Maratsos, Jane Monroe, Elissa Newport, Richard Sanders, Nancy Stein, Tom Trabasso, Owen Whitby, Richard Wojcik, and Robert Wozniak. Others who helped with one or another aspect of data processing included Vera Baviskar, Miao Chiao Chung, Carol Mangano, Lisa Rodke, Barbara Schecter, Lydia Soifer, Ellen Tanouye, and Takashi Yamamoto.

Financial support for the research was provided through Public Health Service Fellowship F1-MH-30,001, Research Grant HD03828 from the National Institutes of Health, and Research Grants SOC-24126, SOC-28126, BNS-15528, BNS-07335, and BNS-19665 from the National Science Foundation. I thank Paul Chapin at NSF and Jim Kavanagh of the National Institute of Child Health and Human Development at NIH for their interest in the research.

If one can thank institutions, I thank Teachers College, Columbia University, for providing the physical context for our work: first in the drafty Dodge "penthouse" and then in that special place, 1055A Thorndike. I thank my colleagues at Teachers College who provided the personal context: John Broughton, Herb Ginsburg, Harvey Hornstein, Deanna Kuhn, Eleanor Morrison, Roger Myers, Sy Rigrodsky, and the late Edward Mysak and Ira Ventry.

This is probably as good a time as any to acknowledge a considerable debt I owe Jim Geiwitz, who, in a memorable hour at the Center for Advanced Study in the Behavioral Sciences in 1982, taught me how to write (although I expect he would still find much to improve upon). For encouraging this book and for their comments on an early draft of Chapter 1, I thank Richard Beckwith, Kathleen Bloom, Peg Lahey, Patsy Lightbown, and Bambi Schieffelin (who also suggested the idea for the jacket design). Support for the preparation of the book was provided by a James McKeen Cattell Sabbatical Award in Psychology. Preparation of the Postscripts at the end of each chapter was facilitated by the Iowa State University/CHILDES Bibliographic database, compiled by Roy Higginson, and the diligence of Tamara Loring and Glenn Maciag. The efforts of Heidi Douglass, who assembled the final manuscript, and Erin Tinker, who prepared the index, are warmly appreciated.

Finally, I am fortunate in having had the loving support of my parents, Estre and Jack Masket, my brother, Ed Masket, and my many friends – especially Rosalie Renbaum, whose friendship has been a sustaining force in my life since our high school years. My daughter, Allison, tolerated the infringement on my time and energy and still managed to grow into the quite wonderful person she is. My husband, Robert H. Bloom, has my gratitude always for this life we have shared and for our love.

Easton, Connecticut
August 25, 1990

1

Introduction

"I'm a teacher . . .
I was teaching you all the time."
Kathryn, 3 years old

Most children begin the year between their second and third birthdays with a fairly sizable vocabulary of words, at least 50 words by most counts. Many have even begun to combine words to form their first phrases and simple sentences. But the age of 2 marks the beginning of a year of great linguistic effort. By the end of this year, most children will have acquired much of what they need to know for forming sentences and making conversation. They will go on from there to acquire the linguistic complexities and subtleties that make a mature language user, and these later acquisitions will continue well into the school years. But they learn the basics in the year from 2 to 3. The papers brought together in this volume have to do with that period before 3 years of age when children acquire their basic knowledge of semantics, syntax, morphology, and discourse.

These studies, originally published between 1970 and 1989, are the result of the longitudinal research program begun in *Language Development: Form and Function in Emerging Grammars.*[1] The chapters are organized into three sections. The first consists of the studies of simple sentences and includes the acquisition of constituent structure and meaning relations (Chapters 2 and 3) and three kinds of complexity in simple sentences: negation (Chapter 4), verb inflection (Chapter 5), and *wh*-questions (Chapter 6). The second section consists of the studies of complex sentences; these are studies of the acquisition of syntactic connectives and clausal meaning relations (Chapter 7), complementation (Chapters 8 and 9), and complex sentences that express causality (Chapters 10 and 11). The two papers in the third section pertain to process and interaction in language development. One is a study of the role of imitation in learning words and constituent structure (Chapter 12); the other is a study of contingency in discourse (Chapter 13). Together, the chapters in this book tell a developmental story of language acquisition from 2 to 3 years. At the beginning of this period, the children we studied were learning to say simple sentences; by the end of the period they had begun to acquire the structures of complex sentences. It was a noteworthy time in their lives. They learned to talk, to express what they had in mind, and to use language to influence the beliefs and actions of themselves and other persons.

Four children – Eric, Gia, Kathryn, and Peter – appear in all the studies, and six others appear in one or two studies. Although the information in this book is largely about child language and its acquisition between 2 and 3 years, we actually began the research when the children first started to combine words, before they were 2 years old. In the studies of early simple sentences (Chapter 2), negation (Chapter 4) and imitation (Chapter 12), for example, the children were observed from about 18 to 25 months of age.

They were born in the 1960s and are the firstborn children of white, college-educated parents who lived in university communities in New York City. Their parents were native speakers of American English, and their mothers were their primary caregivers. They were, then, children from a fairly well defined cultural context. They were chosen as subjects with these qualifications in what turned out to be, in retrospect, a naive effort to come up with a 'homogeneous' population. Since parent education, birth order, ethnicity, and economic differences among children had been found to be sources of individual differences in speech and language, these were the minimal 'controls' that seemed feasible to ensure that the children would be similar in their language learning. However, as we will see, one result of these studies was that despite the similarities among them, the children were nonetheless different from one another, in rate as well as in other aspects of their language learning.

The children were each visited in their homes, and the data were collected in the context of daily activities and informal play with a familiar adult (one or two of the investigators) and, less often, with their mothers. The same toys were brought to all the sessions, for the different children and for each child throughout the study, in an effort to establish consistency in the home contexts among the children and over time. The observations were audio recorded, and the transcriptions included all speech by the child and adults, along with descriptions of nonlinguistic context and behavior.[2]

The papers that make up these chapters have been changed from their original published form only for purposes of clarification and to reduce their length somewhat. Each chapter begins with an introductory section that expands and replaces the abstract in the original publication. A Postscript has been added at the end of each chapter to point the reader to subsequent research in the literature that was influenced by or is otherwise relevant to the results and conclusions reported here.[3]

The purpose of this introductory chapter is to place these studies in the context of contemporary child language research. I begin with a brief description of three dominant perspectives that influence current research and theory in language acquisition. These are the *developmental* perspective, the *learnability* perspective, and the *cross-cultural* perspective. Then I discuss the contributions from this research program to several conceptual themes in current acquisition research and theory. A central theme is the importance of *verbs* for learning syntactic structures: How these children acquired syntax was influenced by the verbs they learned. The other themes are the role of meaning in syntax acquisition, the importance of context for the child learning language and for the researcher studying the child learning language, the relationship of language learning to other aspects of the cognitive development of the young child, and individual differences among children learning the same language.

PERSPECTIVES ON LANGUAGE ACQUISITION RESEARCH

The Developmental Perspective

The studies in this book originated in what has come to be called the 'developmental point of view.' The broad outline of this developmental point of view comes from the theoretical work of Heinz Werner, but we owe the details of its formulation to the monumental work of Jean Piaget.[4] The human infant begins life in an essentially global and undifferentiated state. The bounds between self and other, subject and object – if they exist at all in the first few days of life – are blurred and indistinct. Development is a process of change that leads to increasing differentiation of self and other and, as a result, successive changes in the forms and content of action and thought. On the one hand, developmental change is additive and cumulative. The mental capacities of infants increase as they acquire more and more information about different domains of world knowledge. On the other hand, developmental change is also qualitative as infants think about these content domains in substantively different ways.

The key to qualitative developmental change is the capacity for representation and, ultimately, the development of the symbolic capacity. Actions and feelings in the first year are very much tied to internal conditions and immediately perceivable objects, persons, and events in the environment. In the second year, the infant comes to think about objects that are removed in time and space when events in the situation cue their recall. And in the third year, infants develop the ability to mentally act on the representations they have in mind, instead of acting on the objects directly. The bounds between self and other are defined in this process as infants become able to think about objects and persons in relation to each other and in relation to the self, apart from their perceptions and actions. This development marks the transition from infancy to childhood. The ability to recall prior experiences in relation to present events and to anticipate new events increasingly informs the child's beliefs, desires, and feelings.

Language enables the child to make these thoughts known to other persons through expression and to attribute such thoughts to others through interpretation.[5] Language is acquired in the service of acts of expression and interpretation; it is not an end in itself. This means that how language is acquired depends very much on how children think and what they know. The effort to understand language acquisition, then, depends on understanding the importance to the child of such things as perceivability and repeated encounters that render things familiar and allow for the detection and appraisal of novelty. Most importantly, explaining acquisition depends on understanding that the symbolic capacity develops to make absent objects and events present in the child's thought for expression and interpretation.

The mental notation system for this representation in adult thinking is the subject of speculation and debate. For example, theorists differ on whether the required notation systems are componential (consisting of symbols and procedures for assembling them) or holistic (propositional or imagistic formats).[6] But regardless of the form of these mental contents, what the child has 'in mind' determines *what* the child says (and interprets of what others say).[7] *How* the child expresses these mental objects depends on learning words and syntax. It follows, then, that what children can hold in mind helps determine what they take from the input language and events in the context for learning the language.

The study of language development, in this view, is essentially a bottom-up approach that begins with the child and assumptions about the cognitive capacities children bring to the language learning task. In particular, explaining language development depends on understanding what the child has learned of the language at a particular time and how this knowledge changes from one time to another in progress toward the adult language. Each of the studies in this book addresses a different aspect of language as it develops in the period from 2 to 3. Although each study examines a different question about a basic aspect of language, all started with the same central goal: to discover what children learning language *do* and how what they do can tell us what they *know*.

The aim of each of these studies, then, was to discover something about the children's grammar. Because a grammar is not itself accessible, we looked at the children's language – their use of the grammar – and how that changed over time. In several instances, we began with a rather neutral, pretheoretical question such as 'How did the children acquire syntactic connectives?' (in Chapter 7). Other questions were theoretically motivated. For example, in the study of imitation (Chapter 12) the questions we asked came from competing theoretical views in the literature regarding the part played by imitation for language learning. In the study of *to* complements (Chapter 8), we juxtaposed Otto Jespersen's theory of the origin of the *to* complementizer with Joan Bresnan's theory that *to* is a meaningless semantic marker.[8] In studies of the development of constituent structure (Chapters 2 and 3), we pursued the theory that semantic categories of verbs are central to acquiring grammar.

We inferred what the children knew about language from evidence of the regularities in their language behaviors, since we could not tap their intuitions about language by asking them to tell us directly what was possible or acceptable to them linguistically. Accordingly, a systematic distribution among large numbers of linguistic events was taken as evidence for a principled organization underlying language behavior. A sizable and coherent shift in the regularity of behavior across time, from one observation to a later observation, was seen as developmental change. We approached the data by first reading through an annotated transcription of child speech to form an initial hypothesis about what that child did with a particular aspect of the language. We then tested this first hypothesis by going through the transcript again and judging whether and how each utterance was relevant. Relevance was judged initially on the basis of form, for example, the use of *no* and *not* in the study of negation and the use of *because* and *so* in the studies of causality. The criteria for relevance were expanded to include interpretive evidence regarding content, and our interpretation revealed, for example, the use of anaphoric reference in negation, and sentences with *and* that expressed temporal and causal connections. The initial passes through the data usually caused us to revise our original hypothesis and repeat the process again, and often again, until all relevant instances were identified and accounted for. The result was a pattern of the regularities and consistencies in the child language data, that is, categories that described the form, content, and use of language. Examples are the semantic categories of verbs in early sentences (Chapter 2), the semantic–syntactic configurations in sentences with subcategories of verbs (Chapter 3), categories of discourse contingency (Chapter 13), and so forth. Using the pattern obtained with one child as a heuristic, we repeated the process, first to establish generalizability with samples of speech from the other children at a comparable time (according to similarity in average length of utterance) and then to evaluate change over time in the subsequent observations.

The relative frequency of utterances in different categories, the change in relative frequency over time, and the advent of new categories provided the evidence we used for answering questions about development and proposing a theory of the child's language. The development of sentence negation (Chapter 4) is an example. Interpretation of negative sentences in relation to the contexts in which they occurred revealed three semantic categories of negation with the meanings nonexistence, rejection, and denial. Early on, sentences expressing nonexistence were most frequent; expressions of rejection were less frequent; and expressions of denial were rare. As the children grew older, the frequency of sentences expressing rejection and then denial increased, in that order. Correspondingly, the syntactic form of negation changed, first for nonexistence – for example, from "no wagon" to "a can't find a saucer" – then for rejection – for example, from "no go outside" to "I don't want to comb hairs" – and, eventually, for denial, from "no truck" to "that's not a apple."[9] The relative frequency of the semantic categories of negation at different times and the pattern of change in both their frequency and syntactic form were the evidence used to infer the developmental sequence for sentence negation: nonexistence > rejection > denial.

Our approach is a dialectical one in which we use principles derived from relevant theories in developmental psychology and linguistics to help us understand what we cannot observe directly.[10] In *Form and Function in Emerging Grammars,* for example, I proposed early child grammars using principles from Chomsky's "standard theory" of transformational grammar[11] and the sorts of cognitive constraints that we know influence early development. In *Structure and Variation* (Chapter 2), differences among languages that are synthetic versus analytic helped us understand similar differences among the children in their early tendencies to combine verbs with either nouns (an analytic strategy) or pronouns (a synthetic strategy). In "Variation and Reduction as Aspects of Competence" (Chapter 3) we used a variable-rules model[12] to account for the probablistic nature of relative sentence length and completeness. In short, in order to develop theories of child language and language acquisition, we approach the child data with whatever resources we have in both linguistics and psychology.

In doing this research we observed and described what children did, using audiotaped records of their conversations. The children obliged us by saying well over 100,000 multiword utterances in our sessions with them. The procedural question was how to decide which of these were diagnostic of developmental change. Tapping one's intuitions about language is the mainstay in research with adults and older children, but it doesn't work with 1- and 2-year-olds, as everyone knows by now. Instead we rely on children's 'telling' us what they know by using the forms of language. Such procedures raise problems of sampling: How many utterances and how many children? One pertains to the size of a corpus of utterances for analysis and the other, to the number of children to study. These two decisions necessarily are trade-offs. If the research questions require large longitudinal samples of speech for detecting developmental trends, as was the case in this research, then the inevitable restrictions on time and money mean that fewer children can be studied.[13]

The longer we visited a child, the larger the corpus of speech we could collect, and the more likely we would hear more and different forms. But no one, to my knowledge, has satisfactorily solved the problem of how many data are enough. Everyone agrees that a scrupulous record of all a child's utterances, with contextual notes, is the ideal. It is also an impossibility. A devoted investigator might be able to catch what the child said, but also to record the discourse and other context at the same time would be a prodigious task. Accordingly, we have to sample children's speech. Sampling decisions include the length of sessions and the intervals between sessions, and there are no rules. Both the requirements of evidence and the pragmatics of data collection enter into the decision. For example, in the days before videotape, we could afford to collect large samples of 6 to 8 hours of child speech because an audio record is a drastically reduced record of interaction, which meant that transcription was a relatively manageable task. In the research reported in these studies, we opted for roughly 8-hour samples every 6 weeks for Eric, Gia, and Kathryn. For the sake of comparing sample size and interval differences, we saw Peter for 5 hours every 3 weeks. This yielded a total of roughly 290 hours of observation over a 1-year period. A videotape preserves much more information, and so its transcription is proportionately more demanding and time-consuming. In a second longitudinal study, begun in 1981 with videotaped observations, we observed children for 1 hour every month but increased the size of our subject sample to 14 children. This yielded a total of 178 hours of observation for one year: fewer data from more children.[14] These decisions are not prescriptive, but they have served the purposes of the two different research projects.

Once we have what we believe is a sample of speech that 'represents' what a child does on any given day, what criteria do we use for our conclusions about developments in language? A very conservative criterion for productivity would be a relatively large number, say 10 or 15, tokens of a target behavior. Such a large number would cast a narrow net, and we would come up with those language forms and functions that the child knows well. But we would lose those that are infrequent, either because they are also relatively infrequent in the adult language or because they are forms and functions that the child knows less well or is in the process of learning. A very liberal criterion would be a single instance: For example, the first time a child asks one *why* question or says one negative sentence, we might attribute knowledge of *why* questions or negation. This would cast a very wide net but run the risk of overestimating what the child actually knows or is learning. A single instance could have been memorized, part of a routine, a phrase that the child associates with only a particular situation, or even an error in transcription (as could happen especially in the study of inflections and the small functor forms such as connectives and prepositions). The criteria for productivity in the studies presented here varied according to the aspect of language being studied but was not less than three or more than five instances of a target form, depending on our intuitions regarding expected relative frequency in the adult language. In studies that used smaller samples of speech, these numbers could be too conservative.

In sum, the small number of children in these studies was dictated by the nature of the questions we asked and the methods we used in the research to answer the questions. Small numbers of children require that research results be tested by other researchers, with other children, in order to establish their generality. Such replication is necessary for extending the findings to larger populations. But in evaluating such attempts at replication, we need to keep in mind that different sampling methods and procedures raise problems for comparison. For example, results based on a single instance may differ from results based on a criterion reference for productivity. Issues such as these deserve more discussion in the acquisition literature.

Learnability-Theoretic Research

Whereas the focus in developmental research is on the child learning the language, an alternative approach in acquisition research begins with one or another linguistic theory of the adult grammar. Formal theories of acquisition, as in learnability research, are the result of a top-down approach that begins with a theory of the adult grammar and asks how that theory is learned. For example, how children learn the standard theory of generative transformational grammar was addressed by Wexler and Culicover.[15] Steven Pinker proposed a theory of how children learn the lexical functionalist grammar of Joan Bresnan.[16] More recently, Nina Hyams offered an acquisition theory based on parameter setting in the revision of standard theory known as *government and binding*.[17] Such formal theories of acquisition differ from one another in their presumptions of how much children use the speech they hear for data about the adult language and how much they depend on inborn principles and constraints. But these language acquisition theories share the basic assumption that an explanation of how the child learns language depends on an explicit theory of the end state: the adult grammar that is acquired.

The learnability enterprise was motivated initially by research and learnability proofs in machine learning.[18] Given sentences as input and a set of possible grammatical hypotheses, the learner's task is to determine the correct grammar for generating the input sentences. In the child's case, the input must be relatively simple because of limited processing capabilities, but the output will be the structures of the adult language. This places a heavy burden on the set of hypotheses that the child uses for evaluating the input in order to arrive at the correct grammar. In addition, children are ordinarily not corrected for whatever grammatical mistakes they make, so when they do make a mistake they do not know that they are wrong or how they are wrong. This places yet another burden on the child's learning mechanism. And finally, children are supposedly in a hurry and have to learn the grammar fairly fast. These (and other) assumptions have led researchers to conclude that acquiring language could not be possible unless the child comes to the language-learning task with a strong biological endowment for overcoming these burdens. Usually a set of principles that constrain the possible grammatical hypotheses and a good part of the learning mechanism (what Chomsky originally called LAD, ''the language acquisition device'') must be innate.

Learnability proofs are elegant, and arguments for the innate aspects of language have been presented with a certain eloquence. Those who disagree have the task of demonstrating how the child might have learned whatever is claimed to be unlearnable without the proposed innate component. It is worth pointing out, however, that learnability proofs do not ordinarily operate with the data that children actually receive as input. Moreover, one of the biggest misconceptions in the literature might be that language acquisition is 'quick and easy.' In fact, children work hard at learning language. The studies in this book demonstrate that they have learned quite a lot by the time they are 3 years old, but 3 years is a long time and they still have much to learn.

Another argument for innatism is found in the 'child as linguist' analogy.[19] Children acquire a language by learning the grammar that generates sentences in the language and not by hearing and remembering the sentences themselves. Of course the young child does hear sentences and, supposedly, a lot of noise in the form of nonsentences as well. But the principles and procedures of the grammar to be acquired are nowhere accessible because they are hidden in the minds of those who use them. In short, children hear sentences, but they learn a grammar. The questions for the child are, what is the grammar and how do I learn it?

At the same time, the job of adult linguists is to discover what the grammar of a language consists of. The questions for the linguist are, what is the grammar and how do I figure out what it is? The assumption is that if linguists can answer these questions, they not only will have learned what the grammar is but also will have discovered how children learn it. But linguists have great difficulty answering these questions. Speakers of a language know what is acceptable and unacceptable as a sentence, but linguists cannot agree on just how they know. In fact, they have not been able to agree on the form of the rules, procedures, or principles of grammar. Ray Jackendoff pointed out that several hundred very smart linguists have been working at what a generative transformational grammar might look like for the last 30 years. Because the task has proved to be so difficult for linguists and because the principles and procedures for language that the child needs to learn are not themselves accessible in the environment, learnability theorists assume that children must have a 'head start.' This head start takes the form of innate linguistic constraints that guide the child in discovering what the grammar might be.

But child and linguist are really very different. The most fundamental difference between them is, quite simply, that one already knows the language and the other does not. Given how they start out, the procedures of child and adult cannot be the same or even similar. Children start with one word at a time and work on the problem step by step. Because they don't yet know the language, they don't have to figure out the whole grammar for the language from the beginning. Little feet take small steps. Each step leads to another problem to work out which, once they have solved it, lets them take another step, and so on. Linguists not only have bigger feet, they also know quite a lot more about the world. They are smarter, in part, because they have lived longer. But also knowing the language is a big help in learning about the world. The linguist, then, starts out knowing the language already and knowing a great deal else besides. The child starts out knowing far less.[20]

In sum, the learnability-theoretic approach begins with the adult, a theory of the grammar that the adult knows, and a theory of how that grammar might be learned. If one begins by explaining how the child learns what the adult knows about grammar, then the task for the child is indeed formidable without a 'head start.' But in the developmental approach, one begins with the child, what the child knows, and how what the child knows changes over time. From the child's naive perspective, the task is a more tractable one.

These two traditions, inherited by contemporary research from the 1970s, were summarized by Norman Freeman as follows:

On the one hand, linguistics had generated vast sets of computationally-unspecified rules supposedly curbed by innate constraints which switched themselves in, by some unspecified means, inside the hypothetical child. . . . On the other hand, starting with real child's talk, psychology inherited a vast number of partial "child grammars and lexicons," which could be cobbled together to yield a recognizable shadow of the steady state only by a vast number of contingent assumptions. . . . From these two lines, the 'eighties have seen an encouraging degree of convergence.[21]

In moving toward convergence, learnability research has made increasing use of the data of children's talk for empirically testing theories of acquisition.[22] At the same time, the questions asked in developmental research have been increasingly informed by changes in linguistic theory and learnability research.[23]

The Cross-Cultural Perspective

We have yet a third perspective in child language research, one that is closer to the developmental tradition but has its origins in anthropology and the study of cultural and social differences. Children in other parts of the world not only learn different languages, they also learn different ways of living. From an anthropological perspective, linguistic inquiry is closely tied to the cultural and social contexts of the lives of language users. In this view, the nonlinguistic factors that make effective language users are as important as the language itself. Children need to learn, for example, when talk is acceptable or unacceptable in a situation, in addition to learning how to judge whether or not their sentences are grammatical. Thus, knowing language includes knowing what one can and cannot say to different people in different circumstances and even knowing when one can talk or not talk at all. Bambi Schieffelin and Elinor Ochs persistently remind us that learning language is closely tied to learning how to think and how to feel, as well as to learning what to say as a member of a larger social group.[24]

At the same time that learning language depends on learning about culture, learning the culture depends on learning language. Language is a means of transmitting knowledge about social and cultural practices. Thus, language both contributes to socialization and is the result of socialization.[25] This perspective can be found in the study in Chapter 11 of the meanings of early expressions of causality. Although not a cross-cultural study, we report how sociocultural practices, judgments, and feelings contributed to subjective meanings in the children's expressions of causality. These meanings were an instance in which aspects of the culture were learned through language in the context of learning the language.

Because language and culture inform each other, explanations of language that are based on only a single cultural experience may be misleading. Children learning language in different societies can have different 'developmental stories.'[26]

Summary

The papers reproduced here originated in the developmental tradition. The children we studied came from a single cultural context in New York City and were few in number. The research is similar, in this respect, to cross-cultural ethnographies and cross-linguistic acquisition studies.[27] The focus on the child and the child's point of view in developmental research is a culturally relevant perspective and allows the inclusion of both process and interaction in the research. Our research differed from learnability-theoretic research because it was motivated by questions about aspects of the language the children were learning without assuming that those aspects are formalized by the grammar in a particular way. This means that one can evaluate the data from alternative theoretical perspectives rather than from only a single theory of adult grammar. Both traditional and contemporary theories of language influenced the questions we asked and our interpretation of the results in these studies.

A developmental perspective assumes that children play an active part in acquiring language. They are, in effect, 'the agents of their own development.'[28] Children learn from the language around them by attending to what they hear in contexts they can recognize and understand. They evaluate the input according to what they know about objects, events, and relations in the situation and according to what they have heard before in similar situations. They process language input and compare what they hear at one time with what they have heard at another time. They use frequently heard language forms in deciding what is more or less important to learn to begin with. Moreover, they pay particular attention to what they are currently learning: When children imitate the speech they hear, they imitate the words and/or the syntactic forms they are in the process of learning; they do not imitate what they already know well or forms they know nothing about (see Chapter 12). In contrast, in most learnability research the child is essentially passive. The emphasis is on principles of universal grammar that are innately specified and on input sentences that 'trigger' the acquisition of instantiations of these principles in a particular language.

The three perspectives on research and theory in language acquisition differ in what Stephen Pepper described as fundamental hypotheses about the world, or "world view."[29] The world view of anthropologically motivated, cross-cultural research is contextualism, with its emphasis on history and the totality of changing events. Most learnability-theoretic research has an essentially mechanistic world view, in which language depends on inborn, specifically linguistic constraints triggered by relevant instances in the input. Developmental research and theory has an organismic world view, with an emphasis on change, integration, and process. Pepper tells us that these different world views are mutually exclusive, virtually by definition, because they originate in how we think about the world and we cannot think about the world in two different ways at the same time. Nevertheless, developmental theory has moved toward embracing both organicism and contextualism,[30] which brings the developmental perspective closer to the cross-cultural one. Finally, the three perspectives have the explanation of language acquisition as their common goal, and for this reason the learnability perspective is ultimately related to both. Research in the coming decades could make those connections explicit for informing the research that we do.

CONCEPTUAL THEMES — *three*

Several themes in these studies will be discussed in this chapter to provide a framework for the chapters that follow. These themes continue to influence research and theory today, in new and elaborated forms.

Meaning in Child Language

The studies in this volume have their roots in the renaissance of child language research of the early 1960s. The landmarks in the research of that period are the studies by Martin Braine, Roger Brown and his colleagues, and Wick Miller and Susan Ervin-Tripp.[31] These researchers were moved by the first rumblings of the profound shift in linguistic theory that began in the preceding decade with the work of Zellig Harris and Noam Chomsky.[32] The generative transformational framework that resulted from this shift was to have a lasting influence on all subsequent theories of language. Linguistic inquiry was explicitly cast in terms of the knowledge people have for speaking and understanding sentences, and so the enterprise of specifying that knowledge became a psychological inquiry as much as a linguistic one. The boundaries between the disciplines of psychology and linguistics were thereby loosened irrevocably, and the new terms *psycholinguistics* and *developmental psycholinguistics* proclaimed their integration. The future direction of child language research took shape when Chomsky framed the central problem for linguistic theory as the explanation of how the child acquires knowledge of language structure.[33]

In standard generative transformational theory, grammar was "best formulated as a self-contained study independent of semantics," and meaning was not used to investigate linguistic forms.[34] Meaning in language comes from what we know about the world, which is limitless. For this reason, in addition to the problems of multiple interpretation, meaning could not be a suitable topic for linguistic inquiry.[35] Correspondingly, questions of meaning were ignored in the studies of syntax acquisition in the 1960s as well. However, in *Form and Function in Emerging Grammars* I suggested that semantics could not be ignored in the effort to understand syntax acquisition, because children use the meaning relations between words to discover the categories and rules of syntax. First, children learn the syntax of simple sentences for expressing a core of basic meanings, and subsequently, they learn the syntax of complex sentences to express the meaning relations between the propositions underlying their simple sentences (Chapter 7). The evidence I cited for the original proposal was the data I collected from Eric, Gia, and Kathryn at 19 to 27 months of age. At the same time, but independently, I. M. Schlesinger reported an analysis of semantic categories and relations in the data from the subjects in the earlier studies by Braine, Brown, and Miller and Ervin-Tripp.[36]

The idea that meaning is important to learning syntax soon took hold, helped in large measure by Roger Brown when he applied the meaning relations in *Form and Function in Emerging Grammars* and in Schlesinger's study to data from children in several different studies. The result was a description of the basic meanings of early sentences in what he called "Stage I speech."[37] The importance of semantics for syntax acquisition has since been extended and formalized in contemporary acquisition theory as "semantic bootstrapping,"[38] and the idea is now virtually taken for granted.

The early meaning relations identified in *Form and Function in Emerging Grammars* were of two kinds. Certain meanings were expressed by particular words that the children used often in their early phrases. These included, for example, the relational meanings of recurrence (with *more*) and nonexistence, rejection, and denial (with *no*). Other meanings were described as "grammatical meaning," including the genitive ("Mommy sock") and the locative ("sweater chair"). Most important, however, were the grammatical meanings in sentences with the constituents subject–verb–object, utterances like "Mommy pigtail," "read book," and "Baby do it." Whether only two or all three of these constituents were actually realized in utterances, the majority of the children's sentences expressed action relations between animate nouns as actor or agent subjects and inanimate objects affected by the action.

The semantics of the grammatical meanings in early sentences were later described by Melissa Bowerman in terms of Fillmore's case grammar categories of agent, action, and patient.[39] She suggested (as had Schlesinger[40]) that the evidence from early sentences supported attributing semantic but not syntactic knowledge to the young child. In contrast, I had proposed originally (in *Form and Function in Emerging Grammars*) and argued subsequently (in the papers reproduced here as Chapters 2 and 3) that children learn syntax and semantics together. Once verbs are productive in word combinations, the constituent structure of children's sentences has a semantic–syntactic basis. The assumption that children's early sentences are syntactically motivated is now consistent with virtually all contemporary acquisition theories[41] and has since been embraced by Bowerman as well.[42]

The syntactic–semantic relations in early sentences were defined in the two 1975 papers according to categories of verb meaning. In the first, *Structure and Variation in Child Language* (Chapter 2), we distinguished between (1) verbs that did and did not name a movement: *action* and *state* verbs and (2) whether the goal of an action or state was a location of an object: *locative-action* and *locative-state* verbs. In the second, "Variation and Reduction as Aspects of Competence" (Chapter 3), we identified the different constituent relations that occurred with action verbs and subcategories of locative verbs. We proposed that the children learned grammar by learning semantic categories of verbs that determine the argument structure of sentences (as we shall discuss later in regard to the centrality of verbs). The children were learning different sentence configurations for these verb categories, and this led to the further claim that they were also learning the grammatical categories *subject* and *object*. The evidence for the category subject was the different arguments that occurred with different categories of verbs in the same syntactic (subject) position. The preverbal constituent of the children's sentences differed in semantic role according to the meaning of the verb in different categories of action and locative-action verbs. Sentence-subjects were agents or actors of transitive or intransitive action verbs respectively, and patients (the affected-object) or movers (both agent and affected-object) of intransitive locative verbs. In sum, these semantic roles licensed assigning the pre-verbal constituent of the children's sentences to the grammatical category sentence-subject.

The semantic roles of the constituents in these early sentences derive, for the child, from the two conceptual notions *movement* and *location.* The importance of these concepts has precedence in both developmental psychology and linguistics. In his several infant books, Piaget stressed again and again that children learn about objects in the world by acting on them and perceiving them in different places.[43] Young infants move objects from place to place and discover them anew in different places. Through these perceptions and actions (hence "sensory motor intelligence") in the first 2 years of life, children come to know that objects continue to exist in time and space even though they can no longer see them or act on them. The semantics of their early sentences builds on the conceptual knowledge acquired in infancy through appreciation of the effects of movement and location.[44] In linguistics, "the semantics of motion and location provide the key to a wide range of further semantic fields."[45] In particular, Jackendoff proposed a theory of semantics in which the meaning expressed through the lexical and grammatical systems of language is closely tied to conceptual structure. The ontological categories in this conceptual structure correspond to the categories of projected semantic entities in the constituents of adult sentences. These include, for example, action, thing, and place, which are consistent with the categories in children's early sentences.[46]

In sum, in the studies reproduced here, meaning is the thread that led the children to discover the forms of language. The meanings that were particularly important were action, state, and location (Chapters

2 and 3), negation (Chapter 4), and tense and aspect (Chapter 5) in simple sentences; and in complex sentences, additivity, time, and causality (Chapters 7, 10, and 11), and the psychological attitudes named by verbs of volition, directedness, perception, and knowing (Chapters 8 and 9). In addition, the notion of topic relatedness or shared meaning between sentences guided their discourse acquisition (Chapter 13).

The phrase "rich interpretation" was used by Roger Brown to characterize the practice of attributing meaning to children's speech.[47] Some have questioned its legitimacy,[48] but rich interpretation has remained a powerful instrument in the toolbox of acquisition research. The study of semantic relations in children's sentences in the 1970s[49] resurfaced in the 1980s in the emphasis in learnability-theoretic research on thematic roles and relations in adult grammar for the input children receive. Rich interpretation has been a relatively conservative enterprise so far, because attributions based on what children say are ordinarily restricted to attributions of linguistic meaning in words and combinations of words. More recently, we have begun to extend the practice of rich interpretation in making attributions of the representations in the states of mind that underlie children's expressions.[50] Language expresses what the child has in mind, and these representations are the contents of their beliefs, desires, and feelings. Meaning in language depends on these representations,[51] and so the developments that contribute to the child's having such mental representations also contribute to language acquisition.

The systematic appeal to meaning led to two other themes in *Form and Function in Emerging Grammars* that continue in contemporary child language research. One of these is the importance of the context for the child learning language and for the researcher studying how children learn language. The other is the relationship between language development and developments in other aspects of cognition.

Context and Child Language

Context is important for two reasons: We as researchers use the child's context to discover meaning in the child's language, but more important, the young child uses context to discover meaning in the language.

Rich interpretation required information from the context for interpreting the child's meaning. All this meant is that one can look to the child's focus of attention and use what the child is doing and seeing to infer something of what an utterance is about. The idea was not new.

The fact that children speak "very much in the here and now" was noted by Roger Brown and Ursula Bellugi.[52] Before that, Werner Leopold reported using the "aid of the situation" in inferring the meanings of his daughter's speech.[53] And well before that, Grace de Laguna observed that "even a member of the family often fails to grasp the significance of what the baby is saying if he does not see what the baby is doing."[54] Parents and other caregivers rely on the cues from context and situation to figure out the child's meanings in their everyday activities of daily living. This is because 1- and 2-year-old children talk about what they are doing, what they are about to do, and what they want someone else to do in a way that adults do not. For example, a young child who gets on a tricycle will announce the fact: "I ride bike!"[55] In contrast, when adult speakers know that their listeners can see what they can see, they do not ordinarily tell them about it.

Two things were new. The first was methodological. Studies of early syntax in the 1960s had looked only at the words children said and how those words were combined with one another (in distributional analyses). In *Form and Function in Emerging Grammars* I proposed that one could systematically exploit the child's 'here and now' talk to form hypotheses about meaning and that regularities in meaning could be used to discover the syntax of sentences. The "evaluation of an utterance in relation to the context in which it occurred provided more information for analyzing intrinsic structure than a distributional analysis of the recorded corpus."[56] The example that I used to make this point was the pair of utterances Kathryn used that sounded the same but differed in meaning: "Mommy sock." In one instance of "Mommy sock," Kathryn pointed to Mommy's socks in a pile of dirty laundry. In the other instance of "Mommy sock," Mommy was fashioning a sock on Kathryn's foot out of toilet paper to entertain her as she sat on the toilet seat. The two utterances were the same, but the interpretation of their meaning from the contexts in which they were said revealed different structural relations between the constituents "Mommy" and "sock" in the two instances.

The systematic use of context was an insight 'whose time had come.' Moreover, once the door to context was opened, researchers soon discovered not only that context was a resource for studying the semantics of child speech but also that one could study what the child was learning about the pragmatics of language use.[57] Thus, the first point made about context and child language was methodological: Context could be a systematic resource for linguistic analysis.

The second point made about context and child language in *Form and Function in Emerging Grammars* was conceptual. Not only is context useful to the adult who is studying the child, but it also is crucial to the child learning the language:

The importance of the child's awareness and cognizance of nonlinguistic experience in relation to language in [the] environment, in the course of development, should not be underestimated. . . . children learn to identify certain grammatical relationships and syntactic structures with the environmental and behavioral contexts in which they are perceived and then progress to reproducing approximations of heard structures in similar, recurring contexts. In order to use a structure in a new situation, the child must be able to perceive critical aspects of the context of the situation. Thus, the sequence in which syntactic structures are learned by the child may be influenced as much by [the] ability to differentiate aspects of situational context and recognize recurrent contexts as by such factors as frequency of exposure to structures or their relative complexity.[58]

This idea has since been made increasingly explicit in other research. For example, Dan Slobin proposed that certain scenes "regularly occur as part of [the child's] frequent and salient activities and perceptions, and thereby become the organizing points for later [acquisition of the forms of language]." He cited, in particular, what he called the "prototypical" "manipulative activity scene" that leads children to acquire transitive sentences.[59] However, children learn other sentence frames in addition to transitive action sentences in this period of time, especially for intransitive action verbs, transitive and intransitive verbs with locative arguments, and state verbs (Chapters 2 and 3). They learn these in the context of other kinds of 'scenes' so that action scenes for transitive sentences are not necessarily privileged or 'prototypical.' Richard Beckwith showed that the sentence types children heard their mothers use – indexed with the situational contexts in which they were said – predicted the sentence alternations the children subsequently learned.[60] In short, the speech the child hears is optimal for language learning when it relates to what else the child is attending to at the same time.[61] However, what the child attends to in the situation is determined by developments in perception and cognition.

Cognition and Child Language

It does little good to hear sentences spoken in relation to events if these events are not themselves recognized and understood. Linguistic and nonlinguistic inputs are data for a child only when their appraisal is within the child's perceptual and cognitive abilities. The second fallout from introducing meaning into the study of syntax acquisition is this question of how developments in other aspects of cognition contribute to learning language. Young children express a small core of meanings, and some of these are expressed more frequently than others are. Moreover, certain meanings in the adult language occur infrequently or not at all in early child sentences, for example, comparative constructions, conditionals, identity ("Mommy *lady*"), and the instrumental role of an object in an action ("cut *knife*"). The fact that some relations are infrequent, others are frequent, and some do not occur at all means that the semantic relations expressed in early sentences are not simply a random sampling of the possible meanings the language can express. Rather, children select from the meanings available in the speech they hear only those that fall within their cognitive understanding.

Again, this idea is not new. The relationship between thought and language has been debated through the centuries. The linguist Edward Sapir proposed in 1921 that a "speech element [such as the word *house*] is the symbol first and foremost . . . of a 'concept', in other words, of a *convenient capsule of thought that embraces thousands of distinct experiences and that is ready to take in thousands more*."[62] But students of child language had rarely gone beyond words and sentences to ask how acquiring concepts relates to acquiring language.[63] Even Piaget's *The Language and Thought of the Child* is really a study of egocentric thought and has little to say about language or its development.[64]

The inquiry into cognitive developments and language in the last two decades of child language research has had, by and large, two aims. One is the focus on the child's knowledge base and one or another version of the traditional child language 'mapping problem': how children attach the forms of language to what they know about objects, events, and relations in the world.[65] The importance for language of object concepts and knowledge of events is, by now, virtually self-evident. Most simply, children learn to talk about what they know at least something about. The second cognitive focus in child language research is on development of the capacities and processes of thought that make possible the acquisition of concepts, event knowledge, and language itself.[66] These processes include the development of a symbolic capacity and such Piagetian constructs as object permanence, means–end relations, and operational thought. They also include developments in memory, recall, computational capacity, and automaticity.[67]

We have, then, two cognitive perspectives in child language research. One focuses on acquiring knowledge in general and knowledge of the correspondence between language forms and meaning in particular. The other focuses on the development of the capacities and processes of thought needed to acquire this knowledge. The consequence is that we now have some idea of how cognitive developments contribute to the acquisition of words and the forms of language in the period from 1 to 3 years of age.

At issue, however, is how language originates in the brain. This issue was placed in sharp focus by the historic debate between Jean Piaget and his followers, and Noam Chomsky and his followers, at the Abbaye de Royaumont near Paris in 1975.[68] The question was whether language is a separate cognitive faculty apart from other aspects of cognition and innately specified, as Chomsky argued, or one part of general cognition and attributable to learning and cognitive principles, as Piaget argued. When the dust had settled, both parties of the debate claimed victory. At the least, each had presented the clearest statement so far of their separate views. Jerry Fodor, one of the participants in the Chomsky camp at the debate, subsequently extended the argument that language is represented separately in the brain, and 'modularity of mind' has been picked up and extended in both psychology and linguistics.[69] In contrast, since Piaget's death in 1980, his views have been represented with considerably less force in studies of language and acquisition.

These two positions on language and mind continue to influence research and theory today. The difference between them comes down to what determines cognitive development: how children learn to think, with an emphasis on process, or what their thinking is about, with an emphasis on content. The emphasis in the modularity position is on content. Cognition encompasses developments specific to separate content domains such as language, as in learnability-theoretic research, but also to such domains as object perception,[70] mathematics,[71] and biology.[72] These content domains are separate because each has its own domain-specific constraints and principles of learning.

Piaget's influence is more apparent in research in the developmental tradition, with its emphasis on general principles of learning and organismic change. In this view, developments in different domains can be related to one another because they depend on and derive from the same developments in underlying thought. This is true, for example, in the case of learning words and play with objects in the single-word period. Both depend on learning about objects in general and learning concepts for particular objects.[73] Further, what is learned in one domain can inform what is learned in another. Learning the semantic relations actor–action and action–affected-object and the constituents subject–verb–object in simple sentences depends on knowing the corresponding roles and relationships in action events.[74] In addition, in the domain of language, developments in subdomains inform one another for acquisition. How and what children learn of the structure of sentences depend on their lexical learning and participation in discourse exchanges with other persons. Semantics, syntax, and discourse are not separate for children learning language. Rather, they learn these aspects of language together, from the beginning. For these reasons, the studies in this book have an integrative perspective and address the contact among semantics, syntax, and discourse in the course of acquisition.

The difference between an integrative, cognitive perspective and a strictly linguistic perspective on explanation in acquisition research can be illustrated with the following example: Children's early sentences very often lack sentence-subjects, and they say such null subject sentences as "read book," "ride train," and "no fit." Even after they begin to say sentences with subjects, like "man making muffins" and "this no fits," null subject sentences continue to occur. Why? One linguistic explanation comes from the theory of parameter setting.[75] In Chomsky's government and binding theory, whether or not sentences have subjects is a "parameter" of universal grammar that is "set" differently in different languages. The parameters in universal grammar have a range of values; in this case, subjects are required or not, and these are the two values of the *pro-drop* parameter. Italian is a language that does not have to have sentence-subjects; they are optional. English, in contrast, is a language in which sentence-subjects are obligatory, which is why children's null subject sentences attract attention. The linguistic explanation, according to Nina Hyams and others, is that young children learning English have not yet gotten the information they need from the input language for setting or resetting the pro-drop parameter. They do not yet know that subjects are required, and so they act as children do who are learning Italian. This explanation is a strictly linguistic one, based as it is on an innate principle of universal grammar in government and binding theory.[76]

An alternative explanation of why null subject sentences occur in early child speech (in Chapter 3) draws on the cognitive processing requirements for language learning. What young children know about the structure of sentences can underdetermine what they actually say because of general constraints on cognitive functioning. In *Form and Function in Emerging Grammars,* I suggested that children have a fuller understanding of the constituent structure of sentences than is actually realized in the sentences they say. Others have since made the same observation.[77] When children show they have knowledge of constituent relations and argument structures by producing these in separate sentences – for example "Daddy read," "ride car," and "Mommy pigtail" – then one can attribute to the child the knowledge for fuller sentences – for example, "Mommy make pigtail" or "Daddy read book."[78]

However, the demands on the young child's cognitive resources include recalling words from the lexicon, responding to something someone else says in discourse, or adding syntactic complexity (like "Daddy read *airplane* book" and "Mommy *no* make pigtail." Complexity, lexical, and discourse requirements compete with one another for the child's limited resources. This means that recalling words that are newly learned and less automatic than known words, or adding negation or attribution to a sentence, 'cost' the child, and so something has to give. Thus, negative sentences are shorter than affirmative sentences and lack sentence subjects initially, because negation in a sentence 'costs' the child extra cognitive effort (see Chapters 3 and 4). These cognitive requirements are more systematic in their effects than are the performance factors that Chomsky described, such as fatigue, distractions, and shifts in attention and interest.[79]

The study reported in Chapter 3 reveals which factors competed for the young child's limited resources to reduce sentence length and also which factors facilitated and increased the probability that longer sentences would occur. For instance, the children were more likely to construct longer sentences with verbs that were relatively well known and when part of the sentence had already appeared in the discourse. Null subjects are also a function of semantic role and verb category, which we shall discuss in regard to the centrality of verbs in children's early grammars. In sum, some sort of probability model captures the likelihood that child sentences will be complete. Children omit the subject (or some other sentence part) when their cognitive processing abilities are exceeded, for example, when they use new verbs, nouns, or pronouns or add negation or attribution to the sentence.

The two explanations of subjectless sentences – the cognitive-load hypothesis and the parameter-setting hypothesis – independently converge on a particular feature of language acquisition. Certain kinds of added complexity like negation and two-part verbs reduced sentence length, but one sort of complexity that did not reduce the children's sentences was verb inflection (Chapter 3). The children were not more nor less likely to lexicalize subjects when the verb was inflected. In the linguistic explanation motivated by principles of universal grammar and the pro-drop parameter, Hyams observed that children learn the adult setting for the pro-drop parameter (that subjects in English are obligatory) at about the time they begin to use verb inflection and auxiliaries.[80] Other evidence has since shown that children discover the obligatory subject requirement when they have learned the distinction between tensed and untensed verbs.[81] These findings underscore the close connection between sentence-subjects and verb inflection, a connection that is endogenous in the language and less vulnerable to the more general cognitive processing constraints.

Individual Differences

Children do not progress at the same rate, as is well known, but they also do not progress in their language learning in the same way. Such differences among children from the same social group, learning the same language, were first described in *Form and Function in Emerging Grammars*. The distinction among the children was in whether they initially lexicalized the arguments of verbs as nouns or pronouns. This difference in individual learning was likened to the basic analytic–synthetic distinction among languages in general (see Chapter 2). Synthetic languages like Russian and Finnish mark contrastive meanings or functions by adding affixes to noun and verb stems, much as Eric and Peter in these studies added pronouns like *it, there,* and *this* to their verbs. Analytic languages like English combine lexical items for contrastive meaning, much as Kathryn and Gia learned to combine categories of nouns with verbs. The nominal–pronominal difference has since been replicated in other studies and characterized in terms of analytic and holistic strategies for language learning.[82]

The nominal–pronominal difference is similar to other differences observed subsequently among the children in that it had to do with the form of their speech. Differences were not observed among them in aspects of language content. For example, the children also differed in the sequence in which they learned the different syntactic connectives after *and* (*because, so, when,* and the like), but not in the sequence in which they learned the meaning relations between clauses in complex sentences (Chapter 7). They also differed in the order of clauses that express causality: effect–cause or cause–effect (Chapter 10), but not in the meanings of causality (Chapters 10 and 11). Furthermore, the differences among them in acquisition of form are also differences in the target language. Adult speech shows shifting pronominal–nominal reference, and both effect–cause and cause–effect orders are used in expressions of causality with different connectives (*because* and *so,* respectively).

This raises the question of variation in the input that different children receive. We have come to recognize that the input to children learning language provides a number of options and that these can lead to more or less important differences among them. We do not know the extent to which differences among children may really be differences in the way their caregivers talked to them. We also do not know whether they are differences that make a difference, that is, differences that are important to understanding language learning. These are questions for further research, but such research presents a variety of problems, as discussed by Elizabeth Bates and her colleagues.[83]

The Centrality of Verbs

A theme repeated throughout these studies is that verbs are central to learning grammar and discourse. In *Form and Function in Emerging Grammars,* I pointed out that nouns predominate in presyntactic speech and that children begin to acquire syntax by selecting the verbs, prepositions, and adjectives that combine with the nouns they already know. Because there are no inflections, they cannot be used formally to mark grammatical categories. I suggested that early grammatical categories are marked instead by the selection of verbs, prepositions, and adjectives in ordered relationships with nouns. "The grammatical categories in early child language are selectional rather than inflected. They can only be marked by patterns of order and selection so that membership in categories cannot be reliably determined until lexical items occur in syntactic constructions."[84] This use of "patterns of order and selection" was consistent with standard theory in which grammatical relations are determined by context-sensitive subcategorization rules that define "a *selectional relation* between two positions in a sentence – for example . . . the position of the Verb and that of the immediately preceding and immediately following Noun."[85]

In the later studies, much of what these children learned about grammar and how they learned to participate in discourse were determined by the verbs they learned. In standard theory, the syntactic component of a grammar articulated with actual words in the lexicon through lexical rules that operated only after the syntax of the base structure of a sentence was derived. However, the developmental data repeatedly pointed to the conclusion that children discover the syntax of sentences by learning the verbs in the language. Since that time, and independently of the acquisition data, the contribution from verbs in the lexicon to the syntax of sentences has become increasingly prominent in linguistic theory.[86]

The two 1975 papers (Chapters 2 and 3) were studies of the acquisition of argument structure and underscored the importance of verbs for acquisition. The terminology we used then is different from terms used now, and I will make the connections to current research and theory here. We proposed that the children learned semantic categories of verbs that determined the argument structures and configurations in their sentences. A major distinction in those studies was between verbs that do and do not take locative arguments, the difference between what we called *action* and *locative-action* verbs. In the first study (Chapter 2) we pointed out that when the goal of movement was a change in place of the affected-object, the verb was a locative one. Verbs like *go* and *put* are locative-action verbs that license place as an argument, for example, "go *home*" and "put it *there*." In contrast, when objects were affected by a movement that did not have change of place as a goal, the verb was a simple action, nonlocative verb. When place occurred with action verbs like *eat* and *read*, it was a sentence adjunct (what we called action and place) and not an argument of the verb, for example, "eat *in the kitchen*." Although some of the children's early sentences with action verbs included locative adjuncts (for example, "orange chair read a book"), they were rare. The occurrence of place as an argument of locative verbs was far more frequent.

The acquisition of subcategories of locative verbs that determined different argument structures and sentence configurations was described in subsequent research (Chapter 3). Constituent meaning relations were different with action and locative verbs and with different locative verbs. The semantic role of the sentence-subject was as agent with transitive-action verbs and locative verbs such as *put;* patient with locative verbs such as *go* and *fit* that did not license an agent argument (for example, *"car* goes here" as the child puts the car on the train); and mover with verbs that named an action in which the object that changed location was also the cause of the action (for example, *"Mommy* go store"). Thus, sentences differed according to the syntactic placement of the noun or pronoun that lexicalized the object affected by the movement toward a goal. The affected-object followed locative verbs that took an agent (*put*) but occurred before verbs that did not take an agent (*go* and *fit*). Moreover, verb alternations occurred when the same verb appeared in two different categories with different argument structures. For example, the locative verb *fit* occurred in both transitive ("fit the piece in the puzzle") and unaccusative intransitive ("the piece fits here") alternations.

The semantic roles and relations we identified in the children's sentences are consistent with thematic relations in interpretive semantics[87] and more recent linguistic theories.[88] The notion of thematic relations, introduced originally by Gruber and developed by Jackendoff, has led most recently to work in linguistics having to do with lexical semantics. An integrative survey of this work with a focus on semantic categories of verbs in lexical knowledge has been provided by Beth Levin.[89] In her account, lexical knowledge includes semantic categories defined according to the argument structures they share and the realization of those arguments in the syntactic structure of sentences. Argument structure is determined by the semantics of the verb and its 'affectedness' on entities. For example, an object that changes position is the 'theme' with verbs like *slide;* an object that changes state is the patient with verbs like *cut.* Our description of children's early verb categories and the role of those verb categories in their syntax acquisition anticipated the structural outline of adult lexical knowledge that Levin described, as well as recent learnability-theoretic research on argument structure.[90]

In addition to the configuration data, the evidence for early verb categories included the relative frequency of constituents in the children's speech (Chapter 3). These data were the result of analyses to determine which factors contributed to the lexicalization of constituents and the relative length and completeness of sentences. The most frequently lexicalized constituent was the verb. The second most frequently lexicalized constituent in the children's sentence was the object affected by the movement named by the verb ('affected-object,' or 'theme'). Further evidence of the reality of the children's verb categories was the finding that null subjects were not independent of thematic role and verb category (in addition to the effects of cognitive load already discussed). The probability that a subject would be lexicalized was greatest when it was the affected-object that changed place (with a locative verb). Thus, the sentence-subject was most likely to occur when it was the theme of a locative verb: either the patient with verbs that did not license an agent – for example, *"car* go here," *"this* fits here" – or mover that was both agent and affected-object – for example, *"Mommy* go store."

An alternative explanation is that locative sentences with patient and mover subjects have shorter predicates and, therefore, less cognitive weight than do locative sentences with *put,* which include both object and place in the predicate.[91] However, predicate length with simple (nonlocative) action verbs was the same as predicate length with patient and mover locative verbs, but agent subjects of action verbs were more likely to be null than were patient and mover subjects of locative verbs.

In addition to predicting argument structures and lexicalized subjects, these categories of verbs in the children's sentences also predicted verb inflection (Chapter 5). Verb inflection was not independent of the semantics of verbs: whether (1) relevant movement occurred (the action/state distinction), (2) the goal of movement was a change in place (the action/locative-action distinction), and/or (3) the object that changed place was also the agent of the movement (the distinction among mover, patient, and agent with locative verbs). For example, more inflections occurred with action verbs than with verbs in the other categories, but given how often sentences with action verbs occurred, the proportion of inflections with action verbs was less than predicted. In contrast, the proportion of inflections with patient–locative verbs was greater than was predicted by the relative frequency of sentences in that category. At the level of the particular inflections, *-s* was learned originally with patient–locative verbs, whereas *-ing* and irregular past were learned originally with action verbs.

These semantic categories of verbs also predicted the complex sentences that the children learned. The three complex sentence structures learned with syntactic connectives in this developmental period were conjunction > complementation > relativization, in that sequence. Each of these developed with essentially different populations of verbs. Conjunction occurred overwhelmingly with action and locative verbs; relativization was acquired with the copula; and complementation occurred overwhelmingly with state verbs, with semantic subcategories of state verbs acquired sequentially (Chapters 8 and 9).

Finally, the children learned to participate in discourse by building on the verb in a prior utterance (Chapter 13). The major development in discourse was the increase in contingent messages that shared the topic of a prior utterance with added information. This increase in contingency was characterized primarily by expansions, in which the verb of the prior utterance was repeated and something was added to it: Either major sentence constituents (SVO) were added or modified, or a *wh*-form was replaced by a word or a phrase.

Thus, the verbs in the language were central to how these children acquired grammar and learned to participate in discourse. Different categories of verbs determined differences in argument structure, sentence configurations, and verb inflection in simple sentences and the different structures and connectives in complex sentences. The results of these studies, taken together, led to the following conclusions:

Lexical verb development and grammatical development appear to be mutually dependent, with the result that the child's verb lexicon is not simply part of a mental dictionary with all the words that a child knows, including nouns. Rather, the results of the studies described here suggest that the verb system in child language may consist of a categorization of verbs on several levels of rules of grammar, with a network of attachments to a noun lexicon. . . . and children's knowledge of language structure [is] probably never independent from the different verbs that they know.

The categorization of verbs that has emerged from our studies includes large, molar categories – action/state; locative/nonlocative; durative/nondurative; completive/noncompletive; volitional/epistemic/notice/communication states, etc. The claim for the psychological and linguistic reality of these semantic categories rests on their being coextensive with major grammatical developments in the children's language or on their sequential development. There has been no evidence that more molecular semantic categories – such as verbs of locomotion (*run, walk, skip, fly*, etc.) or verbs of ingestion (*eat, drink, swallow, slurp, chew*, etc.) – have the same psycholinguistic status in these children's early language learning. Such potential molecular categories appear to be represented in the early speech data by only one or a few instances (e.g., *eat* for the larger category of ingestion; *ride* and *run* for the larger category of locomotion; and *say* and *tell* for the larger category of communication, etc.). Thus, . . . the children had learned the relevant linguistic form or structure with a few verb exemplars and the high-frequency pro-verbs, such as *do* and *go,* which they used generally, as they learned a wider range of more semantically specific verbs. Knowing the structure, the children then would be able to fill in and expand the verb categories to form more molecular categories.[92]

The children's early verb categories included a variety of verbs, but in fact, only a few verbs occurred frequently, the all-purpose verbs that we called *pro-verbs*[93] because of their functional similarity to pronouns. They were primarily the action verb *do* and the locative verb *go,* and they occurred in place of a great many other, more descriptive verbs like *chew* and *drive* that the children had presumably not learned as yet. In sum, the children whom we studied acquired syntax by learning a small number of semantic verb categories. These categories consisted of the highly frequent, all-purpose pro-verbs and a few exemplars of more semantically specific, descriptive verbs. Having learned the verb categories and the structures they determine, the children could learn new descriptive verbs that meet the semantic and syntactic conditions in each category.

This account is consistent, in part, with the theory of "syntactic bootstrapping" proposed by Barbara Landau and Lila Gleitman, whereby children use their syntactic parsing of input sentences for learning the meaning of individual verbs.[94] Once children know how to parse sentences into constituents, they can use this syntactic knowledge to learn the argument structures for other verbs that have the same thematic roles and constituent relations. But do they learn how to parse sentences, or do they already have this ability to begin with? According to Landau and Gleitman, a syntactic parser is part of the linguistic endowment that the child brings to acquiring a language. Our view is that children use their knowledge of the syntax of simple sentences to learn more and different verbs but that knowledge of the constituent structure of simple sentences is learned. Constituent structure is learned originally in the context of acquiring verb categories with a small number of general, all-purpose pro-verbs like *do* and *go* and a few descriptive verbs. Having learned something of the argument structures, verb inflections, *wh*-questions, and complex sentences that the verb categories determine, a child can learn other verbs that are more descrip tive in their meanings (verbs like *chew, jump,* and *drive*) with the same syntactic privileges in these categories.

SUMMARY

The purpose of this introductory chapter was to provide a context for the studies described in the volume. We have seen, in particular, how this research project originated in the developmental perspective in child language, with its explicit focus on the child. Several conceptual themes emerged: meaning in child language, the relevance of other developments in cognition, the importance of context, and the existence of individual differences in acquiring aspects of form, if not content. Most important, however, is that the results of these studies have repeatedly pointed to the centrality of verbs in language learning. Each of these themes will surface again in the chapters that follow.

NOTES

1 Bloom, L. (1970). *Language development: Form and function in emerging grammars.* Cambridge, MA: MIT Press. This was originally my Ph.D. dissertation, 1968, Columbia University.

2 These procedures are described in greater detail in Chapter 2 and in Bloom, *Form and function in emerging grammars* (pp. 234–9). See also, Conventions for transcription of child language recordings, app. A, in Bloom & Lahey (1978). In order to avoid redundancy, descriptions of the procedures used to collect and transcribe the data have been omitted or abbreviated after Chapter 2. The speech samples from Eric, Gia, and Kathryn (and a fourth child, Jane) were collected and transcribed by Lois Bloom. The speech samples from Peter were collected and transcribed by Lois Hood and Patsy Lightbown, who took turns interacting with Peter and taking notes on the situational context and behavior. The data from David, Mariana, Paul, and Steven were collected and transcribed primarily by Lois Hood. The transcriptions from Eric, Gia, Kathryn, and Peter are stored in two places and can be made available to other researchers. One is the Special Collections at the Milbank Memorial Library, Teachers College, Columbia University, and the other is the Child Language Data Exchange System at Carnegie-Mellon University (thus far, only the transcripts from Peter are part of the computerized corpora in the CHILDES database.)

3 The citations included in these postscripts are not meant to be exhaustive, and I regret that important studies were undoubtedly missed.

4 Werner (1948) and Piaget's 'infant books,' for example, Piaget (1937/1954), and (1947/1960).

5 Danto (1983); Taylor (1979).

6 See, for example, the papers in Pylshyn & Demopoulos (1986).

7 See, for example, Fauconnier (1985).

8 Jespersen (1964); Bresnan (1970).

9 Examples from Kathryn in Bloom (1970).

10 This characterization was suggested to me by Richard Beckwith.

11 Chomsky (1965).

12 Labov (1969); Sankoff (1974).

13 I have addressed procedural issues in language acquisition research in several places, for example, Bloom (1974a), Bloom, (in press b) and Bloom & Lahey (1978).

14 The research from this longitudinal study is reported elsewhere, for example, in Beckwith (1988); Bloom & Beckwith (1989); Bloom, Beckwith, Capatides, & Hafitz (1988); and Lifter & Bloom (1989).

15 Wexler & Culicover (1980).

16 Bresnan (1978); Bresnan & Kaplan (1982); and Pinker (1984).

17 Chomsky (1982); Hyams (1986).

18 The canonical citation for the origins of learnability research is Gold (1967). An excellent history can be found in Morgan (1986).

19 As offered originally by Chomsky (1965) and echoed more recently by, for example, Jackendoff (1987).

20 Arguments against the 'little linguist' analogy have been made by others, for example, Braine (1971b); Hyams (1986); and White (1981).

21 Freeman (1989).

22 Examples of how the data and results of the developmental studies in this book have been used to 'test' learnability theories can be found in Hyams' (1986) use of the simple sentences data in Chapter 2 to argue for her theory of pro-drop in early sentences, and Pinker's (1984) use of the results of the study of *to* complements in Chapter 8 to argue how children might learn lexical functionalist grammar.

23 See, for example, Beckwith (1988); Leonard (1989); and papers in MacWhinney (1987).

24 Schieffelin (1979, 1990); Ochs (1988); Ochs & Schieffelin (1983).

25 Schieffelin & Ochs (1986).

26 Schieffelin & Ochs (1983).

27 The validity and generalizability of such studies depend on the extent to which the results are replicated by other researchers studying other children, from the same and different cultural contexts. Subsequent studies that addressed similar questions with other populations of children are reported in the Postscript to each of the chapters.

28 MacMurray (1957); Piaget (1937/1954). For discussion of this fundamental point in developmental theory, see, for example, Lerner (1986).

29 Pepper (1942).

30 Reese & Overton (1970).

31 Braine (1963); Brown & Fraser (1963, 1964); Miller & Ervin (1964).
32 Harris (1957); Chomsky (1957).
33 Chomsky (1965, 1968).
34 Chomsky (1957, p. 106).
35 See, for example, Bloomfield (1933).
36 Schlesinger (1971b).
37 Brown (1973).
38 Grimshaw (1981); Pinker (1984).
39 Fillmore (1968); Bowerman (1973a).
40 Schlesinger (1971a).
41 See, for example, Gleitman, Gleitman, Landau, & Wanner (1988); Hyams (1986); Landau & Gleitman (1985); Pinker (1984); and Valian (1986).
42 Bowerman (1987).
43 Piaget (1936/1952); Piaget (1951/1962).
44 Bloom (1973).
45 Jackendoff (1983, p. 188), citing Gruber (1965).
46 In fact, Beckwith (1988) successfully used Jackendoff's categories in a simulation study that showed how children learn argument structure from the linguistic input provided by their mothers.
47 Brown (1973).
48 Howe (1976). For a rebuttal, see Bloom, Capatides, & Tackeff (1981) and Golinkoff (1981).
49 For example, Bloom (1970); Bowerman (1973a); Brown (1973); Leonard (1976); and Schlesinger (1971a).
50 Bloom, Beckwith, Capatides, & Hafitz (1988). The theoretical rationale for this practice is discussed in Bloom (in press a).
51 Fauconnier (1985).
52 Brown & Bellugi (1964).
53 Leopold (1939–1949, vol. 3, p. 31).
54 de Laguna (1927/1963, p. 267).
55 Example from Gia, in Bloom (1970).
56 Bloom (1970, p. 10).
57 In particular, see Bates (1976), Dore (1975), and Ervin-Tripp (1970).
58 Bloom (1970, p. 233).
59 Slobin (1985, p. 1175). Slobin cited Fillmore's (1977) use of scenes in regard to meaning in adult language.
60 In Beckwith (1988).
61 For demonstrations of this on the level of word learning, see, for example, Masur (1982) and Tomasello & Farrar (1986).
62 Sapir (1921, p. 13, emphasis added).
63 Exceptions include earlier work by Roger Brown, for example, (1956) and (1958).
64 Piaget (1923/1926).

65 See for example, Bloom (1970, 1973); Gopnik & Meltzoff (1987); Mervis (1984); Nelson (1974, 1985); and many others.

66 See, for example, Bates (1976); Bloom (1973); Bloom, Lifter, & Broughton (1985); Brown (1973); Gopnik & Meltzoff (1984); Kelly & Dale (1989); Lifter & Bloom (1989); McCuhn-Nicolich (1981); Tomasello & Farrar (1984); and others.

67 Case (1978, 1985); Pascual-Leone (1987).

68 Piattelli-Palmarini (1980).

69 Fodor (1983); Gardner (1983).

70 For example, Spelke (1987).

71 For example, Gelman & Meck (1987).

72 Carey (1985).

73 Bates, Benigni, Bretherton, Camaioni, & Volterra (1979); Lifter & Bloom (1989).

74 A related assumption is captured by "semantic bootstrapping" in learnability research.

75 Hyams (1986).

76 I cannot do justice here to the full logic of the theory, and I refer the reader to Hyams (1986) for a thorough and readable account.

77 For example, Pinker (1984).

78 We are talking here about sentences that are neither imperative (in which subject omission is the rule) nor reduced by elision to avoid redundancy in discourse contexts.

79 Chomksy (1965, p. 3).

80 The two studies are not independent, as Hyams (1986) used the data in Bloom (1970) and Bloom, Lightbown, & Hood (1975; Chapter 2) for testing her acquisition theory. However, she also cited consistent data from other research projects.

81 O'Grady, Peters, & Masterson (1989).

82 Bates, Bretherton, & Snyder (1988); Nelson (1975b); Peters (1977); Ramer (1976).

83 Bates, Bretherton, & Snyder (1988).

84 Bloom (1970, p. 29).

85 Chomsky (1965, p. 113).

86 See especially J. Bresnan (1978); Bresnan & Kaplan (1982); and Chomsky (1982).

87 Jackendoff (1972). For the source of "the fundamental semantic notion . . . [of] *Theme* of a sentence" (p. 29), Jackendoff cites Gruber (1965).

88 Especially our identification of affected-object and (1) the notion of grammatical theme as "that argument which undergoes the motion or change in state denoted in the predicate," Bresnan (1982, p. 24); and (2) the macrorole *undergoer* in Foley & Van Valin (1984).

89 Levin (1985).

90 Bowerman (1987); Pinker (1984, 1989).
91 This is essentially the explanation put forth by P. Bloom (1990) to account for 'subjectless' sentences.
92 Bloom (1981 p. 169).
93 Called "general purpose verbs" by Clark (1978). Clark pointed out the communicative function such verbs share with the heavily used deictic terms *this* and *that* to talk about actions and objects for which children have not yet learned more different words.
94 Gleitman, Gleitman, Landau, & Wanner (1988); Landau and Gleitman (1985).

POSTSCRIPT

The Postscripts at the end of each chapter refer to later works that cited the research in the chapter or were otherwise relevant to it.

The following references cited a few or more of the studies in this book in a survey of the field.

Anisfeld, M. (1984). *Language development from birth to three*. Hillsdale, NJ: Erlbaum.

de Villiers, J., & de Villiers, P. (1985). The acquisition of English. In D. Slobin (Ed.), *The crosslinguistic study of language acquisition* (vol. 1, pp. 27–140). Hillsdale, NJ: Erlbaum.

Gleason, J. (Ed.) (1985). *Language development*. Westerville, OH: Merrill.

Ingram, D. (1989). *Language development*. Cambridge: Cambridge University Press.

Kuczaj, S. (1982). On the nature of syntactic development. In S. Kuczaj (Ed.), *Language development: Vol. 1. Syntax and semantics* (pp. 37–72). Hillsdale, NJ: Erlbaum.

Maratsos, M. (1983). Some current issues in the study of the acquisition of grammar. In J. Flavell & E. Markman (Eds.), P. Mussen (Series Ed.), *Handbook of child psychology: Vol. 3. Cognitive development* (pp. 707–86). New York: Wiley.

In addition, the results of this research have been used in assessment and intervention programs for children with delayed language development and language disorders.

Bloom, L., & Lahey, M. (1978). *Language development and language disorders*. New York: Wiley.

Lahey, M. (1988). *Language disorders and development*. New York: Macmillan.

Part I

Acquisition of Simple Sentences

As children begin to tap into the verb system of adult language, they learn the structures and alternations that are determined by categories of verbs in the language. The meaning and form of simple sentences in these studies were determined largely by the verbs the children were learning. The acquisition of categories of verbs proved to be the foundation for their acquisition of grammar. The first two chapters in this section are studies of the verb categories the children learned and how those categories determined the structure of their sentences. Their simple sentences became more complex as they learned negation, verb inflections, and how to ask questions, and these are addressed in the remaining chapters in this section.

2

Categories of Verbs and Simple Sentences

"Open de buttons."
"This go there."
"I hear childrens!"

Children begin to put words together tentatively, often beginning by combining words they had already learned to say singly. For example, "more" and "juice" become "more juice." Certain meaning relations between words in the earliest two- and three-word sentences come from the meaning of particular words, for example, sentences with *more* mean recurrence, and sentences with *no* mean nonexistence. Children also begin to repeat certain phrases they've heard often, like "go bye-bye," "all gone," and "fix it," as 'large words' rather than true combinations. But the word combinations that soon come to predominate are the result of combining nouns the child already knows with new words, primarily verbs and prepositions, and combining verbs with pronouns. In this study, "verb relations were of central importance in the children's language learning" (p. 43). The period of development covered here began with the earliest word combinations and continued until mean length of utterance was approximately 2.5 morphemes. The purpose of the monograph was represented in its title: to determine the structure of early sentences and possible variation in acquisition among the children.

THE STRUCTURE OF EARLY SENTENCES

A major issue addressed with these data was whether the children's sentences could be described in syntactic as well as semantic terms. The conclusion that I reached in *Form and Function in Emerging Grammars* was that children are learning grammar once verbs are productive in their speech. This claim was challenged by those who proposed, instead, that the structure of early sentences was only semantic.[1] The argument presented here for early syntax was based on the assumption that "the existence of a structure in child language needs to be justified by a test of the child language data and not by tests that apply to adult speech data. The critical issue is whether there is a syntactic structure – a system of rules for combining words – in the children's speech, and not whether one can identify adult syntax in child sentences" (pp. 168–

9). The tests applied to the data included tests of distribution and relative frequency to determine what the children were in the process of learning. These yielded child categories that were continuous with later syntax, but the categories we identified were not yet the categories of adult grammar.

The children were similar to one another in the developmental sequence of semantic–syntactic regularities and categories of verb relations. The three principal categories of verbs were action ("Open de buttons"), state ("I hear childrens!"), and locative ("This go there"). Sentences with action verbs appeared before sentences with state verbs for all four children. Locative sentences appeared later than did nonlocative sentences for two children and at the same time for the other two. Other, separate semantic relations were possession, attribution, recurrence, negation, dative, and instrumental relations. With development, these separate relations eventually appeared in verb arguments or were otherwise subordinated to the argument structure of sentences.

VARIATION AMONG THE CHILDREN

The variation among the children was in the lexical realization of the arguments of verbs. For two of them, Eric and Peter, the early development of syntax was characterized by a synthetic, *pronominal* strategy; they started out using pronominal forms in their early sentences (*"This* go *there"*). In contrast, Gia and Kathryn used an analytic, *categorization* strategy with categories of nominal forms having different grammatical functions in relation to the verb categories ("Open de *buttons"*). For all the children, the semantics of their sentences was the same; they talked about the same kinds of things and in the same sequence in the course of development. But they did not use the same linguistic means for expression: Two children used pronouns to refer to persons and objects in verb relations most often, and the other two used categories of nominative forms relative to verbs most often.

With development, each child proceeded to learn the other system. They thereby acquired the capacity for switching pronominal and nominal reference so that they could learn how to mark the situational and interpersonal contingencies that shift in discourse. By the time mean length of utterance reached 2.5 morphemes, the four children were no longer different. Regardless of how they started out, sentence-subjects (agents and actors) were primarily pronominal, and predicate objects (affected-objects) were primarily nominal. The strategy differences among the children have since been replicated in other studies, which are listed in the Postscript at the end of this chapter. The importance of verbs for syntax acquisition discussed in Chapter I surfaces repeatedly in the chapters that follow.

Structure and Variation in Child Language

Lois Bloom, Patsy Lightbown, and Lois Hood

INTRODUCTION

Research in child language to date has resulted in a consensus about the semantics of early two- and three-word sentences. Studies of children learning English and certain other languages (Bloom, 1970, 1973; Bowerman, 1973a; Brown, 1973; Schlesinger, 1971b; Slobin, 1971a) have revealed that the semantics of early sentences have to do with ideas about objects that originate in the development of sensorimotor intelligence in the child's first 2 years. During this period children learn that objects exist, cease to exist, and recur; that objects can be acted upon and located in space; that people do things to objects or are otherwise associated with objects. It should not be surprising that these are the kinds of things that children first learn to talk about. However, the linguistic means that children learn for the representation of such notions, the sequence of development in child grammar, and the relation of systems of child language to the adult model remain to be determined.

Descriptions of Child Language

Certain claims that have been made thus far for what children learn in order to say sentences have been based upon observed evidence – for example, that children learn relative word position (Braine, 1963) and that children learn semantic distinctions for reference to objects and events (Bloom, 1970; Bowerman, 1973a; Brown, 1973; Schlesinger, 1971b). Other claims for the origin of the child's early linguistic system have been derived from such linguistic theories as generative transformational grammar (e.g., Chomsky, 1965; McNeill, 1966, 1970) and case grammar (e.g., Greenfield & Smith, 1976; Ingram, 1971). There has been an impressive consistency among subjects in different investigations in the use of word order and in the semantics of early sentences. It has also been possible to use one or another linguistic

Reprinted from the Monographs of the Society for Research in Child Development, 1975, serial no. 160, vol. 40, no. 2, with permission from The Society for Research in Child Development.

theory to describe something of both aspects of early child speech. However, it has become increasingly apparent that there is variation in child language as well – variation in the speech of the same child across time as a function of development, as one would expect, but also variation in the speech of different children learning the same language when average utterance length is held constant (Bloom, 1970). The variation among different children is such that in the several longitudinal studies of small numbers of children (usually less than five) in the 1960s, investigators were cautious about pooling the speech data from different children, and results were usually reported for subjects individually.

Two descriptions of early child speech came out of the research in the early 1960s: "pivot grammar" (Braine, 1963) and "telegraphic speech" (Brown & Fraser, 1963). Pivotal utterances were those in which a constant function form such as *more* or *there* was juxtaposed with many different substantive forms, such as *cookie, read,* and *airplane.* Telegraphic utterances contained two or more substantive forms and omitted the linking morphemes (e.g., "Mommy chair"). The two descriptions of early child speech appeared to be contradictory in that function forms were of central importance for defining pivot speech, whereas telegraphic speech was described as consisting only of substantive forms. However, it now appears that these superficial descriptions of early child speech may reflect both the structure of child language and the variation that exists within and among child speakers.

Structure in Child Language

In the present study, speech data from four children were examined in order to discover (1) categories of semantic–syntactic relations between words in the earliest multiword utterances and (2) the lexical representation of sentences in different categories – without attempting to tie the data to one or another theoretical framework. The results that are presented here suggest that the ability to say sentences depends upon learning something of an abstract system of semantic–syntactic structure, a grammar, for representing linguistically what the child already knows about events in the world.

The term *structure* can be defined for child language on three levels according to the results of this study. At the level of the sentence, two or more constituents can be combined so that the meaning of each of the constituents is somehow augmented by their combination, and structure is inferred when that meaning relation is repeated with different constituents and in different situations. Further, structure in the development of a particular child is demonstrated by the predictability of one part of the linguistic system given knowledge of another part – at any one time and in the course of development. Finally, on the most general level, structure in child language is defined by the regularities and consistencies among different children, both at the same time, with mean length of utterance held constant, and in sequential development.

The conclusion that children learn grammatical structure in order to combine two or more words was based upon two kinds of evidence. First, verb relations were of central importance in the children's learning, and the sequence of development of different verb categories was similar for all the children. There were regularities in the ways in which verbs were related to other constituents in sentences, and groups of verbs functioned similarly to one another in their relation to other sentence constituents. For example, one group of verbs (intransitive) was related to animate nouns that specified movers in an action that changed their spatial location (e.g., *go, sit,* etc.), and another group of verbs (transitive) was related to animate nouns that specified agents in an action that affected another object by changing its location (e.g., *put*). The regularity and consistency among utterances with such different verbs as *go, sit, stand up,* and so on, in contrast with other utterances with different verb relations, indicated that the children had made inductions about the possibilities for combining words with similar and different meaning relations between them. Moreover, the fact that the same words (e.g., animate nouns) could function differently in relation to different kinds of verbs (e.g., as agents and movers) was taken as evidence that the children had made higher-order linguistic inductions about superordinate grammatical categories.

Second, there was a systematic variation among the children in the kind of lexical representation in their utterances. Although the speech of all four children was semantically similar – they talked about the same kinds of things and in similar sequence in the course of development – they used either of two alternative strategies for learning syntax in order to represent the same information. The internal consistency in the system used by each child and the predictable development that followed were taken as further evidence that the children's multi-word utterances were derived from underlying rules of grammar.

The description of the emergence of grammar that is presented here is consistent with the view put forth elsewhere (Bloom, 1970, 1973) that children learn language as a means of representing or coding information that they have already acquired about objects, events, and relations in the world. Language development, in this view, follows from and depends upon conceptual development in a logical way – as traditionally argued by Piaget (1954) and Werner and Kaplan (1963) and affirmed more recently by Brown (1973), Schlesinger (1971b), and Slobin (1971a). An extensive argument against the counterclaim that children's linguistic knowledge consists of a set of innate grammatical relations that are there somehow from the beginning to guide and determine linguistic development (as per McNeill, 1970) is presented in Bloom (1973).

The Variation Paradigm

The study of linguistic variation typically has been concerned with describing the effects of linguistic context, or extralinguistic factors that are sociologically or geographically determined, on different aspects of language use (e.g., Bailey, 1973; Labov, 1963, 1969; Sankoff & Cedergren, 1971; and Sankoff & Laberge, 1973). The source of linguistic variation in the child-speech data that have been described so far in the literature (from children of middle-class and generally college-educated parents) is neither cultural nor social. Although it may be environmentally conditioned to the extent that it reflects differences in parent interaction styles (Nelson, 1973), it is more likely that variation in child speech is a function of individual cognitive development in interaction with different aspects of the linguistic code.

Although both the kind of variation to be described here and its conditioning factors are different from those described in studies of sociolinguistic variation (see Sankoff, 1974), the problems are very nearly the same. In both instances it is necessary to observe a large number of behaviors so as to be able to make inferences and to generalize. However, in sociolinguistic studies one generalizes about a particular linguistic community, whereas in child language one makes inferences about the linguistic knowledge of an individual child. Given a large enough sample of observations, it is possible to discover patterns and relationships at one time that can then be compared with observations of the same child at a later time and with observations of other children.

In order to demonstrate the patterns of variability as well as the regularities and consistencies in child speech, it is necessary to collect and process sufficient data to assure that the evidence will be accountable for the resulting descriptions. A single instance of behavior, although interesting in its own right, can assume importance only if it shares certain properties with a large enough portion of all the data. Accordingly, one needs clear evidence, and in sufficient quantity, to allow for meaningful comparisons among behaviors so that similarities and differences can be revealed, both within the language of an individual child and across different children. In presenting the evidence from this study, frequency and proportion measures were used for a taxonomy of semantic–syntactic relations.

SUBJECTS AND PROCEDURES

The subjects of the study – Eric, Gia, Kathryn, and Peter – are first-born children of college-educated parents. They were each visited in their homes at periodic intervals, and their speech was recorded along with descriptions of relevant nonlinguistic context and behavior using the procedures described in Bloom (1970, pp. 234–9). Eric, Gia, and Kathryn were each visited every 6 weeks over several days by Bloom. Peter was visited every 3 weeks by Lightbown and Hood. Figure 2.1 presents a description of the children in terms of mean length of utterance (MLU) (in morphemes); in the time period represented in the present study the children progressed from the period of single-word utterances to mean length of utterance of 2.5 morphemes,[2] and from age 19 months to 26 months. Table 2.1 describes the data base in terms of the numbers of utterances that were processed for each child.

Reliability of Linguistic Interpretation

The recorded observation sessions were transcribed, preserving as much of the information from the original behavioral events as possible. In the analysis to be presented here, a tentative description was made of a portion of the recorded data, and then successively larger and larger portions of the data were examined in order to test the consistency and regularity of the original description. Repeated passes through the recorded data, then, consisted of successive hypothesis testings: As questions were generated, the data were examined in order to answer the questions; the questions were revised; the data reexamined in order

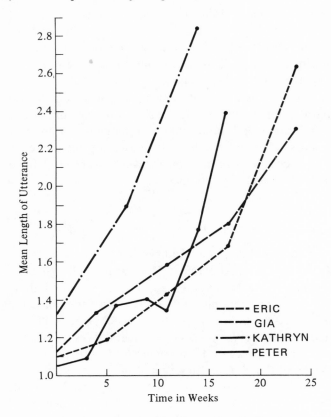

Figure 2.1. Progression of mean length of utterance.

to answer the revised questions; and so on. Bloom (1974a) has discussed the rationale that underlies an analysis in which categories of description are derived from a set of data in this way, in contrast with an analysis that imposes a preconceived scheme for description on data. She pointed out that analysis based on a priori categories of description will necessarily fail to capture important distinctions in the data if distinctions that are present in the data do not correspond to the categories in the preconceived scheme.

Each multiword utterance was examined and the semantic–syntactic relations among words were identified by observing the relationship between the utterance and aspects of the child's behavior and the situational context in which the utterance occurred. Obviously, one cannot be confident that the semantic interpretation given to an utterance by

Table 2.1. *Summary Description of Speech Samples*[a]

Child and Time	Hours	Age (months, weeks)	MLU	Syntactic Utterance Types	Syntactic Utterance Tokens
Eric					
I	4	19,1	1.10	10	16
II	6.7	20,2	1.19	37	48
III	7	22,0	1.42	108	165
IV	8	23,2	1.69	401	504
V	8	25,1	2.63	902	1,056
Gia					
I	7	19,2	1.12	55	100
II	6.7	20,2	1.34	226	341
III	8	22,1	1.58	288	451
IV	8	23,3	1.79	457	671
V	7.5	25,2	2.30	842	1,071
Kathryn[b]					
I	5.5	21,0	1.32	226	284
II	5.5	22,3	1.89	767	896
III	6.7	24,2	2.83	1,443	1,777
Peter					
I	3	21,1	1.04	7	7
II	3.5	21,3.5	1.09	5	7
III	4.5	22,2	1.37	70	150
IV	4.5	23,1	1.41	80	149
V	3	23,2.5	1.33	81	258
VI	4.5	24,1	1.75	243	420
VII	4.5	25,0	2.39	458	643

[a]The total data base consisted of 24,711 spontaneous utterances – both single-word and multiword tokens. Only spontaneous tokens were counted for the present study. See Bloom, Hood, & Lightbown (1974) for comparison of spontaneous and imitative utterances.
[b]The data processed for Kathryn represent only part of the total corpus collected for the longitudinal study and reported in Bloom (1970).

an adult does indeed equal the child's semantic intent. At the least, it is necessary to establish that (1) any utterance can be identified as a separate behavior (from the other linguistic behaviors that occur) by other observers, and (2) given the same information about the utterance and nonlinguistic context and behavior, different observers can assign the same interpretation to it.

The utterances were identified at the level of transcription. All of the transcription was done immediately after the recordings were made.

The linguistic record was transcribed in traditional orthography, with phonetic notation used in cases where speech was not clear. Nonlinguistic information about the context of each utterance was included in the transcription, and a standardized notation convention was used for recording the interaction between utterances and situations. The following procedures were used to establish confidence in the transcriptions. All of the Peter data were transcribed by one investigator (either Lightbown or Hood) and subsequently checked by the other until agreement between them was established in the transcript. In the few cases where agreement could not be reached, the utterance was considered unintelligible. All of the Kathryn, Eric, and Gia data were transcribed by Bloom. Samples of 100 utterances from the data of Kathryn at Time III, Eric at Time V, and Gia at Time V were retranscribed by Hood and then compared with Bloom's original transcription of the same utterances. The proportion of agreement between the two transcriptions (each utterance scored as same or different) was .97 for Kathryn III, .95 for Eric V, and .98 for Gia V.

Interpretation of each speech event was made by at least two of the three investigators for all the data. A comparison was made of the categorization of 100 utterances from Kathryn at Time II by two investigators, with an independent categorization of the same utterances by the third investigator. In the 100 utterances, 110 semantic–syntactic relations were identified, and the proportion of agreement on the categorization of these relations was .89.

RESULTS

The Semantic–Syntactic Categories

The semantic–syntactic relations between two or more constituents could be identified for .88 of all the multiword utterances in the data. Categories of relations emerged with the regular and increasing occurrence of utterances with these relations in the speech of all the children; the categories were not a superimposed a priori system of analysis. By examining each speech event (which included the utterance and behaviors by the child and others relative to the utterance) and considering its relation to other speech events in terms of similarities and differences, it was possible to identify categories of utterances that presumably derived from an individual child's own rule system and were, therefore, functional for the child. Judging the psychological reality of the categorization scheme for each child depended upon the extent to which the individual categories were productive in the linguistic behavior of the child. Accordingly, a criterion of productivity was established to support the assumption that the categories which were derived from the children's behavior did indeed represent their underlying linguistic knowledge: A semantic–syntactic category was considered productive (i.e., derived according to an underlying rule system) if five or more utterance types were observed in the category in the data from a particular child in a particular sample.[3]

Among the categories that emerged from the data were seven categories of verb relations and the category of possession which formed the basis for the present discussion of structure and variation in child language. These were the categories in which reference could be made to relationships between persons and objects and in which a developmental interaction between form and meaning was revealed. In possession, the children made reference to objects that were within the domains of particular persons by virtue of habitual use or association. The criterial features that identified speech events in categories of verb relations were as follows: Verb categories were distinguished (whether or not an actual verb form appeared in the utterance) according to whether or not relevant movement accompanied the utterance (action versus state events) and whether or not place was relevant to either action or state (locative versus nonlocative events). The distinction between action and locative verb relations is similar to the semantic distinction among verbs of motion that do and do not involve change of location for adults described by Miller (1972).

The categories are defined and illustrated below. Further examples from each child at each time are presented in the Appendix to the original publication (Bloom, Lightbown, & Hood, 1975).

Action. Utterances in this category referred to two kinds of movement where the goal of the movement was not a change in the location of an object or person (see Locative Action).

1. Utterances referred to action that affected an object with movement by an agent. At least two of the three components of an action relation (agent–action–object) had to be represented in the utterance in order for the utterance to be included within the category. For example:[4]

		Agent	Action	Affected Object
P VII	(Peter trying to open box)	my	open	that
K III	(Kathryn opening drawer)	—	open	drawer
G III	(Gia going to her bike and then getting on)	⎡Gia ⎣Gia	— ride	bike⎤[5] bike⎦
E IV	(Eric has just reassembled train)	I	made	—

2. Other action utterances referred to movements by actors (persons or objects) in events where no object other than the actor was affected. For example:

		Actor	Action
K II	(Kathryn has just jumped)	Kathryn	jumps
P VI	(Peter watching reels of tape recorder)	tape	go round

Locative Action. Utterances in this category referred to movement where the goal of movement was a change in the location of a person or object.

1. Most locative actions entailed an agent, an affected object or person, and place or the goal of the movement. At least two of the four components (agent–action–object–place) had to be represented in the utterance in order for it to be included in the locative action category. For example:

		Agent	Loc. Action	Object	Place
K II	(Kathryn throwing car and truck in box)	—	put	—	in box
P VI	(Peter putting masking tape on toy car)	—	—	tape	on there
E V	(Eric holds out hand to have Lois put puppet on it)	you	put	—	ə finger
G V	(Gia had put polo shirts on Mommy's bed)	I'm	put	polo shirt	on there

2. Where the agent and affected object or person were the same, the single constituent was designated as mover. For example:

		Mover	Loc. Action	Place
G IV	(Gia wants Mommy to get balloon from ceiling)	Mommy	stand up	ə chair
P VI	(Peter has been playing piano; he stops and turns around on bench)	I	get down	—

Locative State. Utterances in this category referred to the relationship between a person or object and its location, where no movement established the locative relation within the context of the speech event, that is, before, during, or after the child's utterance. Locative states entailed a person or object and a place. At least two of the three components (object–state–place) had to be represented in the utterance in order for the utterance to be included in the locative-state category. For example:

		Object	Loc. State	Place
P VI	(Peter pointing to overhead light in hallway)	light	—	ə hall
G V	(Gia looking for toy bag)	the bag	go	—
K III	(Kathryn looking at picture of dog on chair)	—	sitting	on chair
E V	(Eric on Mommy's chair)	I	sitting	—

Notice. Utterances in this category referred to attention to a person, object, or event, and necessarily included a verb of notice (such as *see* or *hear*), since such events as seeing or hearing could not be identified by aspects of context and behavior. For example:

		Noticer	Notice	Noticed
G IV	(Lois talking to Gia's Mommy)	Lois	watch	Gia
E V	(Eric looking out window)	I	see	two bus come there
K III	(Children shouting in hallway)	I	hear	childrens!

		Noticer	Notice	Noticed
P VI	(Peter looking in mirror box)	—	look at	that!

State. Utterances in this category made reference to transitory states of affairs involving persons or other animate beings: either (1) an internal state, usually with a verb form such as *like, need,* or *want:*

P VI	(Peter standing next to cabinet where pretzels are kept)	I want pretzel
E III	(Lois has said she was going to take Eric's book home)	ə need book
G IV	(Lois asked, "Did Caroline come to your party?")	Caroline sick

or (2) a temporary state of ownership or possession:

K III	(Kathryn taking train from Lois)	I have it
E V	(Eric giving toy to another child)	you have it

Utterances which made reference to external states of affairs included:

G V	(Gia looking out window with sunglasses on)	it's dark outside

Intention. Two verb categories, intention and causality, emerged in the later samples and were distinguished from the others in that each involved two verb forms: a constituent verb in one of the categories already described and a matrix verb that expressed either intention or causality relative to the constituent. Verbs of notice also functioned as matrix verbs in the later data, for example, "I see two bus come there" (E V). The expression of causal relations, for example, "make əm sit down" (K II), did not become productive for any of the children during the period studied.

Utterances in the intention category included variants of such verbs as *want, going to, have to, let's* in combination with an action, locative action, or – occasionally – a state verb. The utterances most often made reference to action or locative-action events which in fact occurred immediately following the utterance or which the child appeared to intend or desire. Almost without exception, the child was the agent of the subsequent event.[6] For example,

K III	(Kathryn picked up lavaliere microphone)	I want ə wear this
G V	(Gia's nose is running; Lois gets a tissue, and Gia is reaching for it)	I want ə blow nose
K III	(Kathryn and Lois having a tea party) (then Kathryn pretends to cut cake)	I gon' cut əs some more

The Remaining Categories. The categories of existence (simply pointing out or naming an object), negation (e.g., nonexistence, disappearance, or rejection of objects or events), recurrence (reference to "more" or another instance of an object or event), and attribution (counting, specifying, or otherwise qualifying objects) included utterances that made reference to objects primarily. Other categories that emerged in the later data were wh-questions and relations that were subordinate to action verb relations: dative (specifying the recipient of an action that also involved an affected object), instrument (specifying the inanimate object that was used in an action to affect another object), and place. The category place included utterances that specified where an action event occurred, for example, "baby swim bath" (E V) and "buy more grocery store" (K II), in contrast with locative action where the goal of the movement was a change in location, for example, "put man block" (K II). The categories that were either not productive or did not manifest systematic developmental change were stereotype, routine, greeting, vocative, manner, time, affirmation, and conjunction. Finally, utterances that could not be assigned to any one category were judged equivocal (when more than one categorization was possible), anomalous (when the relation between utterance and context was contradictory), or otherwise undetermined. The absolute and proportional frequencies of utterance types in each of these categories are presented in the section that follows.

The results of the linguistic analysis consist of (1) the sequence in which the above semantic–syntactic categories appeared in the developmental data and (2) the development of pronominal and nominal lexical representation in multiword utterances. After presenting the results of the sequence of development and the pronominal–nominal variation in development, the findings will be discussed in terms of (1) explanations of sequential development, (2) semantic–syntactic structure in child language, and (3) variation in child language.

Sequence of Development

More than 20 categories of semantic–syntactic relationships in multi-word utterances were identified in the data from the four children in the period from single words to MLU of approximately 2.5 morphemes. Table 2.2 presents the absolute and proportional frequencies of utterance types in each of the categories. An utterance was counted only one time in Table 2.2, regardless of how many times it occurred in a category, if the semantic interpretation of the utterance was the same each time it occurred. If the interpretation was different, the homonymous utterances were counted in different categories. Thus, the frequencies of semantic–syntactic relations in utterance types, not tokens, are represented in the categories in Table 2.2. When two relations occurred in the same utterance (e.g., "eat Mommy cookie"; action–affected-object plus possession), both relations were counted, and the utterance is represented two times in Table 2.2. The proportion of different utterance types with more than one semantic–syntactic relation increased developmentally from none in the earliest samples, to .19 at Eric V, .11 at Gia V, .12 at Kathryn III, and .07 at Peter VII.

The verb categories in combination with the categories of possession, attribution, existence, negation, and recurrence accounted for an average of .77 of the semantic–syntactic relations in the utterances from all of the children. In addition, an average of .04 of the relations were in the categories *wh*-question, instrument, dative, and action-plus-place; an average of .07 were in those categories that showed no developmental change (stereotype, vocative, etc.).

Generally, the absolute frequencies of utterance types increased in all categories for each child across time (see Table 2.2). Proportional frequency tended to increase for the combined verb categories, but proportional frequency tended to decrease for the combined categories existence, recurrence, and negation. Thus, although there were always larger numbers of different utterances as the children matured, utterances that made reference to the interactions between persons and objects or between objects increased proportionally, while there was a proportional decrease in utterances that made reference to an object with respect to itself or its class (except for attributives). Given these proportional interactions, it was concluded that the categories of existence, nonexistence, and recurrence were an earlier development, and the verb categories were a later development for all the children.

The category of possession accounted for .10 or less of the relations

Types, not tokens

Table 2.2. Proportion and Number of Different Semantic–Syntactic Relations in Each Sample[a]

Category	Eric					Gia					Kathryn			Peter						
	I	II	III	IV	V	I	II	III	IV	V	I	II	III	I	II	III	IV	V	VI	VII
Action	.10 (1)	.18 (7)	.20 (22)	.16 (68)	.20 (219)	.06 (3)	.11 (23)	.35 (101)	.35 (173)	.32 (307)	.24 (56)	.21 (174)	.24 (393)	.43 (3)	.40 (2)	.10 (7)	.23 (23)	.35 (28)	.14 (39)	.17 (81)
Locative action	—	.03 (1)	.06 (7)	—	.09 (96)	.06 (3)	.06 (12)	.12 (36)	.13 (67)	.09 (87)	.06 (15)	.13 (108)	.12 (192)	.14 (1)	—	.06 (4)	.05 (4)	.17 (14)	.12 (33)	.15 (71)
Locative state	—	.03 (1)	—	.05 (21)	.02 (24)	—	.00 (1)	.04 (12)	.02 (10)	.03 (30)	.02 (4)	.05 (38)	.04 (67)	—	—	.03 (2)	.01 (1)	—	.05 (13)	.06 (30)
State	—	.05 (2)	.09 (10)	.05 (20)	.07 (81)	.02 (1)	—	.03 (9)	.01 (4)	.03 (26)	.04 (9)	.05 (38)	.06 (106)	—	—	—	.01 (1)	.01 (1)	.01 (4)	.04 (18)
Notice	.10 (1)	.03 (1)	.03 (3)	.01 (5)	.06 (69)	—	.01 (3)	—	.00 (2)	.01 (13)	.01 (3)	.01 (12)	.01 (20)	—	—	.03 (2)	.01 (1)	—	.02 (6)	.01 (3)
Intention	—	—	—	—	.01 (16)	—	—	.01 (4)	.01 (4)	.14 (135)	.02 (5)	.01 (11)	.07 (115)	—	—	—	—	—	—	.01 (7)
Existence	.30 (3)	.15 (6)	.15 (16)	.07 (31)	.06 (64)	.23 (12)	.13 (26)	.06 (19)	.03 (13)	.03 (30)	.04 (9)	.08 (68)	.07 (109)	—	.20 (1)	.07 (5)	.03 (2)	.05 (4)	.04 (10)	.07 (34)
Negation	.10 (1)	.15 (6)	.17 (18)	.05 (24)	.05 (56)	.02 (1)	.02 (4)	.01 (2)	.01 (7)	.04 (42)	.06 (14)	.05 (41)	.03 (54)	—	—	.04 (3)	.05 (4)	.02 (2)	.04 (10)	.02 (9)
Recurrence	—	.05 (2)	.07 (8)	.15 (65)	.03 (31)	.09 (5)	.20 (40)	.06 (18)	.02 (10)	.03 (24)	.08 (19)	.03 (26)	.03 (44)	.14 (1)	.40 (2)	.24 (17)	.16 (13)	.12 (10)	.04 (12)	.06 (31)
Possession	—	—	.03 (3)	.00 (2)	.02 (18)	.02 (1)	.03 (7)	.07 (19)	.08 (40)	.07 (91)	.06 (15)	.06 (51)	.09 (141)	—	—	.07 (5)	.05 (4)	.01 (1)	.04 (12)	.06 (27)
Attribution	—	.03 (1)	.05 (5)	.11 (46)	.10 (113)	—	.03 (6)	.05 (15)	.13 (67)	.10 (95)	.18 (41)	.09 (78)	.07 (116)	.29 (2)	—	.10 (7)	.18 (14)	.12 (10)	.16 (45)	.06 (31)
Wh–question	—	—	.02 (2)	.00 (1)	.05 (54)	—	—	—	—	.02 (19)	—	.03 (23)	.07 (116)	—	—	—	—	—	.04 (12)	.03 (16)
Place[b]	—	.05 (2)	—	.02 (9)	.02 (20)	.02 (1)	.01 (2)	.01 (2)	.01 (6)	.01 (8)	—	.00 (3)	.00 (3)	—	—	.10 (7)	.05 (4)	.05 (4)	.02 (6)	.04 (19)
Action and place	—	—	—	—	—	—	.03 (6)	.01 (2)	.02 (12)	.02 (15)	—	.00 (3)	.00 (8)	—	—	—	—	—	.01 (6)	
Dative	—	—	.01 (1)	.01 (3)	.01 (7)	—	—	—	.01 (4)	.01 (5)	—	.01 (6)	.01 (10)	—	—	.01 (1)	—	—	—	.01 (6)
Instrument	—	—	—	.02 (9)	.01 (14)	—	—	—	—	.01 (5)	—	.00 (2)	—	—	—	—	—	—	—	.01 (3)
Other[c]	.10 (1)	.10 (4)	.02 (2)	.05 (22)	.08 (93)	.30 (16)	.13 (26)	.04 (11)	.06 (31)	.00 (4)	.07 (26)	.06 (50)	.03 (58)	—	—	.03 (2)	—	—	.18 (51)	.11 (56)
Equivocal	—	—	—	—	.00 (4)	.04 (2)	.02 (5)	.04 (11)	.02 (11)	.00 (2)	.01 (2)	.01 (11)	.00 (7)	—	—	.01 (1)	—	—		
Anomalous/undetermined	.30 (3)	.15 (6)	.10 (11)	.16 (66)	.12 (131)	.15 (8)	.20 (40)	.11 (33)	.07 (35)	.01 (12)	.09 (22)	.09 (79)	.05 (83)	—	—	.10 (7)	.11 (9)	.09 (7)	.10 (28)	.10 (48)
Total N of relations	10	39	108	424	1110	53	201	292	499	950	232	833	1642	7	5	70	80	81	281	490

[a] Proportions are rounded to nearest hundredth. Those less than .005 are given as .00.
[b] Multiword utterances that specified only place.
[c] Stereotype, routine, greeting, vocative, conjunction, affirmation, manner, and time.

in each child's speech at each time, and an average of .04 for all the children in all the data. However, this category tended to be less important in the early data and to increase developmentally. The attribution category was different for different children; although absolute frequency tended to increase for all the children, no clear trend emerged for proportional frequencies.

Utterances in the categories instrument and dative emerged only in the later data, as can be seen in Table 2.2. Even though children are no doubt aware that (1) persons can be affected by certain actions that also involve other objects (e.g., as receivers) and (2) there are particular instruments for specific actions (e.g., pencils, crayons, spoons, keys), the children in this study simply did not talk about these kinds of relations in their early syntactic utterances. For the present study, *wh*-questions were identified only by their form; further semantic–syntactic analysis of the children's development of questions in Chapter 6.[7]

In the category action-plus-place, place was not a complement constituent in an action relation as it was in locative relations, since the complement of an action verb does not depend on specifying place to complete the meaning of the verb (e.g., *write* and *play*) as is the case with locative-action verbs (e.g., *go* and *put*). The category action-plus-place did not become productive until after the locative-action category was productive. The children did not produce such utterances as "those children doing there" (K III) or "orange chair read ə book" (G V) until after such utterances as "put man ə block" (K II) and "wrench go there" (E IV) were fully productive. This result is consistent with a report of similar development in Italian by Parisi (1974).

Sequence of the Development of Verb Relations. The development of verbs was central to the elaboration of structure after the emergence of two-word utterances, and the verb relations developed sequentially and similarly among the children. All of the other semantic–syntactic relationships between constituents were eventually subordinated to the verb relations: Possessive, attributive, and recurrence relations were eventually embedded in predicate constituents; place, dative, instrumental, and negation relations were all constituents in verb matrices. The category existence was coded only when no other constituent relations occurred in an utterance.

Given the criterion of productivity, five or more utterance types in a category, the following sequence emerged: Encoding of action events preceded encoding of stative events, and nonlocative relations were generally encoded before locative relations. As can be seen in Table 2.2, the sequential development of verb categories for Eric and Peter was that action verb relations preceded locative-action verb relations and locative action preceded locative-state relations. The sequence of verb relations was somewhat different for Kathryn and Gia: They also learned to encode action events before nonaction (stative) events, but they learned to encode action and locative-action events at the same time. For all the children, there was no developmental difference between the two kinds of action events with transitive (taking an agent) and intransitive (taking an actor) verbs; the number of intransitives was quite small in all instances. There were differences in grammatical complexity between locative-action transitive and intransitive verbs (with agents and movers, respectively) (described in Bloom, Miller, & Hood, 1975, chap. 3), but not in their sequence or relative frequency of occurrence. Accordingly, the two subcategories of action and of locative action were combined here.

The children also differed in their use of the verb *want* for expression of state or intention. Kathryn and Gia used *want* overwhelmingly with a constituent verb (and often affected-object) immediately previous to an action to express intention to act. The category intention was more frequent for Kathryn and Gia than for Eric and Peter both proprotionately and in absolute numbers of utterance types (see Table 2.2). For Peter and Eric *want* was rarely used in combination with a constituent verb to express intention to act. In fact, intention was not a productive category until Eric V and Peter VII, and even in these later samples it comprised only .01 of all the data for each of them (see Table 2.2). Rather, *want* was used by Peter and Eric the way *need* was – with a noun – to express an internal state, such as "I want pretzel."

Kathryn and Gia also used verbs other than *want* as matrix verbs in expressing intention (e.g., *gonna, hafta*), and utterances in the category intention marked the beginning of two kinds of verb complexity. First, they were the first embedded sentences used by the children, and they were primitive in that the child was most often the agent of both the constituent and matrix verbs. Utterances such as "I want Lois button it" (K III) were rare, and utterances such as "I want comb hair" when the child wanted another to be the agent did not occur. The matrix verbs were used most often in situations where the child wanted to or was about to perform the action. Second, it appears that the matrix verbs (*want, gonna, hafta, let's*) in utterances in the category intention were used to express mood (intention to act) and were thus the beginning of the modal system. The only other modals were forms of negation, for example, *can't;* modals such as *will* and *can* did not occur. Notice verbs also began to appear as matrix verbs at the end of this period, for example, "ə see Mommy busy" (K III).

In sum, the sequence of development observed in the present study was as follows: The functional-relations existence, nonexistence, and recurrence preceded development of verb relations. Within verb relations, action events (action and locative action) preceded state events (locative state, state, and notice), and action preceded locative action for two of the children. The categories possession and attribution were variable among the children and appeared to be later developments for Eric and Peter. Other categories developed after the basic verb relations and included specification of instrument, the dative, *wh*-questions, and, for Kathryn and Gia, matrix verbs.

Pronominal–Nominal Variation

Certain relational meanings in early sentences were defined in Bloom (1973) as functional relations: A constant form with specific meaning was combined with a number of different words, and the meaning of the constant form determined the meaning of the relation between the two words in combination. Brown (1973) pointed out that such relations have the form $f(x)$ with a fixed value, f, combined with a variable (x) that can assume many values. Such relational forms make reference across classes of objects and events – that is, many different kinds of things exist, disappear, and recur. Children can talk about such behaviors with respect to many objects and events (such as cookies, airplanes, and tickling) that are themselves otherwise quite different from one another.

These functional relations were observed in the speech of all the children: For example, *no, gone,* or *no more* signaled negation (most often nonexistence), and *more* or *another* signaled recurrence. As observed in Table 2.2, although the absolute frequencies in each of these categories tended to increase developmentally, their proportional frequencies decreased, leading to the conclusion that they were an earlier development than the verb categories for all the children. Indeed, the functional relations were the most frequent in the earlier samples when syntax first emerged.

When mean length of utterance was less than 2.0, Eric and Peter continued the same kind of functional relations to encode particular functions in action, location, and possession relations: the pro-forms *I* or *my* as agent or mover, *it, this one,* or *that* as affected-object, *my* as possessor, and *here* or *there* as place. The structure that Peter and Eric learned, constant forms with constant functions, could be compared to a system of inflectional affixing or case marking which might be schematized as $Ax = X, Bx = X,$ or $Ay = Y, By = Y,$ where x and y are each constant relational forms that always mean the same thing relative to the different forms (A or B) with which they combine to create the relational meaning (X or Y). In this way, Peter and Eric were able to talk about a great many objects in action and locative relations, and syntax did not depend on lexical learning for making particular reference to different objects. However, Peter and Eric knew the names of many objects and persons. They used these nominal forms in single-word utterances and in functional relations with such words as *no* and *more.* There was also a certain amount of variation with the pronominal forms they learned to specify affected-object and place relationships (e.g., "this one" and "it," and "here," "right here," "over there," "there," etc.), as can be seen in the examples in the Appendix. Thus, it was not the case that the pronominal forms with verbs were unanalyzed phrases learned by rote.

The grammatical system that Peter and Eric learned consisted of relations between different verb forms and a number of constant functional forms such as *it, there,* and *my.* Successive verb relations were learned by fitting new categories (such as locative action and then locative state) into the existing system. However, whereas reference to affected-object (with "it," "this one," etc.) and place (with "here" or "there") included many different things and places, Eric and Peter referred only to themselves as agents and possessors (with *I* or *my*) and did not also talk about other people as agents and possessors when MLU was less than 2.0 morphemes.

Within the same MLU period, Kathryn and Gia used the same kind of functional relations – constant forms in combination with many different forms – to represent the notions existence, nonexistence, and recurrence. However, Kathryn and Gia encoded other grammatical relations with categories of nominal forms as agent, affected object, place, and possessor instead of a constant pronominal form for each grammatical relation. Thus, "Mommy," "Daddy," "Baby," "Kathryn," and so on, formed a category agent. Such forms as "book," "cookie," "ball," "toy," "bag," and so forth formed a category affected-object; such forms as "table," "floor," "outside," "bag" formed a category place. The fact that Kathryn and Gia developed action, locative-action, and possession relations at the same time was interpreted as evidence that they had learned the superordinate grammatical categories sentence-subject (including agents, actors, movers, and possessors), predicate-object (including objects of actions, locative actions, and possession), and predicate-complement (place).

The relations between nominal categories in Kathryn's and Gia's speech could be schematized as $A + B = C/D$, where A and B were grammatical categories, and the relations between them, C or D, were superordinate category relationships with specific meaning, such as possession, action, or location. Kathryn and Gia learned an abstract grammatical structure here schematized as $A + B$, which could be used to represent several semantic distinctions, here schematized as C, D. The structure learned by Eric and Peter was different but equally abstract in that it was used to represent a number of semantic distinctions with each distinction dependent upon a linguistic operator or marker. The two systems of pronominal and nominal encoding are aspects of the adult model and, indeed, of language in general. All the children then were quite similar in their semantic knowledge, but there was variation among them in their knowledge of syntax – they were learning two different systems of semantic–syntactic structure that were virtually mutually exclusive in the beginning. There was an impressive consistency within each child and between Eric and Peter on the one hand and Kathryn and Gia on the other when MLU was less than 2.0.

The major development when MLU passed 2.0 was a shift in encoding and the integration of the two alternative systems of pronominal and nominal reference, as presented in Table 2.3 and Figures 2.2 through 2.4. The figures represent proportional frequencies of pronominal encoding for agent and affected-object in action verb relations (Figures 2.2 and 2.3) for the four children, and possessor (Figure 2.4) for Kathryn and Gia.[8] The graphic representation of nominal encoding would, of course, be the mirror image of Figures 2.2 through 2.4. As can be seen, even though the children started out (when mean length of utterance was approximately 1.3) with either one or the other linguistic system, there was a significant shift with development as both systems of reference were gradually integrated for all the children. The occurrence of redundant coding (e.g., "fix it choo-choo train") occurred infrequently and only appeared in the data when MLU passed 2.0.

Table 2.3. *Pronominal and Nominal Encoding of Sentence Constituents*

Child and Time	MLU	Possession–Possessor		Action Agent Actor		Action Affected-Object		Locative Action Agent		Locative Action Mover		Locative Action Affected-Object		Locative Action Place	
		Pro	Nom	Pro	Nom	Pro	Nom	Pro	Nom	Pro	Nom	Pro	Nom	Pro	Nom
Eric															
II	1.19	—	—	—	1	4	2	—	—	—	—	—	—	—	—
III	1.42	2	1	7	1	14	4	—	—	2	2	—	2	1	3
IV	1.69	1	1	12	4	32[a]	33[a]	—	—	2	7	7	11	10	4
V	2.63	16	2	93	28	70[a]	111[a]	20	—	8	25	12	19	42	13
Gia															
II	1.34	1	6	—	8	1	19	—	1	—	6	1	3	—	2
III	1.58	1	18	4	66	14	67	—	7	—	12	—	15	2	11
IV	1.79	7	33	7	106	17	120	—	5	1	31	1	16	15	27
V	2.30	61	30	163	48	79	193	8	4	22	22	8	18	24	44
Kathryn															
I	1.32	2	13	4	19	4	44	—	1	4	1	2	2	—	9
II	1.89	32[a]	34[a]	9	99	41	81	2	12	6	28	22	25	35	37
III	2.83	104	38	123	92	128	212	21	17	15	28	55	49	56	58
Peter															
III	1.37	2	3	—	—	5	2	—	—	—	—	1	3	3	1
IV	1.41	4	—	6	1	17	6	1	—	—	—	1	—	4	—
V	1.33	1	—	3	1	24	3	1	—	—	—	3	5	11	1
VI	1.75	12	—	8	—	23	13	—	—	2	1	7	10	18	4
VII	2.39	23	4	22	7	31[a]	38[a]	8	1	9	5	22[a]	9[a]	36[a]	7[a]

[a] Included here are utterances with redundant coding, for example, "my Kathryn house" and "I fix it choo-choo train."

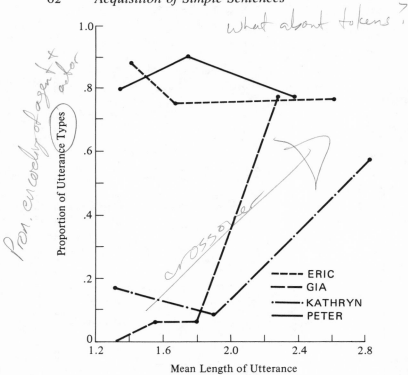

Figure 2.2. Pronominal encoding of agent and actor. The first data point for Peter represents the averaged data from Peter III, IV, and V, when MLU was virtually identical.

Brown (1973) interpreted such utterances as a failure to analyze and segment the *it* from the verb form. However, in the present study, such utterances seemed to represent the children's attempt to learn the alternative forms of pronominal and nominal encoding in making the transition from one form of reference to the other. Also, Gia often said one form and then the other, especially for agents, for example, "Gia lie down/I lie down." Such redundancy, although generally infrequent, occurred equally often in the speech of all the children.

The same developmental trends were apparent in the pronominal–nominal interactions among constituents in locative-action relations. The data in Table 2.3 confirm the distinction between action and locative-action verb relations for Peter and Eric: Action relations took pronominal forms as affected-object, but in locative-action relations Peter and Eric used nominal forms as affected-object (with pronominal

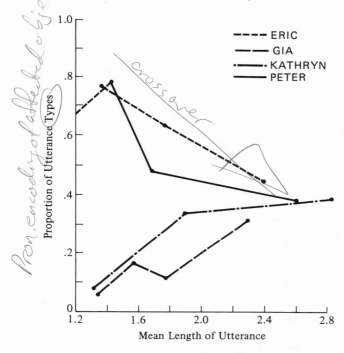

Figure 2.3. Pronominal encoding of affected-object. The first data point for Peter represents the averaged data from Peter III, IV, and V, when MLU was virtually identical.

place). Further, agents (with affected-object) and actors (which were also in a sense the objects affected by the action) were productive in action relations (P IV and E III) before reference to agents (that moved another object) or movers (that were also the objects that moved) became productive in locative-action relations (P VII and E IV), apparently because action relations developed first.

Just before the pronominal–norminal shift there was a decrease in the proportional frequencies of utterances in the combined verb categories (see Table 2.2). This exception to the developmental increase in the proportional frequencies in the verb categories might have been the effect of the transition from the one means of encoding to another.

By the time MLU approached 2.5 morphemes, the variation among the children was greatly reduced. Kathryn and Gia had learned a primitive system of pronominal substitution for nominal categories, and Eric and Peter were learning categories of nominal forms to encode

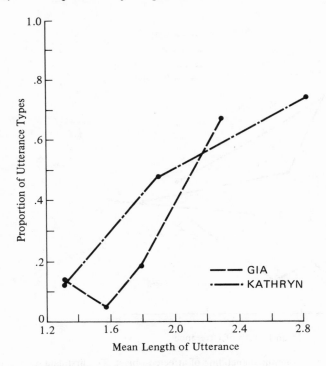

Figure 2.4. Pronominal encoding of possessor.

action, location, and possession. In terms of nominal and pronominal reference, the children were quite similar to one another when MLU approached 2.5 morphemes. No matter how they started out, affected-object was most often nominal, and agent was most often pronominal for all four children. There was a crossover from predominantly pronominal to predominantly nominal encoding of affected object for Eric and Peter, and a crossover from predominantly nominal to predominantly pronominal encoding of agent for Kathryn and Gia.

DISCUSSION

The children in this study learned more than word order and something about the meaning relations between words. The facts of child language appear to translate to case grammar terms in the meanings of word relations, and generative transformational grammar terms in the nature of the grammatical relations between categories. However, it seems to be more profitable to describe such facts of child language on their own terms, by identifying and interpreting speech events according to shared features of situational context and linguistic form rather than in terms of goodness of fit with one or another preconceived system of analysis or linguistic theory.

The findings in the present study will be discussed here in terms of explaining (1) sequential development, (2) semantic–syntactic structure in child language, and (3) variation in child language.

Explaining Sequential Development

There are several possible factors to explore in attempting to account for the sequence of development that was obtained, including relative frequency of exposure, syntactic complexity, semantic complexity, and cognitive complexity.

Frequency of Exposure. One possible explanation for the sequence of development in the children's speech was the relative frequency of utterances in the same categories in the adult speech that the children heard in the course of development. A comparison of relative frequencies of adult and child utterances in the verb categories revealed that they were indeed the same: Action was more frequent than locative action, locative state, and notice, in that order. However, attributive and *wh*-questions were even more frequent than action relations in the adult speech, and these two categories were proportionally far less frequent in the child speech data. Although these interactions were more often between investigator and child than between parent and child,[9] one has the intuitive impression that attributives, *wh*-questions, and the dative are generally frequent in adult speech to children. Parents typically point out different books, toys, articles of clothing, foods, and the like on the basis of relative size, color, amount, or whatever. Parents and other adults also ask children many questions (Broen, 1972; Snow, 1972) and give such directions as "give me the ball" or "show it to Daddy."

The parent–child data that have been reported in the literature indicate that the interaction between frequency of exposure and the sequence of development is quite complicated and that children do not learn different structures simply according to how often they hear them. If sufficient parent speech data had been available in the present study, it might have been instructive to compare frequencies in the parent speech data with the respective children's order of acquisition, as Brown (1973) did for the acquisition of grammatical morphemes. Brown reported that the sequence of development of morphological inflections in his data could not be accounted for by the relative frequency of the same forms in the mothers' speech. Rather than there being a simple causal relation between frequency in adult speech and order of acquisition, it is more likely that children actively search for linguistic forms that can represent what they want to talk about. Once children realize that certain aspects of the environment are relatively constant with respect to their behavior and the behavior of others, they can learn to represent linguistically their conceptualizations of recurring events. No matter how frequently a structure occurs in the speech a child hears, it can be ignored if it is not relevant to the kinds of things the child needs to say (see Bloom, Hood, & Lightbown, 1974, chap. 12, for a discussion of how children actively process linguistic messages for their language learning).

Syntactic Complexity. Brown (1973) invoked a "law of cumulative complexity" (p. 185) to explain the sequence of development in child language: "A construction $x + y$ may be regarded as more complex than either x or y because it involves everything involved in either of the constructions alone plus something more" (p. 407). According to Brown, the order in which grammatical morphemes emerge in child speech can be accounted for in this way. It is also true for progressive syntactic complexity: three-term strings (subject–verb–object) do not appear until after two-term strings (subject–verb, verb–object, subject–object), and recurrence, possession, and attribution do not occur in verb relations until after they are productive separately. The other structures described in the present study were not explicitly accounted for by Brown according to an index of cumulative complexity in what he called Stage I, when MLU was less than 2.0. However, it does appear that syntactic complexity can explain the late emergence of matrix verbs which entail sentence embedding, the dative which entails two different kinds of relations between persons and an object, and the instrumental which entails two kinds of agency. Indeed, these syntactic relations, which the children in the present study acquired later than the basic verb relations, are perfect examples of Brown's "something more" – a new element which must be added to syntactic configurations acquired earlier.

However, there were other aspects of sequential development in the present study that did not fit the cumulative complexity explanation. The theory of cumulative syntactic complexity could neither describe nor explain the sequence of development of the early Stage I semantic–syntactic relations observed in the present study. The "something more" criterion does not appear to explain the fact that verb relations developed after functional relations. Verb relations are quite similar to functional relations in that a particular action such as *eat* can apply across several different objects such as *cookies, meat, pretzels,* just as *more* or *gone* can refer to different objects and events. One might argue that verb relations entail an agent constituent as "something more," but although agents were productive for Gia and Kathryn from the beginning, they were not productive with the earliest verb relations in the Stage I speech of Eric and Peter. For Eric and Peter, then, verb relations, although a later development, were not cumulatively more complex than functional relations. Locative relations involve "something more" (place) than action relations, but action and locative action appeared at the same time in Kathryn's and Gia's speech. The most obvious case in which cumulative complexity did not appear to be a factor was in the sequential development of encoding locative-action and locative-state events. If anything, locative state would seem to entail "something less" in that no agent was involved in affecting the spatial relation between object and place.

Brown did not report a sequence of development of semantic–syntactic relations in Stage I speech. The data he presented were cross-sectional within that period to demonstrate the existence of the "major meanings" of Stage I speech. Although cumulative complexity is descriptive of certain transitions from Stage I to later speech – in particular, those structures that involve conjoining and embedding – there were other syntactic developments in the present study which could not be explained by cumulative syntactic complexity.

Semantic Complexity. Bowerman (1973a) and Schlesinger (1971b) have suggested that children have learned semantic relationships and have not learned grammatical relations when they put two and three words together – that early language learning is semantic rather than syntactic. Bowerman argued that there is insufficient evidence available to conclude that the subject–predicate grammatical relationship exists in early child language and that the distinction involves more abstract linguistic inductions that are probably made later in development. The claim that children are learning only semantic structures, like the similar claim for syntax in early sentences in the 1960s, is only part of the story (see Bloom, 1970). It has become increasingly clear in linguistic theory that semantics and syntax are mutually dependent and inseparable in any theory of grammar, and the two aspects of structure could not be separated in describing the child language observed in this study. Indeed, according to Bowerman (1973b), "The linguistic knowledge which underlies the earliest two- and three-word constructions may be no more complex than simple rules to order words which are understood as performing various semantic functions" (p. 210). Bowerman appears to confuse the claim that children are learning only the semantics of sentences when she fails to consider word-order rules as manifesting knowledge of syntax.

Both Bowerman and Schlesinger argued that evidence of word-order rules is not a sufficient condition for attributing knowledge of the subject–predicate distinction to the child. In particular, Bowerman objected to the assumption of an underlying subject–predicate structure in child language as "too abstract." The kind of evidence that both Bowerman and Schlesinger might accept in order to attribute such knowledge of grammatical relations to the child would be the occurrence of superordinate categories whereby words in the same syntactic position took on different semantic functions relative to one another. Such superordinate grammatical categories were manifest in the system of semantic–syntactic structure that Gia and Kathryn learned. That is, the same words (e.g., *Mommy* or *Baby*) could have different grammatical meanings, such as agent (in an action event), mover (in a locative event), or possessor, and different words (e.g., *chair, floor, box*) could have the same grammatical function (place), and so on. Indeed, the same kind of evidence seems also to appear among Bowerman's own data (1973a, pp. 237–92). Further, the alternative system learned by Peter and Eric, in this same period of time, was no less grammatical. Even though superordinate grammatical categories were not represented in their speech, the patterns of regularity in their speech provided evidence of an abstract linguistic structure that was no less coherent and consistent.

Bowerman pointed out that the syntactic tests of the reality of a subject–predicate distinction in the adult model (e.g., transformations such as the passive that operate the same way on constituents with different semantic functions) are not met in the evidence from child speech. However, the existence of a structure in child language needs to be justified by a test of the child-language data and not by tests that apply to adult-speech data. The critical issue is whether there is a syntactic structure – a system of rules for combining words – in the children's speech and not whether one can identify adult syntax in child sentences.

An important distinction seems to have been blurred in the emphasis on semantic learning by Bowerman, Schlesinger, and others as well – the distinction between semantic development and conceptual development. Children's early language learning is semantic, to be sure, which simply means that they have learned something about the meanings of words and the meaning relations between words. But how they have learned to think about the objects, events, and relations in their experience is something apart from how they have learned to represent such information in linguistic messages. Semantic learning has to do with learning a coding system for representing meaning in natural languages. Semantic complexity cannot be separated from syntactic complexity – both represent the linguistic complexity that influences the course of development. On the other hand, meaning derives from an individual's mental representation of experience. One can look at cognitive complexity apart from linguistic complexity and attempt to specify the conceptual constraints that influence development.

Cognitive Complexity. According to Schlesinger (1971b) and Slobin (1971a) later linguistic developments are semantically more complicated because they are cognitively more complex. To a certain extent, that is obviously true. Cognitive complexity can be defined in terms of the mental operations that result in the mental representation of events (one's experience), and the extent of discrepancy between an original event in reality and the conceptual coding of that event (see the papers in Melton & Martin, 1972, for various accounts of coding systems in human memory). For example, encoding action events occurred before encoding attribution in the present study, and it is reasonable that action on objects was cognitively simpler (involving sensorimotor schemas) than discriminating among similar objects according to relative size, color, or amount (which involves higher-level cognitive processes of categorization and seriation). On the other hand, the fact that encoding locative-state relations did not occur until after encoding locative-action relations would appear to be evidence that relative cognitive complexity was not the only factor operating to determine developmental sequence. Placing an object relative to another point in the context (locative action) would entail the transformation of object *A* from place

B to place *C*. Quite simply, in order to know to change the location of an object, the child would have to be aware that it is already located at *B* and it can be located at *C*. Viewed in this way, a locative state might appear to be less cognitively complex than a locative action.

Knowing about something does not simply translate to being able to talk about it or to understand when others talk about it. Children give every indication that they know the instrumental functions of crayons, keys, spoons, and the like and are aware of the function of persons as receivers in such events as giving, showing, and kissing before these relations are represented in their syntactic speech. Even earlier, before the first sentences appear, children's linguistic behavior presents evidence that they are aware of relations among persons and objects and that objects can be located in space or otherwise acted upon (Bloom, 1973; Greenfield & Smith, 1976). While such awareness is a necessary condition for learning grammar, linguistic development is neither isomorphic with nor a necessary result of cognitive development.

The distinction between cognitive categories and linguistic categories can be easily obscured. As children act on the environment and observe others acting on the environment in similar and different ways, they begin to organize their experiences. The child develops schemata to represent mentally such relations among objects as persons acting on objects, persons habitually associated with objects, the relative location of objects, and persons changing the location of objects. Such cognitive schemata are general and nonspecific to particular persons or objects, having been formed on the basis of many encounters with different persons and objects. With each schema, the child has induced a regularity in the interactions among persons and objects so that future encounters with events can be recognized and incorporated in memory. Such cognitive categories represent the entire relationship among, for example, agent, action, and object, or possessor and possessed.

The child does not need to know anything about words and word meanings in order to form such cognitive schemata. Children learn such abstract object relationships and then need to learn how the words that they hear can take on meanings in relation to one another for more extended messages about particular events. A linguistic category is formed by those words that come together in the language because they can mean the same thing relative to other words, for example, *Mommy, Daddy,* and *Baby* as agent in the relation to *table, chair, floor* as place; or *eat, turn, push* as action in relation to *it* as affected-object. Such differentiated semantic categories as agent, place, and affected object are linguistic inductions that the child has made on the basis of linguistic experience relative to existing cognitive schemata; the meaning relationship between linguistic categories is determined by a semantic–syntactic structure. Although relative cognitive complexity is a factor in explaining linguistic development, it appears to function only in complex interaction with the language that the child is learning. Slobin (1971a) has discussed how cognitive development can interact with linguistic complexity to determine developmental differences and similarities among children learning different languages (see also MacNamara, 1972).

The Cycle of Actions and States in Cognitive-Linguistic Development.
The encoding of action and locative-action relations appeared to be sandwiched between the encoding of two kinds of stative events in the sequence of linguistic development. Existence, nonexistence, and recurrence were often stative and did not necessarily involve action by the child or others; locative state, state, and notice were the stative events that were encoded after action events. However, what appears at first glance to be a discontinuity in linguistic development may result from the primacy of actions over states in the interaction between cognitive and linguistic development. The sequence of linguistic development of semantic–syntactic relations appears to recapitulate the cycle of deriving knowledge of states from knowledge gained through action or the perception of movement.

In early infancy, the child's movements in space result in the beginning mental representation of the spatial context in which objects do not have independent status from the context or from one another. Such static spatial maps provide a background for the more salient objects that move, and moving objects come to be increasingly discriminated from their contexts and from one another. Children might begin to build up the awareness that objects can exist independently from their spatial contexts through a process of recording the location of very familiar particular objects that move or are otherwise involved in actions. Children can be aware of particular objects and their habitual locations from a very early age – perhaps before they begin to know any language at all – through movements that (1) bring such objects into and out of view and (2) serve to emphasize or highlight an object in relation to a static background (see, e.g., Bower, 1974; Tronick, 1972). Specific objects and then objects in general increase in salience in relation to their spatial contexts as the child develops the capabilities for acting on objects in particular ways.

With respect to linguistic development, Huttenlocher (1974) reported that names of a family pet or animal words such as *dog* were among the earliest words that children whose understanding she tested were able to recognize. Other words that the children recognized were similarly objects that moved or objects that were acted on, such as cookies. Clark (1973c) reviewed the diary literature and described movement (and four-leggedness which also involves movement) as among the most common perceptual features that characterize objects frequently named by children's early words. Nelson (1973) reported that for many children, the first words they say make reference to objects that move. The most frequent words in four Czech-speaking children's early vocabularies compiled by Janota (1972) after *Mummy* and *Daddy* were *bow-wow, beep-beep, car, moo-moo,* and *bye-bye* (English glosses given here).

In the sensorimotor period before grammar emerges, children learn about the permanence of objects through their actions on objects and their observations of actions on objects – that is, the child learns that objects exist by acting in ways that make them disappear and recur (Piaget, 1954; Sinclair, 1973). Thus, the notions of existence, nonexistence, and recurrence are action dependent in the single-word utterance period (Bloom, 1973). Children come to an awareness of such object states through their own actions, their observations of the actions of others, and the movements of objects. By the time existence, nonexistence, and recurrence are encoded syntactically, they represent stative events as well as action events.

Subsequently, children encode relations between persons and objects, and encoding most often precedes or accompanies action by the child to bring about those relations. Thus, in the present study, encoding relations between objects and persons or between objects appeared to depend upon an ongoing or intended action by the child or by another at the child's direction. Static relations among objects, in which neither the child nor the child's actions were necessarily relevant to the state of affairs represented in the message, were encoded only after a child learned to encode person–object relations with the support of relevant action.

The ability to talk and understand depends upon the complexity of the language in interaction with the child's strategies for learning it. The variations in sequence of development (Gia and Kathryn learned action, locative action, and possession at the same time, whereas Peter and Eric learned them sequentially) appeared to be determined by the underlying structural systems that the children were learning, as revealed in the two different patterns of grammatical regularity that were represented in the speech of the different children.

Semantic–Syntactic Structure in Child Language

The claim that children are learning grammar does not require that children learn the adult system of grammar or that rules of adult grammar account for child sentences. The children's semantic–syntactic systems were not the same as the adult system, and adult grammar could not have accounted for such systems or their development in any adequate way. Nevertheless, the results of this study strongly support the position that children are learning grammatical structure when they combine two and three words at the end of the second year.

The data presented here provided evidence for the three levels of structure that were defined earlier for child language with respect to sentences, sequence of development, and for child language in general. At the level of the sentence, it was possible to identify semantic–syntactic relationships between constituents for .88 of all the multi-word utterances in the speech of the four children. With few exceptions, word order was consistent within each category, and the speech of each child was consistent with one of two alternative grammatical systems. Second, the longitudinal development of each child mani-fested antecedents and consequences in (1) the sequence in which different categories of semantic–syntactic relationship emerged and developed and (2) the shift from pronominal to nominal or nominal to pronominal encoding, as the children enlarged their original linguistic systems to include both alternatives. Given information about the language of a particular child at a particular time, one could predict other aspects of that child's language at the same time, whether pronominal or nominal reference would predominate, and, at a subsequent time, which categories would appear and the nominal-pronominal shift. Finally, when the children were compared with one another, there was consistency among them in the semantics of their sentences, in the sequence of development, and in the pronominal–nominal shift. One could observe regularities among all four children that were consistent with reports from comparable studies (e.g., Brown, 1973) and conclude that there is a coherent structure in child language.

In judging the grammaticality of child speech, it is necessary to distinguish between the dynamic process of the child's acquisition of grammar and the linguistic description given to that knowledge at any point in time. Judgments of grammaticality cannot be obtained from the child and necessarily depend upon observations of the regularities in the child's speech. The way in which a linguistic description can represent such regularities in children's speech is the issue of formalization that is open to debate at the present time. In Bloom (1970), linguistic descriptions took the form of generative transformational grammars. Since that time, progress in linguistic theory has been such that there is no longer a unified theory of generative grammar and no consensus about the kinds of information to be represented by rules of grammar. The taxonomy of linguistic structures that has been presented here is a linguistic description of speech data that can represent the child's knowledge and changes in the child's knowledge in only a gross way. There is no way of knowing, at the present time, the form in which such knowledge about linguistic structure is represented in the child's mental grammar.

However, it is possible to speak of the emergence of knowledge of grammar when such knowledge is manifested in the child's multiword utterances, with regular and recurring relationships between constituents. That is, if structural features occur often enough and are shared by a large enough number of different multiword utterances, then it is possible to attribute the recurrence of such regular features to the productivity of an underlying rule system (see, e.g., Brown, 1973) and attempt a linguistic description of what the child's system might consist. What such features would be might very well be different for different children speaking the same language (as in the present study), and they most certainly would be different for children speaking different languages.

Variation in Child Language

The two different systems of semantic–syntactic structure when MLU was less than 2.0 morphemes could be compared with the traditional classification of language systems as synthetic–agglutinative or analytic–isolating. The system of pronominal reference that Peter and Eric learned for their early sentences could be described as 'agglutinative,' with a small number of constant morphemes (pronominal *it, there, my,* etc.) added on to other morphemes to signal certain semantic distinctions (affected-object, location, possessor, etc.). In contrast, Gia and Kathryn learned a system whereby many different morphemes were combined to signal the same semantic distinctions, and such morphemes were more isolatable and less dependent on one another. The capacities for both pronominal and nominal encoding (or, put another way, for both agglutinative and isolating linguistic processes) exist among children from the beginning of the use of syntax.

Other studies of child language may be interpreted as confirming the intersubject nominal–pronominal variation observed among the four children in this study. A fifth child, Allison, whose development was reported in Bloom (1973, pp. 233–57), used exclusively nominal forms in her early syntax, as can be seen in the data presented there. In other data from English-speaking children, reported by Huxley (1970) and Nelson (1973), there were children who appeared to use predominantly pronominal forms and other children who used nominal forms in their earliest syntactic utterances. In two unpublished studies by Lightbown (1973) and Vosniadou (1974) of French- and Greek-speaking children respectively, the almost exclusive occurrence of either nominal or pronominal forms was observed in the early syntactic utterances of the different children. It appears that an individual child's first sentences are either nominal or pronominal, and the two systems of reference are not mutually substitutable in the beginning.

The variation among the children in the pronominal and nominal encoding of verb relations and possession can be attributed to the two strategies for syntactic encoding described in Bloom (1973). The first strategy is the linear combination of one word, having the same form and same meaning, with various other words, for example, "fix it," "eat it," "read it," and so on, where *it* operates much like a formal marker. The second strategy is the hierarchical combination of categories of words, with a structural meaning that is essentially independent of the lexical meaning of each word separately. It seems that children can break into the adult linguistic code in one of (at least) two ways: with a system of formal markers or with a system of rules for deriving grammatical categories. Both strategies would provide the child with a means for representing the same semantic information in speech, with greater or lesser lexical specification, and both are aspects of the adult code. The choice of strategy (if there is a choice) as children begin to use syntax would appear to be the result of complex interactions between cognitive development and linguistic experience. Once children recognize the relations among objects and events that recur with different objects in different situations, they can begin to learn a system of syntactic coding that represents such information about events in the speech they hear and in their own speech. The aspects of the system that are learned will be determined at least in part by the kind of linguistic reference that the child hears. Parents may differ from one another in the relative extent to which they use pronominal or nominal forms in their speech to their children.

Children are exposed to systems of deictic reference, with shifting between nominal and pronominal forms, in both the adult-to-child speech they hear and the adult-to-adult speech they overhear. The use of proforms in adult-to-adult speech is governed by a fairly explicit system of deictic reference (see, e.g., Fillmore, 1971). Adults use proforms according to the information that speaker and listener share about events. If an object has already been named or otherwise pointed out in the situation, then the use of pronoun reference occurs with no loss of information because both speaker and listener know, for example, the particular object to which *it* refers, or the place to which *there* refers. Adults use proforms gesturally when they also point out or otherwise indicate the object, action, or person of reference, and anaphorically when the object, action, or person of reference has already been named by either speaker or listener in the situation. Whether one says "eat the spinach" or "eat it" or whether one says "the book is on the table" or "it's over there" depends upon what both the speaker and the hearer already know about the situation and about one another.

This intraspeaker variation forms a part of adult competence and interacts with information about situational and interpersonal contingencies. However, the use of proforms and substantive forms in the children's speech was not a system of shifting deictic reference; the children used either one or the other form of reference. The use of proforms by Peter and Eric was neither gesturally nor anaphorically conditioned. When the pronominal–nominal shift for each of the children occurred, it was not conditioned by deictic constraints from the situation or awareness of the information shared with a listener.

Other kinds of evidence indicate that children less than 3 years old would not know such communication conventions for speaking and understanding that take into account the information shared between speaker and listener for determining message form (e.g., Brown, 1973;

Flavell, 1968; Glucksberg, Krauss, & Higgins, 1975; Maratsos, 1971). It appears then that children learn usage constraints on nominal and pronominal encoding *after* they acquire the formal linguistic means for shifting reference, which the children in this study began to acquire when MLU was approximately 2.5 morphemes and they were approximately 2 years old. How they proceeded to learn to take account of social, cognitive, and linguistic variables as the factors for shifting pronominal or nominal encoding, in their later development, remains to be determined.

Strategies for Language Acquisition. Different investigators have attempted to explain variability in child language behavior in terms of children's strategies for language acquisition.[10] In one context, Bever (1970), Clark (1973b), and Slobin (1971a), among others, have proposed successive strategies of acquisition to explain variability or change in linguistic behavior as a function of development. They each proposed sequences of strategies that children use in the process of learning how to obtain meaning from the words and structure of adult sentences. The strategies proposed by Bever were hierarchically ordered according to the relative complexity or the syntactic constraints of English sentences. The strategies proposed by Slobin and Clark consisted of processing directives that retrospectively accounted for several of the findings in studies of child language and development. Such successive strategies are the steps or rules that children follow for proceeding from one level of development to another, and such strategies, in effect, represent stages in development.

The context in which strategies have been proposed in the present study is the variation observed at the same level of development to explain the two different approaches taken by different children to learning language. While both strategies have to do with learning aspects of the model language, one or the other predominated in the development of different children in the same period of time. The use of strategies in this context is meant to imply an organizational scheme for representing information and taking in new information, based upon the inferences the child has made about the linguistic system. The child's use of this organizational scheme represents a map, or plan – that is, a strategy for linguistic behavior and language learning. Sequential strategies for developmental change would operate within the more general organizational strategy such as the pronominal strategy or the categorization strategy proposed in the present study. One could propose, for example, a set of operating instructions for shifting from nominal to pronominal or from pronominal to nominal representation.

Variation among children has also been described in phonological development by Ferguson. In Ferguson, Peizer, and Weeks (1973), two organizational strategies were described as accounting for different rules used by different children in their early phonological acquisition: one, the choice of consonant–vowel–consonant–vowel models with "assimilation to full reduplication" (p. 61), and an alternative strategy of reducing polysyllabic items to monosyllables. Ferguson (personal communication) has described two different organizational strategies for the acquisition of Spanish liquids: one strategy was first represented by "some kind of lateral" for *l, r, rr,* and intervocalic *d* (*ð*), while the other strategy had "r-quality sounds fairly early." It appears then that in phonological development, as in grammatical development, different children can travel different paths to the same end.

Children differ in how long they use either an initial pronominal or nominal strategy for encoding grammatical relations. In the present study, the four children progressed from their earliest productive syntax (when MLU was approximately 1.3) to the pronominal–nominal or nominal–pronominal shift (when MLU was approximately 2.5) in periods that ranged from 12 to 20 weeks. A child might possibly stay with one or another strategy for only a few weeks (or less) or for a much longer period of time. Indeed, it well may be the case that the strategy shift presents problems for some children, and they may make the shift with difficulty if they make it at all. In a study by Morehead and Ingram (1973), the speech of children whose language was diagnosed as disordered appeared to be quite limited in lexical representation. One could conceivably explain their language disorder as an inability to shift from relations with constant (pronominal) forms to a system of grammatical categories with more varied lexical representation.

CONCLUSIONS

In the present analysis, the regularities and consistencies in the data provided evidence of child language structure that is more like adult grammar than it is different and, furthermore, contains both the analytic and synthetic features of languages in general. The analytic aspects of languages such as English were manifest in the early combinations of categories of nominal forms in the speech of Gia and Kathryn, while the early use of pronominal forms by Peter and Eric was interpreted as similar to processes of affixing as observed in synthetic languages such as Russian and Finnish. The variation observed in the present study helps to explain the apparently contradictory "pivot grammar" and "telegraphic speech" descriptions of child language that were reported in the 1960s. It also helps to explain the fact that some investigators in cross-linguistic research (e.g., Burling, 1959; Park, 1970; Pavlovitch, 1920) have reported exceptions to what has been viewed as a universal in child language, namely, that children use content words in rigid order before they learn to use synthetic features of language (inflections and other functors). McNeill (1970) has suggested that since some languages require rigid word order and few inflections while others use variable word order and obligatory inflections, children can be expected to be influenced by one or the other of these two approaches in their early language learning (see also Brown, 1973, and Traugott, 1973, for further discussion of this issue). In addition, the observed variation can be viewed as the genesis of the capacity for shifting pronominal–nominal reference that is required for usage constraints that depend on situational and interpersonal contingencies.

Until the emergence of the capacity for alternative pronominal and nominal reference, it was possible to conclude that form followed function in the children's language development. When the children first began to use grammar, it was clear that what they were learning to talk about was determined by what they knew about objects and events in the world. Interpretation of their utterances was straightforward because the mapping relation between underlying semantic intent and surface form was quite direct. However, the capacity for alternative pronominal and nominal reference provided the first evidence of function following form in language development. The children had learned that they could refer in sentences to a car as "it" and "car," they could refer to a place as "there" and "floor," and they could refer to possessions as "Kathryn('s)" and "my." However, they had not begun to learn the social and linguistic conventions that govern the use of one or another kind of reference for communication.

The developmental distinctions between action and state events in general, and locative-action and locative-state events in particular, correspond to the grammatical distinctions of 'dynamic' and 'static' aspectual opposition, of which the opposition 'directional' (locative action) versus 'locative' (locative state) is a particular manifestation (see Leech, 1970, pp. 198–201; and Lyons, 1968, pp. 298, 397). Traugott (1973) has discussed the dynamic–static opposition for locative terms in pidgin and creole languages and concluded that the dynamic aspect appears to dominate in the evolution of such languages. The sequence of linguistic development reported here may be a reflection of the more basic dynamic–static distinction in languages in general.

The conclusions offered here are necessarily tentative, awaiting confirmation from studies of more children. The patterns of regularity and variation that have been described here emerged from the data as the result of quantitative comparisons. Just as anecdotal evidence or the description of isolated behaviors is never adequate for justifying an assumption about underlying knowledge, it is also true that the conclusions presented here were based upon performance values that were relative. Indeed, it seems safe to say that there are no absolutes in child language. However, when large interactions in the linguistic data occur, they can be interpreted as important evidence of regularities and patterns of developmental variation in the language of a particular child and, eventually, in the language of larger numbers of children. Other, smaller effects are no doubt a function of other variable factors which will also need to be spelled out eventually.

NOTES

1 For example, Bowerman (1973a); Schlesinger (1971b).
2 Mean length of utterance was used as an index of linguistic maturity so that the children could be compared with one another in the course of the longitudinal study and with other children who have been described in the literature (see, in particular, Brown, 1973). All separable morphemes were counted in the first 100 utterances of each transcription. Immediate self-repetitions, wholly or partially unintelligible utterances, and fragments of songs, rhymes, and games were not counted. Imitative utterances, in which the child repeated an adult utterance with five or fewer intervening child or adult utterances, without changing the model except to reduce it by leaving something out, were not counted or processed in this study but are described in Bloom, Hood, & Lightbown (1974, chap. 12).
3 The criterion of productivity (five or more utterances) was a more stringent requirement in the Peter data than in the data from the other children, inasmuch as the total number of hours at each time was always smaller for Peter than for the other children.

4 Examples of speech events are identified according to the sample in which they occurred: Roman numerals identify successive samples from each of the children, and the children are identified by first initial. Thus, P VII is the sample of speech from Peter at Time VII. Information in parentheses on the left describes the context, and the child's utterance is on the right, here arrayed according to constituents.

5 Note that "Gia bike" might have alternative interpretations. In such cases, preceding and succeeding utterances were examined in an effort to determine the semantic–syntactic category to which the utterance would be assigned. If another utterance in the immediate context appeared to be a completion of the utterance in question or otherwise to disambiguate it, as in this case, the utterance could be assigned to a semantic–syntactic category. If not, it was categorized as equivocal.

6 These complement sentences were the subject of another study (Bloom, Tackeff, & Lahey, 1983, chap. 8).

7 Bloom, Merkin, & Wootten, 1982, chap. 6.

8 Peter and Eric did not make the same transition for possession in this time period because possession was a later development for them (see Table 2.2).

9 The use of investigator–child interaction was a deliberate feature of the research plan and was designed to reduce the variability in the data. It was reasoned that the greatest consistency would be attained in the data if all four children interacted primarily with an investigator (rather than their mothers). For this reason, the intersubject variation in the data is all the more striking. As a result, however, the mother–child data that were recorded were insufficient for extended analyses.

10 See also Bowerman (1974a) for a discussion of strategies for language acquisition.

POSTSCRIPT

For research since Bloom, Lightbown, and Hood (1975) on pronominal–nominal variation and developments in the lexicalization of verb arguments:

Bates, E., Bretherton, I., & Snyder, L. (1988). *From first words to grammar: Individual differences and dissociable mechanisms.* Cambridge: Cambridge University Press.

Bretherton, I., McNew, S., Snyder, L., & Bates, E. (1983). Individual differences at 20 months: Analytic and holistic strategies in language acquisition. *Journal of Child Language, 10,* 293–320.

Furrow, D., Nelson, K., & Benedict, H. (1979). Mothers' speech to children and syntactic development: Some simple relationships. *Journal of Child Language, 6,* 423–42.

Goldfield, B., & Snow, C. (1985). Individual differences in language acquisition. In J. Gleason (Ed.), *Language development* (pp. 303–26). Westerville, OH: Merrill.

Horgan, D. (1978). How to answer questions when you've got nothing to say. *Journal of Child Language, 5,* 159–65.

Horgan D. (1981). Rate of language acquisition and noun emphasis. *Journal of Psycholinguistic Research, 10,* 629–40.

Nelson, K. (1975). The nominal shift in semantic–syntactic development. *Cognitive Psychology, 7,* 461–79.

Peters, A. (1977). Language learning strategies: Does the whole equal the sum of the parts? *Language, 53,* 560–73.

Ramer, A. (1976). Syntactic styles in emerging language. *Journal of Child Language, 3,* 49–62.

For the acquisition of meaning relations in early sentences:

Angiolillo, C., & Goldin-Meadow, S. (1982). Experimential evidence for agent–patient categories in child language. *Journal of Child Language, 9,* 627–43.

Blank, M., Gessner, M., & Esposito, A. (1979). Language without communication: A case study. *Journal of Child Language, 6,* 329–52.

Bloom, L., Capatides, J., & Tackeff, J. (1981). Further remarks on interpretive analysis: In response to Christine Howe. *Journal of Child Language, 8,* 403–11.

Braine, M. (1976). *Children's first word combinations.* Monograph of the Society for Research in Child Development, *41* (serial no. 164).

Budwig, N. (1989). The linguistic marking of agentivity and control in child language. *Journal of Child Language, 16,* 263–84.

Corrigan, R., & Odya-Weis, C. (1985). The comprehension of semantic relations by two-year-olds: An exploratory study. *Journal of Child Language, 12,* 47–59.

Dunlea, A. (1989). *Vision and the emergence of meaning.* Cambridge: Cambridge University Press.

Garman, M. (1979). Early grammatical development. In P. Fletcher & M. Garman (Eds.), *Language acquisition: Studies in first language development* (pp. 177–208). Cambridge: Cambridge University Press.

Golinkoff, R. (1981). The case for semantic relations: Evidence from the verbal and nonverbal domains. *Journal of Child Language, 8,* 413–37.

Golinkoff, R., & Markessini, J. (1980). "Mommy sock": The child's understanding of possession as expressed in two-noun phrases. *Journal of Child Language, 7,* 119–35.

Howe, C. (1976). The meanings of two-word utterances in the speech of young children. *Journal of Child Language, 3,* 29–47.

Kulikowski, S. (1981). Possible word semantics for early syntax. *Journal of Child Language, 8*, 633–9.

Landau, B., & Gleitman, L. (1985). *Language and experience: Evidence from the blind child*. Cambridge, MA: Harvard University Press.

Leonard, L. (1975). The role of nonlinguistic stimuli and semantic relations in children's acquisition of grammatical utterances. *Journal of Experimental Child Psychology, 19*, 346–57.

Leonard, L. (1976). *Meaning in child language*. New York: Grune & Stratton.

McCune-Nicolich, L. (1981). The cognitive bases of relational words in the single-word period. *Journal of Child Language, 8*, 15–34.

McShane, J. (1980). *Learning to talk*. Cambridge: Cambridge University Press.

Miller, P. (1982). *Amy, Wendy, and Beth: A study of early language development in south Baltimore*. Austin: University of Texas Press.

Norlin, P. (1981). The development of relational arcs in the lexical semantic memory structures of young children. *Journal of Child Language, 8*, 385–402.

Retherford, K., Schwartz, B., & Chapman, R. (1981). Semantic roles and residual grammatical categories in mother and child speech: Who tunes into whom? *Journal of Child Language, 8*, 583–608.

Roeper, T. (1987). The acquisition of implicit arguments and the distinction between theory, process, and mechanism. In B. MacWhinney (Ed.), *Mechanisms of language acquisition*. (pp. 309–43). Hillsdale, NJ: Erlbaum.

Schaerlaekens, A. (1975). The two-word sentence in child language development. *Journal of Child Language, 2*, 322–6.

Schlesinger, I. (1982). *Steps to language: Toward a theory of native language acquisition*. Hillsdale, NJ: Erlbaum.

Stockman, I., & Vaughn-Cook, F. (1989). Addressing new questions about black children's language. In R. Fasold & D. Schiffrin (Eds.), *Language change and variation* (Current issues in linguistic theory, vol. 52, pp. 275–300). Philadelphia: John Benjamins.

For further studies of the acquisition of verbs and verb categories:

Behrend, D. (1990). The development of verb concepts: Children's use of verbs to label familiar and novel events. *Child Development, 61*, 681–96.

Bennett-Kastor, T. (1986). Cohesion and predication in child narrative. *Journal of Child Language, 13*, 353–70.

Berman, R. (1982). Verb-pattern alternation: The interface of morphology, syntax, and semantics in Hebrew child language. *Journal of Child Language, 9*, 169–91.

Bowerman, M. (1987). Mapping thematic roles onto syntactic functions: Are children helped by innate "linking rules"? Paper presented to the Child Language Conference, Boston University, Boston.

Cuvelier, P. (1987). The prototypical background in the acquisition process of relational verb meaning properties. In F. Van Besien (Ed.), *First language acquisition*. ABLA Papers, no. 12. (pp. 35–54).

de Villiers, J. (1985). Learning how to use verbs: Lexical coding and the influence of the input. *Journal of Child Language, 12*, 587–95.

Edwards, D., & Goodwin, R. (1986). Action words and pragmatic function in early language. In S. Kuczaj & M. Barrett (Eds.), *The development of word meaning* (pp. 257–73). New York: Springer-Verlag.

Galivan, J. (1987). Correlates of order of acquisition of motion verbs. *Perceptual and Motor Skills, 64*, 311–18.

Gentner, D. (1975). Evidence for the psychological reality of semantic components: The verbs of possession. In D. Normal & D. Rumelhart (Eds.), *Explorations in cognition* (pp. 211–46). San Francisco: Freeman.

Gentner, D. (1978). On relational meaning: The acquisition of verb meaning. *Child Development, 49*, 988–98.

Gentner, D. (1982). Why nouns are learned before verbs: Linguistic relativity versus natural partitioning. In S. Kuczaj (Ed.), *Language development* (vol. 2, pp. 211–46). Hillsdale, NJ: Erlbaum.

Gergely, G., & Bever, T. (1986). Related intuitions and the mental representation of causative verbs in adults and children. *Cognition, 23*, 211–77.

Huttenlocher, J., & Lui, F. (1979). The semantic organization of some simple nouns and verbs. *Journal of Verbal Learning and Verbal Behavior, 18*, 141–62.

Huttenlocher, J., Smiley, P., & Charney, R. (1983). Emergence of action categories in the child: Evidence from verb meanings. *Psychological Review, 90*, 72–93.

Johnson, C., & Wellman, H. (1980). Children's developing understanding of mental verbs – Remember, know, and guess. *Child Development, 51*, 1095–102.

McShane, J., Whittaker, S., & Dockrell, J. (1986). Verbs and time. In S. Kuczaj & M. Barrett (Eds.), *The development of word meaning* (pp. 275–302). New York: Springer-Verlag.

Sudhalter, V., & Braine, M. (1985). How does comprehension of passives develop? A comparison of actional and experiential verbs. *Journal of Child Language, 12*, 455–70.

Tanz, C. (1980). *Studies in the acquisition of deictic terms*. Cambridge: Cambridge University Press.

Weist, R. (1982). *Verb concepts in child language – Acquiring constraints on action role and animacy*. Tübingen: Gunter Narr (Benjamins).

For discussions of individual differences:

Bates, E., Bretherton, I., & Snyder, L. (1988). *From first words to grammar: Individual differences and dissociable mechanisms.* Cambridge: Cambridge University Press.

Bretherton, I., McNew, S., Snyder, L., & Bates, E. (1983). Individual differences at 20 months: Analytic and holistic strategies in language acquisition. *Journal of Child Language, 10,* 293–320.

Furrow, D., & Nelson, K. (1984). Environmental correlates of individual differences in language acquisition. *Journal of Child Language, 11,* 523–33.

Nelson, K. (1975). Individual differences in early semantic and syntactic development. In D. Aronson & R. Rieber (Eds.), *Developmental psycholinguistics and communication disorders* (pp. 132–9). New York: New York Academy of Sciences.

Nelson, K. (1981). Individual differences in language development: Implications for development and language. *Developmental Psychology, 17,* 170–87.

Wells, G. (1986). Variation in child language. In P. Fletcher & M. Garman (Eds.), *Language acquisition: Studies in first language development* (2nd ed., pp. 109–39). Cambridge: Cambridge University Press.

3

Verb Subcategorization and Linguistic Covariation

"This under bridge /
lamb /
Kathryn make under bridge."

Nothing like the full sentence "Kathryn make this lamb [go] under bridge" occurred at the time she said each of the parts of the sentence separately.

The study of verb categories and the structure of simple sentences continued with this investigation into the reasons for the discrepancy between the underlying knowledge of grammar and the form of child sentences, a discrepancy that is evident in an apparent constraint on the length of early sentences. Even after children begin to say three- and four-word sentences with subject–verb–object, two-word sentences continue to occur with the omission of constituents. This fact – that the sentences children say are not an accurate reflection of what they actually know about sentence structure – was the focus of the research in this chapter. The period of development studied here extended the data base used in the previous study, in Chapter 2, to mean length of utterance of approximately 3.0 morphemes. In the results, several factors are described that either constrained or facilitated sentence length.

The major thesis in this study was an elaboration of the grammatical complexity hypothesis originally proposed in *Form and Function in Emerging Grammars:* that children have a fuller knowledge of hierarchical grammatical structure than is apparent from the sentences they say, and that utterance length increases with developments in control of lexical, syntactic, and discourse covariation. Two main features of the analyses reported here were the argument structures of subcategories of action and locative-action verbs and the probabilistic effects of grammatical, lexical, and discourse factors on the length of child utterances. As mentioned in Chapter 1, these results are particularly relevant to current efforts in the acquisition literature to explain children's 'subjectless sentences.'[1]

THE ARGUMENT STRUCTURE OF SUBCATEGORIES OF VERBS

Sentences with action verbs and three subcategories of locative-action verbs presented different patterns of constituent relations in sentences. The four predominant sentence configurations for the four verb categories were action verbs: agent–verb–object; agent–locative-action verbs: agent–verb–object–place; mover–locative-action verbs: mover–verb–place; and patient–locative-action verbs: patient–verb–place. The full realization of these argument structures in the children's sentences varied developmentally and with verb category, and these results are shown in Figures 3.1 to 3.4.

The claim for a fuller underlying structure than was actually realized in sentences meant that the constituents were represented as obligatory in the children's grammars rather than optional (as others had previously suggested).[2] If the constituents were optionally represented, then the distribution of arguments in the children's sentences would have been random, which it was not. The difference between the observed distribution of arguments in the different verb categories and their expected selection probabilities was statistically significant. We concluded, therefore, that the variation in utterance length was systematic, and so we set about determining the factors that contributed to whether constituents were or were not realized in sentences.

COVARIATION EFFECTS ON SENTENCE LENGTH

Constituents were more or less likely to be omitted or, conversely, more or less likely to be realized in sentences in relation to certain lexical, discourse, and grammatical variables. Only a handful of the potentially many aspects of these variables that could have influenced sentence length were investigated. And in addition to the separate effects of each of the factors investigated individually, there were no doubt interactive effects as well that were beyond the scope of this study. Most importantly, however, these effects were systematic competence effects on the cognitive requirements for saying sentences; they were not the kinds of accidental performance factors that might have interfered with competence, such as fatigue, memory lapses, or other attentional distractions.

Grammatical complexity that reduced sentence length included negation, embedded relations in the predicate (e.g., "eat chocolate cookie"), and verbs with particles (e.g., "put heater up"). In contrast, complexity within nominal and verb constituents, such as inflections, auxiliaries, determiners, demonstratives, and articles, had no effect. These occurred as often with longer sentences as with shorter sentences. Lexical factors had both facilitating and constraining effects. Constituents were more likely to be omitted when relatively new verbs were used and more likely to be realized in sentences when old, well-known verbs were used. Discourse support in the form of a preceding, related child or adult utterance favored longer utterances. The full sentence was more likely to occur if the child had already said part of the sentence, and shorter sentences were more likely to be the first utterance in a succession of related utterances. Several explanations had been offered in the literature to explain variable sentence length. The relative adequacy of these alternative pragmatic, semantic, action-based, and grammatical theories is discussed.

The results led to two main conclusions. First, the structure of sentences is mediated by the meaning of the verb, and children operate with a fairly well defined notion of constituent structure. Second, the distribution of constituent relations was not random, as one might expect if their grammatical representation were optional rather than obligatory. However, several factors were shown to vary regularly with utterance length, and this systematic covariation was a reflection of the child's underlying linguistic competence and not simply performance error.

Variation and Reduction as Aspects of Competence in Language Development

Lois Bloom, Peggy Miller, and Lois Hood

An explanation of what children know about language when they begin to use multiword utterances is a central concern in the study of child language. Two specific aspects of early sentences were investigated in this study: apparent constraint on length and the developmental interaction among grammatical complexity, lexical and discourse factors. In early child speech, first sentences are two words long, and sentences get longer as the child's acquisition of grammar increases. However, although utterance length is correlated with increased grammatical maturity up to a ceiling of about 4.0 morphemes, utterance length per se is not an index of the complexity of child sentences. Two-word utterances, for example, can represent a variety of relationships between constituents – compare "a book," "Daddy book," "new book," "read book," and "book table." It is reasonable that an explanation of why the child is limited to two or three words at a time and how circumstances that influence sentence length and complexity change over time

Reprinted from A. Pick (Ed.), *Minnesota Symposia on Child Psychology* (vol. 9, chap. 1, pp. 3–55). Minneapolis: University of Minnesota Press, 1975, with permission from The University of Minnesota Press.

so that longer utterances occur will contribute to an understanding of the linguistic system that children learn.

There are three main issues in the present study. The first has to do with the relative adequacy of different explanations of child language – pragmatic, semantic, action-based, or grammatical – in accounting for the variable length of child sentences. Braine (1974) and Schlesinger (1974) have explained early sentences in pragmatic terms; Bowerman (1973a), Greenfield & Smith (1976), Kates (1974), Park (1974), and Schlesinger (1971a) have explained the structure of early sentences in semantic terms; Bruner (1975), Dore (1975), and McNeill (1975) have proposed that the child's sensorimotor (action) patterns prefigure and thus determine sentence patterns; and the proposals of Bloom (1970), Bowerman (1973b), and Brown (1973) have centered on the nature of early rules of grammar. The thesis that will be presented here is an elaboration of the grammatical complexity hypothesis proposed originally in Bloom (1970): that utterance length is a function of development of the capacity for realizing the underlying grammatical complexity of sentences.

The second issue deals with the relative adequacy of different representations of grammar in child language. The specific questions are (1) whether there are categories such as subject, verb, and object in child language and, (2) if so, whether the representation of such categories in a child language grammar is optional, indicating that constituents may or may not be basic to sentences (Brown, 1973) or obligatory, indicating that such constituents are basic to sentences, whether or not words that represent them actually occur in particular sentences (Bloom, 1970). The evidence suggests that neither of the earlier formulations of optional or obligatory constituents was adequate. The model that will be presented here retains the concept of obligatory constituents, with the addition of probability factors that predict the frequency with which constituents are realized under different linguistic conditions. This variable-rules model is within the paradigm for grammatical formulations proposed by Labov (1969) and by Cedergren and Sankoff (1974) for variation in adult language, and suggested by Brown (1973) for the development of grammatical morphemes.[3]

One consequence of Labov's variable-rules model has been a reformulation of the competence–performance distinction. In the traditional view, competence consisted of a speaker's knowledge of language in the form of categorical rules for generating sentences. The actual production and comprehension of speech (performance) reflected competence interacting with, and distorted by, extralinguistic favors such as memory and attention limitations. In contrast, Labov's version of competence encompasses systematic variation among linguistic elements. He argues that a speaker's knowledge of language includes both categorical rules and variable rules which operate with particular probabilities in particular linguistic environments. Cedergren and Sankoff (1974) pointed out that "the power of this [Labov's] approach lies in the uniquely well-defined and economical relationship which it posits between a probability distribution and a sample, or between a model and a simulation" (pp. 352–3).

The third issue, then, concerns which of the two notions of competence/performance best accounts for the variable length of child utterances. Bowerman (1973a) has suggested that the length of child utterances is constrained by performance factors, as traditionally defined. More specifically, Brown (1973) and Bowerman (1973a) have explained children's continued use of two-constituent sentences when they are able to produce three-constituent and four-constituent utterances as casualties of performance – in effect, linguistic mistakes.[4] Yet Bowerman expressed uncertainty about the status of performance constraints and decided that some constraints were important enough to be represented in grammatical rules, that is, optional verb deletion transformations. Similarly, Brown proposed a categorical grammar in which subject and predicate constituents are represented as obligatory (p. 232) but elsewhere implied that constituents are optionally represented in competence (p. 238). It appears that attempts to apply the traditional competence/performance distinction have resulted in confusion about whether certain influences on child language reflect competence (and therefore should be represented in grammatical rules) or performance. The position taken here is that the length of child utterances is systematically related to several linguistic factors and that this covariation reflects linguistic competence.

Situational and intrapersonal performance factors that are nonsystematic, free-variation may well influence the length of child sentences. However, it is necessary to determine the extent to which variance in the length of utterances can be accounted for by systematic constraints on the child's knowledge, before judging the free or residual variability of constituent relations. In the present observational study of children's language behavior, speech events were examined to determine the distribution of constituent relations, and how factors related to grammatical, lexical, and discourse development covaried with the occurrence of two-, three-, and four-constituent relations as mean length of utterance increased from 1.0 to approximately 3.0 morphemes.

SUBJECTS AND PROCEDURES

The observations in the present study were made when the children were, approximately, between 20 and 28 months old. In an earlier study (Bloom, Lightbown, & Hood, 1975, chap. 2), approximately 25,000 utterances were processed in the period when mean length of utterance increased from 1.0 to about 2.5 morphemes. The results of that study included the sequence of development of the verb relations that were observed in multiword utterances. Two of these verb relations were the dynamic categories (involving movement) of action and locative action. In action events the movement affected an object in ways other than to change its location. In locative-action events the goal of the movement was to change the location of an object. Utterances in these two verb categories formed the corpus for analysis in the present study because (1) these were the semantic–syntactic categories that occurred most frequently for each child and (2) these categories of verbs developed for each child with increasing complexity within and between constituents.

The procedure that was followed was to examine each of the transcriptions from the four children with mean length of utterance less than 3.0 morphemes to identify the speech events that included multiword utterances with action and locative-action constituent relations. Because the investigation concerned the relative frequency of different constituent relations when more than one constituent relation was theoretically available, all imperatives (whether or not agent was expressed) and all intransitive action utterances were omitted from the analysis. Action intransitives exclude objects, and imperatives can exclude agents, so that each of these could not be compared with the relative occurrences of agent–verb and verb–object when the fuller agent–verb–object constituent structure was theoretically possible.

The second level of processing consisted of successive hypothesis-generating and hypothesis-testing procedures to explore the developmental relation among utterances with two, three, and four constituents, to determine how grammatical, lexical, and discourse development interacted with utterance length. Each utterance was multiply coded to identify (1) the meaning relations between the words,

Table 3.1. *Summary Description of Speech Samples[a]*

Child and Time	Hours	Age	Mean Length of Utterance	Number of Syntactic Utterance Tokens
Eric				
III	7.1	22,0	1.42	165
IV	8.0	23,2	1.69	504
V	8.0	25,1	2.63	1,056
VI	8.0	26,3	2.84	1,575
Gia				
II	6.7	20,2	1.34	341
III	8.0	22,1	1.58	451
IV	8.0	23,3	1.79	671
V	7.5	25,2	2.30	1,071
VI	6.0	27,1	2.75	1,286
Kathryn				
I	5.5	21,0	1.37	284
II	8.0	22,3	1.89	1,303
III	9.0	24,2	2.83	2,385
IV	7.8	26,1	3.30	1,655
Peter				
IV	4.5	23,1	1.41	149
V	3.0	23,2	1.33	258
VI	4.5	24,1	1.75	420
VII	4.5	25,0	2.39	643
IX	4.5	26,1	2.62	793
Total				15,010

[a]Only spontaneous utterances were counted in the present study. See Bloom, Hood, and Lightbown (1974) for a comparison of spontaneous and imitative utterances.

(2) the addition of any grammatical marker or other complexity within or between constituents, (3) the lexical variability of verbs and the occurrence of nominal or pronominal forms, and (4) the relation between successive utterances.

RESULTS

Table 3.1 presents a description of each sample of language behavior from the four children and includes information about age, mean length of utterance, time, and numbers of utterances in each sample. The roman numerals in the table (and in the text) were used only for convenience; they merely identify the successive samples from each child. Accordingly, Eric III, Gia III, and Kathryn III have in common the fact that the sample was the third in the longitudinal study of each. The roman numerals that identify the Peter data are higher because samples were collected from Peter more frequently, with shorter intervals between each sample. The important variable that established comparability among the children was, by design, the range of mean length of utterance. It happened that the children were also similar in age during this period.

The results consist of (1) the sequential development of the categories of action and locative-action verbs and the subcategories of locative-action verbs that were identified; (2) the relative distribution of constituent relations in sentences and the developmental change in the distribution of constituent relations within each category and subcategory; and (3) the grammatical, lexical, and discourse factors that covaried with the distribution of constituent relations.

Categories of Verb Relations

The categories of action and locative-action verbs identified in Bloom, Lightbown, and Hood (1975, chap. 2) were the following:[5]

1. *Action.* Utterances referred to movement by an agent that affected an object where the goal of the movement was not a change in the location of an object or person (see Locative action). At least two of the three components of an action relation (agent–action–object) had to be represented in the utterance in order for the utterance to be included within the category.

P VII	(Peter trying to open box)	my open that.
K III	(Kathryn opening drawer)	open drawer.
G III	(Gia going to her bike, and then getting on)	Gia bike. Gia ride bike.
E IV	(Eric has just reassembled train)	I made.

2. *Locative action.* Utterances with locative-action verbs referred to movement where the goal of movement was a change in the location of a person or object.

In the present study, the following three locative-action relationships were identified in the data according to whether the agent of the action was also the object that was affected by the action.

a. *Agent–locative action.* Utterances in this category specified a movement by an agent that caused another object to change place, and the pre-verbal constituent, whether or not expressed, was the agent.

E V	(Eric puts disks on bed)	I put ə up here.
G IV	(Gia bringing lambs to toy bag, then drops them into bag)	Gia away ə lamb.
P VII	(Peter holding recording tape)	put this down.

b. *Mover–locative action.* Utterances specified a movement in which the agent of the action was also the object that changed place, and the pre-verbal constituent, whether or not expressed, was the mover.

K IV		I sit down there.
	(then Kathryn sits on chair)	
G V	(Gia stands up on large stuffed dog)	stand ə wow wow.
E III	(Eric getting up from chair)	I get down.

c. *Patient–locative action.* Utterances in this category specified a movement by an agent that caused another object (patient) to change place, and the pre-verbal constituent, whether or not expressed, was the patient. Patient–locative-action utterances were semantically similar to agent–locative-action utterances but formally similar to mover-locative-action utterances.

E IV	(fitting disc into block)	ə fits here.
P V	(Peter putting tiny car under finger puppet's skirt)	goes on there.
K II	(Kathryn pushing lamb through windows of doll house)	lamb go in there.

The distinction among agent–, patient–, and mover–locative-action utterances was not imposed on the data at the outset but, rather, emerged during the course of the analysis. The categories were distinguished further in that agent–locative-action utterances shared one population of verbs and mover– and patient–locative–action utterances shared a second population of verbs. As can be seen in Table 3.2, the two populations of verbs overlapped only slightly.

Sequence of Development

The proportion of utterances in each of the four verb categories (one action and three locative action) is presented in Table 3.3. Action was

Table 3.2. *Rank Order of Most Frequent[a] Verbs in Three Locative-Action Categories (data combined for all children, all samples)*

Agent–Locative Action		Mover–Locative Action		Patient–Locative Action	
Verb	Frequency	Verb	Frequency	Verb	Frequency
put	287	go	132	go	285
take	48	sit	95	fit	65
away	26	go bye-bye	28	sit	34
turn	10	come	25	fall	30
out	9	get	18	bye-bye	11
get	7	fall	15	stand	6
fit	7	stand	11		
do	6	climb	9		
dump	6	jump	7		
sit	5	move	6		
		away	5		

[a] Includes verbs with frequencies of ≥5.

always more frequent that locative action, and for Eric and Peter, action appeared before locative action. Within the subcategories of locative action: Gia and Peter learned agent first; Eric learned patient first; and Kathryn learned mover first. As mean length of utterance approached 3.0, there was more consistency among the children: agent–locative action was the most frequent for Gia, Kathryn, and Peter, and patient–locative action was most frequent for Eric.

Relative Distribution of Constituent Relations

The relative frequency of two-, three-, and four-constituent relations is presented in Tables 3.4 through 3.7 for the four children. As can be seen, the three- and four-constituent utterances increased, but the two-constituent utterances continued to occur. The frequencies of the individual constituents in each category were combined for the four children at four mean-length-of-utterance levels in Figures 3.1 through 3.4. (See Table 3.8 for individual constituent data.) Verbs were the most frequent constituent in all categories. There was a strong tendency for the constituent that referred to the object affected by movement to be the second most frequent constituent in each category (movers, patients, and objects).

Table 3.3. *Proportional Distribution of Multiword Utterances in Action and Locative-Action Categories*

| | | | Action | | Locative Action | | | | | |
| | | | | | Agent | | Mover | | Patient | |
Child and Time	MLU[a]	N	Prop.	Freq.	Prop.	Freq.	Prop.	Freq.	Prop.	Freq.
Eric										
III	1.42	30	1.00	30	—	—	—	—	—	—
IV	1.69	134	.65	87	.01	2	.02	3	.31	42
V	2.63	310	.65	203	.15	46	.11	33	.09	28
VI	2.84	606[b]	.65[b]	394[b]	.11	66	.08	51	.16	95
Peter										
IV	1.41	56	1.00	56	—	—	—	—	—	—
V	1.33	76	.88	67	.08	6	0	0	.04	3
VI	1.75	111	.70	78	.15	17	.05	6	.09	10
VII	2.39	172	.48	82	.27	47	.07	12	.18	31
IX	2.62	200	.45	90	.28	55	.09	18	.19	37
Gia										
II	1.34	39	.51	20	.36	14	.10	4	.03	1
III	1.58	177	.81	144	.14	25	.01	2	.03	6
IV	1.79	231	.65	151	.09	21	.13	30	.13	29
V	2.30	392	.77	301	.06	22	.10	40	.07	29
VI	2.75	489[b]	.72[b]	352[b]	.12	58	.12	61	.04	18
Kathryn										
I	1.32	80	.70	56	.05	4	.21	17	.04	3
II	1.89	400	.73	291	.11	45	.04	16	.12	48
III	2.83	684	.58	399	.22	148	.10	70	.10	67
IV	3.30	619[c]	.58[c]	360[c]	.23	143	.14	87	.05	29

[a]Mean length of utterance (morphemes).
[b]Number of action utterances estimated on the basis of average number at Times IV and V.
[c]Number of action utterances estimated on the basis of average number at Times II and III.

The notion of optionality (Braine, 1974; Brown, 1973) supplied the null hypothesis for testing the independence of the individual constituents in constituent relations. Two versions of the optionality model – one a homogeneous model and the other a heterogeneous model – were tested to determine whether the obtained distributions were randomly generated. In both models the unconditional probabilities of individual constituents were combined to produce the conditional probability of the various constituent relations, given that the utterances contained at least two constituents.[6] The homogeneous random generation model assumed equal selection probabilities for each of the individual constituents. This probability was estimated by the method of maximum likelihood and was used to predict the distribution of constituent relations in action, mover–locative-action, patient–locative-action, and agent–locative-action utterances. The observed distributions (Tables 3.4 through 3.7) were then tested statistically (by chi-square) for goodness of fit with the predicted distributions. The null hypothesis of no difference between the expected and observed distributions was rejected in 47 out of 48 testable trials, $p<.05$ in 9 trials, and $p<.001$ in 38 trials. This result could mean either that (1) the constituents were independently generated but the selection probabilities were not equal or (2) the constituents were not independently generated.

Homogeneous Model

Assuming equal probability of each constituent, in the three-term case, the three possible two-term constituent relations each had

$$p_2 = \frac{p^2(1-p)}{[p^3+3p^2(1-p)]}$$

and the three-term constituent relation had

$$p_3 = \frac{p^3}{[p^3+3p^2(1-p)]}$$

In the four-term case, the six possible two-term constituent relations each had

$$p_2 = \frac{p^2(1-p)^2}{c}$$

the four possible three-term constituent relations each had

$$p_3 = \frac{p^3(1-p)}{c}$$

Table 3.4. *Eric: Frequency Distribution of Constituent Relations in Action and Locative-Action Categories*[a]

Constituent Relations	Eric III (1.42)[b]		Eric IV (1.69)[b]		Eric V (2.63)[b]		Eric VI (2.84)[b]	
	Prop.	Freq.	Prop.	Freq.	Prop.	Freq.	Prop.	Freq.[c]
Agent–Action–Object								
Agent–Verb	.03	1	.03	3	.12	25		
Agent–Object	—	—	.01	1	0	1		
Verb–Object	.65	20	.85	74	.46	93		
Agent–Verb–Object	.33	10	.10	9	.41	84		
Total Frequencies		31		87		203		
Agent–Locative-Action–Object–Place								
Agent–Verb	—	—	—	—	.17	8	.21	14
Agent–Object	—	—	—	—	—	—	—	—
Agent–Place	—	—	—	—	—	—	—	—
Verb–Object	—	—	—	1	.17	8	.27	18
Verb–Place	—	—	—	—	.17	8	.05	3
Object–Place	—	—	—	—	.07	3	.09	6
Agent–Verb–Object	—	—	—	—	.09	4	.21	14
Agent–Verb–Place	—	—	—	1	.24	11	.03	2
Agent–Object–Place	—	—	—	—	.02	1	—	—
Verb–Object–Place	—	—	—	—	.04	2	.03	2
Agent–Verb–Object–Place	—	—	—	—	.02	1	.11	7
Total Frequencies		—		2		46		66
Mover–Locative-Action–Place								
Mover–Verb	—	—	—	2	.76	25	.59	30
Mover–Place	—	—	—	—	.03	1	—	—

Verb–Place	—	—	—	1	.12	4	.04	2
Mover–Verb–Place	—	—	—	—	.09	3	.37	19
Total Frequencies				3		33		51
Patient–Locative-Action–Place								
Patient–Verb	—	—	.55	23	.32	9	.40	38
Patient–Place	—	—	.19	8	—	—	—	—
Verb–Place	—	—	.19	8	.29	8	.24	23
Patient–Verb–Place	—	—	.07	3	.39	11	.36	34
Total Frequencies				42		28		95

[a] Intransitive verbs (that did not involve action on affected-object) and imperatives (whether or not sentence-subjects were expressed) were not counted.

[b] Mean length of utterance (morphemes).

[c] This analysis was not done for Action verb relations because data were estimated at Eric VI.

Table 3.5. *Gia: Frequency Distribution of Constituent Relations in Action and Locative-Action Categories*[a]

Constituent Relations	Gia II (1.34)[b]		Gia III (1.58)[b]		Gia IV (1.79)[b]		Gia V (2.30)[b]		Gia VI (2.75)[b]	
	Prop.	Freq.	Prop.	Freq.	Prop.	Freq.	Prop.	Freq.	Prop.	Freq.[c]
Agent–Action–Object										
Agent–Verb	.15	3	.25	36	.17	26	.08	23	.09	5
Agent–Object	.15	3	.13	20	.15	23	.03	8	.02	1
Verb–Object	.65	13	.26	38	.37	56	.28	85	.02	1
Agent–Verb–Object	.05	1	.35	50	.30	46	.61	185	.22	13
Total Frequencies		20		144		151		301		
Agent–Locative-Action–Object–Place										
Agent–Verb	—	—	.20	5	.14	3	.05	1	.10	6
Agent–Object	—	—	.04	1	—	—	—	—	.02	1
Agent–Place	—	—	.12	3	—	—	—	—	.02	1
Verb–Object	.93	13	.44	11	.33	7	.05	1	.22	13
Verb–Place	.07	1	.12	3	—	—	—	—	.10	6
Object–Place	—	—	.04	1	.29	6	.27	6	—	—
Agent–Verb–Object	—	—	—	—	.19	4	.18	4	.28	16
Agent–Verb–Place	—	—	.04	1	.05	1	.18	4	.12	7
Agent–Object–Place	—	—	—	—	—	—	—	—	—	—
Verb–Object–Place	—	—	—	—	—	—	.14	3	.07	4
Agent–Verb–Object–Place	—	—	—	—	—	—	.14	3	.09	5
Total Frequencies		14		25		21		22		58
Mover–Locative-Action–Place										
Mover–Verb	—	3	—	1	.43	13	.33	13	.43	26
Mover–Place	—	1	—	—	.03	1	—	1	—	—

	No.	Prop.	No.	Prop.	No.	Prop.	No.	Prop.	No.	Prop.
Verb–Place	—	—	1	—	8	.27	5	.13	6	.10
Mover–Verb–Place	—	—	—	—	8	.27	22	.55	29	.48
Total Frequencies	4		2		30		40		61	
Patient–Locative–Action–Place										
Patient–Verb	5	.83	9	.31	4	.14	14	.78		
Patient–Place	1	.17	—	—	6	.21	—	—		
Verb–Place	—	—	5	.17	19	.66	—	—		
Patient–Verb–Place	—	—	15	.52	—	—	4	.22		
Total Frequencies	6		29		29		18			

[a] Intransitive verbs (that did not involve action on affected-object) and imperatives (whether or not sentence-subjects were expressed) were not counted.

[b] Mean length of utterance (morphemes).

[c] This analysis was not done for Action verb relations because data were estimated at Gia VI.

Table 3.6. *Kathryn: Frequency Distribution of Constituent Relations in Action and Locative-Action Categories*[a]

Constituent Relations	Kathryn I (1.32)[b]		Kathryn II (1.89)[b]		Kathryn III (2.83)[b]		Kathryn IV (3.30)[b]	
	Prop.	Freq.	Prop.	Freq.	Prop.	Freq.	Prop.	Freq.[c]
Agent–Action–Object								
Agent–Verb	.13	7	.10	30	.05	19		
Agent–Object	.18	10	.02	6	.01	3		
Verb–Object	.59	33	.54	156	.46	183		
Agent–Verb–Object	.11	6	.34	99	.48	194		
Total Frequencies		56		291		399		
Agent–Locative-Active–Object–Place								
Agent–Verb	—	—	.04	2	.06	9	.03	5
Agent–Object	—	—	—	—	—	—	—	—
Agent–Place	—	—	.09	4	.01	1	—	—
Verb–Object	—	1	.29	13	.35	52	.21	30
Verb–Place	—	—	.13	6	.03	4	.03	5
Object–Place	—	3	.31	14	.01	1	.01	2
Agent–Verb–Object	—	—	.02	1	.32	48	.37	53
Agent–Verb–Place	—	—	.02	1	.05	7	.06	9
Agent–Object–Place	—	—	.02	1	.01	1	—	—
Verb–Object–Place	—	—	.04	2	.08	12	.14	20
Agent–Verb–Object–Place	—	—	.02	1	.09	13	.13	19
Total Frequencies		4		45		148		143
Mover–Locative-Action–Place								
Mover–Verb	.06	1	.50	8	.29	20	.31	27
Mover–Place	—	—	—	—	—	—	—	—

Verb–Place	.88	15	.19	3	.23	16	.24	21
Mover–Verb–Place	.06	1	.31	5	.49	34	.45	39
Total Frequencies		17		16		70		87
Patient–Locative-Action–Place								
Patient–Verb	—	3	.48	23	.43	29	.48	14
Patient–Place	—	—	—	—	—	—	—	8
Verb–Place	—	—	.25	12	.13	9	.28	7
Patient–Verb–Place	—	—	.27	13	.43	29	.24	7
Total Frequencies		3		48		67		29

[a] Intransitive verbs (that did not involve action on affected-object) and imperatives (whether or not sentence-subject were expressed) were not counted.
[b] Mean length of utterance (morphemes).
[c] This analysis was not done for Action verb relations because data were estimated at Kathryn IV.

Table 3.7. Peter: Frequency Distribution of Constituent Relations in Action and Locative-Action Categories[a]

Constituent Relations	Peter IV (1.41)[b]		Peter V (1.33)[b]		Peter VI (1.75)[b]		Peter VII (2.39)[b]		Peter IX (2.62)[b]	
	Prop.	Freq.	Prop.	Freq.	Prop.	Freq.	Prop.	Freq.	Prop.	Freq.
Agent–Action–Object										
Agent–Verb	—	—	—	—	.03	2	.22	18	.11	10
Agent–Object	—	—	—	—	.03	2	—	—	—	—
Verb–Object	.88	49	.96	64	.87	68	.60	49	.54	49
Agent–Verb–Object	.13	7	.04	3	.08	6	.18	15	.34	31
Total Frequencies		56		67		78		82		90
Agent–Locative-Action–Object–Place										
Agent–Verb	—	—	.17	1	—	—	—	—	.13	7
Agent–Object	—	—	—	—	—	—	—	—	—	—
Agent–Place	—	—	—	—	—	—	—	—	—	—
Verb–Object	—	—	.33	2	.18	3	.25	12	.25	14
Verb–Place	—	—	.17	1	.24	4	.28	13	.20	11
Object–Place	—	—	.33	2	.50	7	.13	6	—	—
Agent–Verb–Object	—	—	—	—	—	—	.09	4	.15	8
Agent–Verb–Place	—	—	—	—	—	—	—	—	.07	4
Agent–Object–Place	—	—	—	—	—	—	—	—	—	—
Verb–Object–Place	—	—	—	—	.18	3	.23	11	.13	7
Agent–Verb–Object–Place	—	—	—	—	—	—	.02	1	.07	4
Total Frequencies		—		6		17		47		55
Mover–Locative-Action–Place										
Mover–Verb	—	—	—	—	.67	4	.83	10	.61	11
Mover–Place	—	—	—	—	—	—	—	—	.06	1

Verb–Place	—	—	—	—	.33	2	.17	2	.22	4
Mover–Verb–Place	—	—	—	—	—	—	—	—	.11	2
Total Frequencies						6		12		18
Patient–Locative-Action–Place										
Patient–Verb	—	—	—	—	.20	2	.06	2	.05	2
Patient–Place	—	—	—	—	—	—	—	—	—	—
Verb–Place	—	—	—	1	.80	8	.74	23	.49	18
Patient–Verb–Place	—	—	—	2	—	—	.19	6	.46	17
Total Frequencies				3		10		31		37

[a]Intransitive verbs (that did not involve action on affected-object) and imperatives (whether or not sentence-subjects were expressed) were not counted.

[b]Mean length of utterance (morphemes).

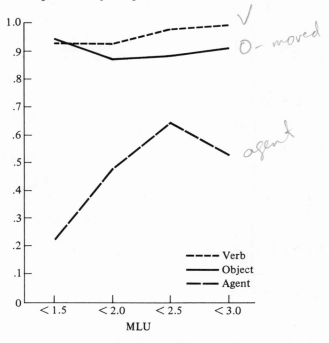

Figure 3.1. Action verbs: proportion of utterances that include the individual constituents, for all children at four MLU points.

and the one possible four-term constituent relation had

$$p_4 = \frac{p^4}{c}$$

where

$$c = p^4 + 4p^3 (1-p) + 6p^2 (1-p)^2$$

The *heterogeneous* random generation model was used to explore further these alternatives. This model assumed unequal selection probabilities for the individual constituents. Unfortunately, the model could not be applied to the action, mover–locative-action, and patient–locative-action data since only four events were observable in each of these categories. For example, the observed events for action utterances were agent–verb, verb–object, agent–object, and agent–verb–object. Because only four events were observable, there were two few degrees of freedom to permit the testing of the heterogeneous model. However, this model could be tested with the agent–locative-action

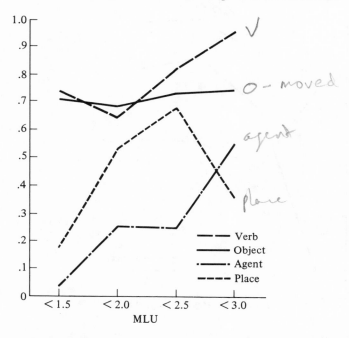

Figure 3.2. Agent–locative-action verbs: proportion of utterances that include the individual constituents, for all children at four MLU points.

data in which 11 events were observable. Accordingly, using the observed distribution, the individual constituent probabilities (agent, verb, object, and place) were estimated by the method of maximum likelihood and were used to predict the distribution of constituent relations.[7] Again, the observed distribution was tested against the predicted distribution, using the chi-square goodness of fit test. Of the 11 samples tested, six differences were significant with $p < .05$, and two approached significance with $p < .07$. It was concluded, therefore, that the individual constituents in agent–locative-action utterances were not independently selected.

Heterogeneous Model
Assuming unequal probabilities of each constituent:

$$p(n_1, n_2, n_3, n_4) = \frac{p_1{}^{n_1} q_1{}^{m_1} p_2{}^{n_2} q_2{}^{m_2} p_3{}^{n_3} q_3{}^{m_3} p_4{}^{n_4} q_4{}^{m_4}}{c}$$

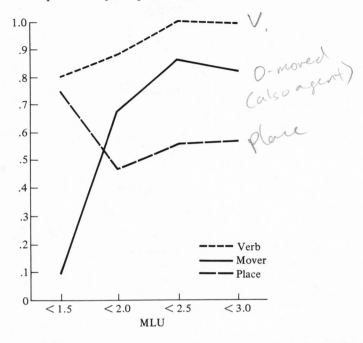

Figure 3.3. Mover–locative-action verbs: proportion of utterances that include the individual constituents, for all children combined at four MLU points.

where

$n_i = 1$ if the ith component is present
    0 if the ith component is absent
$m_i = 1 - n_i$

and c is the constant required to make the probabilities of the 11 observable cells sum to one and may be computed as

$$c = 1 - [p_1 q_2 q_3 q_4 + q_1 p_2 q_3 q_4 + q_1 q_2 p_3 q_4 + q_1 q_2 q_3 p_4 + q_1 q_2 q_3 q_4]$$

The null hypothesis of optional representation of each constituent – as tested by both the homogeneous and heterogeneous models – was rejected. Since the observed distributions were significantly different from the expected distributions, it was concluded that the variation among the constituent relations was systematic. The question then became one of accounting for the variation of the constituent relations and attempting to determine why the two-constituent utterances continued to occur.

The two random generation models tested here fall within the para-

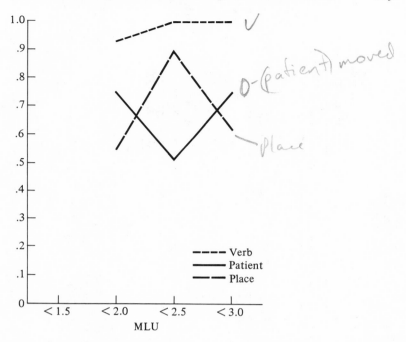

Figure 3.4. Patient–locative-action verbs: proportion of utterances that include the individual constituents, for all children combined at four MLU points.

digm for "probabilistic grammars" proposed by Suppes (1970). Suppes attempted to construct a probabilistic grammar for the noun phrases in a corpus of speech from a child, Adam, collected by Roger Brown and his associates at Harvard. Suppes suggested that only a probabilistic grammar could account for "the distribution of length of utterance, and the relatively sharp bounds on the complexity of utterances" in natural languages. The variable-rules paradigm presented here goes beyond Suppes's analysis; it attempts to capture the relative effects of different aspects of a speech event in determining the probability with which individual constituents will co-occur.

Grammatical, Lexical, and Discourse Covariation with Constituent Relations

The two-constituent relations that continued to occur could not have been intransitives in action utterances (agent–verb) or imperatives (verb–object) because these were not included in the analysis. The extent to

Tabel 3.8. *Individual Constituent Frequencies Presented as Proportion of Utterances in a Category Having the Constituent Expressed*

Child and Time	Action			Agent–Locative Action				Mover–Locative Action			Patient–Locative Action		
	Agent	Verb	Object	Agent	Verb	Object	Place	Mover	Verb	Place	Patient	Verb	Place
Eric													
III	.37(11)	1.00(31)	.97(30)	—	—	—	—	—	—	—	—	—	—
IV	.15(13)	.99(86)	.97(84)	—	—	—	—	—	—	—	.81(34)	.81(34)	.45(19)
V	.54(110)	1.00(202)	.88(178)	.54(25)	.87(40)	.41(19)	.57(26)	.88(29)	.97(32)	.24(8)	.71(20)	1.00(28)	.68(19)
VI	—	—	—	.56(37)	.91(60)	.71(47)	.30(20)	.96(49)	1.00(51)	.41(21)	.76(72)	1.00(95)	.60(57)
Gia													
II	.35(7)	.85(17)	.85(17)	(0)	1.00(14)	.93(13)	.07(1)	—	—	—	1.00(6)	.83(5)	.17(1)
III	.74(106)	.86(124)	.75(108)	.40(10)	.80(20)	.52(13)	.32(8)	—	—	—	.83(24)	1.00(29)	.69(20)
IV	.63(95)	.85(128)	.83(125)	.38(8)	.71(15)	.81(17)	.33(7)	.73(22)	.97(29)	.57(17)	.79(23)	1.00(29)	.80(25)
V	.72(216)	.97(293)	.92(278)	.55(12)	.73(16)	.77(17)	.73(16)	.88(35)	1.00(40)	.68(27)	1.00(18)	1.00(18)	.22(4)
VI	—	—	—	.60(35)	.97(56)	.67(39)	.40(23)	.90(55)	1.00(61)	.57(35)	—	—	—
Kathryn													
I	.41(23)	.82(46)	.88(49)	—	—	—	—	.17(2)	1.00(17)	.94(16)	—	—	—
II	.46(135)	.98(285)	.90(261)	.22(10)	.58(26)	.71(32)	.64(29)	.81(13)	1.00(16)	.50(8)	.75(36)	1.00(48)	.52(25)
III	.54(216)	.99(396)	.95(380)	.53(79)	.98(145)	.86(127)	.26(39)	.77(54)	1.00(70)	.71(50)	.87(58)	1.00(67)	.57(38)
IV	—	—	—	.60(86)	.99(141)	.87(124)	.38(55)	.76(66)	1.00(87)	.69(60)	.72(21)	1.00(29)	.52(15)
Peter													
IV	.13(7)	1.00(56)	1.00(56)	—	—	—	—	—	—	—	—	—	—
V	.04(3)	1.00(67)	1.00(67)	.17(1)	.67(4)	.67(4)	.50(3)	—	—	—	—	—	—
VI	.13(10)	.97(76)	.97(76)	(0)	.59(10)	.76(13)	.82(14)	.67(4)	1.00(6)	.33(2)	.20(2)	1.00(10)	.80(8)
VII	.40(33)	1.00(82)	.78(64)	.11(5)	.87(41)	.72(34)	.66(31)	.83(10)	1.00(12)	.17(2)	.26(8)	1.00(31)	.94(29)
IX	.46(41)	1.00(90)	.89(80)	.42(23)	1.00(55)	.60(33)	.47(26)	.78(14)	.94(17)	.39(7)	.51(19)	1.00(37)	.95(35)

which grammatical, lexical, and discourse factors could account for the variance in utterance length was explored before judging the extent to which the obtained distribution was owing to residual variability of the constituent relations (as suggested by Brown, 1973; and Bowerman, 1973a).

Grammatical Covariation

There were two levels of analysis to determine the effect of added complexity on utterance length. In the first analysis, any addition to a constituent (inflections or modifications) or anything inserted between or after constituents (prepositions, adverbs, possessives, etc.) was counted as complexity added to the constituent structure. (See Table 3.9 for definitions of types of complexity.) If added complexity was more frequent in two-constituent utterances than in three-constituent utterances, there would be two equally plausible interpretations. Either the children could not add complexity to three or four constituents, or they necessarily deleted one of the constituents with added complexity, because of (1) a *length* constraint – they could not say more than just three (or four) words (or morphemes), or (2) a *grammatical* constraint – they could not generate the full constituent structure with added complexity.

In the first level of analysis, the frequency of any complexity was compared in two- and three-constituent relations. Complexity occurred more often with two constituents than with three constituents. The hypothesis that kinds of complexity were equally distributed among two- and three-constituent relations in the samples from the four children (for action, mover–locative action, and patient–locative action) was tested by sign tests. In 15 out of 19 action samples, more object or other complexity occurred in two-constituent relations than in three-constituent relations. In 16 of 23 patient–locative-action samples there was more patient, place, or other complexity in two-constituent relations than in three-constituent relations. The probability of these results, using a one-tailed test, was less than .05 in both cases. In the mover–locative-action samples, mover, place, or other complexity was equally distributed in two- and three-constituent relations. Similarly, verb complexity and prepositions were equally distributed between two- and three-constituent relations in all three categories.

The results for the individual children reached statistical significance (by chi-square) in only 5 of 12 trials for Kathryn and in only 5 of 16

Table 3.9. *Kinds of Complexity*

Verb Complexity
  1. All inflections for tense, for example, *ing, -s, ed*
  2. The contracted copula
  3. Modals, signaling intention most often, for example, "gonna," "want," "hafta," "lets," "lemme," and "shall"
  4. Adverbs of (a) manner, for example, "like this," "this way"
                  (b) time, for example, "now," "right now"
                  (c) recurrence, for example, "again"
  5. Two-part verbs where the preposition did not signal direction of movement, for example, "put heater up," "turn light on"

Object, Place, Mover, Patient, and Agent Complexity
  1. Inflection for plural
  2. Definite article *the*
  3. Demonstratives *this, that, these, those*
  4. Embedded relations (a) Possessor noun or pronoun
                  (b) Attributives, for example, "tiny," "red," "three"
                  (c) Recurrence ("more" or "another")

Other Complexity
  1. Negation, for example, "I can't open it"
  2. Place (when not a constituent of a locative verb, for example, "orange chair read a book")
  3. Dative, for example, "Mommy give them milk and sugar"
  4. Instrumental, for example, "Mommy lock ə keys"
  5. Coordinate and subordinate relation with another clause, for example, "I want go door see my mommy"
  6. Affirmative, for example, "all right," "okay"
  7. Vocative, for example, "shall go in there, Lois"
  8. Introducers, for example, "and," "then"

Prepositions, counted as a separate complexity in locative relations, specified
  1. Direction toward and away from place
  2. Direction toward and away from speaker

trials for Gia (where a trial was defined as a possible comparison between two- and three-constituents, when at least five tokens of each constituent relation occurred and at least three instances of complexity occurred) for action utterances (Table 3.10). There were only occasional significant effects (by chi-square) for Peter and Eric in the action category. In the locative-action category, the interactions could be statistically tested less often, and the significant effects were fewer. In the agent–locative-action subcategory, only the data from Kathryn resulted in more than occasional significant effects.

Verb complexity was observed more often when there was a pre-

Table 3.10. *Summary of Differences Between Kinds of Complexity in Two- and Three-Term Action Constituent Relations*

Child and Time	Agent–Verb/ Agent–Verb–Object Complexity			Verb–Object/ Agent–Verb–Object Complexity			Agent–Object/ Agent–Verb–Object Complexity		
	Object	Verb	Other	Object	Verb	Other	Object	Verb	Other
Eric									
III	—	np	np	nt	ns	nt	np	—	np
IV	—	np	np	nd	ns	ns	np	—	np
V	—	$2{>}3^b$	ns	ns	ns	ns	np	—	np
Gia									
III	—	$2{>}3^b$	nt	ns	ns	nt	ns	—	nt
IV	—	$2{>}3^b$	nt	ns	nt	ns	$3{>}2^a$	—	ns
V	—	ns	$2{>}3^b$	$2{>}3^b$	$2{>}3^b$	ns	ns	—	ns
Kathryn									
I	—	nt	nt	ns	nt	nt	ns	—	nt
II	—	$2{>}3^b$	$2{>}3^a$	ns	$2{>}3^a$	ns	np	—	np
III	—	$2{>}3^b$	ns	$2{>}3^b$	$3{>}2^a$	ns	np	—	np
Peter									
IV	—	np	np	nt	nt	nt	np	—	np
V	—	np	np	np	np	np	np	—	np
VI	—	np	np	nt	ns	ns	np	—	np
VII	—	ns	nt	ns	ns	$2{>}3^a$	np	—	np
IX	—	ns	$2{>}3^a$	ns	ns	ns	np	—	np

nd = no difference; np = not productive (<5 tokens in category); ns = not significant; nt = not testable (<3 instances of complexity).
> = direction of difference between number of constituents.
[a]significant at .05 level. [b]significant at .01 level.

verbal constituent, so that agent–verb, mover–verb, and patient–verb utterances generally included more verb complexity than did verb–object and verb–place utterances. Further, the form of the verbal complexity varied in relation to whether the pre-verbal constituent was agent, mover, or patient. For example, third person singular -*s* occurred overwhelmingly with patients; irregular (and then regular) past occurred with agents and movers and, except for Kathryn, did not occur with patients (see Bloom, Lifter, & Hafitz, 1980, chap. 5, for this analysis and discussion). Prepositions (in locative-action categories) occurred more often when place was mentioned. The other interactions in the data from Gia and Kathryn appeared to be as follows: In the action utterances, agents occurred less often with complex objects than with simple objects, and objects occurred less often with complex verbs than with simple verbs. These results reached statistical significance in Kathryn II for verb complexity and Kathryn III for verb and object complexity (chi-square, $p<.05$), and for verb complexity in Gia III and IV (chi-square, $p<.001$).

The result of the first analysis of complexity was that when any morpheme added to a constituent relation was counted as complexity, two-constituent sentences could not be convincingly differentiated from three-constituent sentences, except for Kathryn and Gia, as indicated in Table 3.10. Two conclusions were possible, given this result. The first conclusion was that there was no absolute limit on utterance length per se; the children did not use more two-constituent relations than three-constituent relations because it was difficult for them to say more than two words at a time. The second conclusion was that if there was a grammatical constraint, it was a more discriminating effect than could be observed by counting any and all additions to utterances as added complexity. The data were then examined at a second level of analysis, to determine whether particular kinds of additions within and between morphemes would differentiate sentences with two- and three-constituent relations.

There were too few instances of complexity to permit separate statistical analysis of each sample for each child. Accordingly, data from the four children were combined. The five more frequent kinds of complexity with action verbs were (1) verb inflections, (2) two-part verbs, (3) definite articles and demonstratives, (4) embedded relations (possession, recurrence, and other attribution), and (5) plural *-s*. The data were analyzed for each of these separately, and the samples were combined according to these criteria: All samples were combined that contained two or more instances of a complexity type, with frequency of subject–verb–object less than the frequency of subject–verb or verb–object. The data base was different for each of the five types of complexity. Grouping the samples in this manner yielded a relatively large number of samples which met the criteria for verb inflections (10 action samples from the four children). In contrast, only 7 (somewhat later) samples met the criteria for plural *-s*. Object complexity was an earlier development than was verb complexity for Gia and Kathryn (who used nouns more than pronouns), and verb complexity was an earlier development than was object complexity for Peter and Eric (who used more pronouns than nouns). See Bloom, Lightbown, and Hood

(1975, chap. 2) for a description of the nominal–pronominal development of the four children.

When the frequency of each type of complexity was compared in two- and three-constituent action relations, there was no significant difference (chi-square test) for verb inflections, the definite article and demonstratives, and plural -*s*. Each of these factors, then, did not increase the complexity of a sentence to differentiate between the number of constituents that could occur. The frequency of two-part verbs was significantly greater in two- than in three-constituent relations (chi-square $= 3.96, p < .05$), and the frequency of embedded relations was greater in two- than in three-constituent relations, but the difference was not significant (chi-square $= 2.58, p < .10$). This last result is more meaningful, however, when the frequency of each of the same relations (possession, recurrence, and other attribution) occurring alone is taken into account. For all the children, when mean length of utterance reached 3.0, these relations were generally frequent but were infrequently embedded in action relations.

The categories with three-constituent relations were combined in order to compare other kinds of complexity (action, mover–locative action, and patient–locative action). Negation was significantly more frequent in two- than in three-constituent relations (chi-square $= 12.28, p < .001$). However, there was no significant difference between two- and three-constituent relations with occurrence of the dative or clausal subordination and coordination.

Thus, the results of the two analyses of grammatical complexity revealed that different kinds of complexity had different effects on utterance length: Verb inflections, prepositions, noun inflections, and determiners occurred as often with two- as with three-constituent relations; negation, two-part verbs, possession, recurrence, and other attribution occurred more often with two-constituent relations than with three-constituent relations.

Lexical Covariation

Verbs. There was greater action and locative-action verb variability (the ratio of number of different verbs to number of utterances) in two-constituent relations than in three-constituent relations, for all the children. All verbs were classified as old (having occurred in any previous sample) or new (having not occurred in a previous sample), and a comparison was made between the occurrence of old and new verbs in two- and three-constituent relations. A sign test of the hypothesis that old and new verbs were equally distributed among two- and three-constituent relations was performed. In 20 out of 31 samples there were more new verbs in two-constituent relations than in three-constituent relations. The probability of this result, given the hypothesis of no difference between old and new verbs, was less than .05.

Nouns. The relative occurrence of nouns and pronouns was compared in two- and three-constituent relations. In an earlier study (Bloom, Lightbown, & Hood, 1975, chap. 2) we reported a developmental shift from nouns to pronouns in the sentences of Gia and Kathryn, and a shift from pronouns to nouns in the sentences of Eric and Peter. In the present study, objects tended to be pronouns more frequently than nouns in three-constituent relations for all the children except Gia at Time IV. Gia at Time IV used pronouns more frequently in two-constituent relations (agents or objects) than in three-constituent relations. For Peter and Eric, objects were nouns more frequently in verb–object than in subject–verb–object. It appeared that nouns as objects represented a lexical constraint for Eric and Peter and that pronouns represented a lexical constraint for Gia at the time of the shift from nouns to pronouns.

Further, when mean length of utterance was less than 2.0, Eric and Peter used a pronominal system for encoding verb–object and agent–verb–object constructions. They did not produce agent–verb utterances until after they had begun to use noun forms as objects (when mean length of utterance exceeded 2.0). In contrast, Gia and Kathryn initially used a nominal system for encoding verb–object and agent–verb constructions. After they began using pronominal forms (mean length of utterance greater than 2.0), the proportion of agent–verb utterances decreased. Thus for all four children, nominal objects and agent–verb constructions tended to covary. It was also possible that relative recency of nouns (old or new) was a factor that influenced the occurrence of two- and three-constituent relations, but an analysis of old and new nouns comparable to the verb analysis was not performed.

Discourse Covariation

Patterns of discourse consisted of formal and semantic relations among successive child or child and adult utterances. Utterances that were successive shared the same topic (in the sense of "topic" discussed by

Hymes, 1964) and were always semantically related to one another by definition, and sometimes formally related as well. The most frequent kind of formal relationship was an expansion of the within-clause structure in successive utterances; semantic relationship was a continuation of meaning (talking about the same topic) from one utterance to another, without necessarily maintaining the same structure (see Bloom, Rocissano, & Hood, 1976, chap. 13). Some examples were:[8]

1. Formal expansions:

K III	(Kathryn closing basket)	close it/I close it.
G IV	(Lois is reading magazine to Gia) Lois: Read?	you read.
		read that magazine/you read that magazine.
P VII	(Peter comes over to tape recorder to press button)	get ə button/I'm gonna get ə button.

2. Semantic relations:

K II	(Mommy had been ironing)	Mommy iron shirt/fresh ə nice.
P IX	(Peter's sister Jenny is in her cradle drinking her bottle).	Jenny she's drinking ə bottle.
	Patsy: Is she?	be quiet.
E V	(Eric makes toy dog and cat kiss) Lois: Who's kissing who? (Eric making them kiss again) Lois: Yes. That's right.	the dog's kissing cat. not crying.

Two- and three-constituent relations in action utterances in the last two samples from each child (Eric IV, V; Gia IV, V; Kathryn II, III; and Peter VII, IX) were compared according to whether or not they occurred successively. The proportion of successive utterances (1) was similar in two- and three-constituent relations, (2) was always high in both (at least .50, except for subject–verb–object at Peter VII) and increased developmentally for the four children (for example, at Peter IX, .71 of the subject–verb–object utterances were successive).

Each successive utterance was considered in terms of its relation to a preceding utterance and its relation to a subsequent utterance. The possible relations to a preceding utterance were (1) first in sequence–

that is, no preceding utterance, (2) a formal expansion, (3) a semantic relation, and (4) other – including repetitions, recodings, and the like. Relative to subsequent utterances, a particular successive utterance could be (1) last in sequence – that is, no subsequent utterance, (2) formally expanded, (3) semantically related, or (3) other.[9]

It was possible to compare successive two- and three-constituent utterances on these variables. Among the successive utterances, three-constituent relations were more often formal expansions of a previous child utterance than were two-constituent relations. For the combined samples, this difference was significant (chi-square = 49.92, $p < .001$) using the chi-square statistic for combining significance probabilities (Fisher, 1967). Semantic relations (not formally related) occurred less frequently than formal expansion and occurred more often in two-constituent relations than in three-constituent relations, but this difference is not significant ($p = .06$, by sign test).

More two-constituent relations than three-constituent relations in the eight samples were subsequently expanded and formally related to subsequent utterances, and this difference was significant (chi-square = 33.42, $p < .025$), as tested by the chi-square statistic for combining significance probabilities. Successive utterances that were subsequently expanded included those that were the first utterance in a sequence. In seven of eight samples, more two-constituent relations than three-constituent relations were first utterances. There were other kinds of relations represented among successive utterances, including repetition and recoding, but these were relatively infrequent and did not differentiate between two- and three-constituent relations.

Grammatical ellipsis. The final hypothesis that was tested in order to explain the variation in utterance length was the possibility that two-constituent relations could be attributed to grammatical ellipsis (described by Halliday & Hasan, 1976, as "texting"); that is, the children could be taking into account prior linguistic reference by themselves and others, thereby eliminating redundant elements in their own speech. For example, "Mommy's going to the store. Daddy's going to the store" could be reduced in natural speech to "Mommy's going to the store. Daddy's going, too." Similarly, an answer to the question "Who's reading the book?" is "Mommy is reading the book," which could be reduced to "Mommy reading."

In order to explore the role of ellipsis, the relation between child utterances and preceding adult utterances was examined in all the data (action and locative-action verb categories). All child utterances whether successive or nonsuccessive, were classified as contingent or noncontingent. A contingent utterance was formally or semantically related to the preceding adult utterance (see Bloom, Rocissano, & Hood, 1976, Chap. 13, for a more extended analysis of contingency in adult–child discourse). A necessary but not sufficient condition for ellipsis is that the elliptical utterance be contingent upon a previous utterance. If the proportion of contingency in two-constituent relations were greater than the proportion of contingency in three-constituent relations, then one might conclude that the children were using ellipsis in responding to adult speech. However, although the proportion of contingent utterances increased developmentally for the four children, the frequency of contingency was not different in two- and three-constituent relations.

Finally, contingent-action utterances in the last sample from each child were examined directly to determine (1) if the two-constituent utterance was elliptical, for example,

P IX   Patsy: What are you looking for?

look for my pencil.

and (2) if the three-constituent utterance occurred in an elliptical condition (that is, where the child utterance was at least partially redundant), for example.

P IX   Lois: What are you gonna do?

I'm gonna fix it.

For Kathryn and Eric there were more three-constituent relations in elliptical conditions than there were two-constituent relation elliptical utterances, whereas for Peter and Gia the opposite was found. However, none of these differences was significant (by chi-square test). It was concluded that grammatical ellipsis, as it operates in adult speech, was not yet productive in the children's speech and could not be a factor accounting for the variable length of utterances. In contrast, the important conclusion that followed from the several analyses of discourse variation was that discourse, that is, the preceding related utterances by the child or an adult, influenced the length of the children's utterances by providing memory support to facilitate the occurrence of three-constituent relations.

DISCUSSION

The major result of this study of grammatical complexity and constituent relations was the variable influence of grammatical, lexical, and discourse factors on increasing utterance length. No one factor emerged as clearly and consistently accounting for the variable occurrence of two-, three-, and four-constituent relations. Rather, each of the factors examined exerted an influence on some of the children some of the time, but none of the factors operated consistently for all of the children all of the time. Moreover, factors operated in both directions, to facilitate as well as to constrain sentences. At the conclusion of this study, there still remained the possibility that other, as yet unidentified, factors operated to affect utterance length in addition to those examined here and in addition to the nonsystematic effect of inherent variability. The interactions described here demonstrate the enormous complexity of the task of language acquisition, and cast immediate doubt on any simplistic explanations of child language that do not take such covariation of factors into account.

The model of child language that will be proposed here is a variation model, within the paradigm developed by Labov (1969), Cedergren and Sankoff (1974), Sankoff (1974), and Bailey (1973) and implicates, without actually specifying, the variable rules in children's knowledge that account for their behavior. The major difficulty in specifying the form of such variable rules is the conflicting influence from several sources on language behavior during development. On the one hand, there are influences, such as certain kinds of complexity and lexical novelty, that constrain utterance length and account, at least in part, for the occurrence of two-constituent utterances. At the same time, there are those developmental influences, such as lexical familiarity and the apparent aid to memory with successive discourse, that facilitate utterances and account for the occurrence of three- and four-constituent relations.

Before presenting the variation model, some of the alternative theories that have been proposed will be reviewed in light of evidence from the present study, and in relation to the original question of what children know about sentence structure. The three issues to be dealt with have to do with (1) the adequacy of pragmatic, semantic, action-based (sensorimotor), and grammatical theories of child language; (2) optional versus obligatory representation of major constituents in rules of grammar; and (3) the extent to which variation in child language is a reflection of underlying grammatical competence.

Alternative Explanations of Child Language

The Pragmatic Argument. Braine (1974) rejected the notion of reduction of a fuller underlying structure than is represented in child speech (Bloom, 1970) and proposed an alternative model to account for the disproportionate distribution of two- and three-word utterances. He suggested that the small number of three-word utterances in early speech reflects the probability with which two expansion rules may co-occur (such as the first rule that the sentence consists of a noun phrase and a verb phrase, and the second rule that the verb phrase includes a noun).

Unfortunately, this model is theoretically untestable. The events that must occur in Braine's model include the single constituents subject, verb, and object, in addition to the combinations subject–verb, verb–object, subject–object, and subject–verb–object. Braine's model predicts the occurrence of an action utterance given an action event and would thus have to include the probability of obtaining any utterance (whether an action verb relation or not, for example, "more cookie" or "my cookie), as well as the probability of no utterance at all. The problems in identifying single constituents that have already been pointed out (footnote 6, p. 140) are further compounded in Braine's model by the problem of identifying action events. Virtually all of the child's early utterances occur in dynamic (that is, action) events involving some kind of movement.

As an explanation of the probabilistic nature of the distribution of nouns and verbs in sentences, Braine proposed that the child's choice of words (or "lexical insertion") is "pragmatic, and not determined by syntactic or semantic structure" – a "process of construction by selecting a word that singles out something pragmatically salient" (1974, p. 455). The only direct evidence of such context saliency is the fact that such words and word combinations occur, and the resulting argument is unfortunately circular. Braine asserted that his formulation established continuity with the earlier single-word period since the same process of "lexical insertion" on the basis of "saliency" accounted also for "holophrasis." At the same time, however, Braine's formulation and pragmatic explanations in general establish a serious discontinuity with later development. Such claims fail to contribute to explanations either of (1) how the child eventually learns grammatical structure or (2) the systematic (semantic–syntactic) regularities that are manifest among the earliest multiword utterances. However, the idea that the use of linguistic rules is probabilistically determined is important and is basic to the model proposed here.

Pragmatic explanations – that what the child mentions in sentences is determined by practical considerations in the situation – have been suggested by a number of investigators (for example, Brown, 1973; Park, 1974; Schlesinger, 1974). To a certain extent there is obvious truth in the claim; the words that children learn, and the words they use, are the words that are practical and useful, as well as meaningful for them. Pragmatics in philosophical theory is concerned with the origin, uses, and effects of signs (Morris, 1964). According to Rudolph Carnap, "the acceptance or rejection of abstract linguistic forms . . . will finally be decided by their efficiency as instruments, the ratio of the results achieved to the amount and complexity of the efforts required" (quoted in Morris, p. 46). Some pragmatic force no doubt does operate to determine the linguistic forms accepted or rejected by the child – motivating greater complexity in order to achieve greater results, while at the same time allowing less complex forms to be maintained when these require less effort to achieve the same results. But what is the operational explanation of "acceptance of a linguistic form" in development? One is still left with the problem of explaining what it means to accept (that is, to learn) the linguistic forms corresponding to pragmatically salient events.

Linguistic forms (words and structures with meaning relations) are not immediately and automatically given along with events; the linguistic forms that need to be learned necessarily transcend individual events. The child must learn words and how to combine words in consistent ways – regardless of the particular referents presented in all possible events. The child might use "read book" in one situation and then use "Mommy read book" in another because of a better result. But the use of "Mommy read book" is consistent with the use of "Daddy eat apple" and "Baby ride bike," and it is the essence of that regularity among many such utterances that must be explained.

Saliency alone does not determine what children talk about, given the fact that child sentences represent only a limited set of the possible relations in events. For example, two notable omissions in the taxonomy of semantic–syntactic structures that have been identified in early child sentences are the dative (giving or showing something to someone) and the instrumental (using some means, such as forks, crayons, or keys to achieve some end) (Brown, 1973). Salience arguments simply use the result to explain the result; there is no independent verification of what constitutes saliency in events. The result is that children do not encode certain relations in early sentences, but the fact is that such relations are obviously salient in action events because the child performs or demands their occurrence. However pragmatic such aspects of events may be (when a child wants to draw, crayons are more salient than other objects), the children studied so far in this investigation and others use the corresponding linguistic forms only rarely (in this case the structural relation between such words as *crayon* or *fork* and action verbs). The relative complexity of linguistic forms contributes to determining the kinds of information that children are able to represent in their messages (Bloom, Lightbown, & Hood, 1975, chap. 2; Slobin 1971a).

The Semantic Argument. Although there are different versions of the semantic explanation, the essential argument specifies what children are not doing as an apparently important part of specifying what they are doing: (1) Children are learning semantic relations between words and word-order rules to express semantic relations in sentences, and (2) children are not learning an abstract grammatical structure, that is, subject–predicate.

Kates (1974) was more explicit than Schlesinger (1974) in emphasizing how contextual saliency contributes to the child's "semanticity." She proposed that early two- and three-word sentences, as well as single-word utterances at an earlier time, derive from "focus-defined semantic categories" that depend upon the focusing experience of "some paradigm case," an initial event that focuses the child's attention on entities or relations between more than one entity. Such focus-defined categories are initially quite broad and only gradually are narrowed down, perhaps not until puberty, to adult (logic-defined) semantic roles such as agent or possessor. Kates suggested that "syntactic patterns and some grammatical morphemes may simply be matched (associated) with certain [focus-defined] semantic categories and relations," and "once the form of the (predicative) sentence is acquired, and after the child is able to form logic-defined categories" the form of the predicative sentence can be used to express a propositional predication.

Kates's position is similar to the arguments presented by Bowerman

(1973a) and Schlesinger (1971a, 1974). The emphasis on semantics as the basis for learning sentences is well placed (see Bloom, 1970). However, grammatical morphemes and the rules of word order that encode information about objects and events are part of grammar, and grammar is both semantic and syntactic. The question at issue concerns the nature of the child's linguistic knowledge that underlies the ability to use syntactic patterns of word order with consistent semantic function, that is, the form of predicative sentences. Whatever that linguistic knowledge is at age 2 years, it neither has the same form nor serves the same functions as the linguistic knowledge of the adult. However, the evidence indicates that the child's linguistic knowledge differs more in degree than in kind from that of the adult. The question is, What does the child's knowledge of sentences consist of?

In the present study, there were two semantic contrasts represented in the relations of nouns to verbs. The first had to do with the force of the effect of an action on the different objects involved in the action, and the second was the distinction between animate and inanimate objects. With respect to the first semantic contrast, the relative frequency of verb–object in action relations was matched by the relative frequency of verb–object in agent–locative action, mover–verb in mover–locative action, and patient–verb in patient–locative action. In addition, when the relative frequencies of the separate constituents in all the categories were compared, the result was that the object, mover, and patient constituents occurred less frequently than verbs but more frequently than the agent and the place constituents. This result – that the object affected by movement (whether an object, mover, or patient) was mentioned more frequently regardless of the verb category – reflected an important semantic function and could be seen as support for the claim that sentence relations are semantic. However, although the semantic functions of objects, movers, and patients were similar, they differed in their positions relative to verbs: Objects were post-verb constituents with action and agent–locative-action verbs, and movers and patients were pre-verb constituents with mover- and patient–locative-action verbs.

Further, patients in patient-locative-action utterances and objects in agent-locative-action utterances had essentially the same semantic function: The child (or someone else) was the causative agent in both. Thus, when referring to the same event the children could (and often did) say "put lamb here" and "lamb go here," but they did not say *"go lamb here" or *"lamb put here."[10] It was not clear what the children's semantic understanding of "lamb go here" was: Whether they distinguished the lamb moving from the lamb being moved. However, even if the children had not yet sorted out the semantic relations, they were quite clear about the syntactic relations of such semantic functions: They consistently put the moving object (patient or mover) in pre-verb (subject) position with certain verbs and in-post verb (object) position with other verbs. Although the children were learning semantic relations, the fact that words serving the same semantic function varied syntactically in relation to different classes of verbs was evidence against the claim that sentence relations are only semantic relations.

The second semantic contrast, between animate and inanimate nouns, has been reported in the studies by Bloom (1970), Bowerman (1973a), Brown, Cazden, and Bellugi (1969), and de Villiers and de Villiers (1974). Sentence-subjects have been described as almost exclusively animate or pseudoanimate (e.g., bears and dolls); affected-objects in action relations have been mostly inanimate. This result has been confirmed in the acquisition of German by Park (1974), leading to his claim that "animacy" is a strong semantic feature in early sentences with the resulting "rule" that animate objects are always mentioned first in sentences. However, in the present study, patients were often inanimate (trucks, blocks, wheels, puzzle pieces, etc.) which was evidence that pre-verb constituents were not only semantically determined (on the basis of "animacy") but were also syntactically determined with respect to the functions of nouns in relation to different verbs, regardless of "animacy."

The reason why animate nouns predominate as agents and movers should be self-evident: Actions and movements that affect objects are performed by persons or other animate beings. But, if it is self-evident why agents and movers in action events are animate, it is still necessary to explain why the animate–inanimate opposition is coded by word order with certain categories of verbs. There is a time, in the single-word-utterance period before syntax appears, when children do not differentiate between agents and objects in terms of the word order they use, and they are as likely to say "juice. Mommy." as "Mommy. juice." in successive single-word utterances (Bloom, 1970, 1973; Smith, 1970). Learning syntax involves learning to make the animate–inanimate distinction a regularity through the use of word order relative to different verbs. Children learn the predicative function of different verbs which, if not the function of a *logical* predicate (in the sense of affirming or denying a property of or relation to a subject), is a *grammatical* predicate in the sense that it completes the meaning of the verb expressing an action by a subject or a state of a subject. If non–English speaking children do not learn word order to signal the difference between functions of nouns relative to verbs, then they will learn whatever other linguistic devices are available to express such regularities.

Different verbs mean different things, but there are also regularities among verbs that have different meanings, so that they form categories of superordinate meaning. Children learn such categories of verbs that share superordinate meaning and that are also similar in structure (e.g., action verbs taking object as a complement; mover–locative-action and patient–locative-action verbs taking place as a complement; and agent–locative-action verbs that take both object and place to complete the verb meaning). That linguistic induction is a powerful one, as knowledge of relations among objects, knowledge of words as referring to events, and growing awareness of discriminable linguistic features (such as phoneme contrasts, word order, intonation, and stress) all come together in the insight that sentences are regularly occurring events with consistent relations between parts. However close the semantic regularities among sentences are to the conceptual regularities of experience, that insight is a linguistic insight about the structure of language. It is not an insight that functions as an abstract object for the child to be aware of or talk about, nor is it the same as the adult intuitions about the nature or functions of sentences. But it is at once a part of what the child knows and a part of what adult language consists of.

The Sensorimotor Argument. The influence of Piaget is apparent in those explanations of child language that emphasize the importance of movement and action in determining which objects and events children first talk about. However, a much more explicit claim about the correspondence between actions and sentences was made by Bruner (1975) and by McNeill (1975). Both concluded that the pattern of child sentences is isomorphic with the pattern of child actions. Bruner specified that interaction between child and parent is a necessary condition for the relationship between sentences and actions to occur. McNeill suggested that the same sensorimotor action patterns that underlie child sentences underlie adult sentences as well through a process of "semiotic extension" (extension from the child to adult systems). Greenfield, Nelson, and Saltzman (1972) analyzed children's actions with nesting cups and referred to actions that follow certain principles of occurrence as a "grammar" of actions.

There is a correlation between the kinds of actions that children perform and some of the action sentences they learn to say. However, it is difficult to see how one can demonstrate anything more than a correspondence between regularities in action events(in that they involve a movement by an agent to affect an object) and regularities in the sentences children use to talk about action events, in that they represent agent, action, and object. Certainly, such a correspondence does not explain the child's linguistic knowledge. The task remains to find what the alignment mechanism (for matching, mapping, or coding speech with action) might be. Finally, if word order in English is a direct printout of the sequential components of an action event, as McNeill claimed, then one wonders why those same relationships are not expressed in the same way in all languages.

The Grammatical Argument: Reduction

When mean length of utterance was less than 1.5, Kathryn could say "read book," and "Mommy book," but full subject–verb–object strings, such as "Mommy read book," were rare. Similarly, at the same time, Kathryn could say "no read" and "no book," but *"Mommy no read" or *"no read book" did not occur. There were two sources of evidence in those data for concluding that action relations and negation were represented more fully in their underlying structure than in their surface structure: (1) the fact that the semantic interpretation of such utterances was, for example, *Mommy read book* or *Mommy no read book* and, more important, (2) the fact that among all the utterances in a particular sample, all the possible partial relationships occurred – subject–verb, verb–object, subject–object. That is, from a large enough sample of the different constituent relations in her speech, one could infer that Kathryn knew the fuller structural relationship subject–verb–object. The explanation of these data in Bloom (1970) was that the child's knowledge of phrase structure operated only in conjunction with a reduction transformation that systematically deleted major constituents in actual sentences.

Several objections have since been raised against the reduction transformation indicating, at least in part, that the analysis and argument in Bloom (1970) were not sufficiently clear. One objection has been that the proposal of a fuller deep structure was the result of analyzing the child utterance in terms of the adult model and attributing to the child system what would be necessary for describing the utterance if an adult had said it (e.g., Bowerman, 1973a; Schaerlaekens, 1973). However, only evidence from actual child utterances was used to infer underlying structure. The effect of reduction was to delete constituents that were included in the child grammar because of their productivity in a large sample of utterances. Forms that did not occur at all or occurred only rarely in the child's speech could not be described as reduced, and many aspects of the adult model were entirely missing. For example, such forms as the auxiliary or possessive -*s* were not grammatically reduced or deleted in the child grammar; they simply were never there to begin with, so reduction was not offered as an explanation of telegraphic speech or as an explanation of the non-occurrence of aspects of adult speech. Further, the same analysis (fuller underlying structure and a reduction transformation) could not be applied to the data from Eric with similar mean length of utterance – even though the semantics of Eric's sentences were quite similar to the semantics of Gia's and Kathryn's – precisely because Eric did not represent all the same separate constituent relations in his speech. Thus, child utterances were reduced with respect to their fuller underlying structure in the child grammar and not with respect to the structure of the adult model.

Both Schlesinger (1971a) and Bowerman (1973a) contested the claim in Bloom (1970) of a subject–predicate structure underlying child sentences and argued that such a claim would follow only from an analysis of child sentences that is based too closely on the adult model of grammar. Bowerman argued against the use of distributional evidence – the relative frequency of verb–object and subject–verb constituent relations – and this issue will be discussed below, in light of evidence from the present study. Bowerman (1973a) also pointed out that the syntactic tests of the reality of a subject–predicate distinction in the adult model (for example, that transformations such as the passive operate in the same way on constituents with different semantic functions) are not met in the evidence from child speech, since children do not use such transformations. But this argument turns on claims made for the adult grammar and could be faulted for the same reason that Bowerman presented the argument in the first place. The existence of a structure in child language needs to be justified by a test of the child speech data.

Part of the problem in making clear the rationale for the reduction transformation seems to have been that the model of grammar used in Bloom (1970) was the generative transformational grammar proposed originally by Chomsky (1957, 1965) for a fragment of adult English syntax. However, generative transformational grammar represents a theory of language, any language, including adult language but not excluding child language. The analysis in Bloom (1970) proceeded from the child speech data to generative transformational grammar as a theory of language for representing certain facts of child language. The use of the theoretical orientation to explain child language did not presume that whatever the theory represented in adult language would be found also in child language.

Brown (1973), Park (1974), and others criticized the reduction transformation because it appeared to be a linguistic rule that dropped out and so made the child grammar more complex in its earlier stages than in its later stages. However, rather than drop out, the process of reduction undergoes its own development and changes as the child grammar approaches the adult grammar. Further, the fact of reduction is implicit in adult grammar and operates in conjunction with many derivational and transformational constraints. Thus, rather than being an expediency for explaining the interpretation of utterances, the reduction that occurs in the child grammar is a linguistic process that interacts with the organization of categories and rule relations in the linguistic system.

There is a difference between reduction, attributed to a limitation on linguistic programming span for sentences, and two other kinds of linguistic omission or deletion. First, Brown and Fraser (1963) described early child sentences as "telegraphic": Children leave out the linking grammatical morphemes that adults would include if they produced the same sentences. For example, in the sentence "Mommy *is* driv*ing the* truck," the italicized forms would not occur in the corresponding child sentence. Second, there is the process of ellipsis that occurs with adult sentences to eliminate redundancy.

The operations of reduction and grammatical ellipsis are each the result of underlying grammatical processes that account for sentences. In contrast, the notion of "telegraphic" speech is only a static description of the surface form of children's utterances when these are compared with adult sentences (Brown, 1973). The morphemes that are left out in child speech characterized as "telegraphic" are often those forms, such as verb inflections, that the child gives no evidence of having learned as yet. In contrast, the constituents deleted in the process of reduction and grammatical ellipsis are derived from complex structures that the child knows or is learning, according to other behavioral evidence. Further, the analysis of discourse in the present study revealed that rules for grammatical ellipsis are learned by children only after they have learned the rules for generating the fuller, pre-elliptical forms.

The conditions for reduction were not spelled out in Bloom (1970) except to point to limitations in both lexical representation (the child did not know enough words) and syntactic complexity (the child could not get all of the sentence together) as probable constraints on relating deep structures to surface structures. Bowerman (1973b) offered a version of the reduction transformation that specified obligatory constituents with optional deletion of verbs to account for the occurrence of subject–object strings. She emphasized that the constraint was not lexical, because the children she studied used what would be the appropriate verbs in other linguistic contexts. However, the evidence in the present study of the differential occurrence of old and new verbs indicated that lexical constraint was indeed a factor. Knowing a lexical item involves more than being able to use that item in one or another context.

Brown (1973) offered a counterproposal for formally accounting for the same facts of limited utterance length, partial constituent relations, and such discontinuous relations as agent–object (as in "Mommy sock"): that constituents are optional in their underlying representation rather than obligatory and then reduced. Brown did not spell out the conditions for exercising options in generating sentences. A serious objection to optionality, as Brown observed, is that it allows for the production of more complex utterances than occur, if all options are exercised. Further, it could imply that all constituents are equally likely to occur.

Cedergren and Sankoff pointed out that

> Whereas an obligatory rule operates on all input strings that satisfy its structural description, an optional rule may or may not apply to a satisfactory input string. In these terms, no accounting is or can be made of the fact that the option is subject to regular constraints revealed through patterns of covariation with elements of the linguistic environment and with non-language factors such as age, class, and social context. (1974, p. 333)

A third formulation then (after obligatory constituents with reduction, and freely optional constituents) would specify the probability of deletion as determined by the conditioning factors under which it operates, in much the same way as the variable rules proposed by Labov (1969) accounted for contraction and deletion of the copula in English (see also Cedergren & Sankoff, 1974). In the present study, comparisons were made of the linguistic conditions under which constituents were more or less likely to be represented in child speech. In this way, it was possible to specify the conditions under which a constituent did or did not occur (its covariations) and the likelihood that it would occur in one or another linguistic context.

In the original reduction argument, it was assumed that combining the partial constituent relations in producing the full constituent structure subject–verb–object exceeded a complexity limit. The observation that the negation marker *no* occurred with a verb (e.g., "no sit"), or with a noun (e.g., "no chair") but did not occur with both (e.g., "*no sit chair") indicated that negation was an added complexity factor. The expectation in the present study was that any added complexity would be more likely to occur with two-constituent relations than with three-constituent relations. Negation and two-part verbs occurred significantly more often with two-constituent relations than with three-constituent relations, and there was a clear but nonsignificant trend in the same direction with embedded relations (object modification) in action events. However, other additions within and between constituents occurred as often (proportionately) with three-constituent relations as with two-constituent relations. Although grammatical morphemes added "something more" to constituent relations and amounted to "cumulative grammatical complexity," as described by Brown (1973), grammatical morphemes did not represent added complexity in the same way that negation, two-part verbs, and embedded relations added complexity to sentences by constraining the realization of the full constituent structure. More important, however, other conditioning factors that were related to the lexicon and to discourse operated in conflicting directions to determine the likelihood that constituents would be represented in utterance.

The next step would be to specify (1) the interaction among the variation factors and (2) the form of the constituent structure of sentences in an attempt to provide a variable-rules model that includes the factors that accounted for the nonrandom distribution of two- and three-constituent relations in the children's early language.

The Grammatical Argument: The Variation Model

The model of variation in the children's sentences with mean length of utterance >1.0 and <3.0 morphemes included four factors: (1) a grammatical complexity factor (C); (2) a lexical access factor (L); (3) a discourse interaction factor (D); and (4) a factor to account for the as-yet unaccounted-for variation, a residual variability (performance) factor (V).

Factor C was grammatical complexity that operated to constrain the constituent structure of sentences and consisted of another semantic–syntactic relation embedded or subordinated to the verb relation, including negation, possession, recurrence, and other attribution.

Factor L concerned the accessibility of words in the child's dictionary, in terms of a word's relative familiarity in (1) its reference function – access to the word in new situations – and (2) its syntactic function – access to the word in new linguistic contexts. Children learn words in their referential sense, with some representation of the constancy or regularity of figurative content, regardless of the particular situation to which the word may refer. But children also learn words in their operative sense with potential variation in the meaning of a word as a function of its linguistic context.

Factor D was the effect of discourse, utterances from the child or another person that occurred successively with an utterance by the child. Factor V consisted of whatever nonsystematic forces operated to influence the length of a sentence.

In the present study, the complexity, lexical, and discourse factors operated with different effects: either to facilitate or increase the probability of realizing one or another constituent relation, signified by an ↑ in the matrix below, or to constrain or reduce the probability of realizing one or another constituent relation, signified by an ↓ in the matrix below. Presumably, the V factor operated with two conflicting (↑ and ↓) effects as well, but since these were not directly observed in this study, their interaction could not be interpolated in the matrix.

The matrix (Figure 3.5) presents the schematic interactions among three factors: Complexity was a constraining factor (↓); discourse was a facilitating factor (↑); and lexical access was either a constraining (↓) or a facilitating (↑) factor. Presented in this way, it was possible to rank the cumulative effects of the factors in their interactions, according to the results of this study. Thus, the most constraining condition would be one without D ↑ in which both L and C were ↓ – the interaction between a new word (verb or noun) and complexity, resulting in reduction (or nonrealization) of one or another constituent. The least constraining condition would be one without C ↓ and with L↑ and D ↑ – familiar lexical items and support from discourse –

	L↓	L↑	D↑
C↓	1	2.5	4.5
L↓		2.5	4.5
L↑			6

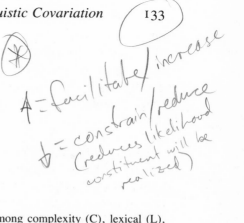

Figure 3.5. Matrix of the interactions among complexity (C), lexical (L), and discourse (D) factors in the generation of sentences: 1 is the strongest constraint = reduction and 6 is maximum support = realization.

with resulting maximum support for realizing the full constituent structure.

The concept of reduction, then, is not an expedient for explaining semantic interpretation and partial constituent relations in child sentences. Rather, reduction is a grammatical process that changes with respect to the conditioning factors under which it operates and in relation to other developments in the child's linguistic system. The reduction transformation (Bloom, 1970) was one linguistic scheme for representing these phenomena; the variation paradigm proposed here appears to offer a more informative scheme for representing the same phenomena.

Constituent Structure in the Variation Model

What are children learning when they learn to combine words to form sentences? The results of this investigation of action and locative-action sentences indicate that children are learning the constituent structure of sentences, with variable probabilities for realizing individual constituents. Verbs are central to the constituent structure: Distributionally, they occur more frequently than other constituents; semantically, they specify the meaning relationship between the subject and complement forms; syntactically, they order subject and complement forms relative to each other. The occurrence of two nouns in an agent–object relationship was relatively rare; for only Kathryn and Gia did agent–object sentences account for more than .10 of the action utterances. Such sentences were never productive for Eric and Peter. The frequency of agent–object sentences decreased substantially when mean length of utterance exceeded 2.0 and with rare exceptions, they did not include any complexity. A lexical explanation of their occurrence seems most reasonable: The children did not know a particular verb or did not know enough about the syntactic function of a particular verb.

Further evidence of the importance of verbs to constituent structure was the fact that the partial constituent relations (for example, agent–verb and verb–object or mover–verb and verb–place) were integrally related to one another. Although such semantic–syntactic relations as possession, recurrence, and attribution seemed to be separate relations and unrelated to one another, the relations of verbs to preceding and succeeding nouns (for example, agent–verb and verb–object) were not separate semantic–syntactic relations. The partial constituent relations were integrated into three- or four-constituent relations before mean length of utterance reached 2.0, and when verb complexity and certain other kinds of complexity appeared, they were included in three-constituent relations as often as in two-constituent relations. In contrast, the other semantic–syntactic relations were embedded in verb relations only with difficulty, appearing more often in two-constituent relations than in three-constituent relations, but occurring most frequently in the data as separate utterances, even as mean length of utterance approached 3.0.

The constituent structure of action and locative-action verb relations included a pre-verb constituent with different semantic functions, that is, agent, mover, and patient, and a post-verb constituent with different semantic functions, that is, affected-object and/or place, both in relation to different categories of verbs. The question of what the pre-verb subject and post-verb complement consist of has been raised often, particularly by those who have argued that children learn separate semantic relations rather than a superordinate grammatical relation such as subject–predicate. The evidence in the present study indicates that they are not separate concepts but, rather, relations within a schema. Diagramatically, these schema relationships could be represented by a phrase structure tree diagram (keeping in mind that phrase structure trees are only hypotheses about mental grammar). This version of phrase structure represents the following information about the linguistic knowledge of the four children in this study learning English.

1. The constituent structure is a linguistic schema that entails relationships between subject and complement forms.

2. The meaning relationship between the subject and complement forms is mediated by the meaning of the verb.

3. The form of the verbal auxiliary (verb complexity) is determined by the meaning relation between the subject and the verb.

4. The subject–verb–complement constituents are obligatory in the linguistic schema, but the complement can be variously represented as affected-object or place or, as with agent–locative action, both object and place.

5. The constituent structure can be complemented in a sentence by another linguistic schema, here represented only indefinitely by the dummy symbol $\triangle$. This second linguistic schema can be an adverb, or recursive, that is, a second constituent structure that is subordinate or coordinate with the first. In any event, its occurrence in the sentence does not affect, that is, constrain, the constituent structure.

6. There is no longer reason to assume that verb–complement is a more unified grammatical relation than is subject–verb, on distributional grounds. In the present study, although verb–object was more frequent than agent–verb in action utterances (as reported also by Brown, 1973), mover–verb and patient–verb were more frequent than verb–place. In addition to the distributional evidence, there was also the finding that the form and function of the verbal auxiliary was determined by whether the subject functioned as agent, mover, or patient: Intention modals and progressive -*ing* occurred with agents; third-person singular occurred with patients and so on (see Chapter 5).

Bowerman (1973a) cited the distributional evidence in her data as supporting a closer unity between subject–verb than between verb–object and suggested, on those grounds, that distributional evidence alone is insufficient to support a subject–predicate distinction. There is a strong tendency for intransitive action verbs and what might have been mover–verb or patient–verb utterances to appear among the subject–verb utterances reported by Bowerman: .58 of the subject–verb utterances reported for two children from whom data were collected when mean length of utterance was less than 1.5 (our analysis of the first two samples from Kendall and the first sample from Seppo in appendixes in Bowerman, 1973a). Intransitive verbs would not be relevant to an analysis of the relative distribution of two-term action relations, inasmuch as no apparent affected-object is involved and the

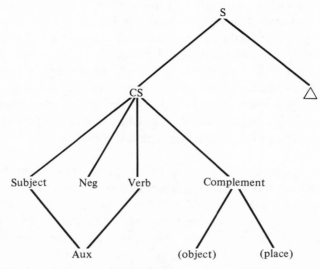

Figure 3.6. Diagram of the constituent structure (CS) of sentences (S): △ is another subordinate or coordinate relation, for example, an adverb or another constituent structure.

two other possible two-term relations (verb–object and subject–object) were precluded from occurring. The difference between the children in Bowerman's study as compared with the children in the present study may have been a situational difference in which events that happened to include either largely intransitive or transitive actions, respectively, were tapped.

7. The negative marker and verbal auxiliary (verb complexity) are distinct and separate from one another. Verb complexity was more likely to occur when the subject was represented, and it occurred as often in three-constituent relations as in two-constituent relations. In contrast, negation rarely occurred when sentence-subjects were expressed, and negation was represented significantly more often in two-constituent relations than in three-constituent relations.

8. Finally, the subject constituent was always the least complex constituent in any of the categories. There was virtually no agent or mover complexity, and patient complexity consisted of only occasional demonstrative pronouns.

The phrase structure tree in Figure 3.6 only describes the results of this study; it is not explanatory. It differs from the formulation in Bloom (1970) that described the data when mean length of utterance was less than 1.5 and before the distinction was made among the patient, mover and agent–locative-action verb categories.

The Role of Memory. Two kinds of coding occur during the first two years: conceptual coding for representing information about objects and events in memory and linguistic coding for talking about and understanding when others talk about objects and events in the world. This study has investigated schemas and processes for linguistic coding, with the implicit assumption that linguistic schemas and processes represent (code, map, etc.) ideas (concepts, knowledge, etc.) about the world. Linguistic competence entails the ability to access the linguistic code – to remember the schema – relative to the child's attention to some element of experience. The variable rules in the model of child grammar suggested here are, in some essential sense, related to the development of memory processes.

Olson (1973) pointed out that increase in utterance length is not explained by increase in immediate memory span; rather, there is a simple correlation between increasing utterance length and increasing memory span (that is, for digits, as classically measured) because both are the result of the development of some higher order cognitive function: "The classical findings on memory span reflect the development of the child's ability to handle verbal information rather than changes in memory or information processing capacity *per se.* . . . Mean utterance length is not a performance restriction due to a simple memory-span limit" (pp. 151, 153). These remarks are addressed to the issue of short-term memory and its relation to utterance length; the issue in the present study has to do with access to linguistic schemas in long-term memory.

Olson (1973) pointed to another factor underlying the increase in mean length of utterance: the use of "preprogrammed routines" or phrases which are actually a "single label" rather than a programmed structural representation – what Leopold (1939–1949) and others have called "stereotype" phrases. Indeed, at Kathryn I, of the six subject–verb–object action sentences that were reported, only one included nominal agent and object ("man ride bus"). In contrast, the others included pro-forms (for example, "Mommy do it," "Baby do it," "I comb my pigtail") at the same time when there were no pronouns in any other utterances. Kathryn did not produce pronoun objects or agents in two-constituent relations until mean length of utterance approached 2.0 morphemes at Time II (see Bloom, Lightbown, & Hood, 1975,

Chap. 2, for the account of pronominal–nominal development). Thus, the fact that three-constituent relations were not proportionately less complex than two-constituent relations at Time I may have been due, in part, to the stereotyped nature of some of the longer utterances (see also R. Clark, 1974).

Access to an underlying rule system is a function of the relative strength of linguistic forms and structures in interaction with the elements of content that they code. Such relative strength is determined by a number of factors, for example, recency of learning, frequency of application, or lexical familiarity. The child's use of a partial constituent relation can also function as an assist, or memory prompt, for supporting the fuller constituent structure, as was apparent when two- and three-constituent relations occurred successively. The increase in utterance length reflects increased access to the fuller constituent structure that is represented in long-term memory – through lexical and discourse factors as well as other possible mnemonics that result from cognitive development. The conclusion in this study is that the structure of sentences is mediated by the meaning of the verb, and the constituent verb relations are schematized according to the relations among obligatory subject–verb–complement constituents.

Competence and Performance. Brown (1973) suggested that children have grammatical knowledge of constituent structure but that they utilize this knowledge freely, thereby producing utterances of varying lengths. Not yet knowing the rules of discourse, children overgeneralize from the elliptical and truncated adult speech they hear and form the impression that it does not matter how much of a full sentence one says. The child may produce a full agent–verb–object sentence, any single constituent, or any correctly ordered combination of two constituents. In terms of the competence–performance issue, Brown's account of the length of child sentences implies that children's knowledge of language (competence) would enable them to produce full constituent utterances, but their inadequate knowledge of discourse (performance in Brown's terms) prevents them from doing so. The resulting child speech is characterized by an "oscillating, apparently lawless optionality" (p. 241).

Cedergren and Sankoff (1974) criticized the notion of optionality for "fail[ing] to capture the nature of the systematic variation which exists even on the level of the grammar of a single individual" (p. 333). They argue that so-called optional possibilities are distributed in

regular ways in the speech of individuals and speech communities and
that such regularities constitute linguistic competence. The results of
the present study fit well into this conceptual framework. Contrary to
Brown and others, the distribution of constituent relations in the children's speech was not random. For example, verbs were consistently
the most frequently expressed constituent; the constituent that referred
to the object affected by movement occurred second most frequently.
Certain combinations such as agent–place rarely or never occurred.
Moreover, the evidence was strong for concluding that children operate with some fairly well-defined notion of constituent structure but
that knowledge is not categorical. Rather, particular linguistic and
nonlinguistic factors have been shown to regularly vary with utterance
length. Two-part verbs, embedded relations, negation, new verbs, and
subsequently expanded child utterances all occurred more often with
two-constituent utterances than with three-constituent utterances. It is
hard to imagine how these results could be explained in terms of "lawless optionality." Instead, this systematic covariation reflects the child's
underlying linguistic competence.

In conclusion, it is apparent that none of the existing explanations
of early child sentences has been adequate, but neither have these attempts to explain children's linguistic knowledge been entirely wrong.
Clearly, semantic considerations are integral to the schemas that children learn for representing information in messages. Pragmatic considerations enter into determining which linguistic forms are most useful
to be learned. Action schemas function to provide the content for many
of the child's sentences. However, the child comes to a linguistic induction about regularities in the relations between words that are, at
once, both semantic and syntactic – having to do with the consistent
ways in which words are ordered relative to one another in relation to
some aspect of experience. That is the beginning of grammar; to what
extent the child grammar can be captured by linguistic theories that are
transformational or case oriented is less important than the fact that
certain regularities among sentences have been captured and represented by a linguistic schema – a schema that is less categorical than
it is variable but that is certainly systematic.

NOTES

1 P. Bloom (1990); Hyams (1986); O'Grady, Peters, & Masterson (1989).
2 Braine (1974); Brown (1973).

3 The issue of writing formal rules has not been addressed here. The analysis of the child language data has been treated, thus far, apart from the problem of formalization. Labov's variable rules deal with constraints in the linguistic and nonlinguistic environments that favor or disfavor the application of certain syntactic and phonological rules. In our data, we identified variation in the occurrence of major sentence constituents in child speech – a more radical variation than has been treated so far in variability paradigms, although one that appears to be within the formal extension of variable rules proposed by Cedergren and Sankoff (1974). In particular, in the application of probability theory to linguistics, Sankoff (see also Suppes, 1970) proposed that probability weightings of constituents in phrase structure rules is a realistic scheme for accounting for the actual production of sentences (W. Labov, personal communication). Such an application of probability theory is particularly attractive for child language data, as it allows for an explanation of the transitions between successive child grammars in terms of how the probabilities of rule application change over time and relate to different factors in the child's linguistic and other cognitive development.

4 *Constituent* refers to a major category term such as agent, verb, object, or place, and *constituent relation* refers to a relationship between two or more constituents.

5 Only a few examples of the categories are given here, but the Appendix in Bloom, Lightbown, & Hood (1975) contains an extensive sampling of all the categories of semantic–syntactic relations found in the time period reported in that study.

6 Single-word utterances were not assigned to semantic–syntactic categories because they are ambiguous with respect to potential constituent function. The problem of assigning a single-word utterance to a constituent relation is discussed at length in Bloom (1973, pp. 133–41), where it was pointed out that one cannot know if a child intends a linguistic function (such as agent or mover or possessor) with only a single word (such as *Mommy*). Interpretation of linguistic structure requires linguistic evidence (at least two constituents in relation to one another in an utterance) to disambiguate the child's intent, and rich interpretation of contextual evidence alone is insufficient. One can identify action events, but different kinds of linguistic events can occur within action events as, for example, when the child eats another cookie and says "eat cookie" or "more cookie" or "my cookie." Utterances expressing recurrence or possession were counted in the present study only when they were embedded in an action-verb relation (e.g., "eat more cookie").

7 The computer program used to test the random generation model with four constituents was written by Owen Whitby.

8 One subset of formal expansions is what Braine (1971b) called "replacement sequences."

9 Most utterances were similar to the following Example 1, in that the three-constituent utterance was an expansion of a two-constituent utterance, and conversely, the two-constituent utterance was expanded to a three-constituent utterance. However, there were utterances, such as Example 2, in which the three-constituent utterance was not expanded from a two-constituent utterance, and Example 3, in which the two-constituent utterance was not expanded to a three-constituent utterance.

1.	(Gia pulling out her tricycle)	ride bike/Gia ride bike
2.		man ride car
	Lois: Where is he?	
	(Gia looking around for him)	man ride the car
3.	(Gia opens box of recording tape	open/tape
	trying to take tape out of box)	open tape stuck

10 An asterisk next to an utterance indicates that it did not occur in the corpora.

POSTSCRIPT

For studies since Bloom, Miller, and Hood (1975) that have supported the claim that young children have a fuller knowledge of grammatical structure than is realized in their actual sentences:

Bloom, P. (1990). Subjectless sentences in child language. *Linguistic Inquiry*, 21, 491–504.

Gerkin, L. (1989). Children's subjectless sentences – Competence or performance? Unpublished manuscript.

Goldin-Meadow, S. (1978). Structure in a manual communication system developed without a language model: Language without a helping hand. In H. Whitaker & H. A. Whitaker, *Studies in neurolinguistics* (vol. 3, pp. 125–206). New York: Academic Press.

Goldin-Meadow, S. (1985). Language development under atypical learning conditions. In K. Nelson (Ed.), *Children's language* (vol. 5, pp. 197–245). Hillsdale, NJ: Erlbaum.

Hyams, N. (1986). *Language acquisition and the theory of parameters*. Dordrecht: Reidel.

Pinker, S. (1984). *Language learnability and language development*. Cambridge, MA: Harvard University Press.

Valian, V. (1990). Null subjects: A problem for parameter-setting models of language acquisition. *Cognition, 35*, 105–22.

Valian, V. (in press). Syntactic subjects in the early speech of American and Italian children, *Cognition*.

For studies of covariation:

Bloom, P. (1990). Subjectless sentences in child language. *Linguistic Inquiry, 21*, 491–504.

Bock, J. (1982). Toward a cognitive psychology of syntax: Information processing contributions to sentence formulation. *Psychological Review, 89*, 1–47.

Camarata, S., & Leonard, L. (1986). Young children pronounce object words more accurately than action words. *Journal of Child Language, 13*, 51–65.

Limber, J. (1976). Unravelling competence, performance and pragmatics in the speech of young children. *Journal of Child Language, 3*, 309–18.

Pea, R. (1979). Can information theory explain early word choice? *Journal of Child Language, 6*, 397–410.

Speidel, G., & Herreshoff, M. (1989). Imitation and the construction of longer utterances. In G. Speidel & K. Nelson (Eds.), *The many faces of imitation in language learning* (pp. 181–97). New York: Springer-Verlag.

Shatz, M. (1978). The relationship between cognitive processes and the development of communication skills. In C. Keasey (Ed.), Nebraska symposium on motivation 1977: Social cognitive development (pp. 1–42). Lincoln: University of Nebraska Press.

Valian, V. (1990). Logical and psychological constraints on the acquisition of syntax. In L. Frazier & J. de Villiers (Eds.), *Language processing and language acquisition* (pp. 119–45). Dordrecht: Kluwer.

For studies of early syntactic categories:

Braine, M. (1987). What is learned in acquiring word classes – A step toward an acquisition theory. In B. MacWhinney (Ed.), *Mechanisms of language acquisition* (pp. 65–88). Hillsdale, NJ: Erlbaum.

Ihns, M., & Leonard, L. (1988). Syntactic categories in early child language: Some additional data. *Journal of Child Language, 15*, 673–78.

Maratsos, M., & Chalkley, M. (1981). The internal language of children's syntax: The ontogenesis and representation of syntactic categories. In K. Nelson (Ed.), *Children's language* (vol. 2, pp. 127–214). New York: Gardner Press.

Pinker, S. (1987). The bootstrapping problem in language acquisition. In B. MacWhinney (Ed.), *Mechanisms of language acquisition* (pp. 399–441). Hillsdale, NJ: Erlbaum.

Valian, V. (1986). Syntactic categories in the speech of young children. *Developmental Psychology, 22*, 562–79.

4

Sentence Negation

"Mommy no play 'corder."

Negation was one of the earliest complexities the children added to simple sentences, and we have already seen, in Chapter 3, the effect of negation on the length of early sentences. The study reprinted here is of early sentence negation from *Form and Function in Emerging Grammars,* and spans the developmental period in mean length of utterance from 1.1 to 2.8 morphemes. Two findings, in particular, are noteworthy. One is the fact of sentence internal negation, and the other is the relation between form and meaning in negative sentences.

SENTENCE INTERNAL NEGATION

The position of *no* in child sentences has been at issue since the 1960s. In *Form and Function in Emerging Grammars,* I proposed that negation was sentence internal and attached to the verb in accord with the scope of negation from the beginning. The fact that children's negative utterances typically begin with *no* and *no more* gives the appearance that negation is external and is misleading. The test case is the occurrence of sentence-subjects with *no.* Most early negative sentences in this study, as in other studies, were subjectless (for reasons discussed at length in Chapter 3 and later). This is why early negative sentences typically begin with *no,* for example, "no fit." When sentences did occur with *no* before the subject in this study, in every instance but one the sentence was an affirmative one, not negative. The *no* was anaphoric and negated something in the context or a previous utterance. For example, Kathryn said, "no, Kathryn playing self." In this instance, the sentence "Kathryn playing self" asserted Kathryn's intention to play with her own toys; the *no* was a refusal to play with my toys.

One meaning of anaphoric *no* in these sentences with subjects was rejection, as in "no [play with your toys], Kathryn playing self." Another meaning was denial. For example, Kathryn had been looking for a book about dragons, picked up a book about bears, and then dropped it as she said, "no, that's a bear book.'' Thus, when sentence-subjects occurred with sentence-initial *no,* the proposition expressed in the sentence was not within the scope of negation.

The original argument against of sentence external negation, in *Form and Function in Emerging Grammars* (this chapter), was directed at the conclusion reached by Ursula Bellugi in her 1967 study of the negative sentences of Adam, Eve, and Sarah from the Roger Brown corpus.[1] Consistent with acquisition research at that time which had ignored meaning, she concluded from the surface distribution of *no* that early negation was external to the sentence. She did not look at the context to see what the negative sentences had meant and so had not done the critical analysis. That analysis was subsequently performed by Peter and Jill de Villiers. When they reanalyzed the early negative sentences of Adam, Eve, and Sarah, they found very few instances in which the subject was expressed and the negative element was nonanaphoric. They concluded that ''these results provide little support for the idea that the use of NEG + S negatives represents a general stage in the acquisition of negation.''[2]

Nonetheless, they allowed that individual differences might exist, citing data they collected from their son Nicholas, when he was between 23 and 29 months old and said initial-*no/not* sentences with the subject expressed. However, all except one expressed the polite form of rejection, and the *no* was an emphatic. An example is ''no Mummy do it,'' in which the scope of negation is actually an unexpressed first-person matrix verb *want* and ''Mommy do it'' is its complement sentence. The resulting meaning is ''[I] no [want] Mommy do it.'' Indeed, Nicholas subsequently used the polite form 'I don't want S'' or ''I don't like S.'' Children differ in their preferred forms for expressing rejection. Kathryn, like Nicholas, used the polite form with first-person matrix subjects (these were null initially, for example, ''no want this,'' but eventually expressed '*I* don't want to comb hairs''). Kathryn also expressed anaphoric rejection frequently. Eric and Gia, in contrast, expressed rejection with the second-person negative imperative most often (''don't touch my block!''). However, these differences among children might be traced to differences in the ways their caregivers talked to them. From a study of the input sentences in the Brown corpus and in their own recorded utterances to Nicholas, the de Villierses found that differences among children in the use of polite, versus imperative, forms of rejection corresponded to differences in the negative sentences the children heard.

In sum, a stage of sentence external negation in early acquisition is a myth.[3] When *no* occurs at the beginning of an utterance, it is most often a negative sentence with the sentence subject omitted. Otherwise, the *no* at the beginning of a sentence is either anaphoric or an emphatic. (I may have inadvertently contributed to the myth myself because of the way I originally reported these utterances, without a comma to separate the anaphoric *no* from the rest of the sentence. My notation system in *Form and Function in Emerging Grammars* for presenting instances from the data was consistent with the pretheoretical notation system I had used for the original transcription. However, I have since added the necessary commas in the examples and in Table 4.2.)

DEVELOPMENT OF FORM–FUNCTION RELATIONSHIPS IN NEGATIVE SENTENCES

Three semantic categories developed in the sequence of nonexistence > rejection > denial in the children's negative sentences. The sequence was based on their order of emergence, relative frequency, and developments in form. The earliest sentences expressed nonexistence at the same time that the meanings of rejection and denial were expressed with the single word *no*. When sentences began to express other meanings – first rejection and then denial – their structure was similar to the earlier learned sentences that expressed nonexistence. At first, sentences in the three semantic categories were not different. They consisted typically of *no* or *no more* and another word, for example, "no fit," "no pocket," "no more 'chine.' " When the new functions (rejection and denial) appeared, they had the same syntactic form learned earlier to express nonexistence. New functions, then, were learned originally with old forms. Subsequent development consisted of learning new forms for expressing what were, by then, old functions. This developmental finding that old forms were used to express new functions and new forms first used to express old functions is consistent with the "basic developmental principle pertaining to *form–function relationships*" in development that Heinz Werner had proposed years earlier: "Novel function is first executed through old, available forms; sooner or later, of course, there is pressure towards the development of new forms which are of a more function -specific character, i.e., that will serve the new function better than the older forms.'"[4] This principle was subsequently included as one of the "operating principles" for learning the surface forms of language proposed by Dan Slobin.[5]

Several investigators have since pointed out that the meanings nonexistence, rejection, and denial are too general and that finer distinctions are possible: for example, nonoccurrence and disappearance in the nonexistence category; refusal and prohibition in the rejection category.[6] Others have reported that the relative frequency of utterances in the different categories is different in single-word speech from their frequencies in sentence negation. Typically, the earliest meaning of *no* as a single word is rejection and is expressed more frequently than other meanings in the single-word period.[7]

The meanings of negation, and developments in the forms for expressing these meanings, have been the focus of much research – not only in English but in other languages as well. These studies are listed in the Postscript at the end of the chapter.

Syntactic and Semantic Development of Early Sentence Negation

Lois Bloom

The children's use of negative sentences provided a particularly fruitful opportunity to study the correlation of linguistic expression with semantic intent. Negation was usually signaled in the children's utterances by a linguistic marker (such as *no, no more, not*), with corresponding nonlinguistic evidence of negation in the immediate context of the speech events. The relationship between the syntax and semantics of negation provided important insight into the question of the relative development of language and cognition.

The syntax of negation in adult English has been described at length in the traditional grammar of Jespersen (1917; 1961, pp. 426–67), and in generative transformational terms by Klima (1964). Of greater significance to this study is the extensive description of the syntactic development of negation in children's language by Bellugi (1967). She described the sequence of developmental changes in the syntactic form of three children's negative sentences from the age of approximately 2 years, over a period of from 1 to about 2 and 1/2 years – until the structure of the children's sentences approached the adult model. Bellugi provided a formal linguistic description of the acquisition of negation but did not inquire into the inherent semantics and syntax of negation that underlie the formal account.

The rule that Bellugi proposed for the earliest negative sentences in the first phase of development, Period A, placed the negative element outside the sentence. This rule implies that there are no constraints on sentence complexity or sentence length with the operation of negation – if the choice of negation simply adds an element to an otherwise affirmative utterance. But in the texts of Kathryn, Eric, and Gia, the negative utterances were among the least syntactically complex, and there was strong evidence that the inclusion of the negative element constrained length and complexity of surface form. Also, specification

Reprinted from *Language Development: Form and Function in Emerging Grammars*, 1970, Chaps. 6 and 7, pp. 148–65, 170–220, with permission from The MIT Press, Cambridge, MA.

of the negative particle outside the sentence is inconsistent with sentence negation in the adult model of English. Negation is an inherent semantic fact of English sentences and is marked by the attachment of the negative particle to the verbal auxiliary *within* the sentence.

The term "cognitive clutter" was used by Slobin (1966) to describe the child's early development of negation in the light of the Bellugi account. He went on to say that the child "develops negation systems of unwieldy complexity – systems that are presumably too complicated to deal with and must be abandoned or seriously modified" (p. 91). But is this indeed the case? The question of the semantic and cognitive aspects of negation appeared worth pursuing in an effort to describe the underlying syntax of early sentence negation.

In addition to Period A, Bellugi described a second stage, Period B, as one in which the negative element occurs after the sentence-subject and has different forms, including *no, not, don't,* and *can't.* The data to be presented here – from the observations of Kathryn I to III, Eric II to VI, and Gia IV to VI – coincided with the Periods A and B that Bellugi described for the three children she studied.

THE SYNTAX OF EARLY NEGATION

A description of the structure of the children's negative sentences was straightforward, for two reasons: (1) The semantics of negation was relatively clear in the annotated transcriptions, so that the nonrealization of constituents in the surface structure of sentences could be demonstrated, and (2) negation was a syntactic operation that entered the grammars at a time when the development of the system was under way, so that its effects on the system could be examined.

All the syntactic constructions with a negative marker (*no*) from the Kathryn I text are presented in Table 4.1.[8] Looking at these negative utterances and the contexts in which each occurred, there appear to be two broad classes of sentences (excluding (15) "no milk," which could not be interpreted). These can be distinguished according to the relation of the surface constituents of the utterance to the negative predication: (1) sentences in which the negative particle preceded an element that was clearly being negated:

(1)   no pocket.
(2)   no pocket in there.
(3)   no sock.
(4)   no fit.

Table 4.1. *All Negative Sentences Produced by Kathryn at Time I*

Description of Speech Event	Kathryn's Utterance
(1) (K unable to find a pocket in M's skirt)	> no pocket.
(2)	⎡ > no pocket in there. ⎤
(3) (K waiting for M to make 'pretend' socks for her feet)	no sock.
(4) (K unable to nest blocks or fit lambs into blocks; 7 instances of utterance in similar situations)	> no fit.
(5) (K standing in unzipped boots)	> no zip.
(6) (K unable to turn plastic screw in washer)	> no turn.
(7) (K unable to close box)	> no close.
(8) (K picked up clean sock)	⎡ this sock. ⎤ ⎣ dirty. ⎦
Oh that's not a dirty one. That just has a big hole in it.	hole.
It has a big hole in it.	> no dirty.
(9) (K pushing away a piece of worn soap in the bathtub, wanting to be washed with new pink soap)	> no dirty soap.
(10) (K pulling sock off her foot)	> no sock.
(11) (K pulling away from L, who had offered to comb her hair)	> no Mommy.
(12) (K protested taking a bath, wanted to go outside)	> no outside.
(13) (K put lamb into block upside down; head was not in round window like the other lambs)	
He can't see out of the window.	
Can he see out of the window?	> no window.
(14) (K pushed lambs off the chair)	
Now why did you do that? They wanta sit on the chair.	
(K trying to climb on the chair)	ə wanta sit down chair.
(M putting lambs on chair)	no!
(K pushing lambs off chair)	
They wanta sit on the chair.	no. no.
(K pushing lambs off)	> ə no chair.
(15) (Indeterminate utterance; M washing K's face after lunch)	milk
Clean your nose.	> no milk.

(5)   no zip.
(6)   no turn.
(7)   no close.
(8)   no dirty.
(9)   no dirty soap.
(10) no sock.

and (2) sentences in which the *no* occurred and the remainder of the sentence was clearly not being negated directly:

(11) no Mommy.
(12) no outside.
(13) no window.
(14) ə no chair.

With "no pocket," there was no pocket; with (3) "no sock," there was no sock; with "no zip," the boots were not zipped; with "no dirty soap," Kathryn did not want the dirty soap. However, with "no outside," Kathryn wanted to go outside; with "no window," there was a window; and with "ə no chair," Kathryn wanted to sit on the chair.

There were two alternative explanations for the occurrence of *no* in utterances where the segment after *no* was clearly not negated. In (11) "no Mommy" and (12) "no outside," the *no* was anaphoric and applied to a prior utterance (Lois, not Mommy, offering to comb Kathryn's hair, and Mommy telling Kathryn it was bath time, respectively). Anaphoric *no* in these sentences occurred in juxtaposition with an affirmative utterance that expressed a positive alternative to something said by someone else. Although only two such examples occurred at Kathryn I, this type of utterance increased in frequency in subsequent samples. For example, the following are two of the eight occurrences of the sentence type *no plus affirmative sentence* at Kathryn II:

(16) K II

(Kathryn, looking for a
book about dragons, picked
up a book about bears) $\left[\begin{array}{l} \text{this.} \\ > \text{no, that's ə bear book.} \end{array}\right]$

(and dropped it)

(17) K II

(Kathryn, unable to
connect the train, giving the
cars to Lois)   no, Lois do it.

Prosodic features of juncture or stress did not assist in interpreting these sentences. There was not a pause after *no,* and *no* did not receive differential stress. Acoustically, these sentences did not differ from negative sentences – for example:

(18) K II

    (Kathryn looking at Lois's bare head)   Lois no hat.

where *no* occurred after the sentence-subject and before a negated constituent. Superficially, such sentences as "no that's ə bear book" and "no Lois do it" were ambiguous, and only the nonlinguistic cues of context and behavior were available to resolve the ambiguity.

The second explanation of *no* in juxtaposition with a segment not being negated applied to (13) "no window," (14) "ə no chair," and the example that follows, in which the surface structure is, at first glance, paradoxical:

(19) E II

    (Eric pointing to the tape recorder as Mommy entered the room, after being told he could not play with it)   no 'chine.

Looking at these utterances – (13), "no window," (14) "ə no chair," and (19) "no 'chine" – without knowing the accompanying behavior and context in which they occurred, the adult could be misled into interpreting them to mean that there was no window, no chair, and no machine. But the children had demonstrated the ability to express non-existence – for example, "no pocket" when there was no pocket and "no more noise" (at Eric II) when the noise had stopped. It appeared that the same superficial form was used to express a more complex negative-syntactic relation.

For each of these sentences – "no window," "ə no chair," and "no 'chine" – a semantic interpretation would depend on an underlying structure that specified a semantic relation between the negative element and a constituent intervening between *no* and the sentence-complement. In these sentences the negative element had immediate effect on an aspect of the sentence that was not produced in its surface structure. A similar analysis could be made with (9) "no dirty soap" and (10) "no sock," where the semantic correlates of negation were different; for example, the dirty soap was being negated, but indirectly in that Kathryn was negating 'using' or 'wanting' the dirty soap.

Such utterances as (13) "no window," (14) "ə no chair," and (19) "no 'chine" were the reduced forms of an implicit, more complex underlying structure. This postulation of reduction in linguistic expression of negation was supported by the following observations. First, the children had learned something about the semantics and syntax of negation; that is, they used the negative particle as a syntactic operator, with semantic effect on immediate constituents, as Kathryn did in (1) "no pocket," (3) "no sock," and (5) "no zip." If Kathryn knows that *no* plus a substantive element signals negation of that element, as in "no pocket," then it is reasonable to assume that her use of that same superficial syntactic structure with different intent, as in "no window," 'means' something else. "No pocket" signaled direct negation of "pocket," but "no window" did not signal negation of "window" in quite the same way. Second, the semantic interpretations of these negative sentences, given the speech events of which they were a part, depended on the postulation of unrealized constituents in more complex syntactic structures than were actually produced. Otherwise, the utterances could not be interpreted as negative in the same sense that other utterances with *no* were interpretable at the same time. In each instance, there was negation of a predicative structure but there was expression of only the object complement. "Window," "chair," and "'chine" functioned grammatically as predicate objects in relation to unrealized constituents that were obligatory in the inherent structure of the sentences.

The children had to have produced a syntactic construction (conjoining two or more constituents with an inherent relationship between them) in order to postulate the operation of reduction. In the texts of the three children there was frequent occurrence of *no* as a single-word utterance, and there were also instances in which the child produced a single word with apparent negative intent, although a negative element was not expressed – for example:

(20) K I

(Kathryn taking off the lavaliere
microphone, not wanting to wear it)   necklace.

An argument for the operation of reduction in these two instances – that is, the occurrence of *no* alone or single-word utterances such as "necklace" – would be necessarily weak. The response *no* is an acceptable elliptical response to yes–no questions or imperatives, and grammatical ellipsis is necessarily distinguished from reduction. In the other instance, "necklace," the nonlinguistic evidence of negative semantic intent was strong, but so was the possibility for ambiguity. Kathryn could have intended the fuller sentence "off necklace" (an utterance that actually occurred in another identical speech event at Kathryn I) as easily as the negative sentence "no necklace," and the context and behavior could support both interpretations.

There were instances of sentence reduction with deletion of the negative element – for example:

(21) K II
    (Lois had said "coffee store?";
    Kathryn was reminded of
    having the "coffee 'chine"
    fixed and then said, shaking her
    head negatively)   > me like coffee.
    (no longer shaking her head)   Daddy like coffee.
    (shaking her head)   Lois ə no coffee.

(22) E III
    (Eric unable to find a
    particular block and giving up)   ə find it.

However, the possible deletion of the negative element was less interesting – and somewhat more difficult to evaluate – than the reduction that occurred in the remainder of a sentence when the negative element was expressed. Sequential utterances in a single speech event – where the child subsequently expanded or changed an utterance and reduced it at the same time – provided clear-cut evidence of the effect of the syntactic operation of negation on sentence complexity, as in "Lois ə no coffee." In the utterances "no window," "ə no chair," "no 'chine," the semantic correlates of negation provided evidence of the nonrealization of constituents. However, a more important question with respect to the effect of negation on syntactic complexity was how all the negative sentences compared in syntactic structure with the affirmative sentences that also occurred in the same texts. Was there any evidence that negative utterances were syntactically different?

The form of the first negative sentences was a negative particle before nominal or predicate forms. There were certain missing elements in these negative utterances that were irrelevant; for example, the fact that no verb and noun inflections occurred was immaterial because verb and noun inflections were not realized in the early grammars at all. However, other structural omissions in the negative utterances were significant because they set the negative sentences apart from the other, affirmative sentences that occurred.

First, there was no expression of sentence-subject in any of the sentences, except "no Mommy" (in which, it turned out, "Mommy" was not the subject of a negative predication). However, at the same time, nominal subjects were expressed in more than 60 of the total of 397 utterances analyzed in the text of Kathryn I, excluding the occurrence of pre-verbal /ə/. Second, there were no occurrences of both a predicate complement and a verb in a single sentence with *no*, although Kathryn expressed such 'complete' verb phrases in more than 40 of the 397 utterances, and verb–object phrases were among the most productive constructions in the texts of all three children. These omissions of subject, verb, or object complements were not attributable to lack of vocabulary; Kathryn 'had' the words in her lexicon – for example, "want," "see," "boot," "box," "lamb," "Mommy," "Kathryn."

Looking at the rest of the surface structure of these sentences, it was apparent that without the *no*, they were comparable to the most primitive utterances that Kathryn produced. However, the more complex underlying structures for these sentences, which would account for their semantic interpretation – for example, "no window": roughly, "*X* no *Y* window" (where *X* and *Y* represent inferred underlying category symbols with the grammatical functions of sentence-subject and predicate) – could be accounted for by the same grammar that would generate the affirmative sentences that also occurred.

A number of affirmative sentences in the data could be considered the affirmative forms of certain of the negative sentences that also occurred, for example, at Kathryn I: "no turn" and "this turn"; "no dirty" and "this dirty." But the negation of "this turn" and "this dirty" did not result in *"this no turn" or *"this no dirty," nor *"no this turn" or *"no this dirty." At Kathryn II there were two examples of an immediate denial of an affirmative statement in which the affirmative sentence was reduced with the operation of negation:

(23) K II
      (Kathryn sticking out her
      tongue)
      Whose tongue do I see?
      Who?   that ə Wendy.
                        >no Wendy.
                        Kathryn. no Wendy.

(24) K II

(Kathryn going into the
bathroom)   ə make plop.
                                                 >no plop.

("plop" was Kathryn's word
for "defecate"; Kathryn
subsequently urinated)

The following example from the text at Gia V illustrated the comparative simplicity of a negative utterance in an extended sequence with more complex utterances, several of which appeared to be plausible positive correlates of the negative. At this time Gia produced sentence subjects (usually pronoun forms) frequently, but none appeared in the negative sentences that also occurred at Gia V.

(25) G V

Do you wanta read "Mop
Top"? (Gia's newest book)   yes
(Lois picking up the book;
Gia reaching for it)   > no Mop Top.
Hm?
(Gia reaching for it)   Móp Tòp.
What?   /mǽdɑ̀p/
(Lois going to the sofa with it;
Gia following, holding out
her arms for the book)   read ə m__/æ · æ^w/.
                                                 I wanta read new /mɑ́də̀/.
(whining)   I wanta read ə my book.

                                    . . .

(Lois gave Gia the book;
after 'reading' it, Gia
giving it to Lois)   you read wə__Móp Tòp.

In sum, exercising the option to include the element of negation in a sentence operated to increase the syntactic complexity of the sentence. To negate a sentence it was necessary to reduce it at the same time; the syntactic operation occasioned the reduction. Further support for the notion that the operation of negation *within* a sentence increased its complexity, and thereby necessitated reduction in the surface structure, was the fact that affirmative sentences with anaphoric *no* (the sentence type *no plus affirmative sentence*) were more structurally 'complete' in all the texts, when compared with the negative sentences that occurred at the same time. Thus, the inclusion of *no* did not affect sentence length when *no* was anaphoric and without effect on the internal syntax of the sentence.

The account of the operation of negation just presented differs from Bellugi's description of the first of five stages in the development of the syntax of negation (Bellugi, 1967; Klima and Bellugi, 1966). In the first stage described by Bellugi, Period A, the mean lengths of utterance of the three subjects she studied were 1.96, 1.80, and 1.74. However, text collection began with Kathryn, Eric, and Gia somewhat earlier in terms of mean length of utterance, which was less than 1.5 for all three children.[9]

Period A was described by Bellugi as "negation outside the sentence nucleus," where a negative element is attached to a "rudimentary sentence." The grammar of the "rudimentary sentence" or its relation to the children's nonnegative sentences was not specified. Negative sentences were described as having "little internal structure, consisting only of noun phrases or unmarked nouns and verbs."

The negative sentences that Bellugi reported – for example, "no heavy," "no the sun shining," "no sit there," "no more string," "no Mommy read," "no no put glove" – are similar in surface form to the sentences of Kathryn, Eric, and Gia over the course of several observations. The more complex sentences, such as "no the sun shining" or "no no put glove," are comparable to the surface form of utterances in the texts of Kathryn II, Eric V, and Gia V.

In the phrase structure for the text of Kathryn I, the negative element was an optional semantic choice within the internal structure of the sentence:

$$K\ I\quad S \rightarrow Nom\ (Ng) \begin{Bmatrix} NP \\ VP \end{Bmatrix}$$

In contrast, Bellugi described the operation of negation in terms of an element "outside" the sentence "nucleus":

$$``\left[\begin{Bmatrix} no \\ not \end{Bmatrix} - \text{Nucleus} \right] \text{S or [Nucleus}-no]\ \text{S}"$$

Bellugi has characterized this first syntactic operation of negation as a "primitive abstraction which later drops out, having been replaced by a much more complex system of negation" and "not the primitive version of some later structure which adds constituents to form longer sentences.'' The principal evidence Bellugi provided for placing the negative element 'outside' the sentence nucleus was the observation that the ''children seldom place the negative morpheme in an internal position in the sentence structure'' (for example, ''no Mommy read,'' ''no the sun shining''), and here Bellugi was describing surface structure only. No evidence of the function of negation or of the relation of the negative element to the rest of the sentence, in terms of content, was presented: ''We have stripped the speech of paralinguistic features . . . of information arising from discourse relations by omitting interchanges, and of information from the setting or situation.'' However, when this kind of information was taken into account in analyzing the texts of Kathryn, Eric, and Gia, semantic interpretation of negative sentences was possible in most cases. Interpreting the semantics of these sentences made it possible to analyze the internal structure of the syntax – revealing that inclusion of the negative element operated to replace or delete other forms.

In the earliest sentences, the negative element did occupy the initial position in the surface of sentences (except for the few occurrences after /ə/), as also observed by Bellugi. However, this occurred as a consequence of the omission of other constituents, that is, sentence-subjects, in the earliest negative sentences. In the subsequent texts (Kathryn II, Gia V, and Eric V) there were sentences that contained both sentence-subject and the negative particle. Table 4.2 presents all the sentences that contained both sentence-subject and a negative element in the texts of Kathryn II, Gia V, and Eric V (such sentences did not occur in the earlier texts). These sentences happened to include the most complex sentences the children produced – precisely because of the inclusion of sentence-subjects.

Differentiation of the negative element had not begun at Kathryn II; the only form was *no*. Gia, at Time V, produced a few sentences with the form ''can't,'' and Eric, at Time V, had begun to use the forms *didn't* and *doesn't* – but the primitive forms *no* and *no more* were far more frequent in both children's texts. Thus, Kathryn's and Gia's sentences in Table 4.2 could be described as having occurred in Bellugi's Period A – before the use of different forms of the negative element, which characterized the second stage, Period B, in Bellugi's account. Eric's sentences might be characterized as transitional – occurring somewhere between Periods A and B. Eric's sentences with *didn't* and *doesn't* were not included in Table 4.2.

In these sentences, *no* occurred both before and after the sentence-subject. However, when the contexts of the speech events of which the utterances were a part were studied, these sentences were seen to fall into two distinct groups. In the first group, (N), the *no* occurred before a predicate that was clearly being negated – for example, "Lois no hat" (Lois was not wearing a hat), "Kathryn no shoe" (Kathryn was not wearing shoes), "Mommy no picture there" (Mommy was reading a novel), "Kathryn no fix this" (Kathryn could not fix the train). In the second group, (A), the *no* was clearly anaphoric and did not apply to the remainder of the sentence, which was an affirmative statement: "no, Kathryn playing self" (Kathryn did not want to play with the slide and went into the playpen to play alone), "no, Lois do it" (Kathryn was giving the train to Lois to fix), "no, man ride *this* tank car" (Gia was pointing to a different car for the man to ride), "no, doll sleep" (Gia wanted to put the doll to sleep).

The only exception to this clear distinction between the (N) negative sentences, where the negative particle followed the sentence-subject, and (A) affirmative sentences, where the negative particle preceded the sentence-subject was the utterance "no Daddy hungry," which occurred as follows:

(51) K II

    (Kathryn looking at a
    picture of a family at a dinner
    table; in the picture the
    mother and children are
    seated at the table and the
    father is walking toward the
    table carrying a platter of
    food)

    hungry. hmmmmm.
    girl hungry.
    Daddy hungry. . . .
> no Daddy hungry.
    Daddy up.
    Mommy hungry.
    boy hungry.

If the distinction between the two kinds of sentences with sentence-subject and a negative element in the texts of Kathryn, Gia, and Eric did not exist in the Bellugi data, it represents an important difference in the development of negation in the two groups of children. In a personal communication to William Labov at Columbia University

Table 4.2. *Utterances with* no *and Sentence-Subjects*

(N) Negative Sentences

   (26) K II Lois no hat. (L not wearing a hat)

   (27) K II Kathryn no shoe. (K pointing to her bare feet)

   (28) K II Mommy no picture there. (M reading a novel)

   (29) K II man no go in there. (K holding her toy clown; watching L pack up toys to leave)

   (30) K II Kathryn no /fɪk/ this. (K unable to snap blocks)

   (31) K II Kathryn no fix this. (K unable to snap blocks)

   (32) K II Kathryn no like celery. (K watching M eat celery after not taking celery when M offered it to her)

   (33) K II Lois ə no coffee. (in sequence (21): "me like coffee, Daddy like coffee, Lois ə no coffee.")

   (34) K II this ə no goes. (K trying to fit puzzle piece into the wrong space)

   (35) E V you no bring ə choo-choo train? (E disappointed because L had not brought the train)

   (36) E V I no reach it. (E pointing to the window blind, which he wanted L to open for him)

   (37) E V I no like to. (M had asked E if he wanted to go on a roller coaster again)

(A) Affirmative Sentences

   (38) K II no, Lois do it. (K, unable to connect the train cars, given them to L to connect)

   (39) K II no, Kathryn want play with self. (K didn't want to play with the slide; L asked, "Shall I do it myself?"; K climbing into her playpen to play with her toys)

   (40) K II no, Kathryn playing self. (In sequence with (39))

   (41) K II no, my have ə this. (In response to "Kathryn'll have two and I'll have two"; K refusing to give wheel to L)

   (42) K II no, I my have ə this. (In response to "Lois'll have this"; L reaching for K's snap block; K holding on to it)

   (43) K II no, that's ə bear book. (K, looking for her book about dragons, picked up a book about bears, then dropped it)

   (44) E V *no,* car going there. (E insisting that he sees a car in a picture in the animal book)

   (45) E V no, this Daddy. (E had called the boy figure "Daddy"; L asked "Is this Daddy?"; E pointing to the Daddy figure)

   (46) E V no, this ə Mommy. (E had named all the figures; L pointed to the baby, asked "Is this Mommy?"; E pointing to Mommy figure)

   (47) E V no, this Mommy Daddy. (E pointing to Mommy and Daddy on the form board, in response to "Is this Mommy?")

   (48) G V no, man ride *this* tank car. (G pointing to a different car for the man to ride on)

Table 4.2 *(cont.)*

(49)	G V	no, now I do ə /dɪt/. (G had completed a puzzle; L asked "Now can I do it?"; G refusing to let L do the puzzle; did it again herself)
(50)	G V	no, doll sleep. (G had pretended to sleep; getting up and taking her doll to put to sleep)
(51)	K II	no Daddy hungry. (This utterance is presented with the context of the speech event in which it occurred in the following discussion)

Note: The comma has been added to the affirmative sentences in this table to indicate their anaphoric function.

(1967), Bellugi described the nonlinguistic context that accompanied the utterance "no I see truck" in a published "section from Adam's first record" (Brown & Bellugi, 1964, p. 135) that would support characterization of the sentence as negative; that is, Adam could not see the truck.

The account of the operation of negation proposed here – that additional structure in a sentence, such as including the element of negation in its base form, has a limiting effect on production – contradicts the Bellugi account. If the negative element is outside the sentence in its underlying structure, then it should not affect the internal structure of the sentence. Such was the case in sentences with preceding anaphoric *no*, where the negative element was without effect on the sentence. However, the rule Bellugi proposed implies that there are no constraints on sentence complexity or sentence length with the operation of negation – if the choice of negation simply adds an element to an otherwise affirmative utterance. But in the texts of Kathryn, Eric, and Gia, the negative utterances were otherwise among the least syntactically complex when compared with affirmative utterances. There was strong evidence that the inclusion of the negative particle reduced surface form.

Finally, the specification of the negative particle outside the sentence is inconsistent with sentence negation in the adult model of English, where negation is an inherent semantic fact of English sentences. In the fully realized system of negation in the adult grammar of English, the "structural position of the negative element in the sentence" is related to the "scope of negation (i.e., the structures over which the negative element has its effect)" (Klima, 1964, p. 316). And, indeed, the constituents that were most often deleted in these early negative sentences were sentence-subjects, which were not within the immediate scope of negation.

Bellugi (1967) suggests that in Period A, negation outside the sentence represented a syntactic structure that has no relation to the adult model of the language – "a primitive abstraction which later drops out." In contrast, the development of Kathryn, Eric, and Gia suggested that the earliest system of negation was more similar to the adult model than it was different – but it was a much simpler, fragmented, and far more generalized system.

The evidence for this conclusion included the following observations:

1. The relation of the negative element to the content of the rest of the surface structure of sentences was direct or else, in some utterances, appeared to be semantically paradoxical (for example, "no 'chine," "no window") unless an unrealized element was postulated between the adjacent constituents "no" and " 'chine," "no" and "window," on which the negative element would have direct effect in the internal structure of the sentence.

2. The negative element never occurred before the subject of a negative sentence. In the earliest examples, there was no occurrence of sentence-subject in negative sentences, although sentence-subjects were fully productive in affirmative sentences in the texts of Kathryn and Gia. Indeed, even at Time V, when Gia produced the sentences in Table 4.2 with anaphoric *no* and an affirmative sentence that included sentence-subjects, she did not produce any negative sentences with sentence-subjects at the same time. When at a subsequent stage, subjects were expressed in negative sentences, the negative element always followed the subject – preceding the negated predicate.

3. The negative element occurred after /ə/, when a possible source for /ə/ might have been *I* or *it*.

The latter two observations correspond to the attraction of the negative element to the essential verb of a sentence in the adult model. When "the whole combination of a subject and a predicate is negativized – the negative element [is] joined more or less closely to the finite verb" (Jespersen, 1961, p. 438). An objection to this interpretation could be raised when the finite verb did not occur. But it was just this nonoccurrence of the verb – for example, *want* or *use* in "no dirty soap," "play" in "no 'chine" – that was an effect of the constraints that operated to reduce the surface structure of the children's early sentences. The sentences could not otherwise be interpretable as negative sentences, given the facts of behavior and context in the speech events in which they occurred.

Negative sentences could not be construed as simply a positive sentence with a negative sign attached, outside the sentence. Rather, the negative element was intrinsic to the structure of the sentence and as such operated to increase its complexity, as in adult grammar. This account has attempted to show that the earliest system of negation in the children's grammar differed from the account of the adult system only in the fact of its essential immaturity.

CONSTRAINTS ON THE FORM OF CHILDREN'S SPEECH

So-called pivot and telegraphic sentences were often the reduced forms of more complex underlying structures. The results of an experimental study by Shipley, Smith, and Gleitman (1969) provide support for the contention that children's speech may not be isomorphic with what they know about linguistic structure. They reported that "children whose speech is telegraphic readily obey well-formed commands, and less readily obey telegraphic commands" (p. 336), indicating that the children know more about grammatical structure than their speech would indicate.

When the total distribution of sentences in a text was examined, sentences were incomplete (in terms of basic subject–verb–object representation), but the pattern was variable. There were subject–verb, subject–object, and verb–object strings, but subject–verb–object strings did not occur. Leopold (1949, vol. 3, p. 28) observed the same restriction on the production of sentences in his daughter's development at the time (20 to 23 months) that "sentence span was limited to two words." He observed that "where the standard [the adult model utterance] required at least three words because the predicate was not a simple verb, the child was forced to omit one of them." It might be argued that inclusion of *no* in such strings simply increased sentence length beyond the 'permitted' two morphemes – that constraint on complexity *is* a constraint on length. But it appeared that reduction was the result of something more than a production limitation on sentence length. The evidence presented here suggests that some sort of cognitive limitation in handling structural complexity (such as accompanies sentence negation) underlies the constraint on length of children's utterances – that the constraint on sentence length reflects an inherent limitation in linguistic operations. It was clear that the earliest negative sentences did not simply add a negative marker or operator to an otherwise affirmative sentence. Rather, the linguistic operation of negation had a limiting effect on structural complexity and length of utterances.

In sum, with an increase in the underlying complexity of a sentence, something had to give in its production. The factors that operated to influence the production or omission of particular forms in a sentence were related to the nature of the language the child was learning (linguistic constraints) and the basic facts of the immaturity of the cognitive system (cognitive constraints) (as discussed in chapter 3).

SEMANTIC CATEGORIES OF NEGATION

Utterances were considered negative if (1) they contained a negative element, such as *no, no more, not,* or *don't,* that signaled negative intent, and/or (2) they were produced with clearly negative intent (as evidenced, for example, by shaking the head, pushing an object away, or refusing to follow a direction). Twelve of the 15 utterances with "no more" (including 4 instances of "no more" in isolation) at Eric II shared the same semantic feature: the nonexistence of the referent in the context of the speech event. When Eric said "no more noise," the noise had stopped; when he said "no more cleaner," the cleaner was gone; when he said "no more juice," he had finished his juice. Thus, the linguistic and contextual features shared by these 12 utterances were the expression of a negative element (*no more*) and the nonexistence of the referent. The semantic interpretation of 2 of the 15 utterances could not be determined, and 1 utterance had a different interpretation.

At the same time, Eric II, there were 76 occurrences of *no* in the text as a single word, and it was possible to interpret the use of *no* in 41 instances. In only 3 instances did *no* signal nonexistence of a referent unequivocally. However, in 33 instances where *no* occurred, the referent did exist in the context. The interpretation of these utterances as negative was based on Eric's behavior as he indicated rejection – by pushing away or turning away from an object or otherwise opposing the occurrence of an event. Five occurrences of *no* were interpreted differently.

Clearly, Eric used the negative marker *no more* to signal nonexistence and the single word *no* to signal rejection. Most of Eric's first negative sentences, at Time II, referred to the nonexistence of objects with *no more*. However, at the same time, he expressed rejection of something that existed in the context, and he did so by using the isolated word *no*.

But whereas the expression of nonexistence and rejection was distinguished formally at Eric II, the same categories were not distinguished formally at Kathryn I:

(1) K I

    (Kathryn not finding a pocket in
    Mommy's skirt, which had no pocket)   no pocket.

(9) K I

    (Kathryn pushing away a sliver of
    worn soap in the bathtub, wanting to be
    washed with new pink soap)   no dirty soap.

The same form signaled nonexistence, "no pocket," and rejection, "no dirty soap." Furthermore, at Kathryn II, a third semantic category, denial, was distinguished on the basis of function, and the form of expression of *denial* was not different from "no pocket" and "no dirty soap":

(52) K II

    (Kathryn, Mommy, and Lois look-
    ing for the truck)

    Where's the truck?

    (Mommy picking up the car, giving it to
    Kathryn)

    Here it is. There's the truck.   no truck.

Thus, three semantic categories of negation characterized the children's earliest negative sentences: nonexistence – the referent was not manifest in the context, where there was an expectation of its existence, and was correspondingly negated in the linguistic expression (examples included [1] "no pocket" and sentences with "no more" at Eric II); rejection – the referent actually existed or was imminent within the contextual space of the speech event and was rejected or opposed by the child, as in "no dirty soap"; denial – the negative utterance asserted that an actual (or supposed) predication was not the case. The negated referent was not actually manifest in the context as it was in rejection, but it was manifest symbolically in a previous utterance; "no truck" denied the expressed identity of the car as a truck.

In a paper that discussed the acquisition of negation by one child learning Japanese as a first language, McNeill and McNeill (1968) raised the issue of the semantic interpretation of negation in Japanese. They reported that the facts of negation in Japanese are accounted for by four different forms of the negative element organized on the basis of three dimensions or contrasts. These forms are not syntactically different – each occurs in sentence-final position, after the predicate phrase. However, the shape of the negative element varies according to semantic function. The three semantic dimensions described were "Existence–Truth, Internal–External, and Entailment–Nonentailment." From the descriptions provided, these three dimensions appear to correspond generally to the semantic categories of negation proposed for Kathryn, Eric, and Gia: nonexistence, rejection, and denial. Although the data presented by McNeill and McNeill were incomplete, they reported that the three negation contrasts in Japanese were acquired by their subject in the order given above.

Negation in the adult model of English can also be organized in terms of the three semantic categories identified in the children's speech; certainly the adult grammar allows expression of the contrastive notions – existence–nonexistence, acceptance–rejection, and affirmation–denial. But whereas in Japanese the semantic categories are neatly signaled by morphological markers, their linguistic expression in English is less efficient. Indeed, the thorough account of the syntax of English negation by Klima (1964) presented only the syntax of negation and ignored the semantic issues: "The analysis . . . offers . . . no interpretation of notions like *negative* that appear as designations of grammatical symbols" (p. 247).

The semantic differences in the early negative sentences of Kathryn, Eric, and Gia were exemplified by the differences among "no pocket," "no dirty soap," and "no truck." It appeared reasonable to approach the inquiry into the children's acquisition of negation by determining whether the three semantic categories of negation – nonexistence, rejection, and denial – were differentiated in the course of development in terms of (1) sequence of development and (2) structural differences in linguistic expression.

PHASE I IN THE DEVELOPMENT OF NEGATION

The first phase in the development of sentence negation was the earliest meaningful and productive use of a negative element in syntactic contexts. This occurred in the texts of Eric II, Kathryn I, and Gia IV.

Eric I to III

In the first text collected, Time I, mean length of utterance was 1.10, and Eric produced *no* as a single-word utterance 13 times. In four instances, the utterance occurred in response to a yes–no question – for example, "Does it fit?" – but the use of *no* was inappropriate in one instance and indeterminate in the other three. There were four spontaneous occurrences of *no* – not in response to a yes–no question – that were indeterminate; it was not clear from the context or behavior whether negation was intended. Five spontaneous occurrences of *no* were appropriate, and all occurred at different times but in the same context: Eric was unable to fit the vacuum cleaner pipe and hose together.

The following paradigmatic sequence also occurred:

(53) E I

    (Eric closed the lid of his toy chest)   all gone.

                                               no more.

                                               make all gone.

This occurrence of "no more" was the only instance of "no more" in the text. "All gone" occurred elsewhere four times – once after Eric dropped his lollipop stick into the radiator grille and I commented, "It's gone." This took place just before the "all gone, no more, make all gone" sequence, with ten intervening adult utterances and three intervening utterances by Eric. The three other instances of "all gone" were indeterminate.

The evidence was limited for postulating the rudimentary beginning of the linguistic expression of negation at Eric I – the sequence in (53) was semantically appropriate, and there were five occurrences of *no* as a single word in an appropriate context signaling negation. But the data were too meager at Time I to determine with conviction if Eric knew the 'meaning' of *no*. There were many more yes–no questions to which he did not respond with *no*, and the word *yes* never occurred. All that could be said at Time I was that the form *no* occurred as a single word and that its interpretation was indeterminate more often than not.

There were 76 occurrences of the single word *no* in the subsequent Eric II text. These instances of *no* have been categorized – where there was sufficient evidence to permit unequivocal classification – as expressions of nonexistence, rejection, or denial and are presented in Table 4.3, along with the functional distribution of *no* at Time III. As

Table 4.3. *Functional Distribution of* no *as a Single Word,*
Eric II and III

	Nonexistence	Rejection	Denial	Indeterminate
Eric II	2(1)	30(3)	(5)	20(15)
Eric III	2	11(11)	0	14(4)

Note: Numbers in parentheses refer to utterances that occurred after a prior question or comment. Utterances were interpreted (and classified as to semantic category) only when the contextual and behavioral evidence was clear. Nearly half the occurrences of *no* could not be interpreted; these occurred often while Eric played alone – for example, when stacking the blocks or connecting the train. At such times what Eric said *(no)* did not appear to relate to what he was doing. There were also instances that could not be interpreted because of insufficient information at the time of transcription.

at Time I, the word *yes* or its equivalent did not occur at Eric II or III. Aside from the indeterminate utterances, *no* was used most frequently to express rejection. At the same time, *no more* occurred in isolation and signaled nonexistence four times at Eric II and eight times at Eric III; *no more* was not used to express rejection. Thus, it appeared that variation in the form of nonsyntactic expressions of negation (*no* and *no more* as single words) corresponded to variation in function – *no* signaled rejection, and *no more* signaled nonexistence at Eric II and at Eric III.

The text at Time III was 2 and ½ hours longer than at Time II, but the number of instances of *no* as a single word decreased from 76 occurrences at Time II to 42 at Time III. Corresponding to the marked decline in the use of *no* as a single word, the number of interpretable syntactic expressions of negation increased from 11 sentences at Time II to 35 sentences at Time III, and mean length of utterance overall increased from 1.19 to 1.42 morphemes. The use of *no* as a single word decreased at Time III with the use of *no* in syntactic expression of negation.

Syntactic Negation at Eric II. The negative sentences at Eric II are presented in Table 4.4. At this time, Eric used syntactic negation to express nonexistence most often – in 9 of the 11 speech events. In order to express rejection he used *no* as a single word – in 33 of the 41 interpretable instances of *no*. Syntactic expression of rejection was marginal, and there was no syntactic expression of denial.

Two utterances with unique structure in Table 4.4, "ə don't want

Table 4.4. *Categorization of Negative Utterances, Eric II*

Nonexistence		Rejection	Indeterminate
no more noise	(4)	ə don't want baby	no more noise
no more light	(2)	no more noise	
no more juice			
no more cleaner			
no 'chine			
no more	(4)	no (33)	no (35)
no	(3)		no more

Note: Numbers in parentheses refer to the number of times the utterance occurred in the text, discounting immediate repetitions.

baby'' and ''no 'chine,'' were sentences not generated by the Eric II grammar (see Bloom, 1970, chap. 5). The forms *don't* and *want* did not occur elsewhere in the text at Time II, and *don't* did not occur subsequently at Time III. Eric said ''ə don't want baby'' as he dropped a doll he had been holding.

The utterance ''no more noise'' occurred five times in appropriate contexts and in one context in which interpretation was indeterminate:

(54) E II

    (Eric and Lois had put
    the wire man on Eric's peg
    bench; Eric started to whim-
    per)   Mommy. Mommy. Mommy.

    O.K. Show Mommy.

    (Eric began to cry; Lois stood
    up)

    Let's go find Mommy in the
    kitchen.   no.

    No?

    (Eric refusing to leave)   no more.
                                           > no more noise.

It was not possible to understand what Eric wanted, but he appeared to be using his negation repertoire – ''no,'' ''no more,'' and ''no more noise'' – to express negation of something. The anomalous occurrence of ''no more noise'' may have been the most readily available syntac-

Table 4.5. *Categorization of Negative Utterances, Eric III*

Nonexistence		Rejection	Denial
no more noise	(13)	no train	no more birdie
no more light	(2)	no more dumpcar	no more blocks
no more car	(2)	ə want any shoes	
no more seal			
no more airplane		no (22)	
no more round			
no more apple			
no more dumpcar			
ə no more			
no go in			
no goes			
no ready go			
no fit			
no it won't fit			
ə find it			
/jə/ find it			
no more	(8)		
no	(2)		

Note: Numbers in parentheses refer to the number of times the utterance occurred in the text, discounting immediate repetitions.

tic construction for expressing a negative notion that Eric was unable
to express otherwise. That is, "no more noise" – the most frequent
syntactic construction – may have been generalized as a negative 'whole'
comparable to "no" and "no more."

Whereas "ə don't want baby" was not related structurally to any
other utterances at either Eric II or Eric III, the utterance "no 'chine,"
anticipated a developmental change that did occur subsequently, at
Time III.

Syntactic Negation at Eric III. Table 4.5 presents the categorized distribution of the negative sentences at Eric III. There was a substantial
increase in the number of negative sentences; syntactic negation expressed nonexistence most productively – in 30 of the 35 negative
sentences that occurred. Thus, although the number of sentences increased substantially, the functional distribution was essentially the
same as at Eric II – Eric was able to express nonexistence syntactically, but rejection was signaled most often by isolated *no*.

However, two developments occurred that distinguished the data at

Eric III from the earlier data at Eric II. First, Eric began to express both rejection and denial syntactically, although occurrence of sentences with these functions was marginal. In addition, there was a differentiation in the form of the negative element in syntactic contexts. Whereas "no 'chine" at Eric II was the only instance of *no* as a negative operator, this form became productive at Eric III. Further, the two forms of the negative element – *no more* and *no* – were in complementary distribution. *No more* occurred in syntactic contexts with noun forms where the noun referent was negated directly – for example, "no more airplane," "no more noise," "no more apple." Moreover, *no more* was used in contexts where negation signaled nonexistence of objects that had occurred previously – the negation of recurrence.

In contrast, the form *no* occurred as a negative operator in syntactic contexts before predicate structures. Thus, the negative element had the form *no* in contexts before verbs – for example, "no go in," "no goes," "no ready go" (referring to sliding the wheels) – and also before nouns that had the grammatical function predicate–object with unexpressed verbs, for example, the sentence "no train" as Eric took the wire man off the train as it was being pushed. Earlier, at Time II, the sentence "no 'chine" had occurred after Eric was told he couldn't play with the tape recorder. When his mother subsequently entered the room, Eric pointed to the tape recorder saying "no 'chine." In both instances, " 'chine" and "train" were not negated directly but were negated with respect to their function as predicate objects. Thus, the negative particle *no* appeared only in predicative constructions, in complementary distribution with *no more,* which appeared with nouns.

Again, as in Eric II, "no more noise" occurred more frequently than any other negative sentence. On one occasion "no more noise" occurred when the bridge collapsed; one occurrence of the sentence was anomalous – as beads were being retrieved for the slide. There was one unique 'stereotype' structure: "ə want any shoes." In addition, there were two sentences – "ə find it" and "/jə/ find it" – that appeared to occur with negative intent, although the negative element was not expressed; Eric produced both sentences when he was unable to find a block he had been looking for.

In summary, negation was a meaningful cognitive–semantic concept for Eric at Time II and at Time III. The mechanism for the linguistic expression of negation had emerged as a productive syntactic operation, although its function was limited, for the most part, to expression of nonexistence, with *no more* used as syntactic operator. Earlier Eric had used two different negative forms contrastively as single words to signal two different semantic functions (*no more* signaled nonexistence, and *no* signaled rejection). When he first began to express rejection and denial syntactically he used the same, first-learned syntactic operator *no more* that he used syntactically to express nonexistence, so that semantic differences were not differentiated structurally.

Thus, although Eric had learned something about the different semantic categories of negation, the development of syntactic expression was limited, at first, to syntactic constructions that expressed only one – nonexistence – at the same time that the other categories were expressed by isolated *no*. Syntactic expression of rejection and denial began to emerge toward the end of the first phase, but the introduction of the syntactic expression of rejection and denial was not accompanied by developmental advance in the form of their linguistic expression. Rather, the differentiation of structure that represented the developmental difference between linguistic expression of negation at Time II and Time III was the syntactic occurrence of *no* and *no more* in complementary distribution in the syntactic expression of the category nonexistence – the first semantic category expressed syntactically.

Gia I to IV

Negation did not appear to have been learned yet as a concept that could be expressed syntactically in the first two texts, Gia I and II. An explanation for the absence of syntactic expression of negation in the early texts obtained from Gia was problematical. It may be the case that there is an element of 'choice' in what is learned – that children choose to learn certain structures and concepts (perhaps on the basis of such notions as 'need' or 'frequency of exposure') and that the number of structures that can be learned or practiced at any one time is necessarily limited. There was no evidence that could be used to decide the relative 'need' for sentence negation in the experience of the three children. There was no apparent reason why Eric and Kathryn would need to express negation more than Gia would. Also, the data did not reveal the extent of exposure to negative sentences in the speech the children heard.

At Time III, Gia produced 4 syntactic constructions with a negative element but only one utterance expressed negation unequivocally:

Table 4.6. *Functional Distribution of* no *as a Single Word,*
Gia I to III

	Nonexistence	Rejection	Denial	Indeterminate
Gia I	2(1)	9(1)	0	3
Gia II	2(1)	8(2)	(9)	2
Gia III	(1)	2(5)	0	4(3)

Note: Numbers in parentheses refer to utterances that occurred after a prior question or comment from someone else.

(55) G III
    (Lois had freed Gia after she had
    gotten stuck climbing onto a chair)   no more stuck.
                                           no more.

Other sentences that contained a negative element, and *no more* as a single word, were not contrastive – they did not necessarily signal negation. For example, Gia said "no more" as she was stacking blocks, and there was no evidence for an interpretation of negation. She produced the utterance "*nat/*" while eating lunch and shaking her head negatively; her mother interpreted this at the time as "not hot." The following occurred several minutes later:

(56) G III
    (Gia eating lunch at 1:00
    P.M.; Mommy and Lois in kitchen
    with her)   morning. morning.

    Good morning.   >no morning.

Gia might have referred to the fact that the time was early afternoon and not morning, but it was more likely that the reference was fortuitous or otherwise associated with Gia's eating lunch rather than breakfast. These four utterances were the only constructions with a negative element at Time III. The syntactic expression of negation was marginal at the time of the first three observations.

Gia used *no* as a single word to express negation in the first three texts; the functional distribution of occurrence of *no* is presented in Table 4.6. Generally, Gia used isolated *no* to signal rejection most often. However, at Time II 9 instances of *no* signaled denial in response to questions about the identity of familiar objects. For example, a clown was held up, and Gia was asked "Is this a cookie?" Gia's response *no* was classed as a denial. The reason for attempting to test the reliability of yes–no responses was the fact that *yes* was a far more frequent utterance than *no* in the second and third texts: 13 occurrences of *yes* at Time I, 145 at Time II, and 137 at Time III.

Gia tended to respond *yes* to almost all yes–no questions. She also responded *yes* to repetitions of her utterances that were presented with rising intonation contour – a question form that attempted to verify what she had said – for example:

(57) G II

(Gia had picked up the train and it came apart)	----train. more.
(giving the train to Lois)	more.
What?	more train.
More train?	> yes.

In similar situations, Eric would produce a subsequent utterance or, less often, repeat his previous utterance – for example:

(58) E II

(Eric watching a cloud of dust on the building lot across the street)	hot. hot.
Hot?	> hot. hot.

Occasionally, Gia said *yes* as a direction – for example, giving me the train to fix, saying *yes*. The *yes* responses to questions were sometimes inappropriate; in 14 of the 145 *yes* responses at Gia II, the context of speech events appeared to call for expression of negation instead. For the most part, *yes* responses had an almost 'automatic' aspect; hearing a rising intonation contour triggered a *yes* response. However, *yes* was often the only appropriate response, as, for example, when Gia's utterance was repeated to her for verification. But in those situations where Gia was given a choice – for example, "Do you want to read this book?" – Gia responded *yes,* whether or not she subsequently complied. In the same situation, Eric simply complied – without expressing agreement – or said "no."

Syntactic Negation at Gia IV. Gia produced five negative utterances at Time IV; these are presented in Table 4.7.

Table 4.7. *Categorization of Negative Utterances, Gia IV*

Nonexistence	Rejection	Denial	Indeterminate
no more pictures	no more		not here
no open it (2)			
no open the wallet	no (15)	no (4)	no (4)

Note: Numbers in parentheses refer to the number of times the utterance oc-curred, discounting immediate repetitions.

It was not clear at the time what was meant by ''not here,'' but the other utterances were interpretable and signaled negation. The data at Time IV were no less meager than data obtained in the earlier sessions, but interpretation of these few sentences was unequivocally expression of negation for all but one utterance (''not here'').

The functional distribution of *no* in isolation included 15 instances of rejection, 4 instances of denial, 4 utterances that were indetermi-nate, and no instances of *no* expressing nonexistence.

In summary, negation was not expressed syntactically in the first three texts collected from Gia. She did use *no* as a single-word utter-ance, expressing rejection most often, but the occurrence of *no* as a single-word utterance was far less frequent than the occurrence of *yes* at Time II and Time III. In the fourth text, it was possible to draw the tentative conclusion that Gia was able to use syntactic expression of negation, but the structure was only marginally productive. Although not tested, there was evidence that Gia understood negative sentences – she generally attended to negative directions, but evidence of a sim-ilar competence in linguistic expression was slight.

Even though the numbers of utterances were small, the four negative sentences in Table 4.7 signaled nonexistence, so that the anticipated order of emergence of linguistic expression of the three semantic cat-egories of negation appeared, tentatively, to match the order observed in Eric's early development of negation.

Kathryn I

The categorization of the negative sentences Kathryn produced at Time I is presented in Table 4.8.

Kathryn used syntactic negation to express nonexistence most fre-quently. She had also begun to express rejection and denial syntacti-

Table 4.8. *Categorization of Negative Utterances, Kathryn I*

Nonexistence	Rejection	Denial
no pocket	no dirty soap	no dirty
no pocket in there	ə no chair	
no sock	no sock	
no fit (7)		
no zip		
no turn		
no close		
no window		
ə no		
no (11)	no (24)	no (3)

Note: Numbers in parentheses refer to the number of times the utterance occurred in the text, discounting immediate repetitions.

cally; these sentences were few in number and did not differ in structure from negative sentences that signaled nonexistence.

Two utterances at Time I were not classed as negative sentences: "no Mommy" and "no outside." These sentences were extracted from the text and included in the original analysis of sentences for semantic categorization because they appeared, superficially, to be negative sentences – they included a negative marker and they lacked final contour or open juncture after *no*. As already discussed, once the contexts in which these utterances occurred was evaluated, it turned out that the negative marker *no* was an anaphoric, external element. This anaphoric *no* did not have effect on the rest of the utterance with which it was juxtaposed. Neither "Mommy" nor "outside" were being negated – Kathryn wanted Mommy to comb her hair; Kathryn wanted to go outside.

Kathryn also used *no* as a single-word utterance; the distribution of *no* in terms of function was 11 instances of nonexistence (4 in response to questions), 24 instances of rejection (15 in response to questions or comments), 3 instances of denial (2 in response to comments), and 17 indeterminate instances of *no* (6 in response to questions). As was true with Eric and Gia, *no,* when interpretable, signaled rejection most often.

Whereas Gia used *yes* far more frequently than *no* and Eric did not use a contrasting form at all, Kathryn used two contrasting forms – *no* and affirmative *O.K.* There were 55 instances of *no* and 43 instances of *O.K.* (including 1 expression of *yes*). When questioned about Kathryn's use of *O.K.* rather than *yes,* her mother reported that this was a 'new stage' – earlier, Kathryn had used only *yes.*

Comparison of the Three Children and Summary of Phase 1

The fact that Gia rarely expressed negation was the important difference among the children. Negation was still a marginal structure at Gia IV, but the constructions that did occur could be interpreted as negative and tended to be appropriate. Although Gia evidently understood negative sentences in the speech she heard, negative constructions were not productive in her own speech. In contrast, Eric and Kathryn each had developed a productive system of syntactic negation that was primitive in structural complexity and did not differentiate semantic function. The children's general linguistic maturity, as measured superficially by mean length of utterance, was essentially similar, although Gia's utterances were somewhat longer than either Eric's or Kathryn's. An account of development in the three semantic categories by the three children in Phase 1 is presented in Figure 4.1.

The structural form of these first negative sentences was a negative marker before nominal or predicate forms. Sentence-subjects were not expressed, even though the children produced affirmative sentences that included sentence-subjects. Negated predicates were reduced, and verb or object forms were deleted when one or the other occurred in production, even though verb–object phrases were the most productive constructions in the texts of all three children. The syntactic operation of negation served to increase sentence complexity, which resulted in a reduction of the surface structure of sentences – as discussed in Chapter 3 and previously in this chapter. The existence of the constituents in the underlying structure of the reduced sentences was postulated on the basis of (1) behavioral and contextual evidence, which revealed that the negative element actually had effect on unexpressed intervening constituents in such sentences as "no window," "no chair" in Kathryn's texts, and "no 'chine," "no more dumpcar," and "no train" in Eric's texts; and (2) the productivity of sentence-subjects in the Kathryn I text.

The grammars for Kathryn and Eric (in Bloom, 1970) accounted for the operation of negation, although the syntactic mechanism was different for each. In Kathryn's phrase structure, the negative ele-

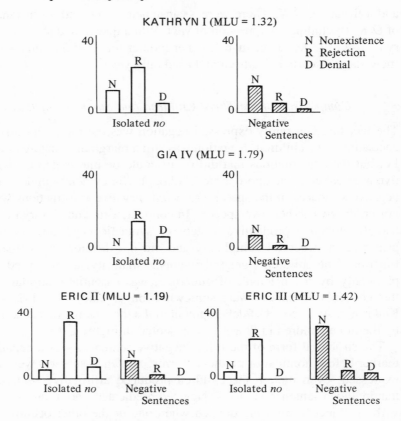

Figure 4.1. Phase I in the development of negation: frequency of isolated *no* and negative sentences in the semantic categories nonexistence (N), rejection (R), and denial (D).

ment appeared as a syntactic operator before the major category constituents – predicate NP and VP – and it was possible to infer an unrealized underlying structure with the grammatical function sentence-subject.

In Eric's phrase structure, evidence was limited for postulating the occurrence of a subject node before the negative element; subject forms were less productive at Eric III than at Kathryn I and did not occur at Eric II. Interpretation of negative sentences did not depend on the representation of an underlying constituent with the grammatical function sentence-subject.

All three children used *no* as a single word to signal rejection most often. Eric did not use a reciprocal form *yes;* Gia used *yes* far more frequently than *no;* and Kathryn used both affirmative *O.K.* and negative *no*.

The earliest negative sentences expressed nonexistence most often. Kathryn and Eric had begun to express rejection and denial syntactically, but sentences signaling nonexistence were far more frequent. Both children, although they had begun to differentiate negative sentences semantically, used the same syntactic structure for sentences with different semantic intent. Even though Eric had differentiated two negative forms in isolation, *no more* and *no,* in earlier expressions of nonexistence and rejection, respectively, he did not differentiate these same semantic categories in the earliest syntactic constructions. The negative sentences that Gia produced expressed nonexistence.

At the close of Phase I in the semantic and syntactic development of negation, the children knew something about three different semantic categories of negation – they were able to express nonexistence, rejection, and, less often, denial. They were able to produce syntactic constructions that signaled nonexistence, but for the most part, expression of rejection and denial was limited to the single-word utterance *no*.

STRUCTURAL DIFFERENTIATION OF SEMANTIC
CATEGORIES OF NEGATION: PHASE 2

The children had begun to use sentences that expressed semantic notions of rejection and denial in Phase 1, but the syntactic structure was not different from sentences that signaled nonexistence and occurred far more frequently. The syntactic differentiation of semantic categories was the major achievement in Phase 2.

The first phase occurred in those texts of Kathryn (Time I) and Eric (Time III), in which mean length of utterance was less than 1.5 morphemes, and in the text of Gia (Time IV), in which mean length of utterance was 1.79 morphemes. At the conclusion of Phase 2, mean length of utterance was 2.83 at Kathryn III, 2.84 at Eric VI, and 2.75 at Gia VI.

The distinction between Phase 1 and Phase 2 was most apparent in a comparison of the negative sentences produced by Kathryn at Time I with those at Times II and III.

Table 4.9. *Categorization of Negative Sentences, Kathryn II*

Nonexistence	Rejection	Denial
no skirt	no bear book	no Wendy (2)
no cup	no meat	no candle
no wagon	no slide away	no tire
no books	no go outside	no truck
no driver in the car		no ready
no hat	no put in there	no plop
all gone magazine	no make ə truck	no Jocelyn
Lois no hat	no ə house lambs	
Kathryn no shoe (2)	no want	this ə no Lois
Mommy no picture there	no want this	
	ə no want ə go now	no Daddy hungry
no fit (8)		
no fit here		
no stand up		
no under		
no go in		
no go first		
no go in there (2)		
no lock ə door		
no find ə tank		
no have ə this		
no like celery, Mommy		
this ə no goes		
man no go in there		
Kathryn no /fɪk/ this		
Kathryn no fix this		
Kathryn no like celery		
Kathryn not quite through		
Lois ə no coffee		
me like coffee		
Kathryn have ə socks on		
can't see (2)		
ə can't see		

Note: The underlined words are those that occurred in an immediately preceding utterance produced by someone else. Utterances within brackets are those that could be accounted for by the grammar at Kathryn I. Numbers in parentheses refer to number of occurrences in the text, discounting immediate repetitions.

Syntactic Negation at Kathryn II

The number of interpretable negative sentences increased from 19 at Kathryn I to 62 at Kathryn II; these have been categorized in terms of function and presented in Table 4.9. Several developmental changes distinguished the sentences at Time II from those that had occurred at Time I.

First, syntactic expression of all three semantic categories was productive at Kathryn II. Although sentences expressing nonexistence were most frequent, the number expressing rejection and denial increased substantially.

Structurally, 34 of these 62 sentences (the bracketed sentences in each category – for example, "no skirt," "no fit," "no truck") were similar to the negative sentences at Time I. The inclusion of a negative element (*no*) in the underlying structure of a sentence at Time I necessitated reduction in its surface structure. Sentence-objects were omitted, and complexity after the negative element – such as inclusion of verb and complement – was also reduced. Having chosen to express negation, there was an obligatory structural constraint on production of the sentence at Time I.

The remaining sentences in Table 4.9 could not have been generated by the Kathryn I grammar because of two important changes: (1) Production of the negated predicate was more structurally complete with inclusion of both the verb and predicate complement – for example, "no lock ə door," "no find ə tank"; and (2) sentence-subjects were expressed – for example, "Kathryn no shoe," "Kathryn no like celery."

However, these changes in the allowed structural complexity of produced sentences applied only to sentences that signaled nonexistence; not only did these sentences occur with greatest frequency in the corpus, but they were also the most structurally complete. There was no production of sentence-subject in expression of rejection, although the understood subject was Kathryn, and "Kathryn" (or "me") occurred as sentence-subject in six sentences that expressed nonexistence. The most grammatically primitive sentences were those that signaled denial – these were most similar in form to the early negative sentences at Kathryn I and were generally only two morphemes.

Three-term subject–verb–object strings occurred in affirmative sentences but occurred only in that category of negative sentences that had been most productive in the preceding corpus – sentences that signaled nonexistence – and not in the categories rejection and denial, which had not been productive. As pointed out in chapter 3, more recently learned structures (in terms of their productivity in performance) were most vulnerable to deletion. This constraint on structural complexity was demonstrated in the three sentences "Kathryn no shoe" (two occurrences) and "Kathryn have ə socks on," which occurred in similar speech events – Kathryn was barefoot. Similarly, the verb *want* was productive and occurred frequently in affirmative sentences – it had also occurred at Kathryn I – but it was expressed in only three sentences that signaled rejection, although its occurrence in the underlying structure was easily postulated from the contextual and behavioral data. For example, Kathryn did not *want* the bear book; Kathryn did not *want* to make a truck. The negative sentences at Time II were among the least structurally complex sentences that occurred.

Another productive sentence type at Kathryn II that had only marginal occurrence at Kathryn I was the expression of anaphoric *no* with an affirmative sentence – for example, "No, Kathryn want play with self" and "No, Lois do it." These sentences were discussed at length earlier, but it is pertinent here to point out again that *no-plus-affirmative-sentence* sentences were more structurally complete than the great majority of the negative sentences that occurred at the same time. The negative element did not apply semantically to the sentence and so did not affect (that is, reduce) its surface form.

The form of the negative element was invariant in Kathryn II. As at Kathryn I, the form was *no* with marginal instances of *can't* in two sentences expressing nonexistence.

In summary, there was a marked increase in the number of negative sentences at Kathryn II. The functional distribution of these sentences followed the distributional trend observed at Kathryn I: The greatest number of sentences that occurred signaled nonexistence. But whereas rejection and denial were marginal at Time I, syntactic expression of these categories was productive at Time II. Nonexistence – the only category that was productive at Kathryn I and the category that occurred most frequently at Kathryn II – was also the category that was most structurally complex in performance. Sentences expressing denial – the category that was least productive, with only one instance at Time I – were also the least complex negative sentences at Time II.

The syntactic placement of the negative element depended upon the scope of negation within the sentence. The negative element occurred immediately previous to the structure over which it had immediate effect – in prepredicate position, following the sentence-subject. In those sentences where the negative element preceded the sentence-subject, with only one exception, the behavioral and contextual interpretation revealed that the negative reference was anaphoric, and such sentences were actually affirmative.

Kathryn's negative sentences at Time II, as at Time I, could be described as having occurred in Period A in Bellugi's (1967) account of negation: Mean length of utterance was still below 2.0 morphemes; the shape of the negative element was limited to one form – *no;* and there was no inflection of nouns and verbs. However, contrary to Bellugi's observation that the negative element was not positioned within the sentence, expression of sentence-subject in Kathryn's negative sentences always preceded expression of the negative element. Where the negative element preceded the subject of a sentence, the sentence was affirmative.

Syntactic Negation at Kathryn III

Syntactic Expression of Nonexistence. Fewer sentences expressing nonexistence occurred at Kathryn III – 25 sentences, as compared with 42 at Kathryn II; these are presented in Table 4.10.

A few sentences were similar in structure to the earliest negative sentences at Kathryn I: "no boy" and "no children." The remaining sentences were similar to the sentences that expressed nonexistence at Kathryn II in the inclusion of sentence-subjects and predicate complement constructions with verbs. But the sentences in Table 4.10 also differed from those that expressed nonexistence at Kathryn II, in two important respects. The pro-forms "I," "this (one)," or "that" replaced the noun forms that had occurred with the same grammatical function, sentence-subject, at Kathryn II. Further, the form of the negative element was variable. In addition to *no* – the only form at Kathryn I and II – there were alternative forms: *not, do* (with negative intent), *don't, doesn't,* and *can't.*

In contrast to the syntactic placement of the negative element in all the sentences discussed so far, there were two sentences in which *no* occurred in sentence-final position. These appeared to be pro-forms analogous to *none* in the adult model:

Table 4.10. *Negative Sentences That Signaled Nonexistence, Kathryn III*

no boy	ə doesn't fit
no children	this not fits!
no more choo-choo train	this one don't fit
no part that	this one do fits (2)
ə no hand there	this one don't fits (2)
	this one don't
no bring lambs	that's not ə turn
no stand up	Kathryn not go over here
not going away (2)	ə can't find ə saucer
	I can't open it
this one ə no	I don't go <u>sleep</u>
this one have no	Mommy no play 'corder

Note: Numbers in parentheses refer to number of occurrences in the text, discounting immediate repetitions.

(59) K III

(Kathryn had discovered
a label on the underside of one of
the blocks; she picked up a
different block to see if it had a
similar label, which it did not)   >this one ə no.

(60)

(Picked up a third block as in
(59); block did not have a label)   >this one have no.
(Picking up fourth block and
seeing label on it)   this one have!

There was no immediately apparent motivation for the variation in the form of the negative element in expression of nonexistence. All were present tense forms. The verb *fit* (the most frequent verb in previous negative sentences at Time I and Time II) occurred with *not, don't, do,* and *doesn't* (but not with *no* which had always negated *fit* previously).

The sentences expressing nonexistence in Table 4.10 are similar to the sentences in the second stage in the acquisition of negation, Period B, described by Bellugi (1967), where the negative element occurred with alternative forms. But as observed also by Bellugi, the different forms of the negative element *don't, doesn't, can't* were not transforms of the auxiliary formatives *do* or *can*. The form *do* functioned only as a main verb.

However, in two respects, the children described by Bellugi in Period B appeared to be linguistically more mature than Kathryn was at Time III. First, Kathryn had not learned the person and number paradigms for personal pronouns, as had the subjects Bellugi studied in Period B. The only productive personal pronoun forms she used in affirmative sentences were the first-person alternants *I, me, my,* and *mine*. Second, although progressive -*ing* was productive at Kathryn III in affirmative sentences, it was marginal in negative sentences. This second distinction was important because Bellugi reported that the newly introduced alternative forms of the negative element, *don't* and *can't*, were restricted in her data to occurrence before nonprogressive main verbs, whereas *no* and *not* were used before verbs with -*ing*. With rare exceptions, however, progressive verbs were affirmative at Kathryn III.

The remaining negative sentences at Kathryn III in the categories rejection and denial are presented in Table 4.11. While both categories continued to be productive at Time III, the number of sentences that signaled denial – previously the least productive category – far exceeded the number that expressed rejection. Syntactic expression of denial occurred as frequently as expression of nonexistence.

In each category, a few sentences were similar to the earlier syntactic structures at Time I and Time II: "no put it back" and "no Eric." However, the great majority of the sentences expressing rejection and denial were substantially different in syntactic structure from the sentences with the same functions at Kathryn II. In both categories, more complex structures replaced the simpler structures observed earlier, and the sentences within each category were remarkably similar in form. The sentences arranged in Table 4.11 confirmed Bellugi's (1967) observation of "across-the-board appearances of some aspects of grammatical systems in the language, often accompanied by a great rise in frequency of structural types."

Syntactic Expression of Rejection. Just as there were progressive changes in the development of expression of nonexistence at Time II, there were significant developmental changes in the form of expression of rejection at Time III.

First, sentence-subjects were produced in sentences that expressed rejection. Whereas at Time II the understood subject (on the basis of context and behavior) was Kathryn, sentence-subjects never occurred in the production of sentences that signaled rejection – even though

Table 4.11. *Negative Sentences That Signaled Rejection and Denial, Kathryn III*

Rejection	Denial
no going home	no Eric
no <u>put it back</u>	not making muffins
	ə not <u>break it</u>
don't <u>get my room</u>	I not <u>tired</u>
don't want go in other room	I not have some fruit
	this <u>man</u> not brother
I ə not go in bathroom	not magic
I don't want play with Lois	that not " 'body home''[a]
I don't want <u>get</u> those ə my <u>room</u>	that not cat
I don't want to comb hairs	that not <u>ə pot</u>
I don't <u>want those shoes</u>	that's not <u>tea</u>
I don't need pants off	that's not <u>scramble</u>
ə don't like that	this not ə pancake
	this not ə doughnut
	that's not <u>ə apple</u>
	that's not apple
	that's not ə man
	this ə not brother
	that not ə sister
	this not ə boy
	that's not <u>ə sister</u>
	that's not <u>ə lady</u>
	that not <u>baa-baa black sheep</u>
	that not ə ugly
	<u>that</u> not ə rabbits <u>house</u>
	that not blue one
	that's not ə pink one
	that not brother
	that not

[a] Kathryn was referring here to the title of the book *Anybody at Home?* which she always referred to as "Body Home."
Note: The underlined words are those that occurred in an immediately preceding utterance produced by someone else.

the first person subject was expressed in those sentences that signaled nonexistence at the same time. At Time III, the understood subject was Kathryn in all but two of the sentences that signaled rejection and was expressed (as in expressions of nonexistence) with the pronominal form *I*.

A second development in the expression of rejection was the expression of the matrix verb, *want* or *need*, on which the negative element had direct effect. Such a matrix form had been postulated as a deleted intervening constituent at Kathryn II; *want* had been productive in affirmative sentences but occurred marginally in expression of rejection at that time.

However, in the two least complex sentences that expressed rejection – "no going home" and "no put it back" – there was no expressed sentence-subject, no matrix verb, and the form of the negative element was the primitive *no* (rather than *don't,* as in all other sentences in the category). It was also the case that these two sentences were negative imperatives involving negation of an event in which someone other than Kathryn was actor-agent. That is, I was the one who was going home and putting something back. Thus, Kathryn learned syntactic expression of rejection first to express negation of her own desire or wish to have or to do something. This was true of all the previous sentences that signaled rejection at Time II and most such sentences at Time III. As a result, development of the linguistic expression of rejection proceeded toward expression of the first person sentence-subject and the operation of negation on a matrix verb in the predicate at Time III. After gaining a certain competence with this structure, Kathryn began to use the negative imperative to express rejection of an event that involved someone else as actor-agent. In doing so, she reverted to the earlier, more generalized syntactic structure – as in "no going home" and "no put it back." It would be expected that the form of this sentence type in the subsequent texts would approach the adult form of the negative imperative "don't go home" and "don't put it back," where the sentence-subject is the unexpressed *you.* But at Kathryn III, use of the negative element *don't* was restricted, in expression of rejection, to those sentences in which Kathryn was the subject of the matrix verb (on which the negative element had effect) and the complement verb as well.

This interpretation of Kathryn's development of rejection coincides with the description of the semantic contrast "internal–external" proposed by McNeill and McNeill (1968): The negative element in Japanese, "*iya* . . . conveys the idea of 'I don't want,' and its use, therefore, depends on *internal desire,* or the lack of it." McNeill and McNeill concluded that this was the second category of negation acquired by their Japanese subject after "existence-truth." This was also the second category of negation that Kathryn acquired – after nonexistence.

Syntactic Expression of Denial. The linguistic expression of the semantic category denial developed last – after nonexistence and rejection. There had been only one instance of denial at Kathryn I, and although there was an increase in frequency, with ten sentences at Time II, the structure of the ten sentences was the same as the one sentence that signaled denial at Time I.

At Kathryn III, denial was the most productive category of negative sentences that occurred. It should be pointed out that the substantial increase in the number of these sentences was not contrived. That is, there was no attempt to 'test' Kathryn's ability to express denial (as described subsequently in the attempt to 'test' Gia's responses to yes–no questions at Gia V).

In addition to the substantial increase in the frequency of sentences expressing denial, significant changes occurred in structural complexity as well. The syntactic structure Kathryn had used to express denial at Times I and II was the same as the first example at Time III in Table 4.11: "no Eric." However, this was the only instance of the primitive structure in the 29 sentences that signaled denial at Time III. In all the other sentences, there was only one form of the negative element: *not*. Nominal subjects occurred: "I not tired," "I not have some fruit," and "this man not brother." In 3 other sentences, sentence-subject was expressed. But in all the remaining 22 sentences, the sentence-subject was a form of the demonstrative pronoun: *This, that,* or *that's.*

At Kathryn II, the occurrence of demonstrative pronouns in sentence-initial position with a predicate nominative had been one of the most productive constructions. Examples of the 308 occurrences of this sentence type included "this ə slide," "that ə baby," "this is my tiger book." Only one of these 308 sentences expressed negation at Kathryn II; all were affirmative sentences except for "this ə no Lois," which occurred in response to the question "Is this Kathryn's, or is this Lois's?" At the time when this sentence type was one of the most productive structures in her grammar, Kathryn never used it to express negation as she did productively six weeks later, at Time III, to signal denial – for example, "that not ə sister," "this not ə doughnut."

This restriction on the use of demonstrative pronouns and negation at Kathryn II was not simply a constraint on sentence length; such sentences as "this ə my Kathryn toys ə floor," "this ə Mommy's fuzzy sweater" occurred at Time II. The fact that *no* was not one of the 'permitted' number of words in an utterance could not be attributed simply to some sort of memory limitation. Although at Time II Kathryn expressed the semantic concept of denial in such utterances as "no candle," "no Wendy" and used demonstrative pronouns in affirmative sentences, the linguistic structure and the cognitive semantic concept were not joined in production until Time III. Thus, the semantics of denial (meaning) and the ultimate structure that signaled denial (form) existed at Time II but did not exist in concert until Time III.

Progressive Differentiation of the Negative Element. Of the variants of the negative element in the speech Kathryn presumably heard, she chose one form, *no,* as the negative element for the earliest syntactic expression of negation: to signal nonexistence. At Time I and Time II, when negative sentences began to express rejection and denial, Kathryn used the same negative element, *no,* in the syntactic expression of all three semantic categories. Subsequently, when she began to differentiate the form of the negative element and *not, don't, can't,* and *doesn't* appeared in negative sentences, *don't* was used almost exclusively to signal rejection, and *not* was used exclusively in sentences that signaled denial. All the variants appeared in the group of sentences that expressed nonexistence.

Expression of rejection is not limited, in adult speech, to constructions with *don't,* and expression of denial is not limited to constructions with *not.* It may be true that rejection of a desire to do or to have something is most often expressed by the structure "I don't want," but there are alternatives – for example, "I won't." Virtually all Kathryn's sentences that signaled denial referred to statements of identity (for example, "that's not scramble" in response to "doesn't that look like scrambled egg?" referring to the yellow wheel on a plate). The same structure would occur in contradiction of a statement of identity in adult speech, but again, there are alternatives – for example, "It isn't a scrambled egg," or the adult might respond to the question with "it doesn't" (look like a scrambled egg).

The form of the negative element in adult speech depends upon the structure of the verbal auxiliary and the notions of tense, aspect, and agreement with subject number and person. Kathryn's linguistic expressions of rejection and denial were limited, in most cases, to only one dimension (or none) of each of these notions. For example, present tense prevailed in all the sentences; Kathryn was the agent of rejection; and a form of the demonstrative pronoun was the subject in expressions of denial.

The status of the verb in expressions of denial and rejection was quite simple. The verb on which the negative element had effect in expression of rejection was limited to a stative matrix verb – *want.* In most of the expressions of denial, there was no verb (exceptions were "not making muffins," "ə not break it," "I not have some fruit"). A form of *be,* on which the negative element would have effect in the adult structure, was not included in any of the sentences expressing denial.

The relatively homogeneous structures used for statements of rejection or denial limited the form of the negative element as well. Kathryn learned a particular form (*don't* or *not*) as the negative element in a particular structure (for expression of rejection or denial, respectively). In contrast, expression of nonexistence involved a number of alternants. In addition to nominal negation in reference to objects that did not exist, predicate negation expressed nonoccurrence of events. In predicate negation, there was reference to both first- and third-person agents and negation of predicates with both action and stative verbs. Kathryn also attempted to express variation in the form of the negative element in expression of nonexistence with the modal forms *don't* and *can't*.

It was also possible that the homogeneous structures and forms of the negative element that Kathryn learned for expressing rejection and denial were the most frequent structures with these functions in the negative sentences she heard. However, there is no available count of most frequent structures in adult speech or, more specifically, in the speech Kathryn heard.

The effect may also have been developmental. Because linguistic expression of nonexistence was differentiated and learned first and rejection and denial were learned subsequently, the negative sentences at Time III may have reflected the fact that Kathryn also recognized the potentiality for variation in structure and attempted to express it in nonexistence before recognizing possibilities for variation in the forms of rejection and denial.

The important fact was that the differences in the form of the negative element observed at Time III, after occurrence of a single form *no* at Time I and Time II, was not simply a matter of free variation. On the contrary, progressive differentiation in the form of the negative element was functionally motivated and directly related to the linguistic expression of the three semantic categories – nonexistence, rejection, and denial.

In summary, Kathryn learned the syntactic expression of the semantic categories of negation in the order (1) nonexistence, (2) rejection, (3) denial. Although she had already begun to express rejection and denial in negative sentences at the time of the first observation, the fact that nonexistence was expressed most frequently at Time I and subsequently developed in syntactic complexity before the other two categories at Time II provided evidence for the conclusion that nonexistence was the first category expressed syntactically.

At Time II the occurrence of sentences signaling rejection was as frequent as sentences that expressed denial, but there was an accompanying increase in structural complexity in rejection while the structure of denial at Time II was most primitive – the same structure used initially to express nonexistence. Subsequently, at Time III, although the number of sentences expressing rejection remained constant, these increased in structural complexity. However, the most significant change at Time III was a 200% increase in the number of sentences that expressed denial – accompanied by a substantial change in structural complexity.

The conclusions that have been drawn from the data collected from Kathryn were confirmed by the data collected over a longer period of time from Eric and Gia. But just as the children differed in their rates of acquisition of syntactic negation, there were substantive, although relatively minor, differences among them as well.

Syntactic Negation, Eric IV to VI

The fourth, fifth, and sixth observations of Eric approximated the same developmental period that has just been described as Phase 2 in Kathryn's development of negation.

Eric IV. All the negative sentences that occurred at Time IV have been categorized and are presented in Table 4.12. Sentences expressing nonexistence continued to occur most frequently in the text, and expression of denial was still marginal, with only one instance (a decrease from three occurrences at Eric III). The significant development at Time IV was the emergence of rejection as a syntactically productive category. However, sentences that expressed rejection were not differentiated formally from negative sentences that signaled nonexistence.

Eric continued to use two forms of the negative element *no* and *no more* in complementary distribution as at Time III: *No* operated in predicative constructions, and *no more* appeared with nouns.

There were no changes in the produced structural complexity of negative sentences, although mean length of utterance increased from 1.42

Table 4.12. *Categorization of Negative Sentences, Eric IV*

Nonexistence	Rejection	Denial
ə no more	no more tank	no, not <u>blue</u>
ə no more cleaner	no more train	
no more light (2)	no more book	
no more lights	no more noise	
no more cleaner (2)	ə no <u>read ə book</u>	
no more pieces (2)		
no more choo-choo train		
no more 'chine		
no more people		
no more man		
no fit /tu/		
no ↑ ·i fit		
no wheels		
no ə think so		
train wheels /tu/ none		

Note: Numbers in parentheses refer to number of occurrences in the text, discounting immediate repetitions. The underlined words are those that occurred in an immediately preceding utterance produced by someone else.

at Time III to 1.69 at Time IV. Even though sentence-subjects and verbs with predicate complements were fully productive in affirmative sentences, they were not yet expressed in negative sentences.

There were also several unique negative structures, as in all the previous texts from Eric: "no ə think so" (an attempt at a familiar phrase), "train wheels / tu / none" (an attempt at the negative pronominal form in response to the question "Does the train have wheels?"), and "no, not blue," the only occurrence of *not* (to signal denial.)

Eric V. The number of negative sentences increased from 24 at Time IV to 56 at Time V; the sentences produced at Time V are presented in Table 4.13.

There was no difference between Time IV and Time V in the relative frequency of negative sentences in the three semantic categories. Sentences signaling nonexistence occurred most often, and rejection was expressed less often, but productively, while denial was still not productive. But whereas there was no change in the status of the three

Table 4.13. *Categorization of Negative Sentences, Eric V*

Nonexistence	Rejection	Denial
no more ball	no more cluck-cluck	no fire engine
no more tank	no bib	no more fire engine
no more 'chine (3)	no piece ə clay nose	ə no piggies
no more birdie		
no more water	no flush	
no more water, Mommy	no have it	
no more lamb	no throw it (2)	
no more bridge	don't throw it	
no more fire	no in there	
no more pigeon		
no more man	no lollipop	
no more book		
ə no more light (2)	no, I didn't go back roller coaster	
no more fire engine	I no like to	
no more tank	no, I didn't	
no fire engine (3)		
oh no fire engine!		
no fire car		
ə no ice cream		

you no bring ə choo-choo train?
I no reach it
ə no fall down
and ə no sit down

not here
not crying

doesn't fit
oh doesn't fit!
ə doesn't fit (2)
I didn't do it
I didn't crying
ə didn't have it

I can't
I didn't
no, I didn't

Note: Numbers in parentheses refer to number of occurrences in the text, discounting immediate repetitions. The underlined words are those that occurred in an immediately preceding utterance produced by someone else.

categories in terms of relative productivity, there were important changes in the complexity of sentences expressing nonexistence and rejection.

For the first time, sentences expressing nonexistence included expression of sentence-subject – most often the pronoun *I*. However, except for the occurrence of *it* after verbs, there was only one instance of predicate complement construction with verbs: "You no bring choo-choo train." Even though these sentences were longer than the negative sentences at Time IV, with inclusion of sentence-subject, they were still among the least complex sentences that occurred in the entire text. One of the first sentence structures Eric used, at Time II, was verb–object, but he still did not use this structure productively in negative sentences at Time V.

The two forms *didn't* and *doesn't* replaced the form *no* in seven sentences with predicate negation. The corresponding affirmative forms *did* and *does* never occurred in the text – *doesn't* and *didn't* appeared to be uniquely negative formatives in the same sense as *no* and *no more*. Among the sentences that signaled nonexistence, many were structurally the same as those that occurred in each of the earlier observations – for example, "no more ball," "no more tank," "no more bridge." However, in the sentences "no fire car," "no fire engine," and "ə no ice cream," the *no* affected the noun form directly and signaled its nonexistence.

This use of *no* and *no more* at Time V may have been analogous to the use of the two forms in adult speech: "no bananas" and the partitive "no more bananas." That is, Eric appeared to distinguish between the nonexistence of something he had experienced previously – for example, "no more fire engine" (Eric was pushing a truck under the bridge and the bridge collapsed on it) and "no fire engine" (Eric looking out the window, not seeing any fire engine on the street). However, it was also the case that *no more,* which was the earliest, primitive form of the negative element in Eric's texts, no longer occurred in the subsequent text at Time VI. The use of the form *no* at Time V – to express simple nonexistence of objects that were not also predicate objects – may have represented a transitional stage, before Eric relinquished *no more* as a negative marker.

Syntactic expression of rejection used the form *no* most often, with only one occurrence of the primitive *no more*. Three sentences included the subject *I* (two of these with *didn't* as the negative element), and these sentences differed from all but one of the rest of the sentences that signaled rejection. The last four sentences listed in the cat-

egory rejection in Table 4.13 – "no lollipop," "no, I didn't go back
roller coaster," "I no like to," and "no, I didn't" – signaled Eric's
not wanting to do or to have something – the same kind of rejection
used productively by Kathryn. The sentences "no, I didn't go back
roller coaster" and "I no like to" occurred in the following sequence:

(61) E V

    (Eric had been on a roller
    coaster the previous weekend;
    Mommy was prompting Eric
    to tell Lois about it)
    Would you like to go again
    on the roller coaster?   > no, I didn't go back
                                             roller coaster.
                                             no!
    (Eric shaking his head)   like to. like to. like to.
    You don't want to go again?   > I no like to.

However, the remaining nine sentences were negative directions with
the second person subject as agent understood. For example, "no more
cluck-cluck" (Eric wanted Mommy to stop imitating a chicken), "no
flush" (Eric didn't want Mommy to flush the toilet until he was out of
the way). Only one sentence used the adult form of the negative imperative *don't*.

There were more indeterminate sentences than occurred previously,
and it was possible to infer semantic intent in some of these utterances,
but only tentatively – for example:

(62) E V

    (Eric standing next to the
    baby's bassinet looking at the
    bottle of shampoo)   no good.

(63)

    (Eric had picked up the shampoo
    and held it, then remonstrating
    to Lois, who was watching him)   > no had it.
                                           /e/ had it, Bloom.
    (Eric put the shampoo back)

It appeared, in (62), that Eric was referring to not being allowed to
play with the baby's shampoo, and in (63) he appeared to be acting
out this reproof with me.

The three sentences that signaled denial used the same structure as negative sentences that had occurred in earlier texts: "no fire engine," "no more fire engine," "ə no piggies." The syntactic expression of denial was still nonproductive, and the utterances that did occur were among the least complex negative sentences at Time V.

Eric VI. The 55 negative sentences in the text at Time VI are presented in Table 4.14. Sentences signaling nonexistence continued to occur most frequently, and these sentences were more structurally complex than at Time V. The developmental changes that had begun to emerge at Time V were fully productive at Time VI.

Only 4 of the 20 predicate negations occurred without sentence-subjects, and in 3 of these sentences the phonological element (/i/ or /ə/) might be interpretable as a rudimentary pronoun form. In addition to the first person *I,* the sentence-subject constituents included *you, it, they,* and the nominal forms "Eric" and "choo-choo train." The person and number paradigms for pronouns were productive in affirmative sentences at Eric VI, whereas they had not begun to emerge at Kathryn III.

The predicate phrase structure with inclusion of verb and complement was productive for the first time in negative sentences at Eric VI – for example, "I couldn't find ə choo-choo train" and "they can't go on the door."

Significant changes occurred in the form of the negative element used in expressions of nonexistence. The primitive form *no more,* which had been used most often in all the previous texts, occurred only once at Time VI. The prevailing form of the negative element that signaled nonexistence of objects was *no.* The differentiation observed earlier between simple nonexistence and nonexistence of something that had occurred previously was no longer tenable. "No choo-choo train" and "no apple" referred to nonexistence after previous existence, and "no more lollipop" was the only instance of partitive *no more.*

A second important change in the negative element was the consistency of the form used in negated predicate constructions. Whereas the earlier variants *didn't* and *doesn't* occurred less often than at Time V, the three forms *can* (with negative intent), *can't,* and *couldn't* were used in all the remaining predicate negations. Moreover, the forms were contrastive: *Couldn't* always signaled previous events – the perfective or past tense; *can* and *can't* signaled events that occurred during the utterance or immediately previous to and during the utterance.

Table 4.14. *Categorization of Negative Sentences, Eric VI*

Nonexistence	Rejection	Denial
no more lollipop	I think no more	that not lollipop
no Daddy		that's ə not bridge
oh no Daddy!	no playing (2)	no, not ə <u>yellow</u>
no apple (3)	don't cry (2)	no, that's ə not
no choo-choo train (4)	don't touch it	<u>choo-choo</u>
oh no choo-choo train (2)	don't eat it	<u>train</u> (2)
no choo-choo train tonight	don't fall down	
	don't fall down, little man	
<u>have</u> no <u>shoes</u>	don't drag it next time	
	don't take ə choo-choo train home	
nothing	no, don't touch it (2)	
nothing there		
didn't see choo-choo train		
it doesn't go		
it doesn't fit in here		
I can't		
I can't climb up		
/i/ can't fit on		
I can't fit in (2)		
I can't eat it		
ə can't go in		
I can't find the bridge		
they can't go on the door		
choo-choo train <u>can't</u> go <u>anyplace</u>		
you can have it. no.		
you can have it		
ə couldn't see ə duck		
Eric couldn't see ə duck		
and I couldn't see piggies		
I couldn't see them		
I couldn't find ə choo-choo train		

Note: Numbers in parentheses refer to number of occurrences in the text, discounting immediate repetitions. The underlined words are those that occurred in an immediately preceding utterance produced by someone else.

The positive alternatives of these forms – *can* and *does* – never appeared in the text.

Syntactic expression of rejection continued to be productive, and the structure achieved the form that had been anticipated in the earlier texts: the negative imperative, with *don't* as the form of the negative element and the sentence-subject unexpressed but implied as the listener. The only expression of rejection where Eric was the agent was "I think no more" – Eric had played with a puzzle and was leaving it to play with the train. Thus, Eric and Kathryn differed in acquisition of the linguistic expression of rejection. Eric acquired the form of the negative imperative to express rejection first. Kathryn expressed rejection in terms of her not wanting to do or to have something and ultimately expressed the first person subject with *want*.

Although syntactic expression of denial was only marginally productive, the negative element was *not,* with a demonstrative pronoun as subject in all but one of the sentences – the same structure used by Kathryn at Time III. Earlier, Eric had used *no more* or *no* as the negative element in expression of denial. At Time VI "no more lollipop" occurred in expression of nonexistence, but "that not lollipop" was used at the same time to express denial.

Thus, the developmental changes that characterized Phase 2 in Kathryn's development of negation had begun to emerge or were anticipated at Eric IV and V and became productive at Eric VI. The sequence in which the syntactic expression of the three semantic categories of negation developed was (1) nonexistence, (2) rejection, (3) denial – the same developmental sequence that was observed in the negative sentences produced by Kathryn.

Syntactic Negation, Gia V and VI

The development of negation was slowest in the texts obtained from Gia. In the first three texts, syntactic expression of negation was indeterminate in interpretation more often than not. In the fourth text, the number of negative sentences was so small that only tentative conclusions were possible. The syntactic expression of negation was marginally productive at Time IV and signaled nonexistence.

Gia V. The number of negative sentences increased from 6 at Time IV to 20 at Time V, and all but 1 of the 20 could be interpreted. The syntactic expression of negation could be considered productive at Time V. All the negative sentences at Gia V are presented in Table 4.15.

There were only two syntactically productive categories – nonexistence and rejection – and a similar number of sentences occurred in each. There was only one instance of denial, and it was not strictly

Table 4.15. *Categorization of Negative Sentences, Gia V*

Nonexistence	Rejection	Denial
no more cookie	no want that	no, not
no <u>draw</u> ə cushion	no <u>watch</u> (2)	
no play ə matches	no take home	
can't doed it (3)	no MopTop	
can't open door	no pinch ə cheek (2)	
can't reach it	not that book	
can't reach pretzel	don't break it	

Note: Numbers in parentheses refer to number of occurrences in the text, discounting immediate repetitions. The underlined words are those that occurred in an immediately preceding utterance produced by someone else.

syntactic – "no, not" (in response to the question "Is the doll cold?"). There were also ten utterances (not presented in Table 4.15) that were interpreted as anaphoric *no* preceding an affirmative statement. In six of these, a single word followed the anaphoric *no*. These utterances were elicited in an attempt to 'test' Gia's competence in expressing denial. For example, I held up the figure of a boy and asked, "Is this the baby?" or held up the figure of a man and commented, "This is a girl." In each instance, Gia said *no* and named the figure correctly, rather than denying the identity suggested by the question or comment. Syntactic expression of denial was not present at Gia V.

The negative sentences were among the most structurally primitive sentences that occurred at Time V, with no expression of sentence-subject, even though expression of sentence-subjects had been productive in affirmative sentences since Time II.

There was variation in the form of the negative element; *can't* occurred only in expression of nonexistence, and *no* occurred in expression of nonexistence and rejection. Other forms – *no more, don't,* and *not* – each had unique occurrence.

Expression of rejection, as in Eric's texts, were negative imperatives, except for one sentence ("no want that").

The development of syntactic negation at Gia V was distinguished by two factors: (1) Gia had learned the cognitive–semantic notion of negation as a concept that could be expressed syntactically, and (2) two semantic categories of negation were syntactically productive –

nonexistence and rejection. The two categories of negative sentences were structurally differentiated only in the use of *can't* exclusively as a negative element before verbs in expression of nonexistence.

Gia VI. Any doubt about the status of negation in Gia's grammar was dispelled at Time VI, when 121 negative sentences occurred and only 3 of these were uninterpretable. The proportion of sentences in the categories nonexistence and rejection was the same as at Time V, with a similar number of sentences (49 and 45) in each category at Time VI. But whereas only one expression of denial occurred at Time V, 24 sentences signaled denial at Time VI, so that all three categories of negation were fully productive in syntactic expression. All these sentences are presented in Table 4.16.

In addition to the 500% increase in the number of negative sentences, a substantial difference was observed in the produced structural complexity of the sentences at Time VI in comparison with sentences with the same functions at Time V. Whereas sentence-subjects had been omitted in negative sentences at Time V, at Time VI sentence-subjects were expressed in every utterance except one ("no pockets"). The form of the subject was the pronoun *I* most often, but *you, it, this,* and *there's* also occurred.

The only instances of expressed sentence-subject in sentences that signaled rejection were "I no make duty in the potty!" "I don't ə microphone," and "no! I don't want it," and each referred to Gia's not wanting to do or to have something. All the remaining sentences expressing rejection were negative imperatives. Thus, Gia and Eric were similar in the development of syntactic rejection – both children learned the structure and function of the negative imperative first. The form of rejection in Kathryn's texts – the negation of desire with expression of the matrix verb and subject *I* – was only a marginal structure in the texts of both Gia and Eric.

Most of Gia's sentences that signaled denial included the form *it's* as subject – a form that was not used by either Kathryn or Eric. In addition, Gia used the subject forms that Kathryn and Eric used: *that, that's,* and *this.* There did not appear to be a motivated difference between *it's* and other forms. Expression of denial, as with Eric and Kathryn, negated statements of identity most often.

Finally, as observed in the negative sentences of Kathryn and Eric at the culmination of Phase 2, there was a functionally motivated differentiation in the form of the negative element. Except for the utter-

Table 4.16. *Categorization of Negative Sentences, Gia VI*

Nonexistence	Rejection	Denial
no pockets	I no make duty in the	I didn't (2)
there's no more	potty!	no, I didn't (3)
there's ə no <u>money</u>	I don't ə microphone	
it's not in the bag	no! I don't want it	I not
		I'm not <u>unhappy</u>
I can (19)	no soap cup	I not <u>smell</u>
I can't (8)	no, not my button	
I can put here	don't (10)	it's not (3)
I can't put this here	don't! I say no!	it's not ready
I can put this pussy cat here	don't go (2)	it's not stop
I <u>can't doed it</u>	don't <u>scare</u>	it not <u>all wet</u>
I can't get out	don't stay (4)	it's not ə <u>big spoon</u>
I can't see it	don't say that! (2)	no, it's not <u>raining</u>
I can't fix it	no, it's not my button	
I can't get it	don't take chair!	it's not cold out
I can't reach	don't take it	no, it's not <u>the</u>
I can't ə put ə lamb in	don't read it!	<u>teddy bear</u>
it don't fit	don't push two	no, it's not yours
no, it don't fit	don't touch this one	
this don't fit in	don't touch ə big one	this not my stick
and this don't fit in too	don't touch my block! (3)	that's not mines
you don't make duty in	don't turn the page	that not Mommy
your diaper	don't hold on ə seesaw	that's not little
I didn't make dirty __/	don't stay in my room	/ðɣ/ not yours
no duty in my diaper	don't take your	
	microphone	
no, I not	don't stand <u>over it</u>	
no, it <u>don't go in this box</u>	don't take the belt out	
	don't take my diaper	
	don't pull my pants down	
	don't go in the room	
	don't go in here until	
	few minutes	
	no, don't here	

Note: Numbers in parentheses refer to number of occurrences in the text, discounting immediate repetitions. The underlined words are those that occurred in an immediately preceding utterance produced by someone else.

ance "I didn't," which expressed Gia's denial of having done something, the negative element *not* was used in all expressions of denial. Except for the single occurrence of each of the forms *no, not,* and *no more,* the negative element in all expressions of rejection was *don't.*

The negative element was variable in expressions of nonexistence with occurrence of *no, not,* and *don't,* in addition to the most productive form, *can't* (which alternated with *can* produced with negative intent). There did not appear to be a meaningful difference among the forms that occurred – for example, "this don't fit in" and "I can" occurred in similar speech events. As observed also with Kathryn and Eric, the auxiliary forms *can, do,* or *did* never occurred in affirmative sentences. Rather, the forms *can't, don't,* and *didn't* appeared to have been learned as variants of the forms *no* and *not.* Although progressive *-ing* was fully productive in affirmative sentences, there was no occurrence of progressive verbs in negative sentences, so that the observation by Bellugi (1967) that the forms *don't* and *can't* were restricted to occurrence with nonprogressive main verbs in her data did not apply to the data collected from Kathryn, Eric, and Gia.

Comparison of the Three Children and Summary of Phase 2

The sequential appearance of syntactic expression of rejection and denial – after the appearance of nonexistence in Phase 1 – was one important aspect of Phase 2. Although sentences expressing nonexistence continued to occur most frequently in most of the texts, expression of rejection and then expression of denial became productive. A schematic account of the proportional distribution of negative sentences in terms of function in Phase 1 and Phase 2 is presented in Figure 4.2.

Just as sentences in semantic categories appeared sequentially in the order nonexistence, rejection, denial – subsequent, progressive increase in the produced structural complexity of each category followed the same order. Expression of sentence-subject and the occurrence of the verb and complement constituents of predicate phrases were evident in sentences expressing nonexistence before these same forms were expressed in rejection or denial. When the syntactic structure of sentences expressing rejection subsequently increased in complexity, the most primitive syntactic form was used in the expression of denial.

A second important aspect of Phase 2 was the development of different but relatively homogeneous structures for the expression of the different semantic categories. The syntactic structure of expression of denial developed last and was similar in the sentences of the three children – the pronominal subject *this, that's,* or, in Gia's sentences, *it's* before the negative element. The complement was a single word – a noun form most often, but adjective forms also occurred ("that's not little" at Gia VI). Generally, there was no verb in these sentences. Final *-s* occurred with *that* and *it,* but the inflectional paradigm of *be*

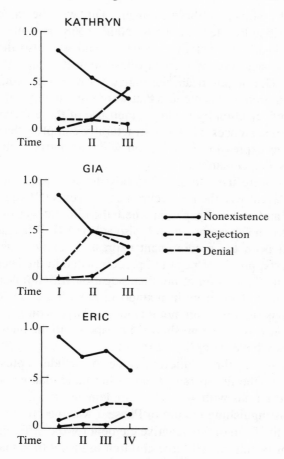

Figure 4.2. Development of negation, Phases 1 and 2: Proportional distribution of negative sentences in the semantic categories nonexistence, rejection, and denial.

was not yet productive in the affirmative sentences in the texts. There was no evidence that *it's* or *that's* represented contractions with the copula *be*.

There were two forms of rejection (the second category in the developmental sequence), and the children differed in their use of each; either one or the other was productive in the negative sentences of each child, but not both. Kathryn expressed rejection of something that she didn't want to do or to have. The ultimate structure she used at Time III included expression of the sentence-subject *I* and *want* or *need* before a predication that involved Kathryn as agent. This was the same form of negation described by McNeill and McNeill (1968) as "internal–external" – the "lack" of "internal desire" – and was also the second form of negation acquired by their Japanese subject.

However, Eric and Gia acquired an alternative form of rejection. Although both children produced sentences that were functionally similar to the expression of rejection by Kathryn, their use of these forms was marginal, and such sentences were less structurally complete than the negative imperative expression of rejection without matrix verbs and no expression of sentence-subject.

Two sentence types were used to signal nonexistence – predicate negation where the referent was the nonoccurrence of events ("I can't climb up" at Eric VI) and nominal negation where the referent was the nonexistence of objects ("no choo-choo train," also at Eric VI). Whereas nominal negation had been the predominant expression of nonexistence in the earliest texts, predicate negation predominated in the later texts of all the children. Expression of nominal negation was simplest – most often the negative element *no* in juxtaposition with a noun or noun phrase. These constructions were not included in larger constructions; the one exception was "have no shoes" in response to the question "Does the little boy have shoes?" at Eric VI.

Predicate negation, for all three children, came to include expression of sentence-subject (the first-person *I* most often) and elaborated predicate phrase constructions with verb and complement forms.

Finally, the third distinguishing feature of Phase 2 was the progressive differentiation in the form of the negative element for the different semantic categories of negation. All three children used *not* to signal denial. Although the function and structure of the expression of rejection differed among the three children, the same form of the negative element, *don't,* was used. Expression of nonexistence occurred with several negative forms.

At the time that negative sentences first began to be differentiated on the basis of function, that is, when negative sentences were used with different semantic intent, the syntactic structure used for each was the same. When the children subsequently developed more complex syntactic expression of nonexistence, the syntactic structure of the earliest sentences that occurred at the same time with different functions – that is, rejection and then denial – was invariably the same as the primitive form of the first sentences that had expressed nonexistence.

Thus, it was not necessary for the children to learn a new or different structure in order to express a new or different semantic intent. Initially, there was one meaning (m_1) of negation and one form (f_1). Subsequently, when two meanings were interpretable, (m_1) and (m_2), it was not the case that the appearance of (m_2) corresponded to the appearance of a second form (f_2), as might have been expected:

Time A: $(m_1) \underset{\downarrow}{} (f_1)$

Time B: $(m_1) \overset{\downarrow}{} (f_1)$
            $(m_2) {} (f_2)$

Rather, the appearance of a different form was associated with the first meaning (m_1), while at the same time the earlier form (f_1) was used to express the second meaning:

Time A: $(m_1) \underset{\downarrow}{} (f_1)$

Time B: $(m_1) \overset{\downarrow}{} (f_2)$
            $(m_2) {} (f_1)$

The acquisition of linguistic expression did not proceed hand in hand with cognitive – semantic development. Learning to express a new semantic category of negation did not involve learning a new structure for its linguistic expression at the same time. Neither was it the case that certain linguistic forms were productive in the children's speech before they knew something about the corresponding underlying cognitive notions. New, more complex structures developed for semantic categories only after expression of the categories with simpler, familiar structures had become productive in the texts.

In summary, even though there were differences in their rates of development and relatively minor formal and substantive differences in their linguistic development, the fact that the three children learned to differentiate the semantic categories in terms of structure in the sequence nonexistence, rejection, denial was the dominant feature of Phase 2 in their acquisition of syntactic expression of negation.

EARLY SENTENCE NEGATION: SEQUENTIAL DEVELOPMENT AND INTERPRETATION

On the basis of the relative frequency of sentences in the different semantic categories of negation, and the progressive developments in the syntactic complexity of these sentences, the order of acquisition for all three children was specified as nonexistence, rejection, denial. This sequence is similar to the sequence that McNeill and McNeill

(1968) anticipated in the development of negation by their Japanese subject, with two differences: a minor difference in the specification of the function of rejection, and a more substantial difference in their specification of the first semantic contrast. In the first contrast they observed, their subject marked the "correctness and incorrectness of statements" in addition to "nonexistence of objects and events."

Because the same sequence occurred in the acquisition of negation by the three children in this study, and there is some evidence for postulating a similar sequence of development in Japanese, it is reasonable to speculate on a rationale underlying this sequential development. Several reasons can be advanced to account for children learning certain syntactic structures before others. The factors of structural complexity and frequency of exposure or the child's experience with specific structures are two factors that are usually suggested; certainly, they play some part in the fact that use of passive sentences, for example, occurs late in the course of development.

However, considering the structural complexity of the ultimate linguistic expression of the three semantic categories, expression of denial appeared to be least complex. The shape of the negative element was constant; there was no expression of a main verb; the complement structure on which the negative element had direct effect was a single word most often; and there was the use of a relatively constant, familiar pro-form as sentence-subject. In contrast, expression of nonexistence was ultimately most complex with expression of different sentence-subjects, variable verbal constituents with predicate complement constructions, and wide variation in the forms of the negative element. But expression of denial developed last, whereas syntactic expression of nonexistence developed first.

However, it was also true that in nonexistence the negative element had direct effect on the nominal or predicate form – for example, "no pocket" and "no fit." Expression of rejection involved negating the child's wanting to have or to do something, for example, "no (want) dirty soap"; or negating wanting someone else to do or to have something, for example "(you) no flush" and "(you) no have it" – with an implication of more complex underlying structure.

As has been pointed out, there was no way of determining which syntactic structures were most frequent in the speech the children heard. It is a matter of speculation as to whether statements of nonexistence occurred more often than statements of rejection or statements of denial in the speech that the parents of the children addressed to them. In Bellugi's (1967) analysis of the negative sentences that each of the mothers of the children in her study used in a period of four hours, "basic sentence negation . . . 'you can't do that,' 'that isn't right,' 'he doesn't want it' " occurred most often, and negative imperatives occurred less frequently.

One reasonable explanation for early attention to syntactic expression of nonexistence before rejection was the adequacy of *no* as a single-word utterance (with appropriate behavior) in expressing rejection; *no* worked in expressing rejection, whereas *no* or even the more explicit *no more* (and appropriate behavior) communicated little information about nonexistence. The fact that the referent was not manifest in the context necessitated its inclusion in expression in order to transmit the information of nonexistence. In contrast, the fact that the referent was present – actually in rejection situations and symbolically in denial situations – made reference somewhat redundant. Thus, the children 'needed' to express nonexistence syntactically in order to transmit information, whereas syntactic expression of rejection and denial was less necessary.

The fact that denial involved a symbolic referent – the child had to interpret the referent in something said – probably accounted in part for the fact that denial developed last. As will be seen in Chapter 13, the children's earliest utterances tended to occur infrequently in relation to another utterance (from someone else or from themselves). Further, McNeill and McNeill (1968) observed that statements of denial usually entailed alternative affirmative statements – for example, "that's not mines. that's dolly's" at Gia VI (whether or not the alternative affirmative statement was actually expressed). Their suggestion is reasonable that "Entailment–Non-entailment" (denial) "requires a child to hold in mind two propositions at once" and so would be acquired after contrasts that involve only one proposition (as in nonexistence and rejection).

In summary, Kathryn, Eric, and Gia approached the task of learning negation – which, in the adult model, is a complex, explicitly differentiated grammatical subsystem – systematically and similarly. It was possible to trace their acquisition of syntactic structure in relation to the meaning of their negative sentences. Further, by studying the acquisition of each of the three children individually and then comparing the obtained sequences of development, both similarities and individual differences were revealed.

The findings presented here complement the description of the acquisition of syntactic structure in early sentence negation proposed by Bellugi (1967). The descriptions of the form of negative sentences in

Bellugi's data were generally similar to the surface features of the sentences of Kathryn, Eric, and Gia. The negative sentences produced by the three children in the development stages described as Phases 1 and 2 could be described as having occurred in the earliest developmental periods that Bellugi described. However, when information about the semantics of the sentences was considered, it was possible to study the syntax of negation more deeply and to inquire into the underlying motivation of syntactic form.

NOTES

1 Bellugi (1967); see also Klima & Bellugi (1966).
2 de Villiers & de Villiers (1979).
3 The only disagreements with this conclusion I know of are in Wode (1977) and Van Valin (in press). Wode's analysis was seriously faulted on methodological grounds by Park (1979), and Wode's conclusions were refuted by, for instance, de Villiers & de Villiers (1979), Park (1979), and, most recently, Weissenborn, Verrips, & Berman (1989). Wode (1984) himself appears to have changed his account; in this later work he describes Neg V, but not Neg S in early sentences. Van Valin discussed instances of Neg S and S Neg reported in the literature (especially in Polish and languages with negative affixing) in terms of scope considerations and functionalist linguistic theory.
4 Werner & Kaplan (1963, p. 60).
5 Slobin (1973).
6 For example, Brown (1973); see also Bloom & Lahey (1978).
7 Belkin (1975); Pea (1980, 1982).
8 For the purpose of this presentation, the negative sentences from Kathryn at Time I, in Table 4.1, will be used as examples. The discussion and conclusions apply as well to the negative sentences in the data from Eric and Gia as well.
9 Bellugi's Period A was based on a 10-hour speech sample from each child, obtained over a 10-week period for two of them and over a 20-week period for the third. The individual observations of Kathryn, Eric, and Gia were spaced over a period of a few days, every 6 weeks. Thus, the period discussed as the first stage (Period A) by Bellugi overlaps the first several observations of Kathryn, Eric, and Gia.

POSTSCRIPT

For studies of the meaning categories in early sentence negation since Bloom(1970):
Choi, S. (1988). The semantic development of negation: A cross-linguistic longitudinal study. *Journal of Child Language, 15,* 517–31.

Crosby, F. (1976). Early discourse agreement. *Journal of Child Language,* *3,* 125–6.

Pea, R. (1980). The development of negation in early child language. In D. Olson (Ed.), *The social foundations of language and thought: Essays in honor of Jerome S. Bruner* (pp. 156–86). New York: Norton.

Pea, R. (1982). Origins of verbal logic: Spontaneous denials by 2- and 3-year olds. *Journal of Child Language, 9,* 597–626.

For studies of negation meanings in single-word speech:

Belkin, A. (1975). Investigation of the functions and forms of children's negative utterances. Ph.D. diss., Teachers College, Columbia University.

Gopnik, A., & Meltzoff, A. (1985). From people, to plans, to objects – Changes in the meaning of early words and their relation to cognitive development. *Journal of Child Language, 9,* 495–512.

For studies of form–function relationships in acquisition of negation:

Clancy, P. (1985). The acquisition of Japanese. In D. Slobin (Ed.), *The crosslinguistic study of language acquisition* (vol. 1, pp. 373–524). Hillsdale, NJ: Erlbaum.

Keller-Cohen, D., & Gracey, C. (1979). Learning to say no: Functional negation in discourse. In O. Garnica & M. King (Eds.), *Language, children, and society* (pp. 197–211). Elmsford, NY: Pergamon.

Park, T. (1979). Some facts on negation: Wode's four-stage development of negation revisited. *Journal of Child Language, 6,* 147–51.

Todd, P. (1982). Tagging after red herrings: Evidence against a processing capacity explanation in child language. *Journal of Child Language, 9,* 99–114.

Van Valin, R. (in press). Functionalist linguistic theory and language acquisition. *First Language.*

Wode, H. (1977). Four early stages in the development of L1 negation. *Journal of Child Language, 4,* 87–102.

For studies of negation at later ages:

de Boysson-Bardies, B. (1977). On children's interpretation of negation. *Journal of Experimental Child Psychology, 23,* 117–27.

de Villiers, J., & Tager-Flusberg, H. (1975). Some facts one simply cannot deny. *Journal of Child Language, 2,* 279–86.

Hopmann, M., & Maratsos, M. (1978). A developmental study of factivity and negation in complex syntax. *Journal of Child Language, 5,* 295–309.

5

Verb Subcategorization and Inflections

"I broke a bridge."
"Tape recorder goes in there."
"I writing circles."

Verb inflections are one of the earliest modifications in children's simple sentences and were studied here as mean length of utterance increased from 1.5 to 3.0 morphemes. Previous studies had considered the meanings of the morphemes themselves to be the major factor that influenced their acquisition. However, in the study of the influence of syntactic complexity, discourse, and lexical factors on sentence length (Chapter 3) we had observed that verb inflections covaried with the subcategories of verbs the children learned. Accordingly, in this study we set out to determine how the semantics of verbs influenced the acquisition of verb inflections. A second issue addressed in the study was the developmental relationship between aspect and tense marking. In linguistic theory, the phrase *aspect before tense*[1] has been used to capture the configurational result when languages use different inflections for coding tense and aspect: Aspect marking takes precedence over tense and is closer to the verb stem. We appropriated the notion of aspect before tense to capture the general finding that aspectual distinctions are developmentally salient and lead the child in discovering tense distinctions.

CATEGORIES OF VERBS AND VERB INFLECTION

The inflections *-ing, -s, -ed,* and the irregular past emerged in the children's speech at the same time but occurred selectively with different categories of verbs. This finding was relevant at two levels of verb subcategorization. The first was the different semantic–syntactic sentence configurations with subcategories of action, locative-action, and state verbs. The argument structures with different verbs determined whether the verb was inflected and, to some extent, which inflections occurred. Given how frequently sentences occurred with different categories of verbs, the frequency of inflection was less than expected with the action and agent–locative-action verbs, and more frequent than expected with patient–locative-action verbs. Moreover, third-person *-s* was used only with patient–locative-action verbs when it first appeared, and

-ing and the irregular past were used with action verbs. With development, the use of inflections increased; the inflections were used with other verb categories; and different inflections were used within categories.

The different inflections also covaried with the lexical meaning of the verbs themselves. Certain all-purpose pro-verbs (e.g., *do, go*) occurred with all the inflections virtually from the beginning. Other, more descriptive verbs, however, took different inflections according to their inherent aspectual meaning. The two aspectual oppositions that guided the emergence of the different verb inflections in the children's speech were the contrasts durative–nondurative and completive–noncompletive. Nondurative events with a completed end state were most likely to occur with *-ed* and irregular past; events that lasted over time and did not have a clear completion were most likely to occur with the progressive *-ing*. The conclusion was that the aspectual contour of an event was a strong influence on how the children acquired the inflections for verb tense. This result was consistent with a number of studies of tense–aspect in the literature.[2]

ASPECT BEFORE TENSE

The finding that verb aspect was developmentally salient was subsequently replicated in a host of studies of children learning a wide variety of languages. These are listed in the Postscript that follows this chapter. The finding was challenged, however, in a study by Richard Weist and his colleagues of the acquisition of verb inflection in Polish.[3] But, in a statistical reanalysis of their own data Lorraine Harner and I were able to show that children learning Polish are no less influenced by aspectual distinctions in learning tense markers than are children learning other languages.[4] In the spontaneous speech of children at about 2 years of age – with mean length of utterance less than 3.0 morphemes, aspectual contour, and, in particular, the relative duration and completeness of an event – are powerful determinants of how a verb is marked with inflections. However, as we pointed out:

The principle of aspect before tense is relative and not absolute in its application to development in the child language data. Although strongly influenced at the beginning by event-aspect, children are no doubt learning tense relations at the same time; they do not learn tense only after they learn aspect. (p. 233 below)

The Semantics of Verbs and the Development of Verb Inflections in Child Language

Lois Bloom, Karin Lifter, and Jeremie Hafitz

The purpose of this study was to explore the relationship between the semantic organization of verbs used in early sentences and the emergence of the inflections of the verb auxiliary (*-ing, -s, -ed/irreg*). In discussions of the acquisition of grammatical morphemes by Brown (1973), de Villiers & de Villiers (1973), and others, only the syntax and semantics (along with environmental frequency) of the individual morphemes themselves have been seriously discussed as contributing to the order in which they are acquired. However, the results of the present study suggest that the semantic organization of the verb system that children learn is at least as important as the meanings of the verb inflections for determining their acquisition.

BACKGROUND

There have been few studies of the semantics of verbs in children's early sentences. Bloom, Lightbown, and Hood (1975, chap. 2) observed developmental differences between verbs of action and state, and between locative and nonlocative actions and states. Bloom, Miller, and Hood (1975, chap. 3) extended the categorization of locative verbs and described three semantic–syntactic categories of locative verbs that differed according to the relationship between a verb and its pre-verb and post-verb constituents (subject–verb and verb–complement). Bowerman (1974b) used 'error' data to describe the emergence of causative verbs in her 2-year-old daughter's language. The implication of these studies is that children learn the verbs of the language as a system and that verbs do not enter children's vocabularies one at a time, as a function only of events in the context. This implication is supported by results of the study reported here.

There have been many and varied studies of children's acquisition of grammatical morphemes. Most have been experimental, exploring children's knowledge of morphological rules for adding affixes to non-

Reprinted from *Language*, 1980, 56, 386–412, with permission from The Linguistic Society of America.

sense words, in the tradition of Berko (1958). Other studies have been observational (e.g., Brown, 1973; Cazden, 1968; and de Villiers & de Villiers, 1973), describing correlations between use of particular morphemes and increase in utterance length. The implications of these studies are that the grammatical morphemes are learned sequentially and apply in general to all of a child's verbs. These implications are not supported by the results of the present study. Brown (1973) discussed the possibility that different verb inflections might be learned for different categories of verbs, for example, 'process' and 'state' verbs; and Antinucci and Miller (1976) observed that past tense first appears only with certain verbs in the acquisition of Italian and English. In experimental studies – of French-speaking children by Bronckart and Sinclair (1973) and of American English-speaking children by Harner (1981) and C. Smith (1978) – event–aspect influenced the inflections that children used in describing actions in elicited production tasks.

After a description of the subjects and procedures for the present observational study, the emergence of verb inflections in the children's sentences will be described. These results will then be discussed in terms of (1) the semantics of verbs in relation both to aspect and syntax in child language and (2) the nature of the rules that children learn for verb inflection.

SUBJECTS AND PROCEDURES

Subjects

The observations of Eric, Gia, Kathryn, and Peter that provided the corpus of utterances for the present study began when verb inflections had begun to appear and the mean length of utterance (MLU) was $\geq$ 1.5 but < 2.0; the study continued until MLU was $\geq$ 2.5 but < 3.0. These observations consisted of 94 hours of naturalistic (nonelicited) language behavior – three times each with Eric and Gia, two with Kathryn, and seven with Peter (see Figure 5.1). The 15 observations were grouped into three successive periods on the basis of consistency in MLU, as indicated in Table 5.1; these periods coincided with MLU Stages I, II, and III of Brown (1973). The results of the study will be reported for these developmental stages, except where intersubject variation precluded grouping the data.

Each speech event with an utterance that included a verb relation was examined to observe (1) the frequency of occurrence of the linguistic/nonlinguistic contexts in which the inflections should have oc-

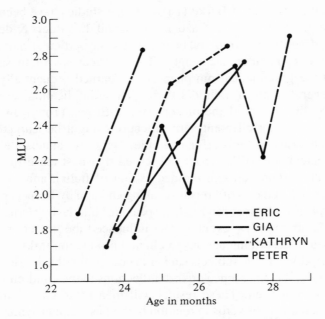

Figure 5.1. Progression in mean length of utterance (MLU) according to age.

curred (obligatory context) or could have occurred (optional context); (2) the frequency of occurrence of each of the verb inflections (*-ing, s, ed/irreg*); and (3) the conditional use of the inflection, that is, the occurrence of the inflection in a given context. Only verbs that appeared in a particular child's speech in both uninflected form and with at least one inflection were included in the analyses. That is, a verb used only in its inflected form by a particular child was not counted as inflected for the morpheme by that child. (In fact, less than .03 of the children's verbs occurred only in their inflected forms.) In all, about 7,000 speech events with verb relations were examined. As will be seen, the use of verb inflections in the period was far short of the criterion Brown (1973) had used to establish acquisition, that is, 90% occurrence in obligatory contexts; the verb inflections were just emerging in the children's speech.

Obligatory and Optional Contexts

Following Brown (1973), both linguistic and nonlinguistic criteria were used for determining the contexts for inflections in speech events. There were three criteria for obligatory contexts:

Table 5.1. *Description of Stages*

Stage	MLU Range	Age Mean	Range	Number of Observations
I	≥ 1.5 < 2.0	23,2	22,3–24,1	4
II	≥ 2.0 < 2.5	25,2	25,0–25,3	3
III	≥ 2.5 < 3.0[a]	26,3	24,2–28,2	8[a]

[a]The sixth observation of Peter was included in Stage III, even though MLU dropped to <2.5, because MLU had been >2.5 for the two preceding observations (see Figure 5.1), and because the data in this observation were more continuous with Stage III than with Stage II.

1. The linguistic context of the verb in the child's own utterance required the use of an inflection (e.g., "I'm go outside," where -*ing* was obligatory but was not used).

2. The prior linguistic context (child or adult) required the use of an inflection (e.g., Adult: "What are you doing?"/Child: "I eat it," where -*ing* was obligatory but was not used).

3. The nonlinguistic context of the speech situation required the use of an inflection (e.g., the book had just fallen off the table: "Book fall down," where *irreg* was obligatory but was not used).

Brown's fourth criterion of subsequent linguistic context, where succeeding adult expansions of the child utterance would require the occurrence of the inflection, was not used because the evidence was not always clear as to whether the adult expansion and the child's prior semantic intent were indeed the same.

Optional contexts were observed for the occurrence of -*ing* and -*s* where the nonlinguistic context of the speech situation would allow either to occur, that is, the use of either inflection (involving third-person singular subjects) as a comment about ongoing activity. (For example, the child is putting a peg figure into a car: "Man go car," where either *going* or *goes* could have occurred.) When the context could not be determined, the utterance was considered ambiguous for a particular inflection; an average of .06 of the utterances were ambiguous and not included in the analyses reported here.

To establish reliability, two independent judges examined 100 utterances that were selected across the four children and across four verb categories. There was high agreement between the two judges and between each judge and the original context coding: The average proportion of agreement was .85 with a range of .80 to .90 for the different contexts and the different judges.

There were two levels of analysis. First, all the speech events that included syntactic utterances with verbs were examined. The occurrence of contexts for the inflections, the occurrence of the inflections, and their conditional use, given optional and obligatory contexts, were determined for different categories of verbs in a first, structural, verb typology based upon the syntactic relations in the children's sentences. Then a distributional analysis of the inflections was used to obtain a second, lexical, verb typology based upon the inherent aspectual meanings of the verbs themselves.

RESULTS

While there was no developmental change in the occurrence of contexts for inflections (an average of .36 of the utterances occurred with contexts for one or another inflection in each of the three periods), there was developmental change in the use of inflections given a context (from an average of .19 in the first observations to .54 in the last observations of each child). The major results of the study were that the verb inflections *-ing, -s,* and *irreg* emerged in the children's speech at the same time, but the inflections were distributed selectively with different populations of verbs.

Verb Typology According to Semantic–Syntactic Structure

Three superordinate categories of verbs had been identified in the children's utterances in previous studies according to sequence of development and/or semantic–syntactic structure: action, locative action, and state. Action and locative-action verbs were distinguished semantically and syntactically; both appeared developmentally before state verbs (Bloom, Lightbown, & Hood 1975, chap. 3; Bloom, Miller, & Hood 1975, chap. 2).

Certain events the children talked about involved movement, with an agent that brought about the movement or 'did' the action – and, most often, an object that was affected by the action. As a hypothetical example, all the utterances "Gia ride," "Ride bike," "Gia bike," and "Gia ride bike" are about the transitive action (*ride*) and the relation between Gia (the agent) and the bike (an affected object). The verb *ride* was an action verb in the sentence context

(1)   # agent _____ object #

Here the object could be optional or not, depending on whether the action verb was transitive. State events did not involve a movement named by a verb in the utterance; for example, the utterance "Baby sleep" is about a nonmovement event and the relation between the baby (an entity) and sleeping (its state). The verb *sleep* was one kind of state verb in the sentence context

(2)   # entity _____ #

The verb *like* was another kind of state verb in the sentence context

(3)   # entity _____ object #

(This difference among state verbs is discussed below.) Action verbs, then, named movement events such as *eat, ride, throw, make,* and *go,* and state verbs named nonmovement events such as *want, know, like, sleep,* and *see.*

Action events were further differentiated according to whether the action verb named a movement toward (or, less often, away from) a place. Locative-action verbs, for example, *put, go, sit,* named movements in which the goal of the movement was a change of place.[5] Locative-action (but not other action) utterances were further differentiated according to the relationship between the pre-verb constituent and the verb.

In mover–locative-action utterances, the pre-verb constituent represented the object that was both the initiator and the recipient of the action named by the verb. Thus, the verb *go* in "Mommy go store" was a mover–locative-action verb in the sentence context

(4)   # mover _____ place #

Two kinds of locative-action events involved two objects – one that changed place and another that caused the change of place. In patient–locative-action utterances, the pre-verb constituent represented the patient, that is, the object that changed place, and the agent was not specified; for example, the verbs *go* and *fit* in sentences like "Tape recorder goes in there" (as Peter put the recording tape into its box) and "Here one fits" (as Kathryn put a lamb into a box) were patient–locative-action verbs in the sentence context[6]

(5)   # patient _____ place #

In agent-locative-action utterances, the pre-verb constituent represented the agent of the movement named by the verb, and the object that changed place was part of the verb complement. Thus the verb *put* in "I put a car under bridge" was an agent–locative-action verb in the sentence context

(6)   # agent ____ object–place #

There were, then, categories of verbs that were distinguishable according to the semantic relation between verb and subject, whether or not all the constituents in the canonical sentence contexts were indeed expressed:

$$(7) \quad \# \left\{ \begin{array}{l} \text{agent} \\ \text{entity} \\ \text{mover} \\ \text{patient} \end{array} \right\} \text{verb-complement} \#$$

Here complement is object, place, object–place, or null, depending on the meaning of the verb. The locative-action categories described here were learned sequentially – although the sequence was different for the different children – and so were distinguished developmentally as well as structurally (see Bloom, Miller, & Hood, 1975, chap. 3).

Occurrence of Inflections in Relation to Semantic–Syntactic Structure

If the semantics and syntax of sentences were not factors in learning verb inflection, then one could expect that the different verb inflections would be distributed among the utterances in the five verb categories in the same way the utterances themselves were distributed within the categories. That is, the relative distributions of the inflections and utterances should be the same across the verb categories if they were independent of each other. However, the two distributions would not be the same if there were an interaction, that is, a dependency relation, between the occurrence of inflections and verb category.

The relative distributions of inflections and utterances were compared across the verb categories, for each of the three developmental periods, in order to test the null hypothesis of no difference between them (see Table 5.2).[7] Significant differences were observed between

Table 5.2. *Comparison of Relative Distributions of Utterances and Inflections in Verb Categories*

Stage		Action	State	Patient–Locative Action	Mover–Locative Action	Agent–Locative Action	N	p^a
I	Utterances	.69	.08	.13	.04	.04	795	<0.01
	Inflections	.54	.09	.27	.09	.00	67	
II	Utterances	.60	.14	.08	.09	.09	1006	<0.001
	Inflections	.52	.11	.32	.04	.01	111	
III	Utterances	.51	.23	.07	.09	.11	4848	<0.001
	Inflections	.47	.14	.21	.15	.03	834	

Above columns Action through Agent–Locative Action are under the heading **Verb Category**.

$^a p$ = Significance level for 2 × 5 chi-square test of equality of the distributions.
Note: Unmarked past and ambiguous utterances were excluded from the analysis.

the distributions, in each period, when tested by chi-square analysis $(x^2_{(4)}; p \leq 0.01)$.[8]

As can be seen in Table 5.2, the proportion of inflections that occurred in action and agent–locative-action categories was less than anticipated when expectation was based on the proportional occurrence of utterances in those categories. In contrast, the proportions of inflections in patient–locative action was greater than expected. The relations between inflections and utterances in state and mover–locative action were less clear; with development, fewer inflections occurred than expected in the state category. Thus, the distribution of inflections was not independent of the verb categories; rather, there was a dependency relation between the occurrence of inflections and the semantic–syntactic structure of sentences within each developmental period. Differences diminished for action and increased for state. Thus, not only was there an interaction of inflections with the semantic–syntactic structure of sentences within each developmental period, but also a shift in this interaction over time.

The results at this first level of analysis suggested that the occurrence of inflections was not independent of verb meaning differentiated according to whether (1) relevant movement occurred (the action–state distinction); (2) the goal of movement was a change in place (the action–locative-action distinction); and/or (3) the object that changed place was also the agent of the movement (the distinction among mover, patient, and agent–locative action).

Emergence of Inflection Use

The use of morphemes was defined as the occurrence of a morpheme, given a context for it (after Brown, except that both optional and obligatory contexts were considered). Three analyses were performed: (1) the use of the individual inflections by each child at each observation; (2) the rank order of inflection use for the children combined, in the three developmental periods; and (3) the use of inflections according to the verb typology.

Individual Use of Inflections. As seen in Figure 5.2, three of the morphemes emerged at the same age for three of the children (Peter used -*s* before the other morphemes); regular -*ed* appeared later than *irreg*; and the use of the individual morphemes varied in relation to one another, both across time and among the children (*irreg* was generally the most frequent for Eric, Gia, and Kathryn while -*s* was always most frequent for Peter).

Rank Order of Use. Overall use was greatest for *irreg,* and least for -*ed* in the three developmental periods. The sequence of acquisition of grammatical morphemes has been reported elsewhere according to the rank order in which each morpheme was used in 90% of obligatory contexts, in longitudinal sampling of the same subjects by Brown (1973) and by Cazden, (1968), and in cross-sectional sampling of subjects at different language levels by de Villiers & de Villiers, (1973). The acquisition sequence for the verb inflections reported in those studies was *ing* < *irreg* < -*ed* < -*s*. In the present study, the emergence of grammatical morphemes has been described prior to acquisition or the achievement of 90% use. The rank order of the relative use of the different morphemes for the three developmental periods was used to compare the emergence of the morphemes in the present study with the acquisition sequence reported in the literature. For each child, each inflection was assigned a rank order according to its magnitude of use. When more than one observation of a particular child was included in a developmental period, the average of the ranks was used as that child's contribution to the rank. The rank orders for the three developmental periods are presented in Table 5.3 (averaged across children

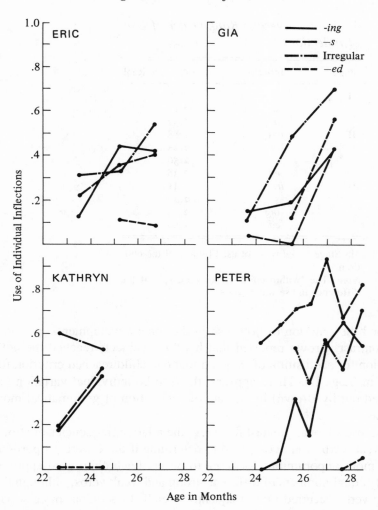

Figure 5.2. Emergence of inflections based on use in optional and obligatory contexts.

within each developmental period). Use was greatest for *irreg* and least for *-ed*. Thus, with respect to the early use of verb inflections (before acquisition as defined above), the three inflections *-ing, -s,* and *irreg* emerged at the same time. However, the rank order of the relative use of the morphemes as they emerged differed from the acquisition order reported elsewhere. Except for Peter's use of *-s* in one sample, no child

Table 5.3. *Average Rank Order of Use of Inflections*

Stage	Inflection	Average Rank
I[a]	*irreg*	1.50
	-s	2.12
	-ing	2.37
II	*irreg*	1.88
	-ing	2.25
	-s	2.50
	-ed	3.38
III	*irreg*	1.41
	-s	2.47
	-ing	2.63
	-ed	3.50

[a] In Stage I, *-ed* was not used by any of the children.
Note: The 'within child' ranks were split if the difference in use was ≤ 0.05.

reached the criterion of 90% use in the three developmental periods. (In contrast, Brown reported that his three subjects reached the 90% criterion for acquisition of *-ing* and that one child reached criterion for *irreg* in Stage II). There appears, then, to be individual variation (as pointed out by Brown) in the rate of acquisition of grammatical morphemes.

Because use was greatest for *irreg,* the relative frequencies of strong and weak verbs were compared to determine if there were proportionately more opportunities for *irreg* to occur. Each child used approximately equal numbers of different strong and weak verbs, although the strong verbs occurred more frequently overall. In addition, more strong verbs (approximately .06) were inflected than weak (less than .01). Thus, in general, there were more opportunities for *irreg* to occur because strong verbs were more frequent and the strong verbs were also inflected more often than were weak verbs.

Morpheme Use and the Semantic–Syntactic Categories of Verbs. The use of the individual morphemes with each of the verb categories in the three developmental periods is presented in Table 5.4. The three morphemes *-ing, -s,* and *irreg* emerged together in Stage I; *-s* was used only with patient–locative action, while *-ing* and *irreg* were used with

Table 5.4. *Use of Inflections in Verb Categories*

Stage	Verb Category	Inflection			
		-ing	*-s*	*irreg*	*-ed*
I	Action	.15 (22/147)[a]		.30 (7/23)	
	Agent Locative				
	Mover Locative				
	Patient Locative		.18 (17/93)		
	State				
II	Action	.24 (36/149)	.17 (2/12)	.50 (19/38)	
	Agent Locative				
	Mover Locative				
	Patient Locative	.14 (3/22)	.45 (29/64)		
	State				
III	Action	.54 (220/410)	.23 (12/53)	.56 (151/271)	.14 (11/76)
	Agent Locative	.11 (20/179)		.24 (7/29)	
	Mover Locative	.62 (89/144)		.60 (34/57)	
	Patient Locative	.20 (13/64)	.67 (154/230)		
	State	.72 (39/54)	.57 (34/60)	.76 (39/51)	

[a]Ratios in parentheses represent absolute frequencies of inflections in relation to contexts.

Note: Empty cells indicate that the inflection did not occur, or that the use of the inflection was nonproductive within a category (i.e., fewer than 5 contexts for an inflection), or that the use of the inflection was productive for only one child.

action. As the children developed, inflection was extended to other categories of verbs; the use of each inflection increased within each category, and more different inflections were used within a category. As can be seen, although use was often greater for *irreg* and *-s* than for *-ing,* the overall, absolute frequency of *-ing* was greater in all three periods.

Selective Co-occurrence of Inflections and Verbs

The occurrence of different inflections coincided with lexical differences among the children's verbs having to do with their inherent aspectual meaning. Verb aspect is the temporal value inherent in the activity or state named by the verb, such as relative duration or punctuality (Friedrich 1974). The co-occurrence of inflections and verb aspect will be described first for action and locative-action verbs and then for state verbs.

Table 5.5. *Stage I: Verbs Used with Inflections*

Semantic–Syntactic Category	Co-occurrence of Inflections and Verbs[a]						
	-ing		*-s*		*irreg*		*-ed*
Action	eat	4	cook	2	break	2	
	hide	3	knit	2	do	2	
	dance	2	try	2	make	2	
	fold	2	go	1	take off	1	
	wash	2	ride	1			
	clean	1					
	cook	1					
	cry	1					
	fix	1					
	fly	1					
	knit	1					
	play	1					
	read	1					
	write	1					
Agent–Locative Action							
Mover–Locative Action	go	1			come	4	
	stand	1					
Patient–Locative Action	come	1	go	12			
			fit	5			
State	hide	2	go	1	come	1	
	sleep	2					

[a] Here and in Tables 5.6 and 5.7, the frequency of occurence of inflection with verb is presented after each verb.

Action Verbs. The inflections tended to occur selectively with different populations of verbs within and across the semantic–syntactic categories of action and locative-action verbs (see Tables 5.5, 5.6, and 5.7). Certain verbs occurred almost exclusively with *ing,* certain others almost exclusively with *-ed/irreg,* and still others with *-s.* There was distributional overlap among a small group of the most frequently used action verbs; each occurred with two or three of the three inflections that were possible.

The most frequent verbs that occurred predominantly (and often exclusively) with one or another inflection shared certain aspectual values. The action verbs that occurred with *-ing* named durative events that extended over time and tended to be noncompletive, in that there was no immediate and clear result. Thus *play, hold, ride,* and *write* were among the clearest instances of verbs that named durative, non-

Table 5.6. *Stage II: Verbs Used with Inflections*

Semantic–Syntactic Category	Co-occurrence of Inflections and Verbs			
	-ing	*-s*	*irreg*	*-ed*
Action	*write* 14	*go* 2	*do* 12	*turn* 1
	do 6		*get* 2	
	make 6		*buy* 1	
	ride 3		*draw* 1	
	cook 2		*find* 1	
	read 1		*make* 1	
	take 1		*tear* 1	
	touch 1			
	try 1			
	wipe 1			
Agent–Locative Action	*take* 1			
Mover–Locative Action	*go* 2		*come* 1	
			fall 1	
Patient–Locative Action	*go* 3	*go* 29	*come* 2	
			fall 2	
State	*sleep* 1	*go* 7		
		hurt 3		
		need 1		

completive events, and such verbs occurred almost exclusively with
-ing. The verbs that occurred with *-ed/irreg* named nondurative, momentary events that tended to be completive, with a relatively clear
result. Thus *find, fall,* and *break* were among the clearest instances of
such verbs, and these occurred exclusively with *-ed/irreg*. The most
frequent verbs that occurred with *-s* (primarily *go,* in the sense of "This
goes here") named events that were both completive with an end result
(as in the events *go, fit, open, sit, stop*) and durative (in the sense of
continuing after completion). The most frequent of these verbs, *go* and
fit, named actions toward the place to or at which some object (the
patient) logically 'belongs' and appeared to be used by the children in
the sense of an assignment of that object to a place. This use of *-s* can
be described as generic in the sense of Lawler (1972). It was also the
case that patient–locative-action utterances occurred exclusively with
third-person subjects, by definition; this may have been another, syntactic factor that influenced the occurrence of *-s*. However, third-
person subjects occurred frequently with mover–locative-action and,
less frequently, with action verbs, but *-s* occurred minimally with these

Table 5.7. *Stage III: Verbs Used with Inflections*

Semantic–Syntactic Category	Co-occurrence of Inflections and Verbs							
	-ing		*-s*		*irreg*		*-ed*	
Action	do	24	go	7	find	39	comb	3
	play	21	stop	2	do	33	jump	3
	eat	20	make	1	get	32	fix	2
	hold	14	sit	1	say	10	call	1
	get	12	step	1	break	7	finish	1
	try	12			have	5	touch	1
	fix	10			bring	4		
	ride	9			make	4		
	make	8			buy	3		
	cry	7			bite	2		
	look	7			eat	2		
	take	7			send	2		
	go	5			write	2		
	drive	4			feed	1		
	have	4			leave	1		
	read	4			lose	1		
	work	4			take	1		
	blow	3			tear	1		
	write	3			throw	1		
	carry	2						
	draw	2						
	dump	2						
	help	2						
	jump	2						
	kiss	2						
	listen	2						
	skate	2						
	sleep	2						
	throw	2						
	walk	2						
	bake	1						
	bounce	1						
	button	1						
	clean	1						
	comb	1						
	drink	1						
	fly	1						
	hurt	1						
	push	1						
	put	1						
	scream	1						
	sew	1						
	sweep	1						
	talk	1						
	tie	1						

Table 5.7. *(cont.)*

Semantic–Syntactic Category	Co-occurrence of Inflections and Verbs			
	-ing	*-s*	*irreg*	*-ed*
	use 1			
	wait 1			
	wave 1			
	wear 1			
	wipe 1			
Agent–Locative Action	*put* 11		*do* 4	
	take 9		*bring* 1	
			get 1	
			take 1	
Mover–Locative Action	*go* 60	*come* 1	*come* 13	*jump* 1
	go bye-bye 17	*go* 1	*go bye-bye* 9	
	sit 7		*go* 7	
	come 1		*fall* 3	
	fly 1		*fly* 1	
	get 1		*leave* 1	
	lay 1			
	stand 1			
Patient–Locative Action	*go bye-bye* 6	*go* 143	*fall* 3	
	go 5	*fit* 9	*come* 2	
	come 2	*come* 2	*go* 1	
			go bye-bye 1	
State	*sit* 8	*go* 15	*say* 26	*look* 1
	sleep 5	*say* 7	*see* 7	
	lay 4	*fit* 5	*find* 2	
	watch 4	*want* 2	*forget* 1	
	cry 3	*belong* 1	*go bye-bye* 1	
	look 3	*like* 1	*have* 1	
	carry 2	*ride* 1	*tell* 1	
	go 2	*stand* 1		
	hold 2	*work* 1		
	open 2			
	take nap 2			
	wait 2			
	have 1			

two categories. The co-occurrences of inflections and lexical aspect resulted in a semantic typology with three verb types. The three verb types coincided with three of the four intersections formed in a matrix of the two semantic oppositions basic to analyses of verb aspect: durative–nondurative, and completive–noncompletive (see Figure 5.3).

The semantic distribution of the majority of the children's action verbs, according to these aspectual oppositions, was coextensive with the selective use of one verb inflection or another. This distribution is presented in Figure 5.3 for the four children and three developmental periods combined. The typology of action verbs according to verb aspect in Figure 5.3 was based strictly upon the distribution of the verb inflections: The completive–durative verbs occurred with -*s;* the non-completive–durative verbs occurred with -*ing;* the completive–non-durative verbs occurred with -*ed/irreg.* In each cell, the verbs that occurred with the distinguishing inflection are listed, along with the frequencies with which they were inflected, as either best or marginal instances. Thus all the verbs are listed in a cell, first of all, on the basis of their co-occurrence with the particular inflection, and in addition, best instances can be identified as those verbs in each cell with clear lexical aspect, as defined by the intersection in the matrix. Marginal instances are those verbs in the typology that occurred with the distinguishing inflection, but with less clear lexical aspect. Thus *find* and *break* were clear in their reference to completive–nondurative actions, whereas *comb* and *write* named events that were only approximately completive–nondurative; indeed, they occurred in noncompletive–durative events as well. There is a clear sense in which verbs like *eat, take, write* could name events that were either completive–nondurative or noncompletive–durative. However, the virtually exclusive use of -*ing* with these verbs was the formal regularity used to classify them among the best instances of durative–noncompletive verbs and among the 'marginal' instances of completive–nondurative verbs.

Pro-Verbs. The action verbs that occurred with more than one inflection included the most frequent verbs *go, do, make,* and *get,* which seemed to function as general, all-purpose verbs, or pro-verbs. Such pro-verbs seemed to 'stand in' for more descriptive verbs in that they named events with different aspectual contours. Other verbs that occurred with more than one inflection included the more specific descriptive verbs *eat, sit, ride, and fix,* but each of these occurred predominantly (at least .80 of the time), with one of the inflections. As seen in Tables 5.5 through 5.7, overlap among the verbs developed over time, in that verbs tended to be used with only one inflection to begin with. The proportion of each of the inflections that occurred with the pro-verbs, *do, go, make,* and *get* is presented in Table 5.8. As can be seen, there was an increase in the use of inflected pro-verbs from Stage I to Stage II, and a decrease from Stage II to Stage III, as more

	DURATIVE

DURATIVE

Verbs with *-s*

Best Instances:

go	195	cook	2	try	2
fit	14	knit	2	sit	1
come	3	stop	2		

Marginal Instances:

make	1
ride	1
step	1

COMPLETIVE

NON-DURATIVE

Verbs with *irreg/-ed*

Best Instances:

do	51	go	8	call	1
find	40	make	7	finish	1
get	35	buy	4	lose	1
come	22	jump	4	take off	1
go bye-bye	10	bite	2	throw	1
say	10	leave	2	touch	1
break	9	send	4	turn	1
fall	9	tear	2		

Marginal Instances:

bring	5	fix	2	feed	1
have	5	take	2	fly	1
comb	3	write	2		
eat	2	draw	1		

Verbs with *-ing*

Best Instances:

go	76	look	7	sleep	2
do	30	read	6	walk	2
eat	24	drive	4	wash	2
go bye-bye	23	work	4	bake	1
play	22	cook	3	drink	1
write	18	fly	3	knit	1
take	17	hide	3	scream	1
hold	14	carry	2	sew	1
make	14	clean	2	sweep	1
get	13	dance	2	talk	1
try	13	draw	2	use	1
ride	12	help	2	wait	1
fix	11	listen	2	wave	1
cry	8	skate	2	wear	1
				wipe	1

NON-COMPLETIVE

Marginal Instances:

put	12	jump	2	hurt	1
sit	7	kiss	2	lay	1
come	4	throw	2	push	1
have	4	bounce	1	stand	1
blow	3	button	1	tie	1
dump	2	comb	1	touch	1
fold	2	hit	1		

Figure 5.3. Distribution of verbs according to intersection of verb aspect.

descriptive verbs were inflected (except for *-ing*, the inflection that occurred least frequently with pro-verbs).

The children used pro-verbs (particularly *do* and *go*) with great frequency, not only with different inflections as in the study reported

Table 5.8. *Proportion of Inflections with* do, go, make, *and*
get

| | Inflections | | |
Stage	*-ing*	*-s*	*irreg*
I	$\frac{1}{29}$ (0.03)	$\frac{14}{26}$ (0.54)	$\frac{4}{12}$ (0.33)
II	$\frac{17}{43}$ (0.40)	$\frac{38}{42}$ (0.90)	$\frac{15}{25}$ (0.60)
III	$\frac{140}{384}$ (0.36)	$\frac{167}{202}$ (0.83)	$\frac{93}{240}$ (0.39)

here, but also with other structures, such as *wh*-questions (see Bloom, Merkin, & Wootten, 1982, chap. 6). The children learned at least these structures of language (verb inflection and *wh*-questions), largely with these general pro-verbs to begin with. As the children gained experience with these different grammatical forms and as they learned more different verbs, they used the inflections with more different verbs (see also Harner, 1981).

State Verbs. The action–state distinction was phenomenological rather than intuitive: Action verbs named events that co-occurred with movement. State verbs named events that did not co-occur with movement. In addition, action and state verbs were also distinguished developmentally: Action verbs were used by the children earlier than state verbs (Bloom, Lightbown, & Hood 1975, chap. 2). The action–state distinction has been described as basic to the semantics of verbs by others as well (Lakoff, 1966; Macaulay, 1971).

State verbs named internal states and perfective states. Among the most frequent internal state verbs were *want, like, need, think,* and *feel.* These were 'private' states that were not perceptible, phenomenological, or capable of being shared (see Allen, 1966; Joos, 1958). Such verbs were inflected infrequently (usually with *-s*) or not at all. When they were inflected, internal-state verbs occurred selectively with one or another inflection, with few exceptions. For example, *say* occurred with both *-s* and *irreg,* but different children inflected *say* with the different forms. The verb *say* was used by Kathryn in an attributive, generic sense (e.g., "Cow says 'moo' "), while Peter and Eric used *said* in reporting (e.g., "Daddy said 'no' "; see note in Table 5.9).

The largest number of state verbs that were inflected also appeared

Table 5.9. *Distribution of Inflections with Perfective and Internal State Verbs*

Stage	Shared (perfective) State				Nonshared (internal) State			
	-ing	*-s*	*irreg*	P[a]	*-ing*	*-s*	*irreg*	P[a]
I	hide sleep	go	find	1.0				
II	sleep	go		.67		hurt need		.33
III	carry cry hold lay look open sit sleep take nap want go[c] have[c]	belong fit ride stand work go[c] say[c]	find go bye-bye say[c] have[c]	.83	watch look[b,c]	like want	forget see	.17

[a] Proportion of inflected state verbs that were either shared or nonshared.
[b] Only *look* also occurred with *-ed,* in Stage III.
[c] *Say* and *look* were inflected with the two forms by different children; *have* was used only by Peter and with both inflections; *go* was used with more than one inflection only by Eric.

as action verbs in the data, the difference being whether relevant movement accompanied the utterance, for example, the ubiquitous *go* and also *sit, sleep, fit, find,* and *break;* see Tables 5.5 through 5.7 for the distribution of inflections with these different state verbs. Such verbs are aptly described as perfective in the sense of Friedrich (1974, p. 16), who defines perfect as ''a state of the subject resulting from a realization of the process referred to by the verb.'' Further, these verbs named states that were phenomenological or 'public' and capable of being observed or 'shared' by others. These perfective verbs were the first state verbs that were inflected, and each was used with only one inflection (see Tables 5.5 through 5.7). In contrast, the internal state verbs like *want, like,* and *forget* were most often uninflected. For all the state verbs, then, the use of the different inflections was, in general, mutually exclusive (see Table 5.9).

In sum, the results of this second level of analysis were, first, that inflection was selective with different populations of action verbs that were distinguishable according to lexical aspect: *-ing* occurred overwhelmingly with events that were durative–noncompletive, *-ed/irreg* with events that were nondurative–completive, and *-s* with events that were durative–completive. But further, the coextensive distribution of inflections and lexical aspect was more characteristic of descriptive verbs than the pro-verbs that were widely used. In addition, the state verbs that named internal, nonshared states (e.g., *want* and *like*) were rarely inflected; other state verbs that named phenomenological, perfective outcomes were inflected more often and with more different inflectional forms.

DISCUSSION

The semantics of the verbs the children were learning was the major influence on their learning verb inflections, as revealed on two levels of analysis. On the first level of analysis, as had been observed by Bloom, Miller, & Hood (1975, chap. 3), the distribution of inflections was not independent of the distribution of utterances that occurred with action, state, and different locative-action verbs. The differential occurrence of inflections and utterances, and the selective use of inflections with different categories of verbs, provided evidence that verb relations influenced the acquisition of inflections. In particular, the relation between the verb and the sentence-subject (agent, mover, patient, entity) determined whether a verb was inflected and often which inflection was used. On the second level of analysis, selective occurrence of inflections also was coextensive with distinctions of verb aspect. Thus the presence of inflections (and, to some extent, which inflections) was determined in part by the syntax of sentences, but the selective use of the different inflections was largely determined by the inherent aspectual meaning of the individual verbs.

Aspect Before Tense

Verb inflections are used to mark both aspect and tense in English; both of these are temporal notions. Aspect is the temporal contour of particular events, for example, an action that is momentary in time (*hit* or *jump*), in comparison with a durative action that lasts over time (*eat* or *play*). Linguistic tense is a deictic relation between the time an action or state occurs (event-time) and the time when an utterance that refers to that event occurs (speech-time). Linguistic tense transcends the aspect of events in that any event, in general, can be spoken about as it happens, after it happens, or before it happens.

Though other languages (e.g., Finnish and Russian) have separate linguistic devices to code distinctions of tense and aspect, the two systems are confounded in English (cf. Lyons, 1968). The same inflections that code tense in English, for example, "She swam" (in the past) and "She is swimming" (now), also code differences in aspect, such as the contrast between "She swam" (for some definite period of time, and finished swimming) versus "She was swimming" (for some definite period of time). In the adult language, the tense and aspect morphemes are used contrastively in these ways with the same verb stem (*swims, swimming, swam*), but they were not used contrastively by the children who were just learning verb inflection in the present study. Most verb stems occurred with only one or another morpheme.

While aspect can be coded by inflectional forms (inflectional aspect) or by the relations between verbs and adverbs (synthetic aspect), the events themselves that are named by verbs have inherent aspectual meaning (lexical aspect).[9] The inherent lexical aspect of verbs can be described intuitively in terms of whether the events named by verbs (1) do or do not last over time – durative events, (e.g., *sing, write*) versus momentary or nondurative events (e.g., *cough, find*) – and (2) do or do not involve an end result – noncompletive events (e.g., *sing*, which can go on indefinitely or be broken off at any point) versus completive events (e.g., *throw*, which has a definite end point). The terms durative–nondurative and completive–noncompletive are here borrowed from Friedrich (1974) but the same contrasts of verb aspect are frequently discussed in the literature (cf. Bronckart & Sinclair, 1973; Bull 1960; Comrie, 1976; Dowty, 1972; Lyons, 1968; Miller & Johnson-Laird, 1976; Ryle, 1949; Smith, 1978; Vendler, 1967; and Woisetschlaeger, 1976). The distinction between durative–noncompletive events and nondurative–completive events observed in the present study is similar to the distinctions made by Ryle and by Vendler between 'activities' and 'achievements,' and by Miller and Johnson-Laird between 'processes' and 'events.'

According to Friedrich, the oppositions stative–nonstative, durative–nondurative, and completive–noncompletive are the three basic features of aspect. It is precisely these distinctions that appeared to guide the emergence of the different inflectional forms in the children's speech. The stative–nonstative opposition was a superordinate prime; state verbs were inflected less often than action verbs (see Table 5.2), and the verbs that named internal nonshared states were rarely inflected. In contrast, the stative aspect identified by Friedrich (1974, p. 16) as "realization of the process referred to by the verb" (see also Lyons), was identified in those state (nonmovement) verbs that also occurred in the data as action (movement) verbs; these were inflected, for example, *sleeping, sitting,* and *broke.* The durative–nondurative opposition distinguished action verbs with *-s* and *-ing* from those with *-ed/irreg,* and the completive–noncompletive opposition distinguished action verbs with *-s* and *ed/irreg* from those with *-ing* (see Figure 5.3).

As pointed out by Dowty (1972) and others, synthetic aspect is the use of adverbs and devices of syntax and discourse to mark aspectual meaning. The children in our study had not yet begun to use synthetic aspect; neither did they appear to be using inflections to mark aspectual contrasts. Rather, the children's use of inflections to code aspect was essentially redundant in relation to the inherent lexical aspect of the verbs themselves. The use of inflections with different verbs had just begun in the third developmental period described in the present study and was no doubt preliminary to their contrastive use.

The importance of aspect in the acquisition of verb inflection was also observed by Bronckart and Sinclair (1973) in an experimental study of French verb forms by children between the ages of 2 years, 11 months, and 8 years, 7 months. Using toys, they presented children with enactments of actions that varied according to the type of result, frequency, and duration of action, and they asked the children to tell about the action. Examples were a horse jumps over a fence; a truck slowly pushes a car toward a garage; and a fish swims in a basin. Even though the children were asked to tell about the action after they saw it performed, the younger children used different verb forms for different kinds of action: "Actions that obtain a clear result are mostly described in the passé composé, actions without an intrinsic aim are described in the present or the passé composé, and actions that do not lead to any result are described in the present" (p. 125). Bronckart and Sinclair concluded that children use the French verb inflections to code aspect distinctions, and not tense, until about age 6. Similarly, both Harner (1981) and Smith (1978) reported experimental evidence to indicate that American English-speaking children are also strongly influenced by event aspect in the use of inflections until about 8 years of age.

In an observational study, Antinucci and Miller (1976) classified the verbs of children learning Italian and English according to whether they named 'end states' and then observed the distribution of past-tense morphemes; past tense in both languages was used first with 'end state' verbs. Although their methodology differed from ours, the results are essentially compatible with the study reported here and the experimental studies. However, Antinucci and Miller did not report the use of any inflections other than past tense. The children in the present study used the three inflections (-*ing, -s, irreg*) from the beginning and were clearly influenced by the aspectual contours of the actions rather than only their end states.

In an observational study of Turkish, Aksu (1978) reported several results that are consistent with the present study. For the three subjects that she studied in the age period of 21 to 30 months, inflections emerged at the same time for past tense *di,* present progressive *iyor,* and optative (intentional) *sin.* Moreover, these inflections were used selectively with verbs that differed according to their inherent aspectual meanings. The results of the present study, together with results reported by Aksu, Antinucci and Miller, Bronckart and Sinclair, Harner, and Smith, are consistent with the general principle of aspect before tense that has been offered for the analysis of verbs in the adult model by Woisetschlaeger (1976, p. 13: "The aspectual suffix is closer to the stem than the tense suffix"). Jakobson (1957/1971, p. 505) observed that in Russian, the shifting deictic forms of tense are suffixed to the stem of the verb, whereas the nonshifting forms of aspect "operate with the stem" directly. Differences among children learning languages that differ according to the linguistic devices used to code aspect and tense would be instructive in evaluating this principle developmentally. Where tense and aspect are coded differently, as in Russian and other Slavonic languages, the expectation is that aspect would be learned before tense. In this regard, according to Radulovic (1975), aspect is used early in Serbo-Croatian acquisition, and such distinctions as perfect–imperfect are acquired before tense is marked; this is consistent with the principle of aspect before tense.

The principle of aspect before tense is relative and not absolute in its application to development in the child language data. Although strongly influenced at the beginning by event-aspect, children are no doubt learning tense relations at the same time; they do not learn tense only after they learn aspect. Although the 2-year-olds in the present study did not appear to be using the inflectional morphemes as tense markers, it is probably not true that such learning would wait until age 6, as claimed by Bronckart and Sinclair. Experimental studies are quite circumscribed with respect to speaker–listener roles and the relations between event-time and speech-time. While supporting the principle of aspect before tense, their results appear to be an underestimation of how and when children learn to encode time. In fact, both Harner and Smith reported that older children began to encode tense reliably before the age of 5. The evidence that children are encoding tense would consist, in part, of (1) the occurrence of different inflections with the same verb (as had already begun to happen in the third developmental period described in the present study), and (2) inflection of auxiliary *be*. In this regard, Brown (1973) reported that past and present tense forms of *be* occurred at the same time (and after *-ing* had been acquired) at about 3 years of age in his longitudinal data. Similarly, the 3-year-olds that Harner observed were already using variants of *be* (both *is* and *was*) with *-ing*, primarily with durative–noncompletive actions.

The fact that children distinguish semantic categories of verb aspect is consistent with other distinctions that have been observed in the development of the verb system. The aspectual distinctions durative–nondurative and completive–noncompletive appear to be basic semantic components, along with action–state and locative–nonlocative, in the development of verb categories (see Bloom, 1978, 1981).

Learning Linguistic Rules

One final issue concerns the nature of the linguistic rules that children learn for verb inflection. There has been a general consensus that the acquisition of grammatical morphemes provides the best single example of rule learning in child language. There have been repeated demonstrations, since Berko (1958), that children can apply the appropriate inflections to novel (nonsense) words in appropriate contexts (e.g., *zib/zibbing*), with the conclusion that children are not learning inflected forms as separate lexical items.

Studies of inflectional processes in child language have been of several kinds. The present study, like those by Antinucci and Miller (1976) and Kuczaj (1977), is concerned with the earliest emergence of inflections in the speech of young children (Brown's Stages I–III). Both Brown (1973) and Cazden (1968) described the eventual acquisition of inflections by somewhat older children (Stages II–V), and their results were replicated in a cross-sectional study by de Villiers and de Villiers (1973). Berko (1958) studied even older children, ages 4 to 7 years, in an experimental paradigm to investigate children's ability to generalize inflectional forms to novel instances. What do these various studies of children, at various points in development, contribute to understanding how verb inflections are learned?

The results of the present study provide indirect evidence that bears on the question of rule learning. Most of the children's verbs occurred with only one variant, for example, *fit/fits, play/playing,* and *break/ broke.* The children might have learned *fit* and *fits,* or *play* and *playing,* as separate lexical items, just as they had to learn *break* and *broke* as two separate words. *Irreg* was the first ranked inflection (in extent of use; see Table 5.3). This result indicates a tendency toward word-by-word learning, especially when we compare the rank orders of emergence (in the present study) and acquisition (as reported elsewhere) of the same morphemes. The sequence of acquisition of morphemes reported by Brown (1973) and by de Villiers and de Villiers (1973) was the order in which the criterion of 90% use in required contexts was met, and the rank order they reported was *-ing, irreg, -ed, -s.* While they reported that *irreg* was the second-ranked morpheme in acquisition, *irreg* was ranked first in emergence in the present study. This may indicate that children learn inflected forms as separate lexical items when the inflections are emerging, before they are acquired.

Additional evidence indicates that the early use of inflections reflects lexical rather than grammatical learning. In a study of the same four children described here, Bloom, Miller, and Hood (1975, chap. 3) reported that the addition of inflections to verbs and nouns did not constrain the length of sentences. There was no difference in the frequency of two- and three-constituent sentences with and without inflections. In contrast, when the children added negative markers to the verb and attributive forms to NP constituents, they were significantly more likely to produce a two-constituent (reduced) sentence than a three-constituent sentence. Thus it appeared that there was no cognitive cost in the use of inflections, indicating that inflected forms were learned as lexical items.

What evidence would support the assumption that learning the inflections of the verb entailed learning a rule of grammar? Two potential sources of evidence were not yet manifest in the data described here. One would be encoding speech-time/event-time tense relations, regardless of verb aspect. The other would be the regularization of irregular forms, but the children in our study had not yet begun to regularize irregular forms (e.g., *goed, falled*). However, the fact that the different inflectional forms (with the exception of the synonymous forms *-ed/irreg*) emerged together in the children's speech (as also observed by Aksu) may indicate that the children had begun to learn a general rule for verb inflection, with variable probabilities for using the different inflections with one or another verb. Such variable rules for child language have been suggested by Bloom, Miller, and Hood (1973, chap. 3) and by Brown (1975). With development, the probability of using different inflections with one or another verb would change, as children learn to consider deictic information from the relations between event-time and speech-time to code tense.

To conclude, lexical and grammatical learning inform one another and are complementary rather than mutually exclusive processes. Learning verb inflection appears to be facilitated by the semantics of the verb and the syntax of sentences. If the aspect before tense interpretation of the early use of morphemes is correct, and inflection is initially redundant with the aspectual semantics of the verbs children learn, then it is necessary to consider the semantic organization of the verb system in child language, along with the semantics and syntax of the inflections themselves, in attempting to explain their acquisition.

NOTES

1 Woisetschlaeger (1976); Jakobson (1957/1971).
2 Antinucci & Miller (1976); Bronckart & Sinclair (1973); Brown (1973).
3 Weist, Wysocka, Witkowska-Stadnik, Buczowska, & Konieczna (1984).
4 Bloom & Harner (1989).
5 The locative constituent place in locative-action utterances was more specific than the locative case in Fillmore's (1968) case grammar, in which locative case "identifies the location or spatial orientation of the state or action identified by the verb." The locative constituent place in locative-action utterances in this study specified the goal of movement when some object or person located at one place is moved to another place. This is what Fillmore referred to, somewhat ambiguously, as "orientation." The aspect of Fillmore's locative case that identifies "the location . . . of the state or action" was represented in utterances in this study as the place in which the simple (nonlocative) action, such as *write, play, ride, build,* and *eat* occurred (e.g., "riding on the playground," "eating in the kitchen") rather than a place that was the goal of movement with such locative-action verbs as *put, go,* and *sit* (e.g., "riding to the playground," "going to the

store''). Developmentally, the adverbial (adjunct) place, in or on which a simple action occurred, was a later development and not observed in the children's speech until after locative-action utterances with place as the goal of movement were fully productive. They did not say such sentences as ''Those children doing there'' or ''Orange chair read a book'' until after such locative-action sentences as ''Put man block'' and ''Wrench go there.'' The same sequence of development with locative action before action-plus-place was reported for Italian children by Parisi (1974); also see Bloom, Lightbown, & Hood (1975, Chapter 2).

6 The sentence contexts presented here are intended to be descriptive of the semantic–syntactic relations between words in sentences, not prescriptive of word order. In fact, word order was most often canonical, as in ''Tape recorder goes in there'' but occasionally not, as in ''Here one fits.''

7 Utterances with contexts for unmarked verbs (e.g., *put, hurt, let go*) were not included in Table 5.2. These represented .01 or less of the utterances overall for the individual children, and less than .05 of the utterances in any category, with the following exceptions: .11 of agent–locative action for Eric and .05 of agent–locative action for Kathryn. In addition, ambiguous utterances – in which a context for one or another morpheme could not be determined – were excluded from the analysis; these represented less than .10 of the sample.

8 The individual observations of each child were also tested for equality of the distributions. For the first seven observations (Stages I and II), there were generally too few frequencies per cell to test reliably the distributions of inflections and contexts. For the remaining eight observations (Stage III), all the individual comparisons of the distributions were significantly different. Thus, grouping the data for statistical analysis was justified.

9 See Macaulay (1971) for a discussion of the historical importance of lexical aspect.

POSTSCRIPT

For studies of the acquisition of inflections and aspect marking since Bloom, Lifter, and Hafitz (1980):

Bamberg, M. (1987). *The acquisition of narratives: Learning to use language*. Berlin: Mouton de Gruyter.

Cziko, G., & Koda, K. (1987). A Japanese child's use of stative and punctual verbs. *Journal of Child Language, 14,* 99–111.

Fletcher, P. (1981). Description and explanation in the acquisition of verb-forms. *Journal of Child Language, 8,* 93–108.

Gathercole, V. (1986). The acquisition of the present perfect – Explaining differences in the speech of Scottish and American children. *Journal of Child Language, 13,* 537–60.

Gerhardt, J., & Savasir, I. (1986). The use of the simple present in the speech of two three-year-olds: Normativity not subjectivity. *Language in Society, 15*, 501–36.

Harner, L. (1982). Immediacy and certainty: Factors in understanding future reference. *Journal of Child Language, 9*, 115–24.

Johnson, C. (1985). The emergence of present perfect verb forms: Semantic influences on selective imitation. *Journal of Child Language, 12*, 325–52.

McShane, J., & Whittaker, S. (1988). The encoding of tense and aspect by three- to five-year-old children. *Journal of Experimental Child Psychology, 45*, 52–70.

Smith, C. (1980). The acquisition of time talk – Relations between child and adult grammars. *Journal of Child Language, 7*, 263–78.

Weist, R., Wysocka, H., Witkowska-Stadnik, K., Buczowska, E., & Konieczna, E. (1984). The defective tense hypothesis: On the emergence of tense and aspect in child Polish. *Journal of Child Language, 11*, 347–74.

Evidence has accumulated in many languages to show that children initially associate past tense with perfective aspect:

Aksu-Koc, A., & Slobin, D. (1985). The acquisition of Turkish. In D. Slobin (Ed.), *The crosslinguistic study of language acquisition* (vol. 1, pp. 839–78). Hillsdale, NJ: Erlbaum. (Turkish)

Antinucci, F., & Miller, R. (1976). How children talk about what happened. *Journal of Child Language, 3*, 167–89. (Italian and English)

Berman, R. (1985). The acquisition of Hebrew. In D. Slobin (Ed.), *The crosslinguistic study of language acquisition* (vol. 1, pp. 255–371). Hillsdale, NJ: Erlbaum. (Hebrew)

Bloom, L., & Harner, L. (1989). On the developmental contour of child language: A reply to Smith & Weist. *Journal of Child Language, 16*, 207–16. A reanalysis of the data in Weist, R., Wysocka, H., Witkowska-Stadnik, K., Buczowska, E., & Konieczna, E. (1984). The defective tense hypothesis: On the emergence of tense and aspect in child Polish. *Journal of Child Language, 11*, 347–74. (Polish)

Clark, E. (1985). The acquisition of Romance, with special reference to French. In D. Slobin (Ed.), *The crosslinguistic study of language acquisition* (vol. 1, pp. 687–782). Hillsdale, NJ: Erlbaum. (French)

de Lemos, C. (1981). Interactional processes in the child's construction of language. In W. Deutsch (Ed.), *The child's construction of language* (pp. 57–76). New York: Academic Press. (Portuguese)

Harner, L. (1981). Children talk about the time and aspect of actions. *Child Development, 52*, 498–506. (English)

Stephany, U. (1981). Verbal grammar in modern Greek early child language.

In P. Dale & D. Ingram (Eds.), *Child language: An international perspective* (pp. 45–57). Baltimore: University Park Press. (Greek)

For discussions of the acquisition of aspect–tense marking:

Bowerman, M. (1985). What shapes children's grammars? In D. Slobin (Ed.), *The crosslinguistic study of language acquisition* (vol. 2, pp. 1257–1319). Hillsdale, NJ: Erlbaum.

Cziko, G. (1989). Children's acquisition of verbs. *First Language, 9,* 1–31.

Lahey, M., Liebergott, J., Chesnick, M., Menyuk, P., & Adams, J. (1990). *Variability in the use of grammatical morphemes: Implications for understanding language impairment.* Manuscript submitted for publication.

Rispoli, M. (1990). Lexical assignability and perspective switch. The acquisition of verb subcategorization for aspectual inflections. *Journal of Child Language, 17,* 375–392.

Rispoli, M., & Bloom, L. (1985). Incomplete and continuing: Theoretical issues in the acquisition of tense and aspect. *Journal of Child Language, 12,* 471–4.

Slobin, D. (1985). Crosslinguistic evidence for the language-making capacity. In D. Slobin (Ed.), *The crosslinguistic study of language acquisition* (vol. 2, pp. 1157–1256). Hillsdale, NJ: Erlbaum.

Smith, C., & Weist, R. (1987). On the temporal contour of child language: A reply to Rispoli and Bloom. *Journal of Child Language, 14,* 387–92.

Van Valin, R. (in press). Functionalist linguistic theory and language acquisition. *First Language.*

For replication of the observation that early inflections occur primarily with high-frequency verbs:

Bates, E., Bretherton, I., & Snyder, L. (1988). *From first words to grammar: Individual differences and dissociable mechanisms.* Cambridge: Cambridge University Press.

6

Wh-Questions

"Where all the people go?"

The acquisition of *wh*-questions was studied in seven children's speech until mean length of utterance was 4.5 morphemes and they were 3 years old. The sequence in which these children learned to ask the forms of *wh*-questions with verbs was *what, where,* and *who* before *how, why,* and *when.* The same sequence, observed in other studies of both comprehension and expression, has often been attributed to development from concrete to abstract thought in cognitive development. The assumption has been that *what* and *where* questions are learned first because they are less abstract than *why* and *when* questions. In this study, however, other factors, which are primarily linguistic, were shown to covary with the sequence of acquisition and contribute to the cognitive requirements for learning *wh*-questions. The three kinds of linguistic constraints that differentiated among the question forms were (1) the syntactic functions of the *wh*-words, (2) the selection of verbs with the different question forms, and (3) the use of questions in discourse.

THE SYNTAX OF *WH*-QUESTION WORDS

The questions learned early in the sequence differed syntactically from those learned later. The first *wh*-words used with verbs were *what, where,* and *who,* and we described these as *wh*-pronominals that ask for the major sentence constituents they replace, usually verb arguments. Thus, the first questions learned were argument questions. In contrast, *how, why,* and *when,* which emerged later, are sentence adjuncts rather than the arguments of verbs. We described these later developing questions as *wh*-sententials with semantic scope that extends over the whole proposition expressed in the sentence. Finally, two other forms that occurred rarely and only at the end of the period, when the children were 3 years old, were the adjectival forms *which* and *whose.* The sequence of development, then, corresponded to syntactic differences among the questions.

THE VERBS IN *WH*-QUESTIONS

The earliest questions, with *what, where,* and *who,* occurred with the copula or a small group of pro-verbs, which were the children's most frequent verbs: *do, go,* and *happen.* Thus, just as the children learned inflections with pro-verbs, as described in Chapter 5, they also learned to ask questions initially with the copula and the pro-verbs. In contrast, the *wh*-questions acquired later in the sequence were more likely to occur with semantically more complex descriptive verbs like *sing, jump,* and *break.* The sequence of acquisition, then, also covaried with categories of verbs: the copula, pro-verbs, and descriptive verbs.

WH-QUESTIONS IN DISCOURSE

The discourse adjustments the children made were different for early and later appearing questions. *What, where,* and *who* showed a pattern of increasing verb ellipsis. In contrast, *how* and *why* questions presented a pattern of increasing expansion of utterance length with expression of verbs that were optional in the discourse context. The children's *wh*-questions were infrequently contingent on a prior utterance from someone else (see also Chapter 13). This meant that in general their questions were more likely than not to introduce the topic of discourse. However, *why* questions were more likely as a group to be linguistically contingent than were any other kind of question.

In sum, the children learned to ask *wh*-questions in a particular order, but in the context of learning the syntactic function of the *wh*-words, the syntax and semantics of verbs, and the requirements of discourse. Such linguistic factors as these, together with other conceptual and pragmatic factors, determined the cognitive requirements for learning to ask questions.

Wh-Questions: Linguistic Factors That Contribute to the Sequence of Acquisition

Lois Bloom, Susan Merkin, and Janet Wootten

The sequence in which children learn to ask and answer questions with *wh*-forms has been explained most often as resulting from constraints on abstract thought in cognitive development (e.g., Ervin-Tripp, 1970; Fahey, 1942; Smith, 1933; Tyack & Ingram, 1977). That is, the questions that are acquired late in the sequence, *why* and *when*, refer to more abstract, less tangible ideas than do *what* and *where* questions, which are learned first. However, recent studies of second language acquisition (e.g., Felix, 1976; Lightbown, 1978) have shown that older children learning to speak a second language acquire questions in the same developmental sequence as do children learning a first language at an earlier age. There are also experimental tests of children's comprehension of questions (Ervin-Tripp, 1970; Tyack & Ingram, 1977) in which transitive and intransitive verbs influenced comprehension differentially with different *wh*-words. In addition, then, to the relative abstractness of the meaning of the different *wh*-forms that may contribute to their developmental sequence, there are other important linguistic factors that operate as well.

In the present study, several sources of influence on how and when children learn to ask *wh*-questions were investigated. Progress in the development of language depends upon the integration of semantics, syntax, and pragmatics (discourse) and integration of these specifically linguistic factors with nonlinguistic conceptual factors more generally (Bloom, 1976; Bloom, Lahey, Hood, Lifter, & Fiess, 1980, chap. 7; Bloom, Miller, & Hood, 1975, chap. 3). Such an integrative model is extended here to a new linguistic form, *wh*-questions, because the only explanations for their acquisition that have been seriously offered consist of the reduction of linguistic development to a single dimension of thought (i.e., the trend from concrete to abstract thought), or to a single dimension of language structure (i.e., the sequential application of

Reprinted from *Child Development, 53,* 1982, 1084–92, with permission from The Society for Research in Child Development.

transformational rules of grammar) (Brown, 1968). Both no doubt influence the acquisition of *wh*-questions, but together with each other as well as with still other aspects of language that are learned concurrently. An ultimate explanation of language development will depend upon an understanding of how different aspects of language come together for the child in the process of its acquisition. Accordingly, for the purposes of the present study, it was hypothesized that the *wh*-forms learned later in the sequence of acquisition would differ from the *wh*-forms learned early in the sequence in their (1) syntactic function relative to the rest of the question, (2) use with verbs that were semantically more complex, and (3) use in different discourse environments. A demonstration that acquiring the forms and structures of language is not reducible simply to one or another dimension of thought or language ought to contribute to understanding processes of education and remediation as well as processes of development.

PROCEDURES

For each of the analyses reported here, the development of each of seven children (three girls and four boys) was examined separately in order to justify combining the data for a group result. Comparison of the results from the individual children assured their similarity to one another in their patterns of development, so that the data were combined with confidence. Given (1) the small number of subjects, (2) the variation among the subjects in frequency and duration of the observation sessions, and (3) the sometimes small number of question tokens per cell in one or another analysis, statistical determination of similarity among subjects would be specious. Where there were differences within the group, the individual trends are indicated. The data from seven children were combined on the basis of increase in average utterance length. For this purpose, mean length of utterance (MLU) was computed for each text from each child according to procedures modified from Brown (1973) and described in Bloom and Lahey (1978, p. 42). The texts were grouped into four MLU periods that corresponded, essentially, to the four MLU Stages II through V identified by Brown. The MLU ranged from 2.00 to 2.30 (mean = 2.14) in Period A, from 2.68 to 3.00 (mean = 2.83) in Period B, from 3.37 to 3.64 (mean = 3.45) in Period C, and from 3.68 to 5.03 (mean = 4.55) in Period D. These periods are not discrete; they simply provide a developmental index based on increasing utterance length that proved to be convenient for observing substantive changes in the acquisition of *wh*-questions.

The children asked a total of 7,877 *wh*-questions in the period from approximately 22 to 36 months of age. There were four major analyses performed on this corpus of questions. First, the relative frequencies of questions with different *wh*-words were observed, and their developmental sequence of acquisition was inferred from the average rank order of frequency in relation to average age of emergence for the seven children. Only the *wh*-forms that were used productively (with productivity defined as the use of at least three different questions with a particular *wh*-form) by at least five of the seven children were included in computing the rank order of emergence. In order to determine how the *wh*-questions learned early in the sequence differed from those learned later, the second analysis consisted of inspection of the questions to determine the syntactic function of the *wh*-question words, and the third analysis consisted of identifying the range and variation of verbs used with the different *wh*-question words.

Since the sequence of acquisition was found to covary with both syntactic and lexical (verb) factors, a fourth analysis was performed in order to explore the intersection of these factors with discourse. Three aspects of discourse were investigated: (1) the occurrence of ellipsis (i.e., the deletion of part or all of the question except the *wh*-word); (2) patterns of adjacency (i.e., questions occurring within approximately 30 sec of a prior utterance) and contingency (i.e., adjacent questions with a constituent or referent of a constituent that was shared with a prior adult utterance occurring within five previous turns in topic-related discourse); and (3) verb cohesion (i.e., the instances where the verb in a child question was the same verb as in the prior adult utterance). The criterion for contingency was based upon the results of an earlier study of the development of contingency relations in the children's discourse (Bloom, Rocissano, & Hood, 1976, chap. 13). The interobserver reliability of the interpretive discourse analysis was assessed in a random sample of 51 questions; the percent agreement was .92 for adjacency, .88 for contingency, and .92 for verb cohesion.

For each of these analyses except syntactic function, two populations of *wh*-questions were identified: One consisted of all of the child's questions, and the second population was the subset of only those questions that included a verb; 72% of the *wh*-questions included a verb. There were two kinds of questions without verbs: incomplete questions (e.g., "What that?") and elliptical questions (e.g., "Why?" or "What block'" in response to an utterance such as "Get the block").

RESULTS

Developmental Sequence

Two sequences of emergence were distinguished: a sequence for only the *wh*-questions that included verbs, and a sequence for all *wh*-questions with and without verbs. The order of acquisition of those questions that included verbs was *where* and *what* at average age 26 months, then *who* at average age 28 months, then *how* at average age 33 months, and *why* at average age 35 months. *Which, whose,* and *when* questions occurred rarely, even at age 36 months when the study ended. The order of emergence for the total population of all *wh*-questions was quite similar, except that *how* emerged before *who,* because *how* occurred without verbs (e.g., "How 'bout this?") several months before *how* appeared in questions with verbs. The only exception to the sequence of acquisition among the seven children was one child who learned *what* before *where;* the other children acquired *what* and *where* at the same time.

Syntactic Function of Wh-*Forms*

There were structural differences among the questions that were acquired sequentially. The first *wh*-forms that emerged with verbs, *what, where,* and *who,* are *wh*-pronominals that ask for the major sentence constituents that they replace. As such, they are relatively simple syntactically. For example, for the sentence "Peter ate a cookie," the *wh*-pronominals ask for the object constituent, *what* (cookie); the subject constituent, *who* (Peter); and the verb phrase constituent, *what do* (ate cookie). Similarly, for the sentence "That's a cookie," *what* asks for *cookie,* and for the sentences "The cookie's gone" or "The cookies are in the bag," *where* asks for *gone* or *bag.*

In contrast, *why, how,* and *when,* which emerged later, are *wh*-sententials that do not replace major sentence constituents but, rather, ask for information that pertains to the semantic relations among all the constituents in a sentence. For example, for the sentence "Peter ate a cookie," the *wh*-sententials ask for *why* (Peter ate the cookie), *how* (Peter ate the cookie), or *when* (Peter ate the cookie). The answers to the *wh*-sententials specify a reason, a manner, or the time that the entire event encoded in the sentence occurs. And finally, *which* and *whose* are adjectival forms that specify something about an object constituent (*which apple* or *whose car*). *Which* and *whose* were used rarely, and neither form was productive in questions with verbs for any child over the course of the study. The sequence in which the *wh*-forms were acquired, then, reflected the relative syntactic complexity among the different *wh*-forms. The pronominal forms *what, where,* and *who* were learned before the sentential forms *why, how,* and *when,* which were learned before the adjectival forms *which* and *whose.*

The *wh*-pronominals *what, where,* and *who* can function as constituents of the copula (the forms of *be,* i.e., *is, are,* etc.) to ask for the identities of objects, places, and persons as in such questions as "What's this?" "Where's the girl?" and "Who's that?" These identifying questions are different from those which ask for a sentence constituent of a main verb (e.g., "What's Peter eating?" or "Who breaked that?"). When *what* questions first appeared, they overwhelmingly functioned as identifying questions with the copula and only much later asked for the object constituents of main verbs. Similarly, the children's early *where* questions asked for the locations of absent objects and persons in copular questions and only later asked about locations of objects and persons in questions in which *where* pronominalized the place constituent of verbs such as *go* and *take.* When *who* questions, which were acquired later, first appeared, they asked for both identities and sentence constituents (both subject and object), although they asked for constituents more frequently. Thus, in Period A, *what* and *where* questions were almost always identifying questions; in Period B, *what, where,* and *who* questions also asked for sentence constituents.

Selective Distribution of Verbs with Wh-*Forms*

Along with questions with the contracted and uncontracted copula (forms of *be*), a small group of verbs, *do, go,* and *happen* were the most frequent verbs that the children used. They seemed to stand in for other more descriptive verbs such as *sing* or *fix* and as such functioned as general, all-purpose pro-verbs. For example, one can do many things, such as fix, stir, shake, turn, jump, and throw, and talk about them with *do,* without naming them specifically. Similarly, one can *go* to many places, in many ways (e.g., leave, ride, walk, run, swim, fly, etc.), and talk about it with *go.* The pro-verbs, then, are very general

Table 6.1. *Distribution of Descriptive Verbs and Pro-Verbs*
with Wh-*Questions*

	Pro-Verbs		Descriptive Verbs	
	Frequency	Proportion	Frequency	Proportion
Where	2,010	.94	131	.06
What	2,323	.85	397	.15
Who	165	.63	96	.37
How	69	.49	72	.51
Why	80	.25	238	.75
Which	10	.42	14	.58
When	4	.31	9	.69
Whose	7	.78	2	.22
Total	4,668	.83	959	.17

in reference: The pro-verb *do* can refer to activities in general, the pro-verb *go* can refer to locative actions in general, and *happen* can refer to completed actions or events in general. In contrast, other verbs are more narrow in reference: One can only *sing* or *draw* or *fix* a few things. Such verbs are also descriptive in that they specifically name activities, and, as a result, are more semantically complex than pro-verbs in that (1) they carry more information; (2) they involve more restrictions on the selection of other parts of the sentence (e.g., subject and object); and (3) they involve many more conditions for the appropriateness of their use (see Fillmore, 1971, for discussion of these factors of semantic complexity).

The *wh*-forms differed according to the frequencies with which they were used with either the semantically more complex descriptive verbs, or the more general copula and proverb forms: (1) *what, where,* and *who* questions, which accounted for approximately three-fourths of all the questions with verbs, occurred with the copula or with pro-verbs eight times out of 10; (2) *why* and *how* occurred most often with descriptive verbs (see Table 6.1).

The great majority of all *wh*-questions with verbs (.83) occurred with the small group of general, all-purpose pro-verbs (the copula, *do, go, happen*). However, the descriptive verbs that did occur were distributed selectively among the questions with different *wh*-forms. The *wh*-questions that were acquired later in the sequence were more likely to occur with descriptive verbs than with pro-verbs (except *whose,* which was infrequent). This was due only in part to the fact that the children learned more different descriptive verbs over time, since (1) all of the descriptive verbs that the children used in their questions were used in previous observation sessions in utterances that were not questions, and (2) developmentally, while the proportion of questions with descriptive verbs increased with *why* (from .55 to .78), there was less increase with *what* (from .09 to .23), no increase at all with *where* or *who,* and a decrease with *how* (from .65 to .46). More important, there was a strong relationship between the syntactic function of the individual *wh*-forms and the semantic complexity of the verbs used with each form. The pronominal *wh*-forms that asked for sentence constituents (*what, where, who*) occurred predominantly with pro-verbs, whereas the sentential *wh*-forms (*how, why, when*) tended to be used with descriptive verbs primarily. Thus, the order of acquisition of *wh*-forms and the kind and variety of verbs that occurred with the different *wh*-forms were covarying factors. In addition, each of the descriptive verbs that each child used tended to occur with only one of the *wh*-question forms. The proportion of verbs used exclusively with only one *wh*-form ranged from .65 to .94 for the seven children (mean = .774 and SD = .089).

In sum, the children learned to ask *wh*-questions with descriptive verbs with those *wh*-question forms that were acquired late in the developmental sequence. The verbs that the children used tended to be restricted in their occurrence to one of the *wh*-question forms.

Discourse Adjustments with Wh-*Questions*

The final analyses were concerned with the ways in which the children's *wh*-questions were related to preceding adult utterances in discourse contexts. Three kinds of discourse adjustments differentiated among the *wh*-questions with development: verb deletion, linguistic contingency with constituent relations shared with a prior utterance, and verb cohesion where the child question repeated a verb from a prior adult utterance.

Verb Deletion. Wh-questions without verbs accounted for .28 of the children's questions overall and were of two kinds: (1) incomplete questions in which a verb would be obligatory in the adult language but was not used in the child's utterance, for example, ''What that?'' or ''Where dog?'' and (2) elliptical questions in which a verb would

Table 6.2. *Elliptical Verb Deletion in Questions*

	Proportion of All Wh-Questions			
	Period A	Period B	Period C	Period D
Where	.01	.02	.07	.15
What	.03	.07	.19	.34
Who	.00	.04	.09	.15
How	np	.70	.51	.35
Why	np	.89	.74	.36

Note: np indicates *how* and *why* were not productive in Period A.

not be expected, for example, contingent questions such as "Why?" or "What?" or "What book?" in response to "Give me the book."

Across all *wh*-forms, incomplete questions in which an obligatory verb did not occur decreased over time as utterance length increased and as the children learned more of the formal requirements for asking questions. At the same time, as can be seen in Table 6.2, there was a gradual increase in the occurrence of elliptical questions without verbs, but only for *what, where,* and *who* (the earliest and most frequent questions the children asked). In contrast, the occurrence of *how* and *why* questions without verbs, where the verb was not obligatory, showed a decrease over time. The discourse adjustments that the children made then, with respect to whether a verb was expressed, were different for the different *wh*-forms; *what, where,* and *who* questions presented a pattern of increasing verb ellipsis or shortened utterance length; *how* and *why* questions presented a pattern of increasing expansion of utterance length with expression of nonobligatory verbs.

Linguistic Contingency. In order to further explore the selective occurrence of verbs with different *wh*-forms, a subset of the corpus of *wh*-questions with verbs was examined for evidence of contingency on previous adult utterances in the discourse context. This subset consisted of only those questions with verbs that were adjacent to a prior utterance in connected discourse, by virtue of occurring within approximately 30 sec of the prior utterance: 812 questions that represented 14.4% of the children's 5,627 questions with verbs. (The 3,719 questions with the copula and the *why don't* questions asked by one of the children, which appeared to function as a directive to act rather than

Table 6.3. *Frequency of Adjacent Questions and Adjacent Questions That Were Contingent*

| | Mean Questions per Hour | | | | | |
| | Period B (N = 259) | | Period C (N = 212) | | Period D (N = 341) | |
	Adja-cent	Contin-gent	Adja-cent	Contin-gent	Adja-cent	Contin-gent
Where	1.47	.46	.74	.19	2.14	.75
What	.90	.33	.89	.27	1.82	.64
Who	.28	.11	.21	.09	.45	.14
How	.60	.19	.36	.05	.75	.16
Why	.23	.06	.28	.13	1.07	.57

Note: There were no contingent questions in Period A.

as true *why* questions, were not included in this analysis. An adjacent utterance was considered contingent if it maintained the topic of conversation and shared any constituent, or the referent of a constituent, with a prior adult utterance that occurred within five previous turns in connected discourse. The following examples are typical of the children's contingent questions with verbs:

(1)   Adult: Let's see what I can *find*.
       Child: What can you *find*?

(2)   (Baby sister is crying)
       Adult: Let's go see why she's *crying*. Maybe we can get her to stop *crying*.
       Child (to baby):   Why are you *crying*?
       Adult: Why is she *crying*?
       Child: Why is this baby *crying*?

(3)   (Child and adult reading a story about swimming)
       Adult: Why are they not *coming*?
       Child: Why they not *coming* in the water?

Because of the substantial differences among the *wh*-questions in relative frequency and the fact that observation sessions with the different children varied in duration from 5 to 8 hours, adjacency and contingency were computed in terms of the average rate of adjacent questions and the average rate of linguistically contingent questions per hour. There were too few contingent questions in Period A for this

Table 6.4. *Proportion of Questions per Hour That Were Contingent*

	Mean Proportion of Adjacent Questions per Hour		
	Period B (N=259)	Period C (N=212)	Period D (N=341)
Where	.31	.26	.35
What	.37	.27	.35
Who	.39	.41	.30
How	.32	.15	.21
Why	.25	.47	.53

Note: There were no contingent questions in Period A.

analysis; the contingency of questions began in Period B and increased in frequency from Period B through Period D.

In terms of the rate of questions asked per hour, *what* and *where* questions were the most frequent questions and also presented the highest rates of adjacency and contingency, as seen in Table 6.3, averaged for the seven children. However, when considering the proportional rate of adjacent questions per hour that were contingent, *why* questions showed the highest proportion of linguistic contingency; *how* questions showed the lowest proportion of contingency; and only about one-third of the *what, where,* and *who* questions were contingent; see Table 6.4. In terms of the rate of questions asked per hour, then, given that a child asked any *wh*-question, it was most likely to be a *what* or *where* question, and given that a child asked a linguistically contingent question, it was still most likely to be a *what* or *where* question. But given that a child asked a *why* question, that question was more likely to be linguistically contingent than if the child were to ask any other kind of *wh*-question. Thus, *why* questions occurred most often with descriptive verbs and were also linguistically contingent more often than were questions with the other *wh*-forms. However, the relatively low frequency with which any of the *wh*-forms were contingent indicated that the children's questions, in general, were more likely to introduce the topic of discourse (the noncontingent questions) than to produce a question in response to what someone else said (see also Chapter 13).

Verb Cohesion. Because (1) *why* questions were proportionately more often contingent than the other *wh*-questions and also occurred most

Table 6.5. *Verb Cohesion: Repetition of Descriptive Verbs from Prior Adult Utterance*

	Proportion of Contingent Questions with Descriptive Verbs		
	Period B ($N = 87$)	Period C ($N = 139$)	Period D ($N = 280$)
Where	.12	.11	.33
What	.18	.20	.24
Who	.18	.21	.27
How	.20	.09	.17
Why	np	.42	.40

Note: np indicates *why* was not productive in Period B.

frequently with descriptive verbs, and (2) each of the descriptive verbs occurred infrequently, it was hypothesized that the source of descriptive verbs in the children's *why* questions might have been the prior adult utterances. All adjacent questions with descriptive verbs were examined for verb cohesion: the proportion of questions that repeated a verb from a prior adult utterance. When a verb was repeated, it was almost always an exact repetition (as in the examples of contingency), or else an inflected verb was repeated without its inflection.

The questions analyzed for verb cohesion were a subset of the questions analyzed for linguistic contingency, consistenting only of those adjacent, linguistically contingent questions that occurred with descriptive verbs ($N = 506$). The remaining questions ($N = 306$) that were also analyzed for linguistic contingency (reported in Tables 6.3 and 6.4) contained the pro-verbs *do, go,* and *happen.* The results reported in Table 6.5 should be interpreted with some caution, since in some cells only one or two of the children contributed to a group mean. For all of the question forms except *how,* there was an increase in the extent to which children made use of descriptive verbs from the adult discourse context. Further, *why* questions shared the adult verb more frequently than any other *wh*-question, but still only about .40 of the time. *How* questions, on the other hand, with the second most frequent use of descriptive verbs, displayed the least amount of verb cohesion with prior adult utterances in the last two MLU periods. Thus, verb cohesion was greatest with *why* questions, which were also most often linguistically contingent, indicating that the source of linguistic contingency was often the verb in the prior adult utterance.

DISCUSSION

The children in this study learned to ask *wh*-questions in the same developmental sequence – *what, where,* and *who* questions were learned before *why, how,* and *when* questions – as has been reported in previous studies of first language acquisition (e.g., Brown, 1968; Ervin-Tripp, 1970; Labov & Labov, 1976; Lewis, 1938; Smith, 1933) and second language acquisition (e.g., Felix, 1976; Lightbown, 1978). Cognitive complexity has been cited most often as the factor responsible for determining the sequence in which children learn *wh*-questions. However, the cognitive hypothesis as it has been presented so far in the literature has been concerned only with the polarity of concrete and abstract thought. As such, it is only a *post hoc* explanation that is, as yet, unsupported by independent evidence, and in fact, there is evidence to dispute it. First, children who learn a second language at age 5 or 6 acquire *wh*-questions in the same order as has been observed in first language learning (Lightbown, 1978). The capacity for relative abstract thought could not be the only factor that determines sequence of acquisition in a second language for a 5-year-old child who already has the conceptual ability to ask all of the same questions in the first language.

Of greater relevance to the present study, however, is the fact that the conceptual notions that are encoded by later appearing questions, time (*when*) and causality (*why*), were encoded reliably at an earlier age in other linguistic structures that these same children learned. Specifically, in the acquisition of complex sentences with syntactic connectives reported in Bloom, Lahey, Hood, Lifter, Fiess (1980, chap. 7), causally interpretable relations were encoded with *and, because,* and/or *so* before the children asked *why* questions, and temporal relations were encoded with *and then,* and *when* long before the children asked *when* questions. In fact, causal and temporal interclausal meaning relations and the syntactic connectives that encode them were among the most frequent meaning relations and connectives in the children's complex sentences, beginning at about 26 months of age. Thus, these children had begun to know temporal and causal semantic notions but not for the syntax of *wh*-questions; that is, a child can know something about semantics but still need to learn the particular syntax.

In the present study, a number of factors interacted with one another to determine the relative conceptual requirements of *wh*-questions and, as a result, their sequence of acquisition. At least three factors contributed to the linguistic complexity of *wh*-questions and helped to determine sequence of acquisition: the syntactic function of the individual *wh*-forms, the relative semantic complexity of different verbs, and contingency relations in discourse.

The earliest learned *wh*-question forms *(what, where, who)* were used overwhelmingly with the copula or the pro-verbs *do* and *go*. Since *what, where,* and *who* are *wh*-pronominals that stand for major sentence constituents, they could be combined with the copula and general pro-verbs such as *do* or *go* without the more complex semantic and syntactic requirements of more specific descriptive verbs. In contrast, *why, how,* and *when,* which were acquired later, are the *wh*-sententials that do not replace major sentence constituents; the scope of the meaning of these *wh*-forms was the sentence, and they were used with descriptive verbs primarily.

Descriptive verbs tended to be used only in one or a few different *wh*-questions, even though these same verbs were used more freely and productively in the children's nonquestion statements. The implication is that learning the meaning and syntax of individual verbs covaried with learning the meaning and syntax of the different *wh*-question forms.

The fact that descriptive verbs tended to occur infrequently, and only with one or another *wh*-question word, might have suggested that the children's questions were learned as routines. Certain of the children's early questions were most probably unanalyzed; that is, the *wh*-word was not separable from the rest of the question in the child's view (e.g., "What's that?" "What X doing?" "What happened?" "Where X go?"). If *why* and *how* questions were also being learned in routines in the same way, then one might expect that they too would occur with only a few descriptive verbs used with great frequency (as *do, happen,* and the copula were used with *what,* for example). But they did not, which was taken as evidence that *why* and *how* with descriptive verbs were not learned as routines in the same way as early questions with *what* and *where* might have been.

Another possibility was that there were many different, but infrequent, descriptive verbs with *why* and *how* because the children were repeating these verbs from prior adult utterances and thereby learning *why* and *how* with descriptive verbs in discourse routines. However, *why* and *how* differed from each other in their relation to prior adult utterances, so that the same explanation for the use of descriptive verbs would not apply to both. The children were learning to ask *why* questions with many descriptive verbs, in the context of contingency relations with the prior adult utterance, and they repeated the verb from the adult utterance about 40% of the time. However, a large number of descriptive verbs occurred with *how*, but *how* questions rarely repeated a prior verb, indicating that the children were not depending only upon the linguistic context for the source of their use of descriptive verbs. It appears, then, that shared verbs in discourse is only a part of the explanation of the differential occurrence of descriptive verbs with *wh*-forms. *Why* and *how* occurred most often with descriptive verbs but functioned differently in discourse: *Why* questions were responsive to topics initiated by someone else; that is, they were contingent; *how* questions introduced new topics.

In an earlier study of the development of discourse skills (Bloom, Rocissano, & Hood, 1976, chap. 13), linguistic contingency was observed to increase developmentally between 2 and 3 years of age, but linguistically contingent questions were a late development. In the present study, child questions were contingent less than half the time, and only the contingency of *why* questions increased developmentally. Thus, these children were most likely to ask a question with a topic of their own, and the ability to use the topic of a prior utterance for formulating a responsive question had only begun to develop during the time period of this study.

Several aspects of the results reported await further investigation of still other factors, most notably contextual and other pragmatic factors, that contributed to the sequence of development of the two groups of *wh*-questions: *what, where,* and *who* before *how, why,* and *when*. For example, it is not clear, from the present data, why *who* questions emerged later than *what* and *where* and why *when* questions emerged later than *how* and *why*. One possible explanation is the relative frequency of contextual events in which children would hear and have occasion to use *who* and *when* questions. For example, young children are usually in the company of familiar others. There are many more objects and places than persons they could ask about which might have contributed both to the late appearance of *who* and the fact that there were relatively fewer identifying questions with *who* than questions that asked for sentence constituents (compared with *what* and *where*).

To conclude, the results of the present study emphasize linguistic complexity and, in particular, the semantic–syntactic functions of verbs as major factors that contributed to the sequence of acquisition of *wh*-forms (see Bloom, 1981). Children learn to ask *wh*-questions in a particular order, but in the context of learning the syntactic function of *wh*-words, the syntax and semantics of verbs, and the requirements of discourse. Such linguistic factors as these, together with other conceptual and pragmatic factors, determine the cognitive requirements for learning *wh*-questions.

POSTSCRIPT

For studies of acquisition of different question types since Bloom, Merkin, and Wootten (1982):

Clancy, P. (1989). Form and function in the acquisition of Korean *wh*-questions. *Journal of Child Language, 16*, 323–47.

Erreich, A. (1984). Learning how to ask: Patterns of inversion in yes/no and *wh*-questions. *Journal of Child Language, 11*, 579–92.

Hsu, J., Cairns, H., & Bialo, N. (1987). When-questions – A study of how children linguistically encode temporal information. *Journal of Psycholinguistic Research, 16*, 241–55.

Klee, T. (1985). Role of inversion in children's question development. *Journal of Speech and Hearing Research, 28*, 225–32.

Lindholm, K. (1987). English question use in Spanish-speaking ESL children: Changes with English proficiency. *Research in the Teaching of English, 21*, 64–90.

Parnell, M., Amerman, J., & Harting, R. (1986). Responses of language-disordered children and *wh*-questions. *Language, Speech, and Hearing Services in the Schools, 17*, 95–106.

Parnell, M., Patterson, S., & Harding, M. (1984). Answers to *wh*-questions: A developmental study. *Journal of Speech and Hearing Research, 27*, 297–305.

Stromswold, K. (1988). Linguistic representations of children's *wh*-questions. In *Papers and Reports in Child Language*, Department of Linguistics, Stanford University.

For studies of the functions of *wh*-questions:

James, S., & Seebach, M. (1982). The pragmatic function of children's questions. *Journal of Speech and Hearing Research, 24*, 2–11.

Part II

Acquisition of Complex Sentences

Once children have learned something about simple sentences, they begin to combine the structures underlying their simple sentences to form complex sentences. Complex sentences, then, include two verbs. In the first of these studies, in Chapter 7, sentences with syntactic connectives were studied to determine how children acquire the connectives for meaning relations between clauses. With all complex sentences considered together, whether or not connectives were expressed, complementation and conjunction were the earliest and most frequent structures the children learned. In the next four chapters, the children's acquisition of these two structures is explored more fully. The details of the acquisition of complementation are presented in Chapters 8 and 9. In these two studies, in particular, we see that verbs continued to be central for acquisition of complex sentences, as they were for the acquisition of simple sentences, inflections, and *wh*-questions. The acquisition of expression of causality, one meaning of conjunction in complex sentences, is described in Chapters 10 and 11.

7

Connectives and Clausal Meaning Relations

"And he look out a window and say 'Hello'."

The development of complex sentences begins between 2 and 3 years of age as children acquire syntactic connectives and learn to express different meaning relations between clauses. This study of the emergence of complex sentences with syntactic connectives spanned the developmental period in mean length of utterance from 2.0 to 4.2 morphemes. The principal results of the study pertained to sequence of acquisition and discourse cohesion.

SEQUENCE OF ACQUISITION

The first syntactic connective the children learned, *and,* was also the most general. *And* was used to express conjunction with all the different conjunction meaning relations: additive, temporal, causal, and adversative. The other, semantically more specific connectives were learned subsequently with these different categories of meaning relations. For example, *and then* and *when* were learned with temporal relations and *because* and *so* with causal relations – another instance of learning new forms for old functions. The earliest connectives learned were those that did not also have nonconnective functions: *and, then,* and *because.* The connectives that were homonymous, *what, where,* and *that,* were learned later. *What* and *where* were acquired as connectives only after they had been acquired in their nonconnective contexts as *wh*-questions (see Chapter 9) and *that* was acquired long after its use as a determiner and demonstrative pronoun. *And* was the first connective acquired by all the children, but the children differed in the order of acquisition for the remaining connectives. The structures of complex sentences with connectives were acquired in the order conjunction < complementation < relativization. Complementation with connectives and relativization were learned after conjunction, in part because both required pronominalization with *wh-* or *that* connectives, which were homonymous forms.

Whereas the order of emergence of the connectives was variable among the children (except for *and*), the children were consistent in the sequence with which they acquired the meaning relations they expressed in complex sentences. The consistency in acquisition of meaning relations with variation in the order of connectives echoed the pattern in simple sentences: consistency among children in acquiring content and variation in acquisition of form (Chapter 2). The conjunction meaning relations were acquired in the order additive < temporal < causal < adversative. Cumulative semantic complexity explained this sequence of conjunction meanings: Temporal relations were also additive; causal relations were both additive and temporal; and adversative relations were also additive, temporal, and often causal. In sum, in the development of complex sentences the children first juxtaposed two simple sentences without a connective, then joined two clauses with the general connective *and*, and then joined clauses with the cumulative semantic meanings additive > temporal > causal > adversative and their explicit connectives.

Finally, the children differed in the onset and rate of their acquisition of complex sentences. Ages of acquisition were highly variable among the individual children, whether rank order of acquisition was consistent among them (as with the clausal meaning relations) or not consistent (as with the different connectives).

DISCOURSE COHESION

Three patterns of cohesion were identified for the connection of clauses in discourse. The syntactic connective was always part of the child utterance, but the clauses they connected sometimes crossed utterance boundaries within and between speaker turns. When the child spoke both clauses, either within one utterance or across two consecutive child utterances, the cohesion was child–child. When the clauses before and after the connective occurred across two or more different speaker turns, the cohesion was either adult–child or child–adult–child. The only meaning relations with cohesion that involved an adult utterance more than 20% of the time were causality and adversative conjunction. All the other complex sentences occurred with child–child cohesion at least 90% of the time, on the average. These results mean that the children did not learn complex sentences by connecting their own utterance to a prior adult utterance to form the two clauses of a complex sentence.

The research in this chapter led to the succeeding studies of the acquisition of complex sentences that follow. Two studies of complementation are reported in Chapters 8 and 9, and two studies of expressions of causality are presented in Chapters 10 and 11.

Complex Sentences: Acquisition of Syntactic Connectives and the Semantic Relations They Encode

Lois Bloom, Margaret Lahey, Lois Hood, Karin Lifter, and Kathleen Fiess

INTRODUCTION

Children begin to combine simple sentences to form complex sentences in the period from 2 to 3 years of age, and development of complex sentences involves learning aspects of form (syntactic connectives and syntactic structures); content (semantic relations between propositions); and use (discourse cohesion). The focus of the study reported here was on the acquisition of connective forms in complex sentences that theoretically combine the structures that underlie two simple sentences.[1] Previous studies of the development of complex sentences have dealt most often with the forms of complex sentences (e.g., Limber, 1973; Menyuk, 1969). Few studies (e.g., Clancy, Jacobsen, & Silva, 1976; Clark, 1970) have dealt with the intersection of linguistic form with semantic content, and none has considered the intersection of linguistic form with content and use in discourse. Further, most studies have described the language of children older than 3 years of age, who already have considerable knowledge of complex sentences (e.g., Bates, 1976; Clark, 1970, 1973a; de Villiers, Tager-Flusberg, & Hakuta, 1977; Ferreiro & Sinclair, 1971; and Lust, 1976). The present study is concerned with the developmental interactions between connective forms and meaning relations and between these form–content interactions and the discourse environments in which they occurred.

METHODS

The data base consisted of five observations of Eric, five of Gia, five of Kathryn, and seven of Peter, beginning with the first observation at

Reprinted from the *Journal of Child Language*, 7, 1980, 235–61, with permission from Cambridge University Press.

Table 7.1. *Summary Description of Speech Samples*[a]

| Child | Age Range (months, weeks) | Mean Length of Utterance | | |
		Range	Mean Increment	S.D.
Eric	25,1–36,0	2.63–3.49	.22	.58
Gia	25,2–34,2	2.30–3.71	.47	.55
Kathryn	24,2–35,1	2.83–4.23	.35	.40
Peter	25,3–38,0	2.00–3.57	.22	.53

[a]The mean increment and the standard deviation were included in this table to indicate the variability of MLU in this development period.

which connectives were produced and using approximately every other observation until the child's third birthday. Information about the children's age and mean length of utterance (MLU) in these observations is presented in Table 7.1. The total number of utterances in these observations was 15,713 for Eric, 20,443 for Gia, 20,025 for Kathryn, and 19,024 for Peter.

All child utterances that contained conjunctions, relative pronouns, and *wh*-pronouns provided the corpus for analysis. Sentence relations that extended cohesion across utterance boundaries (either in the same speaker turn, for example, "# I carry this / and you carry that #," or in two or more turns of different speakers, for example, "# Your Mommy gave you a bottle? # yes # why? # because I'm a little baby #"), were included in the analysis if the child used a connective form (/ indicates utterance boundary; # indicates turn boundary). All the speech events were examined and coded according to their (1) connective forms, (2) semantic relations, (3) syntactic structures, and (4) cohesion relations between connected clauses.

The procedures for identifying the connective forms and the discourse environments for cohesion relations were relatively straightforward because they depended upon identifying formal regularities in the data; that is, whether or not one or another connective was said and whether or not two connected clauses extended across utterance boundaries. On the other hand, the identification of semantic relations between clauses was an interpretive process. Interpretation was centered on the question, What is the meaning of two clauses in relation to each other, given

(1)   The meaning of a first clause,
        /maybe you can bend the man –
(2)   the meaning of the second clause,
        – he can sit /
(3)   the fact that the two clauses are connected by *so* in the sentence /
        maybe you can bend the man *so* he can sit /
(4)   the fact that the child was trying to bend a wire figure and subsequently put it on a train car.

This process of interpreting the semantic relations between clauses in complex sentences is a continuation of the procedures used in earlier studies of the semantic relations between words in children's simple sentences. In earlier child language data, when MLU progresses from 1.0 to 2.0, the semantic relations between words in simple sentences can be inferred from information in the situational context. For example, "Mommy pigtail," in which Mommy is combing the child's hair, can be interpreted as the semantic relation agent–object. The categories of semantic relations in early sentences, such as recurrence, possession, agent–object, and action–object (described in Bloom, 1970; Brown, 1973; Schlesinger 1971b) were derived from the child language data in this way, on the basis of inferences from contextual cues, rather than being imposed upon the child language data on the basis of inferences from the adult model. Similarly, the semantic relations between connected clauses in complex sentences were interpreted, in the later child language data described in this study, on the basis of the relation between what was said and the situational context in which utterances occurred, rather than according to the forms the children used (i.e., connectives or verbs) and their meanings in adult speech. Although certain semantic relations were expected in the data, for example, causality and temporal relations – in part because the children were using such connectives as *because* and *and then* – the meanings of these connectives were not always transparent. The meanings of the semantically more general connectives, that is, *and, that,* and *what,* were even less transparent. After repeated passes through the data, certain meaning relations between clauses emerged as being more consistent and developmentally relevant than others, and these categories of meaning relations form the major results of this study.

Two methodological issues bear on the results reported here: ambiguity and/or equivocal interpretation, and subcategorization. The first issue, ambiguity and/or equivocal interpretation was perhaps the most problematic. The procedures for interpretation followed a general rule of cumulative semantic complexity (after Brown, 1973): If an utterance (A) contained the same relation as another utterance (B) plus something more, then the utterance (A) was interpreted in terms of that something more. For example, the utterance "You push up and it turn" was said as the child played with a toy with parts that could both be pushed up and turned. Only a dependency relation that was temporal between the clauses "you push up" and "it turn" could be inferred with confidence; that is, pushing was neither necessary nor sufficient for turning, and so the utterance was categorized as temporal rather than causal. In the utterance "Maybe you can bend him so he can sit," there was a temporal relation between the clauses plus something more, a causal dependency relation; that is, the man could not sit unless he was bent. The utterance was categorized as causal rather than temporal, based upon the cumulative principle.

Ultimately, the reliability of judgments of interpretation was decided by consensus. Once the final semantic categorization was obtained (the eight semantic relations reported below), the reliability of coding was tested as follows: A sample of 100 utterances was drawn from each of two observations from each of the individual children and coded independently by three of the investigators. The proportions of agreement between independent codings ranged between .80 and .90.

The issue of subcategorization had to do with the fact that several categories of semantic relations were not themselves homogeneous. Even finer distinctions were observed in addition to the major meanings that formed the results of this study. Several of these subcategorizations are described in separate studies. For example, causal utterances expressed both cause–effect and effect–cause orders (as described in Hood & Bloom, 1979, chap. 10). The relations in causal utterances could also be described as either objective or subjective (Bloom & Capatides, 1987, chap. 11). With other subcategorizations, procedures for coding have not yet been worked out. For example, temporally related clauses were either simultaneous or sequential or some overlapping combination of the two, but these distinctions could not always be reliably determined. Still other subcategorizations either occurred too infrequently to be considered important or showed no developmental change.

Given these two qualifications on the interpretation of meaning relations (ambiguity and/or equivocal interpretation, and subcategorization) it was possible to identify the major semantic relations between clauses in an average of .87 of the children's complex sentences. The semantic relations that were either anomalous or otherwise uninterpretable made up the remaining .13 of the data (range .08 to .18 for the several observations of the four children).

In order to establish that a form (i.e., a connective or syntactic structure) or a meaning relation or a connective–meaning relation interaction was acquired, a criterion of productivity was set in advance: The occurrence of five or more different utterances in each of at least two successive observations of a particular child was counted as evidence of productivity for the child (see Bloom, Lightbown, & Hood, 1975, chap. 2; and Bloom & Lahey, 1978, for discussions of productivity and criterion-referenced descriptions of language acquisition, respectively).

RESULTS

Connective forms were used primarily in three different ways. First, nonconnective use involved the use of certain homonymous forms, such as *what, where, that,* and *like* in nonconnective contexts, such as "What doing, where doggie, that my shoe," and "like this." Such homonymous forms have both connective and nonconnective uses. They were learned first in their nonconnective contexts, and with the exception of *what,* they were the last forms to be used as connectives. In contrast, other connective forms, such as *and, then,* and *because,* were nonhomonymous and were the first forms used as connectives.

Second, contextual use involved the use of *and* to chain a child utterance to a nonlinguistic event that was either something the child did or saw in the context, for example:

(1)   K IV
        (K had opened a box of fig-
        ures and taken them out; pick-
        ing up box of furniture)   *and* let's see dis.

(2)   E VI
        (E picks up puppet, puts it in
        box with other puppets)   *and* I close them.

The third use of connectives was the focus of the present study: the use of syntactic connectives to either connect two constituents within a sentence phrase (phrasal structures) or to connect two related clauses (sentential structures). Most frequently, the constituents in phrasal structures were the noun phrase of the predicate complement, for example:

(3)   G VIII
(Mother and Lois talking
about redecoration in Gia's
home)   and Mommy's gonna get me
chair *and* table.

The use of *and* in sentence subject phrases was relatively rare, for example:

(4)   G VII
(telling Lois about yesterday's
visit to Grandma's)   Uncle Paul *and* Grandma no
there.

The distribution of contextual, syntactic, and other[2] uses of connectives is presented in Table 7.2. The children began to use contextual *and* and syntactic *and* at the same time, except for Kathryn who used contextual *and* before using connectives syntactically. The syntactic use of connectives in phrasal and sentential structures is described in the results that follow.

Syntactic Connectives

The connective forms (conjunctions, *wh*-pronouns, and relative pronouns) used most frequently by the four children combined were *and*, *because*, *what*, *when*, and *so*; the less frequently used connective forms were *and then*, *but*, *if*, *that*, and *where* (see Hood, Lahey, Lifter, & Bloom, 1978). The sequence in which the connectives became productive for each child individually is presented in Figure 7.1, according to age. The developmental sequence was rank ordered for each child. When two or more connectives became productive in the same sample, ranks were determined according to proportional use, and the ranks were split if a difference in proportion was $\leq .05$. The rank orders were averaged across the four children, for only those connectives that were used productively for at least two of the children. The average rank order is plotted in Figure 7.2 in relation to average age of connective productivity,[3] with indication of the range in age of emergence among the children. When a connective was not productive for a child, although it occurred, that connective was assigned a later rank than the forms that were productive for that child. Spearman rank-order correlations

Table 7.2. *The Frequency of Structures with Connective Forms*

Child and Time	Age (months, weeks)	Total Number and Proportion of Utterances	Proportion of Utterances with Connectives		
			Syn-tactic	Con-textual	Other
Eric					
V	25,1	9 (.003)	.22[a]	.44[a]	.33[a]
VI	26,3	169 (.046)	.57	.17	.27
VIII	29,3	296 (.12)	.54	.19	.26
X	33,0	234 (.11)	.66	.21	.13
XII	36,0	361 (.10)	.65	.14	.20
Gia					
V	25,2	20 (.007)	.80	—	.20[a]
VI	27,1	122 (.04)	.52	.02[a]	.46
VII	28,2	76 (.04)	.63	.02[a]	.35
VIII	30,0	224 (.05)	.71	.06	.23
XI	34,2	347 (.08)	.66	.10	.24
Kathryn					
III	24,2	7 (.002)	—	1.0	—
IV	26,1	69 (.02)	.71	.10	.19
VI	29,1	181 (.06)	.78	.13	.09
VIII	32,1	213 (.08)	.90	.01[a]	.08
X	35,1	615 (.12)	.73	.06	.20
Peter					
X	27,0	60 (.02)	.53	.07[a]	.40
XII	28,2	33 (.01)	.42	—	.58
XIV	30,0	86 (.04)	.65	.10	.24
XVI	31,2	94 (.04)	.65	.09	.27
XVIII	33,3	128 (.05)	.72	.05	.23
XIX	35,0	338 (.14)	.61	.10	.29
XX	38,0	234 (.10)	.77	.03	.21

[a] = nonproductive.

were computed by comparing the rank orders of connective emergence for all combinations of pairs for the four children. Of the six correlation coefficients computed (range .45 to .84), only one comparison was significant, which confirmed the variation among the children in the rank order of emergence seen in Figure 7.1. For example, *then* was productive early for Kathryn and Gia and never became productive for Eric and Peter; *where* was productive early for Kathryn, late for Eric, and never became productive for Gia and Peter; *what* became productive very early for Peter and later for the other children. Thus, the

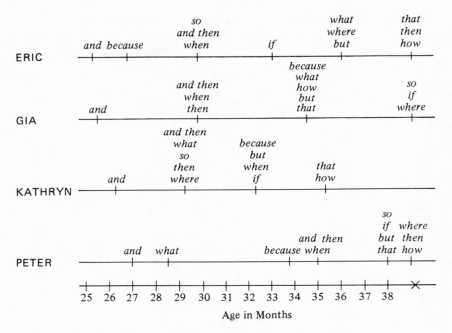

Figure 7.1. Sequence of emergence of syntactic connectives for individual children. (Those connectives listed above the X were not productive within the age period studied.)

graph in Figure 7.2 is intended only as a general summary measure of average rank order and average age of emergence of connectives. There was considerably more variation in age of emergence than in rank order. *And* was the first connective to emerge, and the remaining connectives, by and large, emerged subsequently, although at different ages for different children.

Semantic Relations

Eight major meaning relations were observed;[4] these are described below, with examples.

Additive. In additive relations, two events and/or states were joined without an added dependency relation between them. Each clause was meaningful by itself; the combination of the two clauses did not create a meaning that was anything other than the meaning of each clause

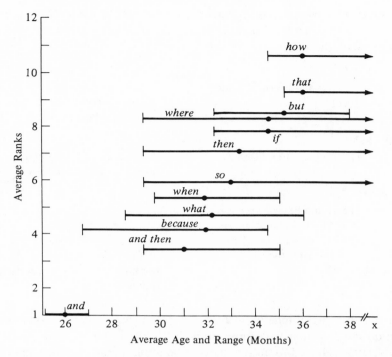

Figure 7.2. Developmental rank order of connective forms. (X on the abscissa indicates the expectation that the connective became productive for the remaining child(ren) eventually, although not within the time span of the study reported here.)

separately. Additive relations were expressed when the child carried out successive actions and chained each clause with each action.

(5) K VI
     Lois: Can you carry this for
     me very carefully?   maybe you can carry that *and*
                                           I can carry this.

(6) E VIII
     (looking at picture in book)   They're taking a vacuum
                                           cleaner to wipe *and* puppy
                                           dog's running.

Temporal. In a temporal relation there was a dependency between events and/or states which involved temporal sequence or simultaneity. The utterance was not chained to successive actions, as could be the case in additive sentences; that is, at least one of the events was not concurrent with the utterance.

(7)   K IV
(talking about visit to friend,
Jocelyn)   Jocelyn's going home *and* take her sweater off.

(8)   K VI
(pushing car to hall)   I going this way to get the groceries *then* come back.

(9)   P XX
(Peter and Patsy looking for
blue block; Patsy suggests
that it's under Peter; Peter
looks; it isn't there)   it's not anywhere/you better look for it/*when* you get back home.

Causal. In a causal relation there was a dependency between two events and/or states which was most often intentional and/or motivational. One clause referred to an intended or ongoing action or state, and the other clause gave a reason or result (see Bloom & Capatides, 1987, Chapter 11; Hood & Bloom, 1979, chap. 10).

(10)   K VI
(giving bendable man to Lois)   maybe you can bend him *so* he can sit.

(11)   E VIII
(going toward disks)   get them *cause* I want it.

(12)   P XX
(telling about a friend who
hurt her foot)   She put a band aid on her shoe *and* it maked it feel better.

Adversative. In this category the relation between two events and/or states was one of contrast. Most often the relation between the clauses was one of opposition, in which one clause negated or opposed the other, or of exception, in which one clause qualified or limited the other.

(13)   P XVIII
(trying to get trunk part in
car)   it can't.

(trying to fit hood part which
fits)   *and* this can go here.

(14)   K X
(telling and demonstrating
how she sleeps on the sofa)   cause I was tired/*but* now I'm
not tired.

Object Specification. In this category the two clauses combined described an object or person mentioned in the first clause. The most common descriptions of the object or person concerned function, place, or activity.

(15)   G XI
(Gia using toy telephone)
Mommy: Who'd you call?   the man *who* fixes the door.

(16)   K X
(K comes into room with fishing pole)
Lois: What's that?   it looks like a fishing thing
and you fish with it.

Epistemic. The dependency relation in utterances in this category involved certainty or uncertainty on the part of the person named in the first clause (the child most often) about a particular state of affairs named in the second clause.

similar to subjunctive?

(17)   E XII
(playing with family figures)
Lois: What do you think this
baby's name is?   I don't know *what* her name
is.

(18)   K VI
(referring to living room of
dollhouse)   I think *that* that's where the
baby will go.

Notice. Utterances in this category called attention to a state or event named in the second clause.

Table 7.3. *Proportional Distribution of Utterances in the Categories of Clausal Meaning Relations*

Category	Subjects and Samples									
	E V	E IV	E VIII	E X	E XII	G V	G VI	G VII	G VIII	G XI
Additive	np[a]	.57	.50	.44	.34	1.00	.81	.60	.41	.26
Temporal	—	.21	.19	.08	.05	—	.13	.23	.36	.23
Causal	—	.13	.17	.30	.36	—	np	.08	.14	.27
Adversative	—	np	.05	.05	.06	—	—	np	np	.03
Manner specification	—	—	np	—	np	—	—	—	—	np
Object specification	np	.05	.06	.06	.06	—	np	.05	.03	.7
Epistemic	—	—	.03	.06	.12	—	—	—	.04	.05
Notice	—	—	—	—	np	—	—	—	—	.05
Other complement	—	—	—	np	np	—	—	—	—	.02
Total	2	96	161	155	234	16	64	111	160	229

[a]np = nonproductive; — = relation did not occur.

(19)   K X
         (putting finger puppet on her
         toe)   watch *what* I'm doing.

(20)   G XI
         (showing Lois some candy)   look *what* my Mommy got
                                                          me.

Other. These were complements, other than epistemic and notice complements, with verbs of communication or the copula primarily.

(21)   K VIII
         (after showing Lois how to
         turn and fall)   that *what* you can do.

(22)   E XII
         (Eric had just awakened,
         when Lois entered room)   tell Iris *that* I wet my bed.

The relative frequency of these semantic relations at each observation is presented in Table 7.3 for the individual children. The sequence of emergence of the meaning relations is plotted for each child individually, according to age, in Figure 7.3. The sequence in which the meaning relations first became productive was rank ordered for each child. When more than one relation was productive within a sample, rank order was decided according to relative proportion, and ranks were split if a difference in proportion was <.05. The average order

Subjects and Samples											
K IV	K VI	K VIII	K X	P VIII	P X	P XII	P XIV	P XVI	P XVIII	P XIX	P XX
.80	.43	.23	.17	np	.78	.43	.80	.43	.60	.47	.22
.16	.23	.17	.13	—	np	—	np	.20	.08	.17	.10
—	.16	.43	.40	—	—	—	np	.11	.22	.19	.29
np	.04	.05	.17	—	—	—	—	np	np	.06	.03
—	—	np	np	—	—	—	—	np	—	np	np
np	.06	.09	.05	—	np	np	—	np	—	np	.04
—	.04	np	.02	—	—	.50	.11	.18	np	.08	.28
—	.05	np	.04	—	—	—	—	—	np	np	np
—	—	np	np	—	—	—	—	—	—	—	np
49	142	192	450	2	32	14	56	61	92	206	179

of acquisition for the four children was determined by averaging the individual rank orders for those categories that were productive for at least two of the children. This average rank order is plotted in Figure 7.4 in relation to average age,[5] with indication of the range in age of emergence among the four children.

Although the acquisition order was based on the meaning relations that became productive for at least two of the children, all the meaning relations were observed (although they were not necessarily productive) in the speech samples for each child. When a category of relations was not productive for a child, that category was assigned a later rank than the productive categories for that child. Spearman rank-order correlations were computed by comparing the rank order of emergence for all combinations of pairs for the four children. Six correlation coefficients were computed; they ranged from .75 to .95, with $p < .05$ for four of the six comparisons. The largest differences occurred in the rank order of the epistemic relation; it emerged much earlier for Peter than for the other children. With epistemic eliminated from the rank order, pairwise comparisons yielded correlation coefficients ranging from .87 to .95, with $p < .05$ for all six comparisons. Thus the children were quite similar to one another in terms of order of emergence of the meaning relations, although the meaning relations emerged at different ages for the different children. Thus, the meaning relations were acquired sequentially over the course of 10 months, with far more similarity in rank order of meaning relations than in rank order of connectives.

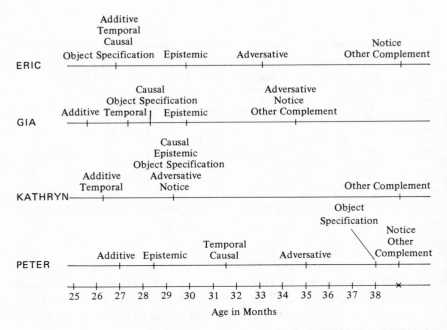

Figure 7.3. Sequence of emergence of semantic relations for individual children. (Those connectives listed above the X were not productive within the age period studied.)

Intersection of Connectives and Semantic Relations

Eight meaning relations were expressed with the 12 connectives that were productive in these complex sentences. Although it was statistically possible to have 96 intersections of content (the meaning relations between clauses) with form (the syntactic connectives used to connect clauses), only 45 intersections actually appeared in the data. However, only 10 of these intersections were productive for at least three of the children, and 15 were productive for at least two of the children. Two of the connectives, *where* and *how,* were productive overall but did not become productive with particular meaning relations.

The development of the intersection of connectives with semantic relations is presented in Figure 7.5. The average ages of emergence of the connectives are displayed along the horizontal axis. The X indicates the average age of the intersection of a connective with a mean-

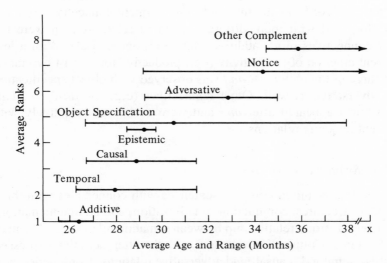

Figure 7.4. Developmental rank order of semantic relations. (X on the abscissa indicates the expectation that the meaning relation became productive for the remaining child(ren) eventually, although not within the time span of the study reported here.

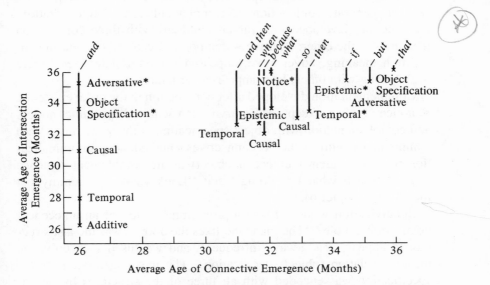

Figure 7.5. The development of the intersection of connectives with semantic relations. (*Where* and *how* did not become productive with any semantic relations. *Intersections that were productive for only two out of the four children.

ing relation. *And* was the first and most frequent connective used and was also used with more different meaning relations than were the other connectives (e.g., additive, temporal, and causal). With a less stringent criterion of productivity (i.e., productive for at least two rather than three of the children), *and* was observed with object specification and adversative as well. Other connectives (e.g., *because, so, but, when,* etc.) appeared after *and* and were each used selectively with different meaning relations.

Syntactic Structures

The children acquired complex sentences with connectives with three syntactic structures: conjunction, relativization, and complementation. There was a strong relationship between semantic relations and syntactic structures. Conjunction was used with the utterances that expressed additive, temporal, causal, and adversative relations. Conjunction was also used occasionally to express object specification. Complementation was used with utterances that expressed epistemic and notice relations and occasionally for object specification. Relativization was used only to express object specification. The sequence of acquisition was, in general, conjunction < complementation < relativization. Conjunction developed first for all children, with three conjunction meanings in the order: additive < temporal < causal. The fourth conjunction meaning, adversative, appeared 4 months later (see Figure 7.4),[6] along with other, later-appearing structures.

Complementation developed after conjunction in the order epistemic < notice < other, except for Kathryn, who acquired epistemic, notice, and complementation with object specification at the same time. Verb complements with syntactic connectives entailed *wh*-pronominalization of a constituent (subject or object) in the complement sentence (e.g., "Watch what I'm doing" and "Look what my mommy got me") (see Chapter 9).

Relativization with *that* or *wh*-pronominalization of an antecedent noun, for example, "The man who fixes the door," was the last structure to appear, was always infrequent, and was used with only one meaning relation (object specification). The meaning relation object specification was encoded with all three of the structures by one or another of the four children: Gia and Peter used only relativization; Eric used conjunction first and then relativization; Kathryn used all three in the order complementation < relativization < conjunction.

Table 7.4. *Frequency of Sentential Structures in the Semantic Relations of Conjunction*

Child and Time	Additive		Temporal		Causal		Adversative	
	N	P	N	P	N	P	N	P
Eric								
VI	55	.36	20	.35	12	.83	np[a]	—
VIII	80	.63	30	.50	27	.85	8	1.0
X	68	.44	13	.38	46	.98	8	.88
XII	80	.56	11	.82	84	.90	15	.80
Gia								
V	16	.13	—	—	—	—	—	—
VI	52	.08	8	.50	np	—	np	—
VII	67	.31	26	.42	9	.67	np	—
VIII	66	.32	57	.95	22	.73	np	—
XI	59	.56	52	.89	61	.92	8	.75
Kathryn								
IV	39	.46	8	.25	np	—	np	—
VI	60	.63	33	.70	23	.87	5	.80
VIII	44	.57	33	.73	82	.91	9	1.0
X	78	.56	59	.80	182	.97	78	.96
Peter								
X	25	.24	np	—	—	—	—	—
XII	6	.50	—	—	np	—	—	—
XIV	45	.69	np	—	np	—	—	—
XVI	26	.35	12	.50	7	.57	np	—
XVIII	55	.36	7	.71	20	1.0	np	—
XIX	96	.54	34	.68	39	.84	12	.83
XX	40	.35	17	1.0	52	.93	6	.83

[a]np = nonproductive; — = relation did not occur.

On another level of syntactic structure, within conjunction, both phrasal structures (connected constituents within a phrase) and sentential structures (connected clauses within a sentence) were distributed differentially across the four meanings of conjunction, and these results are presented in Table 7.4. Both phrasal and sentential structures were acquired at the same time, with additive conjunction, for all the children except Gia, who acquired phrasal structures first. While the relative frequencies of phrasal and sentential structures in additive conjunction remained essentially the same across time, there was a developmental increase in the proportion of sentential structure in temporal conjunction. Sentential structures predominated at all times with all the children for causal and adversative conjunction.

Cohesion Relations in Discourse

While the syntactic connective was always part of a child utterance, the connective was sometimes used to connect relations that extended across utterance boundaries. When both parts of the relation occurred within one or across two consecutive child utterances, the cohesion was child–child. That is, both parts of the meaning relation, before and after the connective, were said by the child, for example, ''And there's my eye/ and there's my feet.'' For two of the conjunction meanings (additive and temporal), for object specification, and for complementation, cohesion was child–child .90 of the time, averaging across samples and across children.

When the two parts of the semantic relation before and after the connective occurred across two or more different speaker turns, the cohesion was either adult–child or child–adult–child, for example, ''# Maybe he'll ride the horse # Yeah, when he comes in #.'' The only two meaning relations with cohesion that involved an adult utterance more than 0.20 of the time were causality and adversative (see Figure 7.6). For all children, the first appearance of the causality meaning relation occurred with child–child cohesion at least twice as often as with adult cohesion. The first appearance of the adversative relation occurred with child–child cohesion at least twice as often for two of the children; of Gia's first three adversative utterances, two were child–child, and Peter's first two utterances were one of each.

A second cohesion analysis was performed with causality and adversative utterances to determine the use of the different syntactic connectives with the different cohesion patterns. With causality, as seen in Table 7.5, more different connectives were used with child–child cohesion. The most frequent connective used with adult–child and child–adult–child cohesion was *because* (most often in response to a *why* question). However, *because* was used in both the child–child cohesion and cohesion involving an adult utterance from the beginning by Eric and Kathryn. Peter's first two instances of *because* were used in adult cohesion, but in the next sample, *because* was used as often in child as in adult cohesion. While Gia's first instances of

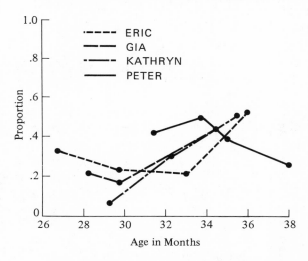

Figure 7.6. Proportion of the combined causality and adversative relations with cohesion involving an adult speaker turn.

because were used in adult cohesion, the connective was not used at all in the next sample and was used frequently in both cohesion patterns by Gia XI. Thus, for all the children, the first productive use of *because* was in both cohesion patterns. All the other connectives were used overwhelmingly with child–child cohesion. With the adversative relation, as seen in Table 7.6, child cohesion was most frequent; *and* and *but* were used with child cohesion first or with both cohesion patterns from the beginning.

DISCUSSION

The first syntactic connective the children learned, *and*, was also the most general: Syntactically, *and* was used in both contextual and syntactic structures; semantically, *and* was used to encode conjunction with all the different conjunction meaning relations in the order additive < temporal < causal < adversative.[6] Other syntactic connectives were learned subsequently, with different syntactic structures, and were semantically more specific. These results will be discussed in terms of form, and relative linguistic complexity in the adult model; content, and the intersection of form with conceptual and semantic factors affecting acquisition; and use, in terms of discourse cohesion.

Table 7.5. *Frequency of Occurrence of Causal Connectives According to Child and Adult Cohesion*

Period[a]	Child and Observation Number	Causal Connective by Cohesion Patterns							
		because Child	Adult	*so* Child	Adult	*and* Child	Adult	Other Child	Adult
A	Eric VI	3	3	2	—	4	—	—	—
	Gia VII	—	2	2	—	4	—	—	—
	Kathryn VI	3	1	8	—	4	—	5	—
	Peter XVI	—	2	—	—	3	—	1	—
	Totals	6	8	12	—	15	—	6	—
B	Eric VIII	2	7	5	—	5	—	5	1
	Gia VIII	—	—	2	0	10	—	8	—
	Kathryn VIII	19	17	17	3	4	1	14	—
	Peter XVIII	6	7	—	—	5	—	—	—
	Totals	27	31	24	3	24	1	27	1
C	Eric X	4	9	7	—	5	—	6	—
	Gia XI	17	25	3	—	7	—	7	—
	Kathryn X	75	30	21	2	9	1	36	—
	Peter XIX	13	9	1	—	6	—	3	1
	Totals	109	73	32	2	27	1	52	1
	Totals overall	142	112	68	5	66	2	85	2

[a] Periods A, B, and C include the first, second, and third observations in which the causative semantic relation was productive.

Table 7.6. *Frequency of Adversative Connectives According to Child and Adult Cohesion*

Period[a]	Child and Observation Number		*but* Child	Adult	*and* Child	Adult	Other Child	Adult
A	Eric	VIII	2	2	3	—	—	—
	Gia	VII	—	—	1	1	—	1
	Kathryn	VI	5	1	—	—	—	—
	Peter	XVIII	—	1	1	—	—	—
	Totals		7	4	5	1	0	1
B	Eric	X	3	1	2	—	2	—
	Gia	VIII	—	—	3	—	—	—
	Kathryn	VIII	5	7	—	—	—	—
	Peter	XIX	3	1	4	2	1	—
	Totals		11	9	9	2	3	0
C	Eric	XII	5	3	5	—	1	—
	Gia	XI	3	3	2	—	—	—
	Kathryn	X	19	49	—	—	—	—
	Peter	XX	4	1	—	—	1	—
	Totals		31	56	7	0	2	0
	Totals overall		49	69	21	3	5	1

Table spanning header: *Adversative Connective by Cohesion Pattern*

[a]Periods A, B, and C include the first, second, and third observations, respectively, in which the adversative semantic relation was productive.

Form of Complex Sentences

Two factors related to connective forms appeared to influence the developmental sequence of connectives and syntactic structures observed in this study. First, there seemed to be a conceptual constraint on learning syntactically homonymous forms (see also Bever, 1970). The first connectives the children learned were nonhomonymous (*and*, *then*, and *because*). The homonymous connectives except for *when* (*what*, *where*, *that*, and *like*), were learned in their nonconnective contexts first. *When*, in contrast, was learned as a connective long before it was learned as a *wh*-question form (see Bloom, Merkin, & Wootten, 1982, chap. 6).

The second factor had to do with the pronominalizing function of *wh*-forms. Harris (1957) described two functions of *wh*-forms in complex sentences: The forms *who*, *what*, *where*, *when*, *which*, as well as *that* can appear as pronominalizing connectives in the structure S_1–Wh–S_2, and either (1) pronominalize an antecedent S_1 noun, as in relativization (e.g., "There's a great hole where the bunny rabbits live") or (2) pronominalize a subject or object constituent of S_2, as in complementation (e.g., "I don't know what this color is"). However, in the present study, *when* was the first *wh*-form to appear and functioned as a conjunction in temporal relations (as in "I'll get my slippers when I come out") rather than as a pronominalizing form. *When* functioned in the same way as *and; because, so,* and *but* functioned in additive, causal, and adversative sentences. The children in the present study learned the S_1–Wh–S_2 connective forms in the order *when* conjunction < *wh*-complement < *wh*-relative.

Of the class of complementizing morphemes discussed by Rosenbaum (1967) in his analysis of predicate complementation – *that, for, to,* and possessive *-ing* – only *that* (e.g., "Tell Iris that I wet my bed") and *to* were observed in the children's speech. *That* was never a productive complementizer (although *that* was productive as a relative pronoun). See Bloom, Tackeff, & Lahey, 1984, chap. 8, for a description of the development of *to* complementation. The children did use pronominal *wh*-complementizers, which were not dealt with in Rosenbaum's analyses (see Bloom, Rispoli, Hafitz, & Gartner, 1989, chap. 9).

Syntactic Structures. Relativization, which occurred primarily with the main clause and required pronominalization of an antecedent noun, was the last structure the children learned. Complementation, which also involved pronominalization (of an S_2 constituent) was learned before relativization and after conjunction (which did not involve pronominalization). The children learned complementation per se originally in the context of certain matrix verbs that took sentence complements without connectives (e.g., *see, tell, want, know*) and that appeared early in their speech along with simple sentences (see also Limber, 1973). For example, "see Mommy busy," "tell him wake up" and "I want man stand up" occurred before or at the same time as the first syntactic connective, with the use of *and* to code additive conjunction (see Chapter 9).

The complementation the children learned with pronominalization was constrained by a small set of semantically specific state verbs, including *know, think, see, watch,* and *tell,* which were similar to verbs in the examples of child sentences reported by Limber (1973) and by

Table 7.7. *Complement-taking Verbs*

	Epistemic	Notice	Communication
Child verbs (Eric, Gia, Kathryn, Peter)	know think	see look show watch	tell ask teach explain
(from Limber, 1973)	*all of the above &* guess remember wonder decide forget	*all the above*	*all the above &* say
Adult verbs (from Rosen- baum, 1967)	*all of the above &* understand believe convince surprise doubt worry imagine trust recognize	*all the above &* hear observe	*all the above &* admit boast promise demonstrate defy persist remind

Rosenbaum (1967) for adult complementation. A semantic distribution of the children's complement-taking verbs is presented in Table 7.7 along with verbs reported by Limber and by Rosenbaum (see also Bloom, 1978). The children's later acquisition of epistemic, notice, and other verb complements with connectives appeared to be a formal development involving pronominalization.

With respect to conjunction, there are two hypotheses in transformational grammar for the derivation of phrasal conjunction, for example, "I want a green book and a pink book." In the more traditional analysis, phrasal conjunction is transformationally derived from an underlying basis that contains two sentential structures, $S \rightarrow S_1$ *and* S_2 (or $NP_1 VP_1$ *and* $NP_1 VP_2$) with a general transformation that deletes the second NP_1 (e.g., Chomsky, 1957; Gleitman, 1965; Stockwell, Schacter, & Partee, 1973). This first hypothesis suggests the possibility that phrasal conjunction, which is transformationally more complex than sentential conjunction because of the deletion transformation, would be acquired by children after sentential conjunction (i.e., "I want a green book and I want a pink book"). This possibility has been supported in studies by Slobin and Welsh (1973) and Lust (1976). However, in the present study, phrasal structures appeared at the same time as (for three of the children) or before (for one of the children) sentential conjunction (as reported also by Bates, 1976, for Italian children, and by de Villiers, Tager-Flusberg, and Hakuta, 1977, and Lust and Mervis, 1980, for American children). These results are consistent with the second hypothesis concerning the derivation of phrasal conjunction: that the phrasal conjunction is itself basic in the underlying structure of the sentence (Stockwell, Schacter, & Partee, 1973). Such phrases as "green book and pink book" are apparently learned as basic sentence constituents.

Content of Complex Sentences

A fuller explanation of the results of this study appears in the intersection of form with the semantic factors (the meaning relations between clauses and the meaning of connectives) and conceptual factors that affected acquisition. The children appeared to learn the connective *and* to begin with in order to express that two events simply go together in both phrasal structures (e.g., "I want to do a boy and a man") and sentential structures (e.g., "You do one and I do one"). The additive use of *and* was followed developmentally by sentences that combined clauses with different meaning relations between them – that is, temporal, causal, and adversative conjunction.

The developmental sequence of conjunction observed in this study cannot be compared with the results reported by Clancy, Jacobsen, and Silva (1976) because the two studies differed in methodology. They reported that coordination (additive conjunction) was always acquired first in the four languages they studied, but the sequence of antithesis (adversative), sequential, and causality was variable in the four languages (although antithesis always preceded causality). The sequence they reported for English was coordination < sequence < antithesis < causality. Although language-specific factors no doubt influence the sequence of development, Clancy and her colleagues reported sequences of "complex meaning" whether or not a connective was expressed and reported only the first instance of a category, without a criterion of productivity. Also, the categories they described were not consistent with the categories in the present study; most notably, they considered that "the child's earliest notion of antithesis involves the rejection of one proposition and the assertion of an alternative" (p.

74). An example they gave was *Nei, pot,* meaning "no compote" in German, as the child rejected soup that was offered. Such instances of anaphoric negation (see Chapter 3) would not have been included as instances of conjunction in the study reported here.

The general cumulative principle that was used to decide on semantic interpretation proved to characterize the developmental sequence in which the semantic subcategories of conjunction appeared (see Brown & Hanlon, 1970, for discussion of syntactic cumulative complexity; and Brainerd, 1978, for discussion of cumulative complexity in cognitive development). In the developmental sequence additive < temporal < causal < adversative, the temporal, causal, and adversative sentences were all additive in that two events or states were joined; causal was both additive and temporal; some of the adversative sentences were additive, temporal, and quasi-causal (e.g., "I was trying to get my crayons but I fell" – meaning "I couldn't get my crayons because I fell"). Adversative sentences included the new meaning of opposition or contrast (e.g., "I have a puppet/but not a real puppet").

The sequence of semantic development also has an analogue in children's conceptual development: Children learn to form collections of things (e.g., Sinclair, 1970) before they learn to form series of things that are ordered relative to one another (e.g., Inhelder & Piaget, 1959/1964). The children in this study learned to talk about things that go together (additive conjunction) before they learned to talk about things that go together in ordered relationship (temporal, causal, and adversative conjunction).

Cohesion of Complex Sentences

The cohesion analysis in the present study provided evidence that learning increasingly complex structures is not dependent upon or otherwise the result of reciprocity in discourse, as has been claimed, for example, by Greenfield and Smith (1976). The two clauses with complex meaning relations that have been described were expressed most often by the child (child–child cohesion). Adult–child or child–adult–child cohesion, which occurred most often in expressions of causality or adversative relations, was always less frequent than child–child cohesion with the same semantic relations and increased developmentally. The development of adult–child cohesion reflected the children's increasing ability to participate in discourse, using newly or already learned linguistic forms, rather than the learning of linguistic forms through discourse. It appears that children have to learn something about the forms of language before learning the situational and interpersonal constraints on using such forms, as has previously been suggested with respect to children's alternating nominal and pronominal forms (Bloom, Lightbown, & Hood, 1975, chap. 2) and temporal deixis with the use of verb inflections (Bloom, Lifter, & Hafitz, 1980, chap. 5).

CONCLUSIONS

The considerable difficulty involved in learning complex sentences can be inferred from the length of time covered by the results of the study reported here. Evidence of sudden insight or 'across the board' learning was not apparent in the present study. On the contrary, approximately 8-week intervals (for Peter) and 12-week intervals (for Eric, Gia, and Kathryn) separated each of the observations that provided the data for analysis, and the linguistic gains observed were small, although consistent, across the entire time span of this study. Although there were intervening observations available (since approximately every other observation was used), the data for these observations did not appear (on the basis of cursory scanning) to conflict in any way with the general picture of slow but steady progress toward the acquisition of complex sentences. Moreover, this acquisition can be described only in terms of emergence, as the children presented evidence of learning something about the forms and functions of complex sentences, rather than in terms of achievement. The procedures used for inferring acquisition were considerably more conservative than those used in other studies (inasmuch as criteria for acquisition included more than use of a single instance of a structure by a single child, as had been the case in other studies; e.g., Bates, 1976; and Clancy, Jacobsen, & Silva, 1976). Nevertheless, it was clear that the children had only just begun to learn about the use of syntactic connectives and meaning relations in conjunction, complementation, and relativization structures.

There was consistency among the children in the sequence in which the different meaning relations emerged and were expressed in complex sentences, but variation among them in the sequence in which they acquired different connectives to encode these meanings. This result – variation in form with similarity in content in the development of individual children – is consistent with reports of other aspects of these children's language acquisition (see Bloom, Lightbown, & Hood,

1975, chap. 2, on nominal/pro-nominal variation and early sentence relations; Hood & Bloom, 1979, chap. 8, on clause order in expressions of causality; and Bloom, Lifter, & Hafitz, 1980, chap. 5, on acquisition of -*ed*/irregular verb inflections). The variation in age of emergence (of connectives and meaning relations) that was observed is consistent with the consensus in the child language literature that age alone is a poor predictor of acquisition.

To conclude, at least three factors influence the acquisition of syntactic connectives and the sequence of development of complex sentences with these connectives: the pronominalization of major constituents, the use of homonymous forms, and cumulative semantic complexity. Additionally, the children did not learn complex sentences by connecting their own utterance with a prior adult utterance to form the two clauses of a complex sentence. Rather, the informational requirements of the content of the children's messages appeared to be a stronger influence than discourse requirements for determining the form of the children's complex sentences with syntactic connectives.

NOTES

1 Because the focus of this paper was on the acquisition of syntactic connectives and the meaning relations they encode, complex sentences without connectives (e.g., "That's the bed Mommy bought me") and complementation (e.g., "Watch me draw a circle") were not included in the analyses in this study. Sentences without connectives were included in two later studies of complementation (in Chapters 8 and 9). In addition, because the connective *to* has special status by virtue of its relation to verb stems in their nonfinite forms (Jespersen, 1961, vol. 5), *to* complements are described in a separate study (in Bloom, Tackeff, & Lahey, 1984, chap. 8).

2 Other uses of connectives included idiomatic verb phrases such as "come and go," "go and get," and "stand and wait" and sentence fragments such as "red and blue" and "milk and cookies."

3 The age at the last sample was used as an estimate of age of emergence for those connectives that occurred in the data but did not become productive.

4 One other semantic relation was observed but never became productive for any of the children: *manner,* for example, "I wanta do it like you did."

5 The age at the last sample was used as the estimate of age of emergence

for those meaning relations that occurred in the data but did not become productive.
6 The terms used for the four meanings of conjunction conform with the terminology used by Halliday & Hasan (1976).

POSTSCRIPT

For studies of the acquisition and uses of syntactic connectives since Bloom, Lahey, Hood, Lifter, and Fiess (1980):

Bassano, D., & Champaud, C. (1989). The argumentative connective *même* in French: An experimental study in eight- to ten-year-old children. *Journal of Child Language, 16*, 643–64.

Durkin, K. (1983). Children's comprehension of complex sentences containing the preposition *between. Child Study Journal, 13*, 133–47.

French, L., & Nelson, K. (1985). *Young children's knowledge of relational terms: Some ifs, ands, and buts.* New York: Springer-Verlag.

Peterson, C. (1986). Semantic and pragmatic uses of "but." *Journal of Child Language, 13*, 583–90.

Peterson, C., & McCabe, A. (1987). The connective "and": Do older children use it less as they learn other connectives? *Journal of Child Language, 14*, 375–81.

Peterson, C., & McCabe, A. (1988). The connective *and* as discourse glue. *First Language, 8*, 19–28.

Scott, C. (1984). Adverbial connectivity in conversations of children 6 to 12. *Journal of Child Language, 11*, 423–52.

Townsend, D., & Ravelo, N. (1980). The development of complex sentence processing strategies. *Journal of Experimental Child Psychology, 29*, 60–73.

Tyack, D., & Gottsleben, R. (1986). Acquisition of complex sentences. *Language, Speech, and Hearing Services in the Schools, 17*, 160–74.

Wing, C., & Scholnick, E. (1981). Children's comprehension of pragmatic concepts expressed in "because," "although," "if," and "unless." *Journal of Child Language, 8*, 347–65.

For studies of the syntax of coordination and conjunction:

Greenfield, P., & Dent, C. (1982). Pragmatic factors in children's phrasal coordination. *Journal of Child Language, 9*, 425–43.

Hakuta, K., de Villiers, J., & Tager-Flusberg, H. (1982). Sentence coordination in Japanese and English. *Journal of Child Language, 9*, 193–207.

Lust, B., & Mervis, C. (1980). Development of coordination in the natural speech of young children. *Journal of Child Language, 7*, 279–304.

The developmental sequence of conjunction meanings additive > temporal > causative in the children's complex sentences is similar to the developmental sequence in storytelling skills and children's understanding of the concept of a story, for example:

Stein, N. (1988). The development of children's story-telling skill. In M. Franklin & S. Barten (Eds.), *Child language, a reader* (pp. 282–97). New York: Oxford University Press.

8

Infinitive Complements with *to*

"I'm trying to get this cow in here."

The acquisition of the connective *to* with infinitive complements was a separate study and not included in the study of complex sentences in Chapter 7 or the study of other forms of complementation in Chapter 9 that follows. Two issues in linguistic theory were addressed in this study of the acquisition of the connective *to* with infinitive complements. The first was the derivational history of *to* complements, and the second was whether *to* was learned as a meaningless syntactic marker. In response to the first question, we concluded that the children learned *to* with the basic structure verb + *to* in the context of a small number of the verbs (and other nonverb forms) in English that are subcategorized in the lexicon for taking infinitive complements. Second, the children learned *to* in these verb contexts with the meaning "direction toward," consistent with the meaning of the preposition *to* and not as a meaningless syntactic marker.

THE BASIC STRUCTURE VERB + *to*

On the basis of both the relative distribution of *to* with matrix and complement verbs and its developmental history, we concluded that the matrix verbs, and not the complement verbs, controlled the emergence of *to*. *To* was acquired differently with different kinds of matrix verbs and occurred more often with new than with old matrix forms. No developmental or distributional regularities were apparent in the use of *to* with complement verbs. Thus, the children learned *to* in the context of the matrix verbs and not as a marker of nonfinite verbs. They learned verb + *to* as the basic structure for complementation rather than a complement structure derived from a fuller underlying sentence structure. As we will see, this conclusion gained support from the subsequent study of other forms of complementation (in Chapter 9).

The Meaning "Direction Toward"

In tracing the historical roots of verbal *to,* Otto Jespersen reported that it
derived originally from the preposition *to* with nouns and originally retained
the prepositional meaning of "direction toward." This meaning was presumably lost, and Jespersen and other linguists have since assumed that the connective *to* is a meaningless form used to mark the nonfinite complement verb
(for example, "I'm trying *to get* this cow in here").[1] However, the data in
this study led us to conclude that children learn the complementizer *to* as a
meaningful form indicating "direction toward," consistent with the meaning
of the preposition *to* and attached to the matrix verb rather than the complement verb (for example, "I'm *trying to* get this cow in here"). Two main
results prompted this conclusion: First, the appearance of *to* occurred in the
children's speech with both nouns and verbs at essentially the same time (for
three of the children) or within successive observations (for the fourth child).
Second, the matrix forms learned with *to* most often had some element of a
continuing-forward meaning or directedness: intentional (*want to, go to*),
inchoative (*try to, time to, ready to*), invitative (*like to, supposed to*), instructive (*show how to, know how to*), and the like.

CHILD LANGUAGE AND LINGUISTIC THEORY

The relationship between child language data and linguistic theory was explicitly
addressed in this study and then highlighted subsequently in an exchange of
'notes' in the *Journal of Child Language.*[2] In particular, Nina Hyams questioned the conclusion that verb + *to* is learned as a grammatical unit, citing
sentences with the matrix verb and *to* separated by the subject of the complement verb (as in "want me to do this").[3] We had reported that these were
rare and appeared late in the data. In reply, Richard Beckwith, Matthew Rispoli, and I pointed out that the strong coreference constraint in the data was
the more important result. One of the strongest findings was that the children's infinitival complements were coreferential with matrix subjects, making unnecessary the claim for a fuller underlying sentence structure for complement structures.

Through the study of the child's tedious working through of the target language, we
can propose principles not derived from linguistic theory that may govern the child's
progress. . . . The phenomena discovered in linguistics are those that the child language researcher must explain, but at the same time the phenomena of child language
must be considered in the search for an adequate syntactic theory.[4]

Learning *to* in Complement Construction

Lois Bloom, Jo Tackeff, and Margaret Lahey

INTRODUCTION

The transition from simple to complex syntax ordinarily begins between 2 and 3 years of age, and the structure of infinitive complements is one of the first complex structures to appear (Brown, 1973; Limber, 1973). Certain other linguistic structures that children begin to acquire in this period have been highly constrained by the kinds of verbs that they know and use, in particular, the acquisition of verb inflections (Bloom, Lifter, & Hafitz, 1980, chap. 5) and *wh*-questions (Bloom, Merkin, & Wootten, 1982, chap. 6). Because sentences with infinitive complements include two verbs, how children acquire infinitive complements is relevant to extending our understanding of the relationship between the acquisition of complex syntax and the development of the verb system in child language. One purpose of this study, then, was to determine whether regularities among the higher verb forms (hereafter referred to as *matrix forms*) or the complement infinitive verbs governed acquisition of *to* as a syntactic marker.

In addition, among the reasons for studying child language is the continuing concern for understanding the nature of language more generally. How children acquire language is relevant to how we attempt to explain language. The study of one or another aspect of language development, then, can be helpful in evaluating alternative theories of language. In the case of the acquisition of infinitive complements, we have several theories but no consensus about their structure in adult language. A second purpose of this study, then, was to evaluate the extent to which child data are consistent with traditional and contemporary theories of infinitive complement structure.

In many linguistic accounts, the connective *to* is presented as part of the larger system of complementation in English, and in particular, *to* complements are contrasted with participial *-ing* complements (e.g., Quirk, Greenbaum, Leech, & Svartvik, 1972; Rosenbaum, 1967). However, *to* complementation was the subject of the separate study

Reprinted from the *Journal of Child Language, 11,* 1984, 391–406, with permission from Cambridge University Press.

reported here because (1) the children in this longitudinal study did not
acquire participial -*ing* complements in the same period (from 2 to 3
years of age), so that *to* complements were not learned contrastively;
(2) *to* complements have recently been singled out in theories of adult
complementation for the theoretical reasons given below. Aspects of
these children's acquisition of other complementation structures have
been described elsewhere (Bloom, Lahey, Hood, Lifter, & Fiess, 1980,
chap. 7; and Bloom, Rispoli, Gartner, & Hafitz, 1989, chap. 9).

In explanations of the occurrence of *to* in infinitive complements in
adult sentences, for example:

(1 a)   I want to go home.
(1 b)   he likes to sleep.

to is considered a meaningless, purely syntactic device. Historically,
verbal *to* was derived from the preposition *to* with nouns and originally
retained the prepositional meaning of direction toward, purpose, or
goal (Jespersen, 1964). Even though "a trace of this meaning" remains
in certain instances (as in the examples "ready to go, I wish to go,")
the meaning has been "gradually obliterated," and Jespersen described contemporary verbal *to* as "a grammatical implement with no
meaning of its own" (1964, p. 330). Similarly, transformational accounts also describe complementizer connectives as semantically empty
(Bresnan, 1970, p. 302). However, Bresnan pointed out that differences in sentence meaning result from the choice of different connectives (e.g., sentences with *for–to* versus *that*), so that they do serve
semantic as well as syntactic functions. In the present study, children's
spontaneous speech was examined to determine whether *to* was learned
as a meaningless syntactic marker or with particular meaning, such as
the prepositional meaning "direction toward" with nouns.

With respect to the syntactic function of *to* in complement structures, Jespersen suggested that "*to* is often felt as belonging more
closely to the preceding verb than to the infinitive" (1964, p. 346).
Virtually all accounts of English grammar subcategorize verb entries
in the lexicon for taking *to* complements. However, two contemporary
theories differ with respect to the underlying syntax of infinitive complements in the adult model (Bresnan, 1978; Koster & May, 1982).
The transformational account by Koster and May is consistent with
standard generative theory in treating all infinitive complements as
sentential and derived from the same underlying sentence structure as
for complementizers. They proposed that sentences like

(2)   John tried to leave.

are derived from the same constituent structure as sentences like

(3)   Mary prefers for John to leave.

with the "superficially absent complementizer and subject," for example, *for* and the subject of the verb *leave* in (2), *John tried [for John] to leave,* "being represented by lexically empty categories" (Koster & May, 1982, p. 116). The child speech data in the present study were examined to determine if *to* was learned originally in sentential contexts with *for* complementizers and sentence subjects, such as (3). In contrast, Bresnan proposed that the "verb + infinitive construction is a basic structure, like the modal + infinitive construction." Both are generated "by means of a phrase structure rule VP → V $\overline{\text{VP}}$," where the lower verb in $\overline{\text{VP}}$ is the infinitive with *to* (Bresnan, 1978, pp. 44–5). The infinitive complement with *to* is itself the basic, underlying structure and is not derived from a more complex underlying sentence structure. In the study reported here, the spontaneous child speech data were used to determine whether *to* was learned originally as a marker of the infinitive or as a complement connective with the higher verb or other matrix forms.

METHOD

Subjects

Eric, Gia, Kathryn, and Peter were the subjects of this study. The texts that were used began when at least four linguistic contexts for *to* with infinitive complement verbs (hereafter identified as CV contexts) were observed. This occurred at between 22 and 25 months for each of the children, and data analysis continued until the last observation of each child at about 36 months. Data from six observation sessions are reported for two children; five observations are reported for a third child; and for the fourth child, who was seen for shorter sessions with shorter intervals between sessions, data are reported for eight observation sessions.

Procedure

Because we cannot tap their intuitions about language by asking them directly to tell us what is possible or acceptable to them linguistically, we need to infer what children know about language from the evidence of the regularities in their language behaviors. Accordingly, a systematic distribution among large numbers of linguistic events is taken as evidence for inferring a principled organization underlying a child's language behavior. A sizable and coherent shift in the regularity of behavior across time, from one observation to a later observation, is taken as evidence of developmental change. In order to establish confidence that the regularities in the children's speech behaviors represented evidence of linguistic knowledge, a criterion of productivity was established in advance. The criterion of four different instances of a linguistic behavior (such as occurrence of *to*) in one text, from one child, was assumed to be minimal evidence for inferring some level of underlying knowledge, at that time, for that child. (See the discussion of productivity criteria in Chapter 1.)

For this study, two complement verb (CV) contexts for *to* were identified. The first CV context was the V–*to*–V context, as in

(4)   I want to see Mommy.

with no intervening noun phrase and with coreferential subject of both verbs, *want* and *see* in (4). The second CV context was V–NP–*to*–V, as in

(5)   I want Mommy get balloon.

where an intervening noun phrase was the subject of the second, complement verb phrase and was not coreferential with the subject of the matrix verb. These CV contexts were extracted from the texts for analysis, whether or not *to* or some phonological variant of *to* (such as [ə]) was expressed. The matrix forms with these CV contexts for *to* included forms that were verbs, such as *want, try,* and *like,* as well as other forms that acted like verbs, such as *ready* and *about.* The estimated total number of utterances in the texts from the four children was 78,986, and 3,798, or .048, of these utterances included a CV context for *to*.

Subsequently, in order to compare emergence and use of *to* in CV contexts with *to* in noun (N) contexts as a preposition, all the children's utterances with a V–*to*–N context, as in

(6)   I'm going to school.

were extracted from the early texts. The texts before as well as after *to* emerged in CV contexts were examined.

All the analyses were performed separately for each observation of each of the children. When a result was the same for the four children, the data were pooled for convenience of presentation. The first step in combining the data from the four children was to consider the last four observations of each of the children (until they were about 36 months old) as four longitudinal periods. These were labeled Periods A, B, C, and D. For example, Period D included the four texts from the four children at about 36 months of age; Period C included the four texts from the immediately preceding observations; and so on. The second step was to include two exceptions: Period A also included the immediately preceding texts from two of the children who began to acquire new matrix forms earlier than the others, and Period D also included the later text from one of these children who was followed for a longer period of time than the others (until 38 months of age).

The Status of [ə] in Verb Contexts

While *wanna, gonna, hafta* are acceptable variants of *to* with *want,* *go,* and *have* in adult American English, the status of the final [ə] in the child forms was initially ambiguous. In contexts with *want,* the function of [ə] was either as a variant of *to* as in (7), a variant of the article *a* as in (8), or *wanna* was an unanalysed lexical item as in (9).

(7)   wanna go playground.
(8)   Gia wanna train.
(9)   wanna more cookie.

In the early texts, [ə] occurred after *want* before a noun phrase and before a verb phrase. For example, in the earliest Gia text that included *want,* [ə] (*wanna*) occurred with a noun or pronoun in 8 out of 50 instances of *want.* Thus it was difficult to support an unequivocal interpretation of [ə]. Further, *want, go,* and *have* occurred primarily with first-person subjects as the apparently unanalyzed forms *wanna, gonna,* and *hafta.* It was only in the later observations, when [ə] began to occur in third-person contexts, for example:

(10a)   he has [ə] go home.
(10b)   she wants [ə] get it.

that it appeared more reasonable to consider [ə] to be a variant of *to.* However, because of the difficulty in supporting an unequivocal interpretation of [ə] in the earlier texts, the use of [ə] and *to* are reported separately in the analyses of CV contexts that follow.

RESULTS

The results of the analyses of the children's utterances with linguistic contexts for the use of *to* consist of (1) the developmental distribution of *to* with different matrix forms in CV contexts; (2) the comparison of the distributional regularities of *to* with old and new matrix forms and complement verbs; (3) the occurrence of *to* in CV contexts with an intervening noun phrase; (4) acquisition of *for–to* complement structures; (5) semantic consistencies among the matrix forms in CV contexts for *to;* and (6) the comparison of the emergence of *to* in CV and N contexts.

Acquisition of to with Different Matrix Forms

Both contexts for and the use of *to* in those contexts increased developmentally, as can be seen in Table 8.1. For all four children, *to* emerged in CV contexts (in that it first became productive, with four different instances) when MLU was about 2.5. After MLU passed 3.5, the children were using *to* or [ə] in at least 75% of CV contexts for *to*.

If the children had learned *to* in the context of complement verbs as a marker of the infinitive form, then any difference in the distribution of *to* would be expected to occur developmentally with complement verbs, and not with the matrix forms. The children initially used a small group of matrix verbs, primarily *want* and *go* and, less often, *got* and *have*. These earliest verbs appeared to function as modal verbs to express the child's mood of wish or intention (see Bloom, Lightbown, & Hood, 1975, chap. 2; Brown, 1973), with a wide variety of different main verbs, for example:

(11a) [ə] want put in there.
(11b) I want open it.
(11c) I gonna get it.

These modal verbs (*want, go, got,* and *have*) were the most frequent matrix forms used by each child; at the time of the first observation, they were the only forms used by three of the children and accounted for 85% of the forms used by the fourth child (Eric). When the modal verbs emerged, they were used primarily without the connective *to* or with some variant of [ə], for example, *wanna, gotta, halfta.*

Nonmodal matrix forms (e.g., *try* and *ready*) appeared after the modals; when they appeared they were used proportionately more often with *to* than without, and they did not occur with [ə]. The use of *to*

Table 8.1. *Distribution of* to *and the Different Contexts for* to

Child and Period[a]	Observation	Age (months, weeks)	MLU	Verb-*to*-Verb			Verb-NP-*to*-Verb		Verb-*to*-Noun[b]	
				Total CV Contexts for *to*	+ *to*	[ə]	Total CV Contexts for *to*	+ *to*	Total N Contexts for *to*	+ *to*
Kathryn										
A	II	22, 3	1.89	32	1 (.03)[c]	2 (.06)	6	—	—	—
	{III	24, 2	2.83	222	*5 (.02)[d]	64 (.29)	20	—	7	1 (.14)
	{IV	26, 1	3.30	328	121 (.37)	35 (.11)	11	—	14	*6 (.43)
B	VI	29, 1	3.35	171	57 (.33)	90 (.53)	3	2 (.66)	38	36 (.95)
C	VIII	32, 1	3.70	211	150 (.71)	41 (.09)	4	3 (.75)	—	—
D	X	35, 1	4.23	306	159 (.52)	128 (.42)	27	*27 (1.00)	—	—
Eric										
	IV	23, 2	1.69	—	—	—	—	—	4	1 (.25)
A	V	25, 1	2.63	47	*16 (.24)	20 (.30)	3	—	6	*4 (.25)
	VI	26, 3	2.84	67	16 (.24)	20 (.30)	3	—	4	3 (.75)
B	VIII	29, 3	3.45	73	56 (.77)	9 (.12)	4	1 (.25)	22	22 (1.00)
C	X	33, 0	4.21	57	41 (.72)	8 (.14)	8	*8 (1.00)	—	—
D	XII	36, 0	3.49	63	45 (.71)	10 (.16)	11	11 (1.00)	—	—
Gia										
A	V	25, 2	2.30	158	2 (.01)	42 (.26)	—	—	16	2 (.13)
B	VI	26, 3	2.75	129	*21 (.16)	51 (.39)	—	—	24	*7 (.29)
	VII	28, 1	3.07	243	29 (.12)	60 (.25)	4	1 (.25)	9	6 (.66)
C	VIII	29, 3	3.64	358	46 (.13)	198 (.55)	2	—	24	23 (.96)
D	XI	34, 2	3.71	268	103 (.38)	145 (.54)	31	*29 (.94)	76	75 (.99)

Peter

	VII	25, 0	2.39	19	—	16 (.84)	—	—	—	—
	VIII	25, 3	2.0	11	—	10 (.91)	—	—	—	—
A {	X	27, 0	2.63	47	*6 (.13)	26 (.55)	2	—	11	*6 (.55)
{	XII	28, 2	2.90	55	3 (.05)	43 (.78)	—	—	15	14 (.93)
B	XVI	31, 2	3.58	286	13 (.05)	263 (.92)	4	4 (1.00)	19	17 (.90)
C	XVIII	33, 3	3.30	105	22 (.21)	83 (.79)	—	—	20	19 (.95)
D {	XIX	35, 0	3.05	276	20 (.07)	248 (.90)	16	*15 (.94)	—	—
{	XX	38, 0	3.57	103	47 (.46)	49 (.47)	7	7 (1.00)	—	—

[a] Period represents texts pooled for presenting group results.

[b] Observations were examined only until *to* was used in at least 95% of obligatory noun contexts.

[c] Numbers in parentheses are the proportional occurrence of *to* in the total contexts.

[d] Starred frequency indicated productivity of *to*.

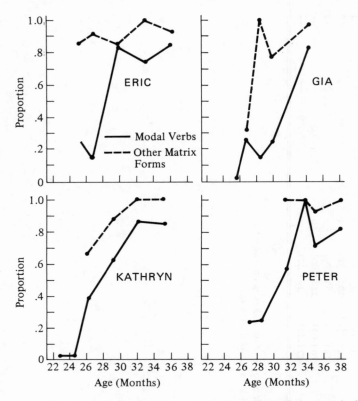

Figure 8.1. Increase in the use of *to* in modal and other matrix forms.

increased substantially with the modals only after *to* was used frequently with these other new matrix forms. This developmental regularity in the use of *to* with different kinds of matrix forms (nonmodals and then modals) is presented in Figure 8.1. (The frequencies in Figure 8.1 represent the frequency of *to* only, with occurrence of [ə] excluded.) In contrast, no developmental patterns were evident among the different verbs used as infinitive complements in these same sentences.

Distribution of *to* with Old and New Matrix Forms

The use of *to* was compared in CV contexts with new and old matrix and complement verbs. Old forms were those that had appeared in any previous observation; new forms were those that had not been observed previously (for each child considered separately).

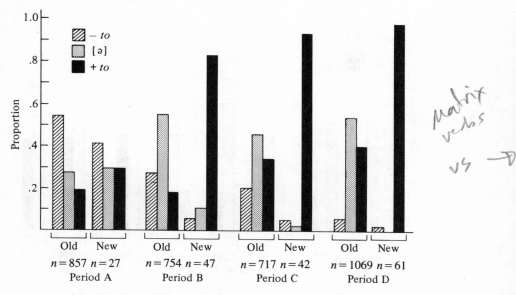

Figure 8.2. Comparison of old and new matrix forms in the use of *to*, in the last four longitudinal periods.

The expression of *to* increased developmentally, as can be seen in Figure 8.2, in the four developmental periods. However, *to* was always more frequent with new matrix forms, and [ə] was more frequent with old matrix forms. These differences were especially pronounced after Period A. This result is not entirely independent of the result presented earlier in Figure 8.1, where *to* emerged with the nonmodal matrix forms first and with the modals later. The modals, which were most frequent, were always among the old forms.

In contrast, each of the children used an average of 100 or more different complement verbs in these same sentences, and there were neither distributional regularity nor developmental differences among the complement verbs in the expression of *to* or [ə]. Moreover, no systematic distribution of *to* occurred among old and new complement verbs, either developmentally or overall, as can be seen in Figure 8.3. Thus the matrix forms and not the complement verbs controlled the emergence of *to*. First, *to* was acquired differently with different kinds of matrix forms, and second, *to* was always more likely to occur with new than with old matrix forms. In contrast, no developmental regularity was observed in the use of *to* with the children's complement verbs.

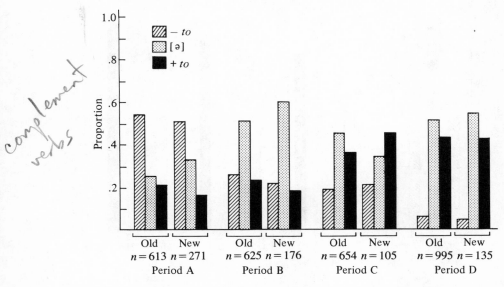

Figure 8.3. Comparison of old and new complement verbs in the use of *to*, in the last four longitudinal periods.

Occurrence of to *with an Intervening Noun Phrase*

The final analysis of the distribution of *to* in CV contexts concerned the context with an intervening noun phrase: V 1–NP–*to*–V 2, where the subject of the second, complement verb was not coreferential with the subject of the matrix form. There were 163 of these contexts for *to* (.04 of all the utterances with a CV context for *to*). With one exception, these CV contexts for *to* with an intervening noun phrase did not occur until after *to* was already expressed in more than .75 of the contexts with modals and MLU was about 3.5. The one exception was Kathryn, who in the earliest texts produced several sentences where the matrix form was the modal verb *want* followed by a sentence without *to* (see Table 8.1), for example:

(12a)   want the man stand up
(12b)   I want Mommy get it.

These contexts then decreased (Observations VI and VIII for Kathryn, Table 8.1). In the last observation, when they were again frequent, *to* was expressed, and the intervening NP was the pronoun *you* most often.

Except for Kathryn, then, CV contexts with an intervening, non-coreferential NP were infrequent early on. When they did eventually become productive for all the children, *to* was used at least 90% of the time (Table 8.1). Only three instances of [ə] occurred in this context – one after and two before the intervening NP; (13a) and (13b) occurred in Kathryn II and (13c) in Kathryn III:

(13a)   want Kathryn [ə] put in [ə] tank
(13b)   [ə] want [ə] Kathryn find [ə] lipstick
(13c)   [ə] want [ə] Kathryn read/read this book.

Sentences with intervening, non-coreferential NP were highly constrained; they were different for the different children; and they were sometimes different for the same child at different times. Five kinds of structures occurred:

(14)   V 1–NP–*to*–V 2, where NP was *me* or *you*, and V 1 was *want* most often:
         (a)   Want me to do it?
         (b)   I'll help you to find the buttons
(15)   V 1–NP–*to*–V 2, where NP was a nominal:
         I want this doll to stay here
(16)   *for* NP *to* phrases, where V 1 was a form other than *want, like,* or *ask:*
         It's hard for you to eat your thing
(17)   intervening NP that functioned as object of both V 1 and V 2:
         (a)   need something to eat
         (b)   I want something to do
(18)   *how to* phrases after verbs such as *show* and *teach:*
         I'll show you how to work it.

(handwritten margin note: seems like — ? S's are same for V₁ + V₂)

The individual children tended to use one or another of these kinds of sentences. Kathryn used (14), and Eric used (17). While Gia used both (15) and (16) and Peter used both (14) and (17), one or another predominated at different times. *How to* phrases, (18), were the least frequent and were used by only two children (Kathryn and Peter).

For–to *Complement Structures*

The children produced *for* complementizer connectives (see 16 above) only rarely and only toward the end of the period under study here. Kathryn produced two; Eric and Peter each produced one. Only Gia produced a sizable number (12), and these occurred in the last observation when she was 34 months, 2 weeks. Moreover, only Peter produced the *for* complementizer after a verb (one instance):

(19)   I wait for you to fix it.

In all the other sentences, the *for* complementizer occurred after nouns or adjectives: ten instances of *time for,* three instances of *hard for,* and one instance of *too early for, enough for,* and *ready for.* It appears, then, that the use of *for* complementizers was lexically specific rather than the result of a generalized syntactic rule for complementation when it first began to appear in these children's speech.

Semantics *of* to

The overwhelming majority of the matrix forms that provided the CV contexts for *to* shared an element of meaning that was best characterized as indicating direction or movement toward the activity named by the complement verb. This semantic consistency, meaning "direction toward," was prefigured by the meaning of the first modals, *want* and *go,* which signaled the child's wish or intention toward performing the action named by the complement verb. Similarly, the next most frequent matrix forms were *like, suppose,* and the inchoative forms *time, try, ready,* and *about,* which also indicated direction toward the activity or state of affairs named by the complement verb. In all, 99% of the instances (i.e., tokens) of the matrix forms that the children used shared the meaning "direction toward." Even when the modals *want, go, have,* and *got* were not counted, 84% of the remaining tokens shared this same meaning.

The 1% of the tokens that did not themselves express direction toward were used most often with complement verbs that expressed a locative action with direction toward, for example:

(20a)   forgot to bring.
(20b)   too far to walk.
(20c)   long way to go.
(20d)   forgot to take.
(20e)   used to go.

These matrix forms appeared to express negation of the meaning direction toward. There were only isolated instances where the interpretation direction toward was not tenable, for example:

Table 8.2. *Matrix Forms That Provided Complement Verb Contexts for* to[a]

Intention (modals)	Inchoative	Invitative	Instructive	Negative
want	try	like	show how	forgot
go	time	supposed	know how	hard
have	ready	get	know what	used
got	about	fun[b]	know where	(too) far
	need	safe[b]	tell	long way
	start[b]	nice[b]	ask	not nice
	be able[b]	easier[b]	teach how[b]	wait
				afraid[b]
				too noisy[b]
				too early[b]
				too ugly[b]
				too big[b]

[a] Listed in order of frequency for all children combined.
[b] Single instance only.

(21a)   forgot to dry.
(21b)   hard to read.

All the matrix forms are listed in Table 8.2, in order of frequency and categorized as expressions of intention, inchoative, invitative, instructive, and negative meaning. This categorization is only suggestive. Obviously, each of the child forms in Table 8.2 is semantically complex, but the taxonomy (intentional, inchoative, invitative, and instructive meanings) is intuitively likely, based upon our adult understanding of the forms. The purpose of the taxonomy is to highlight the interpretation of direction toward, and to demonstrate that the children learned the complementizer connective *to* in the context of that meaning. This interpretation, moreover, is consistent with the historical meaning of the connective *to* derived from the meaning of the preposition *to* with nouns (Jespersen, 1964).

Comparison of to *in Verb and Noun Contexts*

One question that remained was how the acquisition of *to* in CV contexts (e.g., "going to sleep"), related to the acquisition of *to* in noun contexts (e.g., "going to school"). As seen in Table 8.1, *to* was learned in noun contexts either at the same time (by three of the children) or later (by Kathryn) than in CV contexts, and use of *to* increased developmentally in both contexts. Contrary to our intuitive expectations, there were many more CV contexts for *to* than there were N contexts. However, even though the children had more opportunities to use *to* in CV contexts than in N contexts, given an N context, *to* was more likely to occur (overall average .66) than when given a CV context (overall average .28). Further, there was some tendency that given a noun context for *to*, *to* was more likely to occur if that noun was an animate noun than if it was an inanimate noun. Inasmuch as the preposition *to* in noun contexts in the children's speech always meant direction toward, the fact that they learned *to* in verb contexts at essentially the same time that they learned *to* in noun contexts added support to the conclusion that they learned *to* in verb contexts with that meaning.

DISCUSSION

The spontaneous speech data from these four children support the following conclusions regarding *to* in the development of the verb system in their language. First, the children in this study did not learn *to* as a meaningless syntactic marker. The interpretation of *to* as "direction toward" was based upon the meaning of the matrix forms with which *to* was learned. The children's use of *to* was consistent with the historical meaning "direction toward" or "goal" (Jespersen, 1964), and indeed, the appearance of *to* in their speech with both nouns and verbs was closely associated in time.

Second, these 2-year-old children learned *to* as a complementizer connective in the context of a small group of forms that take a verb phrase complement; the basic structure that they learned was verb + *to*. A limited set of matrix forms occurred that took the connective *to*, and a large and varied set of verbs occurred freely as complements. The children did not learn *to* in the context of the complement verbs to mark the infinitive.

The thrust of this conclusion is not diminished by the appearance of an intervening and non-coreferential NP to separate the matrix form and *to* in the surface structure. Utterances with intervening NP were relatively infrequent; the matrix forms were the same forms as in contexts without intervening NP, and the *to* was expressed with intervening NP later and only after the children had learned *to* well enough to use it in more than 75% of the CV contexts. Moreover, the structures with intervening NP were highly constrained: Certain structures were used by only one or two of the children and only with limited lexical–syntactic surface-structure realization. For example, in the later data, when Kathryn used *to* with an intervening NP, she used *want* over-whelmingly with *you* as the intervening NP. The *to* was otherwise part of a fuller connective, for example, *how to* or *for to,* with specific matrix forms (e.g., *show–how to, too hard for–to*). These children were just beginning to acquire the complexities of surface-structure syntax with *to.* Having already established the basic structure of *to* with matrix forms in CV contexts, the children began to learn more complex complementizer structures that were specific to particular matrix forms.

The main result of this study, that the children learned *to* in the basic structure verb + *to,* is consistent with the results of a second study of the acquisition of other complementation structures by the same four children (Bloom, Rispoli, Gartner, & Hafitz, 1989, chap. 9). In the same period, from two to three years of age, the children learned a small number of complement-taking verbs in addition to the verbs with *to:* The most frequent were the perception verbs *see* and *look,* mental verbs *know* and *think,* and communication verbs *say* and *tell.* The complementizer connectives that the children learned were specific to individual verbs, just as *to* was specific to the matrix forms described above, and the basic structure that the children learned was verb + connective. That is, the first verb in a sentence governed whether a connective occurred and, if a connective occurred, which one. For example, as the children acquired the *wh*-connectives, they did not use them in all possible contexts, not even with verbs already established in the lexicons that could be expected to take *wh*-connectives. Other aspects of these children's acquisition of linguistic structure have been verb specific as well – for example, the acquisition of inflections (Bloom, Lifter, & Hafitz, 1980, chap. 5) and the acquisition of *wh*-questions (Bloom, Merkin, & Wootten 1982, chap. 6).

We have identified three hypotheses that converge to explain the acquisition of *to* in the present study. They are complementary rather than mutually exclusive. First, a semantic hypothesis would suggest that syntactic learning is somehow directed to or at least facilitated by semantic categorization (e.g., Bloom, 1970; Slobin, 1973), as in this instance where *to* was acquired with the meaning direction toward. The second hypothesis, a formal one, would predict that *to* is acquired as children come to recognize the distributional regularity of *to* in adult speech (e.g., as Braine, 1976; and Maratsos & Chalkley, 1980, have argued for other linguistic forms in child data). Evidence for this position would be the strong association of *to* with matrix forms and the fact that when sentences with an intervening non-coreferential NP began to appear, the structures were highly constrained in form and different for each of the children. The third explanation is a processing hypothesis: that children begin to use *to* in appropriate contexts as a function of their increasing ability to process longer utterances, unstressed elements, and complement structures. Thus the children learned to use *to* more easily with new forms than with the old forms that were already well established without *to*.

With respect to linguistic theory, the results of this study are more consistent with the lexicalist theory of universal grammar (Bresnan, 1978) than the transformational account (Koster & May, 1982). The child data support Bresnan's view that verb + infinitive and modal + infinitive are basic structures. However, in the present study the evidence indicated that the children learned *to* as a complementizer connective with the higher verb and other matrix forms, and the basic structure that they learned originally was verb + *to*. The children did not appear to learn the same underlying sentential structure for *for–to* and infinitive complements (Koster & May, 1982). The transformational account of simpler structures being derived from more complex underlying sentential structures finds no support. This conclusion is consistent with a similar conclusion regarding phrasal and sentential coordination reported by Bloom, Hood, Lifter, and Fiess (1980, chap. 7), Lust and Mervis (1980), Tager-Flusberg, de Villiers, and Hakuta (1982).

The results of this study support the conclusion that we have drawn elsewhere: The verb system is a determining factor in the acquisition of linguistic structure (see in particular Bloom, 1981; Bloom, Lightbown, & Hood, 1975, chap. 2; Gentner, 1978; and Lahey & Feier, 1982, regarding language dissolution). The subcategorization of verbs exerts a major influence on the acquisition of increasingly complex structures in children's sentences, and the development of the verb lexicon and the grammar are mutually dependent.

NOTES

1 For example, Jespersen (1964); Bresnan (1970).
2 Hyams (1984); Beckwith, Rispoli, & Bloom (1984).

3 She also challenged our interpretation of the derivation of *to* and *for–to* complements, which I have since corrected.

4 Beckwith, Rispoli, & Bloom (1984, p. 687).

POSTSCRIPT

For studies of infinitive complements and the preposition *to* since Bloom, Tackeff, and Lahey (1984):

Crain, S., & Thornton, R. (in press). Recharting the course of language acquisition: Studies in elicited production. In N. Krasnegor, D. Rumbaugh, R. Schiefelbusch, and M. Studdert-Kennedy (Eds.), *Biobehavioral foundations of language development*. Hillsdale, NJ: Erlbaum.

Eisenberg, S. (1989). The development of infinitives by three, four, and five year-old children. Ph.D. diss., City University of New York.

Kim, Y. (1989). Theoretical implications of complement structure acquisition in Korean. *Journal of Child Language, 16*, 573–98.

Pinker, S. (1984). *Language learnability and language development*. Cambridge, MA: Harvard University Press.

Tomasello, M. (1987). Learning to use prepositions: A case study. *Journal of Child Language, 14*, 79–98.

For discussions of infinitive complements:

Beckwith, R., Rispoli, M., & Bloom, L. (1984). Child language and linguistic theory: In response to Nina Hyams. *Journal of Child Language, 11*, 685–7.

Hyams, N. (1984). The acquisition of infinitival complements: A reply to Bloom, Tackeff, & Lahey. *Journal of Child Language, 11*, 679–83.

9

Wh- and Sentence Complements

"Let's go see where Mommy is."
"I think this guy is ready to ride out."

The conclusion reached in earlier studies, that verb subcategorization exerted a major influence on the acquisition of syntactic structures in these children's language, was strongly supported by the results of the two studies of complementation. This was true for verbs that take *to* complements, as we saw in Chapter 8, as well as for the acquisition of complementation with epistemic and perception verbs that take *wh-* and sentence complements. Four epistemic and perception verbs with subordinate complements were acquired by all the children. These were the epistemic verbs *think* and *know* and the perception verbs *look* (*at*) and *see*. These four verbs were the most frequent complement-taking verbs in this as well as other studies reported in the literature. The complement structures the children acquired and the patterns of co-occurrence restrictions in these sentences were conditioned by the particular matrix verbs. In addition, sentences with these different verbs occurred in different discourse environments. These results yielded a lexical typology for complement-taking verbs with three semantic distinctions: epistemic–perception, activity–experience, and certainty–uncertainty.

COMPLEMENT STRUCTURES

The children learned different complement types for the two epistemic verbs: sentence complements with *think* and *wh*-complements with *know*. With verbs of perception, *wh*-complements were more frequent overall, and sentence complements were more frequent with *see* than with *look* (*at*). The children acquired the complementizer connectives for each of the verbs separately. Different (or no) connectives were learned with the different verbs, and when the same connective was learned with two or more verbs it emerged at different times. *That* was used as a complementizer connective only rarely. Finally, the matrix verbs and subordinate verbs in the complement differed in their surface syntax, in both the subjects they took and their inflectional and modal marking. Matrix verbs took first- and second-person subjects only and were rarely inflected. Complement verbs occurred with many more different first-, second-, and third-person subjects and more frequent auxiliary marking for tense and modality.

DISCOURSE CONTINGENCIES

Of the four verbs in the children's sentences, *think* was repeated from a prior adult utterance most often, and *look* (*at*) was repeated least often. *Think* was also most likely, and *look* (*at*) was least likely, to occur with complements that repeated something from a prior adult utterance. This pattern of discourse contingency – with *think* the most frequently contingent verb and *look* (*at*) the least frequently contingent verb – meant that the children used *think* most often to maintain the discourse topic and *look* (*at*) most often to introduce a new topic.

SEMANTIC DIMENSIONS

The first semantic dimension was the superordinate epistemic–perception distinction between the verbs *think* and *know,* and *see* and *look* (*at*), respectively. Two other semantic dimensions also distinguished the verbs within each of these categories. One was the distinction between *look* (*at*) and *see* and between *think* and *know* as verbs of activity and experience, respectively. The activity–experience distinction had been reported for verbs of perception in a typological study of 53 languages by Åke Viberg[1]; it was extended in this study to the children's epistemic verbs. Finally, the patterns of formal and discourse regularities in the children's use of these verbs suggested a third semantic dimension. These children seemed to use these verbs for qualifying the relative degree of certainty–uncertainty of the complement propositions they expressed. This attitudinal distinction was evident within each pair of epistemic and perception verbs, with *know* and *think* expressing certainty–uncertainty, respectively, and *look* (*at*) and *see* expressing certainty–uncertainty, respectively.

The two most clearly differentiated matrix verbs in their syntactic and discourse patterning were *think* and *look* (*at*). They differed, respectively, in their epistemic versus perception superordinate meaning: their functions as first-person statements versus second-person imperatives, and their contingency on prior discourse. *Think* expressed the child speaker's uncertainty and continued a topic introduced into the discourse by someone else most often. *Look* (*at*) expressed a directive with certainty and introduced a new topic that originated with what the child had in mind.

Acquisition of Complementation

Lois Bloom, Matthew Rispoli, Barbara Gartner,
and Jeremie Hafitz

INTRODUCTION

The study reported here is part of a larger investigation into the acquisition of complex sentences by four children between two and three years of age. We have defined *complex sentences* in child speech as sentences with two verbs that express two propositions (Bloom, Lahey, Hood, Lifter, & Fiess, 1980, chap. 7). *Complementation* is the special instance of complex sentences in which one proposition serves as an argument within another proposition (see also the definitions in Quirk, Greenbaum, Leech, & Svartvik, 1972). Those complement-taking verbs that take the *to* complementizer (e.g., *want to* and *have to*) were the subject of an earlier report (Bloom, Tackeff, & Lahey, 1984, chap. 8). For the purposes of the present study, all the remaining complement-taking verbs that this same group of children learned in this period were examined. Verbs were identified as complement-taking verbs if (1) they could take sentential complements (e.g., "*think* I can put him in a house") or (2) they could take *wh*-complementizers with null arguments (e.g., "*Look* at what the little bear's eating").

All the complement-taking verbs in the children's speech are listed in Table 9.1 along with the number of children who used those verbs productively. Productivity was defined as three different sentences with a particular matrix verb. The verbs are categorized here according to their superordinate meaning. Four verbs were chosen for analysis in the present study (*think, know, see,* and *look* [*at*][2]) because these were the only matrix verbs that were productive in the speech of all the children (except the volition–intention verbs that take *to* complements, reported in Bloom, Tackeff, & Lahey, 1984, chap. 8). These same four verbs were also reported in descriptions of the acquisition of complementation in child speech by Limber (1973) and Pinker (1984).

Reprinted from the *Journal of Child Language, 16,* 1989, 101–20, with permission from Cambridge University Press.

Table 9.1. *Lexical Categorization of Complement-taking Verbs*[a]

	Perception	Epistemic	Volition–Intention	Communication	Causative
Four children	*see* *look (at)*	*think* *know*	*want* *like* *go* *have*	—	—
At least two children	*watch* *show*	—	*got* *try*	*say* *tell*	*let* *make*
One child	—	*forget* *wonder* *remember* *bet* *mean* *afraid*	*need*	—	*help* *get*

[a]The productivity criterion for inclusion here was the occurrence of at least three different sentences with a particular verb in one observation session. The volition–intention verbs are the same as those taking *to* complements and are reported in Bloom, Tackeff, & Lahey, 1984, chap. 8.

Complement-taking verbs are developmentally interesting for both linguistic and psychological reasons. Linguistically, they provide the first forms of complex sentences in child speech after the acquisition of simple sentences and questions (Limber, 1973; Bloom, Lahey, Hood, Lifter, & Fiess, 1980, chap. 7; Pinker, 1984). Psychologically, these verbs name internal, mental states rather than actions, and moreover, the mental states they name are directed toward actions or other internal states. The emergence of complementation in child speech is, then, a qualitative development in both linguistic and psychological complexity. The purpose of this study was to investigate factors that contribute to this development.

PROCEDURE

Transcripts of naturally occurring child speech, annotated with descriptions of context and relevant activity, were examined for evidence of (1) the developing productivity of complement-taking verbs, (2) their discourse contexts, and (3) the surface structures of sentences

Table 9.2. *Age and Mean Length of Utterance for Two Developmental Times*

Child	Times[a]	Number of Sessions	Age		MLU	
			Range	Mean	Range	Mean
Eric	1	3	2;1.1–2;5.3	2;3.1	2.63–3.45	2.97
	2	2	2;9.0–3;0.0	2;10.2	3.49–4.21	3.85
Gia	1	3	2;1.2–2;4.2	2;3.2	2.30–3.07	2.71
	2	2	2;6.0–2;10.2	2;8.1	3.64–3.71	3.68
Kathryn	1	3	2;0.2–2;5.1	2;2.3	2.83–3.35	3.16
	2	2	2;8.1–2;11.1	2;9.3	3.70–4.23	3.97
Peter	1	3	2;3.0–2;6.0	2;4.2	2.63–2.90	2.75
	2	4	2;7.2–3;2.0	2;10.2	3.05–3.58	3.37

[a]Times 1 and 2 are the result of grouping data, with Time 1 = MLU < 3.5, and Time 2 = MLU > 3.5.

with matrix verbs, including complement type and complementizer connectives.

Subjects and Methods

For the present study, data are reported for Eric, Gia, and Kathryn from five observation sessions, each lasting approximately 8 hours, at 6-week intervals. For the fourth child, Peter, observation sessions were shorter (approximately 5 hours), with 1-month intervals between sessions, and data are reported from seven observation sessions. A summary description of the children in terms of age and mean length of utterance (MLU) is presented in Table 9.2. In this and subsequent tables and figures, Times 1 and 2 represent a grouping of the data on the basis of MLU, for the purpose of identifying developmental trends. The MLU criterion for distinguishing between Times 1 and 2 was 3.5 morphemes (or its closest equivalent).

The sentences analyzed for this study represented only .007 of all the utterances that the children produced in these sessions between 2 and 3 years of age. The four children produced approximately 79,000 utterances all together. All instances of verbs that could take complements were extracted from the corpus whether or not they occurred with complements and/or complementizer connectives. In all, over 6,000 sentences with such verbs occurred. The acquisition of those verbs that take *to* complements was described in another study (Bloom, Tackeff, & Lahey, 1984). The remaining verbs that could take S- or *wh*-complements and were used in the speech of all four children are the subject of this study: *think, know, see,* and *look (at)*. Approximately 2,600 sentences occurred with these verbs, and in 577 of these sentences the verbs occurred as matrix verbs with complements.

RESULTS

The first result is the distribution of the epistemic and perception verbs, with and without complement structures, in the child data. The subsequent results concern only the sentences with complementation and consist of (1) their discourse contingencies and (2) the subcategorization of complement types, complementizer connectives, and co-occurrence restrictions. As will be seen, these subcategorization phenomena in the course of the children's acquisition were not always consistent with the target language they were learning.

Distribution of Verbs

The frequency with which each verb occurred, both with and without complementation, is presented in Table 9.3. The perception verbs occurred with complements, on average, 12.5% of the time (*see* 14%, *look* 10%). Examples of perception verbs without complements were

(1) E   Doggie is looking up.

(2) K   And nobody can see him.

Examples of these verbs with complements were

(3) G   Look *what my mommy got me.*

(4) K   I'll see *where it is.*

See was the most frequent of these verbs overall; although *see* occurred only 14% of the time with a complement, it was the most frequent matrix verb with complements in the corpus.

Epistemic verbs appeared with complements, on average, 64% of the time (*know* 44%, *think* 83%). Examples of epistemic verbs without

Table 9.3. *Frequencies of Complement and Noncomplement Sentences*

Child	Times		Perception		Epistemic	
			see	*look*	*know*	*think*
Eric						
	1	+COMP	15	13	6	12
		−COMP	349	161	4	2
	2	+COMP	53	8	27	42
		−COMP	96	119	68	5
Gia						
	1	+COMP	1	9	1	7
		−COMP	115	27	4	3
	2	+COMP	23	10	11	5
		−COMP	77	58	14	1
Kathryn						
	1	+COMP	23	7	7	30
		−COMP	174	40	1	4
	2	+COMP	45	4	9	44
		−COMP	223	37	4	41
Peter						
	1	+COMP	17	3	20	3
		−COMP	165	63	6	5
	2	+COMP	30	8	49	35
		−COMP	87	89	16	4
	Totals	+COMP	207	62	130	178
		−COMP	1286	594	117	65

complements included routine phrases like "I don't know," "You know?" "I think so," and "Think so?" but also

(5) E   I don't know that part.

(6) K   I think up on this bed.

Examples of these verbs with complements were

(7) P   Know *what the other ones do?*

(8) G   I think *the children go to bed.*

Thus, except for their routine phrases (e.g., "I don't know") these children used the epistemic verbs largely as complement-taking verbs.

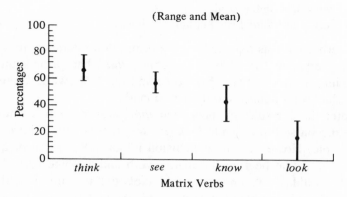

Figure 9.1. Complement contingency.

Discourse Environment

All sentences with complement clauses were examined for evidence of discourse contingency. For this study, *contingency* was defined as the adult's having said something within five prior speaker turns that included either the matrix verb or part of the complement of the child utterance. These two sources of contingency were not mutually exclusive. A sentence could have been said by a child when the adult had already said a sentence with that matrix verb, or some part of the adult's sentence could have become a part of the complement in the child's sentence, or both these things could have happened.

For example, the children's sentences were contingent when an adult utterance introduced a verb or argument that appeared subsequently in the complement of the child sentence, for example:

(9) Adult: Let's see how this one *works*.
    K   You know how it *works?*

The frequency with which the complement in the children's sentences included something from a prior adult utterance is presented in Figure 9.1. Complements with *think* repeated something from a prior utterance most often (66% on average); sentences with *look* (*at*) did so the least (16% on average).

Discourse contingency also included the child's use of a matrix verb when the matrix verb had been used by an adult in a prior utterance, for example:

(10) Adult: I *think* that lamb is cold.
　　　E   He is very cold/I *think* I can put him in a house.

The matrix verb *think* was repeated from a prior adult utterance more often than any other matrix verb. On average, *think* had prior adult introduction into discourse 32% of the time and *see* 11%, while *know* and *look* (*at*) had prior adult use only occasionally.

We interpret these results to mean that *think* was most likely to maintain the discourse topic, while *look* (*at*) was most likely to introduce a new topic. However, this conclusion is not independent of a second conclusion, that hearing the matrix verb and/or some part of what the child would say also made it more likely that the child would use a matrix verb with complementation. *Think,* the verb that was most frequently contingent, was also the matrix verb with the highest proportion of complementation.

Complementation Structure

Complement Type Subcategorization. The two complement types were (1) sentential complements (S-complements), for example:

(11) K   I see *Mommy washing her hands.*

and (2) *wh*-complements, for example:

(12) K   Let's go see *where Mommy is.*

The average frequency of verb + complement types is presented for each verb in Figure 9.2. The development of complementation in this period of time is apparent: Except for sentences with *look,* complementation was more frequent in Time 2 than in Time 1. However, the production of particular complement types was not independent of the matrix verbs.

Think appeared only with S-complements (as expected). S-complements occurred more frequently with *think* than with any other verb for all the children in both time periods. The other epistemic verb, *know,* appeared almost exclusively with *wh*-complements, for example:

(13) G   You know *what's in this bag?*

and rarely with *s*-complements, for example:

(14) E   I know *I open it up.*

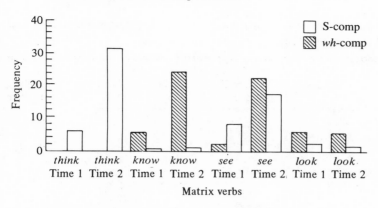

Figure 9.2. Mean frequency of complement types.

Both complement types were used with *see*. Before MLU reached 3.5 (in Time 1), the most frequent complement type with *see* was sentential, while *wh*-complement sentences were less frequent. Once MLU exceeded 3.5 (in Time 2) the balance was reversed, and *wh*-complements were more frequent than S-complements. However, this reversal was due almost entirely to one child, Eric. At Time 1, Eric produced 14 S-complements with *see,* for example:

(15) E   I see *two bus come there.*

and 1 *wh*-complement sentence. At Time 2 he produced only eight sentences with *see* and S-complements, and 45 sentences with *see* and a *wh*-complement, for example:

(16) E   Let's see *what's in the train house.*

S-complements appeared with *look at* (15 instances among the four children), for example:

(17) P   Look at *that airplane coming out the airplane home.*

However, in both developmental periods, *wh*-complements with *look* (as in [3] above) were more frequent.

   In sum, the two epistemic verbs took different complement types: S-complements occurred with *think,* and *wh*-complements occurred with *know.* Overall, *wh*-complementation was more frequent than S-complements with the perception verbs, especially in Time 2, and S-complements were more frequent with *see* than with *look* (*at*).

Table 9.4. *Average Age of Emergence for* Wh-*Question Words and* Wh-*Complement Words*

Wh-Q[a] Words	Average Age	Number of Children[b]	Wh-Comp Words	Average Age	Number of Children[c]
what	2; 2	7	—	—	—
where	2; 2	7	—	—	—
who	2; 4	7	—	—	—
—	—	—	what	2; 6	4
—	—	—	where	2; 7.2	3
how	2; 9	7	how	2; 9.2	3
—	—	—	(if)	2; 10	4
why	2; 11	7	who	2; 11	3

[a] The results for *wh*-question words are from Bloom, Merkin, & Wootten, 1982, chap. 6.
[b] $n = 7$.
[c] $n = 4$.

Acquisition of Complementizer Connectives. Wh-complements were not expected with *think* and were not observed. Otherwise, the complementizers these children learned with *know, see,* and *look (at)* were the same words, except for *if,* that they had acquired earlier in their *wh*-questions (Bloom, Merkin, & Wootten, 1982, chap. 6). *If,* which is not a *wh*-question word, was one of the last of the complementizers they acquired in this period. The order of emergence of *wh*-complementizers resembled the earlier emergence order of *wh*-questions. The two emergence orders are compared in Table 9.4.

The emergence age for *wh*-questions in Table 9.4 is the average for seven children (from Bloom, Merkin, & Wootten, 1982, chap. 6); the emergence age of the complementizers is an average for four of the same children. Consistent with the findings of Bloom, Merkin, and Wootten, emergence was considered the beginning of productivity and was defined as at least three different complements used with a particular *wh*-complementizer. As can be seen, these children asked *what* and *where* questions 4 months (on average) before they used *what* and *where* as complementizers. Two complementizers, *where* and *how,* reached productivity for three children. *How* did not become productive in questions until approximately 7 months after *what* and *where* questions, but unlike *what* and *where, how* emerged as both a question word and a complementizer at about the same time. The last *wh*-word

Table 9.5. *Distribution, Order of Emergence, and Number of Children Using the Different Connectives*

Distribution of connectives		
see–what (4)[a]	know–what (4)	look–what (4)
see–if (4)	know–where (3)	
see–how (2)	know–how (1)	
see–where (1)		

Order of emergence of connectives

$\begin{vmatrix} know–what \\ see–what \end{vmatrix} > look–what$ (3)

know–what > see–what > look–what (1)
know–where > see–where (1)
see–if > know–if (1)

[a] Number of children in parentheses.

to become productive in the children's questions, *why,* was not acquired as a complementizer in the time period covered by this study.

Wh-words are not perceptually salient as complementizers because they occur in the middle of a sentence between the matrix verb and the complement. Their acquisition for complementation may have depended, in part, upon prior segmentation in the more salient, sentence-initial position as *wh*-question words (Pinker, 1984).

Use of the different complementizer connectives was verb specific. This result is presented in Table 9.5. Of the three verbs with *wh*-complementizers, only *see* was productive with all four connectives; *know* was productive with three; and *look* (*at*) was productive only with *what*. The only *wh*-complementizer acquired with all the matrix verbs (except *think*) was *what,* and *what* was used by all the children with each of the three verbs that took complementizers. However, the different connectives did not appear at the same time with the different matrix verbs. The order of emergence is presented in Table 9.5. *What* was acquired with *look* (*at*) only after it had become productive with *know* and *see*. *Where* was productive with *know* before *see,* while *if* was productive with *see* before *know*. These results mean that the acquisition of a complementizer did not promptly generalize to all of the children's matrix verbs that could take that complementizer. Rather, these children acquired the complementizer connectives verb by verb.

That was rare as a complementizer in these sentences. A total of 179 complement sentences with *think* were said by all the children, but only three of these included *that* as a connective, for example:

(18) G   I think *that* he wanna eat this.

These children certainly knew the word; demonstrative pronouns were among the earliest forms in their simple sentences (Bloom, 1970). In addition, *that* appeared with other functions in the complements. *That* appeared 14 times as the subject of the complement verb, in the same deictic sentence frame which had been productive from the beginning of these children's multiword speech, for example:

(19) K   I thought *that was a snacktime.*

(20) E   I think *that is a porkypine.*

In addition, 35 complement sentences occurred with the copula as the matrix verb (not considered in the study reported here), and 25 of these included *that* as a deictic subject, for example:

(21) E   *That* where the butterfly live.

(22) P   *That's* how get them out.

Although *this* was frequent as a determiner in the complement subject, only one instance of *that* occurred in the same position:

(23) K   I think *that* girl is going to dust that that paper away.

(Note also that Kathryn stumbled on the subsequent use of *that* in the same sentence.)

Three factors could have contributed to *that* not being acquired for complementation in the period studied here. First, the plurifunctionality of *that* may have inhibited its acquisition as a complementizer. Since an item with more than one function within a sentence presumably increases perceptual difficulty (Bever, 1970), we might expect an item with several functions in different sentences to be more difficult to acquire. In this instance, then, the prior acquisition of *that* with other functions did not facilitate its acquisition as a complementizer, as had been suggested for the acquisition of the plurifunctional *wh-*forms. A second factor is, of course, input frequency. We do not know how often these children heard *that* as a complementizer with *think, know,* or *see* in this time period.

In addition, Jespersen pointed out that complementation without *that* is especially frequent after such verbs as *think, know,* and *see,* but in these cases "it is historically wrong to say that the conjunction *that* is omitted" (1956/1961, p. 32). Complementation with and without *that* evolved out of independent sentences, for example, (1) "I think that S" and (2) "I think S." Originally *that* in (1) was a demonstrative pronoun object of the verb (i.e., "I think that"). The distinction in this historical argument is relevant to these children's development inasmuch as they did not say sentences like "I think that" or "I know that" and also did not use *that* as a complementizer.

Co-occurrence Restrictions on Matrix and Complement Verbs

Two features distinguished the surface syntax of the matrix and complement clauses. First, the matrix subjects were hightly restricted, while the subjects of complement verbs were varied. Second, matrix verbs were rarely inflected, whereas the subordinate verb in the complement was often either inflected or marked for modality.

Subject Restrictions. Certain restrictions would be expected on the matrix verbs studied here. For example, only animate subjects can see, look, think, and know. However, the differences in variety of subjects of the subordinate and matrix verbs were greater than would be predicted by the target language.

Subjects of Subordinate Verbs. The subordinate complement clauses were copular constructions, with pronominal subjects, in an average of 48% of the sentences with *know,* 35% with *think,* 31% with *see,* and 8% with *look (at),* for example:

(24) K   I think *it's* big enough.

(25) E   Know *what's* in here?

(26) G   I'm going to see if *there's* any more.

Otherwise, a full variety of first-, second-, and third-person subjects occurred in the complements, both nominal, for example:

(27) E   Look at *that donkey* carrying baskets.

and pronominal, for example:

(28) K   I think *we* can put it side of him.

Subjects of Matrix Verbs. In contrast, the subjects of matrix verbs were highly restricted. To begin with, no subjects were expressed with *look;* all were null second person (as in [27]). The matrix verb *think* occurred only with *I* in the speech of three of the children. Only Peter, whose earliest and latest sentences with *think* included only *I*, produced *think* sentences in the interim without *I*. Most of these were null first person, but several were null second person, and one second-person subject was expressed:

(29) P   *You* think it don't belongs to me.

The subjects of sentences with *know* and *see* were only somewhat more varied, and the order of acquisition differed for the different children. Both Gia and Eric began saying sentences with these two matrix verbs first with first-person *I,* and then with second-person *you* both expressed and null. Kathryn and Peter both began to say sentences with *know* and *see* with null second-person subjects (Kathryn also expressed second-person *you*) before they used these matrix verbs with *I.* Neither Gia, Kathryn, nor Peter used any of their matrix verbs with third-person subjects. Only Eric eventually used both of these matrix verbs with third-person subjects, for example:

(30) E   Oh *the bunny rabbit* doesn't know what to do.

In sum, this group of matrix verbs were verbs that named internal mental states and they were acquired to express these states of the child and, to a lesser extent, of the child's discourse partner. They were not used to express the child's attributions of such states to others who were not participants in the discourse (in contrast to the data reported by Shatz, Wellman, & Silber, 1983). On the one hand, the use of these verbs in the children's speech was consistent with accounts that have described limitations on the preschool child's awareness of the mental states of other persons (e.g., Piaget 1923/1955; Wellman, 1985). On the other hand, the fact that these children did not talk about what third persons see, look at, think, or know is not by itself evidence that they could not attribute these internal states to other persons. By the age of 3 years children are able to attribute seeing and looking to other persons (Flavell, 1978). Mothers of children in the same age range as the children studied here have reported that their children use perception words (and significantly more often than epistemic words) in talking about other persons (Bretherton & Beeghly, 1982).[3] Nevertheless, the differences between matrix and subordinate subjects were not entirely predicted by the target language.

Coreference. The children's sentences were examined to determine the coreference of the subject of the complement verb. A total of 332 complements occurred with nominal or personal pronoun subjects, and in only 46 (14%) was the subject of the complement verb coreferent with an expressed subject of the matrix verb. Of these coreferent subjects, 61% occurred with *think,* 28% with *see,* 11% with *know,* and none with *look* (*at*). Thus when coreferent subjects did occur, these were with *think* most often, for example:

(31) K   *I think I*'ll pull the other side.

Sentences with such volition–intention verbs as *want, like,* and *go* were productive with *to* complements in these children's speech about 2 months earlier than complementation with epistemic and perception verbs (reported in Bloom, Tackeff, & Lahey, 1984, chap. 8). In sentences with *to* complements the subject of the matrix verb was also the subject of the complement verb. The children were most often talking about what it was that they wanted to do or were going to do. Non-coreferent subjects appeared in sentences with *to* after MLU 3.5, and this was after non-coreferent subjects appeared with the epistemic and perception verbs. This sequence of development (from Bloom, Tackeff, & Lahey, 1984, together with the present study) was the same sequence that Pinker (1984) also observed. Complementation with subject coreference (with *to* complement verbs and then with *think*) occurred before complementation with non-coreferent subjects.

Morphological Marking. Matrix verbs and subordinate complement verbs also differed in the extent to which they were inflected and/or marked for modality. Again, this difference was not entirely predicted by the target language.

Matrix Verbs. The restrictions on subjects of matrix verbs and the fact that these verbs were state rather than process verbs limited the opportunities for matrix verb inflection. No inflections occurred with *look* (*at*), but none was expected, since *look* (*at*) occurred only with second-person subjects in the imperative. *Know* was limited to either first- or second-person subjects and used frequently with generic co-pular statements in the complement. *Know* was never inflected. *Think* was used almost exclusively with first-person *I*, but only Kathryn used *think* with past tense (6 instances, e.g., [19] above).

See was used with only first- and second-persons subjects. It was never inflected. However, *see* was the one matrix verb that occurred with adverbial or modal marking with any regularity. Twenty-four per-cent of the sentences with *see* as a matrix verb also included an adverb (e.g., *now*) or modal, for example:

(32) P   *Wanna see* I make a ball with my gum?

The children differed in the matrix adverbials and modals used with *see*. Eric used only *let's* ([16] above) and *now;* Gia used *gonna* and *wanna;* Kathryn used *let's* ([12] above); and Peter used *wanna* ([32] above). While the modals would not be expected with *think,* they might have occurred with *know* and *look* but did not.

Subordinate Verbs. In contrast to the matrix verbs, the subordinate verbs in the complement were inflected or occurred with marked mo-dality more than 50% of the time. However, subordinate verbs were used with modals primarily in sentences with *think* and *see* (65% of the modals in complement sentences occurred after *think* and 29% after *see*), for example:

(33) E   I *think* we *should* put this in a house.

Except for Gia, the children used modals with subordinate verbs after *see* and most of these (64% of the modal complement sentences with *see*) were *can* after the complementizer *if,* for example:

(34) K   *See if* it *can* make some sound.

Together, these results lead to the same conclusion offered above with respect to discourse function, complement type, and selection of complementizer connectives: The syntax of sentences with comple-ments was matrix verb specific. Different co-occurrence restrictions on verb inflections, modality, and subjects were observed with the different matrix verbs. In addition, the matrix verbs, as a group, were more restricted in their co-occurrence than were the subordinate verbs in the complement.

DISCUSSION

The results presented here together with the results reported in Bloom, Tackeff, & Lahey, 1984, chap. 8, document the beginning of the ac-quisition of complementation in the year between the ages of 2 and 3. We will discuss these results in terms of two aspects of the acquisition of complementation with perception and epistemic verbs: the use of developmentally prior linguistic forms for acquiring the syntax of complementation, and the meaning function that these complement-taking verbs served in the mental life of the child.

The Origin of the Structures of Complementation

Both complementizers and complement types were based upon structures previously acquired. The children were ready to produce both S-complement and *wh*-complement structures in the first developmental period of this study because they already knew their basic surface structures from earlier learned sentence frames. As observed originally by Limber, "complex sentences will be formed from the child's repertoire of simple sentences" (1973, p. 184).

S-complementation was essentially the addition of a simple sentence after a matrix verb. Sentences with *wh*-complements consisted of a *wh*-question word and a sentence with elision of the element corresponding to the question word. The syntax of *wh*-complements was the same as the syntax of early *wh*-questions. When children first begin to ask *wh*-questions, they often start the questions with a *wh*-word and add a simple sentence (e.g., "What you doing?" and "Where the ball go?"). Similarly, when these children began to produce *wh*-complements, they added the matrix verb to a *wh*-question (e.g., "See what you doing" and "Know where the ball go"). Interestingly, 'errors' like "I don't know what's his problem" are found even among adults (Fay, 1980, p. 117). Thus the developmental origins of both S-complements and *wh*-complements were in the structures acquired at an earlier time for simple sentences and asking *wh*-questions.

However, this process of acquisition consisted of more than the simple addition of forms. For example, while certain co-occurrence restrictions on matrix verbs could have been expected (e.g., lack of tense inflections with second-person subjects in the imperative), others were not (e.g., the lack of modals with subordinate verbs after *know* and *look,* or the occurrence of adverbs and modals in the matrix only with *see,* or the limitations on the subjects of all the matrix verbs). Two factors could explain this pattern of results. One explanation might have been found in the input that the children received, and this is a subject for future research. In addition, however, evidence from psycholinguistic studies of sentence processing has suggested that complement-taking verbs are inherently more difficult than simple transitive verbs for adults to process (Fodor, Garrett, & Bever, 1968). Children might therefore be expected to have greater difficulty in learning co-occurrence restrictions with complement-taking verbs than with the earlier learned transitive and intransitive verbs that appeared as subordinate verbs in complements.

The acquisition of complementation builds on prior acquisition of simpler structures in yet another way. The acquisition of *wh*-complementizers followed their prior segmentation in the more salient sentence-initial question frames. To acquire a word as a complementizer requires that "the word in question must be isolated as a word beforehand" (Pinker, 1984, p. 227). *Wh*-complementizers appeared originally as *wh*-question words. However, the complementizer *to* was segmented as a preposition when it was also acquired as a complementizer (Bloom, Tackeff, & Lahey, 1984, chap. 8). When *to* did appear as a complementizer, with volition–intention verbs, it was not semantically empty. Rather, *to* had the meaning "direction toward" which derived historically from the prepositional meaning. A related analysis to demonstrate that the "complementizers (*for, to*) [are] identical to prepositions" has since been reported with *for*, which was first used as a complementizer only with purposive meaning (Nishigauchi & Roeper, 1987, p. 91).[4] The categorization of a word as a complementizer may be 'given' along with its categorization as a preposition (Pinker, 1984, p. 226). However, we would suggest instead that the knowledge that a word can also be a complementizer is acquired from observing the distributional regularities of matrix verbs with relevant complementizer connectives in the input. Thus one reason why *that*, which was one of the children's earliest and most frequent words, was not acquired as a complementizer in the period studied here, was its perceptual confusability. *That* was learned with several different functions in sentences with matrix verbs.

In sum, the acquisition of complementation began for the four children whom we have studied between their second and third birthdays. This acquisition no doubt continued well into their school years as they learned more different verbs that take complements and more of the lexical, discourse, and syntactic functions of those verbs.

The Meaning Function of Complement-Taking Verbs

These children acquired the structures of complementation with only a handful of the possible verbs that take complements in adult English (Rosenbaum, 1967). Moreover, the majority of the verbs acquired (in

Table 9.1) expressed two superordinate meanings; they were epistemic verbs (e.g., *think* and *know*) and perception verbs (e.g., *see* and *look* [*at*]).

A pattern of lexicalization for the verbs of perception in a sample of 53 languages has been reported by Viberg (1984). Lexical differentiation of the five sensory modalities – sight, hearing, touch, taste, and smell – was hierarchically organized in this typology. The hierarchy is manifested in the extent to which different words name the activity and experience dimensions in each modality. The modalities of sight and hearing in these languages most often have different lexicalizations for activity and experience. In English, for example, the activity verbs are *look* and *listen,* and the experience verbs are *see* and *hear* for sight and hearing, respectively. The modalities of touch, taste, and smell show differentiation between activity and experience much less often, English being an example of a language that does not lexicalize these distinctions (e.g., *taste* in English names both the activity and the experience).

Languages that differentiate activity and experience for only one of the modalities of sight and hearing do so in the sight modality rather than hearing. Sight verbs, then, are at the top of the lexicalization hierarchy for perception verbs, and correspondingly the children in this study differentially lexicalized only sight verbs with complementation. The sight verbs in the speech of all four children were the two basic sight verbs cited by Viberg, *look* (activity) and *see* (experience). Although one or more of the children also acquired other complement-taking perception verbs (in Table 9.1), these were also sight verbs (i.e. the activity verbs *watch* and *show*). The acquisition of complement-taking verbs was thus consistent with the lexicalization hierarchy found for the languages studied by Viberg (1984).

While a similar typology is not available, to our knowledge, for epistemic verbs, the two epistemic verbs the children acquired also distinguished between the activity (*think*) and the experience (*know*). *Think* and *know* were also the most frequent epistemic verbs by far in the longitudinal data reported by Shatz, Wellman, & Silber, (1983).

While few studies have looked at the uses of such verbs in spontaneous speech, several experimental studies of the comprehension of epistemic verbs have been reported with children as young as three years of age (e.g., Johnson & Maratsos, 1977; Abbeduto & Rosenberg, 1985). The conclusion in these studies was that 3-year-olds do not present evidence in comprehension tasks that they understand the differences in the psychological meaning entailments in the terms *think* and *know*. Such understanding was not reported in these studies until age 4. However, in the pattern of results presented here, the 2-year-old children whom we studied used these two verbs differently. Moreover, the differences in use suggested that they used these verbs to express an assessment of the ''degree of reliability'' (Chafe, 1986) of the proposition expressed in the complement of their sentences with *think* and *know*.

These children seemed to have learned *think* and *know* in order to qualify the degree of 'certainty–uncertainty' of the complement propositions in their sentences. The expression of uncertainty with *think* was suggested by the following findings: (1) *Think* was most often contingent on prior discourse, suggesting that the children were expressing new information from the prior discourse that they had not yet fully assimilated (Choi, 1986). (2) The frequent use of modals (e.g., *should, can*) with the verbs in complements of *think* expressed a lack of definiteness in the complement. (3) The complementizer *that*, which indicates certainty with *think* (Jespersen, 1956; Quirk, Greenbaum, Leech, & Svartvik, 1972), was almost entirely absent from the children's sentences with *think*. Likewise, Limber (1973, p. 185) citing Urmson (1963), observed that *think* was ''used parenthetically, especially in the first person, *I,* with the sense of *perhaps* or *maybe*.''

A pattern of certainty for *know* was suggested by other findings. (1) Less contextual and textual contingency occurred with *know* than with *think,* indicating that sentences with *know* expressed what the children already had in mind and were prepared to introduce into the discourse. (2) *Know* occurred most often with the copula as the subordinate verb in the complement, suggesting talk about attributions and generic events. These children, then, differentiated the epistemic verbs with respect to their assessment of the degree of certainty regarding the complement propositions.

Similar attitudinal distinctions could be attributed to the use of the perception verbs *look* and *see,* and *see* was similar to *think* in expressing uncertainty. *See* was second only to *think* in the extent to which the children's sentences repeated something from the prior discourse. *See* was second only to *think* in the frequency of modals in the complement and the only one of the matrix verbs used with modals and adverbs. And finally, *see* occurred with the conditional connective *if* and never with the definite *that. Look,* in contrast, suggested an attitude of definiteness or certainty; it was used exclusively with second-person subjects as an imperative and was contingent on prior discourse least often among all the matrix verbs.

The attitudinal distinctions expressed through the different matrix verbs are best represented by *think* and *look,* the two matrix verbs that were the most clearly differentiated: (1) in their superordinate meaning (epistemic–perception), (2) in their functions (first-person statements/second-person imperatives), and (3) in the extent to which they incorporated elements from the prior discourse. *Think* expressed the child speaker's uncertainty and continued a topic introduced into the discourse most often by someone else. *Look* expressed a directive to the hearer and introduced a new topic that originated with what the child had in mind. *Know* and *see* were intermediate between these two verbs, with *know* closer to *look* in expressing certainty and *see* closer to *think* in expressing uncertainty. This lexical patterning suggests an intricacy in the emerging verb lexicon, derived from the child's view of the world, that has both discourse and syntactic manifestations. It also supports the suggestion that the acquisition of internal state verbs begins with an effort to modify the reliability of statements before the truly cognitive meanings of the terms are acquired (Johnson, 1982).

CONCLUSIONS

The conclusions we draw from these results are consistent with those we have drawn in other studies of these children's language development: Learning the structure of the language is verb dependent (e.g., Bloom, 1981; Bloom, Miller, & Hood, 1975, chap. 3). The study reported here, together with the study of *to* complements in Chapter 8, revealed developments in the subcategorization of complement structures by matrix verbs. The earlier learned volition–intention verbs have the inherent meaning "direction toward" and take complements with *to* (Bloom, Tackeff, & Lahey, 1984). Epistemic and perception verbs, learned later, take S- and *wh*-complements. The acquisition of the syntax of complementation was lexically specific. Rather than learning a general rule for complementation per se, or even separate rules for *wh*-complements, S-complements, *to* complements, *if* complements, and so forth, the children's grammatical knowledge was specific to the matrix verbs. The matrix verbs determined whether a complementizer occurred and, if a complementizer occurred, which one. In the period studied here the children learned this for each matrix verb separately.

This developmental account is consistent with the procedures Pinker proposed for the acquisition of Lexical Function Grammar, whereby children learn that "matrix verbs specify the formal properties of their complements, such as being finite or infinitival, and whether and which complementizers must be present in the complements" (1984, p. 213). However, in addition, we have proposed that procedures for acquisition are influenced by the psychological attitudes that children have toward the propositions they express. In sum, the acquisition of complementation depends upon the child being able to hold in mind two propositions, where one of the propositions is expressible in a simple sentence frame and the other is the mental attitude directed toward the contents of that proposition.

NOTES

1 Viberg (1984).
2 Sentences with *look* were not included in the analyses if (1) they were spoken with segmentation prosody to indicate a sentence break after the matrix verb and/or (2) the sentence complement was a complete sentence with no null constituents (e.g., "Look, my truck got a top"). In both instances, the data were equivocal as to complementation, inasmuch as *look* was potentially a separate sentence.
3 However, the children in our study did not, in fact, use third-person subjects with these verbs even in their simple sentences without complements.
4 We thank Richard Beckwith for calling this analysis to our attention.

POSTSCRIPT

For studies of children's use of mental verbs since Bloom, Rispoli, Gartner, and Hafitz (1989):

Moore, C., & Davidge, J. (1989). The development of mental terms: Pragmatics or semantics? *Journal of Child Language, 16,* 633–41.

Moore, C., Pure, K., & Furrow, D. (1990). Children's understanding of speaker certainty and uncertainty and its relation to the development of a representational theory of mind. *Child Development, 61,* 722–30.

10

Forms and Functions of Causal Language

"Let's all take all the books out so we can read them."

Acquisition of the language for talking about causal connections has an added dimension of interest because of its relevance to theory and research on the development of the concept of causality and causal reasoning. In the study in this chapter, acquisition of the form, content, and use of expressions of causality is described for eight children, spanning the developmental period in average mean length of utterance from 2.5 to 4.53.

THE CONCEPT OF CAUSALITY

The consensus in the literature, from earlier work influenced primarily by Jean Piaget and Heinz Werner, was that true causal understanding develops slowly and is not apparent until age 7 or 8. According to Piaget, young children see two events as merely juxtaposed in time and space without a dependency relation between them. According to Werner, children are aware of the temporal but not the causal relation between events. However, the 2-year-old children in this study gave every indication that they appreciated more than just the additive and temporal relations in causal connections. For example, they expressed both cause–effect and effect–cause orders, regardless of the temporal order of events, and learned the correct connectives for the different orders, *so* and *because,* respectively. Previous research had presented children with tasks to elicit talk about observable sequential actions with physical objects. However, the spontaneous talk by the children in this study, in contrast, was about their causal intentions and motivations in everyday interactions. The results demonstrated that 2-year-old children have an understanding of causal relations between events and/or states and the ability to express these relations. In fact, in his commentary that accompanied the original publication of this monograph, Charles Brainerd commented that "the most important result emerging from [the] analysis, at least from my perspective, is the remarkable precocity and sophistication of [the] subjects' utterances when judged by the claims of cognitive–developmental theories."[1]

THE CONTENT OF EXPRESSIONS OF CAUSALITY

The major categories of content in these causal expressions were *negation, direction,* and *intention.* The children commented on their own intentions to act or requested the listener to act, often with an element of negation. The content of the children's expressions did not change over time; rather, these categories of content accounted for the same proportion of their speech when they were 2 as when they were 3 years of age. The overwhelming majority of their utterances referred to ongoing or imminent situations. Although past and future reference tended to increase somewhat, such reference occurred only in less than 10% of their speech on the average. The one clear development in content was a change in the meaning of the connective *so* from the meaning *so that* to the meaning *therefore.*

THE USE OF CAUSAL EXPRESSIONS IN DISCOURSE

The use of expressions of causality developed in the following order: child statements > appropriate responses to adult *why* questions > child *why* questions. The children learned to respond appropriately to causal questions only after they expressed causality in their own statements and before they began to ask *why* questions themselves. Statements, responses, and questions are fundamentally different discourse events (as discussed at length in Bloom, 1974b). The children were able to say something to express their own semantic intention (in making a statement) before saying something (in a response) that was influenced by what someone else said, which in turn preceded asking about the intention of someone else (with a *why* question). The children progressed from expressing their own intentions when making a causal statement to taking into account the listener's intentions when asking a *why* question. This sequence in the development of causal expressions complemented the explanation of the sequence in which the children learned to ask *wh*-questions (in Chapter 6).

THE FORM OF CAUSAL STATEMENTS

The use of causal connectives increased developmentally (as we also saw in Chapter 7) with three patterns of clause order: predominantly cause–effect, predominantly effect–cause, or a similar use of both orders. The children learned the different connectives with their corresponding clause orders: cause–effect with *so* and effect–cause with *because.* When the clause orders in their mothers' speech were compared for four of the children, each mother tended to be more similar to her own child, and vice versa, than were the mothers to one another or the children to one another.

Finally, except for the variation among the eight children in patterns of clause order and connectives, they were generally similar to one another in their development of expression of causal relations. This pattern of consistency among the children in acquisition of linguistic content with variation among them in acquiring aspects of linguistic form continued the pattern observed previously in their simple sentences (in Chapter 2) and their complex sentences (Chapter 7). [NOTE: Single-word 'Why?' questions were not included in these studies.]

What, When, and How About Why: A Longitudinal Study of Early Expressions of Causality

Lois Hood and Lois Bloom

BACKGROUND

The purpose of this study was to examine the development of causal expressions in children's discourse in the period from 2 to 3 years of age, considering the influence of conceptual, linguistic, and pragmatic factors on language development.

With respect to conceptual development, infants begin to acquire primitive notions of cause and effect in the period of sensorimotor intelligence as they learn to act with schemas of "practical" causality to modify reality to suit their own needs (Bell, 1973; Piaget, 1931/1954, p. 220). It is generally held that the child's causal reasoning continues to be qualitatively different from the adult's until age 7 or 8 (Piaget, 1923/1955, 1924/1968, 1930/1972; Werner & Kaplan, 1963). According to Werner (1948), the young child's causal reasoning is subjective and concrete, with an inability to differentiate cause and effect. Werner and Kaplan (1963) suggested that the child transforms causal and conditional dependency relations into the simpler relations of sequence and simultaneity which mirror perceptions. According to Piaget, development of the ability to understand and express both cause–effect relations (e.g., "the man fell off his bicycle because someone

Reprinted from the Monographs of the Society for Research in Child Development, 1979, serial no. 181, vol. 44, with permission from The Society for Research in Child Development.

got in his way") and logical relations (e.g., "that animal is not dead because it is still moving") depends upon the decline of egocentrism (Piaget, 1923/1955, 1928/1969) and the process of reversibility (Piaget, 1930/1972), among other things. Thus, although there are differing views of the precise nature of the child's conception of causality, the consensus is that truly causal understanding develops slowly and is not apparent until age 7 or 8.

With respect to linguistic development, substantial evidence has been offered to suggest that the understanding and expression of causal and other dependency relationships in language undergo great change from ages 4 to 10 (Johnson, 1972; Katz & Brent, 1968; Laurendeau & Pinard, 1962; Piaget, 1928/1969, 1930/1972; Vygotsky, 1962). Very little is known, however, about the emergence of the expression of causality before the age of 4, that is, how children begin to acquire the linguistic means to express and interpret causal relations in discourse. The use of causative verbs (e.g., *have, make, get, kill, open*) has been described in young children's speech (Baron, 1977; Bowerman, 1974b), and the results from these studies suggest that children have begun to express cause–effect relationships by the age of 3. However, this ability to encode a single causative event in a sentence, such as *"make* the man sit down" or "I *get* it dirty," is conceptually and linguistically different from the ability to encode the causal relation between two events in a sentence, such as "I can't reach to Ria because she's too far away" or "I'm gonna move this (ashtray) away so the fire can't get into your eyes."

At least the following two linguistic variables interact in determining the surface structure of complex sentences that express a causal relation between two events: the order of the clauses, and the conjunction used to connect the clauses. In terms of clause order, one can use a cause–effect order, for example, "the boy was tired so he took a nap"; or one can use an effect–cause order, for example, "the boy took a nap because he was tired." The clause orders appear to be relatively free in English; there is no apparent difference either in meaning or in frequency. However, the clause order and conjunction used to connect the clauses are interdependent. *Because* can only be used with effect–cause order; you can say "the boy took a nap because he was tired," but you cannot say "the boy was tired because he took a nap" (and mean the same thing). Similarly, *so* can only be used with cause–effect order; you can say "the boy was tired so he took a nap," but

Table 10.1. *Summary Description of Speech Samples*

Child	N Observ.	Average Duration Each Observ. (hr)	Age Range[a]	Mean Length of Utterance		
				Range	Mean Increment	SD
David	12	5	29,2–41,1	2.98–5.59	.20	.42
Eric	8	8	25,1–36,0	2.63–4.21	.11	.56
Gia	7	8.4	25,2–34,2	2.30–3.71	.28	.45
Kathryn	8	8.9	24,2–35,1	2.83–5.82	.20	1.03
Mariana	11	5	26,0–36,2	3.10–5.54	.19	.51
Paul	7	5	25,3–32,3	2.13–4.75	.42	.64
Peter	13	4.3	25,3–38,0	2.00–3.58	.13	.45
Steven[b]	6	5	25,3–31,1	2.01–3.06	.21	.30

[a] Age is given in months and weeks.
[b] Steven's family moved away before the study was completed.

you cannot say "the boy took a nap so he was tired" (again, and mean the same thing).

With respect to the pragmatic aspects of expressions of causality, causal statements, causal questions, and responses to causal questions differ according to events in the context that influence language use. In the present study, the development of expressions of causality were studied in terms of the acquisition of these aspects of language use in intersection with aspects of the content and form of causal expressions.

METHOD

Subjects and Procedures

Longitudinal, spontaneous speech data from eight children were analyzed in the period from approximately 24 to 41 months. Four of the children were Eric, Gia, Kathryn, and Peter, and these data consist primarily of investigator–child interactions. The data from the four other children – David, Mariana, Paul, and Steven – included equal proportions of mother–child and investigator–child interaction. Information regarding age, mean length of utterance (in morphemes), and sample size for each child is presented in Table 10.1. The first samples of the children's language behavior that were analyzed for the purposes of this study were those in which the children first began to produce causal utterances. This occurred between 24 months 1 week of age (Kathryn, Time III) and 29 months 2 weeks of age (David, Time I). Earlier data were available from Eric, Gia, Kathryn, and Peter (from approximately 19 months of age), as already indicated. Earlier data were also available from Mariana and David (from approximately 16 months of age).

Criteria for Data Analyses

Utterances were included in the analysis if they met formal and/or semantic criteria. Formal criteria for including an utterance were (1) a "causal" word (e.g., *because, so,*[2] and *why*) in child utterances, whether or not the word unambiguously expressed a causal notion; (2) occurrence of any child utterance following an adult *why* or *how* (meaning "how come" or "how do you know") question, regardless of the semantic or syntactic relationship to the question. Events in which adults asked causal questions that were not followed by a child utterance were also analyzed. The semantic criterion for analysis was an implicit reference to two events and/or states with a causal relation between them. This procedure involved investigator inferences about the causal meaning of child sentences and was essential in order to explore the developmental relationship between the order of causally related clauses and the use of causal connectives. Thus, child utterances without a connective such as "that a piano/don't draw on that," said while Kathryn was pointing to a piece of sheet music, were included in the study.

Coding

Child utterances that met the formal and/or semantic criteria for analysis were coded as statements, responses to adult questions, or questions. Child statements were analyzed in terms of the semantic and syntactic relations between clauses; child responses were analyzed in terms of their semantic and syntactic relations to the adult questions; child questions were analyzed in terms of their semantic and syntactic relationship to prior utterances by adult and/or child.

Child Statements. All spontaneous causal statements were coded (1) for the presence or absence of causal connectives, (2) according to whether the meaning relation between the clauses was causally interpretable or not, and, (3) if causally interpretable, utterances were coded for clause order. Causally interpretable utterances expressed a causal or conditional relation between one event or state and another event or state.[3] The relation was either interpreted as causal by the adult(s) present or was judged so by an investigator retrospectively. The relation did not have to be true or necessarily make sense from an adult point of view to be counted as causally interpretable, for example:

(1) P (25,3)
    (putting pen away and look-
    ing for another pen)   get another one/it dirty.

(2) E (31,2)
    (pretending)   I'm putting medicine on the
                                           lamb's leg cause he had a
                                           boo-boo.

Those utterances that were causally interpretable were then coded according to the order in which the clause expressing "cause" and the clause expressing "effect" were expressed. Examples of cause–effect order were

(3) E (28,1)
    (holding bear on ladder)   hold de ladder [cause] and e
                                           won't fall down. [effect]

(4) M (32,1)
    (running away from picture of
    large knife)   it's gonna cut you [cause]/
                                           let's get away from it. [effect]

Examples of effect–cause order were

(5) K (24,2)   I ə not go in bathroom [ef-
                                           fect]/I did tinkle. [cause]

(6) P (30,3)
    (regarding TV, which is on)
                                           I left it open [effect] because I
                                           wanna watch it. [cause]

Other clause orders were equivocal, that is, both cause–effect and effect–cause interpretations were tenable, for example:

(7) G (29,3)   I don't have any more tape/
                                           it's all used up now.

(8) D (38,0)

(trying to put animals on train)	the animals don't fit
Lois: They don't fit?	no they don't/cause they fall down

Utterances that could not be interpreted in some causal sense included (1) the use of repetition, such as "I'm hungry because I'm hungry"; (2) anomalous utterances where the relationship between the clauses could not be determined; and (3) incomplete and partially unintelligible utterances.

Interjudge reliability for the coding of child statements was obtained for (1) judgment of causal versus noncausal statements; (2) for causal statements only, judgments of causally interpretable versus not causally interpretable statements; and (3) for causally interpretable statements only, judgment of the order of cause and effect clauses. Proportions of agreement of two independent observers with the investigator's original coding ranged from .91 to 1.0 (Hood, 1977).

Responses to Adult Questions. All child responses to adult *how* and *why* questions were coded for the presence or absence of causal connectives and the meaning relationship of the child utterance to the question.

Causally interpretable utterances were those child responses that consisted of a causal explanation in relation to the content of the question. For example:

(9) E (28,1)	there's no more juice for you.
Lois: Why?	
	cause I drink it all.
(10) M (31,1)	take off my socks.
Lois: Why're you taking off your socks?	
	because it's not cold outside/ they're not cold.

Instances where the child's response expressed only some motivation or intention were included. For example:

(11) E (281,)	open it.
Lois: Why?	
	because I want you to open it.

Utterances that could not be interpreted in some causal sense were either instances of (1) no response; (2) the use of "because" alone, for example, "Why is she crying?" "because"; (3) the use of repetition, where the child's response repeated either the previous child's utterance or part of the adult's question; (4) utterances that were anomalous or irrelevant, where the child's response either had no relationship to the adult question or the relationship could not be determined; or (5) incomplete or unintelligible utterances.

In addition to coding the child responses to adult questions, all adult questions were coded as (1) contingent or not on what the child said previously, (2) representing a change in topic, or (3) introducing a new topic.

Child Questions. All *why* questions asked by the children were coded according to their form and the initiator of the topic of the question.[4] With respect to form, child questions were either single-word questions, such as "why?" "cause why?" or, more rarely, "why not?" or multiword questions, for example:

(12) P (38,0)
        (Py is wrapping string around
        doll house)   Why you wrapping it around?

With respect to the topic, child questions were either semantically contingent upon a prior adult utterance and thus continued reference to the discourse topic, for example:

(13) D (39,0)
        (D wants two pieces of ba-
        nana bread)
        Mother: I'll cut it so you'll
        have two.
                      no don't cut them/ why you
                      go an cut them?

or were not contingent on a prior adult utterance and were child initiated, for example:

(14) P (29,2)
        (watching Lois write)   why you gonna do that?

RESULTS

The major findings of this study revealed systematic development in the content, use, and form of the causal utterances of the eight children, and these results are presented in this order: (1) language content (reference and functions expressed in statements, questions, and response); (2) language use (developmental relationships among the discourse categories statements, questions, and responses); (3) language form (clause order–connective relationship); and (4) language input (effects of linguistic context on the content, form, and use of the children's causal expressions).

Frequency of Types of Causal Utterances

The frequencies of causally relevant child statements, child questions, and adult questions are presented in Table 10.2 for each child at each time.[5] As can be seen, except for Steven, there was a substantial increase in each type of utterance for all the children, and in general, there were more child statements than adult questions at each sample. For each child overall, child statements were more frequent than adult questions which were more frequent than child questions (except for Steven, who had fewer child statements than adult questions). Child causal statements and adult causal questions appeared at approximately the same time, between 24 and 26 months; child causal questions were a later development and did not become productive (i.e., five or more different occurrences) until 30 months of age (except for Paul).

Language Content: Reference and Functions

Content analyses of causal utterances revealed similarity among causal statements, child causal questions, and adult causal questions, in that all three utterance types made reference most often to actions or states that were either directions or intentions, often with some negative aspect to the situation. In addition, time reference was most often to ongoing or imminent events or states. Conspicuously absent from the data were utterances that made reference to two sequential actions, independent of intention or direction, such as "the man fell off his bicycle because he hit a tree."

Utterances were considered negative if they referred to the nonoccurrence of an event or to a nonexisting state of affairs. Negation was

Table 10.2. *Frequency of Child Statements, Child Questions, and Adult Questions*

Child and Time	N Causal Statements	N Adult *Why* Questions	N Child *Why* Questions
David			
I	24	12	—
II	22	32	—
III	11	18	—
IV	11	6	—
V	29	11	—
VI	41	11	—
VII	88	22	—
VIII	66	15	1
IX	60	20	4
X	81	24	6
XI	113	12	5
XII	88	28	6
Total	634	211	22
Eric			
(IV)[a]	—	4	—
V	7	8	4
VI	27	18	1
VII	26	12	—
VIII	31	16	2
IX	44	19	—
X	40	12	3
XI	31	46	26
XII	40	65	84
Total	246	200	120
Gia			
(IV)[a]	—	8	—
V	7	5	—
VI	9	24	1
VII	36	54	—
VIII	64	36	7
IX	37	37	10
X	44	30	16
XI	56	47	20
Total	253	241	54
Kathryn			
(II)[a]	—	2	—
III	18	2	—
IV	24	11	—
V	18	16	1
VI	29	12	1

Table 10.2. *(cont.)*

Child and Time	N Causal Statements	N Adult *Why* Questions	N Child *Why* Questions
VII	57	25	3
VIII	60	30	57
IX	156	26	43
X	215	39	49
Total	577	163	154
Mariana			
I	5	7	—
II	7	6	—
III	8	17	—
IV	22	12	—
V	16	18	—
VI	16	26	—
VII	25	15	—
VIII	23	12	—
IX	36	16	1
X	49	24	3
XI	36	17	13
Total	243	170	17
Peter			
(VII)[a]	—	1	—
VIII	9	3	—
IX	22	3	—
X	15	2	—
XI	8	4	—
XII	18	4	—
XIII	10	1	—
XIV	12	4	—
XV	29	4	—
XVI	19	9	—
XVII	33	16	—
XVIII	24	7	4
XIX	37	26	20
XX	56	12	45
Total	292	96	69
Paul			
I	15	15	—
II	17	12	—
III	15	22	13
IV	10	9	21
V	37	19	32
VI	29	13	12
VII	77	10	16
Total	200	100	94

Table 10.2. *(cont.)*

Child and Time	N Causal Statements	N Adult *Why* Questions	N Child *Why* Questions
Steven			
I	I	7	—
II	9	14	—
III	10	10	—
IV	5	14	—
V	6	18	—
VI	9	10	I
Total	40	73	I

[a]The samples in parentheses represent supplementary data. They were not part of the present study, since no child causal statements occurred in them.

most often expressed by a negative function word, such as *no, not, can't, don't, didn't, doesn't,* and *isn't.* However, utterances which referred to a negative situation by the use of other words with negative connotation (mostly verbs and attributives) were also categorized as negative.[6]

Directions and intentions both made reference to imminent actions or states without the expression of negation. Requests for action by the listener were considered *directive;* they expressed the desire on the part of the speaker for some action on the part of the listener. This could be expressed explicitly ("you read this book"; "help me tie my shoe") or implicitly ("I want juice," said in a whining voice). *Intentions* made reference to actions and events which either (1) occurred immediately following the utterance or (2) did not occur, but appeared to be desired by the speaker. Such utterances made explicit reference to intention with a matrix verb, such as variants of *want, going to, have to,* and *let's.* Utterances that could not be categorized as negation, direction, or intention were classified as *other.*

The utterances expressing negation, direction, and/or intention made reference to nine main types of situation. Each situation is identified below, with child statements used as illustrations.

1. Nonoccurrence of an event or state.

(15) P (35,0) it can't go cause it's too little. [negation]

(16) K (32,1)

Lois: Where do you think
she'd like to sit? (doll)
(K holding chair for doll, but
table already has chairs on
four sides of it)

well, there's no room because
there's so many chairs around
there. [negation]

Such utterances were often used in the sense of being stymied or
thwarted.

(17) P (26,2)

(after trying to move high-
chair close to table)

too stuck/I can't do it. [nega-
tion]

(18) E (31,2)

I can't lift this up/oh it's too
heavy. [negation]

2. Request for assistance. Such utterances also referred to a nonoccurrence of an event or state, but they differed in that they explicitly
asked for help.

(19) G (25,2)

(has trouble putting lamb in
block; giving it to L)

can't do it/you do it.
[negation–direction]

(20) M (35,2)

(bringing book to L)

could you read this to me
cause I don't know how.
[negation–direction]

3. Abrupt change in state. Such utterances made reference to a sudden, often unanticipated, change in an object, such as a tower toppling
over.

(21) P (25,3)

(playing with bendable rubber
figure that has no wire in one
arm; arm will not stay at figure's side)

this boy pop/it's broken.
[negation]

(22) E (34,2)

(regarding wheel)   this one didn't go far/it hit
                                           truck. [negation]

4. Rejection. Such utterances expressed the intent or negation of intent of the speaker as agent. Often they contradicted or refuted the previous speaker's suggestion.

(23) E (34,2)
    Lois: Can we read this book?

                                          no.
    Lois: No?

                                            because I want to play rec-
                                          ords. [negation–intention]

(24) K (32,1)
    Lois: You didn't tell me about
    the play.

                                            well/I don't want to.
    Lois: Oh.

                                            I'm too tired. [negation–
                                            intention]

5. Prohibition. Such utterances were negative requests to stop the occurrence of an action by someone else. They differed from rejection in that the action or state negated referred to the listener as agent, not the speaker.

(25) G (33,0)

(regarding tower of blocks)
                                          don't knock this down/I
                                          gonna. [negation–intention]

(26) P (35,0)
                                          don't ring the bell either/
                                          Jenny will wake up. [nega-
                                          tion]

6. Caution. Such utterances made reference to a cautionary action on the part of the child or adult to block the occurrence of an unwanted event.

(27) D (38,0)   you can bring me my puzzle.
    Lois: OK.

                                          very careful so pieces don't
                                        fall·down. [direction–
                                          negation]

(28) E (36,0)   move over/cause the train hurt
                                           you. [direction–negation]

7. Requests for action – self. Such utterances expressed the need for action on the part of others to change the speaker's state or allow the speaker to perform some action.

(29) D (34,0)
        (holding L's pocketbook,
        which he can't open)   you can open it OK? / I'm
                                          gonna look in it. [direction–
                                          intention]

8. Requests for action – other. Such utterances asked for action on the part of others to change the state of someone or something other than the speaker (usually a toy).

(30) G (33,0)
        (regarding bendable figure)   bend her like that and then
                                          she sits down. [direction]
(31) K (30,3)
        (regarding beads)   you put them back on again.
        Lois: OK.
                                          because they dumped out. [di-
                                          rection]

9. Permission. Such utterances expressed the speaker's desire for some object or intended action. In addition to acquiesence, some action by the listener is also intended. For example, if both child and adult are playing in the living room and the child says, "I want a cookie/I'm hungry," the child likely intends the adult to get the cookie.

(32) M (35,2)   I want some milk cause I
                                          have a cold. [intention]

(33) G (25,2)
        (L and G playing in living
        room)   I want go door see my
                                          Mommy. [intention]

There was little development over time in the frequency of these nine types of situations and little variation among the children in their use. The most frequent were nonoccurrence of an event or state, request for action – self, and request for assistance. In addition, there was a slight tendency for prohibition and rejection to become more frequent in the later samples.

Expression of Negation, Direction, and/or Intention. The three categories of meaning expressed in causal utterances – negation, direction, intention – were each examined as they occurred across utterance types for the individual children. Some child statements and some adult question–child response sequences could be double coded, that is, categorized as negation–direction, negation–intention, or direction–intention. The proportion of utterances with negative words, directives, and/or reference to intended actions was consistently over .60, for each of the children, for all three utterance types (see Table 10.3). For all samples combined, negation, direction, and/or intention was expressed in .90 of statements, .81 of adult questions, and .67 of child questions.

The relative frequency of the individual content categories (negation, direction, intention, and other) was determined in its relation to utterance type (child statement, adult question, child question) in three ways. For each utterance type individually, the children were compared to one another in terms of the proportion of utterances in each category. The distribution of utterances in content categories was most similar from one child to another in child statements. The largest proportion of utterances (from .37 for Gia to .50 for Steven) expressed negation, while the smallest proportion of utterances (from 0 for Steven to .11 for Eric) were classified as other. The proportions of direction and intention were similar; except for Paul and Steven, there was less than .05 difference between them. In addition, similarities occurred among the children in the distribution of content categories in child questions. Only for adult questions were the relative proportions of utterances in the categories different from child to child. In other words, the children were similar to one another in the content of their causal utterances, both statements and questions, while there was more variability in adult causal questions.

The remaining two comparisons concerned the interaction of utterance types and content categories. The magnitude of difference in comparisons of the frequency of categories and utterance types varied, depending on the particular category and utterance type being compared. Chi-square tests of differences in the frequency of each content category – negation, direction, intention, and other – across utterance types were performed, and the summary results are presented in Table

Table 10.3. *Proportion of Child Statements, Adult Questions, and Child Questions with Negation–Direction–Intention Content*

Child and Time	Utterance Type		
	Statements	Adult Questions	Child Questions
David			
I	.88	.92	—
II	.95	.97	—
III	.91	.78	—
IV	.82	.83	—
V	.96	.91	—
VI	1.0	.82	—
VII	.91	.91	—
VIII	1.0	.80	1.0[a]
IX	.78	.80	.75[a]
X	.82	.96	.83
XI	.94	.80	1.0
XII	.74	.79	.83
Total	.88	.86	.86
Eric			
V	1.0	.62	.25[a]
VI	.87	.78	1.0[a]
VII	.79	.73	—
VIII	.87	.88	1.0[a]
IX	.85	.79	—
X	.75	.83	.67[a]
XI	.89	.76	.44
XII	.97	.72	.61
Total	.86	.76	.58
Gia			
V	1.0	.50[a]	—
VI	1.0	.91	1.0[a]
VII	.97	.89	—
VIII	.94	.81	1.0
IX	1.0	.73	.70
X	.98	.93	.75
XI	.80	.85	.95
Total	.93	.85	.85
Kathryn			
III	.94	.67[a]	—
IV	.96	.45	—
V	.83	.56	.50[a]
VI	.83	.58	1.0[a]
VII	.98	.92	1.0[a]

Table 10.3. *(cont.)*

Child and Time	Utterance Type		
	Statements	Adult Questions	Child Questions
VIII	.95	.83	.65
IX	.92	.80	.29
X	.87	.82	.68
Total	.90	.76	.56
Mariana			
I	1.0	.86	—
II	1.0	.67	—
III	1.0	1.0	—
IV	.95	.92	—
V	.88	.83	—
VI	.81	.88	—
VII	.96	.87	—
VIII	.91	1.0	—
IX	.86	.88	1.0[a]
X	.93	.91	.67[a]
XI	.78	.65	.69
Total	.89	.87	.71
Paul			
I	.93	.80	—
II	1.0	.67	—
III	1.0	.65	.54
IV	1.0	.90	.90
V	.94	.79	.75
VI	.93	.92	.92
VII	.94	.80	.75
Total	.95	.77	.78
Peter			
VIII	1.0	.33[a]	—
IX	1.0	1.0[a]	—
X	1.0	1.0[a]	—
XI	1.0	1.0[a]	—
XII	.94	.50[a]	—
XIII	.88	1.0[a]	—
XIV	.92	.50[a]	—
XV	.93	.50[a]	—
XVI	.89	1.0	—
XVII	.85	.88	—
XVIII	.95	.86	1.0[a]
XIX	.89	.72	1.0
XX	.88	.54	.55
Total	.92	.75	.72

Table 10.3. *(cont.)*

Child and Time	Utterance Type		
	Statements	Adult Questions	Child Questions
Steven			
I	1.0[a]	.62	—
II	1.0	.79	—
III	1.0	.80	—
IV	1.0	.86	—
V	1.0	.83	—
VI	1.0	1.0	1.0[a]
Total	1.0	.82	1.0
All children combined	.90	.81	.67

[a] Utterance type not productive.

10.4. In the category comparisons, negation was most similar in its distribution across the three utterance types (.23 of the comparisons were different). In the utterance type comparisons, adult and child questions were most similar across content categories, (.36 of the comparisons were different). In summary, adult and child questions were more similar in content than were child statements and adult questions, which were, in turn, more similar than were child statements and child questions.

Time Reference. All causally interpretable child statements were examined to determine the direction of difference between the time of the event (event-time) and the time of the utterance about the event (speech-time). Utterances that referred to ongoing events and to events that were imminent or just about to happen (i.e., direction and intention) were categorized as *present;* utterances making reference to events that were not about to happen were categorized as *future.* Utterances that made reference to any past event or state, including the immediate past (e.g., ''The tower fell down''), were categorized as *past.*

For all the children, reference to past and future events occurred relatively late, was always infrequent, and showed surprisingly little development. In general, utterances which referred to past events were rarer (from 0 for Steven to .16 for Eric) than utterances which referred

Table 10.4. *Number of Statistically Significant Differences (chi-square) in Frequency of Content Categories Across Utterance Type*[a]

Utterance Type Comparison	Negation	Direction	Intention	Other	Total
Child statements: adult questions	1/8	3/8	4/8	6/8	14/32 (.44)
Child statements: child questions	2/7	5/7	3/7	6/7	16/28 (.57)
Adult questions: child questions	2/7	5/7	1/7	2/7	10/28 (.36)
Total	5/22 (.23)	13/22 (.59)	8/22 (.36)	14/22 (.64)	—

[a] $p < .05$.

to future events (from .08 for Eric to .19 for Kathryn). Thus, overwhelmingly, the children's causal statements made reference to ongoing or immediately future events or states.

Language Use: Statements, Questions, and Responses

The developmental relationship among the three utterance types was examined in terms of relative frequency, onset and maintenance of productivity (five or more different utterances), and meaningfulness.

Frequency. Each child (except Steven) increased over time in the frequency of either child statements, child questions, or both (Table 10.2). The frequency of adult questions increased for only four children.

Productivity. The occurrence of five or more different utterances in a sample was used as an index of productivity (see Chapter 1 for a discussion of productivity in child language). As seen in Table 10.2, child statements and adult questions were productive at the same time; child questions were a later development. Where earlier data were available, the sample before the emergence of child statements was examined to see if adult questions had occurred at an earlier time (sample N's in parentheses in Table 10.2). For Eric, Kathryn, and Peter, adult questions occurred but were not productive in earlier samples, while for Gia they were. Adult questions did not occur in the earlier samples from David and Mariana. The general tendency, then, was for adult questions to become productive when child statements also became productive. Child questions became productive much later than statements and adult questions, and, except for Paul and Peter, remained nonproductive for at least two samples after they first appeared.

Meaningfulness. While there was relatively little increase in the frequency of adult questions, there was development in the way the children responded to adult questions. The earliest responses to adult questions were not causally interpretable: They were either no response, repetition, anomalous, or the single word *because.* Causally interpretable responses were compared with child statements classified as either causally interpretable or not, in terms of both absolute and proportional frequencies for each child at each time (see Figure 10.1). The absolute frequencies of causally interpretable statements and responses were nearly equal in the first few samples; however, proportionately, more of the child statements were causally interpretable than were responses to adult questions, even at the beginning. While absolute frequencies and proportions of both increased over time, causally interpretable statements increased more and were always more frequent.

Causally interpretable responses occurred productively between 1½ and 5½ months later than causally interpretable statements. Child questions occurred productively only after both causally interpretable statements and responses were productive for all of the children (except Paul). Thus, the same developmental sequence – statements < responses < questions – was observed for absolute numbers of utterances in each utterance type as well as for the frequency and proportion of utterances that were causally interpretable.

Variation in the Use of Why *Questions.* There were three forms of *why* questions: (1) the single-word "why?" (2) multiword *why* questions, and (3) single-word/multiword *why* sequences in which the child asked "why?" and was queried by an adult "why what?" and then produced a multiword *why* question. For example:

(34) E (36,0)

    Lois: Let's leave your blanket
here/you can't keep your
blanket.

                                      why?

    Lois: Why what?

                              why can't I take my blanket?

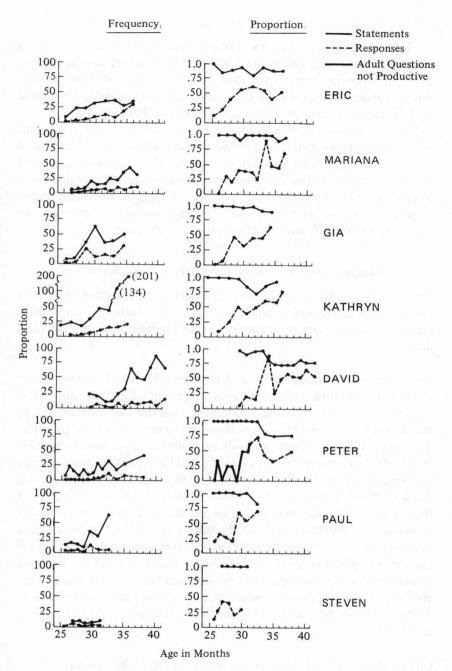

Figure 10.1. Frequency and proportion of statements and responses that were causally interpretable for each child.

Children's questions were most often contingent, that is, related both contextually and linguistically to a prior adult utterance, as in the above example. Noncontingent questions also occurred and were always multiword questions; the proportion of noncontingent questions tended to decrease over time for all the children except Paul.

Single-word *why* questions tended to increase, and except for Paul who asked single-word *why* questions overwhelmingly, when causal child questions became productive, both single-word and multiword questions occurred. The developmental trends were for *why* questions to emerge gradually in the early samples, for single-word and multi-word questions to appear together, for single-word *why* questions to increase, and for noncontingent questions to decrease.

Language Form: Causal Connectives and Clause Order

There was a developmental interaction between connective forms and clause order (effect/cause and cause/effect) in causally interpretable child statements, with both similarities and variation among the children.

Connectives. The proportion and number of causally interpretable statements with different connectives are presented in Table 10.5. The children began making causal statements without connectives; six of the children combined clauses without any connectives to begin with. The proportion of statements without connectives declined steadily, and by the last sample less than .50 of the children's statements (except for Steven) occurred without connectives. In most cases *and* was either the first connective used or the most frequently used connective in the first sample with connectives, and its use declined. More specific connectives were distributed differently among the children, both in terms of emergence and subsequent development (see Chapter 7). Both David and Peter acquired *because* before *so;* Gia, Kathryn, and Paul acquired *so* before *because;* Mariana and Eric acquired *because* and *so* together. By the last sample, *because* was much more frequent than *so* for Gia, Kathryn, David, Mariana, and Paul, but essentially equal to *so* for Eric and Peter.

Clause Order. The absolute frequency and proportion of statements in cause–effect and effect–cause order for each child at each time are presented in Figure 10.2. The children varied in their overall use of the two clause orders, with three predominant patterns. Three children

Table 10.5. *Presence of Different Connectives in Causally Interpretable Statements*[a]

Child and Time	No. Conn.	and	so	be- cause	Other[b]	Total
David						
I	.88(21)	.04(1)	—	—	.08(2)	24
II	.67(14)	.14(3)	—	.14(3)	.05(1)	21
III	.73(8)	.18(2)	—	.09(1)	—	11
IV	1.0(11)	—	—	—	—	11
V	.56(14)	.12(3)	—	.28(7)	.04(1)	25
VI	.31(10)	.06(2)	—	.62(20)	—	32
VII	.09(6)	.06(4)	.04(3)	.76(51)	.04(3)	67
VIII	.20(10)	.08(4)	.14(7)	.51(26)	.08(4)	51
IX	.11(5)	.02(1)	.28(13)	.48(22)	.11(5)	46
X	.21(14)	.03(2)	.26(18)	.49(33)	.01(1)	68
XI	.12(11)	.01(1)	.14(13)	.71(64)	.01(1)	90
XII	.08(6)	.04(3)	.08(6)	.74(53)	.05(4)	72
Eric						
V	1.0(7)	—	—	—	—	7
VI	.48(11)	.35(8)	.09(2)	.09(2)	—	23
VII	.35(8)	.48(11)	—	—	.17(4)	23
VIII	.42(13)	.19(6)	.22(7)	.06(2)	.10(3)	31
IX	.49(17)	.03(1)	.11(4)	.23(8)	.14(5)	35
X	27(10)	.22(8)	.30(11)	.11(4)	.11(4)	37
XI	.56(15)	—	.26(7)	.18(5)	—	27
XII	.20(7)	.06(2)	.34(12)	.31(11)	.09(3)	35
Gia						
V	1.0(7)	—	—	—	—	7
VI	1.0(9)	—	—	—	—	9
VII	.75(27)	.19(7)	.05(2)	—	—	36
VIII	.47(29)	.11(7)	.13(8)	—	.29(18)	62
IX	.78(29)	.03(1)	.14(5)	—	.06(2)	37
X	.50(20)	.08(3)	.18(7)	.20(8)	.04(2)	40
XI	.47(24)	.08(4)	.04(2)	.33(17)	.08(4)	51
Kathryn						
III	.94(17)	.06(1)	—	—	—	18
IV	1.0(24)	—	—	—	—	24
V	.78(14)	.22(4)	—	—	—	18
VI	.55(16)	.03(1)	.24(7)	.10(3)	.07(2)	29
VII	.15(7)	.02(1)	.40(19)	.38(18)	.06(3)	48
VIII	.27(12)	.02(1)	.36(16)	.32(14)	.02(1)	44
IX	.16(21)	.01(2)	.41(55)	.38(51)	.04(5)	134
X	.23(47)	.10(20)	.11(23)	.38(77)	.17(34)	201
Mariana						
I	1.0(5)	—	—	—	—	5
II	1.0(7)	—	—	—	—	7

Table 10.5. *(cont.)*

Child and Time	No. Conn.	*and*	*so*	be- cause	Other[b]	Total
Mariana cont.						
III	.62(5)	—	—	—	.38(3)	8
IV	.70(14)	—	.20(4)	.05(1)	.05(1)	20
V	.81(13)	.06(1)	.06(1)	.06(1)	—	16
VI	.56(9)	.19(3)	.12(2)	—	.12(2)	16
VII	.52(13)	.16(4)	—	.12(3)	.20(5)	25
VIII	.26(6)	.13(3)	.13(3)	.04(1)	.43(10)	23
IX	.26(9)	.11(4)	.06(2)	.20(7)	.37(13)	35
X	.40(18)	—	.11(5)	.33(15)	.15(7)	45
XI	.31(11)	.03(1)	.11(4)	.31(11)	.23(8)	35
Paul						
I	1.0(15)	—	—	—	—	15
II	1.0(17)	—	—	—	—	17
III	.87(13)	—	—	.13(2)	—	15
IV	.70(7)	—	.10(1)	.20(2)	—	10
V	.67(24)	.06(2)	.14(5)	.08(3)	.06(2)	36
VI	.55(16)	.03(1)	.21(6)	.10(3)	.10(3)	29
VII	.11(7)	.03(2)	.23(15)	.61(39)	.02(1)	64
Peter						
VIII	1.0(9)	—	—	—	—	9
IX	1.0(22)	—	—	—	—	22
X	1.0(15)	—	—	—	—	15
XI	1.0(8)	—	—	—	—	8
XII	1.0(18)	—	—	—	—	18
XIII	1.0(10)	—	—	—	—	10
XIV	1.0(12)	—	—	—	—	12
XV	.90(26)	.10(3)	—	—	—	29
XVI	1.0(19)	—	—	—	—	19
XVII	.94(31)	.03(1)	—	—	.03(1)	33
XVIII	.58(11)	.16(3)	—	.26(5)	—	19
XIX	.32(9)	.07(2)	—	.46(13)	.15(4)	28
XX	.30(13)	.07(3)	.30(13)	.26(11)	.07(3)	43
Steven						
I	1.0(1)	—	—	—	—	1
II	1.0(9)	—	—	—	—	9
III	1.0(10)	—	—	—	—	10
IV	1.0(5)	—	—	—	—	5
V	.83(5)	—	—	—	.17(1)	6
VI	.56(5)	—	.22(2)	.11(1)	.11(1)	9

[a] *N*'s on the left in each col. are proportions; frequencies appear in parentheses.
[b] Includes *when, then, to, if, unless*, etc.

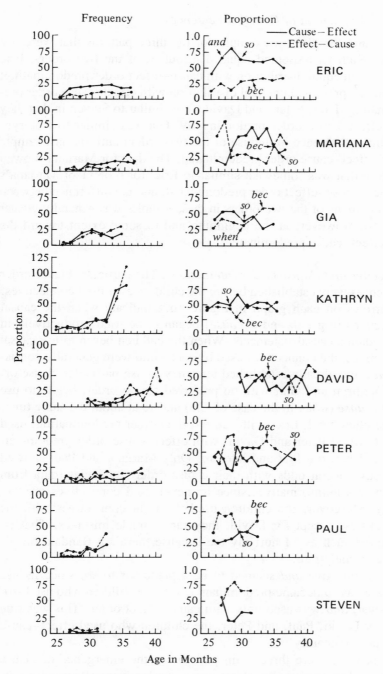

Figure 10.2. Frequency and proportion of child statements in cause–effect and effect–cause order for each child.

represented the clearest examples of the three patterns that were observed: Kathryn presented equal distribution of the two orders; Eric presented unequal distribution with cause–effect order predominating; and Steven presented unequal distribution with effect–cause order predominating. Paul, Peter, and David were similar to Steven in that they used effect–cause order predominantly. Gia was similar to Kathryn, with little difference in the use of the two orders until the last sample where effect–cause order predominated. The data for Mariana showed a pattern that was somewhat similar to Eric; for 6 of 11 of Mariana's samples, cause–effect order predominated, and the difference between the proportions of the two orders in these samples was generally greater than .30. However, at the beginning and to some extent toward the end, effect–cause predominated.

Connective and Clause Order Interactions. The particular clause order differences were established before the children ever used connectives. The arrows on each graph in Figure 10.2 indicate when the causal connectives (e.g., *so* and *because*) began to be used productively in the children's causal statements. When the children began to use causal connectives, the connectives used by each child were generally consistent with the already established tendency to use particular clause orders. Kathryn and Gia, with no preferred clause order, began to use both *because* (*when* in the case of Gia) and *so* at about the same time. On the other hand, Eric, with cause–effect order predominating, used *so* first, while Peter and David, with effect–cause order predominating, used *because* first and later *so*. Only Mariana and Paul showed connective use at odds with their clause order tendencies (data from Steven was uninformative, since he never used connectives productively). Moreover, the children used the right connectives with the right orders; except for David, they rarely made mistakes. That is, utterances such as "I hurt my toe because there's a Bandaid on it" were extremely rare.

The connective *and* seemed to be a precursor to *so,* since its use decreased as *so* became predominant (for those children who used *so*). Moreover, *and* was used only with cause–effect order. This was true even for David, Paul, and Peter, the children who used effect–cause order predominantly.

Thus, there were three main patterns in the emergence of clause order: predominant cause–effect order, predominant effect–cause order, and similar distribution of the two orders. These clause order patterns existed before the children began to use connectives, and the eventual use of a particular connective was consistent with the particular clause order patterns.

Error Analysis of Connective–Clause Order Use. Errors in causal statements – for example, the use of *because* with cause–effect order, or *and* or *so* with effect–cause order – accounted for only .06 of all the children's causal statements. Such errors were restricted in two ways. First, almost all errors consisted of the use of *because* with cause–effect order. (There were four instances of errors with *and,* six with so, and 57 with *because.*) Second, most of the *because* errors occurred with one child, David; 45 of the 57 errors were David's.

There are actually two meanings that *so* can have as a causal connective. It can mean *therefore,* as in "the second book is old so I hafta buy a new one"; alternatively, it can mean *so that* or *in order that,* as in the directive "you put this gate up so the baby can't get in." When all child statements with *so* were examined in terms of these two meanings of *so,* a developmental progression was found – from *so* meaning *so that* to *so* meaning *therefore.* For example, with respect to Eric's *so* statements, those that had a *therefore* interpretation increased from none at Eric VIII to .42 at Eric XII. The other children, except David, showed a similar pattern. However, David's overall proportion of *so* statements meaning *therefore* was lower than any of the other children, especially those who used *so* frequently (.14 for David, in comparison with .69 for Peter, .38 for Kathryn, and .21 for Eric).

Errors in the use of *because* with cause–effect order overwhelmingly had a *therefore* interpretation, for example, "he sick cause I gonna fix him." In only 2 out of 57 occurrences of *because* with cause–effect order did *because* mean *so that.* More important, .89 of David's *because* errors were occurrences of *because* meaning *therefore.* The difference between David and the other children is schematized below.

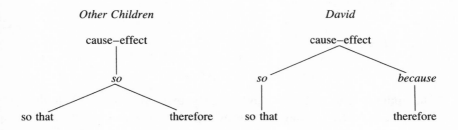

Thus, David's errors in clause order and use of connectives were indeed systematic. Unlike the other children who gradually began to express a *therefore* relationship with *so,* David expressed the *therefore* relationship with *because,* his predominant connective.

Comparison of Mother and Child Clause Orders. One possible explanation for the variation among the children in their use of clause order might have been differences in the speech that the children heard: The children's mothers might have used clause orders differentially. In order to test this hypothesis, mothers' causal statements from David, Mariana, Paul, and Simon (the four children from whom enough mother–child interaction was available for comparison) were analyzed for clause order patterns.

The results of this analysis are presented in Figure 10.3 for mother and child speech. Just as the children were different from one another in their use of the two clause orders, the mothers also were different from one another. However, when each mother was compared with her child, each mother tended to be more similar to her child than to the other mothers. Mariana and her mother showed a sharp increase in cause–effect order followed by a decline. Two of the children with effect–cause patterns, Paul and Steven, had mothers with effect–cause patterns. David showed an effect–cause pattern, while his mother showed a variable pattern of cause–effect and effect–cause orders (rather than a contrary cause–effect pattern).

As a measure of the general consistency of each child's and each mother's clause order pattern, the children were compared with their respective mothers according to the number of samples in which the proportion of statements in cause–effect order was greater than in effect–cause order. These comparative data from the mothers and their children are presented in Table 10.6. As can be seen, except for David, the mothers were similar to their children in terms of the number of samples in which use of cause–effect order was greater than use of effect–cause order.

DISCUSSION

The Content of Causal Expressions

The findings of this study strongly suggest that 2 to 3-year-old children have some understanding of causal relations between events and/or

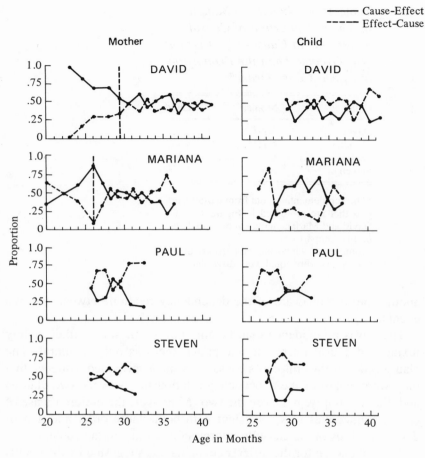

Figure 10.3. Proportion of statements in cause–effect and effect–cause order for four mother–child pairs. Data points to the left of the dotted line on the graphs for David's and Mariana's mothers represent supplementary data from earlier videotaped sessions.

states and that they have the ability to express such relations. This result is in conflict with the views of Piaget (1923/1955, 1928/1969, 1930/1972) and Werner and Kaplan (1963), neither of whom have credited the child with a conception of causality until the age of 7 or 8. According to Piaget, young children see two events as merely juxtaposed in time and space; they are not aware of any sequential relation between the two. According to Werner and Kaplan, children see causal relations as temporal relations; they are aware that one event precedes

Table 10.6. *Number of Samples in which Proportion of Causal Statements in Cause–Effect Order Was Greater Than the Proportion in Effect–Cause Order*[a]

Child	Mother	Child
David	6/11[b]	3/12
Mariana	5/11	7/11
Paul	1/6	0/6
Steven	0/6	1/5

[a] The supplementary data from earlier samples that are presented in Figure 10.3 for David and Mariana have not been included in this comparison.
[b] Samples in which the proportions in the two orders were equal were discounted.

another but are unaware of the dependency relation between the two events.

There was no evidence that the children in this study either merely juxtaposed causal events or interpreted them as only temporal. The clause order of the children's causal statements provided evidence that they were aware of the dependency relationship between two clauses and did not simply juxtapose the two. Moreover, the children's use of causal connectives was consistent with both clause order and dependency relations in the causally interpretable events in the context.

An explanation for the different conclusions suggested by the results of the present study can be found in an examination of what the children were talking about. Piaget (1928/1969, 1930/1972) and Werner and Kaplan (1963) based their conclusions on data concerning how children talk about observable sequential actions that involve physical objects. However, the children in this study simply did not talk about causal events that occurred between physical objects in the world and rarely made reference to sequential actions in their causal statements. They were no doubt aware of events of physical causality as, for example, a cup falling off a table because someone's elbow hit it. Likewise, they probably talked about such events in other ways, for example, with a single-word utterance such as "uh oh," or with an utterance expressing a single relation, such as "cup fall down" or "I knock it down." However, they did not talk about such events with causal utterances. The children did talk about intentions and motivations in their causal utterances which could be support for Piaget's characterization of the child's first causal relations as expressing "motivational" or "psychological" causality. Although the children made reference to intentions and motives in their causal utterances, their linguistic expression of causal relations was no less systematic because it dealt with psychological rather than physical phenomena.

Although the children in this study did not talk about physical causality in their causal statements, physical causality is precisely the type of situation that has been presented to children in experimental studies of the development of causality (e.g., Corrigan, 1975; Hood, 1972; Hood & Mansfield, 1971; Johnson, 1972; Katz & Brent, 1968; Kuhn & Phelps, 1976; Sullivan, 1972). (See Hood, 1977, for a review of this literature.) Subjects in these studies have generally been older than the subjects of the present study. While information about these older subjects' spontaneous causal statements has not been available, the content of the experimental tasks probably differed from the content of their own speech. The traditionally poor performance of older children in such studies may be due in part to the contrast between the content of the causal tasks presented to them and the content of their own spontaneous causal utterances.

In the present study there was little change over time in the content of the children's causal statements. First, the same categories of meaning – negation, direction, intention – accounted for approximately the same proportion of the children's speech at the beginning of the study when they were 2 years old and at the end when they were 3 years old. Second, while there was a slight tendency for reference to past and future events to be a somewhat later development, even at the last samples, such reference accounted for an average of less than .10 of the child statements.

The one development in the content of the children's causal statements was that except for David, the relations expressed in utterances with the connective *so* progressed semantically from a *so that* to a *therefore* relation. While there was also progression from *so that* to *therefore* relations in David's causal statements, he used different connectives to express these different meanings – *so* for *so that* and *because* for *therefore*.

The relatively late emergence of a *therefore* relationship expressed by *so* or *because* in the children's causal statements supports Piaget's idea that *therefore* (*puisque*) represents a more complex type of reasoning than *because* (*parce que*). Piaget based this assumption on his observations that utterances with *puisque* are extremely rare in children younger than 9 or 10, although he did acknowledge that *puisque* is generally an infrequent word in French. A parallel situation exists in English; *therefore* is rare in adult speech and does not occur in child speech. However, in English a *therefore* relationship can be expressed by *so,* a word that is exceedingly common in adult speech and, as was found in this study, also in child speech.

The Form of Causal Expressions

While there was little development in the content of causal expressions, there were major developments in the form of the children's causal statements, causal questions, and responses to adult questions.

Causal Statements. Since six of the eight children had preferred clause order before they ever used causal connectives and since the children rarely made errors in combining connectives with clause order, it seems likely that clause order preference determined connective use. Thus, it is not the case that children become aware of the interdependence of clause order and causal connective at the same time or that the causal connective used determines the clause order.

The results of different clause order patterns and the consistency between clause order pattern and connective acquisition provide little evidence to support either of the alternative hypotheses suggested by Piaget (1928/1969) and Werner and Kaplan (1963) to explain the development of the child's causal reasoning. In Piaget's view, causal events are seen as merely juxtaposed and *because* means *and* to the child. However, six of the eight children expressed clauses in a preferred order, and all the children used the appropriate connectives with whatever orders they used. They did not make mistakes that would suggest that *because* meant only *and* to them. One child, David, did use *because* with cause–effect order. However, there was no evidence that he used *because* to mean *and*. Rather, David appeared to use *because* to mean *therefore,* in contrast with his use of *so* to mean *so that.* A second finding that was inconsistent with Piaget's juxtaposition hypothesis was the use of *and* with cause–effect order exclusively (versus no connective with effect–cause order) in the earliest utterances. This consistent differentiation of the two clause orders would appear to argue against the idea that these children lacked directionality in their causal thinking.

There was also little support for Werner and Kaplan's (1963) hypothesis that causal relations are first expressed in an order that matches the perceived order of events. While it is true that two children, Eric and Mariana, did appear to be using what could be termed a temporal order strategy (i.e., they used a cause–effect order predominantly), the other six children clearly did not: Four of them used the opposite of a temporal order strategy in mentioning the effect before the cause, while the other two children used both orders. (See Hood, 1977, for further discussion of these results in relation to the literature on causal reasoning.)

Responses to Adult Questions. In general, the adults in this study began to ask *why* questions when the children began to make causal statements. For all the children except Kathryn, however, there was at least a 2-month lag between the appearance of adult *why* questions and causally interpretable responses to such questions. The children progressed from giving responses that were largely semantically anomalous and structurally incomplete (or not responding at all) to the point where the majority of their responses were semantically meaningful and structurally complete. This result is in basic agreement with the developmental sequence observed by Blank (1975) and Blank and Allen (1976) in an observational study of one child from 18 to 31 months of age. However, the children in the present study progressed further than their subject by the end of the study; they gave causally interpretable responses more often than not, and they were also older.

Child Questions. The appearance of *why* questions at approximately 30 months of age for the children in this study is consistent with previous reports in the literature (e.g., Brown, 1968; Davis, 1932; Lewis, 1938; Smith, 1933). The result that between .42 and .64 of the children's questions expressed negation or were contingent on prior adult utterances which expressed negation is consistent with other studies that also found negation to be a factor in children's early *why* questions (Blank, 1975; Blank & Allen, 1976; Issacs, 1930; Lewis, 1938).

The children's *why* questions increased in frequency. With the exception of Paul, most of the children had at least one multiword *why* question either before or at the same time as single-word "why," and in the samples when *why* questions were first productive, approximately half the questions were multiword. Seven of the children seemed to be following a different course of development in asking *why* questions than the child studied by Blank (1975) and Blank and Allen (1976). Their subject used the single-word "why" for a relatively long period of time, from 18 to 25 months, before multiword *why* questions appeared. In addition, Blank also reported that her subject's *why* questions progressed from being contingent on previous adult speech to initiating dialogue, but for seven of the children in this study there was a decrease in noncontingent questions. Blank reported a further constraint on *why* questions: Not only were they contingent on a prior adult utterance from 18 to 25 months but that utterance was a negative statement by the adult. Only later, from 28 to 31 months, were *why* questions asked equally often after adult affirmative statements and negative statements. In the present study, in contrast, *why* questions occurred after adult affirmative statements from the beginning.

The Use of Causal Expressions

The children in this study produced spontaneous causal statements before they gave causally interpretable responses to *why* questions, and with one exception, both statements and responses occurred before the children asked *why* questions themselves. Like these children, two of the children described by Brown (1968) also learned to ask *why* questions only after they could give well-formed responses to adult *why* questions. One possible explanation of the sequence – statements < responses – would be if the adult questions were unrelated to the ongoing topic of conversation and situation, so that the message in the question was new to the child. However, the overwhelming majority of the adult questions were contingent on a preceding child utterance, for example:

(35) E (25,1)   baby Nancy crying.
      Mother: Why is baby Nancy
        crying?

Another possible explanation of the sequence – statements < responses < questions – is the explanation often offered in the literature for the late appearance of *why* questions relative to other *wh*-questions in children's speech: that *why* and *when* questions emerge after *what* and *where* questions because they refer to unobservable or intangible events or ideas, in contrast to *what* and *where* questions which have more figurative referents (Blank, 1975; Blank & Allen, 1976; Brown,

1968). However, the same sequence – statements < responses < questions – was also observed for locative *where* questions in the language development of Eric, Gia, Kathryn, and Peter (Bloom & Hood, unpublished data). A similar result was reported by Söderbergh (1974) for the development of *what* questions by a Swedish-speaking child, who did not ask *what* questions until she responded appropriately to *what* questions from adults (and similarly for *why* questions). If the relative tangibility hypothesis to explain the late appearance of *why* questions were to explain the sequence of development, one would not expect the same sequence in language use for *where* and *what* questions as well, which do have identifiable (tangible) referents and are among the earliest questions children ask.

A more general explanation of the sequence – statements < responses < questions – observed in this and other studies is the fact that expressing a spontaneous statement, responding to a question, and asking a question are fundamentally different tasks (see Bloom, 1974b; Bloom, Rocissano, & Hood, 1976, chap. 13). It appears that it was easier for the children to say something based on their own semantic intention (a statement) than to say something based on a semantic intention that was either influenced by the message of another speaker (a response) or was intended by the child to influence the semantic intention of another speaker (a question). In the response context, it is necessary to process both the form and content of the speaker's message in relation to the situation. If the child processed the form of the utterance (i.e., the word *why*) but not necessarily the content, the simplest responses were the single word *because* and/or an imitation of part or all of the adult's utterance. Only when responses to questions became interpretable more often than not was there evidence that the children had indeed taken into account both the form and the content of the previous message. The fact that interpretable responses occurred only *after* the children could express interpretable causal relations in their spontaneous statements suggests that responding to the form and content of a question required at least three things: first, that the child be able to encode causal relations and, second, that the child be able to encode causal relations with a semantic intention that is influenced by the message of the other speaker. Third, responding required the ability to maintain discourse over two or more turns, given that adult causal questions were most often contingent on prior child utterances.

The question context presented additional form and content requirements to the child. Asking causal questions obviously required a new form for encoding causal relations. In terms of question content, the child's semantic intent was both influenced by and influenced the other speaker, in that the child was intending to evoke a semantic intent on the part of the other speaker. The source of the children's semantic intention varied, then, in these ways in the statement, response, and question contexts: In making a statement the semantic intention originated with the child; in responding to another's question the semantic intention was influenced by the other speaker; in asking a question the semantic intention originated with the child but also entailed an inference about the other speaker to evoke a semantic intention. The fact that the children in the present study began to ask "why" only after they were able both to encode a causal relation in a statement and respond appropriately to an adult *why* question refutes the claim of Blank (1975) and Blank and Allen (1976), who looked at questions and responses and concluded that the use of *why* begins with no conceptual understanding at all.

Similarity and Variation in Acquisition

The development of the expression of causal relations was systematic and generally consistent for the eight children. However, there was also variation among them in form (patterns of clause order) and use (one child asked "why?" at the same time as he answered *why* questions appropriately). This variation in language form and use, with consistency in language content, is consistent with other reports of variation in the child language literature (see, e.g., Bloom, 1970; Bloom, Hood, & Lightbown, 1974, chap. 12; Bloom, Lightbown, & Hood, 1975, chap. 2; Clark & Garnica, 1974; Ferguson & Farwell, 1975; Nelson, 1975b; Ramer, 1976). Whereas the variation reported in other studies has been in the development of simple sentences by younger children, the variation observed in the present study had to do with the development of complex sentences by children up to 3 years of age. Thus, variation is not limited to the very earliest stages of development. Similarity in content and variation in form and use may prove to be a continuing pattern, observable whenever new linguistic structures are being learned.

Orientation to Intention of Self and Other

The children in this study were learning to take into account the activities of people other than themselves in their causal statements. However, reference to the listener's actions or states generally took the form of directives in which the child requested the listener to do something. Thus, the children still focused on their own intentions. But the developmental sequence in language use that was observed in this study is suggestive that the children were gradually learning to take the listener's intentions into account and to differentiate their own intentions from those of others. Although the content analysis of child and adult questions did not include a differentiation between intention of child and intention of adult, there is a strong suggestion in the data of developmental differentiations between adult and child intentions and between speaker and listener actions. The developmental sequence – causal statements < responses to adult *why* questions < child *why* questions – also reflects a sequence of three different intentional orientations, as schematized below.

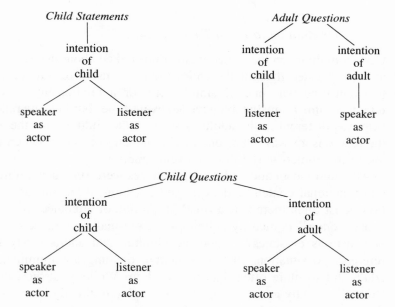

As can be seen, this development in orientation is one of both successive differentiation and expansion. In expressing a causal relation through a statement, the orientation was the child's own intention; reference was to what the child was about to do or wanted the listener to do. When adults asked *why* questions of the child, they made reference to intentions of both the child (the listener) and themselves (as speaker). This situation differs from that of child statements in three ways: (1)

The reference to the child's own intentions is now expressed by another speaker in the form of a question; (2) reference is now also made to the adult's intentions; and (3) reference is also made to different intentions according to whether the speaker or listener was the actor. There was further differentiation with *why* questions: When asking *why* questions, the children made reference to both speaker and listener as actor, whether the intention was on the part of the child or the adult.

Thus, the development from statements to responses to questions may be coextensive with development from referring to actions by self and others as aspects of one's own intentions, to referring to both actions and intentions of both self and others. Such a decentering from oneself has been considered a major aspect of language development as well as cognitive development more generally (e.g., Piaget 1925/1955, 1928/1969).

Orientation to Event Time

Certain findings on the kinds of situations talked about in causal utterances suggested that for the child, the relationship of utterance-time to event-time was one of simultaneity or a relationship in which utterance-time immediately preceded event-time. Further, the relationship was different in the adults' speech to the children; for the adults the relationship was either one of simultaneity or one in which utterance-time immediately followed event-time.

Although most child and adult utterances were similar in referential and functional content and expressed negation, direction, and intention, most often there was a small proportion of utterances in the category "other" (which by definition did not make reference to imminent actions or states). While the children and adults rarely made reference to situations that were neither ongoing nor imminent, the adults did so more often than the children. While what the category "other" actually consisted of was not explored directly in this study, the impression was that for the adults, utterances in the category most often made reference to the immediate past, to what the child or adult had just done. It might be said that the children were anticipatory, while the adults were more reflective. Both had the present as their starting point, but the children looked forward and anticipated events, primarily events that involved their own activities, while the adults looked backward to reflect upon what had just occurred, both in terms of their own and the child's activities. While the children still talked primarily about their own actions, they had begun to talk about the activities of people other than themselves, but such talk was in the form of directives and, in that sense, was still very much tied to the child's own intentions and motivations. However, the possibility that an important development in later language development is the gradual change from an anticipatory to a reflective orientation deserves further study.

NOTES

1 Brainerd (1979, p. 42).
2 Excluded were occurrences of *so* as an intensifier, as in "so big," or as an introducer, as in "so then I ate lunch."
3 The definitions of *causal* and *conditional* are those given in Webster's *Third New International Dictionary:* "Causality – The relation of cause and effect or between certain regularly correlated events or phenomena as a necessary connection or intrinsic bond embedded in the very nature of things; Conditional – Expressing a condition or supposition."
4 Other causal questions besides *why*, for example, "how come you're leaving?" were not intentionally excluded from the study; they just did not occur.
5 Adult questions, rather than child responses, were counted, as a substantial number of adult questions received no linguistic response.
6 The distinction between negative function words *(no, not, can't)* and verbs and attributives with negative connotations is the distinction between nexal and special negation, respectively, made by Jespersen (1961, vol. 5). Nexal negations are those in which the entire predication is negativized; in special negations, some particular word is negativized. Some examples of special negation mentioned by Jespersen are words with the prefixes *no-* (e.g., *nowhere*), *un-* (e.g., *unhappy*), *in-* (e.g., *inhuman*); *scarcely, hardly,* (*a*) *little,* and (*a*) *few.* The attributives with *too* as the intensifier, as in *too big,* appear to be cases of special negation, although Jespersen did not discuss *too* in this way. In addition, many of the verbs the children used could be considered instances of special negation. They occurred in the children's causal statements used in reference to the following sorts of things: (1) toys that did not work, paper that was torn, and the like – *break, broke, wrecked, tore;* (2) objects not present – *missing, lost, empty;* (3) objects that abruptly changed state, most often a tower of blocks, cups, and the like, that was knocked down or that fell over – *fall off, knock over;* (4) finished events or states – *finished, stopped, turn off;* (5) objects that were unattainable – *stuck, locked;* (6) removal of an object in the

sense of getting rid of it – *throw away, take off (clothes), put away;* (7) silence – *be quiet, hush, shut up;* and (8) objects (or sometimes a person) being in a state that impeded action – *too heavy, too tight, too hard, too hot, too small.*

POSTSCRIPT

For studies of causal language since Hood and Bloom (1979):

Bebout, L., Segalowitz, S., & White, G. (1980). Children's comprehension of causal constructions with "because" and "so." *Child Development, 51,* 565–8.

Bretherton, I., & Beeghly, M. (1982). Talking about internal states: The acquisition of an explicit theory of mind. *Developmental Psychology, 18,* 906–21.

Bretherton, I., Fritz, J., Zahn-Waxler, C., & Ridgeway, C. (1986). Learning to talk about emotions: A functional perspective. *Child Development, 57,* 529–48.

Donaldson, M. (1986). *Children's explanations: A psycholinguistic study.* Cambridge: Cambridge University Press.

French, L. (1986). Acquiring and using words to express logical relationships. In S. Kuczaj & M. Barrett (Eds.), *The development of word meaning* (pp. 303–38). New York: Springer-Verlag.

French, L. (1988). The development of children's understanding of "because" and "so." *Journal of Experimental Child Psychology, 45,* 262–79.

Johnson, H., & Chapman, R. (1980). Children's judgement and recall of causal connectives – A developmental study of "because," "so," and "and." *Journal of Psycholinguistic Research, 9,* 243–60.

McCabe, A., Everly, S., Abramovitch, R., Corter, C., & Pepler, D. (1983). Conditional statements in young children's spontaneous speech. *Journal of Child Language, 10,* 253–8.

McCabe, A., & Peterson, C. (1985). A naturalistic study of the production of causal connectives by children. *Journal of Child Language, 12,* 145–59.

Sharp, K. (1982). Preschoolers' understanding of temporal and causal relations. *Merrill–Palmer Quarterly, 28,* 427–36.

11

Causal Meanings and the Concept of Causality

"I was crying because I didn't want to wake up, because it was dark, so dark."

Two major findings from the studies of complex sentences in Chapter 7 and causal expressions in Chapter 10 led to this second study of the acquisition of causal language. One finding was quantitative: the increasing use of syntactic connectives in development of the form of causal statements and responses. The other was the more qualitative finding that the children's causal expressions were primarily about their intentions and motivations for acting. Accordingly, the first purpose of the study in this chapter was to determine the developmental relationship between the acquisition of connectives and the meaning of causal expressions. In addition, the finding that the children talked about intentions and motivations was particularly relevant to developmental theories of the concept of causality. For this reason, the second purpose of the study was to explore further the children's causal meanings in relation to psychological and philosophical theories of causality. This study used the causal statements and responses to *why* questions in the data base from seven of the children in the preceding study (those, except for Steven, who were followed until they acquired the causal connectives).

SUBJECTIVE AND OBJECTIVE CAUSAL MEANING AND CONNECTIVES

The children expressed two broad categories of causal meaning in 94% of their interpretable causal statements. Subjective causal meaning expressed causal connections concerned with personal, emotional, or sociocultural beliefs that were the reasons or results of their actions. Subjective causal connections were not fixed or self-evident; rather, they were social constructions, and they were learned largely from the language the children heard. For example, waking up in the dark can be frightening, and children often cry when they awaken at night. In comforting them, parents provide the language of explanation that socializes the child's experience and expression of emotion. Eventually, this language is reflected in children's own talk about the causes and circumstances of their feelings in events of the same kind.[1]

Objective causal meanings had to do with action-based means–end and consequence relations. These were evident (perceptible or imaginable) and fixed in the physical order of things that resulted from actions in everyday events. Objective meanings were a continuity in language of the kinds of sensorimotor causality experienced in the actions of infancy.[2] For example, from their actions with pull toys, a child learns that a pull toy will roll over a wire in its path leading to the child's saying something like "I'm gonna pick this up so it can't step on the cord."

Acquisition of the syntactic connectives *and, because,* and *so* was associated with objective meaning, even though more of the children's statements expressed subjective meaning overall. The children presumably already knew something about sensorimotor objective causes and consequences from infancy. Thus, learning the linguistic forms was facilitated with familiar and well-established content that was evident and verifiable in the physical context. We discuss this early association of connectives with objective meanings as another instance of 'learning new forms with old functions'.

CAUSAL LANGUAGE AND THE CONCEPT OF CAUSALITY

The concept of causality attributable to these children's thinking, from the evidence of what they talked about, emphasized the actions, feelings, and perceptions of persons in everyday causal events, or intentional causality.[3] They discovered causal connections through their own and others' actions or heard them in everyday discourse about everyday events. Causality for them was neither the 'cement of the universe' that provides the structure of reality nor an innate quality of the mind that determines reality.[4] Rather, the construction of a theory of causality begins in infancy with the emergence of an understanding of the regularities in the relation between change and the actions of oneself and others that bring about change. Before language, perceptible actions and their results are the child's only source of causal understanding. As language is acquired, the child can discover causal attributions through discourse.

Sources of Meaning in the Acquisition of Complex Syntax: The Sample Case of Causality

Lois Bloom and Joanne Bitetti Capatides

The transition in language development from a simple sentence grammar to complex syntax begins between 2 and 3 years of age. As a sample case of this transition to complex sentences that express increasingly complex ideas, we have inquired into how young children acquire the language for expressing their beliefs about causally related events in the world. This study concerns the meanings of children's early causal language: When children begin to combine propositions with a causal connection between them, what kinds of meaning do they express? This question is relevant not only to children's language development but also to the inferences we can draw from their causal language about their underlying concept of causality. How do the meanings of children's early causal statements relate to what we know, first, from psychological accounts of the development of causal understanding and, second, from philosophical theories of causality in the world?

THEORIES OF CAUSALITY AND THE DEVELOPMENT OF CAUSALITY

Three models of causality are relevant to attempts to understand the development of causal understanding: the empiricist model of Hume (1739/1890); the rationalist theory of innate ideas attributed to Kant (1781/1965); and contemporary theories of intentionality, for example, Hart and Honoré (1959) and Searle (1983). According to Hume, inferring a causal connection between events in the world depends on detecting certain observable regularities in the physical world: When two events occur together, one after the other, and consistently in relation to each other, then one can infer that the relation between them is a causal one. In Hume's model, the development of causality depends

Reprinted from the *Journal of Experimental Child Psychology*, *43*, 1987, 112–28, with permission from Academic Press.

upon the child's detecting these empirical regularities of contiguity, order, and constant conjunction in physical and mechanical events. The principles of causal reasoning, then, depend on the structure of events in the world, and the child's task is to detect their regularities.

For Kant, in contrast, causality is an innate property of the mind according to which causal connections are attributed to physical events. The individual's concept of causality determines the structure of reality, conferring the causal connections on events in the world for the regularities that we observe. In this model, the development of causality depends upon an underlying conceptual mechanism for causal understanding. Psychological investigations into the development of causality have proceeded on the basis of one or another of these two philosophical points of view (see, for example, Bullock, Gelman, & Baillargeon, 1982; Sedlak & Kurtz, 1981; Shultz, 1982).

Intentional theories of causality, in contrast, emphasize that actions and perceptions of persons establish causal connections, rather than physical and mechanical regularities in the world or a predetermined mental concept. That is, we discover causality by experiencing it through our actions and perceptions (Searle, 1983). A cause is essentially something that intervenes to change the normal course of events, and the intervention is often a human one (Ducasse, 1929/1969). And in matters of jurisprudence, the two central concepts of causation in the law depend upon (1) a person's manipulating things in order to bring about an intended change, or (2) one person, by word or deed, providing another with a reason for acting (Hart & Honoré, 1959). In this view, the concept of causality develops as children learn to regulate their actions and interactions in the world.

Piaget's developmental account of the foundations of causality in infancy, before language, is consistent with theories that implicate human perceptions and actions in causal attributions. For Piaget (1937/1954) the adult operates with a concept of causality but this property of the mind is not innately determined. Rather, causality is constructed by the child, over time, on the basis of (1) the child's own actions and the actions of others that bring about change, and (2) the child's observations of the regularities and correlations in the world associated with such change.

The essence of sensorimotor causality in infancy is a relation between actions and their physical effects and involves sequences or chains of events that can be perceived directly, for example, pulling a string and watching the toy move. Action and effect gradually became dis-sociated as the infant comes to perceive other intermediary objects, notably persons, that touch one another in the context of such change. Soon the infant uses an adult as an intermediary – grasping the adult's hand and steering it or directing it to perform an action. Development of the concept of causality, then, begins in infancy with the child's own actions that bring about change, and the child's getting other persons to bring about change (Piaget, 1937/1954, 1971/1974).

Causality is at first limited to the data of perception, to what is evident in the context. Gradually, the child becomes able to reconstruct a cause in the presence of an effect, and inversely, given an object, the child can foresee its future effects. A mental construction – involving *new* situations and not merely familiar relationships – supersedes direct contact and action. Such mental representations of events that are not given in the context are, however, mental representations of objective causal connections with perceptible content.

Another source of the development of causal understanding that is not often considered is the information about causal connections in the discourse that the child hears. Language input can lead the child to discover the bases for causal attribution in physical events, for instance, when someone tells the child not to throw a glass "because it will break." And the language that the child hears in interactions is a primary source for learning about causal connections in nonphysical events, for instance, "She is lonely because everyone went away." Once the child begins to participate in conversational discourse, linguistic input can provide the causal connections between antecedent and consequent events that cannot be experienced directly through action. For example, children as young as 3 years of age can complete a narrative sequence about events that are the causes or consequences of emotional states (Trabasso, Stein, & Johnson, 1981).

As will be seen, the children in the present study began to express causal connections in complex sentences with two sources for the meanings of their causal statements. One source was their sensorimotor understanding of objective causal relations, and the other was subjective causal attributions provided in discourse with other persons.

This study of the acquisition of the syntax of causal statements was concerned with the following questions: (1) What meanings are expressed in the causal statements of 2-year-old children, and (2) how do these meanings interact with the acquisition of the syntax of complex sentences? Thus, this study was concerned with *form*, the emergence of conjoined clauses, first without and then with syntactic connectives, in relation to *meaning,* the content of the semantic connection between the clauses and its relation to the underlying concept of causality.

SUBJECTS AND PROCEDURES

The data consisted of all the causal utterances, except the children's *why* questions, from the data base used by Hood and Bloom (1979, chap. 10). The subjects were seven children, three girls and four boys, observed longitudinally from 26 to 38 months of age. Data analysis was begun with those observations in which each child began to produce causally related propositions *without* syntactic connectives and continued until the children were about 3 years old.

Although the analyses were done for each child individually, the children were similar in their profiles of development, so that the data could be pooled for reporting the results. The index that was used to pool the data was the rate of increase over time in the number of causal statements with connectives. As is well known, children differ from one another in onset and rate of development. The children in the present study began to say causal sentences with connectives at different ages (ranging from 26 months, 3 weeks to 31 months, 2 weeks), and they also differed in both the number of causal utterances in their speech and their average utterance length. For these reasons, the data could not be pooled according to age, mean length of utterance, or absolute frequency of causal utterance types or tokens. Accordingly, the individual transcriptions were assigned to developmental periods according to each child's individual rate of increasing frequency of causal statements with connectives. In this way, the children were each compared with themselves, and each served as her or his own control, so that differences between them in rate of development were controlled for.

The first developmental period, Period A, included the texts from all the children before syntactic connectives were productive in their causal statements (with productivity defined as five different causal utterances with connectives). To pool the data according to rate of development thereafter, each child's transcriptions were inspected for at least a twofold increase in the number of causal utterances with connectives from one observation to the next. Where a twofold increase (or greater) was found from one transcription to the next, the two transcriptions were considered to represent different developmen-

Table 11.1. *Description of Four Developmental Periods*

Period	Total Utterances	Sessions	Hours	Age Mean	Age Range	MLU Mean	MLU Range
A	194	13	76.5	26,3	24,2–30	2.80	2.0–3.4
B	228	7	45.5	29,2	26,3–32	3.42	2.8–4.2
C	495	11	68.5	31,3	29,2–35	3.89	3.2–5.0
D	737	8	48.5	35,1	32,3–38	4.11	3.1–5.0
$N = 7$							

tal periods. When less than a two-fold increase occurred, the two transcriptions were included in the same developmental period. Based upon the rate of increase in the frequency of causal statements with connectives, three developmental periods (B, C, and D) were clearly discernible after Period A with no connectives. The number of observation sessions, total number of causal utterances (except *why* questions), age range, and range of mean length of utterance for the four developmental periods are presented in Table 11.1.

Text Analyses

The words *utterance* and *statement* are used throughout this paper as follows: An *utterance* refers to a speech unit, something the child said that is defined by both the discourse frame, that is, its occurrence relative to other utterances, and the limits of its topic. A causal *statement* is any utterance or succession of utterances that expressed a causal relation between propositions and did not have the form or function of a *why* question.

Both formal and semantic criteria were used to decide which utterances to include in the analyses. Formal criteria were (1) a causal word (e.g., *because, so, if*) in child utterances, and/or (2) a child utterance following an adult *why* question. Semantic criteria were based on the proposition as the unit of identification (see Ochs, Schieffelin, & Platt, 1979, for discussion of this criterion). Utterances were included with propositional reference to two events or states with a causal relation between them, whether both propositions were spoken by the child (for example, "I can't eat these because the belly's full") or one proposition was spoken by the child and the other spoken by an adult, for example:

Adult: I have to pack up my toys now.
Child: because you're going home?

Thus, causal statements could extend across utterance boundaries and speaker turns. The unit of analysis was a causal relation between propositions, to distinguish causal statements from causal questions (with *why*), and lexical causatives (the use of such verbs as *make* in single-proposition statements). The research reported here on complex sentences differs, then, from studies of the acquisition of causative verbs in single-proposition statements (Bowerman, 1974b), and periphrastic causative structures (Baron, 1977; Shibatani, 1976).

Every causal statement was coded for form and meaning. The dimension of form was straightforward, whether or not the causal statement included a syntactic connective, that is, *and, so, because,* and *if,* and was coded directly from the linguistic texts. The dimension of meaning was inferential and depended upon an interpretation of what the child said in relation to topic and context. Causal meaning was inferred from the connection between some end state and the change in the context or the conditions that brought about the end state. The interpretive analysis followed the kinds of discovery procedures we have used in our earlier research (e.g., Bloom, 1970; Bloom, Lightbown, & Hood, 1975, chap. 2; see also Bloom, Capatides, & Tackeff, 1981; and Golinkoff, 1981, for discussion of the theoretical rationale for interpretive analysis). Because one does not know in advance which aspects of the child's behaviors will be most relevant to the developmental questions, discovery and resolution go hand in hand. Categories emerge, to begin with, as a result of identifying similarities and differences among speech events, and the categories are revised in the process of "fitting" more and more of the speech events to them, until as many of the data as possible are accounted for (the standard method followed in much of the research in ethology, cultural anthropology, and linguistics, e.g., Beer, 1973; Bloom, 1974a; M. Harris, 1964; Vendler, 1962).

Reliability

Only statements in which the causal meaning relation between propositions was interpretable and unambiguous, as agreed upon by two judges after each interpreted the utterances independently, were included in the analyses reported here. Utterances that were uninterpretable or ambiguous were those that could not be coded for semantic meaning because of insufficient contextual information. For the most part, they were not bizarre, nor were they "animistic" or otherwise similar to the precausality described by Piaget (1923/1955). For example, Eric said "made a bridge under so the man will watch," while he set up a "bridge" with a book; this utterance was not included in the analyses because the context was insufficient for interpreting what he meant. The relative frequency of uninterpretable or otherwise ambiguous statements (with and without connectives) remained constant over time: 13%, Period A; 13%, Period B; 12%, Period C; and 16%, Period D.

The interpretive analysis was done by two investigators working together until the relevant dimensions of meaning were identified and categories of meaning were agreed upon. Subsequently, one of the original investigators recoded all the causal statements according to the meaning categories. A test of reliability was performed by having a third judge code a randomly selected text (consisting of 45 utterances) from one of the children (Mariana). The percentage of agreement between the original coding and the reliability coding was .84. Almost all the disagreements proved to be reconcilable scoring errors rather than judgment differences.

RESULTS

The results consist of description of the children's causal statements in terms of form (the use of connectives), meaning (categories of causal relations between propositions), and the covariation of form and meaning.

Form

The analysis of form was simply an analysis of whether or not the children used a syntactic connective to join two propositions in a causally related sequence, and was relatively straightforward. The children made causal statements without connectives (Period A) before they did so with connectives (beginning in Period B). The relative frequency of statements with connectives increased from 37% of all causal statements in Period B, to 71% in Period C, to 83% in Period D.

Meaning

Two broad categories of causal meaning emerged from the interpretive analysis: objective and subjective meaning. Of the total number of utterances in Table 11.1, 86.5% were interpretable. Subjective and objective meaning accounted for 94% of the interpretable causal utterances.

Objective meaning was evident and fixed in the physical world; the children were talking about events in which the causal relation was transparent and involved a minimum of inference. Statements with objective meaning expressed relations in which the first event or state of affairs and the resulting end state were perceptible, or imaginable if one or both were not part of the immediate context of the speech event. For example:

(1) M   (Mariana picking up a pull
         toy before it rolls over
         microphone wire)   I'm gonna pick this up so it
                                             can't step on the cord.

(2) G   I don't have a Christmas tree.
         Adult: Why?

                                             Because throw it out.

Statements with objective meaning expressed a *means–end* relation (as in Example 1), a *consequence* relation (as in Example 2), or a *condition,* as in the following example:

static
condition

(3) D   (Tiny blue barrel is inside
         other barrels)   You can't see it cause it's
                                             way inside.

Subjective meaning expressed causal relations that were not fixed relations or self-evident. Rather, they were causal connections that were presumably made by the child on the basis of a personal, affective, or sociocultural belief that was either the original state of affairs or the resulting end state. Whereas the causal connection in objective statements was a cause–effect relation that derived from a fixed physical order of events, the causal connection in subjective statements was derived from a constructed social order. For example:

(4) K   (Lois starting to pack up her
         toys and leave)   I'll help you too if you have a
                                             little trouble.

(5) G   (Gia and adult playing with
          doll) Adult: What shall we
          give him?   Nothing.
          Adult: Why?   Because not hungry.

(6) M   (Mariana reading picture
          book; picture with train at red
          stop light)   This one can't go.
          Adult: It can't go?
                                                 No, because that sign doesn't
                                                 say go.

(7) P   (Peter has just shown adult
          his guinea pig)
          Adult: Why do you have him?
          Did you take him home from
          school?   Yeah, cause they don't be-
                                                 long in school.

(8) G   Adult: I want to go home
          now.   Wait my mommy comes.
          Adult: Why?
                                                 Because I will be lonely.

   Both objective and subjective meaning had to do with events that
involved human intervention, either personal or interpersonal. However, the two kinds of meanings were different according to how the
child's statement matched the way events and states are typically associated in the world. Objective meaning had to do with a physical
order in the world that is associated with actions and perceptions. Subjective meaning had to do with a cultural order that is agreed upon
socially. This difference in relational meaning is illustrated in the following pairs of examples. In each pair (9) and (10), similar content
was expressed, but a different causal relation was inferred. In Examples 9(a) and 10(a), the meaning relation is objective – one thing
follows another because of the way they go together in the physical
world. But in 9(b) and 10(b) the meaning relation is subjective – one
thing follows another because of social or cultural custom:

(9a) P   I can't close that one.
          Adult: you can't?   *objective*

                                                 No/because it's broken.

(b) P (Peter, in another context)

This was broken and I gotta fix it.

(10a) G

I gonna step in puddle with sandals on and get it all wet.

(b) K

We didn't go anywhere/just stay home because it was all wet.

The children's causal statements, taken together with and without connectives, most often expressed subjective meanings. Throughout the four periods an average of 62% of their causal statements were subjective: 66% in Period A, 63% in Period B, 57% in Period C, and 63% in Period D.

In sum, in the period from 2 to 3 years of age, when these children were learning to express causal relations between propositions in complex sentences, (1) they acquired the syntactic connectives and the frequency of connectives increased, and (2) they expressed both objective and subjective meanings, with subjective meaning expressed more often overall. Only form, the use of connectives, increased developmentally.

Meaning and Connectives

Although no developmental trend was apparent for meaning taken alone, the emergence of connectives and meaning interacted developmentally. On the basis of the relative frequency of statements with subjective meaning overall, causal statements could be expected to occur primarily with subjective meaning, regardless of whether a connective was expressed. If no fluctuations in this expected pattern of covariation of connectives and meaning occurred over time, then we could conclude that development is *only* quantitative and linguistic, with the only development being an increase in frequency of connectives. In contrast, fluctuations in the pattern of covariation of connectives with subjective and objective meaning could be interpreted as qualitative change in the developmental interaction between linguistic form and underlying conceptualization.

Subjective meaning was always more frequent in sentences without connectives for all the children, with only one exception (in the case of one child, four of his six sentences expressed objective meaning in

Table 11.2. *Frequency of Causal Statements, with Objective and Subjective Meaning, with and without Causal Connectives*

Time	No Connective	Connective	Total
Period B			
Objective	34	45	79
Subjective	99	33	132
Total	133	78	211
Period C			
Objective	37	118	155
Subjective	67	138	205
Total	104	256	360
Period D			
Objective	23	197	220
Subjective	78	302	380
Total	101	499	600
$N = 7$			

Period A). However, in Period B, when connectives first emerged, subjective meaning was less frequent in sentences with connectives than in sentences without connectives, and more than half the causal statements with connectives expressed objective meaning (Table 11.2).

All the children showed the same developmental pattern over time in their acquisition of connectives given subjective or objective meaning. The influences of time and meaning on the acquisition of connectives were tested statistically using the logit form of loglinear analysis (Knoke & Burke, 1980), with the occurrence of connectives as the dependent variable. The data in Table 11.2 are categorical frequency data for the dependent variable of the connective (plus or minus connective in causal statements), in relation to time (Periods B, C, D) and meaning (objective, subjective) as the independent variables. The logit models for these data, presented in Table 11.3, test three hypotheses: (1) that the use of connectives was related to developmental period; (2) that the use of connectives was related to meaning, and (3) that the contingency between the use of connectives and meaning changed over time.

The use of connectives increased significantly over time, difference likelihood ratio $\Delta L^2(2) = 152.66$, $p < .01$). The ratio of sentences with and without connectives increased from less than 1 to 1 in Period B to approximately 5 to 1 in Period D. The use of connectives was also

Table 11.3. *Logit Analysis for Frequencies of Causal Statements in Table 11.2*

Effect	Difference Likelihood Ratio	df
Time × connective	152.66[a]	2
Meaning × connective	24.75[a]	1
Time × meaning × connective	5.96[b]	2
N = 7		

[a]$p < .01$.
[b]$p = .05$.

significantly related to meaning, difference likelihood ratio Δ $L^2(1) = 24.75$, $p < .01$. In sentences without connectives overall, subjective meaning was far more frequent than objective meaning with a ratio of 2.6 to 1. In sentences with connectives, the disparity was not as great, with a ratio of 1.3 to 1.

The relation between meaning and connective changed significantly over time, difference likelihood ratio Δ $L^2(2) = 5.96$, $p = .05$. In sentences without connectives, the ratio of subjective meaning to objective meaning varied from 3 to 1 in Period B, to about 2 to 1 in Period C, and to more than 3 to 1 in Period D. However, in sentences with connectives the ratio varied from less than 1 to 1 in Period B, to about 1 to 1 in C, and to 1.5 to 1 in Period D. In sum, subjective meaning predominated for statements with and without connectives combined; however, the acquisition of syntactic connectives in Period B was associated with expression of objective meaning. By Period D, sentences both with and without connectives expressed subjective meaning primarily.

DISCUSSION

We discuss these results in terms of (1) the relation between these children's concept of causality and theories of causality and (2) the acquisition of increasingly complex language.

Two-Year-Old Causality

The picture of 2-year-old causality that emerged from the results of this study begins to bridge the gap between accounts of early sensorimotor causality and later physical and logical causality. Objective causal meanings in the children's statements represented a continuity in language of the kind of sensorimotor causality displayed earlier on the plane of action, having to do with evidential and action-based means– end and consequence relations. But even though they talked about causal relations that were evident between things in the physical order of the world, these perceptible causal events were not the kinds of physical and mechanical causality between objects that depend on the detection of empirical regularities. Rather, the concept of causality for the 2-year-old children in this study, as reflected in the objective meanings of their causal statements, involved the causes and consequences of their actions in everyday events.

The children talked more often about subjective causal relations, with appeals to affective emotions and drives, personal judgments, and cultural practice that were a part of the social order of the world. One source of subjective meanings was in interactions with others in which the child could see either the affective consequences of an action (for example, seeing father angry when the child pokes the dog) or the behaviors of others in response to expression of emotions and feeling (for example, when the child cries and a caregiver comforts or feeds the child). But other causal connections were imperceptible and could have been learned only from the speech that the children heard (and overheard); for example, "this one can't go . . . because that sign (red stoplight) doesn't say go" and ("Did you take him home from school?") . . . "yeah, 'cause they don't belong in school." The children could not have discovered such relationships as these between events, and the feelings, personal judgments, or cultural beliefs that were causally associated with the events, by acting on the environment. Someone must have told them that red means stop and green means go, that guinea pigs do not belong in school, and so on. Much of what the children knew about subjective causality must have come when adults supplied them with beliefs, reasons, and justifications in past discourse.

Thus, the children learned about certain causal connections by acting and observing others act on the world and learned to express objective meanings that derived from the fixed physical order in such actions. They also learned about other causal connections by interacting with other persons and observing the social consequences of actions or the ways that others behave in relation to the emotional expression of personal feelings. But in addition to their knowledge of causality acquired in the context of their actions and interactions in the world, the children also learned about causality from the language they heard. Discourse is a major source for subjective meanings. Subjective causality, then, was a special instance in which something about the culture – how practices, judgments, affective states, and so forth, are valued as reasons for acting – is learned in the context of learning the language for its expression (Hood, Fiess, & Aron, 1982; Schieffelin, 1990).

Not only did subjective causality from age 2 to 3 differ in this way from earlier sensorimotor causality, it also differed from Piaget's (1924/ 1969) description of psychological causality in preschool children. Piaget (1923/1955) reported that in response to such questions as "Why is there a great and little Salève?" children gave animistic answers such as "Because there is one for little children and the other for big ones" and "Because of people who want to go into the little one or the great one" (pp. 228–9). He described such answers as "precausal" because children attributed psychological motivation to inanimate things out of "confusion between the psychical and the physical order of things" (p. 230). However, the children in the present study, though concerned very much with intentions and motivations, feelings and beliefs, gave no indication that they confused physical causality with the intentions of persons. The difference is they were talking about things they knew something about (Gelman, 1978). The children did not talk about, and adults did not ask them about, such physical phenomena as the sizes of lakes or the movement of clouds. When the children in the present study spoke for themselves, the content of their language and, presumably, their thinking as well centered on events for which their psychological explanations were appropriately causal.

Inherent in Piaget's genetic epistemology is the progressive approximation of the mind of the child to the mind of the scientist (Gruber & Vonèche, 1977). Accordingly, Piaget, as well as more recent psychologists investigating the development of causality (e.g., Bullock & Gelman, 1979; Kun, 1978; Shultz, 1982), inquired into the child's understanding in terms of adult understanding of physical and logical phenomena. The theoretical models of causality tested in the developmental research have been based on correlations in the physical world or concepts of causal mechanism.

However, for the young children in this study, theories of causality that emphasize the actions and perceptions of persons in everyday causal events (e.g., Ducasse, 1924/1969; Hart & Honoré, 1959; Lucas, 1962; Searle, 1983) were most relevant to the concept of causality attributable to them on the basis of the content of their language. The children displayed in their language an awareness of causality in the particular events and the human interactions that formed the contexts of their development. They discovered causal connections through their own and others' actions or heard them in everyday discourse. Causality, for them, was not the Humean "cement of the universe" that provides the structure of reality. Rather, causality was the means whereby they regulated their actions and their interactions in the world.

In sum, the construction of causality begins in infancy with the emergence of (1) an understanding of the relation between change and the actions of oneself and others (Piaget, 1937/1954) and (2) the detection of certain regularities in these events (e.g., Borton, 1979; Golinkoff et al., 1984). Before language, perceptible actions and their results are the child's only source of causal understanding. As language is acquired, the child can discover causal attributions through language. These are the bases – sensorimotor causality and causal attributions in discourse – upon which the 2-year-old child proceeds to construct an increasingly abstract understanding of causality. We propose that using causal language will be a large factor in deepening and extending the dimensions of their causal understanding and strategies for causal reasoning.

Learning the Language of Causality

These children's causal language provided a sample case of the transition in language development from simple to complex syntax. We know, from our earlier research into the acquisition of complex sentences, that the children we have studied acquired the syntax and connectives for connecting two propositions with additive, temporal, and causal meaning relations in the sequence: additive before temporal before causal (Bloom, Lahey, Hood, Lifter, & Fiess, 1980, chap. 7). The fact that the children were already connecting propositions to express additive and then temporal meaning relations, before they connected propositions with causal meanings, is another instance of the observation that children first express new functions (in this case, causality) with old forms. Once a form is acquired with particular meaning, it can be used in acquiring other meanings (Bloom, 1970; Slobin, 1973; Werner & Kaplan, 1963).

Although causal statements expressed subjective meanings first and most often, the children acquired syntactic connectives primarily in *learning connectives, not causality.*

statements with objective meaning. This reversion to the sensorimotor-based, objective causal meanings in learning connectives is another instance of the observation that children frequently learn new forms to express established meanings. The implication here is that an advance in linguistic complexity has a constraining effect on the system (Bloom, Miller, & Hood, 1975, chap. 3; Shatz, 1978). This effect is somehow mitigated when the content is familiar and well established, as means–end and consequence relations presumably were from infancy, as well as evident and verifiable in the context. This constraint on processing capacity, with the use of old forms for expressing new content and resorting to earlier learned content when learning new forms, is an instance of the effects on acquisition exerted from within the child.

We have seen, in these children's acquisition of the language of causality, how language, thought, and society influence one another in development. The closeness of objective meanings to sensorimotor causality provided evidence to support a hypothesis of cognitive priority. At the same time, subjective meanings provided an example of the influence from the language and society on thought. The children heard causal expressions in the speech that was directed to them, and they also participated in exchanges in which an adult's response to what they said was causally related. These were the contexts in which subjective meanings were acquired.

The results of this study are consistent with a model of development in which the child actively constructs both thought, in this instance the concept of causality, and the language. The concept of causality is constructed as the child acquires knowledge of persons, objects, and actions from evidential and linguistic events. Knowledge in memory, along with data from perception, provide the contents of psychological awareness, or intentional states in the philosophical sense, which the child endeavors to express through language and action. Language is constructed in the child's effort to express the underlying representations that are the contents of these states of mind (Bloom & Beckwith, 1986). We have reported elsewhere that the children whom we have studied began using causal statements before they began to ask *why* questions. This means that development proceeded from talking about actions of self and others as expressions of what the child has in mind to the beginning of the ability to inquire into the contents of mind in others with *why* questions (Hood & Bloom, 1979, chap. 10).

To conclude, the contents of the child's mental states give meaning to what the child does and says and direct the child to semantically relevant aspects of discourse for learning the language. This model of language development places the control of acquisition in the mind and action of the child (Bloom, Hood, & Lightbown, 1974, chap. 12; Shatz, 1982), rather than in the events of the external context or the support the child receives in familiar interactions with adults. Events in the external context and the child's interactions are critically necessary, but it is the child's ability to understand and use these external events that is explanatory.

NOTES

1 See Kopp (1989) and Thompson (1990) for discussion of this point. The frequency with which the children talked about personal, social, and culturally determined reasons and results having to do with their actions and feelings was an influence from the language and cultural context on their own language and thought (see Schieffelin & Ochs, 1986).
2 Piaget (1936/1952).
3 For example, Ducasse (1924/1969); Searle (1983).
4 As per the theories of Hume and Kant, respectively.

POSTSCRIPT

For studies of the meanings of early expressions of causality since Bloom & Capatides (1987):
Dunn, J. (1988). *The beginnings of social understanding.* Cambridge, MA: Harvard University Press.

Part III

Studies of Process and Interaction

This final section presents two studies of how discourse contributes to the process of acquisition. The first of these studies of interaction addresses an old problem, imitation and its role in language development. The role of imitation was studied from 18 to 25 months of age as the children made the transition from single-word to multiword speech. In the second study of the development of discourse, imitation was one kind of contingency along with the several kinds of contingency that developed in the period from 2 to 3 years of age. In both studies, the results confirmed the view that children actively seek knowledge of language from the input they receive in interactions with adults.

12

Imitation and Its Role in
Language Development

Patsy: "I think it's pressed plaster."
Peter: "pressed plaster."

Considerable differences of opinion can be found in the historical literature
on whether imitation is important to language learning. At the time this study
was published, psychological theory (both behaviorism and Piaget) and linguistic theory (generative transformational grammar) were at odds on the role
that imitation could have for language acquisition, each seeing imitation as
important or irrelevant, respectively. In this study, the children's naturally
occurring imitative and spontaneous speech were compared to see if imitation
made a difference in their language learning. The first result was that the
children differed in how frequently they imitated the speech they heard. More
important, however, was the finding that when they did imitate, they were
selective in the words and semantic–syntactic relations they repeated from the
input. In this study, mean length of utterance was less than 2.0 morphemes,
and the children were less than 2 years old.

INDIVIDUAL DIFFERENCES IN THE TENDENCY TO
IMITATE

The six children in this study showed wide differences in the proportion of
their speech that was imitated, from about 5% to about 35% of the different
utterances they produced. However, even though the children were different
from one another, each tended to be consistent in the tendency to imitate over
time in the period when mean length of utterance increased from essentially
single words to just under 2.0 morphemes. The original working definition of
imitation set a five-utterance limit between the model adult utterance and the
child's utterance for the child's utterance to be considered imitative. For those
children who imitated frequently, imitations tended to occur immediately after
the model utterance. For those children who imitated rarely, extending the
time to ten utterances did not result in an increase in their frequency of imitation. From the results of this first analysis, then, we concluded that actually
repeating what an adult says is not necessary for learning language; that is,
the children acquired language whether or not they imitated.

but →

SELECTIVE IMITATION

For those children who did imitate, imitation was selective and evidence of learning; it was not merely an automatic echoing of random linguistic events. At the level of individual lexical items, two different populations of single-word utterances were found: those used spontaneously and those that were imitated. This result meant that the children tended to repeat words they did not also use spontaneously and did not imitate those words they said spontaneously. Moreover, over time there was progression in only one direction: Words that were imitated at an earlier time became spontaneous, but not vice versa.

At the level of the structure of multiword utterances, acquisition of semantic–syntactic categories (for example, action-on-affected-object) and developments within categories (for example, nominal or pronominal lexicalization of the affected-object) showed progressive change from imitated to spontaneous occurrences. However, when imitation in a semantic–syntactic category was more frequent than expected on the basis of frequency of imitation overall, spontaneous utterances also occurred at the same time. This was taken as evidence that the children imitated aspects of sentences from the input they were in the process of learning. They did not repeat what they already knew well or what they knew nothing about. Thus, for those children who imitated, imitation was developmentally progressive. In the imitation context, a child has the perceptual support of a model utterance relative to information in nonlinguistic events that may be only partially mapped onto linguistic schemas. Imitating the model utterance provides experience in expressing the relevant aspects of an event, and this experience helps consolidate the pairing of form and content.

However, by imitating what someone else says, children are also learning something about the use of language in discourse. The definition of imitation used in this study was a conservative one. An utterance was defined as imitative if it repeated all or part of a preceding utterance from someone else and did not add to it or change it other than to leave some part out. In fact, one aspect of discourse development is to repeat all or part of a prior message and also change it in some way. This observation led to the study of discourse in Chapter 13.

Imitation in Language Development: If, When, and Why

Lois Bloom, Lois Hood, and Patsy Lightbown

When children say something in response to what someone else says, they can either repeat what they hear or say something that is more or less related to it. The two possibilities, to imitate or not to imitate, are represented in the following speech events from two different children:

(1) P	(age 21 months, 1 week):		
	(Peter opening cover of tape recorder)		open/open/open.
	Did you open it?		
	(Peter watching the tape recorder)		open it.
	Did you open the tape recorder?		
	(Peter still watching the tape recorder)		tape recorder.
(2) A	(age 19 months, 2 weeks):		
	(Allison jumped up, almost hitting her head on overhead microphone; the microphones in the studio had been placed and adjusted by the cameraman before videotaping began; Allison touches the microphone, turns to Mommy)		man.
	Man. That's the microphone. That's the microphone.		
	(Allison pointing to another microphone on lavaliere around Mommy's neck)		Mommy.
	Yeah, Mommy has a microphone.		
	(Allison looks at overhead microphone)		
	That's another microphone.		
	(Allison still looking at overhead microphone)		man.

In the two situations, "tape recorder" and "microphone" were relatively unfamiliar. Peter had not seen tape recorders before; Allison

Reprinted from *Cognitive Psychology, 6,* 1974, 380–420, with permission from Academic Press.

had not seen a microphone since the first video session three months earlier. Peter repeated the word he did not know, whereas Allison named something that was associated with the word she did not know. Both children were processing information about language. In order to determine whether or not imitation is important for processing speech relative to the events to which it refers, it is necessary to determine the extent to which children imitate the speech they hear, when imitation occurs if it occurs, and why it occurs. This study described the extent to which imitation occurred in the speech of six children and explored the function of imitation for lexical and grammatical learning in their early language development.

There has always been considerable disagreement about the importance of imitation for language development. One prevailing assumption has been that children need to repeat the speech that they hear in order to learn it. For example, according to Jespersen, "One thing which plays a great role in children's acquisition of language, and especially in their early attempts to form sentences, is Echoism: the fact that children echo what is said to them" (1922, p. 135). Kirkpatrick (1909) and others believed that children are virtually compelled to imitate and that they imitate not only what they themselves have seen or done previously but also totally novel behavior. Bloch (1921), Guillaume (1926/1968), Lewis (1951), and others described a critical stage of imitation that comes between the stage of comprehension and the beginning of speech. However, Fraser, Bellugi, and Brown (1963) concluded from an experimental study of elicited imitation that imitation preceded comprehension in development, and there were early observers, for example, Meumann (1903) and Thorndike (1913), who discounted the importance of imitation for language development altogether.

The behaviorist view of language learning would expect new behaviors to be imitated before they can be incorporated into an individual's repertoire of behaviors, for example, Mowrer (1960), Jenkins and Palermo (1964), and Staats (1971). In 1941, Jakobson (1968 translation) pointed out the contradiction between behaviorist views of language learning that emphasized the importance of imitation on the one hand and the notion of creativity in rationalist accounts of the nature of language on the other. The contradiction was elaborated by Chomsky (1959) and in recent debates about theories of language development (see, for example, the papers and discussions in Bellugi & Brown,

1964; Dixon & Horton, 1968; Slobin, 1971b; Smith & Miller, 1966). If the child's task is to discover the rules of grammar that make it possible to speak and understand sentences never spoken or heard before, then imitating a sample of utterances would not be very helpful. In the theory of generative grammar (Chomsky, 1957, 1965), underlying sentence structures and not actual utterances themselves are the relevant data, and underlying structure cannot be imitated (see, for example, McNeill, 1970; Slobin, 1968).

Apparently, only two studies have actually compared children's imitative and spontaneous utterances. Ervin-Tripp (1964) compared the word order of imitative and spontaneous utterances in the speech of five children; Kemp and Dale (1973) compared grammatical features in the imitative and spontaneous utterances of 30 children. Both studies concluded that imitative speech was not "grammatically progressive," that is, that neither word order nor grammatical features were more advanced in imitative than in spontaneous utterances. However, other impressions have been contradictory. Bloom (1968), Slobin (1968), and Brown (reported in Slobin, 1968) commented that something more than casual observation of children's speech suggests that imitative utterances are different and somewhat beyond the grammatical level represented in spontaneous utterances. Shipley, Smith, and Gleitman (1969) reported that children who were just beginning to use multiword utterances were more likely to repeat a command that contained a nonsense word (for example, "throw *ronta* ball") than a command with only real words – which led them to conclude that imitation might be a factor in lexical learning.

To the extent that a child must hear a lexical item before using it, one might consider that much of a child's speech is imitative. Leopold (1939–1949, vol. 3), Piaget (1951/1962), and Sinclair (1971) have taken just such a broad view of imitation in development – that as a child incorporates experience in memory, virtually all behavior imitates a model that, if not actually present in the context, would be represented mentally. However, if all behavior in the young child is imitative, then the task of explaining behavior remains, and imitation loses considerable force as a process that might contribute to development. In order to explore the function of imitation as a process in language development, it was necessary to define imitation in a way that made it possible to examine the developmental relationship between behaviors that were and were not imitative.

PROCEDURES

For the purpose of this study, only behavior that followed an actual model was considered imitative. An utterance was *imitative* (1) if it occurred in a natural situation (that is, without the child's being asked or prompted to imitate), (2) if it repeated all or part of a preceding model utterance from someone else, (3) if it did not add to or change the model other than to reduce it by leaving something out, and (4) if no more than five utterances (from the child or others) intervened after the model. The arbitrary limit of five utterances was chosen as intuitively reasonable for establishing an imitative utterance as one that occurred in the context of the model. All other utterances were considered *spontaneous*.[1]

The study focused on the period of language development in which children progress from using only one word at a time (when mean length of utterance is essentially 1.0) to the emergence of grammar and the use of structured speech (when mean length of utterance approaches 2.0).

Data were obtained from six children in this developmental period from single words to syntax: Eric, Gia, Jane, Kathryn, and Peter were each visited in their homes periodically, and their speech was audio recorded as they interacted primarily with an investigator. The interactions with the sixth child, Allison, were video recorded in the audiovisual studio at Teachers College, Columbia University, using the procedures for recording and transcribing described in Bloom (1973, pp. 138–41). The speech samples that were obtained from the six children are described in Table 12.1 in terms of length of sessions, age, mean length of utterance (MLU), and numbers of utterances. In Table 12.1 and throughout this report, the term *type* refers to a particular utterance, and the term *token* refers to an instance of an utterance type. Thus, the utterance "read that book" was one type that, occurring four times in a sample, had four tokens. As a multiword utterance, "read that book" is also a syntactic utterance type. The data for analysis consisted of more than 17,000 utterances from the six children in the period from age 18 months to 25 months.

Three separate analyses were performed. First, the extent and consistency of imitation were determined for each child in terms of the proportion of utterance types that were imitated in each session. Second, the imitative and spontaneous occurrences of lexical item tokens were observed within each session and across successive sessions. Third,

Table 12.1. *Summary Description of Speech Samples*

	Sample Specifications			Number of Utterances			
Child and Time	Length (hours)	Age (months, weeks)	Mean Length of Utterance	Total Types	Total Syntactic Types	Average Types per Hour	Total Tokens
Allison							
I	0.75	16, 3	1.06	49	11	70	283
II	0.75	19, 2	1.02	67	4	77	321
III	0.75	20, 3	1.13	118	19	157	379
IV	0.75	22, 0	1.73	168	94	224	271
Eric							
I	4	19, 1	1.10	96	23	24	296
II	6	20, 2	1.19	179	72	30	615
III	6.7	22, 0	1.42	363	176	52	1043
IV	3	23, 2	1.69	311	185	104	629
Gia							
I	6.7	19, 2	1.12	246	83	37	1045
II	3.3	20, 2	1.34	282	149	85	933
III	5	22, 1	1.58	310	197	65	804
IV	2.1	23, 3	1.79	300	194	143	601
Jane							
I	5	18, 2	1.29	350	82	70	1144
II	2.5	20, 0	1.27	239	111	96	438
Kathryn							
I	5	21, 0	1.32	432	226	86	917
II	1.7	22, 3	1.89	443	303	260	697
III	1.7	24, 2	2.83	474	427	279	642
Peter							
I	3	21, 1	1.04	171	21	59	610
II	3.5	21, 3½	1.09	136	12	39	418
III	4.5	22, 2	1.37	302	119	65	1052
IV	4.5	23, 1	1.41	363	165	82	1166
V	3	23, 2½	1.33	255	129	83	583
VI	4.5	24, 1	1.75	594	424	133	1364
VII	4.5	25, 0	2.39	685	551	152	1195

all multiword utterances were examined for regularities in form and meaning in order to determine categories of semantic–syntactic structure. Imitative and spontaneous utterance types in each category were then compared within each session and across successive sessions.

THE EXTENT AND CONSISTENCY OF IMITATION

The first concern was to determine whether the children imitated the speech they heard and the extent to which an individual child's tendency to imitate was consistent across time. Following this, imitative and nonimitative utterances were compared for each child in order to determine if there were lexical and structural differences between the two kinds of utterances.

Every utterance in each speech sample was coded as spontaneous or imitative according to the working definitions given earlier. The proportions of utterance types that occurred only spontaneously, only imitatively, or both spontaneously and imitatively are presented in Table 12.2.[2] It is immediately apparent that there were differences in the extent to which the children imitated. The proportion of imitation in Allison's speech was never more than .06, whereas the proportion of imitation in Peter's speech was always at least .27. For most of the children, the relative tendency to imitate that was observed in the first speech sample continued until MLU reached approximately 2.0 morphemes.[3] Only Kathryn showed an appreciable change over time. Because the difference between Time I and Time II was so great, Kathryn's speech at Time III was analyzed even though MLU was 2.83 and thus beyond the limits of the study. The lower proportion of imitation at Time II continued at Time III; .09 of the different utterances at Time III were imitative.

There were marked differences then in the extent to which the different children imitated, but each child was consistent in the tendency to imitate across time, as can be seen in Figure 12.1. According to these results, imitation is not required for learning to talk; two children progressed from single-word utterances to MLU of almost 2.0 without imitating the speech that they heard. Part of the confusion in the early literature about the relative importance of imitation for language development may be attributed to the fact that different observers were watching different children, who did or did not imitate.

It might be hypothesized that the nonimitating children were indeed imitating but their imitation was somehow delayed. To explore this possibility, the latency of imitation, in terms of the number of utterances that intervened between the model and its reproduction, was determined for each of the speech samples. The occurrence of imitative utterances was compared in two different conditions: immediate

Table 12.2. *Proportion of Utterance Types That Were Only Spontaneous, Only Imitative, or Both Spontaneous and Imitative*

Child and Time	All Utterances			Only Syntactic Utterances		
	Sp	Im	Sp + Im	Sp	Im	Sp + Im
Allison						
I	.85	.04	.11	.91	.09	—
II	.88	.06	.06	1.00	—	—
III	.92	.04	.04	.95	—	.05
IV	.94	.04	.02	.98	.11	.01
Eric						
I	.71	.17	.12	.69	.22	.09
II	.73	.15	.12	.76	.18	.06
III	.73	.17	.10	.76	.21	.03
IV	.76	.17	.07	.78	.16	.06
Gia						
I	.69	.14	.17	.86	.13	.01
II	.87	.07	.06	.94	.05	.01
III	.88	.06	.06	.92	.06	.02
IV	.96	.04	—	.97	.03	—
Jane						
I	.38	.42	.20	.47	.49	.04
II	.60	.32	.08	.57	.41	.02
Kathryn						
I	.53	.36	.11	.64	.34	.02
II	.86	.11	.03	.88	.11	.01
Peter						
I	.30	.42	.28	.34	.57	.09
II	.48	.31	.21	.59	.33	.08
III	.58	.27	.15	.68	.28	.04
IV	.54	.34	.12	.57	.36	.07
V	.55	.27	.07	.66	.30	.04
VI	.58	.34	.08	.57	.38	.05

imitation with no intervening utterance, and nonimmediate imitation with at least one but not more than five intervening utterances.

The number of imitative utterance types with token frequency of immediate imitation greater than token frequency of nonimmediate imitation was compared with the number of imitative utterances with nonimmediate frequency greater than immediate frequency. The results

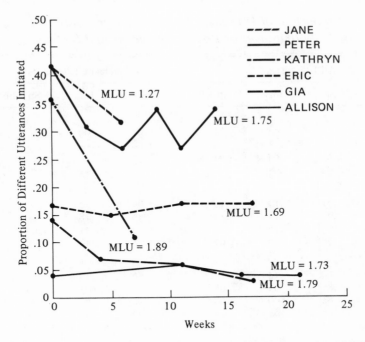

Figure 12.1. Relative extent of imitation. The proportion of different utterances imitated by each child at each Time.

of a sign test of the hypothesis that immediate and nonimmediate imitation were equally likely to occur are presented in Table 12.3. In the first entry in Table 12.3, for example, for Eric at Time I, there were 27 imitative utterance types; two of these had equal numbers of immediate and nonimmediate tokens and were not included in the analysis. Three of the remaining 25 had frequency of nonimmediate imitation greater than frequency of immediate imitation, and 22 had frequency of immediate imitation greater than frequency of nonimmediate imitation. The probability of this result given the hypothesis of no difference between immediate and nonimmediate imitation was less than .01. As can be seen in Table 12.3, there was a significant difference between immediate and nonimmediate imitation ($p < .01$) for the imitating children (Eric, Jane, Peter, and Kathryn at Time I), whose overall proportion of imitation exceeded .15, and for Gia at Time I when the proportion of imitation was .14. Thus, if these children imitated, they tended to do so immediately, with no utterances intervening between an imitative utterance and its model.

Table 12.3. *Comparison of Immediate and Nonimmediate Imitation*

| Child and Time | Number of Utterances | | Proba-bility (less than) |
	Freq. of Nonimm. Greater Than Freq. of Imm.	Freq. of Imm. Greater Than Freq. of Nonimm.	
Eric			
I	3	22	.01
II	11	30	.01
III	30	56	.01
IV	22	46	.01
Jane			
I	8	212	.01
II	15	71	.01
Peter			
I	15	98	.01
II	19	52	.01
III	40	79	.01
IV	37	118	.01
V	21	67	.01
VI	39	200	.01
Kathryn			
I	35	122	.01
II	35	26	.90
Gia			
I	22	47	.01
II	18	20	.44
III	26	12	.99
IV	4	9	.14
Allison			
I	4	2	.89
II	3	3	.66
III	6	5	.73
IV	5	3	.85

However, for the nonimitating children, for whom the overall pro-portion of imitation was less than .15 (Kathryn at Time II, Allison, and Gia), the difference between immediate and nonimmediate imita-tion was not significant (except for Gia at Time I). The nonimitating children might have been imitating a model that was further removed than the original five-utterance limit that had been established in defin-ing imitation for this study. In order to test this, the spontaneous utterances from Allison and Gia were classified again after extending to ten the number of utterances that could intervene between the model and its "imitation." In the four samples of Allison's speech, there were only four imitations of a model that occurred with at least five and no more than ten intervening utterances; in 5.6 hr of Gia's speech (the middle third of each sample), there were ten such utterances. If so few imitative utterances occurred within a ten-utterance boundary, there was no reason to expect that there would be imitative utterances beyond that limit. Indeed, it might well be questioned whether such utterances were even imitative at all or whether they might have occurred in any event.

COMPARISON OF IMITATIVE AND SPONTANEOUS SPEECH

After it was established that the extent of imitation varied from child to child but remained consistent for each child, we determined how imitation functioned for those children who imitated.

There was a clear division between the utterance types a child imitated and those produced spontaneously, as can be seen in Table 12.2. Any utterance type which had at least one spontaneous and one imitative token is included in the Sp + Im column. The number of utterances with both spontaneous and imitative tokens was relatively small for all the children and tended to decrease as MLU increased. When only the syntactic utterances were taken into account, there was an even stronger separation of spontaneous and imitative utterances. Furthermore, many of the utterances represented in the Sp + Im column were high-frequency utterances with many spontaneous tokens and only two or three imitative tokens. For example, at Peter IV, the utterance "in there" occurred 15 times spontaneously and one time imitatively.

Lexical Items

One function of imitation that has often been suggested is that imitation helps children learn new words.

Different Populations of Words. In order to test whether there were two different populations of words in the children's speech at each time, the following procedure was used: The proportion, p, of lexical item tokens which were imitative was calculated for each speech sample, both for single-word utterances and words used syntactically. The entries for words used syntactically were found by separating each syntactic utterance into its "word parts" and counting each word separately. For example, the utterance "need another one" was counted as one occurrence each of "need," "another," and "one." The frequency of imitative versus spontaneous tokens of each word which occurred three or more times within a speech sample was compared with the distribution expected on the basis of the binomial expansion using the value of p for that speech sample. If the two-tailed probability of obtaining the observed split between imitative and spontaneous tokens was less than .05, that word was considered to have an extreme split between imitative and spontaneous use. After the number of words with extreme splits was found, a binomial test with $p = .05$ was applied to ascertain the likelihood of this number of extreme splits occurring in each sample. For example, for Peter at Time I, of 59 single-word utterances that occurred at least three times, 16 of them split in an extreme way between their spontaneous and imitative frequencies; the probability of observing this many extreme splits was $<.001$. Thus, it was concluded that for this sample there were two populations of single-word utterances, those used spontaneously and those used imitatively.[4]

The number of words with extreme splits, the total number of words in the analysis (words that occurred three times or more), and the binomial probability of observing a ratio of words with extreme splits to total number of words at least this extreme is presented in Table 12.4 for those times when the overall proportion of imitation of different utterances was greater than .15.[5] As can be seen, for all the samples except Eric at Times I and IV, the results were significant for single-word utterances and/or words used syntactically. This result means that the children tended to use certain words only spontaneously and certain other words only imitatively. However, explanations for the split between imitative and spontaneous occurrence appeared to be different for single-word utterances and words used syntactically.

Single-Word Utterances. The results for single-word utterances were less than convincing at first glance. The number of words that split in an extreme way in their imitative and spontaneous frequencies was not significant for Peter at Times II, V, and VI, nor for Eric at Times I, III, and IV. However, as can be seen in Table 12.4, for the three samples from Peter that were not significant, the number of words that

Table 12.4. *Summary of Binomial Tests for Two Populations of Words, Imitative and Spontaneous*

Child and Time	Single-Word Utterances			Words Used Syntactically		
	No. of Words with Extreme Splits	No. of Words in Analysis	Proba-bility (less than)	No. of Words with Extreme Splits	No. of Words in Analysis	Proba-bility (less than)
Eric						
I	1	29	.77	0	4	.83
II	8	44	.01	0	14	.49
III	5	67	.24	7	37	.01
IV	3	37	.28	2	49	.71
Peter						
I	16	59	.01	0	3	.86
II	3	44	.38	3	7	.01
III	23	79	.01	6	31	.01
IV	14	89	.01	8	52	.01
V	4	34	.09	7	40	.01
VI	4	49	.23	36	113	.01
Jane						
I	18	101	.01	4	14	.01
II	5	24	.01	2	34	.51
Kathryn						
I	7	64	.05	9	69	.05

occurred three or more times so that they could be counted in the analysis was smaller than in those samples where the results were significant.

Inspection of the data from another perspective – the number of words, regardless of how often they occurred, that split with either no spontaneous and only imitative, or only spontaneous and no imitative occurrence, in the same samples – revealed that Eric and Peter used most words only spontaneously or only imitatively. The proportions of utterances with such splits was at least .75 (and in 4 of the 6 samples at least .85). Thus, it appeared that even in these samples from Peter and Eric, there were indeed two populations of words. A possible explanation of why these samples had so few words with extreme splits was that Peter and Eric simply did not talk very much in these samples, and thus words were not likely to occur frequently, spontaneously, imitatively, or both (see Table 12.1). Thus, the test of significance applied to lexical items was just not sensitive enough for data where the sample of speech was relatively small. The test depended on words occurring with high frequency. When there were enough words occurring often enough, the test of significance impressively supported the observation that single-word utterances tended to be imitative or spontaneous.

Words Used Syntactically. The results for words used syntactically were significant for 8 of the 13 speech samples. The fact that the words the children used spontaneously in syntactic constructions tended to be different from the words used imitatively in syntactic constructions could have two explanations. On the one hand, the differences might be evidence for differentiation of lexical items, as was apparent in the analysis of single-word utterances. On the other hand, when imitating words in a syntactic construction, the children might in fact have been imitating an aspect of the syntax rather than the particular lexical item that was included in the construction. The two kinds of imitation, lexical and grammatical, could not be separated in any analysis that looked at each speech sample separately. For this reason, the samples from Eric and Peter were analyzed in terms of change over time.

Progression from Imitative to Spontaneous Use. If imitation leads to the learning of particular lexical items, then one could expect that those words that were imitative at an early time, if repeated at successive times, would gradually come to be used spontaneously. The hypothesis that a significant proportion of words would progress from mostly imitative occurrence to mostly spontaneous occurrence in the period of study was tested for those children whose overall proportion of imitation was above .15 for more than two sessions. The test was applied for each word that (1) occurred in at least two sessions, (2) was imitated at least once and spontaneous at least once, and (3) showed some change across time, either from imitative to spontaneous or spontaneous to imitative use.

Spearman rank-order correlations were found between the session ranks and the observed ranks of the ratio of imitative occurrences to total number of occurrences. This procedure was applied separately to single-word utterances and words used syntactically. The number of sessions in which a target word occurred varied from 2 to 6 for Peter and 2 to 4 for Eric, and the session ranks changed accordingly. If a word occurred in all 6 sessions from Peter, the ranking of sessions was 1, 2, 3, 4, 5, 6; if a word occurred in only 4 of the sessions from Peter, the sessions in which the word occurred were ranked 1, 2, 3, 4. If the ratio of imitative occurrences to total number of occurrences was the same for more than one session, the average of the ranks was used. For example, for the word *off*, the ratios of imitative tokens to total number of tokens were 1/1 at Time I, 1/2 at II, 0/4 at III, and 0/3 at IV, for Eric. The session ranking (Times I–IV) was 1, 2, 3, 4, and the observed ratio ranking was 1, 2, 3.5, 3.5, with a resulting rho of .50. For the word *foot*, the imitative to total ratios were 0/1 at Time I and 1/6 at Time III, with no occurrences at Times II and IV. The session ranking was 1,2, and the observed ranking was 2,1, with a resulting rho of -1.00. A *t* test was performed on the Spearman rank-order correlations with the null hypothesis that the mean correlation equals zero.

For Peter, there was a significant trend for imitative occurrence of single words to decrease over time. The mean correlation (rho = .323) was significantly different from zero ($t(132) = 5.14$, $p < .001$). This was not the case for words used syntactically (rho = .04, $t(102) = .5012$). For Eric, the reverse was true. For words used syntactically, the mean correlation (rho = .255) was significantly different from zero ($t(51) = 2.329$, $p < .05$), while for single-word utterances it was not (rho = .047, $t(57) = .429$). Thus, there was a progression across time as imitation of a particular lexical item decreased while the spontaneous use of that item increased, for single-word utterances in Peter's speech and for multiword utterances in Eric's speech. These differences between Peter and Eric were consistent with the differences between them in the semantic–syntactic functions of imitation in multiword utterances which will be discussed subsequently.

In sum, imitation played a role in the acquisition of new lexical items for the children in this study whose overall imitation was greater than .15. To the extent that spontaneous use was an index of knowing a word, it could be concluded that the children imitated words that they did not yet know. At any particular time, the children did not imitate words they used spontaneously and did not use spontaneously the words they imitated. Further, there was a clear trend for individual words that were originally imitative to become predominantly spontaneous at later times.

Semantic–Syntactic Structure

Classifying multiword utterances according to the relations between words resulted in a taxonomy of semantic–syntactic categories that allowed several comparisons to be made. Within one sample of speech from an individual child, both the relative frequency of the different relations and the different utterance forms with these relations could be compared in imitative and spontaneous speech. Successive samples of speech from the same child could then be compared to determine the developmental interaction between imitative and spontaneous speech. In this way it was possible to evaluate the role of imitation for semantic learning (between categories) and syntactic learning (within categories) and to demonstrate that imitation did indeed function in the acquisition of grammar for those children who imitated.

The semantic–syntactic categories were identified by observing the relationship between an utterance and aspects of the child's behavior and the context in which the utterance occurred. Although one cannot know the full semantic intention for any particular utterance, that is, precisely what a child means, there was relatively little difficulty in knowing what the children were talking about. Virtually all the utterances occurred in relation to what the children (and the adults) could see, or in relation to what the children had just done, were doing, or were about to do. The semantic–syntactic categories were dependent on (1) the child's utterance occurring in direct reference to the event that was encoded in the utterance and (2) the inclusion of at least two words in the utterance with an identifiable relationship between them. Adult interpretations were very much context- and utterance bound, so that the categories of semantic–syntactic relations were directly derived from the child speech event data rather than being a predetermined system of analysis.

Four of the categories represented verb relations (whether or not an actual verb was one of the words) that were identified in terms of (1) whether or not movement accompanied an utterance and (2) the goal of movement, when movement occurred. These criteria were contextual and distinguished between action and state relations and between locative and nonlocative actions and states. Of all the relations in the children's speech that expressed action, the overwhelming majority entailed action on an affected-object or the goal of a change in location. Such verbs as "get up" and "fall down," which are intransitive in the adult model, were productive as locative-action verbs in the present study; such intransitive verbs as "turnaround" and "dance," which were categorized as actions (without affected-object), did not occur productively (with productivity defined as five different utterances at a particular time).

For several verbs in each of these categories, one could argue for a different classification based on adult introspection. The verb "get" was an example of the dilemma that sometimes arose in distinguishing between action and locative-action events. One could argue that "get" involves movement that changes the location of an object. However, the child's goal in "getting" appeared to be more the act of obtaining than a change in location of the object, and utterances such as "get it" and "get cookie" were classified as action-on-affected-object. The definitions used for categorizing the relations between words in multiword utterances can be found in Bloom, Lightbown, & Hood, 1975, chap. 2.

The relative occurrence of spontaneous and imitative utterances in each of the categories will be reported: (1) for categories in which there were at least five utterance types at a particular time and (2) for those times in which the proportion of different imitative utterances exceeded .15 of the total number of different utterances: Peter, Times I–VII; Kathryn, Time I; Jane, Times I and II; and Eric, Times I–IV. The criterion of an overall proportion of imitation of .15 was used because below that level there were too few different imitative utterances to allow for a meaningful comparison between imitative and spontaneous speech. Utterance types that had both spontaneous and imitative tokens were not included in this analysis; they represented less than .10 of all the syntactic utterance types from all the children, and they did not include any different categories.

The evidence of the interaction between imitative and spontaneous speech for semantic–syntactic learning will be presented as frequency data: the number of imitative and spontaneous multiword utterance types within each category of semantic–syntactic relationship. In all the samples, there were several noncontrastive categories in which there was either little difference in the form of imitative and spontaneous speech, or few imitations.[6] For other categories, spontaneous and imitative multiword utterances could be compared with respect to the development of different linguistic forms (subcategories) within each semantic–syntactic category. For example, in Peter's speech, in the category action-on-affected-object, the subcategories were pronominal and nominal lexicalization of affected-object. In addition to presenting

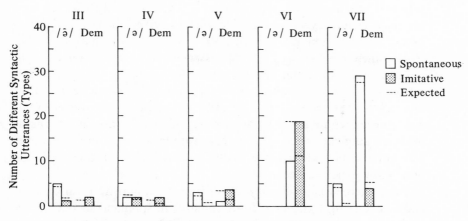

Figure 12.2. Existence. Peter, Times III–VII.

the *observed* occurrence of different utterances, the *expected* occurrences within subcategories will be presented. Expected frequencies were determined from the overall proportion of different *syntactic* utterances imitated at each time (see Table 12.2). The information presented here consists of the observed and expected occurrence of utterance types that were imitative or spontaneous, within categories and across time.

Peter I–VII. There were no productive categories (with productivity defined as five or more different utterances within a category) in Peter's speech samples at Times I and II. Several semantic–syntactic categories reached the criterion of productivity at Time III. As will be seen, the relative occurrence of imitative and spontaneous utterances at Time VI, when MLU was 1.75, forced the decision to consider the next sample, Time VII, when MLU was 2.39 and beyond the original limits of the study.

Existence. In Peter's speech, reference to existence was made by utterances with a primitive form of *a* or *the* or a demonstrative pronoun (the subcategories /ə/ and Dem in Figure 12.2) and a noun. There were few utterances with a demonstrative at Times III, IV, and V, and those that did occur were largely imitative. At Time V there were 1 spontaneous and 4 imitative utterances with a demonstrative. At Time VI there were 10 spontaneous utterances with a demonstrative, but there were 19 utterances that were imitative, which greatly exceeded the expected frequency of imitative utterances, given the overall proportion of syntactic imitation at Time VI. That is, inasmuch as 38% of all Peter's different syntactic utterances at Time VI were imitative, the observed ratio of imitative to spontaneous occurrence was inversely related to the expected ratio, in the Demonstrative subcategory. However, in the next sample at Time VII, the situation was reversed. Only 4 utterances with a demonstrative were imitative, while 29 utterances occurred spontaneously. The observed imitative to spontaneous ratio was in the expected direction, with the observed occurrence of imitation below expected occurrence.

Thus, there was a subcategory shift in the linguistic form of utterances specifying Existence, from imitative to spontaneous occurrence of demonstrative pronouns, between Times VI and VII. Peter learned to use demonstrative pronouns to indicate Existence between Times VI and VII. The imitation data at Time VI provided evidence that he was in the process of learning the form. However, the relation between imitative and spontaneous occurrence at Time VII indicated that he had learned it, to the extent that spontaneous use was an index of learning. Utterances with /ə/ occurred less often, and except at Time IV, they were rarely imitative.

Action-On-Affected-Object. The most dramatic interaction between imitative and spontaneous speech was in the category Action-on-Affected-Object in which the subcategories were Pronominal (Pro) and Nominal (Nom) lexicalization of affected-object. Both a category shift and a subcategory shift from imitative to spontaneous use occurred. As can be seen in Figure 12.3, of the 17 different utterances in the category at Time III, more were imitative than spontaneous, and the observed ratio of imitative to spontaneous occurrence was inversely related to the expected imitative to spontaneous ratio. The category shift occurred between Time III, when Peter was learning the category, and Time IV, when he had learned the category Action-on-Affected-Object, since the observed and expected ratios of imitative to spontaneous occurrence were in the same direction. Subsequently, at Time V, it might be said that Peter consolidated his gains and used the pronoun *it* overwhelmingly to represent affected-object in the category Action-on-Affected-Object.

The pronominal to nominal subcategory shift occurred between Times VI and VII. The observed and expected ratios of imitative to sponta-

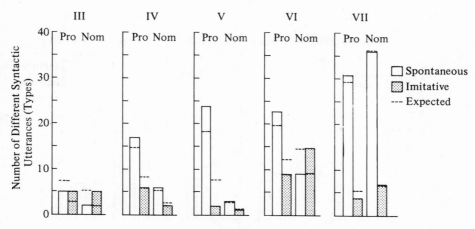

Figure 12.3. Action-on-affected-object. Peter, Times III–VII.

neous occurrence with the pronoun *it* were in the same direction after Time III. However, with nominal objects, the observed and expected ratios changed from an inverse to direct relationship at Time VII, and further, the number of different utterances with a noun-object was greater than the number of utterances with *it* at Time VII. Thus, Peter learned the category between Times III and IV, and learned to use noun-objects in affected-object relation to action verbs between Times VI and VII. The fact that there were more spontaneous than imitative noun-objects at Time IV could not be explained; it was the only instance in all the samples from all the children of a spontaneous to imitative subcategory progression.

Attribution. In the category Attribution (Figure 12.4), the subcategories were "two," in reference to two objects or a second object (a few utterances with "two," with no evidence of duality in the context, were not included in Figure 12.4), and other attributive forms such as *big, nice, dirty,* and *funny.* Peter was learning attributive reference from Time III through Time V, and the evidence of a category shift at Time VI was that Peter had learned to use the word *two* to talk about exactly two objects or a second object, and he rarely imitated such utterances. However, the inverse relation between observed and expected occurrence of imitative and spontaneous utterances with other attributive forms continued from Time III through Time VI. Further, even though the observed and expected ratios of imitative to sponta-

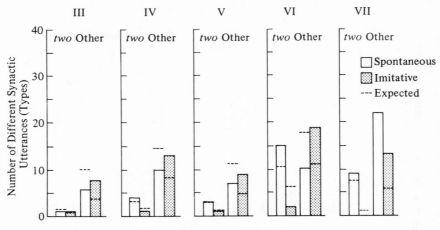

Figure 12.4. Attribution. Peter, Times III–VII.

neous occurrences with other attributives were in the same direction at Time VII, the observed frequency of imitative utterance types was still considerably greater than the expected frequency. At Time VII, Peter had learned a single attributive form (''two'') and no longer imitated that form, but he was still in the process of learning to use a class of other forms for attributive reference at Time VII.

Locative Relations. An example of the interaction between spontaneous and imitative speech in the locative categories is presented in Figure 12.5.[7] Whereas action verbs had been productive since Time III, locative-action verbs did not occur in multiword utterances until Time V. Utterances in the category Place-of-Locative Action (with verb expressed), for example, ''put there'' or ''put car'' were always more frequent than utterances in the category Object-of-Locative Action (with verb expressed), for example, ''put pretzel'' or ''put it.'' Thus, reference to affected-object was more likely to occur when Peter used an action verb than when he used a locative-action verb which could entail two complements: both affected-object and place.

New Categories at Time VI. The proportion of syntactic imitation in Peter's speech decreased markedly between Times VI and VII, (from .38 to .16). It might be argued that the subcategory shifts that have been described did not have to do with semantic–syntactic learning as

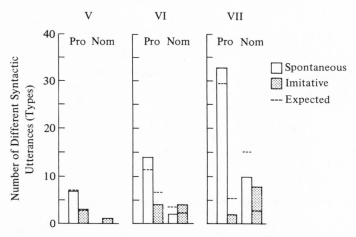

Figure 12.5. Place-of-locative action, verb expressed. Peter, Times V–VII.

much as they were a function of the decrease in imitation in general between Times VI and VII. However, as seen in Figures 12.4 and 12.5, the observed frequency of imitation continued to be greater than the expected frequency of imitation at Time VII. The interaction between imitative and spontaneous speech continued with new categories that first appeared at Time VI, as can be seen in the examples in Figures 12.6 and 12.7.

The data from Peter demonstrated the interaction between imitative and spontaneous speech most explicitly: Imitation occurred within semantic categories and with forms that were just emerging. Peter did not imitate what he knew best, and he did not imitate what he knew nothing about. Whenever imitation exceeded expectation, there were always spontaneous utterances within the same category or subcategory as well. Peter imitated utterances in just those categories and subcategories which were to become fully productive at a subsequent time but which were currently beyond his productive capacity. To that extent, imitation provided evidence of grammatical learning.

Peter imitated more than the other children. Furthermore, the Peter data were collected at three-week intervals, so that the developmental changes in his speech might have been missed if data collection had been more widely spaced. However, the same interaction between imitative and spontaneous utterance types within certain categories was observed in Kathryn I and Jane I and II.

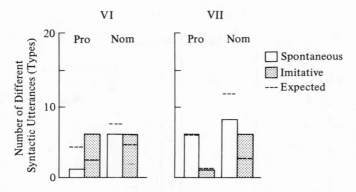

Figure 12.6. State-and-causative-object. Peter, Times VI and VII.

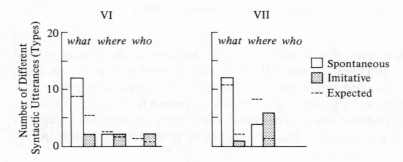

Figure 12.7. *Wh*-questions. Peter, Times VI and VII.

Kathryn I. A comparison of spontaneous and imitative utterances in Kathryn's speech is presented in Table 12.5.[8] As with Peter, the dominant semantic–syntactic category involved action. However, whereas in Peter's speech pronominal reference was always far more frequent than nominal reference, and Peter progressed from pronominal to nominal reference from Time III to Time VII, pronouns occurred rarely in Kathryn's speech and were imitative more often than spontaneous.

Jane I and II. Spontaneous and imitative utterances in Jane's speech are compared in Figure 12.8.

The data collected from Jane were the least satisfying for several reasons. First of all, her family moved away after the second session, so that it was not possible to follow development in those categories

Table 12.5. *Contrastive Semantic–Syntactic Categories: Kathryn, Time I*

	Observed and Expected Occurrence of Spontaneous and Imitative Utterance Types							
	Subcategories							
	Pro				Nom			
Semantic–Syntactic Category	Sp		Im		Sp		Im	
	Obs	Exp	Obs	Exp	Obs	Exp	Obs	Exp
Agent-Action	I	2	2	I	12	8.6	I	4.4
Action-Aff.-Obj.	I	2.6	3	1.4	21	19.1	8	9.9
Place	—	2	3	I	I	3.3	4	1.7
Possession	I	2.6	3	1.4	8	9.2	6	4.8
Attribution	I	2	2	I	28	23.8	8	12.2
		"more"				"another"		
Recurrence[a]	13	8.6	—	4.4	2	4.6	5	2.4
		"Hi"				Notice verb		
Notice	4	2.6	—	1.4	3	5.9	6	3.1

[a] All occurrences of "another" and three occurrences of "more" specified another instance of an object while the first object was still present. The remaining ten occurrences of "more" specified a second object or event without the simultaneous presence of the first.

that were predominantly or only imitative at Time II. Second, even though 6 weeks elapsed between Times I and II, there was virtually no change in mean length of utterance and change in only 3 semantic–syntactic categories: the subcategory shift with Action-on-Affected-Object, and the appearance of two new categories at Time II, Locative-State and Attribution. Finally, there was a relatively large number of nonproductive categories – more than for Peter, Kathryn, or Eric – which gave the impression that Jane had spread herself thin, trying to learn many things at once. However, as with Peter and Kathryn (at Time I), it was possible to conclude that Jane was indeed using imitation in processing information about the semantic–syntactic relations between words as she learned grammar.

Eric I–IV. The data from Eric told a different story about the relationship between imitative and spontaneous utterances: None of the semantic–syntactic categories was contrastive. As can be seen in Fig-

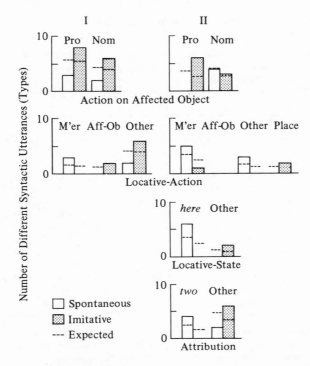

Figure 12.8. Semantic–syntactic categories. Jane, Times I and II.

ures 12.9 and 12.10, imitative multiword utterances were relatively infrequent. The observed and expected imitation in each category was virtually identical, in marked contrast to the differences between observed and expected imitation in the speech of the other children. This observed–expected convergence in Eric's syntactic speech was evidence that his imitative behavior was not motivated by his learning the semantic–syntactic structure of multiword utterances.

As already reported, Eric was apparently using imitation in the process of learning individual lexical items. It appears that Eric's imitation of multiword utterances was also lexically motivated. Individual words that occurred in imitative multiword utterances did not also occur in spontaneous multiword utterances. However, the words in imitative multiword utterances occurred both spontaneously and imitatively as single-word utterances in the same sample. This parallels the finding that for the children whose imitation was evidence of semantic–syntactic learning, utterance types were imitative in semantic–

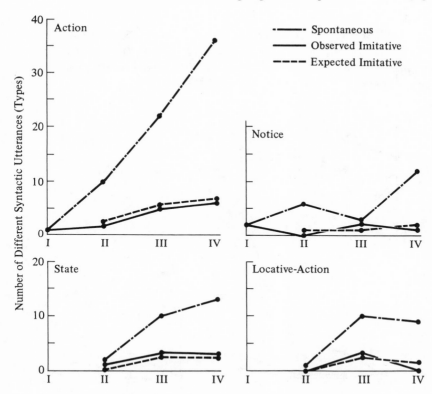

Figure 12.9. Relative frequency of utterances with different verbs. Eric, Times I–IV.

syntactic categories only where there were spontaneous utterance types as well.

The difference between Peter and Eric in progression from imitative to spontaneous use of words reported earlier (the progression occurred in single-word utterances for Peter and in multiword utterances for Eric) corresponded to the differences observed between them in the semantic–syntactic analysis. Peter apparently imitated words that he already knew in semantic–syntactic relations that he was in the process of learning. Eric, however, imitated words he did not yet know that occurred in the semantic–syntactic relations that he already was able to use spontaneously.

The semantic–syntactic categorization of utterances revealed that for Eric, as with the other children, imitation was never random, given the two results: (1) a difference between lexical items that were spon-

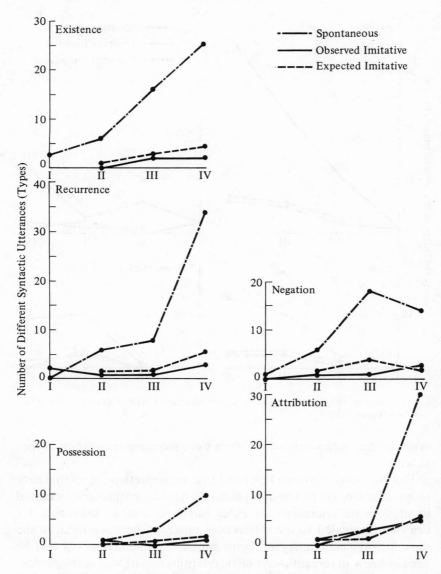

Figure 12.10. Relative frequency of utterances in semantic–syntactic categories without verbs. Eric, Times I–IV.

taneous and imitative in syntactic contexts and (2) that the overall proportion of imitation in his speech predicted the proportion of imitation within each semantic–syntactic category. Thus, Eric imitated new lexical items he heard in speech that encoded the same kind of knowledge as his own multiword utterances. His knowledge of semantic–syntactic relations appeared to structure his processing of new lexical items.

Imitation and Utterance Length. When mean length of utterance (morphemes) was computed separately for spontaneous and imitative utterances, two different trends appeared for imitating and nonimitating children. For those samples where the overall proportion of imitation was less than .15, MLU was consistently higher for spontaneous utterances than for imitative utterances. However, in those language samples where the overall proportion of imitation was greater than .15, the MLU of imitative utterances usually equaled or exceeded the MLU of the spontaneous utterances. The claim that imitation had an important function in the language development of the children who imitated does not require that imitative utterances be longer than spontaneous ones – only that they be different and that the differences be related to developmental change. The lexical and semantic–syntactic analyses made it clear that these differences did exist. The longer MLU of the imitative speech simply represented a superficial index of such differences.

Summary. In the syntactic speech of Kathryn at Time I, Jane, and Peter, certain categories and subcategories that were productive in spontaneous speech were imitated rarely, if at all. However, it was almost always the case that when observed imitation exceeded expected imitation within a category or subcategory, there were spontaneous utterance types as well – evidence that the children already knew something about what they were imitating. This result does not conflict with the earlier finding that different lexical items were only imitative or only spontaneous; both kinds of utterance types (lexical items and multiword) were either imitative or spontaneous, as indicated by the small number of Sp + Im in Table 12.2. However, the lexical analysis was based on token frequencies, whereas for multiword utterances the important analysis was the relative spontaneous and imitative occurrences of utterances types within semantic–syntactic categories. The categories included both spontaneous and imitative utterance types, but each multiword utterance type was either imitative or spontaneous.

Finally, the developmental interaction between imitative and spontaneous speech moved in the same direction – from imitative to spontaneous occurrence – for lexical items (in the speech of Peter and Eric) and grammatical structure (in the speech of Peter, Jane, and Kathryn). Once lexical items and semantic–syntactic categories and subcategories were observed to be predominantly spontaneous, they were never predominantly imitative in subsequent samples. Imitation appeared to function for learning the semantic–syntactic relations in multiword utterances for Peter, Jane, and Kathryn. However, in Eric's speech, the semantic–syntactic relations between words were not different in imitative and spontaneous utterances, and the motivation for imitation in Eric's speech was lexical. Lexical and grammatical imitation in the children's speech was developmentally progressive.

IMITATION AND LANGUAGE DEVELOPMENT

Before discussing the results of this study as evidence of processing information for language development, the results will be compared with two other studies that also examined and compared children's imitative and spontaneous utterances: Ervin-Tripp (1964) and Kemp and Dale (1973), and with other discussion of imitation in the literature.[9]

In the study by Ervin-Tripp, rules of grammar were proposed for the spontaneous utterances in the speech of five children who ranged in age from 22 to 34 months, and then the children's imitative utterances were examined to determine the extent to which they were consistent with the rules of grammar. In the speech of four of the children, both imitative and spontaneous utterances could be accounted for by the same rules. For the fifth child, imitative utterances were shorter and less complex than spontaneous utterances.[10] Ervin-Tripp concluded that imitation was not "grammatically progressive" for the five children. According to the examples of grammars, the rules on which the analysis was based were rules of word order in which three or more optional classes of words were ordered relative to a final required class. The optional classes included articles, demonstrative pronouns, attributives, certain verbs, and such words as *more* and *no*. In some rules the final optional class was virtually identical to the required class, which included such words as noun forms and certain other attributives (for example, color names).[11] This result was consistent with the report by Brown and Fraser (1963) that both imitative and spontaneous child speech preserved the word order of the model language.

In the present study, rules of word order would not have differentiated between imitative and spontaneous utterances either. Demonstratives, articles, verbs, attributives, and such forms as *more* and *no* preceded object nouns in both kinds of speech. Thus, it was not so much the case that the results reported here were inconsistent with Ervin-Tripp's conclusions. Rather, the analysis she reported was simply not sensitive enough to detect the differences that might have existed between the two kinds of utterances in her data.

Kemp and Dale (1973) embedded model sentences in the speech that they addressed to 30 children between the ages of 22 and 36 months during play. They interpreted two results as opposing: (1) On the one hand, since certain grammatical features which occurred in free speech were never imitated, they concluded that imitative speech was even less advanced than spontaneous speech; (2) on the other hand, since other grammatical features occurred in imitative utterances but not in free speech, then imitative speech could be grammatically progressive. Similar results in the present study were interpreted as complementary aspects of the nature of imitation in language development.

To Imitate or Not to Imitate

The variation among the six children in this study with respect to *if* they imitated (their relative tendency to imitate) and *when* they imitated (the lexical and grammatical conditions that accompanied imitation) may explain the confusion in the literature of the last century about the importance of imitation for language development. The more important theoretical issues have evolved about the central question of *why* some children imitate – how imitation may function as a process in language development.

Certain speculations that might explain why some children imitate in the first place cannot be resolved by the data or the results of this study. Such factors as parent–child interaction, personality, or intelligence might well have been important as predisposing factors that determined whether a child was or was not an imitator in the first place. As such, they would appear to be empirical issues that could be tested elsewhere. However, such factors are essentially passive influences on behavior – an individual's intelligence, personality, and parents are not self-determined. Thus, children may not be able to control whether or not they are imitators in the first place. But if they do imitate, it appears that when they imitate and why are self-determined, to the extent that both are based on what the child already knows and is in the process of learning.

Imitation as an Active Process

If certain model utterances had not been available for a child to imitate, then, obviously, they could not have appeared among the imitative utterances, and the fact that they did not occur would have been determined by the environment and not by the child. However, Peter had ample opportunity to imitate both pronominal and nominal reference to affected-objects at Time IV, as revealed by the following analysis. All the adult utterances to Peter that (1) immediately preceded an utterance by Peter and (2) represented Notice or Action-on-Affected-Object were compared with Peter's subsequent utterances, for the first 2 hours (almost one-half) of the sample at Time IV. There were 45 adult utterances that met the criteria, and 20 of these included pronouns as affected-object (2 with *one* and 18 with *it*). Peter imitated only one of these. In all other instances, he either said something related to the utterance or repeated a previous utterance. Yet in his spontaneous speech, pronominal reference occurred far more often than nominal reference. The fact that Peter did not imitate utterances with pronominal reference even though they were present in the input was evidence that Peter determined what he did and did not imitate.

The fact that imitation is selective has been reported frequently, if not actually demonstrated, by Guillaume (1926/1968), Valentine (1930), Jakobson (1941/1968), Aronfreed (1969), and others. However, different factors have been thought to underlie the choice of what is imitated. On the one hand, if each time a child imitates, the relation between a linguistic signal and its referent in a speech event is affirmed, then an intrinsic reinforcement could serve to maintain imitation behavior. In this case, the reward for imitation is learning – a conclusion that would be supported by the data presented here. On the other hand, it is frequently presumed that children repeat the speech they hear because such behavior is rewarded by the environment. Several theories to explain language development have depended on such a chain of events whereby the child hears a stimulus, repeats it, and is reinforced by an adult in the situation who may smile, repeat it again, supply a referent, and so on. (Allport, 1924; Jenkins & Palermo, 1964; Mowrer, 1960; Staats, 1971). While children may well enjoy whatever attention is given to imitating behavior, such pleasure and attention alone would not explain the systematic relationship between imitative and spontaneous utterances in the children's speech that was observed in this study.

The idea that a child's imitation is determined or shaped by reinforcement from the environment is another view of the child as essentially passive with respect to the forces that contribute to and maintain behavior. Similarly, the view of language development that depends upon an independent cognitive structure for organizing linguistic input, such as the "language acquisition device" proposed by Chomsky (1965) and McNeill (1970), places the child in another kind of passive role. Both the behaviorist and the nativist positions result in the conclusion that the child is simply the victim of fate and circumstance in learning to talk. But whatever the nature of children's linguistic knowledge may be at any time, they add to and change that knowledge in relation to experience. The results of this study have emphasized the active interaction of the child in language development: The children appeared to imitate as they processed linguistic and nonlinguistic input from the environment for information about language.

Piaget (1951/1962) distinguished between early sensorimotor imitation in the first two years and later "representative" imitation that begins some time toward the end of the second year. During the sensorimotor period, according to Piaget, imitation is unconscious and comes about through confusion between the movements of others and movements of the self. Because children are unable to differentiate between internal and external states, they cannot distinguish their own actions and movements from those that they see. Sensorimotor imitations are provoked from "direct perceptions." An important change occurs at the end of the second year and continues into the early school years (to about age 7), as the reproduction of a model comes to be preceded by an "imaged representation" of it. It is this reproduction of an image of the model that is characterized by Piaget as "representative imitation" that is "deferred." Although the model is not perceptually present, the child necessarily has an image of the model in mind before reproducing it.[12]

The imitation behavior in the present study would qualify as sensorimotor imitation as described by Piaget to the extent that the model utterances were perceptually present. Indeed, the operating definition of imitation depended upon "direct perception," even though perception and production were sequential (as was the case with the imitative behavior described by Piaget). However, the important result of this study of such perceptual imitation was that the children's behavior was discriminating in that they differentiated among stimuli in a highly systematic way. The imitating children discriminated, first, between their own linguistic behavior and the behavior of others and, second, among the different linguistic behaviors of others. They imitated only words and structures in the speech they heard which they appeared to be in the process of learning. They tended not to imitate words and structures that they themselves either used spontaneously and so presumably knew or did not use spontaneously at all and so presumably did not know. Imitative behavior was not merely acoustic or an automatic echoing of random linguistic events.

In conclusion, when and why the imitating child would imitate depended upon what was already known about the behavior. The important facts were that the children imitated neither linguistic signals that were already well known to them nor structures that were completely absent from their own spontaneous speech. Peter imitated relatively new semantic–syntactic structures that included words that he used spontaneously elsewhere; Eric imitated new words only when they occured in the same semantic–syntactic structures as were represented in his spontaneous speech. Similarly, in the study by Shipley, Smith, and Gleitman (1969), the novel (nonsense) words that seemed to precipitate imitation were embedded in standard sentence frames and in familiar contexts. The conclusion by Fraser, Bellugi, and Brown (1963) that imitation precedes comprehension and production in development was not supported. Rather, the results confirmed the observations of Preyer (1882/1971), Guillaume (1926/1968), Valentine (1930), and others that children imitate only what they already understand to some extent. Piaget (1937/1954) observed that imitation is always a continuation of understanding.

One might explain imitation as a form of encoding that continues the processing of information necessary for the representation of linguistic schemas (both semantic and syntactic) in memory. In the imitation context, the child has the perceptual support of a model utterance relative to events which, while recognized, are only partially mapped onto linguistic schemas. Imitating the model utterance provides experience in encoding the relevant aspects of the situation to which the utterance refers, consolidating the mapping or coding relation between form and content. Although the imitation behavior observed in this study provided evidence of such active processing of linguistic and nonlinguistic information for learning the relation between the form of speech and the nonlinguistic states of affairs to which it refers, it was not clear that the imitation behavior was necessary for such information processing. Further, it was apparent that some processing of the same kind of information input is possible without such supported encoding, certainly for the nonimitating children and perhaps for the imitating children as well.

NOTES

1 Slobin (1968) suggested that the most important function of imitation for language acquisition might be the opportunity for children to imitate adult expansions of their own utterances. Such utterances, which represented less than .01 of the data Slobin examined, were not distinguished from other imitative utterances in the present study. When a child's utterance was expanded or repeated by an adult and the child subsequently repeated the original utterance (either unchanged or reduced), the second utterance was also considered spontaneous.

2 Utterance *types* (each different utterance counted as a type), rather than utterance *tokens* (the number of occurrences of a type), were used for computing these proportions. Item frequency (tokens rather than types) would have resulted in a smaller proportion of imitation in the speech of all the children, because spontaneous utterances occurred more frequently than did imitative utterances.

3 Except for Jane, whose family moved away following the second recording session.

4 This test was devised by Ruth Gold.

5 In those samples in which the proportion of imitation was less than .15 (see Table 12.2), there were too few imitative occurrences of different words to apply the test.

6 These data can be found in the original publication (Bloom, Hood, & Lightbown, 1974).

7 Other examples can be found in the original publication.

8 Data from 5 of the original 7.5 hours of interaction with Kathryn at Time I were processed for the following analysis, and for this reason the numbers of utterances in particular categories do not correspond to the account in Bloom (1970).

9 Some of the issues in the present paper were also discussed by Miyamoto (1973). Ryan (1973) independently presented data that complement the data presented here, with strikingly similar interpretations and conclusions.

10 If children imitate what they do not quite know, then imitations might well be more fragmented and less 'complete' than other speech, as was the case with a few of the samples from the imitating children in the present study.

11 More recently, Ervin-Tripp (personal communication) reported that other grammars not discussed in her original report were more complex.

12 Piaget discussed linguistic imitation only in the context of imitation in general as it functions in the development of symbolic thought.

POSTSCRIPT

For studies that further explored the role of imitation in language learning since Bloom, Hood, and Lightbown (1974):

Clark, R. (1977). What's the use of imitation? *Journal of Child Language, 4*, 341–58.

Coggins, T., & Morrison, J. (1981). Spontaneous imitations of Down's syndrome children. *Journal of Speech and Hearing Research, 24*, 303–8.

Corrigan, R. (1980). Use of repetition to facilitate spontaneous language acquisition. *Journal of Psycholinguistic Research, 9*, 231–41.

Kuczaj, S. (1987). Deferred imitation and the acquisition of novel lexical items. *First Language, 7*, 177–82.

Leonard, L., Chapman, K., Rowan, L., & Weiss, A. (1983). Three hypotheses concerning young children's imitations of lexical items. *Developmental Psychology, 19*, 591–601.

Leonard, L., Fey, M., & Newhoff, M. (1981). Phonological considerations in children's early imitative and spontaneous speech. *Journal of Psycholinguistic Research, 10*, 123–33.

Leonard, L., & Kaplan, L. (1976). A note on imitation and lexical acquisition. *Journal of Child Language, 3*, 449–55.

Leonard, L., Schwartz, R., Folger, M., Newhoff, M., & Wilcox, M. (1979). Children's imitation of lexical items. *Child Development, 50*, 19–27.

Leonard, L., Schwartz, R., Folger, M., & Wilcox, M. (1978). Some aspects of child phonology in imitative and spontaneous speech. *Journal of Child Language, 5*, 403–15.

Moerk, E. (1977). Processes and products of imitation: Additional evidence that imitation is progressive. *Journal of Psycholinguistic Research, 6*, 187–202.

Moerk, E., & Moerk, C. (1979). Quotations, imitation, and generalizations. Factual and methodological analyses. *International Journal of Behavioral Development, 2*, 43–72.

Pearson, B. (1990). The comprehension of metaphor by preschool children. *Journal of Child Language, 17*, 185–203.

Ramer, A. (1976). The function of imitation in child language. *Journal of Speech and Hearing Research, 19,* 700–17.

Reger, Z. (1986). The functions of imitation in child language. *Applied Psycholinguistics, 1,* 323–52.

Rodgon, M., & Kurdek, L. (1977). Vocal and gestural imitation in children under two years old. *Journal of Genetic Psychology, 131,* 115–23.

Schwartz, R., & Leonard, L. (1985). Lexical imitation and acquisition in language-impaired children. *Journal of Speech and Hearing Disorders, 50,* 141–9.

Sloate, P., & Voyat, G. (1983). Language and imitation in development. *Journal of Psycholinguistic Research, 12,* 199–222.

Snow, C. (1981). The uses of imitation. *Journal of Child Language, 8,* 205–12.

Speidel, G., & Nelson, K. (Eds.) (1989). *The many faces of imitation in language learning,* New York: Springer-Verlag.

Stewart, D., & Hamilton, M. (1976). Imitation as a learning strategy in the acquisition of vocabulary. *Journal of Experimental Child Psychology, 21,* 380–92.

Stine, E., & Bohannon, J. (1983). Imitations, interactions, and language acquisition. *Journal of Child Language, 10,* 589–603.

Tager-Flusberg, H., & Calkins, S. (1990). Does imitation facilitate the acquisition of grammar? Evidence from a study of autistic, Down's syndrome, and normal children. *Journal of Child Language, 17,* 591–606.

Whitehurst, G., & Vasta, R. (1975). Is language acquired through imitation? *Journal of Psycholinguistic Research, 4,* 37–49.

13

Development of Contingency in Discourse

Kathryn: "Do you perfer cheddar cheese?"
Mother: "No."
Kathryn: "Why don't you?"
Mother: "Because I like the taste of muenster better."
Kathryn: "Why don't like taste of of cheddar?"

A major goal of language acquisition is for the child to be able to take something from what someone else says and form a contingent message that converts simple turn taking into discourse. The second study in this section built on the study of imitation and was concerned with how these children learned to participate in discourse. Categories of child discourse, their development, and their interactions with aspects of preceding adult utterances were the major results of this study. It turned out that repeating part or all of what an adult said (imitation) was the first way in which the children were able to share the topic of a prior expression. At first they only repeated; then they both repeated and added something to the prior expression; and eventually they repeated, added to, and also changed something in the prior expression.

The study of discourse spanned three periods, defined by increasing mean length of utterance. The first two, one with mean length of utterance less than 2.0 and the second with mean length of utterance between 2.0 and 2.75 morphemes, were at the beginning of the second year when the children were between 21 and 27 months of age. The third period was at the end of the year when the children were about 36 months old and mean length of utterance was about 4.0 morphemes.

CATEGORIES OF CHILD DISCOURSE

The discourse interaction between adult and child was examined in terms of topic sharing and the linguistic and contextual relations between their messages. Child utterances were identified as *adjacent* (when immediately preceded by an adult utterance) or *nonadjacent*. Adjacent child utterances were *imitative* when they shared the same topic and form but did not add new information; *contingent* when they shared the same topic and also added new information to the preceding adult message; or *noncontingent* when they did not share the same topic. Contingent speech, which was the focus of the study, was *linguistically contingent* when the children added either new information with the same verb relation as in the adult utterance or a related clause with a new verb relation. Otherwise, contingent speech was *contextually contingent* when the children shared the same topic but not the form of the adult's utterance. Linguistically contingent speech was further differentiated with subcategories of content, such as expansions and alternatives, and with subcategories of form, such as replacements and modifications.

DEVELOPMENT OF DISCOURSE CATEGORIES

From the beginning, adjacent speech was more frequent than nonadjacent speech. At the time the study began, the children had already learned a basic rule of discourse: to say something after someone else says something. However, child utterances were most often noncontingent in the first two periods of the study, as the children introduced new topics or changed the topic more than half the time. Contingency, in general, and linguistic contingency, in particular, were the major developments in the children's discourse from 2 to 3, as messages increased that shared the topic of a prior utterance, with added information. Linguistic contingency consisted of utterances that either repeated or expanded the verb relation from the prior adult utterance, with replacements, additions, or other modifications (e.g., "Because I like the taste of muenster better'' => *"Why don't like taste of of cheddar?''*). Thus, the children learned to participate in discourse by using the verb in antecedent messages to construct their own contingent messages.

Changes also occurred in the adults' speech. The children's linguistically contingent speech occurred more often after adult questions than after non-questions, and the adults asked proportionately more questions over time as the children's linguistically contingent responses to questions increased. In their own responses to the children, the adults tended to repeat what the child said less frequently and to ask *wh*-questions for expansions more frequently, just as the children were imitating less and expanding more in the period from 2 to 3 years of age. The influence between child and adult was mutual in the course of their interaction.

Two published samples of adult–adult speech were also examined at the conclusion of this study, for the purposes of discussion. In one, which took place in the presidential office at the White House, the adult utterances did not fit the categories of child discourse. We took this to mean that the children we studied still had much to learn about discourse contingencies. In the other sample, a couple were rowing in a boat on a lake, and their talk contained the same sorts of contextual and linguistic expansions we observed in the children. Thus, although the patterns we described are not the final goal in development of discourse, they are patterns available to adults in conversation, depending on the situation and the relationship between the participants.

INTERACTIONS BETWEEN DISCOURSE AND LANGUAGE LEARNING

Children learn language form and content through discourse at the same time they are learning how to participate in discourse. However, language acquisition is not simply additive. In all these studies, but in Chapters 3 and 4 in particular, we saw how learning one aspect of language often has a cognitive cost with an observable effect on another aspect (such as omission of subjects with negation). An example of this in the study of discourse was that the children did not ask contingent questions in the first two periods when mean length of utterance was less than 2.75 morphemes. Although contingency had increased and they were asking many questions in this period of time (as seen in Chapter 6), contingent responses were not questions. The children were asking contingent questions by the time they were 3 years old, but even then contingent utterances were questions only 13% of the time. In the exchange between Kathryn and her mother that introduced this chapter, Kathryn (age 2 years, 10 months) asked, "Why don't like taste of of cheddar?" Her question was contingent, but it also showed some wear and tear, with the omission of *you* and the disfluency *of of*. At the end of the period, then, the children were asking contingent questions, but they were not asking them frequently or easily.

To participate in conversations, children must be able to use the information in a prior message to access something stored in memory, hold that representation in mind, and access the procedures of language for its expression. At the same time they are learning to do this, between 2 and 3 years, they also are acquiring the words and grammar of the language. It isn't easy, and children work hard at it. In these two chapters in this last section, we have seen the active part that children take in working at what and how they learn from the speech they hear.

Adult–Child Discourse: Developmental Interaction Between Information Processing and Linguistic Knowledge

Lois Bloom, Lorraine Rocissano, and Lois Hood

In the beginning of language development, a child's major source of information for formulating messages is nonlinguistic: Young children talk primarily about what they see and do. One of the goals of language development, however, is the ability to obtain information from a prior linguistic signal, relate that information to existing knowledge, and form a contingent message. In the present study, discourse between adults and children was observed, and the content of successive adult and child utterances was described in terms of the semantic and formal relations between their messages. In this way it was possible to determine to what extent, and how, the four children in this study learned to use the information represented in input sentences for formulating their own messages, in their language development from 2 to 3 years of age.

Three sorts of interaction studies in language development are relevant to the development of conversational discourse in child language. Most studies have been studies of input only, in that they have focused on the form of adult speech to children in order to describe the model of speech from which children learn language, for example, Baldwin and Baldwin (1973), Broen (1972), Phillips (1973), Siegel (1963), and Snow (1972). Other studies have been concerned with the conventions of conversation, whereby matters of pacing, pausing, turn taking, initiating, and terminating are controlled by the participants and serve various functions, for example, Dittman (1972), Garvey and Hogan (1973), and Keenan (1974a). The studies most relevant to the research reported here are those that have looked at the aspects of form and content shared by reciprocal messages, such as the studies by Keenan (1974b); Seitz and Stewart (1975); Shapiro, Roberts, and Fish (1970); and Söderbergh (1974); and the study of the function of imitation for

Reprinted from *Cognitive Psychology*, 8, 1976, 521–51, with permission from Academic Press.

lexical and grammatical learning, reported in Bloom, Hood, and Lightbown (1974, chap. 12).

The general question addressed in the research reported here had to do with the source of the information coded in children's messages. There are two sources of information for coding in language: the conceptual representation of experience in memory – the knowledge that the child has of objects and events in the world – and the situation in which the speech event occurs. The particular question addressed in the present study had to do with the ability to use that information in the situation that is presented to the child in the form of an utterance from someone else, for formulating a contingent message.

After describing the procedures of the study, the development of discourse will be described in terms of (1) the extent to which children's speech was contingent on prior adult messages, (2) the semantic and formal interactions between adult speech and contingent child speech, and (3) the influence of the child's linguistic knowledge on these interactions between adult and child speech.

SUBJECTS AND PROCEDURES

The longitudinal data from Eric, Gia, Kathryn, and Peter were sampled for the purpose of this study with a consecutive sample (CS) of 400 utterances from each of the children, at each of three times when the mean length of utterance (MLU) coincided with the periods in language development defined by Brown (1973) as Stage 1, MLU < 2.0; Stage 2, MLU 2.0–2.75 and Stage 5, MLU 3.5–4.0. In these three stages, mean length of utterance progressed from approximately 1.3 to 4.0 morphemes, and the children progressed from approximately 21 to 36 months of age.

The analyses reported here began with samples of 200 consecutive utterances from each child at each time. A second sample of 200 consecutive utterances from each child at each time was analyzed afterwards in order to test the validity of the first analysis. Although there was some variation between two samples from the same corpus in certain instances, the interactions that form the results of the study were the same in all instances with both of the 200 utterance samples from each child at each time. Accordingly, the results for the two samples combined for each child at each time are reported here.

Child utterances were examined in order to determine, first, whether the utterance followed an adult utterance (adjacent speech) and, then,

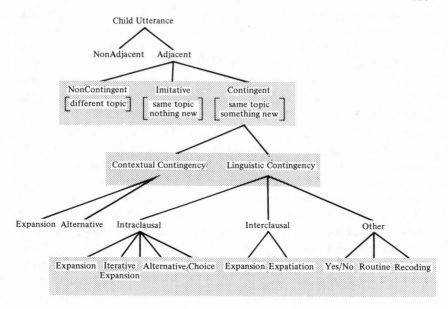

Figure 13.1. Categories of child discourse.

whether the relationship between an adjacent child utterance and a prior adult utterance was a *semantic* relation, with continuity of meaning as determined by nonlinguistic and linguistic contexts and, also, a *formal* relation, with lexical or structural continuities. The child discourse categories that were observed as a result of these levels of analysis, and their interaction, form the results of the study.

RESULTS

Extent of Contingency in Child Speech

Adjacent and Nonadjacent Speech. Whether or not the children took account of a prior adult message for formulating their own message depended, in the first place, upon whether or not an adult said something before the child said something. The first distinction, then, was between speech that was and was not adjacent (see Figure 13.1).

The factor that distinguished between adjacent and nonadjacent speech was pause time. If a definite pause occurred between a child utterance and a preceding adult utterance, then the child utterance was considered not adjacent to the adult utterance. If there was less than a definite pause or no pause between a child utterance and a preceding adult utterance, then the child utterance was considered as occurring within the space of the adult utterance and so adjacent to the adult utterance. The judgment of pause time was subjective and determined from the description of the contexts of events as recorded in the transcriptions. In order to test the reliability of the decisions that utterances were or were not adjacent to prior adult utterances, judgments were made by two independent observers of 150 of the utterances (25 utterances from each of two children at each stage). The agreement of the two independent observers with the original judgment of the investigators was .94 and .86 at Stage 1; .92 and .92 at Stage 2; and .94 and .98 at Stage 5. The question remains whether there were nonadjacent utterances that were actually related to preceding adult utterances and separated only arbitrarily by subjective pause time. The intent, however, was to determine the extent to which child utterances occurred in the time–space context of a prior adult utterance, and not to determine any and all possible relations between child utterances and all previous adult utterances. Accordingly:

Adjacent speech consisted of those child utterances that occurred after an adult utterance.

Nonadjacent speech consisted of those child utterances that occurred without a previous adult utterance or with a definite pause after a previous adult utterance. For example:

(Adult and child sit on floor, child picks up block)	(i) here a block.
Let's build a bridge.	(ii) a big bridge.
(Child and adult building; child picking up a block)	(iii) this block.

In the above examples (i) "here a block" is nonadjacent, having occurred without a previous adult utterance, and (ii) "a big bridge" is adjacent to the adult utterance "Let's build a bridge." The third child utterance (iii) "this block," is nonadjacent, having occurred after a pause during which there was also a shift of focus. There was no independent means of knowing whether (ii) "a big bridge" would have occurred if the adult utterance "Let's build a bridge" had not occurred, or if (iii) "this block" would have occurred if the adult utterance "Let's build a bridge" had not also occurred before it. The distinction between adjacent and nonadjacent speech simply identified those child utterances that occurred in the context of an immediately previous adult utterance.

Table 13.1. *Distribution of Adjacent and Nonadjacent Utterances: Consecutive Sample*[a]

Child and Stage	MLU	Age	Adjacent				Non-adjacent
			Contin-gent	Non-Contin-gent	Imita-tive	Total	
Eric							
1	1.19	20,2	.28	.31	.12	.71	.29
2	2.63	25,1	.29	.23	.05	.56	.44
5	3.83	36,0	.52	.18	.04	.74	.26
Gia							
1	1.12	19,2	.24	.23	.17	.64	.36
2	2.30	25,2	.45	.09	.01	.55	.45
5	4.14	36,0	.53	.25	—	.78	.22
Kathryn							
1	1.32	21,0	.23	.30	.23	.75	.25
2	2.83	24,2	.33	.25	.09	.67	.33
5	4.23	35,3	.39	.13	.01	.53	.47
Peter							
1	1.41	23,1	.10	.39	.18	.67	.33
2	2.62	26,1	.24	.21	.09	.54	.46
5	3.70	38,0	.42	.09	.02	.53	.47

[a] n = 400 utterances for each child at each stage.

The proportions of adjacent and nonadjacent child speech in the CS at each of the three stages, for each child, are presented in Table 13.1. Adjacent speech was always greater than nonadjacent speech, even at Stage 1, although the proportion of adjacent speech decreased from Stage 1 to Stage 2. Between Stage 2 and Stage 5, adjacent speech from Kathryn continued to decrease, but increased for Eric and Gia and remained essentially the same for Peter.

One might suppose that adjacent speech was greater than nonadjacent speech because of the frequency of adult speech; with many utterances from the adult it might seem that few opportunities for nonadjacent speech from the child would occur. To explore this possibility the average frequencies of adult and child speech per hour were compared at all three stages, and the frequency of child speech is plotted against the frequency of adult speech for each child in Figure 13.2.[1] Both adult and child speech increased from Stage 1 to Stage 5, and in 10 of the 12 samples, child speech was more frequent than adult speech – in

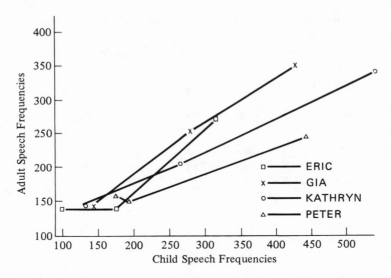

Figure 13.2. Relative frequencies of adult and child speech, average number of utterances per hour.

only the first samples from Kathryn and Eric was adult speech more frequent. Although the absolute frequencies of both adult and child speech increased, the increase in adult speech was not reflected in a proportional increase in adjacent child speech (see Table 13.1). This suggests that the high proportion of adjacent speech was not a function of how frequently the adults talked.

Kinds of Adjacent Speech. Three kinds of adjacent child speech were observed: contingent, noncontingent, and imitative speech (Figure 13.1). Two factors distinguished among these three: first, whether a child utterance shared the topic of the prior adult utterance and, second, if both utterances shared the same topic, whether the child utterance added new information relative to the topic of the prior utterance. All utterances that added new information shared the same topic, but not all utterances that shared the same topic also added new information. The agreement of two independent observers with the original judgment made by the investigators of kinds of adjacent speech was .93 and .95 at Stage 1; .91 and .89 at Stage 2; and .98 and .96 at Stage 5.

Noncontingent speech consisted of those child utterances that did not share the same topic as the preceding adult utterances, for example:

(1) E (Stage 2)

    Alright, put the light on.   cookie.

(2) K (Stage 2)

    (looking out window)

    Where are the children?

    (climbing off window ledge)   want get down.

Imitative speech consisted of those child utterances that shared the same topic with the preceding utterance but did not add information; that is, all or part of the preceding utterance was repeated with no change, for example:

(3) K (Stage 1)

    Take your shirt off.   shirt off.

(4) P (Stage 1)

    She might pinch her fingers.   pinch her fingers.

Contingent speech consisted of those child utterances that both (1) shared the same topic with the preceding utterance and (2) added information to the preceding utterance, for example:

(5) E (Stage 2)

    I see two.   I see two bus come here.

(6) K (Stage 2)

    I'm gonna build a high house.   I wanta build a high house too.

The proportion of contingent, noncontingent, and imitative utterances in the CS are presented in Table 13.1 and in Figure 13.3 for the four children combined. Contingent speech increased developmentally, and imitation decreased for the four children; except for Gia, noncontingent speech decreased.[2]

When the nonadjacent speech was discounted, the average proportion of just the adjacent speech from the four children that shared the topic of a prior adult utterance (that is, contingent and imitative speech) increased from .56 at Stage 1, to .67 at Stage 2, to .76 at Stage 5. Speech that was contingent (that shared the topic *and* added new information) increased from .31 at Stage 1, to .57 at Stage 2, to .73 at Stage 5.

The adult speech the children heard consisted of investigator speech more often than mother speech. In order to determine whether this variable was important, the proportions of imitative, contingent, and noncontingent child speech were compared in the two contexts of mother

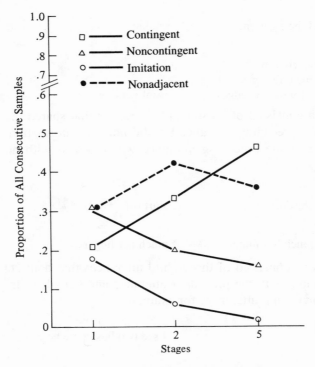

Figure 13.3. Proportional distribution of child utterances in categories of child discourse for the four children combined.

and investigator speech for the four children at Stages 1 and 2. There were 24 comparisons (four children, at two stages, with three discourse categories), and there was no significant difference (by chisquare tests of proportions) between mother and investigator in 20 of the comparisons. In Stage 1, Peter used more imitative speech with his mother (chi square $= 4.968$, $p < .05$); in Stage 2, Gia used more imitative and noncontingent speech with her mother (chi square $= 5.516$ and 4.338, respectively, $p < .05$) and more contingent speech with the investigator (chi square $= 9.926$, $p < .01$).

Formal and Semantic Interaction between Adult Speech and Contingent Child Speech

Categories of Contingent Discourse. Child utterances were distinguished according to how the children used the information in an adult

Table 13.2. *Proportions of Utterances in Categories of Topic-Related Discourse: Consecutive Sample*

Child and Stage	n^a	Yes–No	Contingent Speech						Imitation
			Social Routine	Recod-ing	Self-Expan-sion & Recoding	Expan-sion	Alter-native	Expatia-tion	
Eric									
1	162	.24	.01	.03	.01	.38	.04	—	.30
2	147	.13	—	.05	—	.46	.12	—	.15
5	223	.23	—	.04	.05	.56	.05	—	.08
Gia									
1	167	.05	—	.05	—	.46	.01	—	.42
2	186	.45	.01	.03	.01	.36	.13	—	.02
5	213	.27	—	.04	.02	.51	.13	.03	.01
Kathryn									
1	181	.13	—	.04	.01	.31	.03	—	.50
2	167	.23	—	.07	.01	.43	.06	—	.22
5	162	.20	—	.02	.05	.54	.09	.05	.04
Peter									
1	113	.01	—	.09	—	.16	.10	—	.65
2	130	.35	.02	.05	.03	.22	.07	—	.26
5	176	.32	—	.05	.06	.44	.06	.02	.06

$^a n$ = number of contingent and imitative utterances, at each stage for each child.

message for formulating their own messages. There were different kinds of contingency (as well as imitation) when a child produced an utterance that shared the same topic as a prior adult utterance, and the proportional frequencies of utterances in each of these categories of topic-related speech are presented in Table 13.2. Most simply, the child could respond *yes–no* or produce some sort of social routine like *thank you* or *bye-bye*. Social routines were relatively rare; *yes* and *no* were variable, both longitudinally for individual children and among the children. The *yes–no* variability was difficult to evaluate because it was not always clear if the children used the two forms appropriately. Also, *yes–no* responses often appeared to be a response set at particular times. Because of this tendency toward such a set and because *yes–no* responses provided little insight into how the children used the information in adult messages, they were not explored further. When *yes* or *no* was followed by a succeeding child utterance that shared topic, the succeeding utterance was coded, and the *yes–no* was ignored.

Recodings were child utterances that repeated part or all of the prior adult utterance and changed its form without adding to or altering its meaning. Recodings accounted for less than .10 of the topic-related speech in each sample. Recodings at Stage 1 were predominantly shifts from the nominal coding of predicate objects (in the adult utterance) to pronouns (in the child utterance). At Stage 2, anaphoric deictic recoding began, with pronominal shift for agents, from *you* (in adult utterance) to *I* (in child utterance). Finally, at Stage 5, anaphoric deixis was extended to pronoun shift for objects, *this* and *that,* and place, *here* and *there.* In addition, there were *self-expansions* and *self-recodings* that were contingent on an adult acknowledgment of a child's prior utterance, for example, "hm, you do" or "oh."[3]

The remaining categories were most important developmentally (examples to follow in the subsequent section): the contingent utterances that were *expansions* (that added information about the topic of a prior utterance), *alternatives* (that added information by opposing an aspect of the topic in the prior utterance), or *expatiations* (that added information to the prior utterance and introduced another, related topic). As can be seen in Table 13.2, expansions, where the child added to the adult utterance in several ways, increased. Expatiations were a late development at Stage 5. Alternatives showed no developmental trend and, as a single category, were variable both within and among the four children.

Categories of Linguistic and Contextual Contingency. The sources of semantic contingency were examined in the relationship between adult utterances and succeeding child utterances that were expansions, alternatives, or expatiations. The major distinction observed was between (1) semantic contingency based on situational context only – contextually related utterances – and (2) semantic contingency based on formal criteria as well as possible situational context – linguistically related utterances. Linguistically contingent child speech used the clause structure of the preceding adult utterance and may or may not have been contextually related; contextually contingent speech did not use the clause structure of the preceding utterance. The agreement of two independent observers with the original judgment made by the investigators of the following categories of linguistic and contextual contingency was .98 and .95 at Stage 1; 1.0 and .95 at Stage 2; and .96 and .96 at Stage 5.

Linguistic Contingency. Linguistic contingency consisted of a semantic relation between the child utterance and the preceding adult utterance with structural continuities between the child utterance and the clause structure of the adult utterance. The structural continuities were either intraclausal or interclausal in relation to prior utterances: (1) *Intraclausal relations* were certain expansions and alternatives in which information was added by the child within the same clause structure and with the same verb relation as in the adult utterance; (2) *interclausal relations* were expatiations and one kind of expansion in which information was added by the child with another clause that was grammatically subordinate to the clause of the adult utterance.

Intraclausal expansions preserved the same verb relation as in the adult utterance and consisted of the addition of a major subject–verb–object (SVO) constituent that was missing from the adult utterance, a *wh*-replacement, or the modification of an SVO constituent in the adult utterance, for example:

(7) G (Stage 1)
    Mommy sit.   Mommy stool. (addition of
                                      SVO constituent)

(8) P (Stage 1)
    What's in your hand?   book. (*wh*-replacement)

(9) K (Stage 2)
    Let's take the shoes out.   doll shoes. (modification
                                      within SVO)

Intraclausal iterative expansions preserved the same verb relation as the adult utterance, except that the referent of a major constituent such as agent, object, or place was changed. In the situations in which iterative expansions occurred, the adult's utterance referred to some event that was taking place, and the child's utterance referred to an event that was additional, in that it did not oppose the event referred to by the adult but simply went along with it.

(10) K (Stage 2)
    (pushing doll on slide) She
    climbs up and then she slides
    down.   Kathryn slides too.

(11) K (Stage 1)
(washing Kathryn's shoulder
and arm in the bath tub) Wash
the shoulder. (Mother washes
her hand)   wash hand.

(12) K (Stage 1)
(looking at a book) What are
the children doing? Are they
stretching? (Kathryn
stretches)   baby stretch.

Interclausal expansions added another verb relation that was grammatically subordinate to the verb relation in the adult utterance, for
example:

(13) K (Stage 5)
Does my finger fit?   no
Why?   because it's too big.

(14) E (Stage 5)
Yes. Pussy cat is calling to
wolf. Why?   because he's up in this build-
                                                 ing too tall.

(15) K (Stage 5)
Well I think the bear and the
doggie would like to visit the
donkey.   but he not gonna have a birth-
                                                 day.

Interclausal expatiations added information to the prior utterance
and introduced another related topic, for example:

(16) K (Stage 5)
I can't open it. (lockbox)   yes you can open that one but
                                                 I'm gonna lock it so you can't
                                                 get in.

(17) G (Stage 5)
How did they get there? (ber-
ries on trees)   they just picked them up and
                                                 put them on the hooks on the
                                                 berries and they hang up
                                                 them.

Two kinds of alternatives to a prior adult utterance were linguistically contingent.

Intraclausal alternatives opposed the idea represented in the adult's
utterance while preserving the same verb relation, for example:

(18) P (Stage 1)

You gonna make a house
again? (playing with blocks)   tunnel.

(19) K (Stage 1)

Don't lock it. (Lois and Kath-
ryn playing with lock box)   I'm gonna lock it.

(20) G (Stage 2)

Shall we sit on the sofa and
read my book? (Gia going to
orange chair)   orange chair ə read ə book.

Choice alternatives presented a choice by the child from more than one alternative presented in the adult utterance, for example:

(21) K (Stage 5)

Did you call her a nurse? Or a
stewardess?   a stewardess.

Contextual Contingency. For other contingent discourse, the child's utterance followed from the situation or action in the speech event that included the adult–child interaction. Contextually contingent speech did not use the clause structure of the preceding adult utterance. The child either expanded on or presented an alternative to the idea in the adult utterance with a different verb relation that was not grammatically subordinate to that in the adult utterance.

Contextual expansions added a different verb relation that was contextually related to what the adult said. The most common expansions of this type referred to successive aspects of the situation, for example:

(22) G (Stage 1)

Give it to Lois. (Lois is putting her toys away in her bag)   away.

(23) P (Stage 1)

I'll put my scarf on first.
(Getting ready to leave)   home?

(24) P (Stage 2)

I can't get the bolt off.   need ə screwdriver?

(25) K (Stage 2)

Where's the other sock?   see my sitting on it.

Contextual alternatives opposed the idea represented in the adult utterance, with a new verb relation, for example:

(26) P (Stage 1)
    Why don't you put the box
    back in the bag? (trying to
    open box)   open.

(27) P (Stage 1)
    I think we're gonna leave the
    tape recorder alone.   push.

(28) E (Stage 5)
    Well here's the conductor.
    He's sitting up here on the en-
    gine.   No! Let me take the engine.

(29) G (Stage 5)
    We don't wanna wake him.
    (Gia's brother)   I want go see him.

Development of Linguistic and Contextual Contingency. The distribution of the different kinds of linguistic and contextual contingency is presented in Table 13.3 as proportions of topic-related speech (contingency and imitation). Contextual contingency decreased from Stage 1 to Stage 5. Within linguistic contingency, intraclausal relations increased, and interclausal relations were a late development at Stage 5. The children were similar to one another, and Figure 13.4 presents the data combined for the four children. Linguistic contingency developed as the children progressed from imitating to learning to use the information in prior adult messages. They (1) expanded the same verb relation with a *wh*-replacement, added constituents or modified constituents within a clause, and, later, (2) added a second verb relation that was grammatically subordinate to the verb relation in the adult utterance.

When only contingent speech was examined and imitation was discounted, the proportion of lingusitic contingency was the same at Stage 1 and Stage 2 (.39) and increased only from Stage 2 to Stage 5 (.58). This increase in linguistically contingent speech was a function of the appearance of interclausal contingency at Stage 5, because the proportion of intraclausal contingency was similar at all three stages. Although the proportion of contingent speech that was intraclausal linguistic contingency was the same at Stages 1, 2, and 5, development occurred in the form of linguistic contingency.

Table 13.3. *Proportions of Utterances in Categories of Linguistic and Contextual Contingency*[a]

Child and Stage	Linguistic Contingency									Contextual Contingency		
	Intraclausal Relations					Interclausal Relations			Total Ling. Cont.	Expansion	Alternative	Total
	Expansion	Iterative Expansion	Alternative	Choice	Total	Expansion	Expatiation	Total				
Eric												
1	.25	.01	.03	—	.29	.01	—	.01	.30	.11	.01	.12
2	.35	.03	.07	—	.45	—	—	—	.45	.18	.05	.23
5	.35	.03	.02	.01	.41	.12	—	.12	.53	.06	.02	.08
Gia												
1	.29	.01	—	—	.30	—	—	—	.30	.16	.01	.17
2	.25	.01	.11	—	.37	—	—	—	.37	.10	.02	.12
5	.36	.01	.11	.01	.49	.06	.03	.09	.58	.08	.01	.09
Kathryn												
1	.16	.01	.02	—	.19	—	—	—	.19	.14	.01	.15
2	.19	.05	.04	—	.28	—	—	—	.28	.19	.02	.21
5	.28	.05	.07	.01	.41	.17	.05	.22	.46	.04	.01	.05
Peter												
1	.08	—	.02	—	.10	—	—	—	.10	.08	.08	.16
2	.16	—	.05	—	.21	—	—	—	.21	.06	.02	.08
5	.26	—	.03	.01	.30	.07	.02	.09	.43	.11	.02	.13

[a] *n* = number of contingent and imitative utterances, at each stage for each child, as in Table 13.2; rows sum to total expansions, expatiations, and alternatives, as in Table 13.2.

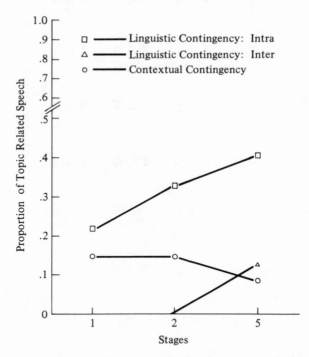

Figure 13.4. Proportional distribution of topic-related child utterances in categories of contingent speech for the four children combined.

Developmental Changes in the Form of Linguistic Contingency

Several kinds of lexical and structural continuity between adjacent adult and child messages shared the same topic. The distribution of the forms of linguistic contingency was similar in the speech of the four children, and this result is presented in Figure 13.5 for the data from the four children combined. Most frequently, and overwhelmingly at Stage 1, the child utterance consisted of a lexical item or a phrase that could function either as an additional consituent, or to replace a constituent in the adult utterance (Add in Figure 13.5), for example:

(30) K (Stage 1)
  Put this on with a pin.   sharp.

(31) P (Stage 1)
  You gonna make a house
  again?   tunnel.

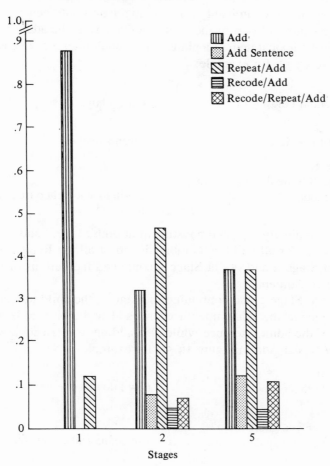

Figure 13.5. Proportional distribution of the forms of linguistic contingency for the four children combined.

Beginning at Stage 2 and continuing in Stage 5, the child utterance could represent an added sentence, for example:

(32) K (Stage 5)
    Well, where's Gary?   he doesn't come to the party.

(33) P (Stage 5)
    Where did you get that?   when Santa Claus came he
                                      bring me my bed and of
                                      course and vacuum cleaner.

At Stage 2, the predominant form of linguistic contingency consisted of a repetition of part of the adult utterance with the addition or replacement of a lexical item or a phrase in the adult utterance (Repeat/Add in Figure 13.5), for example:

(34) P (Stage 2)
     What did I draw?   draw a boy.

(35) G (Stage 2)
     Can I read it?   I wanta read it.

(36) E (Stage 2)
     I didn't bring the choo-choo
     train today.   ə bring ə choo-choo train to-
                                               morrow?

The most frequently repeated constituent at both Stage 2 and Stage 5 was the verb. For all children combined, .66 of all the Repeat/Add utterances at Stage 2 and .55 at Stage 5 contained the verb as one of the repeated constituents.

Beginning at Stage 2 and continuing in Stage 5, the child utterance could both recode the adult utterance and add to it, or recode and repeat part of the adult utterance while also adding to it (Recode/Add and Recode/Repeat/Add in Figure 13.5), for example:

(37) P (Stage 2)
     You do that one.   now I do that one.

(38) P (Stage 2)
     What are you going to do?
     (Peter setting up doll house)   I'm gonna make something in
                                               this.

(39) (Stage 5)
     Where did you get it? (Christ-
     mas tree)   I got it from the Christmas
                                               tree man.

Asking Contingent Questions. The children's linguistically contingent speech included *wh*-questions at Stage 5, but not at Stages 1 and 2, and it appears that the development of linguistically contingent questions did not begin until sometime between Stages 2 and 5. Of the children's noncontingent speech, .11 utterances were questions at Stage 2, and .16 were questions at Stage 5, in comparison with linguistically contingent speech in which there were no questions at Stage 2 and .13 questions at Stage 5. Using the information in a prior utterance to ask a *wh*-question, that is, asking a question that is linguistically contingent, appears to have been more difficult than producing a linguistically contingent statement or asking a noncontingent question. While *wh*-questions occurred in the children's speech at Stage 2, they were not linguistically contingent until after Stage 2.

Discourse in Relation to Questions in Adult Speech

The effect of the adults' use of questions and nonquestions on the children's development of discourse was examined. All *wh*-questions and yes–no questions from the adults were counted as questions, except those that functioned as requests (e.g., "Why don't you sit over here?" or "Will you bring it over?"), which were counted as nonquestions. For this analysis the CS was expanded to include all of those intervening adult utterances to which the children did not respond. The original CS, then, consisted of child speech that was adjacent and nonadjacent to adult speech; the expanded CS included the CS plus all other adult utterances within the same sample. The proportion of adult utterances that were questions increased from .38 at Stage 1, to .49 at Stage 2 and .60 at Stage 5. The results, presented in Table 13.4, were that at all three stages, (1) linguistic contingency, which increased developmentally, occurred more often after adult questions than after nonquestions; (2) imitation and no response, both of which decreased developmentally, occurred more often after nonquestions than after questions; (3) contextual contingency tended to occur more often after nonquestions.

Because linguistic contingency occurred more often after adult questions than after nonquestions and the proportion of adult questions increased, one might hypothesize that the developmental increase in linguistic contingency occurred because the adults tended to ask more questions at Stage 2 and then again at Stage 5. This was clearly not the case, because the number of adult questions in the expanded CS actually decreased for Eric, Kathryn, and Peter from 564 at Stage 1 to 448 at Stage 5 (see Table 13.4).[4] Even though there were actually fewer opportunities for linguistic contingency to occur after questions for three of the children, the number of linguistically contingent utterances increased from 90 to 289. (The number of adult questions did increase for Gia, from 128 at Stage 1 to 228 at Stage 5, but the increase in linguistic contingency for Gia, from 51 to 119, was smaller than for the other children.)

The distribution of the major discourse categories (imitation, lin-

Table 13.4. *Discourse Categories in Relation to Questions and Nonquestions in Adult Speech*

Child and Stage	Adult Speech	Categories and Proportions of Child Speech After Questions and Nonquestions in Adult Speech					
		Linguistic Contingency	Contextual Contingency	Imitation	Non-contingent	No Response	Other[a]
Eric							
1	+Q .51(281)	.13(37)	.04(11)	.05(15)	.22(61)	.47(133)	.09(24)
	−Q .49(273)	.03 (9)	.04(10)	.12(34)	.22 (61)	.51(138)	.08(21)
2	+Q .54(183)	.22(41)	.09(16)	.02 (4)	.27 (50)	.30 (54)	.10(18)
	−Q .46(155)	.12(18)	.08(12)	.10(15)	.26 (41)	.38 (59)	.06(10)
5	+Q .60(190)	.48(92)	.04 (7)	.01 (1)	.18 (34)	.03 (6)	.26(50)
	−Q .40(129)	.19(24)	.08(10)	.12(16)	.29 (38)	.16 (21)	.16(20)
Gia							
1	+Q .32(128)	.29(37)	.04 (5)	.09(12)	.19 (24)	.30 (38)	.08(10)
	−Q .68(275)	.05(14)	.08(23)	.21(58)	.27 (74)	.36 (98)	.03 (8)
2	+Q .56(204)	.27(56)	.04 (8)	.01 (2)	.09 (19)	.20 (40)	.39(79)
	−Q .44(160)	.09(14)	.09(14)	.01 (1)	.09 (15)	.66(105)	.07(11)
5	+Q .67(228)	.40(91)	.03 (7)	— (1)	.22 (50)	.09 (20)	.26(59)
	−Q .33(114)	.25(28)	.10(11)	.01 (1)	.43 (49)	.12 (14)	.10(11)
Kathryn							
1	+Q .38(172)	.12(21)	.06(10)	.17(30)	.24 (42)	.29 (50)	.11(19)
	−Q .62(278)	.04(12)	.06(17)	.22(61)	.28 (79)	.35 (98)	.04(11)
2	+Q .39(124)	.23(29)	.07 (9)	.08(10)	.23 (29)	.06 (8)	.31(39)
	−Q .61(192)	.09(18)	.13(25)	.14(26)	.38 (72)	.21 (40)	.06(11)
5	+Q .54(138)	.49(68)	.05 (7)	.03 (4)	.14 (20)	.06 (8)	.22(31)
	−Q .46(116)	.31(36)	.01 (1)	.01 (1)	.24 (28)	.29 (34)	.14(16)

Peter

1	+Q .29(111)	.06 (7)	.04 (4)	.17(19)	.50 (56)	.22 (24)	.01 (1)
	−Q .71(268)	.01 (4)	.05(14)	.20(54)	.40(107)	.29 (79)	.04(10)
2	+Q .45(144)	.13(19)	.03 (5)	.08(11)	.25 (36)	.23 (33)	.28(40)
	−Q .55(179)	.05 (9)	.02 (4)	.13(23)	.34 (60)	.36 (64)	.11(19)
5	+Q .55(120)	.43(52)	.08(10)	.02 (2)	.13 (16)	.04 (5)	.29(35)
	−Q .45(100)	.17(17)	.11(11)	.08 (8)	.18 (18)	.07 (7)	.39(39)

[a]Other = yes–no, social routine, recoding, self-expansion, self-recoding.

guistic contingency, contextual contingency, etc.) in response to adult questions and nonquestions is presented in Table 13.4. As can be seen, linguistic contingency was more frequent after questions and increased for both questions and nonquestions. However, the proportional increase was greater for nonquestions than for questions. For example, for Kathryn the change in linguistic contingency in response to questions from Stage 1 to Stage 5 was .12 to .49, which represents a fourfold increase, while in response to nonquestions, there were proportionately eight times more linguistically contingent responses (.04 to .31). Thus, although linguistic contingency was always more frequent after questions than nonquestions, with development the children began to give such responses more frequently to nonquestions.

This tendency for responses to become distributed more evenly between questions and nonquestions from Stage 1 to Stage 5 held for the other discourse categories in addition to linguistic contingency. At the same time, however, there was a concomitant trend in the speech of the adults; the proportion of adult utterances that were questions increased from Stage 1 to Stage 5. These two developmental trends acted as competing factors, producing the result shown in Figure 13.6, where the proportion of each of the major child discourse categories that occurred after adult questions is shown for the four children combined. As can be seen, the proportion within each category (imitation, linguistic contingency, contextual contingency, and no response) that occurred after questions was essentially the same at each stage. This constancy in the proportion of the various discourse categories in response to adult questions was a direct result of the competing effects from the proportional increase in adult questions and the proportional increase in child responses to nonquestions.[5] As a consequence, there was an equilibrium maintained between adult and child in their discourse interaction.

Discourse Support from the Child for Linguistic Contingency

The results presented thus far have been based on adjacent adult–child utterance pairs, and one question that remains is how often the adult–child contingency relations actually originated with a preceding utterance from the child, as in the following example:

(40) G (Stage 2)
    (pointing to space for tank on
    tank car)   uh oh missing.

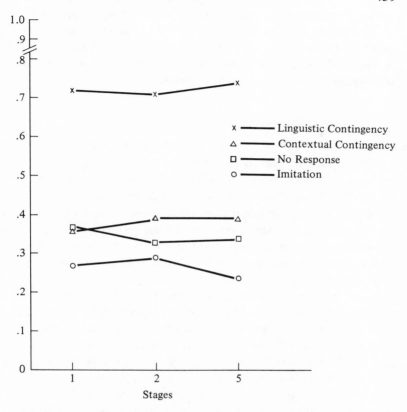

Figure 13.6. Proportions of each of the child discourse categories that occurred in response to adult questions, for the four children combined.

Uh oh what's missing?   missing tank car.

Gia's second utterance is linguistically contingent on the adult utterance, and both are linguistically contingent on the preceding child utterance.

Less than .20 of the children's linguistically related utterances were also linguistically contingent on a preceding child uterance (.15 at Stage 1, .16 at Stage 2, and .19 at Stage 5). More often, then, the children's speech was linguistically contingent when the topic originated with the adult utterance than with a prior child utterance. When the topic originated with a prior child utterance, the intervening adult utterance functioned as a 'prompt' in the form of an imitation or asked for an expansion from the child. Most often, the adult either (1) imitated part or all of the first child utterance and the second child utterance was really a self-expansion or (2) asked a *wh*-question based on the first child utterance and the child responded to the *wh*-question. Imitative adult utterances were most frequent at Stage 1 and decreased to Stage 5; and adult *wh*-questions were least frequent at Stage 1 and increased to Stage 5.

DISCUSSION

Fillmore (1971/1973) has compared the interaction in discourse to a "game of catch" played by throwing balls into the air. Each player comes to the game with a basket of balls and knowledge of the basic rule that only one ball can be in the air at any one time – thus distinguishing the game of catch from other games with balls such as warfare or juggling. Tossing a ball into the air corresponds to contributing something to a conversation, and Fillmore described different versions of the game that are analogous to different kinds of conversation between speakers.

In the first version of the game, one player begins by picking up a ball and throwing it in the air. Another player watches the ball, catches it, and throws it back to the first player, who, in turn, watches the ball, goes to where it will land, catches it, and throws it again to the second player. The ball represents the topic of the conversation and goes back and forth in this way, until either of the players lets the ball fall to the ground or else the first player puts it back in the basket.

In the second version of the conversation game described by Fillmore, one player takes a ball and throws it into the air. The other player waits until it falls to the ground and then picks up another ball and throws it into the air. The other players wait for it to land, and then the first player or someone else throws a ball into the air again. Although the players are taking turns, they are not sharing a topic of conversation.

Fillmore's conversation metaphor is relevant to the major results of this study of adult–child discourse in the following ways: More of the children's utterances were adjacent to an utterance from someone else than they were nonadjacent – that is, they occurred in a context in which someone else had just said something. Already at Stage 1, then, the children had learned the first basic rules of discourse: (1) Only one ball can be in the air at one time, and (2) you throw your ball in the air after someone else throws theirs. Recent research by Stern, Jaffe, Beebe, and Bennett (1975) would indicate that these early rules of discourse are developmental, and learned sometime after the first few months of life. They reported that the largest proportion of the vocalization of the infants they observed was "co-actional" at 3 to 4 months, as children vocalized more often in unison with their mothers than in a "dialogic" or alternating pattern.

However, child utterances were largely noncontingent at Stages 1 and 2, so that although the children knew that talking was reciprocal and they were taking conversational turns, they were playing the second conversation game described by Fillmore about half the time: One player throws a ball in the air, the other player waits for it to fall to the ground and then throws another ball into the air . . . and so on. By the time the children were 3 years old, at Stage 5, they were playing the first version of the conversation game fairly well: The same ball (representing the topic of conversation) went back and forth between speakers, and the children added new information to the topic most of the time.

There were two possible explanations of the children's speech that was either nonadjacent or adjacent but noncontingent: first, that such speech functioned to change the topic of conversation or introduce a topic and, second, an explanation that is not mutually exclusive with the first, that it is easier for children to produce spontaneous speech than to produce contingent speech. The children introduced new topics or changed the topic of conversation with more than half of what they said at Stage 1. By Stage 2, nonadjacent speech had increased in the same proportion that noncontingent speech decreased (Figure 13.3), and for two of the children nonadjacent speech had increased again by Stage 5. Thus, the children were becoming more active in initiating conversational exchanges – no doubt as a result of how adults were responding to them (which was explored in the present study only to a limited extent).

However, even though the children might have chosen to change the topic of conversation, there is also evidence to indicate that it may be more difficult to produce a contingent message than to produce a 'spontaneous' message. First, it was apparently more difficult for the children in this study to ask a *wh*-question in response to a prior utterance from someone else than to ask a *wh*-question spontaneously at Stage 2. At Stage 2, .11 of the children's noncontingent speech were questions, which is consistent with other reports of the frequency of questions in children's speech: .13 of the speech from children in the age range 18 to 72 months studied by Smith (1933) and .14 from children in the age range 36 to 54 months studied by McCarthy (1930). However, questions did not appear in the children's contingent speech until Stage 5. Second, in studies of the development of negation in child language, both McNeill and McNeill (1968) and Bloom (1970, chap. 4) observed that negative sentences that express denial of the truth of a prior statement, for example, "That's not truck" (after "Here's a truck"), develop after negative sentences with other semantic functions, such as nonexistence and rejection of objects and events. In a study by Belkin (1975), expressions of denial occurred more frequently and developmentally earlier after questions than after statements – which is consistent with the results for linguistic contingency reported here.

In addition, the difference between spontaneous and elicited speech provides further evidence of the different processes involved in producing spontaneous and contingent messages, as is evident in the following example from Bloom (1974b).[6] Although Peter imitated often in naturalistic situations and he willingly played 'the game' when asked to imitate sentences, he was unable to reproduce the same sentences that he had said spontaneously on the preceding day. For example, when asked to repeat, "I'm trying to get this cow in there," Peter said, "Cow in here," and when asked to repeat, "You made him stand up over there," Peter said, "Stand up there." It appears, then, that Peter's spontaneous speaking ability, given the support of contextual events and his own intention, exceeded his ability to say sentences that he was asked to imitate without such support, even though they were the very same sentences that he himself had produced at another time (see also Maratsos & Kuczaj, 1975; Slobin & Welsh, 1973).

While increase in linguistic contingency was a major development in discourse in the present study, it still accounted for less than half the adjacent speech the children produced when they were 3 years old. This result and the above observations have implications for the evaluation that is given to children's language performance when assessing their language development. Children's linguistic behavior is often assessed in situations in which speech is elicited from the child – as in experimental tasks that involve question answering and elicited imitation. Such tasks present children with a situation in which they are expected to produce a contingent response, which is fundamentally different from producing a message that expresses their own semantic intention, as the following model would indicate.

Three cognitive components interact with one another and with information from linguistic and nonlinguistic events in the child's con-

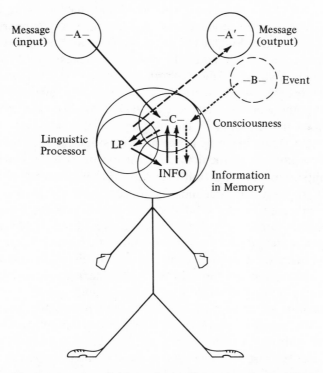

Figure 13.7. A model for understanding and producing information in messages.

text, as the child either produces or understands messages. There is (1) the child's *memory* – the conceptual information about objects and events in the world; (2) the child's scheme for *linguistic processing* for both decoding linguistic forms, in order to obtain information or meaning, and using linguistic forms, in order to represent information in messages to other persons; and (3) the child's immediate *consciousness* – what the child thinks about when producing an utterance or hearing an utterance from someone else. The three components and the interactions that underlie different states of affairs for speaking and understanding in language development are schematized in Figure 13.7.

The two situations in which the child either hears a message (A) that maps onto a contextual event (B) or produces a message (A′) relative to a contextual event (B) are the two situations which predominate in early child language – when children both understand and speak in the 'here and now.' However, from the beginning of child language and with increasing frequency through to adulthood, messages are understood and messages are produced without the necessary support of an encoded event in the context (B) being perceptually available to the child's consciousness (C). When the child hears a message (A) and the only information about the meaning of the message in (A) is available to the child through processing the linguistic signal in relation to information about the world in memory, the task is to create a mental representation of the meaning of the message in consciousness (C). In turn, that represented meaning of the prior message can then be related to some new content in memory to form the basis for a contingent semantic intention – the situation schematized in Figure 13.7, in which the child's message (A') depends upon processing information from input (A, indicated by the solid lines) as a condition for processing information for output (A', indicated by the dashed lines). This capacity is the goal of language development and is the capacity upon which the development of discourse would appear to depend – where the topic of conversation is shared by different speakers. In the present study, observations were made of the formal and semantic relations between contingent child utterances (A'), and prior adult utterances (A), while the extent to which there were corresponding events in the context, possible (B), was not explored directly.

If one considers that the categories of nonadjacent and adjacent speech reported here were exhaustive, that is, all of the CS from each child at each stage was accounted for – then, to the extent that the CS was representative of the children's discourse, the following conclusions appear to follow: First, it seems that certain rules of discourse could function independently of the cognitive processes involved in speaking and understanding. The children knew to say something after another person had spoken. Utterances that did not share the topic of prior messages occurred when the children's knowledge of this basic rule of discourse operated without their necessarily processing the prior message, as they attended to something else or changed the topic. Such messages that introduced a new topic are represented in Figure 13.7 with the dashed lines that indicate how the child would raise some information from memory (with or without an association with some event in the context) to consciousness, forming a semantic intention to express in an output utterance.

In the more complex situations in which the topic of a prior utterance was shared, the children very often shared the topic by saying the same thing – that is, they imitated. This result complements the results of a previous study of imitation in which the function of imitation for lexical and grammatical learning was investigated (Bloom, Hood, & Lightbown, 1974, chap. 12).[7] Imitation was, therefore, one of the earliest strategies available for discourse, as observed also by Keenan (1974a). Considering the cognitive processes for speaking diagrammed in Figure 13.7, it would appear that the easiest way to process the relation between linguistic form and nonlinguistic content in a prior utterance (and maintain the topic of conversation at the same time) would be to either imitate, without needing to recall new forms or content from memory, or add a new form that complemented the form and content of the prior utterance – given some representation of the prior utterance in (C). At Stage 1, the children either imitated or added to adult utterances but did not both repeat and add in the same utterance as they did in Stage 2 (Figure 13.5). Moreover, at Stage 1, imitation occurred most often after statements, and adding (linguistic contingency) occurred most often after questions – which indicated that the children discriminated between questions and statements in adult speech and responded differently to each.

The major development in the children's discourse from Stage 1 to Stage 5 was the increase in messages that shared the topic of a prior utterance with added information. This increase in contingency was characterized primarily by expansions, in which the verb of the prior utterance was repeated and something was added to it: Either major sentence constituents were added or modified, or a *wh*-form was replaced by a word or a phrase. The explanation of this result that is most consistent with the reported function of imitation for language learning at Stage 1 (Bloom, Hood, & Lightbown, 1974, chap. 12) is that children were learning the lexical and grammatical functions of verbs. However, the children were also learning a major device for texting in conversation (Halliday & Hasan, 1976), as the developing discourse between speakers shared the same constituents (see Z. Harris, 1964). While the evidence available so far does not differentiate between these two possible explanations, it seems safe to conclude that discourse develops between adult and child as a function of learning both language use and the relations between language form and content (lexicon and grammar). Social interaction, then, may be complementary rather than primary. Children learn language form and content through discourse as they learn how to participate in conversations.

One important aspect of this study has not been made explicit as yet.

There were changes in the children's speech, and there were also changes in the adults' speech as well. The adults asked proportionately more questions as children's linguistically contingent responses to questions increased. In their own responses to the children, the adults tended to repeat what the child said less frequently and to ask *wh*-questions for expansions more frequently – as the children also were imitating less and expanding more in the time from Stage 1 to Stage 5. The patterns in the development of discourse that have been described no doubt resulted from mutual influences between adult and child, and the feedback that each receives in the course of their interaction. Children pay attention to those aspects of the adult speech that they hear which they are in the process of learning or which they need to learn, and adults progressively modify their speech to children in order to provide a model that is responsive to the child's evolving needs and capacities. An important cue is provided the adult by the kind of response the child gives, and changes in the child's discourse patterns will influence the adults' response patterns. Thus, there were changes in the children's speech that depended presumably upon factors of age and ability, as well as upon complementary changes on the part of the adults in conversation (see also the studies of mother–child interactions by Moerk, 1975; Nelson, 1973; Phillips, 1973; Seitz & Stewart, 1975; Söderbergh, 1974; and others).

Other Studies of Child Discourse. The description of the linguistic exchanges in adult–child dyads can be compared with the results of studies of peer dyads that have been reported by Garvey (1974), Garvey and Hogan (1973), and by Keenan (1974b). Both Keenan (with 29-month-old twins) and Garvey and Hogan (with 3- to 5-year-olds) have emphasized children's use of repetition and routines in peer interactions. In contrast, routines were infrequent in the present study, and imitation per se was an early discourse strategy that virtually disappeared by Stage 5. It would seem then that the development of discourse (at least as defined as the ability to share the same topic and add information to a prior utterance from someone else) depends upon the monitoring by an adult who can provide input in relation to the child's capacities for output. In peer interaction, where such monitored support is presumably not available, children may revert to earlier behaviors for sharing topics in conversation. Moreover, there is some evidence that the topics that are so shared are limited. The exchanges between the 29-month-old twins that Keenan described, in which the children expanded one another's utterances (or both repeated and expanded – Repeat/Add) consisted most often of fragments of songs and nursery rhymes.

Shapiro, Roberts, and Fish (1970) compared the echoing behavior of schizophrenic children (mean age 55 months) and normal children (2 to 4 years of age) and distinguished between exact repetition and "mitigated" or "restructured" echoing (where the children repeated and added, or added to and reduced, a prior utterance). They found that both groups of children produced exact repetitions, but only the nonschizophrenic children also used restructured echoing. Although the schizophrenic children echoed the speech they heard, they did not also produce contingent messages that added information to the topic of conversation. In addition, among the normal children, exact repetition was most frequent among 2-year-olds and restructured echoing was most frequent among the 4-year-olds, which corresponds to the results presented here. Other studies have also reported a higher incidence of imitation among younger children and a decline in imitation with development (for example, Moerk, 1975; Seitz & Stewart, 1975; Shipley, Smith, & Gleitman, 1969; Slobin, 1968). However, when a distinction was made between just imitation, and imitation in combining with recoding and adding, as in the present study, imitation did not actually decline so much as it changed with development, as the children learned to both repeat and add in conversation.

Patterns of Adult Discourse. It is not clear how the adult–child interactions reported here compare with adult discourse, or even if the same categories are applicable. In fact, a preliminary analysis reveals that adult–adult discourse can differ from adult–child discourse in important ways. An attempt was made to apply the discourse categories observed here to transcripts of conversations between adults that have been reported elsewhere: One was the conversations between President Gerald R. Ford and others in his office, published in the *New York Times Magazine,* April 20, 1975; another was the conversations between a married couple on vacation reported by Soskin (1963).

In the presidential transcripts, over .90 of the reported adjacent messages were contingent, as compared with approximately .70 of the children's utterances at Stage 5 in the present study. The adult discourse generally did not fall into any of the categories of linguistic or contextual contingency that characterized the children's discourse. That is, they neither shared the verb relation of the preceding utterance, nor were their utterances related by events in the nonlinguistic context – due to the absence of relevant nonlinguistic events in the immediate context. Rather, utterances were linguistically contingent as a respondent used the information in a prior message and shared the topic of conversation, but did so most often by using another verb relation and, sometimes, by paraphrasing the preceding verb relation and/or elaborating on it with additional verb relations, for example:

1.   Theis: Father Hesburgh, who was a leader of the antiwar movement, strongly suggested we avoid Southeast Asia. The subject of hunger . . .
     Ford: I'm not talking about Vietnam or Cambodia (p. 34).
2.   Ford: As long as he could get some input from you and others besides myself . . .
     Rumsfeld: Sure. He does that all day every day (p. 46).
3.   Ford: My wife and I watch the Miss America contest all the time. We really enjoy that on TV.
     Miss America: I sure hope you saw it this year (p. 32).

Thus, it seems that the kind of linguistic contingency observed for the children is not the final goal in the development of discourse, and development would continue, particularly as the children learned more verbs.

In contrast, in a portion of the Soskin (1963) transcript, the conversation recorded between a husband and wife while they were rowing in a boat was not so different from the patterns of adult–child discourse that have been described. In particular, there were many of the same kinds of contextual and linguistic expansions. The Soskin transcript was situationally quite different from the President Ford transcript – especially in terms of the personal and status relations between the participants, and the extent to which the context supported the topic of conversation, for example, Southeast Asia and the Miss America contest in contrast with the cabins on the lake and the waves from the oars. Also, it is not clear to what extent the presidential transcripts were edited, and the participants in the Soskin transcripts were noticeably self-conscious about the recording procedure. Thus, no claim can be made here about the extent to which each of these transcripts is representative of adult discourse. Simply as illustrations, however, they indicate that while the patterns of conversation between adults and children described in the present study are not the final goal in the development of discourse, they are patterns that are available as well to adults in conversation, depending upon such factors in the situation as personal relationship, context, and topic.

NOTES

1 In computing the frequency of adult speech, clusters of adult utterances unified by topic and not separated by pauses – so that the child could not have responded – were counted as one turn. For example, the series of utterances "They'll be right back. They'll come back soon. They went to buy the paper" was counted as only one turn. Similarly, successive child utterances unified by topic were counted as only one turn.

2 In the figures that present the combined data from the four children ($N = 1,600$ utterances at each stage), the stages along the abscissa represent discrete points in time, so that the lines between points are not continuous functions.

3 When a child utterance followed an adult acknowledgment but changed topic, it was counted as nonadjacent. Also, sequences in which the adult asked the child to repeat because the child had not been heard or understood – for example, by saying "What?" or "What did you say?" – were not included in the CS.

4 The results presented in Table 13.4 showing that the number of adult utterances decreased may appear to contradict the results presented in Figure 13.2, which indicates an increase in adult speech frequency. However, the absolute number of adult utterances spoken in the span of 400 child utterances is presented in Table 13.4, whereas Figure 13.2 represents the average number of utterances per hour. Because the relative increase in adult speech frequency was less than the relative increase in child speech frequency (Figure 13.2), it follows that the absolute number of adult utterances spoken in the span of 400 child utterances would decrease as the time span decreased.

5 The results presented in Figure 13.6 are predictable given the conditional probabilities of each of the discourse categories occurring in response to questions and nonquestions. To illustrate, the following formula predicts the result shown in Figure 13.6 for linguistic contingency:

$$p(q/c) = p(q) \cdot p(c/q)/p(q) \cdot p(c/q) + [1 - p(q)] \cdot p(c/nq)$$

where $p(q/c)$ = the probability that a question preceded a linguistically contingent utterance (i.e., the data in Figure 13.6); $p(c/nq)$ = the probability that a nonquestion preceded a linguistically contingent utterance; and $p(q)$ = the probability that an adult utterance is a question (i.e., the data in Table 13.4). The observed rise in $p(q)$ (from .38 at Stage 1 to .60 at Stage 5), which with age would lead to an increase in $p(q/c)$, and the observed rise in $p(c/nq)$, which with age would lead to a decrease in $p(q/c)$, counteracted each other, leading to the result presented in Figure 13.6.

6 From data collected in collaboration with Patsy Lightbown.

7 In the earlier study (Chapter 12), the children differed in frequency of imitation, with imitation counted for utterance types rather than utterance tokens (as in the present study). The type–token ratios for imitation in the CS at Stage 1 were Kathryn, .91; Peter, .85; Eric, .70; and Gia, .57. Gia, who imitated types least often, had more imitated tokens than did Kathryn and Peter, who imitated types most often. Thus the results of the two studies are not contradictory.

POSTSCRIPT

For studies since Bloom, Rocissano, and Hood (1976) that have explored the uses and extensions of imitation in discourse:

Folger, J., & Chapman, R. (1978). A pragmatic analysis of spontaneous imitations. *Journal of Child Language, 5,* 25–38.

McTear, M. (1978). Repetition in child language. In R. Campbell & P. Smith (Eds.), *Recent advances in the psychology of language* (pp. 293–311). New York: Plenum.

Ochs, E. (1983). Evolving discourse: The next step. In E. Ochs & B. Schieffelin (Eds.), *Acquiring conversational competence* (pp. 40–9). London: Routledge & Kegan Paul.

Ochs, E. (1983). Making it last: Repetition in children's discourse. In E. Ochs & B. Schieffelin (Eds.), *Acquiring conversational competence* (pp. 26–39). London: Routledge & Kegan Paul.

Oshima-Takane, Y. (1988). Children learn from speech not addressed to them: The case of personal pronouns. *Journal of Child Language, 15,* 95–108.

Reger, Z. (1986). The functions of imitation in child language. *Applied Psycholinguistics, 1,* 323–52.

Scherer, N., & Olswang, L. (1984). Role of mothers' expansions in stimulating children's language production. *Journal of Speech and Hearing Research, 27,* 387–96.

Wellen, C. (1985). Effects of older siblings on the language young children hear and produce. *Journal of Speech and Hearing Disorders, 50,* 84–99.

For studies of developments in discourse contingency:

Ackerman, B. (1981). When is a question not answered? The understanding of young children of utterances violating or conforming to the rules of conversational sequencing. *Journal of Experimental Child Psychology, 31,* 487–507.

Bloom, K., Russell, A., & Wassenberg, K. (1987). Turn taking affects the quality of infant vocalizations. *Journal of Child Language, 14,* 211–27.

Loeb, D., & Schwartz, R. (1990). Language characteristics of a linguistically precocious child. *First Language, 10,* 1–18.

Lord, C., & Leimbach, M. (1983). A longitudinal study of form–function relations in a mother's questions and her child's responses. *Developmental Psychology, 19,* 585–90.

Olsen-Fulero, L., & Conforti, J. (1983). Child responsiveness to mother questions of varying type and presentation. *Journal of Child Language, 10,* 495–520.

Pickert, S., & Furth, H. (1980). How children maintain a conversation with adults. *Human Development, 23,* 162–76.

Tamir, L. (1980). Interrogatives in dialogue – Case study of mother and child 16–19 months. *Journal of Psycholinguistic Research, 9,* 407–24.

Van Hekken, S., & Roelofsen, W. (1982). More questions than answers: A study of question–answer sequences in a naturalistic setting. *Journal of Child Language, 9,* 445–60.

Van Kleeck, A., & Frankel, T. (1981). Discourse devices used by language disordered children: A preliminary investigation. *Journal of Speech and Hearing Disorders, 46,* 250–7.

Yoder, P., & Davies, B. (1990). Do parental questions and topic continuation elicit replies from developmentally delayed children?: A sequential analysis. *Journal of Speech and Hearing Research, 33,* 563–73.

For studies of the functions of discourse:

Foster, S. (1986). Learning discourse topic management in the preschool years. *Journal of Child Language, 13,* 231–50.

Hoff-Ginsberg, E. (1990). Maternal speech and the child's development of syntax: A further look. *Journal of Child Language, 17,* 85–99.

Miller, P. (1982). *Amy, Wendy, and Beth: Learning language in south Baltimore.* Austin: University of Texas Press.

Miller, P., & Sperry, L. (1988). Early talk about the past: The origins of conversational stories of past experience. *Journal of Child Language, 15,* 293–315.

Pickert, S. (1985). Functions of repetition in the conversations of preschool children. *Journal of General Psychology, 112,* 35–41.

Wanska, S., & Bedrosian, J. (1986). Topic and communicative intent in mother–child discourse. *Journal of Child Language, 13,* 523–35.

For a review of studies of discourse development:

Shatz, M. (1983). Communication. In J. Flavell & E. Markman (Eds.) & P. Mussen (Series Ed.), *Handbook of child psychology: Vol. 3. Cognitive development* (pp. 841–90). New York: Wiley.

References

Abbeduto, L., & Rosenberg, S. (1985). Children's knowledge of the presuppositions of *know* and other cognitive verbs. *Journal of Child Language, 12*, 621–41.

Aksu, A. (1978). Aspect and modality in the child's acquisition of the Turkish past tense. Ph.D. diss., University of California, Berkeley.

Allen, R. (1966). *The verb system of present-day American English*. The Hague: Mouton.

Allport, F. (1924). *Social psychology*. Boston: Houghton Mifflin.

Antinucci, F., & Miller, R. (1976). How children talk about what happened. *Journal of Child Language, 3*, 167–89.

Aronfreed, J. (1969). The problem of imitation. In L. Lipsitt & H. Reese (Eds.), *Advances in child development* (vol. 4, pp. 210–319). New York: Academic Press.

Bailey, C. (1973). Variation resulting from different rule orderings in English phonology. Unpublished manuscript. Georgetown University.

Baldwin, A., & Baldwin, C. (1973). The study of mother–child interaction. *American Scientist, 61*, 714–21.

Baron, N. (1977). *Language acquisition and historical change*. Amsterdam: North Holland.

Bates, E. (1976). *Language in context*. New York: Academic Press.

Bates, E., Benigni, L., Bretherton, I., Camaioni, L., & Volterra, V. (1979). *The emergence of symbols: Communication and cognition in infancy*. New York: Academic Press.

Bates, E., Bretherton, I., & Snyder, L. (1988). *From first words to grammar: Individual differences and dissociable mechanisms*. Cambridge: Cambridge University Press.

Beckwith, R. (1988). Learnability and psychological categories. Ph.D. diss., Columbia University.

Beckwith, R., Rispoli, M., & Bloom, L. (1984). Child language and linguistic theory: In response to Nina Hyams. *Journal of Child Language, 11,* 685–7.

Beer, C. (1973). A view of birds. In A. Pick (Ed.), *Minnesota symposia on child psychology* (vol. 7, pp. 47–86). Minneapolis: University of Minnesota Press.

Belkin, A. (1975). Investigation of the functions and forms of children's negative utterances. Ph.D. diss., Columbia University.

Bell, W. (1973). The perception of causality in the infant. Paper presented to the biennial meeting of the Society for Research in Child Development, Philadelphia.

Bellugi, U. (1967). The acquisition of negation. Ph.D. diss., Harvard University.

Bellugi, U., & Brown, R. (Eds.) (1964). *The acquisition of language.* Monographs of the Society for Research in Child Development, 29 (serial no. 92).

Berko, J. (1958). The child's learning of English morphology. *Word, 14,* 150–77.

Bever, T. (1970). The cognitive basis for linguistic structures. In J. Hayes (Ed.), *Cognition and the development of language* (pp. 279–352). New York: Wiley.

Blank, M. (1975). Mastering the intangible through language. In D. Aronson & R. Rieber (Eds.), *Developmental psycholinguistics and communication disorders. Annals of the New York Academy of Sciences, 263,* 44–58.

Blank, M., & Allen, D. (1976). Understanding "why": Its significance in early intelligence. In M. Lewis (Ed.), *Origins of intelligence* (pp. 259–78). New York: Plenum.

Bloch, O. (1921). Les premiers stades du language de l'enfant. *Journal de Psychologie, 18,* 693–712.

Bloom, L. (1968). Language development: Form and function in emerging grammars. Ph.D. diss., Columbia University.

Bloom, L. (1970). *Language development: Form and function in emerging grammars.* Cambridge, MA: MIT Press.

Bloom, L. (1973). *One word at a time: The use of single-word utterances before syntax.* The Hague: Mouton.

Bloom, L. (1974a). The acccountability of evidence in studies of child language. Comment on *Everyday preschool interpersonal speech usage: Methodological, developmental, and sociolinguistic studies.* In F. Schacter, K. Kirshner, B. Klips, M. Friedricks, & K. Sanders (Eds.), Monographs of the Society for Research in Child Development, 39 (serial no. 156).

Bloom, L. (1974b). Talking, understanding and thinking. Developmental relationship between receptive and expressive language. In R. Schiefelbusch & L. Lloyd (Eds.), *Language perspectives – Acquisition, retardation, and intervention* (pp. 285–312). Baltimore: University Park Press.

Bloom, L. (1976). An integrative perspective on language development. Keynote address. In *Papers and reports on child language development* (No. 12, pp. 1–22). Department of Linguistics, Stanford University.

Bloom, L. (1978). The semantics of verbs in child language. Address to Eastern Psychological Association, Washington, D.C.

Bloom, L. (1981). The importance of language for language development: Linguistic determinism in the 1980s. In H. Winitz (Ed.), *Native language and foreign language acquisition* (vol. 379, pp. 160–71). New York: New York Academy of Sciences.

Bloom, L. (in press). Representation and expression. In N. Krasnegor, D. Rumbaugh, & M. Studdert-Kennedy (Eds.), *Biobehavioral foundations for language development*. Hillsdale, NJ: Erlbaum.

Bloom, L. (in press). Transcription and coding for child language research. In J. Edwards & M. Lampert (Eds.), *Transcription and coding methods for language research*. Hillsdale, NJ: Erlbaum.

Bloom, L., & Beckwith, R. (1989). Talking with feeling: Integrating affective and linguistic expression. *Cognition and Emotion, 3,* 313–42.

Bloom, L., Beckwith, R., Capatides, J., & Hafitz, J. (1988). Expression through affect and words in the transition from infancy to language. In P. Baltes, D. Featherman, & R. Lerner (Eds.), *Life-span development and behavior* (vol. 8, pp. 99–127). Hillsdale, NJ: Erlbaum.

Bloom, L., & Capatides, J. (1986). Discourse contexts and functions of causal statements. Unpublished data.

Bloom, L., & Capatides, J. (1987). Sources of meaning in complex syntax: The sample case of causality. *Journal of Experimental Child Psychology, 43,* 112–28.

Bloom, L., Capatides, J., & Tackeff, J. (1981). Further remarks on interpretative analysis: In response to Christine Howe. *Journal of Child Language, 8,* 403–11.

Bloom, L., & Harner, L. (1989). On the developmental contour of child language: A reply to Smith & Weist. *Journal of Child Language, 16,* 207–16.

Bloom, L., Hood, L., & Lightbown, P. (1974). Imitation in language development: If, when and why. *Cognitive Psychology, 6,* 380–420.

Bloom, L., & Lahey, M. (1978). *Language development and language disorders*. New York: Wiley.

Bloom, L., Lahey, M., Hood, L., Lifter, K., & Fiess, K. (1980). Complex sentences: Acquisition of syntactic connectives and the semantic relations they encode. *Journal of Child Language, 7,* 235–61.

Bloom, L., Lifter, K., & Broughton, J. (1985). The convergence of early cognition and language in the second year of life: Problems in conceptualization and measurement. In M. Barrett (Ed.), *Children's single-word speech* (pp. 149–80). London: Wiley.

Bloom, L., Lifter, K., & Hafitz, J. (1980). Semantics of verbs and the development of verb inflection in child language. *Language, 56*, 386–412.

Bloom, L., Lightbown, P., & Hood, L. (1975). *Structure and variation in child language.* Monographs of the Society for Research in Child Development, 40 (serial no. 160).

Bloom, L., Merkin, S., & Wootten, J. (1982). *Wh*-questions: Linguistic factors that contribute to the sequence of acquisition. *Child Development, 53*, 1084–92.

Bloom, L., Miller, P., & Hood, L. (1975). Variation and reduction as aspects of competence in language development. In A. Pick (Ed.), *Minnesota symposia on child psychology* (vol. 9, pp. 3–55). Minneapolis: University of Minnesota Press.

Bloom, L., Rispoli, M., Gartner, B., & Hafitz, J. (1989). Acquisition of complementation. *Journal of Child Language, 16*, 101–20.

Bloom, L., Rocissano, L., & Hood, L. (1976). Adult–child discourse: Developmental interaction between information processing and linguistic knowledge. *Cognitive Psychology, 8*, 521–52.

Bloom, L., Tackeff, J., & Lahey, M. (1984). Learning *to* in complement constructions. *Journal of Child Language, 10*, 391–406.

Bloom, P. (1990). Subjectless sentences in child language. *Linguistic Inquiry, 21*, 491–504.

Bloomfield, L. (1933). *Language.* New York: Holt, Rinehart & Winston.

Borton, R. (1979). The perception of causality in infants. Paper presented to the biennial meeting of the Society for Research in Child Development, San Francisco.

Bower, T. G. R. (1974). *Development in infancy.* San Francisco: Freeman.

Bowerman, M. (1973a). *Early syntactic development: A cross-linguistic study with special reference to Finnish.* Cambridge: Cambridge University Press.

Bowerman, M. (1973b). Structural relationships in children's utterances. Syntactic or semantic? In T. Moore (Ed.), *Cognitive development and the acquisition of language* (pp. 197–213). New York: Academic Press.

Bowerman, M. (1974a). Discussion summary – Development of concepts underlying language. In R. Schiefelbusch & L. Lloyd (Eds.), *Language perspectives – Acquisition, retardation and intervention* (pp. 191–209). Baltimore: University Park Press.

Bowerman, M. (1974b). Learning the structure of causative verbs: A study in the relationship of cognitive, semantic and syntactic development. In *Papers and reports on child language development* (No. 8, 142–78). Department of Linguistics, Stanford University.

Bowerman, M. (1987). Mapping thematic roles onto syntactic functions. Are children helped by innate "linking rules"? Paper presented to the Child Language Conference, Boston University.

Braine, M. (1963). The ontogeny of English phrase structure: The first phase. *Language, 39,* 1–13.

Braine, M. (1971a). The acquisition of language in infant and child. In C. Reed (Ed.), *The learning of language* (pp. 7–86). New York: Appleton-Century-Crofts.

Braine, M. (1971b). On two types of models of the internalization of grammars. In D. Slobin (Ed.), *The ontogenesis of grammar* (pp. 153–86). New York: Academic Press.

Braine, M. (1974). Length constraints, reduction rules, and holophrastic processes in children's word combinations. *Journal of Verbal Learning and Verbal Behavior, 13,* 448–56.

Braine, M. (1976). *Children's first word combinations.* Monographs of the Society for Research in Child Development, 41 (serial no. 164).

Brainerd, C. (1978). The stage question in cognitive–developmental theory. *Behavioral and Brain Sciences, 2,* 173–213.

Brainerd, C. (1979). *Commentary.* Monographs of the Society for Research in Child Development, 44 (serial no. 181).

Bresnan, J. (1970). On complementizers: Towards a syntactic theory of complement types. *Foundations of Language, 6,* 297–321.

Bresnan, J. (1978). A realistic transformational grammar. In M. Halle, J. Bresnan, & G. Miller (Eds.), *Linguistic theory and psychological reality* (pp. 1–59). Cambridge, MA: MIT Press.

Bresnan, J. (1982). The passive in lexical theory. In J. Bresnan (Ed.), *The mental representation of grammatical relations* (pp. 3–86). Cambridge, MA: MIT Press.

Bresnan, J., & Kaplan, R. (1982). Grammars as mental representations of language. In J. Bresnan (Ed.), *The mental representation of grammatical relations* (pp. xvii–lii). Cambridge, MA: MIT Press.

Bretherton, I., & Beeghly, M. (1982). Talking about internal states: The acquisition of an explicit theory of mind. *Developmental Psychology, 18,* 906–21.

Broen, P. (1972). *The verbal environment of the language learning child.* ASHA Monographs, 17. Washington, D.C.: American Speech and Hearing Association.

Bronckart, J., & Sinclair, H. (1973). Time, tense, and aspect. *Cognition, 2,* 107–30.

Brown, R. (1956). Language and categories. Appendix to J. Bruner, J. Goodnow, & G. Austin, *A study of thinking* (pp. 247–312). New York: Wiley.

Brown, R. (1958). How shall a thing be called? *Psychological Review, 65,* 14–21.

Brown, R. (1968). The development of *wh*-questions in child speech. *Journal of Verbal Learning and Verbal Behavior, 7,* 279–90.

Brown, R. (1970). The first sentences of child and chimpanzee. In R. Brown, *Psycholinguistics* (pp. 208–34). New York: Free Press.

Brown, R. (1973). *A first language, the early stages.* Cambridge, MA: Harvard University Press.

Brown, R., & Bellugi, U. (1964). Three processes in the child's acquisition of syntax. *Harvard Educational Review, 34,* 133–51.

Brown, R., Cazden, C., & Bellugi, U. (1969). The child's grammar from I to III. In J. Hill (Ed.), *Minnesota symposia on child psychology* (vol. 2, pp. 28–73). Minneapolis: University of Minnesota Press.

Brown, R., & Fraser, C. (1963). The acquisition of syntax. In C. Cofer & B. Musgrave (Eds.), *Verbal behavior and verbal learning: Problems and processes* (pp. 158–97). New York: McGraw-Hill.

Brown, R., & Hanlon, C. (1970). Derivational complexity and order of acquisition in child speech. In J. Hayes (Ed.), *Cognition and the development of language* (pp. 11–53). New York: Wiley.

Bruner, J. (1975). The ontogenesis of speech acts. *Journal of Child Language, 2,* 1–19.

Bull, W. (1960). *Time, tense, and the verb: A study in theoretical and applied linguistics, with particular attention to Spanish.* Berkeley and Los Angeles: University of California Press.

Bullock, M., & Gelman, R. (1979). Preschool children's assumptions about cause and effect: Temporal ordering. *Child Development, 50,* 89–96.

Bullock, M., & Gelman, R., & Baillargeon, R. (1982). The development of causal reasoning. In W. Friedman (Ed.), *The developmental psychology of time* (pp. 209–53). New York: Academic Press.

Burling, R. (1959). Language development of a Garo and English speaking child. *Word, 15,* 45–68.

Carey, S. (1985). *Conceptual change in childhood.* Cambridge, MA: MIT Press.

Case, R. (1978). Intellectual development from birth to adulthood: A neo-Piagetian interpretation. In R. Siegler (Ed.), *Children's thinking: What develops?* (pp. 37–72). Hillsdale, NJ: Erlbaum.

Case, R. (1985). *Intellectual development: Birth to adulthood.* Toronto: Academic Press.

Cazden, C. (1968). The acquisition of noun and verb inflections. *Child Development, 39,* 433–8.

Cedergren, H., & Sankoff, D. (1974). Variable rules: Performance as a statistical reflection of competence. *Language, 50,* 333–55.

Chafe, W. (1971). *Meaning and the structure of language.* Chicago: University of Chicago Press.

Chafe, W. (1986). Evidentiality in English conversation and academic writing. In W. Chafe & J. Nichols (Eds.), *Evidentiality: The linguistic coding of epistemology* (pp. 261–72). Norwood, NJ: Ablex.

Choi, S. (1986). Pragmatic analysis of Korean modal markers in children's speech. Paper presented to the Annual Meeting of the Linguistic Society of America, New York.

Chomsky, N. (1957). *Syntactic structures*. The Hague: Mouton.

Chomsky, N. (1959). Review of B. F. Skinner, *Verbal behavior*. *Language, 35*, 26–58.

Chomsky, N. (1965). *Aspects of the theory of syntax*. Cambridge, MA: MIT Press.

Chomsky, N. (1968). *Language and mind*. New York: Harcourt, Brace, & World.

Chomsky, N. (1982). *Some concepts and consequences of the theory of government and binding*. Cambridge, MA: MIT Press.

Clancy, P., Jacobsen, T., & Silva, M. (1976). The acquisition of conjunction: A cross-linguistic study. *Papers and reports on child language development* (No. 12, December, pp. 71–80). Department of Linguistics, Stanford University.

Clark, E. (1970). How young children describe events in time. In G. Flores d'Arcais & W. Levelt (Eds.), *Advances in psycholinguistics* (pp. 275–84). New York: American Elsevier.

Clark, E. (1973a). How children describe time and order. In C. Ferguson & D. Slobin (Eds.), *Studies of child language development* (pp. 585–606). New York: Holt, Rinehart & Winston.

Clark, E. (1973b). Non-linguistic strategies and the acquisition of word meanings. *Cognition, 2*, 161–82.

Clark, E. (1973c) What's in a word? On the child's acquisition of semantics in his first language. In T. Moore (Ed.), *Cognitive development and the acquisition of language* (pp. 65–110). New York: Academic Press.

Clark, E. (1978). Strategies for communicating. *Child Development, 49*, 953–9.

Clark, E., & Garnica, O. (1974). Is he coming or going? On the acquisition of deictic verbs. *Journal of Verbal Learning and Verbal Behavior, 13*, 559–72.

Clark, R. (1974). Performing without competence. *Journal of Child Language, 1*, 1–10.

Comrie, B. (1976). *Aspect*. Cambridge: Cambridge University Press.

Corrigan, R. (1975). A scalogram analysis of the development of the use and comprehension of "because" in children. *Child Development, 46*, 195–201.

Danto, A. (1983). Towards a retentive materialism. In L. Cauman, I. Levi,

C. Parsons, & R. Schwartz (Eds.), *How many questions? Essays in honor of Sidney Morgenbesser* (pp. 243–55). Indianapolis: Hackett.

Davis, E. (1932). The form and function of children's questions. *Child Development, 3*, 57–74.

de Laguna, G. (1927/1963). *Speech: Its function and development.* Bloomington: Indiana University Press.

de Villiers, J., & de Villiers, P. (1973). A cross-sectional study of the acquisition of grammatical morphemes. *Journal of Psycholinguistic Research, 2*, 267–78.

de Villiers, J., & de Villiers, P. (1974). Competence and performance in child language: Are children really competent to judge? *Journal of Child Language, 1*, 11–22.

de Villiers, J., Tager-Flusberg, H., & Hakuta K. (1977). Deciding among theories of the development of coordination in child speech. *Papers and reports on child language development* (No. 13, pp. 118–25). Department of Linguistics, Stanford University.

de Villiers, P., & de Villiers, J. (1979). Form and function in the development of sentence negation. *Papers and reports on child language development* (No. 17, August, pp. 57–64). Department of Linguistics, Stanford University.

Dittman, A. (1972). Developmental factors in conversational behavior. *Journal of Communication, 22*, 404–23.

Dixon, T., & Horton, D. (1968). *Verbal behavior and general behavior theory.* Englewood Cliffs, NJ: Prentice-Hall.

Dore, J. (1973). The development of speech acts. Ph.D. diss., City University of New York.

Dore, J. (1975). Holophrases, speech acts, and language universals. *Journal of Child Language, 2*, 21–40.

Dowty, D. (1972). Studies in the logic of verb aspect and time reference in English. Ph.D. diss., University of Texas, Austin.

Ducasse, C. (1924/1969). *Causation and the types of necessity.* New York: Dover.

Ervin-Tripp, S. (1964). Imitation and structural change in children's language. In E. Lenneberg (Ed.), *New directions in the study of language* (pp. 163–89). Cambridge MA: MIT Press.

Ervin-Tripp, S. (1970). Discourse agreement: How children answer questions. In J. Hayes (Ed.), *Cognition and the development of language* (pp. 79–107). New York: Wiley.

Fahey, G. (1942). The questioning activity of children. *Journal of Genetic Psychology, 60*, 337–57.

Fauconnier, G. (1985). *Mental spaces: Aspects of meaning construction in natural language.* Cambridge, MA: MIT Press.

Fay, T. (1980). Transformational errors. In V. Fromkin (Ed.), *Errors in lin-*

guistic performance: Slips of the tongue, ear, pen and hand (pp. 111–22). New York: Academic Press.

Felix, S. (1976). *Wh*-pronouns and second language acquisition. *Linguistische Berichte, 44,* 52–64.

Ferguson, C. (1964). Baby talk in six languages. *American Anthropologist, 66,* 103–14.

Ferguson, C., & Farwell, C. (1975). Words and sounds in early language acquisition. *Language, 51,* 419–39.

Ferguson, C., Peizer, D., & Weeks, T. (1973). Model-and-replica phonological grammar of a child's first words. *Lingua, 31,* 35–9.

Ferreiro, E., & Sinclair, H. (1971). Temporal relationships in language. *International Journal of Psychology, 6,* 39–47.

Fillmore, C. (1968). The case for case. In E. Bach & R. Harms (Eds.), *Universals in linguistic theory* (pp. 1–90). New York: Holt, Rinehart & Winston.

Fillmore, C. (1971, 1973). Deixis, I. Unpublished lectures.

Fillmore, C. (1971). Verbs of judging: An exercise in semantic descriptions. In C. Fillmore & D. Langendoen (Eds.), *Studies in linguistic semantics* (pp. 273–89). New York: Holt, Rinehart, and Winston.

Fillmore, C. (1977), Topics in lexical semantics. In R. Cole (Ed.), *Current issues in linguistic theory* (pp. 76–138). Bloomington: Indiana University Press.

Fisher, R. (1967). *Statistical methods for research workers.* New York: Hatner.

Flavell, J. (1968). *The development of role-taking skills in children.* New York: Wiley.

Flavell, J. (1978). The development of knowledge about visual perception. In C. Keasey (Ed.), *Nebraska symposium on motivation 1977: Social cognitive development* (vol. 25, pp. 43–76). Lincoln: University of Nebraska Press.

Fodor, J. (1983). *The modularity of mind.* Cambridge, MA: MIT Press.

Fodor, J., Garrett, M., & Bever, T. (1968). Some syntactic determinants of complexity, II: Verb structure. *Perception and Psychophysics, 3,* 453–61.

Foley, W., & Van Valin, R. (1984). *Functional syntax and universal grammar.* Cambridge: Cambridge University Press.

Fraser, C., Bellugi, U., & Brown, R. (1963). Control of grammar in imitation, comprehension and production. *Journal of Verbal Learning and Verbal Behavior, 2,* 121–35.

Freeman, N. (1989). Review of *Mechanisms of language acquisition* (B. MacWhinney, Ed.). *Journal of Child Language, 16,* 470–5.

Friedrich, P. (1974). *On aspect theory and Homeric aspect.* Chicago: University of Chicago Press.

Gardner, H. (1983). *Frames of mind*. New York: Basic Books.

Garvey, C. (1974). Some properties of social play. *Merrill–Palmer Quarterly, 20,* 163–80.

Garvey, C., & Hogan, R. (1973). Social speech and social inter-action: Egocentrism revisited. *Child Development, 44,* 562–8.

Gelman, R. (1978). Cognitive development. In M. Rosenzweig & L. Porter (Eds.), *Annual Review of Psychology, 29,* 297–332.

Gelman, R., & Meck, E. (1987). The notion of principle: The case of counting. In J. Hiebert (Ed.), *Conceptual and procedural knowledge: The case of mathematics* (pp. 29–57). Hillsdale, NJ: Erlbaum.

Gentner, D. (1978). On relational meaning: The acquisition of verb meaning. *Child Development, 49,* 988–98.

Gleitman, L. (1965). Coordinating conjunctions in English. *Language, 41,* 260–93.

Gleitman, L., Gleitman, H., Landau, B., & Wanner, E. (1988). Where learning begins: Initial representations for language learning. In F. Newmeyer (Ed.), *Linguistics: The Cambridge survey*. Vol. 3, *Language: Perspectives and biological aspects* (pp. 150–93). Cambridge: Cambridge University Press.

Glucksberg, S., Krauss, R., & Higgins, E. (1975). The development of referential communication skills. In F. Horowitz (Ed.), *Review of child development research* (vol. 4, pp. 305–45). Chicago: University of Chicago Press.

Gold, E. (1967). Language identification in the limit. *Information and Control, 10,* 447–74.

Golinkoff, R. (1981). The case for semantic relations: Evidence from the verbal and nonverbal domains. *Journal of Child Language, 8,* 413–37.

Golinkoff, R., Carlson, V., Gibson, E., Harding, C., Sexton, M., Uzgiris, I., & Watson, J. (1984). The development of causality in infants: A symposium. In L. Lipsitt & C. Rovee-Collier (Eds.), *Advances in infancy research* (vol. 3, pp. 125–65). New York: Ablex.

Gopnik, A., & Meltzoff, A. (1984). Semantic and cognitive development in 15- to 21-month-old children. *Journal of Child Language, 11,* 495–513.

Gopnik, A., & Meltzoff, A. (1987). The development of categorization in the second year and its relation to other cognitive and linguistic developments. *Child Development, 58,* 1523–31.

Greenfield, P., Nelson, K., & Saltzman, E. (1972). The development of rulebound strategies for manipulating seriated cups: A parallel between action and grammar. *Cognitive Psychology, 3,* 291–310.

Greenfield, P., & Smith, J. (1976). *The semantics of communication in early language development*. New York: Academic Press (Originally cited as Greenfield, P., Smith, J., & Laufer, B., 1972). Communication and the beginnings of language. Unpublished manuscript).

Grimshaw, J. (1981). Form, function, and the language acquisition device. In C. Baker & J. McCarthy (Eds.), *The logical problem of language acquisition* (pp. 165–82). Cambridge, MA: MIT Press.

Gruber, J. (1965). Studies in lexical relations. Ph.D. diss., Massachusetts Institute of Technology.

Gruber, H., & Vonèche, J. (1977). *The essential Piaget*. New York: Basic Books.

Guillaume, P. (1926/1968). *Imitation in children*. Chicago: University of Chicago Press.

Halliday, M., & Hasan, R. (1976). *Cohesion in English*. London: Longman Group (English Language Series).

Harner, L. (1981). Children talk about the time and aspect of actions. *Child Development, 52,* 498–506.

Harris, M. (1964). *The nature of cultural things*. New York: Random House.

Harris, Z. (1957). Cooccurrence and transformations in linguistic structure. *Language, 33,* 283–340.

Harris, Z. (1964). Discourse analysis. In J. Fodor & J. Katz (Eds.), *The structure of language* (pp. 355–83). Englewood Cliffs, NJ: Prentice-Hall. (Originally published in 1952)

Hart, H., & Honoré, A. (1959). *Causation and the law*. Oxford: Oxford University Press.

Harvard University, Staff of the Computation Laboratory (1955). *Tables of the cumulative binomial probability distribution*. Cambridge, MA: Harvard University Press.

Hood, L. (1972). Comprehension and production of causal and temporal conjunctions. Unpublished manuscript.

Hood, L. (1977). A longitudinal study of the development of the expression of causal relations in complex sentences. Ph.D. diss., Columbia University.

Hood, L., & Bloom, L. (1979). *What, when, and how about why: A longitudinal study of early expressions of causality*. Monographs of the Society for Research in Child Development, 44 (serial no. 6).

Hood, L., Fiess, K., & Aron, J. (1982). Growing up explained: Vygotskians look at the language of causality. In C. Brainerd & M. Pressky (Eds.), *Verbal processes in children* (pp. 268–85). Berlin: Springer-Verlag.

Hood, L., Lahey, M., Lifter, K., & Bloom, L. (1978). Observational descriptive methodology in studying child language: Preliminary results on the development of complex sentences. In G. Sackett (Ed.), *Observing behavior. Vol. 1: Theory and applications in mental retardation* (pp. 239–63). Baltimore: University Park Press.

Hood, L., & Mansfield, A. (1971). The linguistic expression of causality in the child. Unpublished manuscript.

Howe, C. (1976). The meanings of two-word utterances in the speech of young children. *Journal of Child Language, 3,* 29–47.

Hume, D. (1739/1809). *A treatise of human nature*. In T. Green & T. Grose (Eds.), *The philosophical works,* (vol. 1). London: Longmans.

Huttenlocher, J. (1974). The origins of language comprehension. In R. Solso (Ed.), *Theories in cognitive psychology* (pp. 331–68). New York: Halsted.

Huxley, R. (1970). The development of the correct use of subject personal pronouns in two children. In G. Flores d'Arcais & W. Levelt (Eds.), *Advances in psycholinguistics* (pp. 141–65). New York: American Elsevier.

Hyams, N. (1984). The acquisition of infinitival complements: A reply to Bloom, Tackeff, & Lahey. *Journal of Child Language, 11,* 679–83.

Hyams, N. (1986). *Language acquisition and the theory of parameters*. Dordrecht: Reidel.

Hymes, D. (Ed.) (1964). *Language in culture and society*. New York: Harper & Row.

Ingram, D. (1971). Transitivity in child language. *Language, 47,* 888–910.

Inhelder, B., & Piaget, J. (1959/1964). *The early growth of logic in the child*. New York: Norton.

Issacs, N. (1930). Appendix on children's "why" questions. In S. Issacs (Ed.), *Intellectual growth in young children* (pp. 291–349). New York: Harcourt.

Jackendoff, R. (1972). *Semantic interpretation in generative grammar*. Cambridge, MA: MIT Press.

Jackendoff, R. (1983). *Semantics and cognition*. Cambridge, MA: MIT Press.

Jackendoff, R. (1987). *Consciousness and the computational mind*. Cambridge, MA: MIT Press.

Jakobson, R. (1941/1968). *Child language, aphasia and phonological universals*. The Hague: Mouton.

Jakobson, R. (1957/1971). *Shifters, verbal categories and the Russian verb*. In *Selected writings* (vol. 2, pp. 130–47). The Hague: Mouton.

Janota, P. (1972). Development of children's vocabulary. In K. Ohnesorg (Ed.), *Colloquium paedolinguisticum, proceedings of the First International Symposium of Paedolinguistics, at Brno,* 1970. The Hague: Mouton.

Jenkins, J., & Palermo, D. (1964). Mediation processes and the acquisition of linguistic structure. In U. Bellugi & R. Brown (Eds.), *The acquisition of language*. Monographs of the Society for Research in Child Development, 29 (serial no. 92).

Jespersen, O. (1917). *Negation in English and other languages*. Copenhagen: Royal Danish Academy.

Jespersen, O. (1922). *Language: Its nature, development, and origin*. London: Allen & Unwin.

Jespersen, O. (1961). *A modern English grammar on historical principles* (vols. 1–7). London: Allen & Unwin. (Originally published between 1909 and 1949)

Jespersen, O. (1964). *Essentials of English grammar*. Tuscaloosa: University of Alabama Press.

Johnson, C. (1982). Acquisition of mental verbs and the concept of mind. In S. Kuczaj (Ed.), *Language development* (vol. 1, pp. 445–78). Hillsdale, NJ: Erlbaum.

Johnson, C., & Maratsos, M. (1977). Early comprehension of mental verbs: *think* and *know*. *Child Development, 48*, 1743–7.

Johnson, H. (1972). The child's understanding of causal connectives. Ph.D. diss., University of Wisconsin.

Joos, M. (1958). English language and linguistics. Mimeographed edition, Beograd: Institute for Experimental Phonetics (cited in Allen, 1966).

Kant, I. (1781/1965). *Critique of pure reason*. New York: Macmillan.

Kates, C. (1974). A descriptive approach to linguistic meaning. Unpublished manuscript.

Katz, E., & Brent, S. (1968). Understanding connectives. *Journal of Verbal Learning and Verbal Behavior, 7*, 501–9.

Keenan (Ochs), E. (1974a). Again and again: The pragmatics of imitation in child language. Paper presented to the Annual Meetings of the American Anthropological Association, Mexico City.

Keenan (Ochs), E. (1974b). Conversational competence in children. *Journal of Child Language, 1*, 163–83.

Kelly, C., & Dale, P. (1989). Cognitive skills associated with the onset of multiword utterances. *Journal of Speech and Hearing Research, 32*, 645–56.

Kemp, J., & Dale, P. (1973). Spontaneous imitation and free speech: A developmental comparison. Paper presented to the biennial meeting of the Society for Research in Child Development, Philadelphia.

Kirkpatrick, E. (1909). *Genetic psychology*. New York: Macmillan.

Klima, E. (1964). Negation in English. In J. Fodor & J. Katz (Eds.), *The structure of language* (pp. 246–323). Englewood Cliffs, NJ: Prentice-Hall.

Klima, E., & Bellugi, U. (1966). Syntactic regularities in the speech of children. In J. Lyons & R. Wales (Eds.), *Psycholinguistic papers. Proceedings of the Edinburgh Conference* (pp. 183–208). Edinburgh: Edinburgh University Press.

Knoke, D., & Burke, P. (1980). *Log-linear models*. Beverly Hills, CA: Sage.

Kopp, C. (1989). Regulation of distress and negative emotions: A developmental view. *Developmental Psychology, 25*, 343–54.

Koster, J., & May, R. (1982). On the constituency of infinitives. *Language, 58*, 116–43.

Kuczaj, S. (1977). The acquisition of regular and irregular past tense forms. *Journal of Verbal Learning and Verbal Behavior, 16*, 589–600.

Kuhn, D., & Phelps, H. (1976). The development of children's comprehension of causal direction. *Child Development, 47*, 248–51.

Kun, A. (1978). Evidence for preschoolers' understanding of causal direction in causal sequences. *Child Development, 49,* 218–22.

Labov, W. (1963). The social motivation of sound change. *Word, 19,* 273–309.

Labov, W. (1969). Contraction, deletion, and inherent variability of the English copula. *Language, 45,* 715–62.

Labov, W. (1972). Rules for ritual insults. In W. Labov, *Language in the inner city: Studies in the black English vernacular* (pp. 297–353). Philadelphia: University of Pennsylvania Press.

Labov, W., & Labov, T. (1976). Learning the syntax of questions. In R. Campbell & P. Smith (Eds.), *Recent advances in the psychology of language: Formal and semantic approaches* (pp. 1–44). New York: Plenum.

Lahey, M., & Feier, C. (1982). The semantics of verbs in language development and language dissolution. *Journal of Speech and Hearing Research, 25,* 81–95.

Lakoff, G. (1966). Stative adjectives and verbs in English (NSF Report no. 17). Cambridge, MA: Computational Laboratory, Harvard University.

Landau, B., & Gleitman, L. (1985). *Language and experience: Evidence from the blind child.* Cambridge, MA: Harvard University Press.

Laurendeau, M., & Pinard, A. (1962). *Causal thinking in children.* New York: International Universities Press.

Lawler, J. (1972). Generic to a fault. *Chicago Linguistics Society, 8,* 247–58.

Leech, G. (1970). *Towards a semantic description of English.* Bloomington: Indiana University Press.

Leonard, L. (1976). *Meaning in child language.* New York: Grune & Stratton.

Leonard, L. (1989). Language learnability and specific language impairment in children. *Applied Psycholinguistics, 10,* 172–202.

Leopold, W. (1939–1949). *Speech development of a bilingual child* (4 vols.). Evanston, IL: Northwestern University Press.

Lerner, R. (1986). *Concepts and theories of human development.* New York: Random House.

Levin, B. (1985). Lexical semantics in review: An introduction. In B. Levin (Ed.), *Lexical semantics in review. Lexical Project Working Papers 1.* Cambridge, MA: MIT Center for Cognitive Science.

Lewis, M. M. (1938). The beginning and early functions of questions in a child's speech. *British Journal of Educational Psychology, 8,* 150–71.

Lewis, M. M. (1951). *Infant speech, a study of the beginnings of language.* New York: Humanities Press.

Lifter, K., & Bloom, L. (1989). Object play and the emergence of language. *Infant Behavior and Development, 12,* 395–423.

Lightbown, P. (1973). Nominal and pronominal forms in the speech of three French-speaking children. A pilot study. Ph.D. diss. proposal, Teachers College, Columbia University.

Lightbown, P. (1978). Question form and question function in the speech of young French L$_2$ learners. In M. Paradis (Ed.), *Aspects of bilingualism* (pp. 21–43). Columbia, SC: Hornbeam.

Limber, J. (1973). The genesis of complex sentences. In T. Moore (Ed.), *Cognitive development and the acquisition of language* (pp. 169–85). New York: Academic Press.

Lucas, J. (1962). Causation. In R. Butler (Ed.), *Analytical philosophy* (pp. 32–65). New York: Barnes & Noble.

Lust, B. (1976). Conjunction reduction in the language of young children. Paper presented at the Second Annual Boston University Conference on Language Development.

Lust, B., & Mervis, C. (1980). Development of coordination in the natural speech of young children. *Journal of Child Language, 7,* 279–304.

Lyons, J. (1968). *Introduction to theoretical linguistics*. Cambridge: Cambridge University Press.

Macaulay, R. (1971). Aspect in English. Ph.D. diss., University of California, Los Angeles.

MacMurray, J. (1957). *Self as agent*. London: Farber & Farber.

MacNamara, J. (1972). Cognitive bases of language learning in infants. *Psychological Review, 79,* 1–13.

MacWhinney, B. (Ed.) (1987). *Mechanisms of language acquisition*. Hillsdale, NJ: Erlbaum.

Maratsos, M. (1971). The use of definite and indefinite reference in young children. Ph.D. diss., Harvard University.

Maratsos, M., & Chalkley, M. (1980). The internal language of children's syntax: The ontogenesis and representation of syntactic categories. In K. Nelson (Ed.), *Children's language* (vol. 2, pp. 127–214). New York: Gardner Press.

Maratsos, M., & Kuczaj, S. (1974). Evidence from elicited imitation for preproductive competence in a grammatical system. *Papers and reports on child language development* (No. 7, pp. 65–77). Department of Linguistics, Stanford University.

Masur, E. (1982). Mothers' responses to infants' object-related gestures: Influences on lexical development. *Journal of Child Language, 9,* 23–30.

McCarthy, D. (1930). *The language development of the preschool child*. Institute of Child Welfare Monograph Series, no. 4. Minneapolis: University of Minnesota Press.

McCuhn-Nicolich, L. (1981). The cognitive basis of relational words in the single word period. *Journal of Child Language, 8,* 15–34.

McNeill, D. (1966). Developmental psycholinguistics. In F. Smith & G. Miller (Eds.), *The genesis of language: A psycholinguistic approach* (pp. 15–184). Cambridge, MA: MIT Press.

McNeill, D. (1970). *The acquisition of language: The study of developmental psycholinguistics*. New York: Harper & Row.

McNeill, D. (1975). Semiotic extension. In L. Solso (Ed.), *Information processing and cognition – The Loyola symposium* (pp. 351–80). Hillsdale, NJ: Erlbaum.

McNeill, D., & McNeill, N. (1968). What does a child mean when he says "no"? In E. Zale (Ed.), *Proceedings of the conference on language and language behavior* (pp. 51–62). New York: Appleton-Century-Crofts. Also (1967) paper presented to the biennial meeting of the Society for Research in Child Development, New York.

Melton, A., & Martin, E. (1972). *Coding processes in human memory*. New York: Wiley.

Menyuk, P. (1963). A preliminary evaluation of grammatical capacity in children. *Journal of Verbal Learning and Verbal Behavior, 2,* 429–39.

Menyuk, P. (1969). *Sentences children use*. Cambridge, MA: MIT Press.

Mervis, C. (1984) Early lexical development. The contributions of mother and child. In C. Sophian (Ed.), *Origins of cognitive skills* (pp. 339–70). Hillsdale, NJ: Erlbaum.

Meumann, E. (1903). *Die sprache des kindes*. Zurich: Zürcher & Furrer.

Miller, G. (1972). English verbs of motion: A case study in semantic and lexical memory. In A. Melton & E. Martin (Eds.), *Coding processes in human memory* (pp. 335–72). New York: Wiley.

Miller, G., & Johnson-Laird, P. (1976). *Language and perception*. Cambridge, MA: Harvard University Press.

Miller, W., & Ervin, S. (1964). The development of grammar in child language. In U. Bellugi & R. Brown (Eds.), *The acquisition of language,* Monographs of the Society for Research in Child Development, 29 (serial no. 92).

Miyamoto, J. (1973). Imitation and the learning of grammatical rules. In *Papers from the ninth regional meeting* (pp. 398–409). Chicago: Chicago Linguistics Society.

Moerk, E. (1975). Verbal interactions between children and their mothers during the preschool years. *Developmental Psychology, 11,* 788–94.

Morehead, D., & Ingram, D. (1973). The development of base syntax in normal and linguistically deviant children. *Journal of Speech and Hearing Research, 16,* 330–52.

Morgan, J. (1986), *From simple input to complex grammar*. Cambridge, MA: MIT Press.

Morris, C. (1964). *Signification and significance*. Cambridge, MA: MIT Press.

Mowrer, O. (1960). *Learning theory and the symbolic process*. New York: Wiley.

Nelson, K. (1973). *Structure and strategy in learning to talk*. Monographs of the Society for Research in Child Development, 38 (serial no. 149).

Nelson, K. (1974). Concept, word and sentence: Interrelations in acquisition and development, *Psychological Review, 81*, 267–85.

Nelson, K. (1975a). Individual differences in early semantic and syntactic development. In D. Aronson & R. Rieber (Eds.), *Developmental psycholinguistics and communication disorders* (pp. 132–39). New York: New York Academy of Sciences.

Nelson, K. (1975b). The nominal shift in semantic–syntactic development. *Cognitive Psychology, 7*, 461–79.

Nelson, K. (1985). *Making sense: The acquisition of shared meaning*. New York: Academic Press.

Nishigauchi, T., & Roeper, T. (1987). Deductive parameters and the growth of empty categories. In T. Roeper & E. Williams (Eds.), *Parameter setting* (pp. 91–121). Dordrecht: Reidel.

Ochs, E. (1988). *Culture and language development: Language acquisition and language socialization in a Samoan village*. Cambridge: Cambridge University Press.

Ochs, E., & Schieffelin, B. (1983). *Acquiring conversational competence*. London: Routledge & Kegan Paul.

Ochs, E., Schieffelin, B., & Platt, M. (1979). Propositions across utterances and speakers. In E. Ochs & B. Schieffelin (Eds.), *Developmental pragmatics* (pp. 251–68). New York: Academic Press.

O'Grady, W., Peters, A., & Masterson, D. (1989). The transition from optional to required subjects. *Journal of Child Language, 16*, 513–29.

Olson, G. (1973). Developmental changes in memory and the acquisition of language. In T. Moore (Ed.), *Cognitive development and the acquisition of language* (pp. 145–57). New York: Academic Press.

Parisi, D. (1974). What is behind child utterances? *Journal of Child Language, 1*, 97–105.

Park, T. (1970). The acquisition of German syntax. Working paper, University of Muenster.

Park, T. (1974). A study of German language development. Unpublished manuscript, Psychological Institute, Berne.

Park, T. (1979). Some facts on negation: Wode's four-stage development of negation revisited. *Journal of Child Language, 6*, 147–51.

Pascual-Leone, J. (1987). Organismic processes for neo-Piagetian theories: A dialectical causal account of cognitive development. *International Journal of Psychology, 22*, 531–70.

Pavlovitch, M. (1920). *Le langage enfantin: Acquisition du serbe et du français par un enfant serbe*. Paris: Champion.

Pea, R. (1980). The development of negation in early child language. In D. Olson (Ed.), *The social foundations of language and thought* (pp. 156–86). New York: Norton.

Pea, R. (1982). Origins of verbal logic: Spontaneous denials by 2- and 3-year olds. *Journal of Child Language, 9*, 597–626.

Pepper, S. (1942). *World hypotheses: A study in evidence.* Berkeley and Los Angeles: University of California Press.

Peters, A. (1977). Language learning strategies: Does the whole equal the sum of the parts? *Language, 53*, 560–73.

Phillips, J. (1973). Syntax and vocabulary of mothers' speech to young children: Age and sex comparisons. *Child Development, 44*, 182–5.

Piaget, J. (1923/1955). *The language and thought of the child.* London: Kegan Paul.

Piaget, J. (1924/1968) *Judgment and reasoning in the child.* Totowa, NJ: Littlefield, Adams.

Piaget, J. (1930/1972). *The child's conception of physical causality.* Totowa, NJ: Littlefield, Adams.

Piaget, J. (1936/1952). *The origins of intelligence in children.* New York: International Universities Press.

Piaget, J. (1937/1954). *The construction of reality in the child.* New York: Basic Books.

Piaget, J. (1947/1960). *Psychology of intelligence.* Paterson, NJ: Littlefield, Adams.

Piaget, J. (1951/1962). *Play, dreams and imitation in childhood.* New York: Norton.

Piaget, J. (1971/1974). *Understanding causality.* New York: Norton.

Piattelli-Palmarini, M. (Ed.) (1980). *Language and learning: The debate between Jean Piaget and Noam Chomsky.* Cambridge, MA: Harvard University Press.

Pinker, S. (1984). *Language learnability and language development.* Cambridge, MA: Harvard University Press.

Pinker, S. (1989). *Learnability and cognition: The acquisition of argument structure.* Cambridge, MA: MIT Press.

Preyer, W. (1882/1971). History of the development of speech, excerpt from *Die sprache des kindes.* In A. Bar-Adon & W. Leopold (Eds.), *Child language: A book of readings* (pp. 29–31). Englewood Cliffs, NJ: Prentice-Hall.

Pylshyn, Z., & Demopoulos, W. (Eds.) (1986). *Meaning and cognitive structure: Issues in the computational theory of mind.* Norwood, NJ: Ablex.

Quirk, R., Greenbaum, S., Leech, G., & Svartvik, J. (1972). *A grammar of contemporary English.* London: Longman Group.

Radulovic, L. (1975). Acquisition of language: Studies of Dubrovnik children. Ph.D. diss., University of California, Berkeley.

Ramer, A. (1976). Syntactic styles in emerging language. *Journal of Child Language, 3,* 49–62.

Reese, H., & Overton, W. (1970). Models of development and theories of development. In R. Goulet & P. Baltes (Eds.), *Life-span developmental psychology: Research and theory* (pp. 116–45). New York: Academic Press.

Rodd, L., & Braine, M. (1971). Children's imitations of syntactic constructions as a measure of linguistic competence. *Journal of Verbal Learning and Verbal Behavior, 10,* 430–43.

Rosenbaum, P. (1967). *The grammar of English predicate complement constructions.* Cambridge, MA: MIT Press.

Ryan, J. (1973). Interpretation and imitation in early language development. In R. Hinde & J. Stevenson-Hinde (Eds.), *Constraints on learning* (pp. 427–43). New York: Academic Press.

Ryle, G. (1949). *The concept of mind.* New York: Barnes & Noble.

Sankoff, G. (1974). A quantitative paradigm for the study of communicative competence. In R. Bauman & J. Sherzer (Eds.), *Explorations in the ethnography of speaking* (pp. 18–49). Cambridge: Cambridge University Press.

Sankoff, G., & Cedergren, H. (1971). Some results of a sociolinguistic study of Montreal French. In R. Darnell (Ed.), *Linguistic diversity in Canadian society* (pp. 61–87). Edmonton: Linguistic Research.

Sankoff, G., & Laberge, S. (1973). On the acquisition of native speakers by a language. *Kivung* [Journal of Linguistic Society in Papuan New Guinea] *6,* 32–47.

Sapir, E. (1921). *Language.* New York: Harcourt Brace.

Schaerlaekens, A. (1973). A generative transformational model for language acquisition: A discussion of L. Bloom, *Language development: Form and function in emerging grammars. Cognition, 2,* 371–6.

Schegeloff, E. (1972). Notes on a conversational practice: Formulating place. In D. Sudnow (Ed.), *Studies in social interaction* (pp. 75–119). New York: Free Press.

Schieffelin, B. (1979). How Kaluli children learn what to say, what to do, and how to feel: An ethnographic study of the development of communicative competence. Ph.D. diss., Columbia University.

Schieffelin, B. (1990). *The give and take of everyday life.* Cambridge: Cambridge University Press.

Schieffelin, B., & Ochs, E. (1983). A cultural perspective on the transition from prelinguistic to linguistic communication. In R. Golinkoff (Ed.), *The transition from prelinguistic to linguistic communication* (pp. 115–32). Hillsdale, NJ: Erlbaum.

Schieffelin, B., & Ochs, E. (Eds.) (1986). *Language socialization across cultures.* Cambridge: Cambridge University Press.

Schlesinger, I. (1971a). Learning grammar: From pivot to realization rule. In R. Huxley & E. Ingram (Eds.), *Language acquisition* (pp. 79–89). New York: Academic Press.

Schlesinger, I. (1971b). Production of utterances and language acquisition. In D. Slobin (Ed.), *The ontogenesis of grammar* (pp. 63–101). New York: Academic Press.

Schlesinger, I. (1974). Relational concepts underlying language. In R. Schiefelbusch & L. Lloyd (Eds.), *Language perspectives – Acquisition, retardation and intervention* (pp. 129–51). Baltimore: University Park Press.

Searle, J. (1983). *Intentionality: An essay in the philosophy of mind.* Cambridge: Cambridge University Press.

Sedlak, A., & Kurtz, S. (1981). A review of children's use of causal inference principles. *Child Development, 52,* 759–84.

Seitz, S., & Stewart, C. (1975). Imitations and expansions: Some developmental aspects of mother–child communication. *Developmental Psychology, 11,* 763–68.

Shapiro, T., Roberts, A., & Fish, B. (1970). Imitation and echoing in young schizophrenic children. *Journal of the American Academy of Child Psychiatry, 9,* 421–39.

Shatz, M. (1978). The relationship between cognitive processes and the development of communication skills. In C. Keasey (Ed.), *Nebraska symposium on motivation 1977: Social cognitive development* (vol. 25, pp. 1–42). Lincoln: University of Nebraska Press.

Shatz, M. (1982). On mechanisms of language acquisition: Can features of the communicative environment account for development? In E. Wanner & L. Gleitman (Eds.), *Language acquisition: The state of the art* (pp. 102–27). Cambridge: Cambridge University Press.

Shatz, M. (1983). Communication. In J. Flavell & E. Markman (Eds.) & P. Mussen (Series Ed.), *Handbook of child psychology: Vol. 3: Cognitive development* (pp. 841–90). New York: Wiley.

Shatz, M., Wellman, H., & Silber, S. (1983). The acquisition of mental verbs: A systematic investigation of the first reference to mental state. *Cognition, 14,* 301–21.

Shibatani, M. (Ed.) (1976). *Syntax and semantics VI: The grammar of causative constructions.* New York: Academic Press.

Shipley, E., Smith, C., & Gleitman, L. (1969). A study in the acquisition of language: Free responses to commands. *Language, 45,* 322–42.

Shultz, T. (1982). *Rules of causal attribution.* Monographs of the Society for Research in Child Development, 47 (serial no. 194).

Siegel, G. (1963). Adult verbal behavior in "play therapy" sessions with retarded children. *Journal of Speech and Hearing Disorders* (Monograph Supplement no. 10).

Sinclair, H. (1970). The transition from sensory-motor behavior to symbolic activity. *Interchange, 1*, 119–26.

Sinclair, H. (1971). Sensorimotor action patterns as a condition for the acquisition of syntax. In R. Huxley & E. Ingram (Eds.), *Language acquisition: Models and methods* (pp. 121–30). New York: Academic Press.

Sinclair, H. (1973). Some remarks on the Genevan point of view on learning with special reference to language learning. In R. Hinde & J. Stevenson-Hinde (Eds.), *Constraints on learning* (pp. 397–415). New York: Academic Press.

Slobin, D. (1966). Comments on developmental psycholinguistics. In F. Smith & G. Miller (Eds.), *The genesis of language* (pp. 85–91). Cambridge, MA: MIT Press.

Slobin, D. (1968). Imitation and grammatical development in children. In N. Endler, L. Boulter, & H. Osser (Eds.), *Contemporary issues in developmental psychology* (pp. 437–43). New York: Holt, Rinehart & Winston.

Slobin, D. (1971a). Developmental psycholinguistics. In W. Dingwall (Ed.), *A survey of linguistic science* (pp. 267–311). College Park: University of Maryland Press.

Slobin, D. (Ed.) (1971b). *The ontogenesis of grammar: Some facts and several theories.* New York: Academic Press.

Slobin, D. (1973). Cognitive prerequisites for the development of grammar. In C. Ferguson & D. Slobin (Eds.), *Studies of child language development* (pp. 175–208). New York: Holt, Rinehart & Winston.

Slobin, D. (1985). Crosslinguistic evidence for the language-making capacity. In D. Slobin (Ed.), *The crosslinguistic study of language acquisition* (vol. 2, pp. 1157–1256). Hillsdale, NJ: Erlbaum.

Slobin, D., & Welsh, C. (1973). Elicited imitation as a research tool in developmental psycholinguistics. In C. Ferguson & D. Slobin (Eds.), *Studies of child language development* (pp. 485–97). New York: Holt, Rinehart & Winston.

Smith, C. (1970). An experimental approach to children's linguistic competence. In J. Hayes (Ed.), *Cognition and the development of language* (pp. 109–35). New York: Wiley.

Smith, C. (1978). Stages in the acquisition of time talk. Unpublished manuscript.

Smith, F., & Miller, G. (Eds.) (1966). *The genesis of language.* Cambridge, MA: MIT Press.

Smith, M. (1933). The influence of age, sex and situation on the frequency, form and function of questions asked by preschool children. *Child Development, 4*, 201–381.

Snow, C. (1972). Mothers' speech to children learning language. *Child Development, 43*, 549–65.

Söderbergh, R. (1974). *The fruitful dialogue, the child's acquisition of his first language: Implications for education at all stages.* Project Child Language Syntax, Reprint no. 2, Stockholm University, Institution for Nordiska Sprak.

Soskin, W. (1963). *Verbal interaction in a young married couple.* Lawrence: University of Kansas Social Science Studies.

Spelke, E. (1987). The development of intermodal perception. In P. Salapatek & L. Cohen (Eds.), *Handbook of infant perception* (vol. 2, pp. 233–73). Orlando, FL: Academic Press.

Staats, A. (1971). Linguistic–mentalistic theory versus an explanatory S–R learning theory of language development. In D. Slobin (Ed.), *The ontogenesis of grammar* (pp. 103–50). New York: Academic Press.

Stern, D., Jaffe, J., Beebe, B., & Bennett, S. (1975). Vocalizing in unison and in alternation: Two modes of communication within the mother–infant dyad. In D. Aronson & R. Rieber (Eds.), *Developmental psycholinguistics and communication disorders. Annals of the New York Academy of Sciences, 263,* 89–100.

Stockwell, R., Schachter, P., & Partee, B. (1973). *The major syntactic structures of English.* New York: Holt, Rinehart & Winston.

Sullivan, L. (1972). The development of causal connectives by children. *Perceptual and Motor Skills, 35,* 1003–10.

Suppes, P. (1970). Probabilistic grammars for natural languages. *Synthese, 22,* 95–116.

Tager-Flusberg, H., de Villiers, J., & Hakuta, K. (1982). The development of sentence coordination. In S. Kuczaj (Ed.), *Language development: Problems, theories, and controversies* (vol. 1, pp. 201–43). Hillsdale, NJ: Erlbaum.

Taylor, C. (1979). Action as expression. In C. Diamond & J. Teichman (Eds.), *Intentions and intentionality: Essays in honor of G. E. M. Anscombe* (pp. 73–89). Ithaca, NY: Cornell University Press.

Thompson, R. (1990). Emotional self-regulation. In R. Thompson (Ed.), *Socioemotional development. Nebraska symposium on motivation* (vol. 36, pp. 367–467). Lincoln: University of Nebraska Press.

Thorndike, E. (1913). *The original nature of man.* New York: Teachers College, Columbia University Press.

Tomasello, M., & Farrar, M. (1984). Cognitive bases of lexical development: Object permanence and relational words. *Journal of Child Language, 11,* 477–93.

Tomasello, M., & Farrar, J. (1986). Joint attention and early language. *Child Development, 57,* 1454–63.

Trabasso, T., Stein, N., & Johnson, L. (1981). Children's knowledge of events: A causal analysis of story structure. In G. Bower (Ed.), *Learning and motivation* (vol. 15, pp. 237–82). New York: Academic Press.

Traugott, E. (1973). Explorations in linguistic elaboration: Language change, language acquisition, and the genesis of spatio-temporal terms. *First historical conference on historical linguistics,* Edinburgh.

Tronick, E (1972). Stimulus control and the growth of the infant's effective visual field. *Perception and Psychophysics, 11,* 373–6.

Tyack, D., & Ingram, D. (1977). Children's production and comprehension of questions. *Journal of Child Language, 4,* 211–24.

Urmson, S. (1963). Parenthetical verbs. In C. Caton (Ed.), *Philosophy and ordinary language* (pp. 220–40). Urbana: University of Illinois Press.

Valentine, C. (1930). The psychology of imitation with special reference to early childhood. *Journal of Psychology, 21,* 105–32.

Valian V. (1986). Syntactic categories in the speech of young children. *Developmental Psychology, 22,* 562–79.

Van Valin, R. (in press). Functionalist linguistic theory and language acquisition. *First Language.*

Vendler, Z. (1962). Effects, results and consequences. In R. Butler (Ed.), *Analytical philosophy* (pp. 1–15). New York: Barnes & Noble.

Vendler, Z. (1967). *Linguistics and philosophy.* Ithaca, NY: Cornell University Press.

Viberg, Å. (1984). The verbs of perception: A typological study. In B. Butterworth, B. Comrie, & O. Dahl (Eds.), *Explanations for language universals* (pp. 123–49). Berlin: Mouton.

Vosniadou, S. (1974). Strategies in the acquisition of Greek. M.A. Thesis, Teachers College, Columbia University.

Vygotsky, L. (1962). *Thought and language.* Cambridge, MA: MIT Press.

Weissenborn, J., Verrips, M., & Berman, R. (1989). Negation as a window to the structure of early child language. Unpublished manuscript. Max Planck Institute, Nimejgan.

Weist, R., Wysocka, H., Witkowska-Stadnik, K., Buczowska, E., & Konieczna, E. (1984). The defective tense hypothesis: On the emergence of tense and aspect in child Polish. *Journal of Child Language, 11,* 347–74.

Wellman, H. (1985). The child's theory of mind: The development of conceptions of cognition. In S. Yussen (Ed.), *The growth of reflection in children* (pp. 169–206). San Diego: Academic Press.

Werner, H. (1948). *Comparative psychology of mental development.* New York: Science Editions.

Werner, H., & Kaplan, B. (1963). *Symbol formation.* New York: Wiley.

Wexler, K., & Culicover, P. (1980). *Formal principles of language acquisition.* Cambridge, MA: MIT Press.

White, L. (1981). The responsibility of grammatical theory to acquisitional data. In N. Hornstein & D. Lightfoot (Eds.), *Explanation in linguistics* (pp. 241–71). London: Longman Group.

Wode, H. (1977). Four early stages in the development of L_1 negation. *Journal of Child Language, 4,* 87–102.

Wode, H. (1984). Some theoretical implications of L_2 acquisition research and the grammar of interlanguages. In A. Davies, C. Criper, & A. Howatt (Eds.), *Interlanguage* (pp. 162–84). Edinburgh: Edinburgh University Press.

Woisetschlaeger, E. (1976). A semantic theory of the English auxiliary system. Ph.D. diss., Massachusetts Institute of Technology.

Name Index

Abbeduto, L., 329
Abramovitch, R., 374
Ackerman, B., 470
Adams, J., 239
Aksu, A., 233, 236
Aksu-Koc, A., 238
Allen, D., 367, 368, 370
Allen, R., 228
Allport, F., 429
Amerman, J., 256
Angiolillo, C., 82
Anisfeld, M., 36
Antinucci, F., 211, 233, 234, 236n2,
    238
Aron, J., 390
Aronfreed, J., 428
Aronson, D., 85

Bailey, C., 44, 120
Baillargeon, R., 378
Baldwin, A., 437
Baldwin, C., 437
Bamberg, M., 237
Baron, N., 336, 382
Barrett, M., 84, 374
Barten, S., 289
Bassano, D., 288
Bates, E., 26, 34n57, 35n66, 35n73,
    35n82, 81, 84, 239, 261, 284, 287
Bebout, L., 374
Beckwith, R., 20, 33n10, 33n14,
    33n23, 34n46, 34n50, 291, 308,
    309, 332, 392
Bedrosian, J., 471
Beebe, B., 460
Beeghly, M., 324, 374

Beer, C., 382
Behrend, D., 83
Belkin, A., 206n7, 207, 462
Bell, W., 335
Bellugi, U., 19, 125, 144, 146, 147,
    155, 156, 157, 159, 160, 181,
    182, 183, 200, 204, 205, 206,
    206n1, 206n9, 400, 430
Benedict, H., 81
Benigni, L., 35n73
Bennett, S., 460
Bennett-Kastor, T., 83
Berko, J., 211, 234, 235
Berman, R., 83, 206n3, 238
Bever, T., 77, 84, 281, 322, 327
Bialo, N., 256
Blank, M., 82, 367, 368, 370
Bloch, O., 400
Bloom, K., 470
Bloom, L., 32n1, 32n2, 33n9, 33n13,
    33n14, 34n44, 34n48, 34n49,
    34n50, 34n55, 34n56, 34n58,
    35n65, 35n66, 35n73, 35n80,
    35n84, 36n92, 36, 41, 42, 44, 45,
    46, 47, 49, 57, 58, 66, 68, 70, 72,
    74, 75, 80, 81, 82, 88, 89, 91, 92,
    113, 114, 116, 117, 119, 121,
    123, 124, 125, 127, 128, 129,
    130, 133, 136, 137, 140n5, 140n6,
    141, 146, 167, 175, 178, 206,
    206n6, 210, 214, 216, 228, 230,
    234, 235, 236, 236n4, 237, 237n5,
    238, 239, 242, 243, 244, 253,
    255, 256, 261, 263, 264, 265,
    266, 270, 281, 282, 283, 285,
    286, 287, 288, 292, 293, 297,

Bloom, L. (*cont.*)
  307, 308, 309, 312, 313, 315,
  320, 321, 322, 325, 326, 328,
  331, 332, 334, 335, 369, 370,
  374, 377, 380, 382, 391, 392,
  393, 399, 401, 402, 414, 431n6,
  431n8, 432, 437, 438, 462, 465,
  470
Bloom, P., 36n91, 139, 141
Bloomfield, L., 34n35
Bock, J., 142
Bohannon, J., 433
Borton, R., 391
Bower, T., 71
Bowerman, M., 16, 34n49, 36n90, 41,
  67, 68, 69, 80, 81, 83, 89, 90,
  111, 123, 125, 128, 130, 135,
  136, 210, 239, 336, 382
Braine, M., 14, 15, 33n20, 41, 42, 82,
  84, 89, 97, 121, 139, 140n8, 142,
  308
Brainerd, C., 285, 333, 373n1
Brent, S., 336, 365
Bresnan, J., 5, 9, 35n86, 35n88, 293,
  294, 308
Bretherton, I., 35n73, 35n82, 35n83,
  81, 84, 239, 324, 374
Broen, P., 65, 437
Bronckart, J., 211, 231, 232, 233, 234,
  236n2
Broughton, J., 35n66
Brown, R., 14, 15, 18, 19, 34n49,
  34n63, 35n66, 41, 42, 44, 58, 62,
  66, 74, 76, 79, 80, 89, 90, 97,
  111, 122, 123, 125, 129, 130,
  131, 135, 138, 139, 144, 159,
  206n6, 210, 211, 212, 218, 220,
  234, 235, 236, 236n2, 243, 253,
  263, 264, 285, 292, 297, 367,
  368, 400, 401, 427, 430, 438
Bruner, J., 89, 126
Buczowska, E., 236n3, 238
Budwig, N., 82
Bull, W., 231
Bullock, M., 378, 390
Burke, P., 387
Burling, R., 79

Cairns, H., 256
Camaioni, L., 35n73
Camarata, S., 142
Campbell, R., 470

Capatides, J., 33n14, 34n48, 34n50,
  82, 264, 270, 282, 377, 382, 393
Carey, S., 35n72
Carlson, V., 391
Carnap, R., 122
Case, R., 35n67
Cazden, C., 125, 211, 218, 234
Cedergren, H., 44, 89, 90, 120, 130,
  131, 138, 140n3
Chafe, W., 330
Chalkley, M., 142, 308
Champaud, C., 288
Chapman, K., 432
Chapman, R., 83, 374
Charney, R., 84
Chesnick, M., 239
Choi, S., 206, 330
Chomsky, N., 7, 10, 15, 22, 23, 24,
  33n17, 33n19, 34n34, 35n85,
  35n86, 41, 129, 283, 400, 401,
  429
Clancy, P., 207, 256, 261, 284, 287
Clark, E., 36n93, 72, 77, 238, 261,
  370
Clark, R., 138, 432
Coggins, T., 432
Comrie, B., 231
Conforti, J., 471
Corrigan, R., 82, 365, 432
Corter, C., 374
Crain, S., 309
Crosby, F., 207
Culicover, P., 9
Cuvelier, P., 83
Cziko, G., 237, 239

Dale, P., 35n66, 239, 401, 426, 427
Danto, A., 33n5
Davidge, J., 332
Davies, B., 471
Davis, E., 367
de Boysson-Bardies, B., 207
de Laguna, G., 19
de Lemos, C., 238
de Villiers, J., 36, 83, 125, 142, 144,
  206n2, 206n3, 207, 210, 211, 218,
  235, 261, 284, 288, 308
de Villiers, P., 36, 125, 144, 206n2,
  206n3, 210, 211, 218, 235
Demopoulos, W., 33n6
Dent, C., 288
Deutsch, W., 238

Dittman, A., 437
Dixon, T., 401
Dockrell, J., 84
Donaldson, M., 374
Dore, J., 34n57, 89
Dowty, D., 231, 232
Ducasse, C., 378, 390, 393n3
Dunlea, A., 82
Dunn, J., 393
Durkin, K., 288

Edwards, D., 84
Eisenberg, S., 309
Erreich, A., 256
Ervin, S., 34n31
Ervin-Tripp, S., 14, 15, 34n57, 242, 253, 401, 426, 427, 432n11
Esposito, A., 82
Everly, S., 374

Fahey, G., 242
Farrar, M., 34n61, 35n66
Farwell, C., 370
Fauconnier, G., 33n7, 34n51
Fay, T., 327
Feier, C., 308
Felix, S., 242, 253
Ferguson, C., 78, 370
Ferreiro, E., 261
Fey, M., 432
Fiess, K., 242, 253, 261, 288, 293, 308, 312, 313, 390, 391
Fillmore, C., 16, 34n59, 76, 236n5, 247, 460, 461
Fish, B., 437, 467
Fisher, C., 118
Flavell, J., 36, 77, 324, 471
Fletcher, P., 82, 85, 237
Fodor, J., 22, 327
Foley, W., 35n88
Folger, J., 470
Folger, M., 432
Foster, S., 471
Frankel, T., 471
Franklin, M., 289
Fraser, C., 34n31, 42, 129, 400, 427, 430
Frazier, L., 142
Freeman, N., 11
French, L., 288, 374
Friedrich, P., 221, 229, 231, 232
Fritz, J., 374

Furrow, D., 81, 84, 332
Furth, H., 471

Galivan, J., 84
Gardner, H., 35n69
Garman, M., 82, 85
Garnica, O., 207, 370
Garrett, M., 327
Gartner, B., 282, 293, 307, 312, 332
Garvey, C., 437, 466
Gathercole, V., 237
Gelman, R., 35n71, 378, 390
Gentner, D., 84, 308
Gergely, G., 84
Gerhardt, J., 238
Gerkin, L., 141
Gessner, M., 82
Gibson, E., 391
Gleason, J., 36, 82
Gleitman, H., 34n41, 36n94
Gleitman, L., 31, 34n41, 36n94, 83, 161, 283, 401, 430, 467
Glucksberg, S., 77
Gold, E., 33n18
Gold, R., 431n4
Goldfield, B., 81
Goldin-Meadow, S., 82, 141
Golinkoff, R., 34n48, 82, 382, 391
Goodluck, H., 309
Goodwin, R., 84
Gopnik, A., 35n65, 35n66, 207
Gottsleben, R., 288
Gracey, C., 207
Greenbaum, S., 292, 312, 330
Greenfield, P., 41, 70, 89, 126, 285, 288
Grimshaw, J., 34n38
Gruber, H., 390
Gruber, J., 28, 34n45
Guillaume, P., 400, 428, 430

Hafitz, J., 33n14, 34n50, 113, 210, 237, 282, 286, 287, 292, 293, 307, 312, 332
Hakuta, K., 261, 284, 288, 308
Halliday, M., 118, 288, 465
Hamilton, M., 433
Hanlon, C., 285
Harding, C., 391
Harding, M., 256
Harner, L., 209, 211, 228, 232, 233, 234, 236n4, 238

Harris, M., 382
Harris, Z., 15, 281, 465
Hart, H., 377, 378, 390
Harting, R., 256
Hasan, R., 118, 288, 465
Herreshoff, M., 142
Higgins, E., 77
Hoff-Ginsberg, E., 471
Hogan, R., 437, 466
Honoré, A., 377, 378, 390
Hood, L., 35n80, 41, 47, 49, 57, 66,
    80, 81, 88, 91, 92, 114, 116, 117,
    119, 123, 137, 140n5, 141, 210,
    214, 216, 228, 230, 235, 236,
    237n5, 242, 244, 253, 255, 261,
    264, 265, 266, 270, 286, 287,
    288, 293, 297, 308, 312, 313,
    331, 335, 340, 365, 367, 369,
    370, 374, 380, 382, 390, 391,
    392, 393, 399, 414, 431n6, 432,
    437, 465, 470
Hopmann, M., 207
Horgan, D., 82
Horton, D., 401
Howe, C., 34n48, 82
Hsu, J., 256
Hume, D., 377, 391, 393n4
Huttenlocher, J., 72, 84
Huxley, R., 75
Hyams, N., 9, 23, 33n20, 33n22,
    34n41, 139, 141, 291, 308, 309
Hymes, D., 117

Ihns, M., 142
Ingram, D., 36, 41, 78, 239, 242
Inhelder, B., 285
Issacs, N., 367

Jackendoff, R., 11, 17, 28, 33n19,
    34n45
Jacobsen, T., 261, 284, 286
Jaffe, J., 460
Jakobson, R., 233, 236n1, 400, 428
James, S., 256
Janota, P., 72
Jenkins, J., 400, 429
Jespersen, O., 5, 146, 160, 291, 293,
    305, 306, 308, 323, 330, 373n6,
    400
Johnson, C., 84, 238, 329, 331
Johnson, H., 336, 365, 374
Johnson, L., 379

Johnson-Laird, P., 231
Joos, M., 228

Kant, I., 377, 393n4
Kaplan, B., 44, 206n4, 335, 363, 364,
    366, 367, 391
Kaplan, L., 432
Kaplan, R., 33n16, 35n86
Kates, C., 89, 123
Katz, E., 336, 365
Keenan, E., 437, 465, 466
Keller-Cohen, D., 207
Kelly, C., 35n66
Kemp, J., 401, 426, 427
Kim, Y., 309
King, M., 207
Kirkpatrick, E., 400
Klee, T., 256
Klima, E., 146, 155, 159, 164, 206n1
Knoke, D., 387
Koda, K., 237
Konieczna, E., 236n3, 238
Kopp, C., 393
Koster, J., 293, 294, 308
Krasnegor, N., 309
Krauss, R., 77
Kuczaj, S., 36, 84, 234, 374, 432, 462
Kuhn, D., 365
Kulikowski, S., 82
Kun, A., 390
Kurdek, L., 433
Kurtz, S., 378

Laberge, S., 44
Labov, T., 253
Labov, W., 33n12, 44, 89, 90, 120,
    130, 140n3, 157, 253
Lahey, M., 32n2, 33n13, 36, 81,
    206n6, 239, 242, 243, 253, 261,
    265, 266, 282, 287, 288, 292,
    293, 308, 309, 312, 313, 315,
    321, 325, 326, 328, 331, 391
Lakoff, G., 228
Landau, B., 31, 34n41, 83
Laurendeau, M., 336
Lawler, J., 223
Leech, G., 80, 292, 312, 330
Leimbach, M., 471
Leonard, L., 33n23, 34n49, 83, 142,
    432, 433
Leopold, W., 19, 137, 161, 401
Lerner, R., 33n28

Levin, B., 28
Lewis, M., 253, 367, 400
Liebergott, J., 239
Lifter, K., 33n14, 35n66, 35n73, 113,
    210, 237, 242, 253, 261, 266,
    286, 287, 288, 292, 293, 307,
    308, 312, 313, 391
Lightbown, P., 35n80, 41, 47, 49, 66,
    75, 80, 81, 91, 92, 114, 116, 123,
    137, 140n5, 210, 214, 228, 237n5,
    242, 253, 265, 286, 297, 308,
    370, 382, 393, 399, 414, 431n6,
    432, 438, 465, 470
Limber, J., 142, 261, 282, 283, 292,
    312, 313, 327, 330
Lindholm, K., 256
Loeb, D., 471
Lord, C., 471
Lucas, J., 390
Lui, F., 84
Lust, B., 261, 284, 288, 308
Lyons, J., 80, 231, 232

Macaulay, R., 228, 237n9
McCabe, A., 288, 374
McCarthy, D., 462
McCuhn-Nicolich, L., 35n66, 83
MacMurray, J., 33n28
MacNamara, J., 71
McNeill, D., 41, 44, 79, 89, 126, 127,
    164, 185, 202, 203, 205, 401,
    429, 462
McNeill, N., 164, 185, 202, 203, 205,
    462
McNew, S., 81, 84
McShane, J., 83, 84, 238
McTear, M., 470
MacWhinney, B., 33n23, 83, 142
Mansfield, A., 365
Maratsos, M., 36, 77, 142, 207, 308,
    329, 462
Markessini, J., 82
Markman, E., 36, 471
Martin, E., 69
Masterson, D., 35n81, 139
Masur, E., 34n61
May, R., 293, 294, 308
Meck, E., 35n71
Melton, A., 69
Meltzoff, A., 35n65, 35n66, 207
Menyuk, P., 239, 261

Merkin, S., 81, 228, 242, 256, 281,
    292, 307, 320
Mervis, C., 35n65, 284, 288, 308
Meumann, E., 400
Miller, G., 49, 231, 401
Miller, P., 57, 83, 88, 141, 210, 214,
    216, 230, 235, 236, 242, 331,
    392, 471
Miller, R., 211, 233, 234, 236n2, 238
Miller, W., 14, 15
Miyamoto, J., 431n9
Moerk, C., 432
Moerk, E., 432, 466, 467
Moore, C., 332
Morehead, D., 78
Morgan, J., 33n18
Morris, C., 122
Morrison, J., 432
Mowrer, O., 400, 429
Mussen, P., 36, 471

Nelson, K. (Karen), 126, 288
Nelson, K. (Katherine), 35n65, 35n82,
    44, 72, 75, 81, 82, 84, 85, 370,
    433, 466
Nelson, K. E., 141, 142
Newhoff, M., 432
Nishigauchi, T., 328
Norlin, P., 83
Normal, D., 84

O'Grady, W., 35n81, 139
Ochs, E., 12, 33n26, 381, 393n1, 470
Odya-Weis, C., 82
Olsen-Fulero, L., 471
Olson, D., 207
Olson, G., 137
Olswang, L., 470
Oshima-Takane, Y., 470
Overton, W., 33n30

Palermo, D., 400, 429
Parisi, D., 56, 237n5
Park, T., 79, 89, 122, 125, 129,
    206n3, 207
Parnell, M., 256
Partee, B., 283, 284
Pascual-Leone, J., 35n67
Patterson, S., 256
Pavlovitch, M., 79
Pea, R., 142, 206n7, 207
Pearson, B., 432

Peizer, D., 78
Pepler, D., 374
Pepper, S., 14
Peters, A., 35n81, 35n82, 82, 139
Peterson, C., 288, 374
Phelps, H., 365
Phillips, J., 437, 466
Piaget, J., 3, 17, 21, 22, 33n28, 44,
    72, 126, 285, 324, 333, 335, 336,
    363, 364, 365, 366, 372, 378,
    379, 383, 390, 391, 393n2, 397,
    401, 429, 430, 432n12
Piattelli-Palmarini, M., 35n68
Pickert, S., 471
Pinard, A., 336
Pinker, S., 9, 33n22. 34n38, 34n41,
    35n77, 36n90, 141, 142, 309, 312,
    313, 321, 325, 328, 331
Platt, M., 381
Preyer, W., 430
Pure, K., 332
Pylshyn, Z., 33n6

Quirk, R., 292, 312, 330

Radulovic, L., 233
Ramer, A., 35n82, 82, 370, 433
Ravelo, N., 288
Reese, H., 33n30
Reger, Z., 433, 470
Retherford, K., 83
Ridgeway, C., 374
Rieber, R., 85
Rispoli, M., 239, 282, 291, 293, 307,
    308, 309, 312, 332
Roberts, A., 437, 467
Rocissano, L., 117, 119, 244, 255,
    369, 437, 470
Rodgon, M., 433
Roelofsen, W., 471
Roeper, T., 83, 328
Rosenbaum, P., 282, 283, 292, 328
Rosenberg, S., 329
Rowan, L., 432
Rumbaugh, D., 309
Rumelhart, D., 84
Russell, A., 470
Ryan, J., 431n9
Ryle, G., 231

Saltzman, E., 126
Sankoff, G., 33n12, 44, 89, 90, 120,
    130, 131, 138, 140n3

Sapir, E., 21
Savasir, I., 238
Schachter, P., 238, 284
Schaerlaekens, A., 83, 128
Scherer, N., 470
Schieffelin, B., 12, 33n26, 381, 390,
    393n1, 470
Schlesinger, I., 15, 16, 34n49, 41, 44,
    67, 68, 69, 80, 83, 89, 122, 123,
    124, 128, 263
Scholnick, E., 288
Schwartz, B., 83
Schwartz, R., 432, 433, 471
Scott, C., 288
Searle, J., 377, 378, 390, 393n3
Sedlak, A., 378
Seebach, M., 256
Segalowitz, S., 374
Seitz, S., 437, 466, 467
Sexton, M., 391
Shapiro, T., 437, 467
Sharp, K., 374
Shatz, M., 324, 329, 392, 393, 471
Shibatani, M., 382
Shipley, E., 161, 401, 430, 467
Shultz, T., 378, 390
Siegel, G., 437
Silber, S., 324, 329
Silva, M., 261, 284, 287
Sinclair, H., 72, 211, 231, 232, 233,
    234, 236n2, 261, 285, 401
Sloate, P., 433
Slobin, D., 20, 36, 41, 44, 69, 71, 77,
    123, 145, 147, 206n5, 207, 238,
    239, 284, 307, 391, 401, 431n1,
    462, 467
Smiley, P., 84
Smith, C., 125, 161, 211, 231, 232,
    233, 234, 238, 239, 401, 430, 467
Smith, F., 401
Smith, J., 41, 70, 89, 285
Smith, M., 242, 253, 461
Smith, P., 470
Snow, C., 65, 81, 433, 437
Snyder, L., 35n82, 35n83, 81, 84, 239
Söderbergh, R., 369, 437, 466
Soskin, W., 467, 468
Spelke, E., 35n70
Sperry, L., 471
Spiedel, G., 142, 433
Staats, A., 400, 429
Stein, N., 289, 379
Stephany, U., 238

Stern, D., 460
Stewart, D., 433, 437, 466, 467
Stine, E., 433
Stockwell, R., 283, 284
Stromswold, K., 256
Studdert-Kennedy, M., 309
Sudhalter, V., 84
Sullivan, L., 365
Suppes, P., 109, 140n3
Svartvik, J., 292, 312, 330

Tackeff, J., 34n48, 81, 82, 282, 287,
    292, 309, 312, 313, 315, 321,
    325, 326, 328, 331, 382
Tager-Flusberg, H., 207, 261, 284,
    288, 308
Tamir, L., 471
Tanz, C., 84
Tavakolian, S., 309
Taylor, C., 33n5
Thompson, R., 393n1
Thorndike, E., 400
Thornton, R., 309
Todd, P., 207
Topmasello, M., 34n61, 35n66, 309
Townsend, D., 288
Trabasso, T., 379
Traugott, E., 79, 80
Tronick, E., 71–2
Tyack, D., 242, 288

Urmson, S., 330
Uzgiris, I., 391

Valentine, C., 428, 430
Valian, V., 34n41, 141, 142
Van Besien, F., 83
Van Hekken, S., 471
Van Kleeck, A., 471
Van Valin, R., 35n88, 206n3, 207, 239
Vasta, R., 433
Vendler, Z., 231, 382

Verrips, M., 206n3
Viberg, A., 311, 329, 332
Volterra, V., 35n73
Voneche, J., 390
Vosniadou, S., 75
Voyat, G., 433
Vygotsky, L., 336

Wanner, E., 34n41, 36n94
Wanska, S., 471
Wassenberg, K., 470
Watson, J., 391
Weeks, T., 78
Weiss, A., 432
Weissenborn, J., 206n3
Weist, R., 84, 209, 236n3, 238, 239
Wellen, C., 470
Wellman, H., 84, 324, 329
Wells, G., 85
Welsh, C., 284, 462
Werner, H., 3, 44, 145, 206n4, 333,
    335, 363, 364, 366, 367, 391
Wexler, K., 9
Whitby, O., 140n7
White, G., 374
White, L., 33n20
Whitehurst, G., 433
Whitaker, H., 141
Whitaker, H. A., 141
Whittaker, S., 84, 238
Wilcox, M., 432
Wing, C., 288
Witkowska-Stadnik, K., 236n3, 238
Wode, H., 206n3, 207
Woisetschlaeger, E., 231, 233, 236n1
Wootten, J., 81, 228, 242, 256, 281,
    292, 307, 320
Wysocka, H., 236n3, 238

Yoder, P., 471

Zahn-Waxler, C., 374

Subject Index

action, 4, 72, 89, 126–7, 139, 232,
    237–8n5, 247; *see also* causality;
    verbs, action
  on affected object, 16, 29, 43, 49,
    53, 63, 69, 70, 91, 93, 124, 125,
    127, 139, 214, 398, 413–14, 416–
    17, 421, 428; *see also* thematic
    roles and relations, theme
  events, 23, 52, 53, 56–7, 58, 68, 69,
    71–2, 123, 131, 215, 414
  and location, *see* locative
  relations, 16–17, 49–50, 56, 59–60,
    62–4, 65, 71, 93, 95, 97, 111–12,
    114, 115, 117, 119, 121, 125,
    127, 133–4, 135–6, 137, 217
  –state distinction, 29, 30, 49, 79–80,
    215, 217, 228, 232, 234, 413
adjuncts, *see* locative; *wh*-questions,
    syntactic functions
adult
  grammar, 5, 9–12, 13, 17, 18, 21,
    25, 28, 39, 40, 41, 60, 68–9, 73,
    75, 77, 78, 124, 126, 128, 129,
    146, 147, 159, 160, 161, 164,
    185, 188, 205, 231, 248, 263,
    279, 283, 293, 323, 324; *see also*
    negation, adult
  speech, 26, 69, 76, 119, 128, 138,
    187, 188, 192, 205, 307–8, 327,
    334, 362, 366, 372, 435, 437,
    438, 441–2, 459–60; *see also* in-
    put
  see also causality, in discourse (re-
    sponses to *why* questions); dis-
    course, adult–adult; discourse,
    questions

adverbs, 111, 135, 231, 232, 326, 327,
    330
analytic/synthetic distinction, 7, 25, 40,
    74–5, 78–9; *see also* pronominal/
    nominal
animate/inanimate distinction, 16, 124,
    125, 306, 323
argument structure, 17, 24, 27, 28–31,
    40, 49–52, 81, 86–7, 93–4, 134–
    5, 208, 214–16, 240; *see also* con-
    stituent, relations; constituent,
    structure; semantic–syntactic; the-
    matic roles and relations; underly-
    ing structure; verbs, relations;
    verbs, subcategorization
aspect
  event, 79–80, 209, 211, 226, 230–3
  inflectional, 209, 221–30, 231–3,
    237
  lexical, 214, 226, 230, 231, 232
  perfective, 228–9, 230, 238
  synthetic, 231, 232
  and tense, 18, 208, 209, 230–6, 238,
    239
  see also verb typologies
attributive relation, *see* functional rela-
    tions; length of utterance, and
    grammatical complexity

behaviorism, 397, 400, 429

case grammar, 16, 41, 64, 139, 236n5
causality, 1, 6, 18, 52, 260, 333–73,
    373n3, 374, 375–93

and actions, 376, 378–9, 389–91, 392

clause order (of cause and effect), 26, 333, 334–5, 336, 338, 339–40, 342, 356, 360–2, 364, 366, 370

concept of, 253, 333, 335–6, 363, 375, 376, 377–80, 388–91, 392

connectives, *see* connectives

consequences, *see* causality, meaning relations (objective/subjective)

in discourse, 335, 336 (*see also* causality, meaning relations (objective/subjective)); responses to *why* questions, 278, 334, 337, 340–1, 342, 349, 352, 367, 368–70, 371–2, 375; sequence of development, 334, 353–4, 368–70, 371–2, 392; statements, 334, 337, 338–41, 342, 349, 352, 353, 366–7, 368–70, 371–2, 375, 381–2, 392; *why* questions, 251–2, 334, 337, 341, 342, 349, 352, 353–4, 356, 367–70, 371–2, 392

individual differences, 26, 287, 334–5, 356, 360, 362, 370, 380

intentional, 333, 365, 376, 378, 390–1; categories (direction/intention/negation), 270, 334, 342, 345–52, 365, 367–8, 371–3

lexical causatives, *see* verbs

meaning relations, 6, 26, 253, 278, 333, 334–6, 338–40, 362–5, 367, 369–70, 377, 381–3, 384–8, 393 (*see also* semantic, relations (complex sentences)); objective/subjective, 12–13, 22, 264, 364–5, 375–6, 379, 382, 384–8, 389–92

means-end, *see* causality, meaning relations (objective/subjective)

precausality, 383, 390

reasoning, 333, 335, 366, 367, 377–8, 391

sensorimotor, 335, 376, 378–9, 388–9, 390, 391, 392

theories of, 375, 376, 377–9, 390–1

child grammar, 5, 6, 10–12, 13, 24, 39, 41, 42, 48–9, 59–60, 68–9, 73–4, 75–6, 78, 79, 86, 87, 88–91, 120–1, 128–9, 133, 138–9, 144, 146–7, 152–3, 155, 160, 161, 164, 175–6, 179, 183, 186,

211, 234, 236, 292, 295, 308, 331; *see also* knowledge of language; theories of child language

cognitive (or conceptual factors), 10, 13, 17, 20–5, 29, 32, 66, 70–1, 87, 90, 126, 169, 186–7, 197, 205, 240, 241, 242, 253, 256, 279, 284, 369–70, 386, 429, 462–3

cost (or competition), 24, 25, 29, 235, 392, 436; *see also* length of utterance; reduction

decentering, 3, 336, 371–3, 392

development, 3–5, 18, 21–2, 44, 69, 71–3, 76, 137–8, 146, 203, 240, 242, 253, 285, 335–6, 372, 392

processing, 9, 24, 137, 161, 327, 369, 392, 400, 401, 421, 430, 461, 464–5

see also causality, concept of; complexity; constraints; memory; mental

concrete to abstract thought, *see* cognitive, development

competence/performance, 24, 87, 88, 89–90, 121, 137, 138–9, 161, 173, 185

complementation (or subordination), 1, 30, 57, 66, 67, 115, 134, 257, 259–60, 276, 278, 282–3, 286, 290–309, 310–32; *see also* complex sentences, sequence of development; verbs, complement; verbs, matrix

complement types, 310, 314, 315, 318–19, 326, 327; *for-to*, 293–4, 297, 303–4, 308, 309n3, 328; infinitival *(to)*, 5, 33n22, 287, 290–309, 309n3, 310, 312, 315, 325, 331; sentential, 322–6, 327–8, 331; *wh-*, 310, 312, 315, 318–19, 320–1, 327–8, 331

complementizers, 291, 293–4, 303–4, 305, 306–8, 310, 312, 314, 315, 320, 321–3, 326, 327–8, 330, 331–2; *see also* connectives, *that;* connectives, *to;* connectives, *wh-*

complex sentences, 2, 31, 257, 289, 327, 335, 370, 377, 391

individual differences, 260, 273, 287, 303, 308

complex sentences (*cont.*)
    sequence of development: meaning
        relations (additive/temporal/causal/
        adversative), 26, 260, 272–3, 279,
        284–5, 286–7, 289, 391; syntactic
        structures (conjunction/complemen-
        tation/relativization), 30, 257, 259,
        276–8, 282–4, 287
    see also causality; complementation;
        connectives; semantic, relations
complexity, 112t, 134
    cognitive, 65, 69–71, 147, 253, 313,
        366
    cumulative, 66–7, 131, 26c, 264,
        285, 287
    semantic, 65, 67–9, 241, 247, 248,
        254, 260, 264, 283, 287
    and sequence of development, 66–71
    structural, 1, 20, 57, 65, 66–7, 69,
        71, 122–3, 189, 192, 194, 198,
        200, 203–4, 246, 253, 255, 279,
        283, 313, 392
    see also length of utterance; reduction
comprehension, 242, 329–30, 400, 430
conjunction (or coordination), 30, 53,
        67, 115, 134, 257, 259, 262, 265–
        6, 276–8, 279, 282–4, 286, 288;
        see also complex sentences, se-
        quence of development; semantic
        relations, complex sentences
connectives, 259–88
    causal, 253, 259, 334–5, 336, 338,
        340, 342, 356, 360–2, 364, 365–
        6, 375, 376, 379–82, 383, 386–8,
        391–2
    contextual, 265–6, 279
    individual differences, 26, 259–60,
        267–8, 286–7, 334–5, 356, 360
    meaning of, 290–1, 293–4, 304–5,
        306, 307–8, 338, 361–2, 365–6
    sequence of development, 26, 259–
        60, 265–8, 274–6, 279, 281–2,
        286–7, 320–1, 356, 360–2, 365–6
    syntactic, 1, 5, 26, 30, 253, 257,
        259–61, 265, 266–8, 274, 276,
        278, 279, 282, 286–7, 288; *see
        also* connectives, causal
    and, 6, 259, 263, 265, 266, 276,
        278, 279, 281, 282, 284, 356,
        360, 361, 366, 376, 382
    because, 6, 259, 263, 265, 266, 276,
        278, 279, 281, 282, 333, 334,

336, 356, 360, 361, 362, 365,
        366, 369, 376, 382
    but, 266, 276, 282
    if, 266, 320, 321, 326, 330, 382
    so, 6, 259, 266, 276, 282, 333, 334,
        336, 356, 360, 361, 362, 365,
        366, 376, 382
    that, 259, 263, 265, 266, 276, 281,
        310, 322–3, 328, 330
    then, 259, 263, 266, 267, 281
    to, 5, 290–308, 312, 321, 328
    wh-, 259, 263, 266–8, 274, 276,
        281, 282, 307, 312, 320–1, 327–8
constituent(s)
    defined, 140n4
    frequencies (or distribution), 29, 95,
        114, 124, 133, 139
    probability of lexicalization, 7, 24–5,
        86, 87, 89, 97, 106–9, 121, 130–
        1, 132–3, 140n3; *see also* length
        of utterance, lexicalization of con-
        stituents; rules, variable
    relations, 16, 19, 24, 28, 31, 42–3,
        74, 86–7, 93, 95–120, 127, 128,
        135, 138, 210, 215–16, 248
    of sentences, 56, 121, 125, 210, 240,
        245–6, 247–8, 250, 254, 255,
        265–6, 276, 282, 284, 287, 447,
        450, 452, 454, 465
    structure, 1, 5, 16, 24, 31, 42–3,
        131–9, 294
    see also argument structure; length of
        utterance; optional-obligatory; re-
        duction; semantic–syntactic, struc-
        ture; syntactic, structure
constraints, 88, 130, 135
    cognitive, 24, 25, 69, 161–2, 205,
        242, 281, 369
    linguistic (or grammatical), 11–12,
        90, 111, 114, 129, 162, 179, 180,
        186–7, 240, 291
    performance, 24, 87, 90, 111
    see also length of utterance
context
    linguistic (optional/obligatory): for
        connectives *(to),* 294, 295, 297,
        302–6; for inflections, 211–14,
        218, 325
    situational, 3, 4–5, 7, 18–20, 32,
        46, 48, 65, 121–3, 146, 150, 152,
        156, 157, 159, 161, 162–3, 165,
        172, 174, 175, 180, 181, 183,